# DANTE IN CONTEXT

In the past seven centuries Dante has become world renowned, with his works translated into multiple languages and read by people of all ages and cultural backgrounds. This volume brings together interdisciplinary essays by leading international scholars to provide a comprehensive account of the historical, cultural, and intellectual context in which Dante lived and worked: from the economic, social, and political scene to the feel of daily life; from education and religion to the administration of justice; from medicine to philosophy and science; from classical antiquity to popular culture; and from the dramatic transformation of urban spaces to the explosion of visual arts and music. This book, while locating Dante in relation to each of these topics, offers readers a clear and reliable idea of what life was like for Dante as an outstanding poet and intellectual in the Italy of the late Middle Ages.

ZYGMUNT G. BARAŃSKI is Serena Professor of Italian Emeritus at the University of Cambridge and Notre Dame Chair of Dante and Italian Studies at the University of Notre Dame.

LINO PERTILE is Carl A. Pescosolido Professor of Romance Languages and Literatures at Harvard University, and Director of The Harvard University Center for Italian Renaissance Studies at Villa I Tatti, Florence.

# DANTE IN CONTEXT

EDITED BY
ZYGMUNT G. BARAŃSKI
AND
LINO PERTILE

# CAMBRIDGE
## UNIVERSITY PRESS

University Printing House, Cambridge CB2 8BS, United Kingdom

Cambridge University Press is part of the University of Cambridge.

It furthers the University's mission by disseminating knowledge in the pursuit of education, learning and research at the highest international levels of excellence.

www.cambridge.org
Information on this title: www.cambridge.org/9781107033146

© Cambridge University Press 2015

This publication is in copyright. Subject to statutory exception and to the provisions of relevant collective licensing agreements, no reproduction of any part may take place without the written permission of Cambridge University Press.

First published 2015

Printed in the United States of America by Sheridan Books, Inc.

*A catalogue record for this publication is available from the British Library*

*Library of Congress Cataloguing in Publication data*
Dante in context / edited by Zygmunt G. Barański and Lino Pertile.
pages  cm. – (Literature in context)
Includes bibliographical references and index.
ISBN 978-1-107-03314-6 (hardback)
1. Dante Alighieri, 1265–1321.  2. Literature and society–Italy–History–To 1500.  3. Italy–Civilization–1268-1492.  I. Baranski, Zygmunt G., editor.  II. Pertile, Lino, editor.
PQ4353.A2D36 2015
851'.1–dc23        2015022566

ISBN 978-1-107-03314-6 Hardback

Cambridge University Press has no responsibility for the persistence or accuracy of URLs for external or third-party internet websites referred to in this publication, and does not guarantee that any content on such websites is, or will remain, accurate or appropriate.

*For Maggie and Anna*

# Contents

| | |
|---|---|
| *List of illustrations* | *page* x |
| *List of maps* | xii |
| *Notes on contributors* | xiii |
| *Chronology* | xx |
| *Abbreviations and note on translations* | xxiv |

| | |
|---|---|
| Introduction<br>*Zygmunt G. Barański and Lino Pertile* | 1 |

| | | |
|---|---|---|
| PART I: POLITICS AND SOCIETY | | 7 |
| 1 | Empire, Italy, and Florence<br>*William Caferro* | 9 |
| 2 | Economy<br>*William R. Day, Jr* | 30 |
| 3 | Law<br>*Sara Menzinger* | 47 |
| 4 | Justice<br>*Giuliano Milani* | 59 |
| 5 | Men and women<br>*Holly Hurlburt* | 71 |
| 6 | Church and orthodoxy<br>*George Dameron* | 83 |
| 7 | Heresy and dissidence<br>*David Burr* | 106 |

vii

viii                               Contents

8   Daily life                                                     119
    *Edward D. English*

PART II: INTELLECTUAL TRADITIONS                                   135

9   Philosophy and theology                                        137
    *Andrea A. Robiglio*

10  Moral philosophy                                               159
    *Luca Bianchi*

11  Natural philosophy                                             173
    *Edward Grant*

12  Medicine                                                       189
    *Michael R. McVaugh*

13  Islamic and Jewish influences                                  200
    *Luis M. Girón Negrón*

14  Cosmology, geography, and cartography                          221
    *Theodore J. Cachey, Jr*

PART III: LINGUISTIC AND LITERARY CULTURES                        241

15  Linguistic Italy                                               243
    *Mirko Tavoni*

16  Education                                                      260
    *Robert Black*

17  Rhetoric, literary theory, and practical criticism            277
    *Ronald L. Martinez*

18  Classical antiquity                                            297
    *Robert Black*

19  Religious culture                                              319
    *Peter S. Hawkins*

20  Visions and journeys                                           341
    *Eileen Gardiner*

21  Historical and political writing                               354
    *John C. Barnes*

*Contents*      ix

22   Vernacular literatures      371
*Paolo Cherchi*

23   Popular culture      389
*Jan M. Ziolkowski*

PART IV: VISUAL AND PERFORMATIVE CULTURE      399

24   Illumination, painting, and sculpture      401
*Louise Bourdua*

25   Architecture and urban space      427
*Areli Marina*

26   Music      448
*Michael Scott Cuthbert*

PART V: DANTE: LIFE, WORKS, AND RECEPTION      459

27   Life      461
*Lino Pertile*

28   Works      475
*Lino Pertile*

29   Textual transmission      509
*Zygmunt G. Barański*

30   Early reception (1290–1481)      518
*Zygmunt G. Barański*

*Further reading*      538
*Index*      565

# Illustrations

14.1 Giovanni di Paolo (Siena 1398–1482), *The Creation of the World and the Expulsion from Paradise*, 1445. Robert Lehman Collection. Courtesy of The Metropolitan Museum of Art (www.metmuseum.org). *page* 222

14.2 A schematic representation of the Ptolemaic universe. 228

14.3 Map of the earth, based on M. Musa's *Dante's Paradise* (Bloomington: Indiana University Press, 1984). 236

24.1 Gospel of Matthew, 'L' (*Liber generationis*) depicting the Tree of Jesse, *Bibbia sacra c.*1267 (Paris, BN, ms. Lat. 22, fol. 346r.). Reproduced courtesy of Bibliothèque nationale de France. 406

24.2 Gospel of Matthew, 'L' (*Liber generationis*) depicting the Tree of Jesse, *Bibbia vulgata* also known as 'Bible of Charles V', 1285–90 (Gerona, Cathedral chapter library, MS. 10, fol. 391r.). Reproduced courtesy of Gerona Cathedral. 407

24.3 Cimabue, crucifix, Santa Croce, Florence, before 1288. Reproduced courtesy of Quattrone Snc Di De Luise Alba E C. Fotografia Di Arte. 408

24.4 Giotto, crucifix, Santa Maria Novella, Florence, *c.*1290. © Photo SCALA, Florence. 409

24.5 Facade of S. Maria del Fiore, Florence, by Alessandro Nani, after a drawing by Bernardino Poccetti (Archivio dell'Opera di S. Maria del Fiore). Reproduced courtesy of Quattrone Snc Di De Luise Alba E C. Fotografia Di Arte. 416

24.6 Statue of S. Gemignano, tufo, Sant'Anastasia, Verona, 1290s. Reproduced courtesy of Louise Bourdua. 418

24.7 Tomb of Guglielmo Castelbarco, above entrance to the cloister of Sant'Anastasia, Verona, *c.*1320. Reproduced courtesy of Louise Bourdua. 419

## List of illustrations

24.8  *Maestro del Redentore*, Votive portrait of Guglielmo Castelbarco, San Fermo Maggiore, Verona, *c.*1318. Reproduced courtesy of Louise Bourdua. — 420

24.9  Anonymous master, *Procession*, tower of abbey of San Zeno, Verona, *c.*1260. Reproduced courtesy of Louise Bourdua. — 421

24.10  Giotto, *Arrest of Christ*, *c.*1305, Arena chapel, Padua. Reproduced courtesy of Quattrone Snc Di De Luise Alba E C. Fotografia Di Arte. — 424

25.1  Giovanni Toscani (Maestro della Crocifissione Griggs), *Procession of the Palio dei Barberi standards in Piazza San Giovanni*, from a now-dismembered *cassone*, Florence, *c.*1425. Florence, Museo Nazionale del Bargello. Photo: Scala/Art Resource, NY. — 428

25.2  View of Florence, detail from the *Madonna della Misericordia*, fresco, Loggia del Bigallo, Florence, *c.*1342. Photo: Alinari/Art Resource, NY. — 432

25.3  Palazzo dei Priori (or Palazzo Vecchio or della Signoria) and Piazza della Signoria, Florence, begun 1299. Photo: Scala/Art Resource, NY. — 434

25.4  Domus Mercatorum, Verona, begun 1301. Photo: David Nicholls, 2003. — 437

25.5  Detail of the Piazza dei Signori, Verona, *c.*1525, from Niccolò Giolfino, *Gaius Mucius Scaevola Thrusting his Right Hand into the Flame*, tempera on panel, *c.*1525–1550. Photo: Sotheby's; courtesy of Biblioteca Berenson, Fototeca, Harvard University Center for Italian Renaissance Studies–Villa I Tatti. — 439

25.6  Detail, east wall fresco, Ambrogio Lorenzetti, *Effects of Good Government on the Town*. Siena, Palazzo Pubblico, Sala della Pace, 1338–39. Photo: HIP/Art Resource, NY. — 445

25.7  Detail, west wall fresco, Ambrogio Lorenzetti, *Effects of Bad Government on the Town*. Siena, Palazzo Pubblico, Sala della Pace, 1338–39. Photo: Scala/Art Resource, NY. — 446

## Music examples

26.1  Examples of innovations in rhythmic notation arriving (a) *c.* 1200, (b) *c.* 1260, (c) *c.* 1300. — 452

26.2  *Kalenda Maya* with two possible rhythmic interpretations. — 454

# Maps

1   Historical map of Europe during the fourteenth century. From
*The Public Schools Historical Atlas*, edited by C. Colbeck, 1905.
Image courtesy of University of Texas Libraries,
University of Texas, Austin.                          *page* 534
2   Dante's Italy around 1300.                                     535
3   Walls of Florence from Roman times to 1333.             536

# Notes on contributors

ZYGMUNT G. BARAŃSKI is Serena Professor of Italian Emeritus at the University of Cambridge and Notre Dame Chair of Dante and Italian Studies at the University of Notre Dame. He has published extensively on Dante, as well as on medieval and modern Italian literature and culture. Among his books are *'Sole nuovo, luce nuova': Saggi sul rinnovamento culturale in Dante* (1996), *Dante e i segni* (2000); *'Chiosar con altro testo': Leggere Dante nel Trecento* (2001), and, with Theodore J. Cachey, *Petrarch and Dante: Anti-Dantism, Metaphysics, Tradition* (2009). After serving as senior editor of *The Italianist* for many years, he currently holds the same post with *Le tre corone*.

JOHN C. BARNES, prior to his retirement, was for a quarter of a century the Professor of Italian in University College Dublin. The principal area of his work has always been medieval Florentine literature, especially historiography and the writings of Dante. He has co-edited a number of collections of essays on the latter, to be followed in the near future by *War and Peace in Dante* and *Dante and the Seven Deadly Sins*. He has also worked on certain twentieth-century Italian authors, particularly Pirandello, and has for many years been the President of the Society for Pirandello Studies.

LUCA BIANCHI is Professor of History of Medieval Philosophy at the Università del Piemonte Orientale, Vercelli. He is the author of several books on medieval and Renaissance thought, including: *Il vescovo e i filosofi. La condanna parigina del 1277 e l'evoluzione dell'aristotelismo scolastico* (1990); *Censure et liberté intellectuelle à l'Université de Paris* (1999); *Studi sull'aristotelismo del Rinascimento* (2003); *Pour une histoire de la 'double vérité'* (2008). He is the editor of *Christian Readings of Aristotle from the Middle Ages to the Renaissance* (2011).

xiv Notes on contributors

ROBERT BLACK is Professor of Renaissance History at the University of Leeds. His books include *Benedetto Accolti and the Florentine Renaissance* (1985); *Studio e scuola in Arezzo durante il medioevo e il rinascimento* (1996); *Humanism and Education in Medieval and Renaissance Italy* (2001); and *Education and Society in Florentine Tuscany* (2007). His new biography, *Machiavelli* (2013), was a *Times Literary Supplement* book of the year. In 2014 he was Robert Lehman Visiting Professor at Villa I Tatti, the Harvard University Center for Italian Renaissance Studies in Florence.

LOUISE BOURDUA is Reader in History of Art at the University of Warwick and Head of Department. She has published widely on mendicant art, iconography, patronage, the Veneto, and Tuscany, including *The Franciscans and Art Patronage in Late Medieval Italy* (2004) and 'The arts in Florence after the Black Death' in *Florence. Artistic Centers of the Italian Renaissance* (2012).

DAVID BURR is Professor of History Emeritus at Virginia Tech. He was educated at Oberlin College, Union Theological Seminary, and Duke University. In addition to preparing critical editions of works by Peter John Olivi and translating works by Angelo Clareno, he has written several monographs dealing with various aspects of early Franciscan history, including *Olivi and Franciscan Poverty* (1989), *Olivi's Peaceable Kingdom* (1993), and *The Spiritual Franciscans* (2001). He is currently collaborating on an edition of Olivi's Matthew commentary, but is especially interested in groups that exist just inside or just outside the boundaries of orthodoxy, particularly apocalyptic groups.

THEODORE J. CACHEY, JR is Professor of Italian Studies at the University of Notre Dame. His research focuses on Dante and Petrarch, the history of the Italian language, and the literature and history of travel. He has authored and edited several books, including *Le isole fortunate* (1985), *Dante Now* (1995), *Petrarch's Guide to the Holy Land* (2002), *Pigafetta's First Voyage Around the World* (2007), and *Dante and Petrarch: Anti-Dantism, Metaphysics, Tradition* (2009), as well as many essays and book chapters. He is founder and co-editor (with Zygmunt G. Barański and Christian Moevs) of the William and Katherine Devers Series in Dante and Medieval Italian Literature.

WILLIAM CAFERRO is Gertrude Conaway Vanderbilt Professor of Medieval European History at Vanderbilt University. He specializes primarily in economic history and Trecento Italy. He is the author of *Mercenary Companies and the Decline of Siena* (1998), *John Hawkwood: An English Mercenary in Fourteenth-century Italy* (2006), and *Contesting the Renaissance* (2011). He is currently editing a collection of essays devoted to commerce and the global Renaissance.

PAOLO CHERCHI is Emeritus Professor of Romance Languages and Literatures at the University of Chicago where he taught from 1965 to 2003. He was also Professor of Italian Literature at the Università di Ferrara (2003–09). He has published extensively on medieval and Renaissance literature, primarily Italian and Spanish, but also Old French and Occitan. His books include: *Andreas and the Ambiguity of Courtly Love* (1994); *Polimatia di riuso: mezzo secolo di plagio (1549–1589)* (1998); *L'onestade e l'onesto raccontare del 'Decameron'* (2004); *Verso la chiusura: saggio sul Canzoniere di Petrarca* (2008); *La rosa dei venti: una mappa delle teorie letterarie* (2011).

MICHAEL SCOTT CUTHBERT is Associate Professor of Music at the Massachusetts Institute of Technology. He has worked extensively on music of the fourteenth century, computational musicology, and minimalism and other music of the past forty years. His publications include seven articles on computational musicology, *Ars Nova: French and Italian Music of the Fourteenth Century* (2009; with John Nádas), 'Generalized set analysis and Sub-Saharan African rhythm', and 'Free improvisation: John Zorn and the construction of Jewish identity through music'. His current book project covers sacred music in Italy during the Black Death and Great Schism.

GEORGE DAMERON is Professor and Chair of History at Saint Michael's College in Colchester, Vermont. He is the author of *Episcopal Power and Florentine Society, 1000–1320* (1991), *Florence and Its Church in the Age of Dante* (2005), and numerous essays and articles. He is currently working on a history of Florence before the Black Death and a study of the political economy of grain in Tuscany before 1350. A past president of the New England Historical Association (2006–07), he also served as a Peace Corps volunteer in West Africa (Benin) as a grain storage specialist.

WILLIAM R. DAY, JR is an economic historian and numismatist. He completed his Ph.D. on *The Early Development of the Florentine economy, c.1100–1275* at the London School of Economics and Political Science in 1999. His publications include 'The population of Florence before the Black Death: survey and synthesis' (2002) and

'Fiorentini e altri italiani appaltatori di zecche straniere (1200–1600): un progetto di ricerca' (2010). He is also co-author of *Medieval European Coinage 12: Italy (I) North Italy* (2015).

EDWARD D. ENGLISH is Executive Director of Medieval Studies and Visiting Associate Professor of History at the University of California, Santa Barbara. His publications include *Enterprise and Liability in Sienese Banking, 1230–1350* (1988), *The Encyclopedia of the Medieval World* (2005), and *A Companion to the Medieval World: Blackwell Companions to European History*, co-edited with Carol Lansing (2009). He is finishing a book manuscript entitled *Conflict and Consensus: Siena and Its Nobles, 1240–1420*.

EILEEN GARDINER is author of *Visions of Heaven and Hell before Dante* (1989), *Medieval Visions of Heaven and Hell* (1993), *The Pilgrim's Way to St. Patrick's Purgatory* (2010), and *Hell-on-Line* (www.hell-on-line.org), a website on the infernal otherworld in various traditions. With Ronald G. Musto, she is co-founder and co-publisher of Italica Press. She is also a former co-director of ACLS Humanities E-Book and of the Medieval Academy of America, and co-editor of *Speculum: A Journal of Medieval Studies*. With Dr Musto, she is co-author of 'The electronic book' in *The Oxford Companion to the Book* (2010), and of *Digital Humanities: A Primer for Scholars and Students* (2015).

LUIS M. GIRÓN NEGRÓN is Professor of Comparative Literature and Romance Languages and Literatures, and Member of the Committee on the Study of Religion, at Harvard University. A specialist in medieval Iberia, he writes and teaches on the cultural interactions between Muslims, Christians, and Jews, as gauged from the literary history of Arabic, Hebrew, and the Romance vernaculars. He is the author of *Alfonso de la Torre's 'Visión Deleitable': Philosophical Rationalism and the Religious Imagination in 15th Century Spain* (2001), and co-author, with Laura Minervini, of *Las Coplas de Yosef: entre la Biblia y el 'midrash' en la poesía judeoespañola* (2006).

EDWARD GRANT is Distinguished Professor Emeritus of History and Philosophy of Science at Indiana University, Bloomington. He has published over one hundred articles and thirteen books. During 1985–86, he served as president of the History of Science Society. His honours and awards include: Fellow of the Guggenheim Foundation (1965–66); Member, School of Historical Studies, Institute for Advanced Study, Princeton (1965–66; 1983–84); The George Sarton Medal of the History of Science Society (1992); Fellow of the American Academy of Arts and Sciences (elected 1984); Fellow of the Medieval Academy of America (elected 1982).

PETER S. HAWKINS, Professor of Religion and Literature, Yale Divinity School, has long specialized on Dante. His publications include *Dante's Testaments: Essays in Scriptural Imagination* (1999), *The Poets' Dante: Twentieth-Century Reflections*, co-edited with Rachel Jacoff (2001), *Dante: A Brief History* (2006), and *Undiscovered Country: Imagining the Life to Come* (2009). He has also worked in biblical reception history: *Scrolls of Love: Ruth and the Song of Songs* (2006); *Medieval Readings of Romans* (2007). His essays have appeared in *PMLA*, *Critical Enquiry*, *Religion and Literature*, *MLN*, and *Annali d'italianistica*.

HOLLY HURLBURT is Associate Professor of History at Southern Illinois University, Carbondale. Her research focuses on women and power in Venice, the Veneto, and the Mediterranean. Her first book *The Dogaressa of Venice, 1200–1500: Wife and Icon* was published in 2006. In 2007–08 she was a fellow at Villa I Tatti, The Harvard University Center for Italian Renaissance Studies. Her forthcoming book on the last Queen of Cyprus, Caterina Corner, will be published in 2015 by Yale University Press.

MICHAEL R. MCVAUGH is William Smith Wells Professor of History Emeritus, University of North Carolina. He has published *Medicine before the Plague: Doctors and Patients in the Crown of Aragon 1285–1345* (1993) and *The Rational Surgeons of the Middle Ages* (2005), as well as an edition of the *Inventarium* or *Chirurgia Magna* of Guy de Chauliac (1997–98). He is one of the general editors of the *Arnaldi de Villanova Opera Medica Omnia* (1975–), of which thirteen volumes have so far appeared in print.

ARELI MARINA is Associate Professor of Art History and Medieval Studies at the University of Illinois, Urbana-Champaign, and was a fellow at I Tatti during 2010–11. Her research examines the intersections of public rhetoric, political authority, and monumental art production in Italy between the medieval and early modern eras, especially in relation to the spatial arts: urbanism, architecture, and sculpture. Recent publications on architecture and urbanism include an award-winning book entitled *The Italian Piazza Transformed: Parma in the Communal Age* (2012) and 'From the myth to the margins: The patriarch's piazza at San Pietro di Castello in Venice' (2011).

xviii                    Notes on contributors

RONALD L. MARTINEZ is Professor of Italian Studies at Brown University. In addition to some four dozen articles on Italian literature from Cavalcanti's lyrics to Ariosto's *Orlando furioso*, he has collaborated on several projects with Robert M. Durling, including a monograph on Dante's lyric poetry, *Time and the Crystal: Studies in Dante's Rime Petrose* (1990), and on an edition, with translation, notes, and commentary, of Dante's *Commedia* (1996, 2003, 2011). Recent publications include the article on the *Decameron* in *Boccaccio: A Guide to the Complete Works*, a discussion of spectacle in the Italian Renaissance in *A Companion to the Italian Renaissance*, and an account of Petrarch's Latin verse in *The Cambridge Companion to Petrarch*. He is currently preparing a monograph on appropriations of medieval liturgy in Dante's works.

SARA MENZINGER teaches medieval legal history in the Faculty of Jurisprudence at the Università di 'Roma 3'. Her earliest studies were on legal political thought in Italian medieval cities and on the role of lawyers in urban institutions, *Giuristi e politica nei comuni di Popolo* (2006). Editing one of the oldest medieval treatises on public law, the *Summa Trium Librorum of Rolandus of Lucca* (2012) allowed her to study the dialogue between medieval legal doctrine and Roman legal texts. This led her to her current work on medieval theories of citizenship, and especially on the interaction between definitions of citizenship and tax regulations.

GIULIANO MILANI is Ricercatore at the Università di Roma 'La Sapienza', where he teaches medieval history. He works on the Italian city-states from the twelfth to fourteenth centuries, with particular focus on exclusion of political enemies, administration of justice, and practical uses of writing and images. He is the author of *L'esclusione dal comune. Conflitti e bandi politici a Bologna e in altre città italiane tra XII e XIV secolo* (2003), *I comuni italiani: Secoli XII–XIV* (2005), *Bologna* (2012), and some forty essays.

LINO PERTILE is Carl A. Pescosolido Professor of Romance Languages and Literatures at Harvard University, and Director of The Harvard University Center for Italian Renaissance Studies at Villa I Tatti, Florence. He taught in Italy and Britain before joining Harvard in 1995. His research has focused on Dante, the Renaissance, and Italian literature of the twentieth century. His books include the critical edition of *Annotationi nel Dante fatte con M. Triphon Gabriele* (1993), and the volumes *La puttana e il gigante: dal Cantico dei Cantici al Paradiso terrestre di Dante* (1998) and *La punta del disio: semantica del desiderio nella 'Commedia'* (2005). He co-edited with Peter Brand the *Cambridge History of Italian Literature* (1999).

ANDREA A. ROBIGLIO is Associate Professor of the History of Philosophy at the University of Louvain. He specializes in medieval and Renaissance studies with a focus on social thought, and is the author of *L'impossibile volere. Tommaso d'Aquino, i tomisti e la volontà* (2002) and *La sopravvivenza e la gloria. Appunti sulla formazione della prima scuola tomista – sec. XIV* (2008). He is a member of the Groupe d'Anthropologie Scolastique (EHESS, Paris) and of the Aquinas and the Arabs research consortium. A collection of his essays on Dante will be published in 2015 by Longo Editore.

MIRKO TAVONI is Professor of Italian Linguistics at the Università di Pisa. He has directed the DanteSearch Project (Dante's works lemmatized and morpho-syntactically annotated: www.perunaenciclopediadadantescadigitale.eu:8080/dantesearch). His annotated edition and translation of the *De vulgari eloquentia* appeared in 2012 and his book *Qualche idea su Dante* (2015). A further major research interest is linguistic theories of the fifteenth and sixteenth centuries: a collection of essays on this topic, entitled *Renaissance Linguistics in Italy and in Europe*, is also forthcoming.

JAN M. ZIOLKOWSKI is Arthur Kingsley Porter Professor of Medieval Latin, Harvard University, and Director of Dumbarton Oaks Research Library and Collection, Washington DC. Two of his books examine folk tradition and literature: *Fairy Tales from before Fairy Tales: The Medieval Latin Past of Wonderful Lies* (2007) and *Solomon and Marcolf* (2008). In Virgil scholarship he co-edited *The Virgilian Tradition* (2008) and *The Virgil Encyclopedia* (2013). Other volumes deal with Abelard, musical notation of classics, and twelfth-century poetry. He edited *Dante and the Greeks* (2014) and *Dante and Islam* (2014).

# *Chronology*

## 1250–1350

| | |
|---|---|
| 1250 | Death of Emperor Frederick II. |
| 1252 | First gold florin coined in Florence. |
| 1260 | Battle of Montaperti. Banished Florentine Ghibellines defeat Guelfs. |
| 1265 | May/June Dante born in Florence. Charles of Anjou enters Italy. |
| 1266 | Battle of Benevento. Manfred killed. Guelfs return to Florence. |
| 1289 | Florence defeats Arezzo at Campaldino. |
| 1270–73 | Dante's mother, Bella, dies. |
| 1274 | May: first encounter with Beatrice. |
| 1276 | Guido Guinizzelli dies in Bologna. |
| 1277 | 9 February: marriage contract with Gemma Donati. |
| 1282 | Dante's father, Alighiero di Bellincione, dies. |
| 1282 | War of the 'Sicilian Vespers': the Aragonese rulers (Spanish) replace the Angevin (French) in Sicily. |
| 1283 | Dante publishes first poem. Friendship with Guido Cavalcanti. |
| 1285 | Marriage to Gemma Donati. |
| 1286–87 | Dante writes the *Fiore* and *Detto d'Amore*. |
| 1287 | Dante in Bologna? Beatrice marries Simone de' Bardi. |
| 1287 | Birth of first child, Giovanni (?). |
| 1289 | Dante as horse soldier at the battle of Campaldino against Arezzo. Son Jacopo is born (?). |
| 1290 | Death of Beatrice. Son Pietro is born (?). |

## Chronology xxi

| | |
|---|---|
| 1293 | Ordinances of Justice.<br>Dante writes *Vita nova*.<br>Brunetto Latini dies in Florence. |
| 1294 | December, Pope Celestine V abdicates five months after his election. Boniface VIII becomes pope.<br>Construction of Basilica di Santa Croce begun in Florence. |
| 1295 | Dante enrols in the Guild of Physicians and Apothecaries and enters political life. From November he is a member of the Council of Thirty-Six. |
| 1296 | Dante a member of the Council of the Hundred.<br>Construction of new cathedral (Duomo) begun in Florence. |
| 1299 | Daughter Antonia is born (?).<br>Construction of Palace of the Priors (Palazzo Vecchio) begun in Florence. |
| 1300 | Easter week: Dante's fictional journey to the realms of the afterlife.<br>April: Pope Boniface proclaims the Jubilee Year.<br>May: Florentine Guelfs split into Blacks and Whites.<br>May: Dante is ambassador to San Gimignano on behalf of the Guelfs.<br>15 June–15 August: Dante serves as Prior; signs warrant sending Guido Cavalcanti into exile; Guido dies in the summer. |
| 1301 | April–September: Dante member of the Council of the Hundred.<br>October: Sent on a diplomatic mission to Pope Boniface VIII in Rome.<br>November: Charles of Valois enters Florence; Black Guelph *coup d'état*. |
| 1302 | 27 January: While on his way back to Florence, Dante is fined 5,000 florins and excluded from public office for two years; refuses to pay fine.<br>10 March: sentence confirmed; if caught, Dante will be burnt at the stake.<br>Dante joins exiled White Guelfs in a leading position.<br>Boniface VIII's bull *Unam sanctam*, proclaiming supreme authority. |
| 1303 | Dante in Verona, guest of Bartolomeo della Scala. Probably visits Treviso, Venice, and Padua. Begins *Convivio* and *De vulgari eloquentia*. |

| | |
|---|---|
| | French troops humiliate Pope Boniface at Anagni. Death of Boniface. Benedict XI elected October 1303. |
| 1304 | July: Benedict XI dies. |
| | Dante in Arezzo. Letter to cardinal Niccolò da Prato on behalf of the Whites. |
| | Dante in Bologna, works on *Convivio* and *De vulgari eloquentia* (?). Francesco Petrarca born in Arezzo. |
| | 20 July: White Guelfs and Ghibellines defeated at La Lastra, near Florence. |
| 1305 | Bertrand De Got elected pope with the name of Clement V. Giotto paints the interior of the Scrovegni Chapel in Padua. |
| 1306 | Dante in Lunigiana, guest of Moroello Malaspina. |
| 1307 | Dante in Casentino: letter and *canzone* (*Rime* CXVI) to Moroello Malaspina. |
| 1308 | Henry of Luxembourg chosen to be next Emperor. |
| | Dante in Lucca. In this period he starts writing the *Commedia* and continues until 1320/21. |
| 1309 | Henry crowned emperor as Henry VII at Aix-La-Chapelle (Aachen). |
| | Clement V moves the papacy to Avignon, France, where it remains until 1377. |
| | Robert of Anjou, King of Naples. |
| 1310 | October: Henry VII in Italy. Dante in Poppi, near Arezzo, guest of Guido da Battifolle, writes an open letter to rulers and people of Italy urging them to welcome Henry. |
| 1311 | Henry VII crowned in Milan. |
| | 31 March: Dante writes letter urging the Florentines to open the city to Henry VII. |
| | 17 April: Dante writes to Henry VII exhorting him to attack Florence. |
| 1312 | Henry VII crowned in Rome, but not in St Peter's. |
| | Dante settles in Verona as guest of Cangrande della Scala. He writes or begins writing *Monarchia* (?). |
| 1313 | August: Henry dies of malaria in Buonconvento, near Siena. Giovanni Boccaccio is born in Florence (or Certaldo?). |
| 1314 | Completes *Inferno*. Pope Clement V dies. Dante writes open letter to Italian cardinals urging them to elect an Italian pope. Conclave closes for two years. |
| 1315 | Completes *Purgatorio*. June: Amnesty offered to Florentine exiles; Dante rejects offer. |

# Chronology

October: Florence reconfirms Dante's exile and extends it to his children.

Albertino Mussato crowned poet laureate in Padua.

| | |
|---|---|
| 1316 | Conclave reopens in Lyons. Frenchman Jacques Duèse is elected pope as John XXII. |
| 1318 | Dante leaves Verona and settles in Ravenna as a guest of Guido Novello da Polenta. |
| 1319–20 | Dante writes two Latin eclogues to Giovanni del Virgilio and the *Questio de aqua et terra*. |
| 1320 | 20 January: Dante reads the *Questio de aqua et terra* in a public lecture in Verona. Completes *Paradiso* between 1320 and 1321. |
| 1321 | Dante is sent on a diplomatic mission to Venice by Guido Novello. On his return, he dies of malaria in the night between 13 and 14 September and is buried in Ravenna in the Church of San Pier Maggiore, now San Francesco. |
| 1322 | Commentary to *Inferno* in Latin by Jacopo, son of Dante. |
| 1324 | Commentary to *Inferno* in Latin by Graziolo Bambaglioli, Bologna. |
| 1324–8 | Commentary to the full *Commedia* in Italian by Iacomo della Lana, Bologna. |
| 1327 | Milan: Biblioteca Trivulziana, Ms. 1080: first illustrated ms of the *Commedia*. |
| 1328 | The Dominican Guido Vernani writes the *De reprobatione Monarchiae*, a fierce attack on Dante's political treatise. |
| 1329 | According to Boccaccio, the *Monarchia* is publicly burnt as heretical in Bologna. |
| 1333 | Commentary to *Inferno* in Latin by Guido da Pisa, Pisa (?). |
| 1334 | *Ottimo Commento*, full commentary in Italian. |
| 1335 | The *Commedia* is banned by the Dominican order in Tuscany. |
| 1340 | *Comentum* in Latin by Pietro Alighieri, Verona. |
| 1341 | Petrarch crowned poet laureate in Rome by Robert of Anjou, King of Naples. |
| 1343 | Death of Robert of Anjou and end of Angevin dynasty in Naples. |
| 1343–50 | Commentary on the whole poem in Latin by Alberico da Rosciate, Bergamo. |
| 1347–50 | Black Death. |

# *Abbreviations and note on translations*

The following editions and translations are used throughout, unless otherwise stated.

Bible
: *Biblia Sacra iuxta vulgatam versionem*, ed. R. Weber and R. Gryson, 5th edn (Stuttgart: Deutsche Bibelgesellschaft, 2007).
*The New Jerusalem Bible* (New York: Doubleday, 1990).

*Commedia*
: *La Commedia secondo l'antica vulgata*, ed. G. Petrocchi, 2nd edn, 4 vols. (Florence: Le Lettere, 1994).
*The Divine Comedy*, trans. J. D. Sinclair, 3 vols. (Oxford University Press, 1981); slightly adapted.

*Conv.*
: *Convivio*, ed. F. Brambilla Ageno, 3 vols. (Florence: Le Lettere, 1995).
*Dante's Il Convivio (The Banquet)*, trans. R. H. Lansing (New York: Garland, 1990).

*Detto*
: *Il Fiore e il Detto d'Amore attribuibili a Dante Alighieri*, ed. G. Contini (Milan: Mondadori, 1984), pp. 483–512.
*The Fiore and the Detto d'Amore, A Late 13th-Century Translation of the 'Roman de la Rose' Attributable to Dante*, trans. S. Casciani and C. Kleinhenz (University of Notre Dame Press, 2000), pp. 509–39.

*Dve*
: *De vulgari eloquentia*, ed, P. V. Mengaldo, in Dante Alighieri, *Opere minori*, 2 vols. (Milan and Naples: Ricciardi, 1979–88), vol. II, pp. 1–237.
*De vulgari eloquentia*, trans. S. Botterill (Cambridge University Press, 1996).

*Ecl.*
: *Egloge*, ed. G. Albanese, in Dante, *Opere*, 3 vols. (Milan: Mondadori, 2011–), vol. II, pp. 1593–783.
P. H. Wicksteed and E. G. Gardner, *Dante and Giovanni del Virgilio* (Westminster: Constable, 1902).

## Abbreviations and note on translations

xxv

| | |
|---|---|
| *ED* | *Enciclopedia Dantesca*, 5 vols. (Rome: Istituto della Enciclopedia Italiana, 1970–78). |
| *Ep.* | *Epistole*, ed. C. Villa, in *Opere*, vol. II, pp. 1417–592 *Dantis Alagherii Epistolae: The Letters of Dante*, ed. and trans. P. J. Toynbee, 2nd edn (Oxford: Clarendon Press, 1966). *Four Political Letters*, trans. C. E. Honess (London: MHRA, 2007). |
| *Fiore* | *Il Fiore*, pp. 1–467. *The Fiore*, pp. 35–499. |
| *Inf.* | *Inferno.* |
| *Mon.* | *Monarchia*, ed. P. Shaw (Florence: Le Lettere, 2009). *Monarchy*, trans. P. Shaw (Cambridge University Press, 1996). |
| *Par.* | *Paradiso.* |
| *Purg.* | *Purgatorio.* |
| *Questio* | *Questio de aqua et terra*, ed. F. Mazzoni, in *Opere minori*, vol. II, pp. 693–880. *A Question of the Water and the Land*, trans. C. H. Bromby, in A. Paolucci (ed.), *Dante beyond the Commedia* (New York: Published by Griffon House Publications for The Bagehot Council, 2004), pp. 1–32. |
| *Rime* | *Rime*, ed. D. De Robertis (Florence: Edizioni del Galluzzo, 2005). *Dante's Lyric Poetry*, trans. K. Foster and P. Boyde, 2 vols. (Oxford: Clarendon Press, 1967). |
| *Vn* | *La vita nuova*, rev. ed. M. Barbi (Florence: Bemporad, 1932). *Vita nova*, trans. A. Frisardi (Evanston: Northwestern University Press, 2012). |

All translations from classical Latin authors, unless stated otherwise, are taken from the Loeb Classical Library. All other translations are noted in the individual chapters.

# Introduction

### Zygmunt G. Barański and Lino Pertile

The idea for this book came to us as it comes to every university teacher when preparing a list of secondary readings for a course on Dante. One needs to offer a context, namely, an idea of the cultural, historical, intellectual, and geographical conditions in which Dante lived and wrote. What was happening in Florence around the year 1300, and why was Dante banished? Who were the Guelfs and the Ghibellines, and the Whites and the Blacks? And why were the empire and the Church always at loggerheads? How could the Church be so wealthy when St Francis was so poor? There are also trickier questions that one must be ready to answer – questions concerning vernacular and Latin; genre, language, and style; poetry, philosophy, and theology; religion, heresy, and orthodoxy. And questions concerning everyday life: rich and poor; immigration, the expansion of cities, forms of government, and social change; public health, justice, and injustice; literate and illiterate audiences; the condition of women (Dante does not spare them his invectives, yet he is also sensitive to issues of what today we would term gender difference); not to mention family life, lust, and love (why does Dante write so much about Beatrice, and not a word about his wife Gemma?). Answers do exist, but students, and we their teachers, must extract them from scores of scholarly volumes, each dealing with individual aspects of the economy, society, politics, religion, philosophy, art, literature, and music of the time, just to mention the most obvious subjects the knowledge of which would help facilitate an understanding and an enjoyment of Dante's works. In short, there is no single volume, as far as we are aware, either in English or in Italian, that offers a comprehensive overview of the material, cultural, and intellectual world in which Dante became Dante. This book aims to fill this lacuna by providing original essays on a broad array of facets of life in central and northern Italy at the time of Dante Alighieri, roughly between the middle of the thirteenth and the middle of the fourteenth centuries.

Yet despite the range of *Dante in Context*, its treatment of the late medieval Italian world cannot but be partial and fragmentary. There are issues, such as literature written in Latin in the post-classical age, and especially in the thirteenth and fourteenth centuries, that might have merited chapters of their own. Ultimately, editorial decisions needed to be made, and we feel confident that the decisions we took were appropriate. At the same time, literature in Latin in its many forms does appear at various points in the book. To guide the reader through the book, we have introduced some cross-referencing between chapters. However, we believe that consulting the index, which includes selected names, titles, and subjects, will offer a more effective means both to grasp something of the complexity of the medieval world and of the interconnections that defined it, and to begin to appreciate the cultural weight of a figure like Thomas Aquinas or of a text of the calibre of Boethius' *Consolation of Philosophy*. Although far from exhaustive, the index thus expands the book's range beyond the apparent limits imposed by the ostensible subject-matter of its thirty chapters.

A first series of essays introduces the reader to the economic, social, and political realities of life in Italy around the year 1300, casting light too on the life of the Church and of religious movements outside the Church, on law and justice, and on men and women's experience of everyday life. A second section devoted to intellectual traditions maps out major developments in Western thought, including the presence of Jewish and Islamic currents, and explores the practice of medicine and the understanding of geographic and cosmological space in the culture of the time. A third section deals with linguistic and literary cultures, but also offers chapters on all levels of education, visions and journeys to the other world, and popular culture. A fourth section examines the fast evolving urban spaces, and offers a panoramic view of the extraordinary changes that occurred in the fields of art, architecture, and music. Only at this point, within the contextual framework thus reconstructed, did it seem appropriate to present in a final section an up-to-date overview of Dante's life, works, and reception. In this way, it ought to become apparent how Dante's experiences as man, thinker, and writer were in constant dialogue and tension with the historical events, circumstances, and anxieties of his time. In every chapter, the reader is presented with modes of thinking, being, and behaving that Dante supported and longed to see developed, but also with other ways whose development he abhorred and did his utmost to challenge and stifle. The book closes with a critical reflection on the modalities through which the poet's works were transmitted, received, and read, especially in

# Introduction 3

the two centuries after his death, which highlights how Dante's engagement with the world continues, indeed grows, beyond his own time.

The twenty-five scholars responsible for the essays included in the first four sections of this volume represent together a wide range of expertise and critical traditions in Anglo-American and Italian scholarship. Black is the leading authority on education and schooling and a specialist on classicism in the late Middle Ages; Day is an expert on the Florentine economy before Dante; Hurlburt is a medieval historian specializing in women and gender; English focuses on Sienese life in the thirteenth and fourteenth centuries; Menzinger is a researcher in the history of medieval law; Caferro has written extensively and innovatively on economy, war, and a range of aspects of Trecento Italian society; Cuthbert is a musicologist whose interests combine the music of the fourteenth century as well as computational musicology; Milani is the author of a recent innovative and much acclaimed book on the Italian communes; Dameron is an eminent historian with special expertise on Florentine Church power; Burr is a leading scholar of Olivi and Italian Franciscanism; Bianchi is a world-renowned specialist on medieval ethics and Aristotle; Robiglio works on late medieval philosophy from Aquinas to humanism; Girón Negrón is a well-known comparative literature specialist who works on Arabic and Jewish literature and the history of religion; Tavoni is a historian of the Italian language who has recently been making groundbreaking contributions in Dante studies; Bourdua and Marina are art historians of noteworthy originality; Grant is a most distinguished practitioner of the history of science and McVaugh is a prominent historian of medicine; Ziolkowski is a leading authority in medieval Latin studies, and Gardiner has published extensively on the tradition of journeys and visions; finally Barnes, Cachey, Hawkins, and Martinez all have strong international reputations as Dantists, but they also have separate and powerful specialisms in the topics for which they have been selected to write, while Cherchi is an illustrious historian of Romance literatures.

Though at different stages of their careers, these scholars are all specialists in their separate, individual fields, the majority, we should like to stress, are not professional Dantists. This was a deliberate choice on our part. We wanted to avoid as much as possible viewing late medieval Italy *sub specie Dantis*, as inevitably happens when the focus is placed on the great poet. In this volume, the reader will not find chapters on Dante and politics, Dante and justice, Dante and literature, Dante and music, and so on and so forth. Our authors were instructed to write on politics, justice, and literature in Dante's time but largely independently of him.

Only in a very few cases, when it seemed difficult to deal with certain topics outside of Dante's works (see for example the chapter on popular culture), Dante has provided the basic focus, but this has been very much the exception rather than the norm. By coming to Dante from the context, rather than the other way round, we hope to refine, nuance, and sometimes challenge a number of assumptions that are often made and accepted in Dante studies regarding the poet's historical, economic, and cultural background.

This is not then, and is not meant to be, another collection of essays on Dante, but a book that we are confident will *indirectly* cast new light on Dante and his works. 'Indirectly' is the crucial word here. None of the contributions included is about Dante – except of course the first two chapters in the last section – but all are about the world in which Dante lived and out of which his genius arose. Dante is one of those rare writers whose genius cannot easily be explained as a straightforward product of social, intellectual, or even literary forces and traditions. However, the *Commedia*, just to mention the best known of his works, is – perhaps more than any other poem produced in the West – deeply rooted in its place and time, and one can understand it more clearly and effectively by looking at the picture of the world from which it comes. This is the picture this book intends to sketch.

The collection has been conceived with mainly the needs and questions of undergraduate and graduate students in the English-speaking world in mind. It thus provides a large amount of basic information. However, the essays are not mere syntheses of existing scholarship. All the authors have aimed to provide personal, original overviews of their topics, while also offering suggestions for further reflection and debate on the part of specialized scholars, and even of general readers. By suggesting connections across different historical fields and disciplines, it is hoped that, ultimately, the book will encourage and inspire new research into the relationship between material culture, intellectual traditions, and literary and artistic expression in the late Middle Ages.

*Dante in Context* has not been an easy academic and editorial project. We are thus extremely grateful to Linda Bree and Anna Bond at Cambridge University Press for their constant support, advice, and timely efficiency. Most of all we are thankful for their unflagging patience, as we are for our contributors' forbearance. Demetrio S. Yocum is an excellent and sophisticated indexer and James Cotton is an elegant and painstaking translator. The book has been enriched by their contributions. We are also very pleased to express our warmest gratitude to the Institute for

*Introduction* 5

Scholarship in the Liberal Arts at the University of Notre Dame and to the Department of History of Art, University of Warwick, for their generous financial support toward the costs of the index, translations, and some of the illustrations. Our friends Albert Ascoli, Ted Cachey, Simon Gilson, and Giulio Lepschy gave us invaluable advice at crucial moments in the book's development.

*Dante in Context* has had many 'homes' – Cambridge, England and Massachusetts; Chicago and Notre Dame; Reading and Florence – which are, of course, the places where we live and work, and between which we regularly move. In fact, over the past several years, we have very rarely found ourselves in the same place at the same time. And yet, thanks to the unexpected intimacy offered to us by Skype and to the swift efficiency of electronic communication, collaborating has not been difficult. Indeed, it has been a source of satisfaction and pleasure that has further strengthened our close friendship of now many years. We are both extremely fortunate that, wherever we might be, we always have the support, advice, gentle irony, and love of our partners, Maggie and Anna, to whom the book is dedicated.

PART I

*Politics and society*

CHAPTER I

# Empire, Italy, and Florence

## William Caferro

In June 1273 Pope Gregory X (1210–76) travelled to Florence to make peace between the Guelf and Ghibellines factions. The reconciliation took place in a public ceremony near the Rubaconte bridge (now Ponte alle Grazie) before a crowd of notables that included Charles of Anjou (1226–85), ruler of Naples and vicar of Tuscany, and Baldwin of Flanders (1217–73), the deposed Latin ruler of Constantinople. Gregory went next to Lyons, where at an ecumenical church council (1274) he confirmed the election of Rudolf of Habsburg (1218–91) as Holy Roman Emperor and arranged religious peace with Byzantium and its emperor Michael Palaeologus (1223–82), who had retaken Constantinople in 1261. The act united the Greek and Roman Churches.

In quick succession, Gregory appeared to solve many of the most divisive issues of the day. Contemporary Italian writers expressed great hope at the turn of events. The Dominican chronicler Salimbene de Adam of Parma (1221–*c*.1288) credited Gregory with 'renewing the empire' and praised him as 'just, generous and saintly'. The Roman chronicler Saba Malaspina spoke of the start of a 'golden age' that would bring peace and prosperity to Italy, especially to the troubled *Regno* (Kingdom) and the south.[1] Dante's thoughts, however, are unknown. Gregory X and his deeds at Florence and Lyons do not appear in the poet's work. Gregory's efforts, if indeed truly realistic, came to little. He had hardly left Florence when the factions repudiated their accord and began quarrelling anew. Rudolf of Habsburg became mired in intramural battles in the north against a rival claimant, Otto II (*c*.1230–78), King of Bohemia, and failed to take up his Italian inheritance and the imperial crown, which remained vacant until the advent of Henry VII of Luxembourg (*c*.1275–1313) in Italy forty years later (1310). Charles of Anjou and Michael Palaeologus launched mutual attacks against each other in Albania and Epirus, and Anjou's own authority in southern Italy was soon undermined by revolt in Sicily (1282). Meanwhile, Palaeologus' religious accommodation at Lyons was repudiated at home, and when he died in 1282 he was denied Christian burial by angry Greek prelates.

Italy remained 'a ship without a pilot in a great storm' (*Purg.* VI, 76–7). Dante's adulthood and political career coincided with what historians view as a high point in civic discord and upheaval. The contestants included emperors, popes, the French ruling house, local *signori* (lords), Guelfs, Ghibellines, the *popolo*, members of new emerging social groups, and the *magnati* (see below), namely the traditional elite families. The rivalries were played out against a backdrop of demographic and commercial expansion, and of intellectual ferment that included the rediscovery and reintegration of the works of Aristotle that helped initiate new theories of political organization (see Chapter 21). All these issues are evident in Dante's work and provided the basis for his appeal for peace and justice.

The empire cast a large shadow over Italian politics. Frederick II of Hohenstaufen's (1194–1250) dominion over both Sicily and northern Italy gave de facto meaning to the idea of universal Roman empire. His aggressive policies intensified antagonisms among already bellicose city-states and left a legacy of conflict with popes, who excommunicated him twice and deposed him in 1245. It was during Frederick's reign that the labels Ghibelline and Guelf became firmly fixed as part of the Italian political vocabulary. They derived from a contested German imperial election in the twelfth century and in Italy represented allegiance to the emperor and the Church respectively.

The relationship between the empire and the papacy was a central issue during Dante's lifetime. At its core lay the question of primacy of authority: whether the State or Church possessed plenitude of power, an issue that involved all of Christendom (see Chapter 3). Frederick had reinforced his claim to universal empire by means of Roman law, which he introduced into his kingdom in Sicily through his promulgation of the Constitutions of Melfi in 1231. Papal claims were based on the Donation of Constantine, by which the Roman emperor ceded temporal power to the Church in the fourth century, and on the *translatio imperii* (transfer of empire), according to which Charlemagne in the ninth century received the *imperium* from the Greeks through the intercession of the papacy. Pope Innocent III (b. 1160/61; papacy 1198–1216) gave wide currency to the papal position in two important bulls, *Venerabilem fratrem nostrum* (Our Venerable Brother) and *Per venerabilem* (Through our Venerable Brother), issued in 1202. The former asserted the pope's right to intervene in disputed imperial elections; the second allowed the pontiff the right to settle disputes between the French and English rulers. Innocent's

*Empire, Italy, and Florence*

formulation of papal supremacy remained current in Dante's day and was implicit in Pope Gregory X's affirmation of Rudolf of Habsburg at Lyon in 1274. It was restated by Pope Boniface VIII (b. *c*.1235; papacy 1294–1303) in 1303 and by Pope Clement V (b. *c*.1264; papacy 1305–14) in the Promise at Lausanne (October 1310), just prior to Henry VII's descent into Italy.

The ideological struggle between the papacy and the empire was also a territorial one. Northern and central Italy were divided between those lands subject to imperial jurisdiction and those subject to papal jurisdiction. The former, the so-called kingdom of Italy included Piedmont, Lombardy, Veneto, Emilia Romagna, Liguria, and Tuscany; the latter, the papal state, included Lazio, Umbria, and the Marche. The emperor's sovereign rights allowed him the authority to appoint imperial vicars and legitimize lordships. It also gave him the power to validate acquisitions by cities of lands in the countryside, an overlooked but significant prerogative given the hegemonic nature of Italian communes with regard to their rural lands. The papacy extended its influence through appointment of Church officials and rectors in the papal state. Papal patronage had an important financial dimension. The pope's wealth and standing in Christendom and his contacts throughout Europe allowed merchants to gain access to markets and collect debts. A commercial city like Florence gained much in this regard from alliance with the pope.

The empire nevertheless needs to be understood in its broad political context. Like the rest of Europe, the German state experienced demographic growth. It was expanding territorially, moving primarily in the direction of the eastern Slavic frontier. The empire took part in the interplay of international politics that involved England, France, Aragon, Hungary, Poland, Flanders, and Byzantium. But while neighbouring England and France were becoming more centralized states under strong monarchies, the empire remained steadfastly decentralized. It consisted of a series of independent principalities, seven of which held the right to elect the emperor. Dante described the electors in *Monarchia* as 'proclaimers of divine providence' (III, xvi, 14), but in reality they were often corrupt, and the process permeated with graft. Elections were contested and caught up in international dynastic politics. In successive years, Alfonso X, King of Castile (1221–84), and Richard of Cornwall (1209–72), brother of King Henry III of England (1207–72), were respectively elected Holy Roman Emperor in 1256 and in 1257. Cornwall was supported by the Archbishop of Cologne, an elector whose lands had close commercial ties with England. Alfonso X had the backing of the Archbishop of Trier, another elector who was the sworn enemy of the Archbishop of Cologne.

Alfonso also received support from the French king Louis IX (1214–70), who was then at odds with England. Alfonso claimed personal right to the empire through blood ties to the Hohenstaufen clan; his mother was first cousin of Frederick II.

The French were perennial contenders for the imperial crown. They were territorial rivals of the empire in the old middle kingdom of Lotharingia–Burgundy and had competing interests in Hungary and elsewhere. King Philip III of France (b. 1245; reign 1270–85) actively sought the imperial title against Rudolf of Habsburg in 1271, and subsequent French rulers did the same during vacancies in 1291 and 1308. The persistence of French claims is emblematic of its shared heritage with the empire. French kings, like their German counterparts, saw Charlemagne as a founding father and the key figure in the *translatio* by which Roman *imperium* was transferred from the Byzantine east back to the west. In any case, the connection between the German empire and France remained close. Dante's 'lofty Arrigo' (*Par.* XXX, 127), Henry VII of Luxembourg, spoke French and was a vassal of the French King Philip IV (b. 1268; reign 1285–1314). There were current in Italy in Dante's day two prophecies. One, of French origin, popular in Guelf circles, claimed that a French heir to Charlemagne would come forth and bring peace to Italy. The second, of German origin, popular in Ghibelline circles, maintained that Emperor Frederick II, who was still alive, residing at Mount Aetna, would ultimately return to power and revive the empire. German emperors nevertheless remained weak figures. They held small patrimonies at home and were frequently at war with rivals. Indeed, the success of their candidacies depended in part on their inability to dominate the local political scene. Electors chose those who would not challenge their own authority. Adolf of Nassau (b. *c.* 1255; emperor 1292–98) fought his rival Albert of Austria (b. 1255; emperor 1298–1308), who in turn waged war against the King of Bohemia, as Rudolf of Habsburg had done years earlier.

It is important to stress that European rulers were connected by dynastic ties that also included Italian states. Richard of Cornwall, his brother King Henry III of England, King Louis IX of France, and Charles of Anjou were all married to daughters of Raymond Berenguar V of Toulouse (1198–1245) – 'each a queen' as Dante called the women in *Paradiso* VI, 133. Alfonso X of Castile was the father-in-law of the Italian Marquis of Montferrat, William VII (*c.* 1240–92), who married his daughter to the Byzantine emperor, Andronicus Palaeologus (1259–1332). Count Amadeus V of Savoy (1249–1323) in Piedmont was cousin of Emperor Henry VII and served as his vicar general when he came to Italy. Amadeus' lands

*Empire, Italy, and Florence*

stretched north of the Alps into France, bordering those of the Counts of Anjou, which in turn stretched south of the Alps into Italy to the town of Cuneo. Savoyards were active in England, helping King Henry III build his royal offices there.

The career of Charles of Valois (1270–1325), younger brother of King Philip IV of France, illustrates well the international nature of politics at the time. In addition to his holdings in France, Charles possessed, through his first marriage, rights to Sicily, and by his second marriage, rights to Constantinople. In 1285 he was invested with the kingdoms of Aragon and Valencia, in 1297 he fought for France against Flanders, and in 1308 he was a candidate for Holy Roman Emperor. His mission on behalf of Pope Boniface VIII to Florence, to 'pacify' the city in 1301, led directly to Dante's exile (*Purg.* XX, 71–5).

Italian states were closely connected to the broader Mediterranean world, which possessed a basic unity, linking Constantinople to Tunis to Barcelona. The kingdom of Aragon competed with Italian commercial cities for privileges in northern Africa. Pisa opposed Aragonese attempts to control Sardinia (1295) and recognized the claims of Alfonso of Castile as Roman emperor. Venice and Genoa fought for commercial rights in Constantinople and maintained colonies in the Greek east. Florentine merchants were active in Achaia; the Cerchi bank served as collector of papal funds in Morea. The war of the Sicilian Vespers (1282–1302) underscored the wide-ranging forces at work. It began with a popular revolt in Palermo, but soon involved most of Europe, north and south. The Byzantine ruler, Michael Palaeologus, accused with the Aragonese King Peter III (1239–85) of conspiring to initiate the war, emerged as an important and conspicuous figure. He cast himself as the 'new Constantine', an appellation noted by Italian chroniclers and problematic in terms of contemporary notions of empire. The Byzantines considered themselves Romans (*romaioi*) and heirs of the empire, but they were viewed in the west as Greeks. Palaeologus' open association with the Roman emperor who founded the city of Constantinople and first brought the empire east further complicated the issue.

The Italian peninsula is in any case best understood as a diverse and heterogeneous entity, with a variety of cultural and ethnic influences. The most important cohesive force was the papacy. The circumstances in the late thirteenth century conspired, however, to hamper consistent policy, which increased the volatility of Italian politics. Between 1254 and 1294 the average tenure of popes was only three-and-a-half years. There were four popes elected after the death of Gregory X in 1276, and the Holy

See remained vacant for two full years just prior to the ill-fated papacy of Celestine V (1215–96), who abdicated less than a month after his election in 1294. The crusading zeal that had helped project pontifical authority in earlier years had lost its lustre owing to the current practice of calling out crusades against internal enemies within Europe. Popes were involved in the same family feuds and rivalries as secular princes. The pontiffs sought to build up their territorial interests as a hedge against external and internal rivals. Pope Nicholas III (b. *c.*1216; papacy 1277–80), a member of the powerful Orsini clan, appointed his own relatives to key positions in the papal state and the Romagna, for which he earned the contempt of Dante who placed him in Hell with the simoniacs. Boniface VIII, Nicholas' infernal companion, did the same. A member of the less prominent Caetani clan, Boniface waged continual battle with the Colonna family, against whom he called a crusade in 1297. The departure of the papacy from Rome to Avignon (1305) after Boniface's bruising battle with Philip IV of France added another layer of ambiguity and difficulty to pontifical authority in Italy. The 'Babylonian captivity' of the Church (1309–77) damaged the prestige of the papacy, which was widely viewed as being subject to French royal influence. Boniface, who died shortly before the transfer (1303), was subjected by Philip to trial *in absentia* in France (1310–11), and was charged with heresy and demon worship.

The immediate goal of the papacy after the death of Emperor Frederick II in 1250 was to undo Hohenstaufen encirclement. This did not require the defeat of the Hohenstaufens so much as separating Sicily from the rest of the empire. In 1254 Pope Alexander IV (b. 1199 or *c.*1185; papacy 1254–61) attempted to do so by investing Edmund (1245–96), son of King Henry III of England, with Sicily as a papal fief. But the act proved untenable owing to baronial conflicts in England and the growing strength in Italy of Manfred (1232–66), Frederick II's natural son. Fear of Manfred induced Pope Urban IV (b. *c.* 1195; papacy 1261–64), a Frenchman, in 1263 to invite Charles of Anjou, the brother of King Louis IX, to Italy to take possession of Sicily. Charles arrived in 1266, the year after Dante's birth. He defeated Manfred at the Battle of Benevento (1266) and followed with a victory over Manfred's cousin Conradin (1252–68) at the Battle of Tagliacozzo (1268).

The advent of Charles had fateful consequences for Italy. After Tagliacozzo, he consolidated his hold on Sicily and maintained nominal lordships in central and northern Italy, including the title of imperial vicar of Tuscany, bestowed on him by the pope. According to his biographer Saba Malaspina, Charles' victories caused his ambition to soar

*Empire, Italy, and Florence* 15

and, spurred by ' "accursed hunger for gold" (*Aeneid* III, 57) and desire for world monarchy', he became transformed personally from a 'bearer of arms of justice' to the epitome of 'greed and avarice'.[2] Anjou sought to extend his influence over the entire eastern Mediterranean, including recovering the Latin Empire in Byzantium and controlling the Holy Roman Empire. He attempted to do the latter by promoting the candidacy to emperor of his nephew King Philip III.

Anjou's policies polarized Italian politics and stoked Guelf and Ghibelline rivalries. The chronicler Salimbene de Adam, writing in the years 1283–88, saw Ghibelline and Guelf 'parties and divisions everywhere in Italy' – 'in Tuscany and Lombardy, in the Romagna and the March of Ancona, in the March of Treviso'. He found the worst divisions in Tuscany where, paraphrasing the book of Isaiah, he accused both sides of having 'drunk to the dregs the cup of the wrath of God'.[3] To oppose Charles' Angevin and Guelf hegemony, William VII of Montferrat formed a Ghibelline league consisting of numerous cities extending from Turin to Genoa.

Charles' ascent, however, gave the Guelf cause the upper hand, providing it with an added military and economic dimension. Charles relied heavily on Guelf and papal bankers to finance his activities in Italy. In return the bankers received important concessions from Anjou in Naples and Sicily and privileges from the papacy in the international marketplace. Florentines took over the financial organization of the Neapolitan kingdom, from which the city also derived much of its grain. Charles exerted his authority in Florence through control of the office of *podestà* (the official in charge of maintaining peace and justice in the city), and through personal representatives, such as the French nobleman Jean Britaud of Nangis (d. 1278), for whom Brunetto Latini (*c.*1220–93) worked as a notary. Florence and Anjou's allies joined the Guelf league army (after Benevento in 1266), for which each state provided a *taglia* or share of the overall force. It was therefore the case that the Florentine army of the late thirteenth century was not so much an expression of the city's own power as an element of broad Guelf military strength. Florence remained a member of the Guelf league long after Charles of Anjou's death in 1285 and after internal political reforms had changed the nature of the city's government. The Guelf league meanwhile brought to Florence a succession of mercenary captains, some from local feudatories in Tuscany and the Romagna, and some from France, such as Amerigo of Narbonne (*c.*1230–98), who was the author of *chansons de geste*, and, like Dante, fought at Campaldino in 1289, where he was wounded in the face. Dante himself participated directly in Guelf league-related business, travelling in May 1300 to San Gimignano on behalf of Florence to seek an increase of the *taglia* offered by that city. It was as a member of a Guelf league army in 1311–13 that Florence opposed Henry VII when he came to Italy.

For all the use of the terms by contemporaries, the precise meaning of Ghibelline and Guelf is far from clear. They represented in the first instance allegiances to imperial and papal parties respectively. But the simple distinction is inadequate. As we have already seen in the case of Rudolf of Habsburg and Gregory X, emperors and popes were often allied to each other in this period. Conversely, the ties between the papacy and the Angevins wavered during the tenure of different popes. Charles of Anjou's victories had effectively replaced Hohenstaufen domination in Italy with Angevin domination, leaving the pope again encircled. Gregory X's fear of this led him to support Rudolf of Habsburg, from whom he sought the cession of the Romagna to add to the papal state. Gregory's successor Nicholas III pursued a similar policy.

There was a tendency among contemporaries to associate Ghibellines with the nobility and military class, and the Guelfs with more commercial elements. The Dominican rector of Santa Maria Novella, Remigio de' Girolami (d. 1319), implicitly drew on this notion when he described Ghibellines as 'lions' for their bellicose ways, and the Guelfs as 'calves', a meek sacrificial animal.[4] Niccolò Machiavelli (1469–1527), in his *Florentine Histories*, saw the Guelfs and Ghibellines as 'humours' rather than actual parties. He nevertheless, like Salimbene, credited them with 'tearing apart Italy' with their disputes.[5]

Whatever their precise nature, Guelf and Ghibelline represent useful labels, both then and now, to structure the political chaos of late-thirteenth- and early-fourteenth-century Italy. The ruling elite of cities defined themselves according to the terms, and exiled those who took opposing views. The exiles spread the divisions, giving them a supra-communal aspect that one scholar has compared to the modern-day NATO alliance. Guelf exiles of one city would seek refuge with like-minded enemies, thus linking cities together in a chequerboard of conflicting interests. Pisa and Cremona were traditionally Ghibelline, while their neighbours Florence and Milan had Guelf ties. Ghibelline Modena generally opposed Guelf Bologna and Mantua; Ferrara and Padua formed Guelf alliances against Ghibelline Verona. The Guelf–Ghibelline labels often functioned as political markers that had little real connection with the papacy or the empire, and often appeared more as a symptom of factional discords than the cause of them. The labels were in any case easily disposed of by their own proponents for the sake of political expediency. The Guelf ruler Obizzo II Este of Ferrara (b. *c*.1247; reign 1247–93) formed an alliance in 1289 with the Ghibelline ruler Alberto della Scala of Verona (b. *c*.1245; reign 1277–1301) against his Guelf neighbours. This confused the polarities in the region, which became still more muddled when Pope Clement V asserted direct claim over the city of Ferrara in 1308, initiating an infra-Guelf struggle between the papacy and the Este family.

It is nevertheless important to stress that the parties did not encompass all of Italy. They made little headway in Venice, where internal political cohesion was the subject of a self-propagated 'myth'. The Venetian doge and chronicler Andrea Dandolo (1306–54) demonstrated little real understanding of the rivalry, when he described Guelf and Ghibellines as the names of two brothers from Tuscany. Dandolo nevertheless well understood the destructive power of the parties, seeing in them a diabolical spirit, an opinion shared by the Milanese chronicler Pietro Azario (1312–d. after 1366) who claimed that the terms derived from two actual devils, Gualef and Gibel.[6]

What is undeniably clear from contemporary accounts is that the Guelf–Ghibelline controversy was characteristic of the endemic violence that plagued Italy in the age of Dante. It was fuelled in the first instance by the expansionist policies of states closely packed in a small geographic area and by family feuds that were a basic feature of Italian society. Indeed, Italian city-states may be distinguished from their northern urban counterparts by their enduring interest in territorial conquest and by their social make-up, which included an aristocratic landholding class (*magnati*) that was at once rural and urban, with land in the countryside and involvement in commerce and industry in the city. Italian aristocratic families arranged themselves into corporations, *consorterie*, that functioned as kinship groups of mutual assistance. They possessed their own statutes and councils, which allowed them to act independently of political structures. This encouraged rivalries and vendettas and feuds on a grand scale, fought within cities from towers.

The excesses of the aristocracy were opposed by a rising commercial classes of 'new' men or *popolo*. The group is perhaps best understood as a self-appointed counterweight to the elite, against whom they consciously defined themselves and whose penchant for violence in the urban setting they sought to diminish. The *popolo* consisted of those who 'bought and sold'. It was subdivided into those with substantial wealth (*popolo grasso*) and those with more modest means (*popolo minuto*), excluding the poor and humble. The *popolo*, like the magnates, arranged itself into corporations, often craft guilds, through which it extended its political power. A Bolognese civil code in 1282 described the *popolo* and *magnati* in language strikingly similar to that used by Remigio de' Girolami for Guelfs and Ghibellines. It compared the latter to wolves, on account of their martial bearing and violent ways, and the former to meek lambs. Machiavelli spoke of a 'natural enmity' existing between the *popolo* and *magnati*, stemming from the desire of the latter to command and the former not to obey them.[7]

The atmosphere of intense rivalry facilitated the rise of strongmen or lords (*signori*), who pledged to restore order. Frederick II's lieutenant Ezzelino da Romano (1194–1259) from the March of Treviso represented the first wave of such men, establishing dominion over the cities of Verona, Vicenza, and Padua. His aggressive policies and autocratic persona, however, gave lords an enduringly bad reputation. The chronicler Rolandino of Padua (1200–76) compared Ezzelino to the devil, and Dante placed him in the seventh circle of Hell alongside Obizzo II Este of Ferrara (*Inf.* XII, 109–12). Obizzo was likewise described – by Riccobaldo of Ferrara (1245–1318) in his *Chronica Parva Ferrariensis* (Little Chronicle of Ferrara) – as the incarnation of evil. Riccobaldo argued, however, that Obizzo's ability to do evil ultimately made him more powerful than God because the Almighty could do only good.

The 'rise of the *signori*' is a well-worn theme in Italian scholarship, highlighted by Jacob Burckhardt and Joseph Addington Symonds, among others. Apart from the personal characteristics of the lords, what distinguished them, as Riccobaldo suggested, was their power. The lords took charge of the political machinery of the states they dominated, sometimes overtly, sometimes behind the scenes, and in this way brought a degree of order. The Este of Ferrara, like Charles of Anjou, controlled the office of *podestà*; Alberto Scotto of Piacenza (1290–1317) served as captain of the people and rector of the merchant guild; the della Scala of Verona were heads of the *mercanzia* (merchant guild). Gherardo da Camino (1240–1306) assumed the more overt title of *capitano generale* (captain general) of Treviso, which afforded him the right to 'to do and act according to his will'.

The lordships were most developed in Lombardy, Piedmont, Treviso, Emilia, and the Marche. The *signori* themselves came from a variety of backgrounds. Cangrande della Scala of Verona (1291–1329), Dante's patron, who dominated Treviso in the early fourteenth century, was from *popolano* origins. His antagonists, the Este family of Ferrara, sprang from the old nobility. The Della Torre and Visconti, who vied for control of

## Empire, Italy, and Florence

Milan, were *popolo* and *magnati* respectively. Piedmont was dominated by feudal aristocratic houses, including the counts of Savoy in Susa and the Aosta valley and the marques of Montferrat in the upper Po and Varaita valley. The Romagna, the site of continuous warfare (*Inf.* XXVII, 37–8), was home to numerous powerful feudatories, including the Ordelaffi of Forlì, Manfredi of Faenza, and the da Polenta of Rimini. Guido Novello da Polenta (*c.*1250–1310), Manfred Hohenstaufen's former vicar, assumed the lordship of Ravenna in 1275.

Dante lamented the political status quo, complaining in *Purgatorio* VI, 124–5 that 'the cities of Italy are full of tyrants'. The equation of lord with tyrant must, however, be treated with care. For Symonds in the nineteenth century and much of the Anglo-American scholarship that followed, the term was necessarily pejorative. Lordships were a synonym for oppressive rule, despotism, and the antithesis of freedom, liberty, and republicanism that stood as a distant model for modern western democracies. Recent scholarship has, however, softened the distinction, arguing that the difference between lordships and republics was less than supposed. Both shared similar oligarchic structures and restrictions on individual liberty, and sought the same powers to protect property, prevent lawlessness, and acquire revenue. Medieval republics were hardly modern democracies, and 'tyrannical' lords, such as Gherardo da Camino and Cangrande della Scala, were among the most generous patrons of the day. Dante, who benefitted from the largesse of both, displays an ambiguous attitude toward this class of men. He praised 'good Gherardo' in both *Purgatorio* (XVI, 124–38) and *Convivio* (IV, xiv, 12) and lauded Cangrande's virtues in *Paradiso* (XVI, 70–93). But he described Guido da Montefeltro (1220–94), lord of Urbino, as a 'most noble Latin' in *Convivio* (IV, xxviii, 28) and consigned him to the pit of Hell in the *Commedia* (*Inf.* XXVII).

In any case, the lordships of the late thirteenth and early fourteenth century represented a wide range of types of regimes, the details of which scholars have still not entirely illuminated. A few *signori*, such as the Este of Ferrara and the Visconti of Milan, remained in power for the long run. The Guelf and Ghibelline controversy allowed some lordships to grow rapidly into regional entities. But many faded as quickly as they formed. This was the case of William VII of Montferrat, who, in the name of the Ghibelline cause, extended his rule over cities in Piedmont and Lombardy including Como, Vercelli, Alessandria, and Milan. But the constellation fell apart when William died. Similarly, Guido da Montefeltro spread his sway over several communes as leader of the Ghibelline league that opposed papal interests in the Romagna. After victories in 1275 and 1282, however, Guido abandoned the league, sought reconciliation with the Church and joined the Franciscan order in 1296 (see *Inf.* XXVII). The *signori* were thus largely ephemeral. But they nevertheless represented the wave of the future. By the end of the fourteenth century, Italy saw the establishment of more permanent regimes. From these evolved the principalities associated with the Renaissance era.

The city of Florence remained a republic, if a troubled one. 'The divided city' (*Inf.* VI, 61), as Dante called it, was assailed by the same divisive forces operating throughout Italy. It suffered greatly from the Guelf–Ghibelline controversy, which, as contemporaries such as Salimbene de Adam noted, was most fiercely contested in Tuscany. We know much more about the particulars in Florence, however, owing to the numerous extant contemporary accounts, all of which stress the local penchant for violence and civic discord. Brunetto Latini in his *Livres dou Tresor* (Books of Treasure) explained Florence's bellicosity – which led to his own exile – as the consequence of the city's founding on land dedicated to Mars, the god of war. The chronicler Ricordano Malaspini said that the Florentines were 'always fighting battles and war, and when they had no other opponent, they fought among themselves'.[8]

The Guelf–Ghibelline dispute in Florence purportedly originated with the murder of a nobleman, Buondelmonte de' Buondelmonti on Easter Sunday 1215. Buondelmonti was killed at the base of the statue of Mars by members of the Amidei family (*Inf.* XXVIII, 106–8; *Par.* XVI, 140) who, along with other enemies of the Buondelmonti, formed a Ghibelline party in opposition to the political orientation of the deceased and the city itself, which was Guelf. The Florentine Dino Compagni (*c.*1255–1324) began his chronicle with the deed, which he saw as initiating continuous civil war that culminated in the White and Black Guelf controversy that ultimately led to the end of Compagni's political career and Dante's exile. The Buondelmonti story is, however, instructive of the complicated nature of Florentine factionalism. At the centre of the dispute was family rivalry and vendetta, suggestive of the personal nature of civic unrest and party politics in the city, for which the labels Guelf and Ghibelline are insufficient.

The divisions within Florence were accentuated by the presence of a strong commercial sector associated with the *popolo*. The city had grown in the thirteenth century into an economic colossus, the home of international merchant banks and a vibrant wool cloth industry. It attracted new immigrants – the 'confusion of people' that Cacciaguida (*c.*1091–*c.*1148) complains of in *Paradiso* XVI, 67 – it expanded its town walls, widened streets, and undertook new building projects, including at Santa Maria Novella in 1280, the hospital of Santa Maria Nuova in 1286, and the cathedral in 1295. Pope Boniface VIII described Florence as a 'fifth element' that ruled the world along with 'earth, water, fire and air'.[9]

The *popolo* played a critical role in Florentine affairs. Politically, they represented an alternative to the party regimes of Guelf and Ghibelline, although they were not entirely distinct from them. The *popolo* expressed its political power through craft guilds and stood in direct opposition to the interests of the *magnati*, who were associated with knighthood and military power and constituted, in the opinion of the *popolo*, a threat to the common good. The influence of the Florentine *popolo* was so strong that it is evident even in Dante, who, despite his overt antipathy toward the class, used its language and even echoed its views in his condemnation of the factions of the day. Indeed, the force of the *popolo* and its deep-seated antagonism toward the *magnati* has led scholars to interpret Florentine society and politics in distinctly Marxist terms. Gaetano Salvemini famously depicted Florentine political struggles as reflecting class conflict between a feudal landed aristocracy (*magnati*) and a rising commercial bourgeoisie (*popolo*). More recent scholarship has, however, viewed the distinction as too simple. The *popolo* and *magnati* were, upon close inspection, difficult to separate from each other. Not all those designated as *magnati* were in fact from the noble class, nor were all those identified as *popolo* from the mercantile class. It may well have been that the term magnate was employed to brand opponents not unlike the way the term 'communist' has been used in the modern day.

After Charles of Anjou's victory at Benevento in 1266, Florence moved to a more permanent Guelf orientation. Florence's economic might and nearness to papal lands made the city an important part of Angevin and papal strategy. This fact lay behind Gregory X's efforts to settle the divisions in Florence in 1273 and Pope Nicholas III's subsequent attempt in 1280, when he sent his nephew Cardinal Latino Malabranca (d. 1294) to arrange peace in the city. The financial links, initiated during the advent of Charles of Anjou in Italy, grew stronger with the outbreak of the war of the Sicilian Vespers (1282). Florentine bankers heavily subsidized both Anjou and the papacy. Indeed, Boniface VIII did well to praise the economic potency of Florence, for he was particularly reliant on Florentine bankers to finance his activities, including his ongoing battle with the Colonna family.

It was, nevertheless, the war of the Sicilian Vespers that helped to loosen Angevin political influence in Florence. Shortly after the war began, the Florentine *popolo* passed reforms (1282) that shifted power to them and their guilds, and away from the magnates. Chief among the reforms was the establishment of a 'priorate' with executive powers, consisting initially of three men and then six, taken from the twelve major guilds (*arti maggiori*). The measures constituted a significant step in transforming Florentine government and broadening participation in it. But they did not succeed in removing the wealthy magnates from power. Dino Compagni complained bitterly about this, and of the corruption of the new regime that was unable to 'protect the weak from the strong'.[10] Ten years later, under the guidance of Giano della Bella (*c.*1240–*c.*1305; *Par.* XVI, 130–1), a member of the old nobility with wide support from the *popolo*, Florence passed a more sweeping set of reforms, including the famous Ordinances of Justice in January 1293. Employing egalitarian language of representation and popular sovereignty, the Ordinances further broadened the base of the popular regime. It expanded the number of guilds eligible for the priorate and placed additional restrictions on magnates, who were now required to post surety for good behaviour and were effectively deprived of all political rights. A wholly new office, the Standard Bearer of Justice, was established to enforce sentences against magnates without formal trials. Lists of proscribed magnates were drawn up. They included men with both Guelf and Ghibelline ties, representing much of the Florentine economic elite. The lists reinforce the egalitarian nature of the Ordinances that appear aimed at securing participation for lower-level, non-elite guildsmen in the Florentine government.

Giano della Bella's government lasted from 1293 to 1295, but collapsed in March 1295 under the weight of opposition from the magnates. Giano himself was forced into exile. According to Compagni, Florence 'fell into fresh dangers', including a return to factionalism among powerful families.[11] It was at this time that Dante began his political career (1295), two years after the death of Brunetto Latini and the start of the pontificate of Boniface VIII. Dante's political career lasted for seven years. He was elected to the post of prior in 1300 (15 June to 15 August), the fictional year of his journey in the *Commedia*.

Dante's tenure in public office coincided with the outbreak of the great Black and White Guelf dispute that ultimately led to the poet's exile. Ptolemy of Lucca (*c.*1236–1327), who was a prior of Santa Maria Novella at the time, accused the participants of 'fracturing all of Tuscany' with their violent acts, which he noted were accompanied by earthquakes and divine augurs.[12] The Florentine Black Guelfs were led by Corso Donati (d. 1308); the Whites were led by Vieri dei Cerchi (d. 1313). Both men were

*Empire, Italy, and Florence* 23

members of prominent aristocratic families with deep roots in the city. The Donati and their followers represented an older, more established elite; the Cerchi and their followers were seen as more nouveaux riches. But there was in fact no clear distinction between the sides according to economic and social status or even ideology. The disagreement had the aspect of feud and family rivalry, which in turn may help to explain its intensely destructive nature.

Pope Boniface VIII's attempt to mediate the dispute brought the situation to a head. Following the tradition of popes Gregory and Nicholas, Boniface sent envoys to Florence to make peace between the parties. But Boniface's own circumstances were exceedingly precarious at the time. His authority in Italy was threatened by the Colonna clan and by the Spiritual Franciscans and their leader Jacopone da Todi (1230–1306), who supported the Colonna's challenge to the pope's legitimacy. Boniface also faced international pressure: from France, where his battle over plenitude of power with King Philip IV was intensifying; and from the empire and its presumptive heir Albert of Habsburg, whom Boniface would not recognize until he gained imperial rights to Tuscany. In Florence, Boniface gave his support to the Black Guelfs, whose adherence to the papal cause was more steadfast than the independent-minded Whites. After the failure of several initial attempts, in November 1301 Boniface sent Charles of Valois to Florence as his envoy with the title of *paciarius* or peacemaker. Charles of Valois' mission to the city was the first stop on a broader military expedition to Sicily, to support the flagging Angevin efforts there. Remigio de' Girolami gave a public sermon in Florence welcoming Charles and urging him to use his authority to bring the factions together.

Valois' embassy to Florence on behalf of peace ended in war; his expedition to Sicily for war ended in peace (the Treaty of Caltabellotta, 1302). In Florence, Valois sided with the Blacks, who then attacked their opponents and ransacked the city. They sent the White Guelfs into exile, and Dante, who supported the Whites, was condemned as well. The city passed sentence against Dante in January 1302. A little more than a year later, Pope Boniface – his dispute with Philip IV of France reaching its culmination – would be humiliated by the king's men at Anagni. Pope Clement V moved the papacy from Rome to Avignon, where it remained until 1378.

It was in this context of political turmoil that Dante's political views emerged most fully. Dante repudiated the sovereign city-state that had cast him out in favour of universal empire founded on Rome and sanctioned by God. The precise timing of Dante's conversion to 'Ghibelline' doctrine has been the subject of much scholarly speculation. But the endeavour seems of dubious merit given the imprecise and shifting nature of Guelf and Ghibelline ideologies. Dante's political views may be more effectively rendered in generic terms: that he supported the party that lost the struggle for control of Florence, then rejected Florence, and with it the primacy of the city-state as a political form.

For Dante, empire represented universal authority, won by the Romans and extending geographically over the whole world. It regulated the civil order and was necessary for the well-being of mankind in both this world and the next one. Its divinely appointed mission was to restrain cupidity, the chief obstacle to justice and mankind's goal of achieving happiness. Dante drew for his notion of imperial jurisdiction on both Augustine and Aristotle. Empire was a remedy for man's defects, which for Augustine was a result of the Fall and for Aristotle was natural to humankind. Dante's construct also relied upon Virgil, who in *Aeneid* I, 278 has Jupiter proclaim that it is to the Romans that 'I have given Empire without end'. In Dante's schema, the Romans were a chosen people, whose status owed to their nobility and was made manifest by divine signs, including the birth and crucifixion of Christ under Roman rule (*Conv.* IV, v; *Mon.* II, x, 110). The empire existed prior in time to the papacy, which had no right to temporal power. In *Paradiso* VI, in the heaven of Mercury, Dante presents Justinian (527–65) as the ideal figure of the emperor and the proper relationship between the empire and the Church. Justinian restored the empire's universal authority, bringing it and its symbol, the imperial eagle, from the 'bounds of Europe' (*Par.* VI, 5) in the Byzantine east, where it had been taken by Constantine, back to the west, uniting both sides. He did so while moving in step with Pope Agapetus (d. 536), who offered spiritual consultation and correction of religious error. Justinian brought divine justice to the earthly realm through the codification of Roman law.

If Justinian was Dante's ideal Roman emperor of the distant past, Henry VII of Luxembourg represented for him a present-day model and an earthly hope for restoration of the proper political order. Henry was by all accounts an impressive man. Compagni described him (like Dante's Justinian) as 'wise', 'just', 'loyal', 'bold', and 'noble' (though noting that he was 'somewhat cross-eyed'[13]). In his epistle to Italian rulers, Dante enthusiastically welcomed Henry as 'Caesar', 'Roman prince', and 'Sun of peace' (*Ep.* V, 1–2, 7). He compared his mission to that of Moses leading the Israelites from slavery and saw in it the start of a new era of consolation and peace. Compagni claimed that Henry's sojourn represented the will of omnipotent God that Henry should 'come strike down and punish the tyrants of Lombardy and Tuscany, until all tyranny was extinguished'.[14]

Despite initial support from both Guelf and Ghibelline states and Pope Clement V, Henry's impetus in Italy quickly dissipated. His appointment of imperial vicars, repatriation of exiles, and imposition of taxes led to rebellions against his authority, including in Milan, which had first welcomed him. Florence spearheaded the military opposition against Henry, forming a league with the cities of Lucca, Siena, and Bologna and eventually with Robert, ruler of Naples (1278–1343). Pope Clement withdrew his support of Henry in favour of King Robert. Henry made it to Rome, where he received the imperial crown at the Lateran palace from Cardinal Niccolò da Prato (c.1250–1321) in June 1312. But the act meant little. Henry waged war against his opponents in Tuscany and in 1313 died in the town of Buonconvento, south of Siena, and was buried in Ghibelline Pisa. In the end, Henry VII's intervention in Italy only exacerbated the Guelf–Ghibelline disputes he had intended to pacify.

The continuing conflict stimulated much political literature. Indeed, Dante's appeal to empire is best understood in the context of widespread contemporary calls for peace, expressed both in visual and written media, and in works that have not all received close examination from modern scholars. The late thirteenth and early fourteenth centuries were highly productive in terms of medieval political thought and production of political treatises. The writings addressed the rivalry between the papacy and the empire, as well as the conflict between Pope Boniface and Philip IV and the discord among and within Italian cities. The works bear the influence of Aristotle and the scholastic tradition. Ptolemy of Lucca was likely completing Thomas Aquinas' *De Regimine Principum* in Florence at the time of Charles of Valois' advent in the city in 1301. Remigio de' Girolami's two political tracts, *De bono communi* (On the Common Good; 1302) and *De bono pacis* (On the Benefit of Peace; 1304), which grew out of the violence in Florence at that time, employed Aristotle's *Politics* and *Ethics* for the central argument that the good of the whole community must be placed above the advancement of the individual. Meanwhile Giles of Rome (c.1243–1316) used Aristotle in his *De ecclesiastica potestate* (On the Power of the Church; 1302) to help support Pope Boniface's claim to the primacy of spiritual power and right to intervene in secular affairs. John of Paris (c.1255–1306) in turn refuted Giles' assertions, using Aristotle (*De regia potestate et papali* (On Regal and Papal Power; 1302/03) to support King Philip IV's claim that the priesthood was wholly spiritual.

Like Dante, contemporaries argued in favour of the universal nature of empire. Indeed, Manfred Hohenstaufen, just prior to Charles of Anjou's descent into Italy (1265), had penned a manifesto that asserted, as Dante does in the *Commedia* and *Monarchia*, the primacy of the Roman empire above all nations of the world using Scripture and Roman law to support his thesis. The German chronicler and canon of Cologne, Alexander of Roes (d. after 1288), argued in his *Memoriale de prerogativa romani imperii* (Reminder of the Prerogative of the Roman Empire; 1281) that the foundation of the Roman empire was the result of divine providence. He believed, as did Dante, that the empire was necessary for mankind's salvation, and was divinely sanctioned by the incarnation of Jesus Christ under Roman rule. The *imperium* was then transferred to the Germans by way of Charlemagne and the *translatio*. The Benedictine abbot Engelbert of Admont (*c.* 1250–1331), a student of philosophy at Padua, drew on Aristotle and Augustine to argue that the empire was necessary for the well-being of the human race and responsible for the establishment of peace and justice in the world. All rulers were subject to the Roman emperor, who stood at the apex of a pyramid that had the city as its base. Engelbert stated this thesis in *De ortu et fine Romani imperii* (The Origin and End of the Roman Empire), which was written (1307–10) at approximately the same time that Dante's hero, Henry VII, descended on Italy.

Some scholars have dismissed Alexander and Engelbert as intellectual lightweights. But what is clear is that the issue of empire was broadly engaged at this time, in the work of a wide range of contemporary writers. They grappled not only with the conflicting claims of universal authority by the Church and state, but with the precise relationship between Rome and the western claim to empire and Byzantium and the eastern claim to empire. Writers sorted through rival German and French imperial claims, which were in turn linked to emerging notions of state sovereignty that would ultimately extinguish the idea of universal empire altogether. Alexander of Roes purposefully sought to establish a German claim to empire against French counterclaims, which had cast Charlemagne as a French ruler, and the *translatio* by consequence as a transfer of the *imperium* from the Greeks to the French. Brunetto Latini offered a pro-French interpretation of Charlemagne and the *translatio* in his *Livres dou Tresor.*

The actions of Pope Gregory X and his deeds at the Council of Lyons – with which we began this chapter – played a significant role in contemporary discussions of empire. The Venetian chronicler Martino da Canal abruptly stopped his narrative in *Estoires* (Histories; begun in 1267) of the 'notable deeds' of his native city when he reached Lyons. He addressed his readers directly about the question of empire: whether the east or west held priority. He decided that the issue was too big to discuss at length without obscuring the purpose of his chronicle, which was intended only

# Empire, Italy, and Florence

to honour Venice.[15] Marin Sanudo (*c*.1270–*c*.1343), writing some fifty years later, treated Lyons as a dramatic high point of his *Istoria del Regno di Roamania* (History of the Kingdom of Romania; 1328–33). He credited the council with reuniting the eastern and western parts of the 'Roman empire', which had been 'torn asunder' by the *translatio*, after which there was 'no love left between the Greeks and Latins'. Sanudo portrayed the Byzantine emperor Michael Palaeologus as a heroic figure, who, not unlike Dante's Justinian, united the empire, bringing together east and west, after assuming the proper faith.[16]

The east–west dimension of empire is also evident in the writings of Riccobaldo of Ferrara, whose work Dante may have known. Like the poet, Riccobaldo was exiled from his native city, took part in the circle of Cangrande della Scala of Verona, lived for a time in Ravenna, and enthusiastically supported Emperor Henry VII. In *Compilatio chronologica* (Chronological Compilation; 1313) Riccobaldo gave, along with a Dantesque affirmation of the 'good old days' and condemnation of contemporary mores, a history of the Roman *imperium*, which, as in *Paradiso* VI, stressed the primacy of empire over the papacy. But unlike *Paradiso* VI, which treats empire as a wholly western phenomenon, Riccobaldo dwells on the divisions between the two sides. Like Martino da Canal, Riccobaldo addressed his audience directly about the issue. He asserted that the western claim to *imperium* was ultimately more 'worthy' than the eastern one. He described the west as 'the tree and root' of empire, while the east was merely a branch that would shrivel and die without the former.[17] Riccobaldo's careful delineation of eastern claims to *imperium* is all the more noteworthy because he wrote during the reign of the Byzantine emperor Andronicus Palaeologus (b. 1259; reign 1282–1332), who, unlike his father Michael, had largely receded from western affairs. Byzantium had become more interested in its Hellenic past rather than claims to the Roman empire.

Riccobaldo's attitude nevertheless emphasizes the complexity of the contemporary understanding of empire, and particularly of the *translatio* and the role played in it by Charlemagne. The issue was not merely one of Church and State: whether Charlemagne crowned himself or the pope did so. It involved also consideration of whether the *imperium* could be divided between east and west, which involved contemplation of the nature of Charlemagne's relationship with the eastern Empire and the manner in which he received the *imperium*. The importance of this issue has been largely overlooked by modern scholars, who studied empire too narrowly in its western context.

The concern about the nature of the *translatio* is reflected in numerous contemporary treatises produced on the subject. Ptolemy of Lucca wrote two tracts. The first, his earliest surviving work, completed perhaps in 1276–77 was composed on behalf of Pope Nicholas III. The second, believed to have been finished in 1308, was written to reassert papal authority over the empire, on the occasion of Philip IV's attempt to install Charles of Valois as emperor prior to the election of Henry VII in 1308. Ptolemy's treatise served as the basis for Landolfo of Colonna's (*c.*1250–1331) *De translatione imperii* (On the Transfer of Empire; 1324), which employed similar arguments to support Pope John XXII's (b. 1244; papacy 1316–34) claims to universal power against those of Emperor Ludwig of Bavaria (1282–1347). Landolfo's treatise drew response from no less a figure than Marsilio of Padua (*c.*1275–*c.*1342), whose *De translatione imperii* argued the opposite point: that the papacy had no right to involve itself in secular affairs and to interfere with the emperor, and, indeed, played little role in the original *translatio* of the empire to Charlemagne.

The example of Marsilio of Padua takes us beyond Dante's lifetime. It makes clear, however, that the outstanding issues of Dante's day remained unsettled. The battle between the empire and the papacy continued, with Lewis of Bavaria and John XXII cast in the principal roles. Marsilio issued a call for peace and limits to papal authority in his *Defender of the Peace* (1324), which appeared three years after Dante's death. The 'dream' of universal empire was nevertheless rapidly fading. Henry VII had indeed already exposed its limits during his sojourn in Italy. When King Robert of Naples moved against him (1312), the emperor charged Robert with treason and summoned him to an imperial tribunal in Pisa. But Robert refused to go and submitted the case to Pope Clement V, who issued a bull, *Pastoralis cura* (Pastoral Care; 1313), which was in effect the first legal expression of territorial sovereignty. Clement ruled that an emperor could not judge a king, and by implication, that no ruler was subject to another and that public power was territorially confined. By the middle years of the fourteenth century, the empire had effectively lost its claims to universal power. When Emperor Charles IV (b. 1316; reign 1346–78) came to Italy in 1355 and 1363, it was primarily to collect subsidies. What remained, however, was internecine violence and civic discord that continued to afflict the peninsula and the city of Florence.

## Empire, Italy, and Florence

### Notes

1 *The Chronicle of Salimbene de Adam*, trans. and ed. J. L. Baird, G. Baglivie, and J. R. Kane (Binghamton: MRTS, 1986), pp. 498–9, 503; Saba Malaspina, *Rerum Sicularum, Die Chronik des Saba Malaspina,* ed. W. Koller and A. Nitschke (Hannover: Hanschke Buchhandlung, 1999), pp. 239–40.
2 Malaspina, *Rerum Sicularum*, p. 241.
3 *The Chronicle of Salimbene de Adam*, p. 381.
4 Quoted by C. T. Davis, 'An early Florentine political theorist', *Proceedings of the American Philosophical Society*, 105 (1960), 662–76, at 667.
5 N. Machiavelli, *Florentine Histories*, trans. L. F. Banfield and H. C. Mansfield (Princeton University Press, 1988), p. 15.
6 A. Dandolo, *Chronica*, ed. E. Pastorello (Bologna: Zanichelli, 1938), p. 45.
7 Machiavelli, *Florentine Histories*, p. 105.
8 Brunetto Latini, *Li livres dou tresor*, trans. S. Baldwin and P. Barrette (Tempe: ACMRS, 2003), p. 26; R. Malaspini, Storia fiorentina in *Rerum italicarum scriptores*, ed. L. A. Muratori (Milan: Societas Palatina, 1726), vol. VIII, col. 883.
9 Quoted in G. Holmes, *Florence, Rome and the Origins of the Renaissance* (Oxford: Clarendon Press, 1986), p. 36.
10 *The Chronicle of Salimbene de Adam*, p. 9.
11 *The Chronicle of Salimbene de Adam*, p. 22.
12 Ptolemy of Lucca, Annales in *Rerum italicarum scriptores*, ed. L. A. Muratori (Milan: Societas Palatina, 1727), vol. XI, cols. 1249–1306.
13 *The Chronicle of Salimbene de Adam*, p. 86.
14 *The Chronicle of Salimbene de Adam*, pp. 86–7.
15 Martino da Canal, *Les Estoires de Venise*, ed. A. Limentani (Florence: Olschki, 1973), pp. 338–55.
16 M. Sanudo Torsello, Istoria del Regno di Romania in *Chroniques greco-romanes*, ed. K. Hopf (Berlin: Weidmann, 1873), pp. 135–8.
17 Riccobaldo of Ferrara, *Compilatio chronologia*, ed. A. T. Hankey (Rome: Istituto Storico Italiano per il Medio Evo, 2000), pp. 127–32.

CHAPTER 2

# Economy

*William R. Day, Jr*

More than a decade before the birth of Dante in 1265, Florence was already the largest city in Tuscany and the dominant commercial power in the region. According to the Florentine chronicler Giovanni Villani (*c.*1276–1348), the urban population of Florence was twice the size of Pisa's by about the middle of the thirteenth century. The introduction of the gold florin in 1252 and the sustained issue of the new coin over the succeeding decades, despite its initial unpopularity, attest to a build-up of gold reserves among the city's merchant bankers and the extent to which Florentine trade and finance had developed. Of the other Tuscan cities, only Lucca struck a gold coin during the thirteenth century. After two attempts, however, monetary authorities in Lucca abandoned the project, like most governments elsewhere in Europe that either began to strike gold coinage during the two or three decades after the introduction of the florin or else planned to do so (for instance, the kings of England and France, the Roman Senate, Perugia, and Bologna). Only in Florence, along with Genoa and later Venice, were commerce, finance, and industry sufficiently developed and the gold supply dependable enough in the thirteenth century to support the sustained production of gold coins.

As a Guelf city, Florence benefitted from the virtual interregnum that began with the death of Emperor Henry VI (1165–97; sole king of Italy 1190; emperor 1191), and lasted until his son Frederick II (1194–1250) formally became King of Italy in 1218. In political terms, the breakdown of imperial power afforded Florentine authorities the scope to found the Tuscan League within just a few months of Henry's death and to consolidate their position at the head of the League as the dominant Guelf political power in Tuscany. It also gave Florence freedom to deal harshly with competing interests in its own territory without fear of military reprisal. Furthermore, it very likely produced conditions more favourable to Florentine economic expansion by reducing barriers to trade posed by the traditionally Ghibelline cities and seigniorial powers in Tuscany.

*Economy* 31

The accelerated pace of Florentine commercial expansion during the early years of the thirteenth century was evident at the international level by the 1220s. At one end of Europe, Florentine merchants are documented in England from 1223, and their presence there had already reached such proportions by 1234 that King Henry III (1216–72), instead of extending two-year grants of entry to individual Florentines as was usually the case for foreign merchants, issued a general licence of admittance to all Florentines. At the other end of the European world, in the eastern Mediterranean, one Ranieri of Florence was settled in the Levantine port city of Acre, selling cloth out of his *botega* (shop) there in 1224. Whether the cloth that Ranieri was selling was manufactured in Florence is unclear, but Florentine textiles were beginning to appear on foreign markets during this period, first in Venice (1225), then in Palermo (1237), Macerata (1245), Lucca (1246), and Ragusa (Dubrovnik, 1253).

The great wave of demographic and economic expansion that transformed Florence from a second-rate town in Tuscany into one of the dominant commercial centres in Europe and the cradle of the Italian Renaissance actually had its beginnings even earlier, more than a century before Dante's birth. Relations between Florence and Pisa certainly antedated the twelfth century, but the earliest such evidence comes only in 1158, when the two cities agreed to a treaty to end a conflict between Florence and Lucca on the one hand and Pisa and the Guidi Counts on the other.[1] By that time, according to the widely travelled North African geographer Muhammad al-Idrisi (1099–1165/66), Florence (*Flūransah*) was already a populous city.[2] Continued growth necessitated the construction of a new circuit of walls in 1172–75 that more than doubled the enclosed area of the city on the right bank of the Arno. The new walls embraced suburbs that were turned over to new residential property as well as to trade and industry, for example the Borgo della Balla, so named for the bales of cloth that were prepared there for transport, and Campo Corbolino alongside the Mugnone to the immediate west of San Lorenzo, which was covered with workshops.

The Pisans had completed the construction of a new larger enclosure for their city less than a decade earlier, but they never extended their twelfth-century walls, whereas the Florentines continued to expand the enclosed area of the city to accommodate the growing population. In the 1250s the Florentines completed the extension of their walls on the left bank of the Arno across the Ponte Vecchio, which Dante referred to as the 'passage of the Arno' (*Inf.* XIII, 146). In 1284 the Florentines began to build an entirely new and much larger circuit of walls to take in not only the more urbanized areas stretching out beyond the existing enclosure along the major access roads, but also the undeveloped land between them, probably in the expectation of further development. Within the walls, too, the building of public works in Florence exceeded what was taking place elsewhere in Tuscany. By 1252 Florence had four bridges across the Arno within its walls – the Ponte Vecchio plus the Ponte Nuovo or Ponte alla Carraia (1218–20), the Ponte Rubaconte (1237, now Ponte alle Grazie), and the Ponte di Santa Trìnita (1252) – whereas Pisa had only two until 1260. Moreover, the construction of the Rubaconte in Florence was part of a larger public works project that included paving all the roads in the city. In 1255 construction also began on the Palazzo del Popolo, later called the Bargello. Orsanmichele, after having been destroyed by fire, was rebuilt as a public grain market around 1290, and work began on the Palazzo dei Priori, otherwise known as the Palazzo della Signoria or Palazzo Vecchio, in 1299.

Private and ecclesiastical building was also conspicuous in thirteenth-century Florence. Already in the second half of the twelfth century, the urban landscape was punctuated with towers that belonged to the city's wealthiest families and consortia of families. More than fifty of them are attested from the eleventh to the beginning of the thirteenth century. By the middle of the thirteenth century, some were as high as 120 Florentine *braccia*, or about 70 metres. The popular government viewed the towers as physical manifestations of power and sources of civic discord, especially between pro-papal Guelf party members and pro-imperial Ghibellines, but they were also signs of development. In 1250, to promote reconciliation between the parties, authorities of the so-called *primo popolo*, the popular government, ordered that all towers be reduced to a maximum of 50 *braccia*, or about 30 metres, and then used the stones excised from the taller ones towards the construction of the extension of the urban enclosure in the Oltrarno. Around the same time, the new mendicant orders began to construct their churches just beyond the walls where there was still enough open space to accommodate their huge structures and large *piazze*. These churches included Santa Croce (rebuilt 1294/95) of the Franciscans and Santa Maria Novella (begun 1246) of the Dominicans. The new mendicant churches also included Ognissanti of the penitential order of the Humiliati (1256), Santissima Annunziata of the Servites (1250), Santo Spirito of the Augustinians (1250), and Santa Maria del Carmine of the Carmelites (1250).

Building in Florence was symptomatic of the city's commercial development. A year before construction began on the new twelfth-century

*Economy* 33

walls, Florence and Pisa had agreed to an important treaty that entitled Florentine citizens to favoured treatment in Pisa as well as access to the Mediterranean on Pisan vessels on the same terms as Pisan citizens.[3] Before the end of the century, through the port of Pisa, Florentine merchants were established in Sicily and presumably elsewhere in the Mediterranean basin where Pisan traders operated. The sources nevertheless offer only occasional glimpses of Florentine merchants in the Mediterranean because they typically travelled and traded as Pisans, taking advantage of Pisan privileges in foreign markets, using Pisan *fondachi* (warehouses), going through Pisan consuls in their relations with local authorities, and identifying themselves as Pisans. Even as late as 1245, Florentines were among the various Tuscan merchants in Acre who were still trading as Pisans.[4] The 1171 treaty nevertheless suggests that Florentine merchants were already trading in the Mediterranean in the later twelfth century.

The agreement of 1171 was also conspicuously one-sided, which suggests that the Florentines were already negotiating with Pisa from a position of power. The Florentine promise of military support was no doubt critical for the Pisans, who were then at war with Genoa and Lucca. Pisa's willingness to pay such a heavy price for Florentine support might have also hinged upon other factors, for example Pisa's dependence on timber from the Florentine *contado* (the countryside controlled by the city) for shipbuilding. Neither Pisa's shipbuilding industry nor the timber resources in Tuscany and their exploitation are well studied, but an early thirteenth-century epic poem about the second Balearic war (*c*.1114) suggests that the Pisans depended on the forests of the Mugello, especially for the wood used in fashioning the sail yards of their vessels; from the Mugello, the wood was carried on the river currents of the Sieve and Arno to the boatyards of Pisa. As Florentine commerce expanded in the thirteenth century, Florentine merchants secured further conspicuous concessions in Pisa. In 1256, for example, Florence obtained not only exemptions from most customs duties and tolls in Pisa and its territory, but also, significantly, an oath from the Pisans that they would use Florentine weights and measures in their dealings with Florentine merchants even in Pisa.[5] The ability of Florence to gain concessions of this magnitude a generation before the destruction of the Pisan fleet at Meloria in 1284 is probably an accurate barometer of the extent to which the Pisan economy was by then dependent on the commercial traffic through its city and port generated by Florentine traders. Florentine dependence on Pisa for the easiest means of access to the sea of course had its drawbacks. When political relations between Florence and Pisa deteriorated, the Pisans sometimes closed their port to Florentine merchants, forcing them to use one of several hardly satisfactory alternatives such as Talamone and Porto Ercole in the Maremma or Pietrasanta and Versilia in the Lucchesia. Tactics of this sort were nevertheless increasingly self-defeating for the Pisans. When they closed their port to Florentine merchants, they also deprived themselves of an important source of revenue.

The early expansion of the Florentine economy depended in part on access to the sea because it enabled Florentine merchants to obtain raw materials for industry and to reach the foreign markets that soon became important outlets for the city's manufactured goods. Certainly by 1200, and probably earlier, Florentines were exploiting their virtually unlimited supply of running water for industrial purposes to finish and produce woollen textiles. The merchants of the Calimala guild (Arte di Calimala), originally the importers and finishers of northern fabrics in Florence and named after the street on which their guild was based, are first attested in 1192 and had their own distinct measure for woollen fabrics – the *braccio canne Callismale* – by 1205. The wool guild (Arte della Lana) is securely attested for the first time only in 1212, but had probably already been established by 1193, when there is a reference to the seven major guilds to which both the Calimala and wool guilds clearly belonged in the early thirteenth century. By 1264 a Florentine merchant named Clarissimo Falconeri was able to claim that he had been involved in the cloth trade for more than sixty years.[6] Some of the earliest commercial treaties of Florence, with Bologna in 1203 and Faenza in 1204, also show that the Florentine cloth industry was producing woollen textiles for export at the beginning of the thirteenth century and thus suggest that the industry was well established by then.

When the Humiliati arrived in Florence in 1239 and began to finish woollen textiles, they were therefore entering an already well-established industry. Within just a few years of their arrival, if not earlier, the industry was producing its own recognizable fabrics, *pannos Florentinos de lana* (Florentine woollen cloth). Textile manufacturing in Florence attracted surplus labour from the agrarian sector and spurred intense demographic expansion in the city, from a population of probably less than 20,000 in around 1200 to perhaps as great as 120,000 in the early fourteenth century. Concentrated demand for foodstuffs in Florence stimulated growth in agricultural productivity and the development of the trade infrastructure in the *contado*. By about 1308 the industry had some 300 workshops in the city. There were fewer workshops 30 years later, only about 200, and they produced perhaps 20–30 per cent less cloth, but by then, in what was destined to become a recurring pattern of import substitution in Florence, the local industry had begun to produce more valuable high-quality fabrics in imitation of imported English ones, and the industry still sustained more than 30,000 persons in one way or another, at least a quarter of the urban population. While the very early development of the Florentine industry is shrouded in mystery, the city's entry into the commercial manufacturing of woollen textiles for export must have already occurred by the end of the twelfth century. At first, Florentine involvement in the cloth trade consisted in the importation of unfinished fabrics from Northern Europe and raw merino wool mainly from the Algarve and north west Africa, the so-called *lana del garbo* attested in Florentine sources, and the local finishing and manufacture of woollen fabrics from these materials, which then rapidly developed into a thriving industry.

The early trade of Florence was thus characterized by the importation of raw materials for industry and foodstuffs for the burgeoning urban population, partly from within the *contado* but also from further afield, and by the exportation of manufactured products and financial services (see below). This trade initially developed along three main trajectories. In addition to the one along the Arno to the seaport of Pisa, another extended north across the Apennines to Bologna and Faenza (and thence to points beyond), while a third went to the southeast along the Arno to Arezzo and thence to the Tiber and along Rome's river into central Italy. There were of course other lines of Florentine trade but these were the three most important, above all because they enabled merchants to make extensive use of inland waterways to reduce transport costs while facilitating the effective coordination of local, regional, and supraregional trade through interstitial secondary market towns such as Empoli between Florence and Pisa, Figline (Valdarno) and Montevarchi between Florence and Arezzo, and Borgo San Lorenzo between Florence and trans-Apennine destinations. These secondary markets serviced highly productive agricultural areas near the confines of the Florentine *contado* and functioned as centres of transhipment for Florentine imports and exports as well as outlets for Florentine manufactured goods. They also drew in foodstuffs and raw materials from tertiary markets both within the Florentine *contado* and beyond on the edges of neighbouring *contadi*.

An important factor in the early development of the Florentine economy, at least until 1250, was the easing of tension between Florence and the principal seigniorial powers in the Florentine *contado*, both lay and ecclesiastical, especially the Guidi counts, whose numerous possessions were spread throughout north-eastern Tuscany and along both sides of the Apennines between Tuscany and Romagna. Some of the most important Guidi assets were nevertheless positioned along the edges of the Florentine *contado*. Hostilities between Florence and the Guidi reached their height towards the middle of the twelfth century. The main flashpoints were, from 1142 to 1153–54, the Guidi stronghold at Monte di Croce above the Sieve Valley in the hills northeast of Fiesole, and then in 1155, the *castrum* of Marturi on the main route between Florence and Siena where the Guidi were beginning to establish a foothold. After the death of Count Guido VI in 1157, however, both Florence and the Guidi recognized that continued belligerence was counterproductive. The succession to the royal throne of Frederick I Barbarossa (b. 1122; reign 1152–90) and his coronation as emperor in 1155 might have also helped to temper both the antipathies and anxieties that Florentine authorities and the Guidi felt for and about each other. In 1158, as the respective allies of Lucca and Pisa, Florence and the Guidi agreed to a treaty that effectively marked the beginning of a new more congenial phase in their relationship.

There were nevertheless teething problems. The peace was briefly shattered in 1174 when the Florentines attacked Poggibonsi in response to the continued efforts of the Guidi to consolidate their position in the area. Poggibonsi, which Villani later described as 'situated in the navel of Tuscany',[7] occupied a strategic position adjacent to the destroyed *castrum* (castle) of Marturi along the disputed frontier between Florence and Siena. It was also developing into an important interstitial market centre with its own commercial measure for grain. The Florentines regarded it as vital to their interests that it remained free of Guidi control. Within just a few years of the Florentine assault, Siena and the Guidi both recognized Florentine dominion over Poggibonsi and renounced their properties and rights in the town. It was another century before Poggibonsi was fully integrated into the Florentine *contado* and its trade network, but the rapprochement between Florence and the Guidi was complete by 1180 when Count Guido VII (late 1140s–1214) established direct ties with the city. He arranged to have his earlier marriage to Agnese of Montferrat dissolved and then married 'the good Gualdrada' (*Inf.* XVI, 37), the virtuous and well-spoken only child of a prominent Florentine citizen, Bellincione Berti de' Ravignani, who had been the principal Florentine negotiator in the 1176 agreement with Siena and the Guidi. Dante's glorification of 'the lofty Bellincione' (*Par.* XVI, 99) might have stemmed directly from his daughter's pacification of Count Guido and the immense benefit that it brought to Florence in the form of a peace dividend.

*Economy* 37

The importance of cordial relations between Florence and the Guidi lay in the control that the counts exercised at key points along the main arteries of communication in the Florentine *contado*, for example at Empoli and Montevarchi, and the capacity that this afforded them to disrupt Florentine trade. Already in 1182 the citizens of Guidi-controlled Empoli submitted to Florence and granted all Florentine citizens safe passage through the territory of Empoli by land and on the Arno. Their submission was nevertheless a qualified one in so far as they agreed to defend Florence against all adversaries except the Guidi, but the Florentines were probably more concerned about the facility of safe passage through the territory of Empoli and the maintenance of good relations with the Guidi than they were about the outright subjugation of the town. The arrangement probably also benefitted the Guidi and Empoli nearly as much as the Florentines in the revenues generated for them by Florentine commercial traffic between Florence and Pisa.

Internal divisions between the sons of Count Guido VII eventually led them to partition the family patrimony in 1230. Relations between Florence and the Guidi remained amicable, which kept the main corridors of communication open and continued to facilitate the expansion of Florentine commerce and industry. Internal discord nevertheless made it more difficult for the counts to maintain the integrity of their estates and led to the accumulation of enormous debts. By the 1240s the Guidi had begun to dismember their estates to satisfy their creditors. In 1254–55 the heads of three of the four main branches of the Guidi counts were ultimately forced to sell to Florence their quarter shares of their extensive possessions and rights in Empoli and Montevarchi as well as Montemurlo, a hilltop fortress between Prato and Pistoia. Count Guido Salvatico of Dovadola (d. after 1299) held on to the remaining quarter-share for another two decades but was forced to sell it in 1273 to Florence explicitly to satisfy his debts. Seven years later, once again presumably to complete the conveyance, Guido Salvatico also sold a quarter share of the counts' urban properties on the eastern side of Florence in the Sesto Porta San Piero to the Cerchi, one of the families of 'new citizens' so disparaged by Dante's ancestor Cacciaguida (*c.* 1091–*c.* 1148; *Par.* XVI, 65). By the time of Dante, the holdings of the various branches of the Guidi counts were confined largely to the Apennines east and north-east of Florence.

The Guidi were not the only powerful lords with whom Florentine authorities had to contend to keep open the main lines of trade. The Alberti counts were originally associated with the development of nearby Prato, but they lost control of the city early in the twelfth century. By the end of that century, their power was concentrated in the Pesa and Elsa Valleys and in the western Mugello along the frontier between the *contadi* of Florence and Prato. In the later twelfth century the counts developed a new fortified settlement near Certaldo at Semifonte, which posed a significant threat to Florence, particularly its bishops, who held extensive properties in the area. Under intense pressure from the communal government, the Alberti submitted to Florence in 1184 and again in 1200, but the continuing construction of Semifonte and the apparent refusal of Alberti vassals and other investors in the settlement to abide by the submission led the Florentines to raze the stronghold to the ground in 1202. After that, the Alberti largely disappeared from the sources for a half-century, which suggests that relations between Florence and the counts during the interim period were largely peaceful.

The Ubaldini lords were also important because they controlled portions of both the southern and northern escarpments of the Apennines north of Florence along some of the main trans-Apennine routes. In 1200 the Ubaldini lord Fortebraccio di Grecio agreed to safeguard Florentines and their possessions in the territory under his control along some of the main trans-Apennine routes in the usual manner, which suggests that the passage of Florentine merchants through Ubaldini territory was by that time common. In 1217 Ugo di Berlinghiero and other members of the Ubaldini agreed to observe a decision of Vitale degli Ubaldini regarding tariffs on goods sent northwards from Florence. These agreements facilitated the passage of trans-Apennine commercial traffic to and from Florence through Ubaldini territory and also assimilated the Ubaldini networks of distribution and exchange into the broader Florentine market network. The Guidi, Alberti, and Ubaldini networks, as well as the interdependent networks of the many Vallombrosan monasteries scattered across the Florentine hinterland, complemented the extensive urban-oriented network of the Florentine bishops. The overlay and intertwining of these networks not only facilitated the access of Florentine merchants to markets beyond the Florentine *contado* but also promoted economic integration within the *contado*, as attested for example in the standardization of weights and measures in the *contado* on the Florentine standard over the course of the thirteenth century.

After the death of Emperor Frederick II in 1250 and the virtual collapse of imperial power, relations between Florence and powerful forces in the *contado*, both lay lords and rural communes, rapidly deteriorated. The precise source of the new tension is unclear but the pressure most likely came from Florence in an attempt to exploit the imperial power vacuum and to expand the tax base as part of a broader programme of administrative and fiscal reform. Soon after Frederick's death, the Florentines attacked strategically situated Guidi and Ubaldini outposts in the hinterland at Montaio in the upper Arno Valley and at Montaccianico in the Mugello, respectively. In 1252 the Florentines attacked Figline, where Count Guido Novello (*c.* 1227–93) of the Guidi counts had taken refuge with a band of Ghibelline exiles from Florence in rebellion against the city. Two years later, Florence tried once again to secure its hold over Poggibonsi, which for more than three decades had in fact behaved like an independent commune by negotiating a succession of treaties on its own behalf. By the end of the decade the Florentines had also launched assaults on the Alberti strongholds of Vernio and Mangona in the western Mugello. In the short term, conflict between Florence and the dominant seigniorial powers in the territory appears to have contributed to a general breakdown of order and a worsening of the conditions for trade, particularly along the main trans-Apennine routes, where all three of these seigniorial dynasties still controlled substantial territories. This is suggested in the rise of commercial reprisals between Florence and both Bologna and Faenza in the 1250s and several agreements between the cities to limit them. Another sign of deteriorating conditions can be found in the 1258 appeal of the Apennine convent of Santa Reparata near Marradi for Florentine protection against the injustices perpetrated upon it by 'powerful barons, counts and tyrants in its vicinity', which almost certainly refers to one or more of the branches of the Guidi.[8] The antagonism between the popular government in Florence and the Ghibelline aristocracy eventually led to the expulsion of the Ghibellines in 1258, which in turn resulted two years later in the backlash of Montaperti and the establishment of a new Ghibelline regime in Florence under Count Guido Novello.

The Ghibelline government in Florence soon gave way to a new Guelf administration, the so-called *secondo popolo*, but the Guidi continued their opposition to Florence, albeit in more surreptitious ways. Towards 1280, the Guidi took advantage of the rising popularity of the Florentine gold florin for their own illicit gain. Guido and Alessandro di Aghinolfo (1250s–*c.*1338) of the Romena branch of the Guidi counts enlisted a moneyer named Adamo of Brescia, also called Adamo of Anglia, to set up a clandestine mint in their *castello* of Romena in the Casentino to strike false gold florins. The production of florins containing three fewer carats of gold (12.5 per cent) than the virtually pure Florentine florins was discovered in 1281 only after a fire in Borgo San Lorenzo in Florence destroyed the *palazzo* of the Anchioni family and uncovered a large cache of the coins in an apartment leased by a co-conspirator responsible for putting the coins into circulation in the city. The *spenditore* confessed and was burned to death in Florence with Maestro Adamo (*Inf.* XXX, 60–90),[9] while Guido and Alessandro di Aghinolfo made amends for their transgression by joining the Guelf party, thus giving rise to Guelf and Ghibelline factions within the Guidi and further compromising the ability of the Guidi to act in unison.

Factionalism in Florence persisted throughout Dante's lifetime, eventually precipitating the split in the Guelf party between the Cerchi-dominated Whites and the Donati-dominated Blacks that led to the expulsion of the Whites from Florence in 1302 and Dante's condemnation to exile. Dante bemoaned the factional politics of early fourteenth-century Italy and hoped that Henry VII of Luxembourg (*c.*1275–1313; king of Italy 1310; emperor 1312) would succeed in imposing his authority upon the Italian city-states and thereby end the discord, but Henry died before he was able to mend Italy's internal divisions, leaving Dante to conclude that the opposing factions in Italy, and above all in his Florence, were not yet ready for compromise. The extent to which internal discord in Florence and other Italian cities affected commerce is unclear. Some scholars have argued that factionalism in Florence in the later thirteenth and early fourteenth centuries originated in part from rivalries between merchant bankers, but others have pointed out that merchants from opposing Florentine factions often worked amicably side by side in foreign marketplaces, just as merchants from opposing cities, for example Florence and Siena, amicably engaged in trade or other business activity together abroad, sometimes even as partners in the same ventures.

In addition to the pacification of the Guidi counts and other seigniorial powers, two other factors that encouraged the expansion of the Florentine economy were the gradual insinuation of Florentine merchants into international finance, especially papal banking, and the recompense that they received for their support of the papal–Angevin campaign to wrest the kingdom of Naples from Frederick II and his descendants. Like the development of the woollen textiles industry, the advent of Florentine merchants in international finance probably dates back to the later twelfth century. Already in 1177, for example, Florentine bankers were turning up at the papal residence in Anagni near Rome. In the early thirteenth century, they were active in moneylending at the papal court, extending loans and providing exchange services to visiting prelates and other petitioners. Like other Italian merchant bankers at the papal court, they often collected on their loans at the Champagne fairs. Because the transport of specie was risky, however, it was common for the merchants to use the moneys recovered at the fairs to invest back into the credit and exchange markets or to purchase commodities such as wool and unfinished woollen cloth for despatch to Italy. Exactly when Florentine merchant bankers became involved in this trade is unclear, but the accounts of a Florentine moneychanger working in Bologna in 1211 attest to exchanges on northern European currencies such as French *provisini* and *tornesi* that were common at the fairs, thereby suggesting that Florentines were already active by then in the exchange market at the fairs. Certainly by 1235 Florentines were travelling to the Champagne fairs regularly enough that Pope Gregory IX (b. *c.*1145; papacy 1227–41) granted Florentines attending the fairs protection against unjust prosecution in parts of France outside Paris and the Champagne dioceses of Châlons-sur-Marne, Meaux, and Langres, in effect, wherever they did not already have recourse to the institutions of justice.

In the 1230s the merchant bankers handling the transfer of papal revenues from local collectors to the papal treasury were still mainly Sienese, but the position of Florentine merchant bankers at the papal court improved substantially when Sinibaldo Fieschi of Genoa was consecrated Pope Innocent IV (b. *c.*1195; papacy 1243–54) and began his assault on Frederick II. To finance his project to bring down the emperor, the pope appealed especially to Florentine creditors, and when they were unable to meet his prodigious credit needs on their own, the Calimala guild of Florence stepped in and mortgaged its immovable property to mobilize the necessary funds. This no doubt helped to raise the profile of Florentine merchants in Rome, though it was perhaps only during the pontificate of Alexander IV (b. 1199 or *c.*1185; papacy 1254–61) that Florentines began to gain prominence as official bankers of the pope.

The paucity of the data on the early involvement of Florentine merchant bankers in international finance in general and in the transfer of papal revenues in particular makes it extremely difficult to assess the impact of these activities on the Florentine economy before the middle of the thirteenth century when substantial evidence for Florentine international merchant banking first begins to appear. The merchants involved in papal banking nevertheless probably benefitted from the deposits they took from collectors for safekeeping and conveyance to the papal treasury, despite the risks, far beyond their charges for these services. This is because they were often able to retain deposits for periods long enough to invest them profitably on their own behalf before consigning them to the papal treasury. In the fourteenth century the period between the initial deposit of funds with bankers and their consignment to the papal treasury, when specified, varied from about two weeks to nearly three months with most of the transfers completed within seven weeks, but this perhaps reflects the efforts of popes from Boniface VIII (b. *c.*1235; papacy 1294–1303) onwards to limit the time between the deposit of funds with Florentine bankers and their consignment to the papal treasury. In the second half of the thirteenth century the average length of the period between deposit and consignment might have been longer, certainly long enough to permit short-term investment in commodities, above all in raw wool and unfinished cloth for transport to Italy, and in the credit and exchange markets.

In exchange for their financial support of the papal–Angevin alliance, Florentine merchants also received preferential treatment, especially in southern Italy. Florentines were already active in the Italian south, but their presence there took on an entirely different complexion after Popes Urban IV (b. *c.*1195; papacy 1261–64) and Clement IV (b. unknown; papacy 1265–68) beseeched Charles I of Anjou, Count of Provence (b. 1226; reign 1246–85) to assume the throne of Naples, which had been governed by Manfred (1232–66), the illegitimate son of Frederick II, since the death of Frederick's son Conrad IV (b. 1228) in 1254. Two years later Charles arrived in Rome and gained election as senator, and then set out for South Italy, defeating Manfred at Benevento in February 1266. A little more than two years after that, Frederick's grandson Duke Conrad of Swabia (Conradino, or 'little Conrad'; 1252–68) descended into Italy to assert his hereditary rights to the Neapolitan crown, but Charles stamped his authority on the kingdom by defeating Conrad at Tagliacozzo in Abruzzo in August 1268 and executing him in Naples in October.

Some Florentine companies, for example the Frescobaldi, started to request privileges from Charles of Anjou in South Italy even before he had defeated Manfred and was crowned King of Naples. Most other companies waited to see how events unfolded. Before the 1270s only a few companies actually received rights in South Italy, but the ones that did benefitted from privileged access to South Italian commodities, most notably hard-grain durum wheat from Apulia and Sicily, which they exported to northern Italian markets. In all cases, Charles demanded that recipients of commercial rights in South Italy maintain good relations with the Guelf party. The Angevin conquest of South Italy effectively completed what has been called the *guelfizzazione* of the entire peninsula south of Arezzo and Siena, which facilitated the trading relations of the predominantly Guelf Florentine merchant banking companies throughout the region. The South, moreover, lacked its own well-developed textile industries, which ensured Florentine merchants a ready market for the principal manufactures of their city.

Other factors also contributed to and reflected the vitality of the economy in Florence. The earliest fragments of notarial registers of the city and *contado*, which survive from the later 1230s onwards, attest to an active private credit market in which notaries brokered short-term loans between lenders and borrowers, typically for relatively small amounts over periods from 2 to 12 months at 10 to 20 per cent interest. In the hinterland, a significant proportion of the loans were dispersed during the first several months of the year, typically from January through April, to be redeemed in agricultural produce after the forthcoming harvest, often in grain on the feast of the Assumption in August. In the early development of the private credit market, the mediating role of notaries was important in bringing together borrowers and lenders of different social classes. This is because borrowers, mostly small to middling owner-cultivators who most needed access to credit in the late winter and early spring, were unable to obtain loans from within their own social group, since other members tended to have similar credit needs. By the later thirteenth century there are signs that some notaries had begun to specialize in brokering private credit transactions, as attested in some late thirteenth-century registers of urban notaries that contain particularly high proportions of private loan contracts, over half of all acts in some cases. The register of one late-thirteenth-century urban notary, Ser Matteo di Biliotto, was probably more typical; the more than 300 loan contracts recorded in it over a little more than two years accounted for more than one-third of the total number of acts and ran to the value of nearly 12,000 gold florins.[10] If Ser Matteo's register is in any way representative, the nearly 600 notaries working in Florence and its *contado* very well might have redacted loan contracts to the value of more than 2.5 million florins per annum. Notaries also recorded transfers of credits and debits, sometimes on overdue loans. In the early fourteenth century, however, these kinds of credit transactions virtually disappeared from notarial registers as Florentine statutes ordered the acceptance of ledger entries as prima facie evidence for debt.

Merchants' ledgers from about 1250 onwards therefore provide another perspective on the local credit market in Florence. Entries for credit transactions in late-thirteenth-century ledgers suggest that most loans were notarized, but they also show that some were extended without any further record decades before ledger entries alone were regarded as sufficient prima facie evidence for debt. Ledger entries further show that creditors routinely allowed their debtors to offset their debits in the form of credits with a third party, and they likewise offset their own debits by drawing on a credit owed by a third party.

In Prato and Montemurlo around the middle of the thirteenth century, Dante's ancestors routinely invested in the private credit market, charging interest rates between 15 and 20 per cent, sometimes explicitly stated, and even increasing their own patrimony through foreclosure at the expense of clients unable to satisfy their debt obligations. The Alighieri continued to invest in the private credit market throughout the later thirteenth century, but Dante himself appears in the sources mainly as a borrower, which perhaps explains his consignment of usurers to the seventh circle of Hell (*Inf.* XVII, 34–78). For Dante, the most notorious usurers of his time, identifiable in *Inferno* by the family arms on the money pouches that they wear around their necks, were the Guelf Gianfigliazzi and Ghibelline Ubbriachi families of Florence, the 'sovereign knight' (l. 72) usually understood to be a former standard-bearer of justice of Florence named Giovanni Buiamonte de' Becchi (d. 1310), and two moneylenders of Padua, Reginaldo degli Scrovegni (d. before 1289) and the 'great usurer' Vitaliano, who is usually identified as Vitaliano Dente (d. 1309/10).

The credit market in Florence during the thirteenth and early fourteenth centuries still awaits detailed analysis, but evidence indicates that it was more casual and more informal, more conditioned by personal relationships, more permissive of overdrafts and delayed payments, and less disciplined than modern credit markets. The judicial enforcement of loan contracts and the seizure of immovable property from borrowers in default on loans are nevertheless attested in Florence from as early as 1233. The market appears to have been efficient, too, in the sense that recovery rates on outright loans and other extensions of credit might have exceeded 90 per cent. The widespread use of credit in Florence effectively expanded the money supply. It provided investors with the opportunity to gain a reasonable return on their spare capital at relatively low risk, while enabling borrowers to overcome temporary liquidity problems. The credit market also enabled workers in the agrarian sector, who still made up some two-thirds of the population in the territory of Florence and whose income was presumably concentrated at specific times of the year when their main cash crops were harvested, to spread their revenue out over the entire year. Initially, notaries brokered these credit transactions, but entries in merchants' ledgers had already begun to acquire a quasi-legal status in the thirteenth century. By 1325 the statutory acceptance of these entries as prima facie evidence in Florentine courts effectively disengaged the notary from involvement in the kind of relatively modest short-term credit transactions that had previously made up a substantial proportion of his activity. This benefited both borrowers and lenders because it lowered the costs associated with taking on and dispensing loans as well as litigating over them should the need arise.

Still other factors contributed to the efflorescence of Florence in the thirteenth century, some local and others broader and structural. At the local level, the education system and high rates of literacy and numeracy in Florence no doubt helped to shape the city into a commercial powerhouse. Florentine merchants were also precocious in the development of the insurance contract, which reduced the risks associated with long-distance trade. In broader terms, the rise of Florence coincided with the expansion of overland commerce and inland river-bound trade, encouraged by the consolidation of communal government and urban authority over theoretically subject territories – namely, their respective dioceses or *contadi* – across much of north-central Italy. This helped to foster the growth of such inland centres as Orvieto and Perugia as well as the cities on the via Emilia from Milan to Bologna, while enabling communal authorities to negotiate commercial treaties with their trading partners that afforded foreign merchants recourse to local institutions of justice and thereby reduced the scourge of officially sanctioned robbery in commercial reprisals.

When the Florentine Guelf party split into the rival Black and White factions at the end of the thirteenth century and the Blacks, with the support of Pope Boniface VIII, gained control of Florence and then, in 1302, expelled the Whites, including Dante, the city was already approaching maximum expansion. By that time Florence had been undergoing sustained economic and demographic growth for more than a century, from the take-off in the second half of the twelfth century. The Florentine economy probably continued to enjoy modest growth throughout the first quarter of the fourteenth century and possibly into the 1330s, but the city's economy grew most spectacularly during the hundred or so years before the birth of Dante.

### Notes

1 B. Maragone, *Gli annales pisani di Bernardo Maragone*, ed. M. L. Gentile (Bologna: Zanichelli, 1936), pp. 17–18.

46          William R. Day, Jr

2 M. Amari and C. Schiaparelli (eds.), *L'Italia descritta nel 'Libro del re Ruggero'
compilato da Edrisi* (Rome: Tipi dei Salviucci, 1883), p. 91.

3 F. Dal Borgo (ed.), Raccolta di scelti diplomi pisani (Pisa: G. Pasque, 1765),
pp. 307–8; P. Santini (ed.), Documenti dell'antica costituzione del comune di
Firenze (Florence: G. P. Vieusseux, 1895), pp. 5–6, doc. 4.

4 R. Davidsohn (ed.), Forschungen zur Geschichte von Florenz, 4 vols (Berlin:
Mittler und Sohn, 1896–1908), vol. II, pp. 295–8, doc. 2307; R. Davidsohn,
Storia di Firenze, 8 vols. (Florence: Sansoni, 1956–68), vol. VI, p. 751.

5 P. Santini (ed.), Documenti dell'antica costituzione del comune di Firenze:
Appendice (Florence: Olschki, 1952), pp. 189–204, doc. 66.

6 ASF, *Dipl.*, Santissma Annunziata, 5 June 1264.

7 G. Villani, *Nuova cronica*, ed. G. Porta, 3 vols. (Parma: Guanda, 1990–91),
vol. I, p. 468 (VIII, 36).

8 Santini (ed.), *Documenti*, pp. 253–5, doc. 83.

9 P. Pieri, *Cronica di Paolino Pieri Fiorentino delle cose d'Italia dall'anno 1080 al
1305*, ed. A. F. Adami (Rome: Venanzio Monaldini, 1765), p. 43.

10 M. Soffici and F. Sznura (eds.), *Ser Matteo di Biliotto notaio: Imbreviatura.
I. Registro (1294–1296)* (Florence: SISMEL, 2002), pp. lxii–lxiii.

CHAPTER 3

# *Law*

## *Sara Menzinger*

### Uzzah between theological and political interpretation

Dante and Virgil, after toiling up a hard rocky slope, arrive at the first of the seven terraces of Purgatory, where the proud are punished for their arrogance. A wall of marble stands before them, adorned with carvings of the sin of pride of such perfection that their execution surpasses not just the supreme sculptor Polycletus, but Nature herself (*Purg.* X, 28–33). Among the first carvings is one depicting the Levite Uzzah, who, the Bible recounts, joined the procession of Israelites behind the cart carrying the Tablets of the Law to Jerusalem by King David's order. Uzzah stretched out a hand to steady the cart that threatened to overturn because the oxen were restless. That gesture, rather than earn Uzzah divine approval, caused his death. God struck him down on the spot to punish him for his arrogance and irreverence (2 Sam. VI, 4–8).

The ruthlessness of God's judgment did not fail to impress readers of the Bible as far back as the early Middle Ages, when, in Scriptural commentaries, a complex metaphorical interpretation of Uzzah's punishment began to appear – an interpretation that continued to be enriched until the twelfth century, and whose popularity endured well beyond that period. The tale of Uzzah was read as an exemplary case of the relationship between the priesthood and the lay world, and during the many years between Pope Gregory the Great (b. *c.*540; papacy 590–604) and the theological and juridical texts of the twelfth century, it would be interpreted progressively as a reminder of the need for absolute separation between spiritual and temporal power. The fullest expression of that interpretation is to be found in the *Decretum Gratiani* (Gratian's Decree). Compiled by Gratian (*c.*1090–*c.*1150), who is believed to have been a Benedictine monk who taught at the Monastery of Saints Felix and Nabor in Bologna, the *Decretum* is a fundamental work of canon law – the law governing the affairs of the Church, especially the law created or recognized by papal authority – written around 1140 that quickly became a key point of

48 Sara Menzinger

reference for jurists in the city, and then in other Italian and European centres of learning. Basing itself on an extensive account of the story of Uzzah derived from sixth- and seventh-century theological texts, the *Decretum*, with its mix of theology and ecclesiastical rules and principles that typifies it, clarifies the meaning of Uzzah's punishment as follows: the ark of the covenant symbolizes the men of the Church; the Levite Uzzah stands for the laity; the instability of the cart did not, as some had erroneously suggested, represent wrongs done by the clergy, but was caused by the weight of laymen burdening the shoulders of the Fathers and Doctors of the Church; and the unruly oxen were men who had done wrong, putting the ark in danger by causing it to lean and risk falling (*Decretum Gratiani* C. 2 q.7 c. 27).[1] No layperson could accuse a man of the Church of correct actions that were exclusively subject to divine judgment. To do so, would be to intrude into a sphere from which humans were excluded. Such, in essence, was Gratian's view of why Uzzah had been punished.

## The origins of canon law: the ideology of the *Decretum Gratiani*

The above interpretation is one of a number of passages in the *Decretum* that, after its author's death, would remain influential in the political and juridical thought of the thirteenth and fourteenth centuries, since they offered authoritative arguments that dealt with urgent ideological questions. To understand the use Dante made of those arguments helps to explain his complex approach to civil and canon law, fundamentally inspired by his political opposition to Pope Boniface VIII (b. 1235; papacy 1294–1303), and by his uncompromising indictment of the erroneous turn that, in his view, canon legal theory had taken, beginning especially in the mid thirteenth century. Dante often relied on biblical passages to discredit the arguments of the hierocrats, supporters of papal political supremacy (see Chapter 1), and offered technical interpretations – readings of Scripture from a theological-juridical perspective – to counter the most radical theses of the canonists. For example, his refutation of the pope's powers as the vicar of Christ, and thus of the papal ability to unseat the emperor, expressed in a well-known passage of the *Monarchia* (III, vi), is based on an interpretation of Samuel's role in deposing Saul. In his eloquent deployment of the biblical passage, Dante also reveals a close familiarity with civil legal doctrine (*Mon.* II, v, 1; see Chapter 28).

It was precisely the political significance of the biblical tale of Uzzah that made it appealing to Dante; and he drew on it again in one of his most militant epistles to exonerate himself of accusations that he was an enemy of the Church. In 1314 Dante accused the Italian cardinals of leading the Church astray, while presenting himself as showing the right way – seemingly a second Uzzah interfering in ecclesiastical affairs. Nevertheless, the poet also stated that his intention was not to right the ark, for that was God's prerogative alone, but to return the oxen to the straight and narrow path, namely, to correct the prelates, and especially the cardinals, who had distanced the Church from the true path (*Ep.* XI, 9–12).

The use Dante makes of the Biblical story demonstrates that he had direct knowledge of the interpretation circulating in contemporary theological and juridical texts, beginning with the *Decretum*. Although Gratian's interpretation of Uzzah at first sight seems to condemn any lay intrusion into the spiritual realm, it in fact came to stand for the principle of non-interference – a principle that, in the two centuries after Gratian, was energetically defended by opponents of hierocratic doctrine and of the corpus of canon law supporting it. First among these were students of civil law, who appreciated the *Decretum*'s late-antique notion of a division between the lay and ecclesiastical spheres, a notion formalized by Pope Gelasius (d. 496) at the end of the fifth century, and which offered the ideological framework for relations between Church and empire for more than 500 years. 'Gelasian dualism' was founded on the conviction that there were *duae dignitates*, two authorities, each ordained by God and responsible for administering separate spheres through an equal division of tasks, and especially of juridical tasks. The spiritual realm was entrusted to the pope, while the secular realm was the responsibility of the emperor.

Around the middle of the sixth century this view was firmly endorsed by Justinian (*c.*482–565), who in the *Novellae* (Novels) section of the *Corpus iuris civilis* (Body of Civil Law) clearly expressed the view that priesthood and empire, both gifts of God (*dona Dei*), must not act as obstacles to one another, since the first was charged with administering the divine sphere, while the second dealt with the earthly one.[2] Justinian's text thus became an important means for disseminating Gelasian ideas during the early Middle Ages, not least because popularizations of the *Novellae* were relatively well-known, especially when compared to other sections of the *Corpus iuris*, many of which were partial or abridged, while others, like the *Digest*, were forgotten until the twelfth century.

Gratian's endorsement of the early medieval political-juridical division of power also meant that the *Decretum* was in harmony with the views of Bolognese civil law experts (and those beyond Bologna as well) who, from the beginning of the twelfth century, were attentively examining

Justinian legal texts. All the more so because, in many academic circles in central and northern Italy, legal studies were quite eclectic, and Gratian was intensely scrutinized by civil legal experts as well as by canonists. At the university of Bologna, on the other hand, sources that, unlike the *Decretum*, did not adhere to Roman law were viewed with suspicion until the middle of the thirteenth century, since they were thought to risk polluting the philological work done by the school of Irnerius (*c.*1050–*c.*1125), the glossator and teacher who had played a vital role in reviving Roman legal studies in Italy.

Gratian's views on the separation of papal and imperial responsibilities remained surprisingly resistant to Pope Gregory VII's (b. 1020/25; papacy 1073–85) ideas that circulated widely in theological texts between the eleventh and twelfth centuries in France and Italy. Challenging the early medieval equilibrium of empire and Church as complementary powers, Gregory became a tireless supporter of the supremacy and infallibility of papal authority, as testified by his claim in the *Dictatus Papae* (The Dictates of the Pope; 1075), the most famous expression of his thought, that the pope could depose the emperor. In the twelfth century these new hierocratic theories had almost no effect on Gratian's work, since the *Decretum* represented rather a monument to the past than an outpost of emerging canon legal theories. Gratian's ideological framework was shared by those canonists who – prior to the publication of the *Liber Extra* (Additional Book; 1234) by Pope Gregory IX (b. 1170; papacy 1227–41) – made the *Decretum* the focus of their intellectual work, composing commentaries on it for which they earned the title of 'Decretists'. A growing familiarity with Roman legal texts, promoted by among others Huguccio of Pisa (d. 1210), one of the most influential authors of his generation, reinforced the influence of Gelasian ideas on ecclesiastical legal thought, until in many cases it was nearly identical to the civilian standpoint.

## The transformation of canon legal thought during the thirteenth century

Matters relating to canon law were to change radically beginning in the early thirteenth century, when the pronounced hierocratic positions upheld both by Alanus Anglicus (*fl. c.*1190–*c.*1210) and by the political-ideological line followed by Pope Innocent III (b. 1160/61; papacy 1198–1216) made manifest the clear change of tack that had taken place in the collections of 'decretals' – letters on points of common law issued by popes in the wake of Gratian, in which the theological outlook characteristic of Gregory VII had come to predominate. Innocent III's celebrated allegory of the two great lights in the sky, the sun and moon, effectively captures the position that canon thought had embraced by the beginning of the thirteenth century, when a largely horizontal view of the relationship between Church and empire was replaced by a strongly hierarchical model, with the claims of the spiritual world being given clear primacy over those of the secular world. The degree to which the empire was subordinated to the papacy was likened to the distance between the sun and the moon, a distance that during the course of the thirteenth century would begin to be estimated in exact terms on the basis of mathematical-astrological data taken from studies of Ptolemaic texts. The ideological shift that thus took place with the work of the Decretalists marked the end of an era: specifically, the end of the Gelasian balance – born to contain late-antique caesaropapism, moderated during the Carolingian age to encompass a quasi-integrated relationship between Church and empire, and then anachronistically reintroduced in the twelfth century by Gratian and the Decretists – a balance that, bolstered by the rediscovered sources of Roman civil law, had long been the undisputed ideological framework structuring the relationship between Church and empire prior to the eleventh century and the advent of Gregory VII.

In a purely juridical sense, the decline of the Gelasian paradigm led to new theories that, in response to a perceived need to coordinate the two systems, posited complex interconnections between civil and canon law. Against the old idea of separate spheres, the new unitary concept of 'both laws' (*utrumque ius*) held that canon and civil law were addressed to the same subjects: the former dealt with them as the faithful (*fideles*), the latter as citizens (*cives*). It was an effective and functional view; however, it evolved into the extremist hierocratic theories espoused by Pope Boniface VIII, so that the effort to combine Roman law with the Christian tradition tended in effect to mean, following the Decretalistic formulations of the second half of the thirteenth century, that spiritual positions were granted priority over secular ones. The broadening of the category of 'sin', which began to embrace an ever-growing list of transgressions, was, according to civil opponents from Odofredus (d. 1265) to Dante's friend Cino da Pistoia (1270–1336/37), the pretext that allowed ecclesiastical jurisdiction to expand at the expense of secular law.

Between the thirteenth and fourteenth centuries, the Gelasian principle of non-interference took on a political hue that previously had been alien to it. In Italy it began to be invoked by all those political and academic voices that opposed the increasingly ambitious claims of the Church. We cannot really understand the status that Dante grants to Gratian in the *Commedia* without being aware of such underlying tensions. There is thus a direct connection between Gratian's place in the heaven of the Sun and the political opinion expressed in *Purgatorio* XVI, = 103–14 and throughout the *Monarchia*. In open opposition to the Decretalists, Dante proclaimed that the papacy and the empire were two suns shining in Rome with equal and distinct radiance. Not by chance, the poet maintained the same position in the Epistle to the Cardinals, in which he drew on the Gratian interpretation of the story of Uzzah to absolve himself of any charge that he might be considered an enemy of the Church (*Ep.* XI, 21).

There is no doubt that such views, in particular the so-called principle of non-interference, were part of what today are termed 'Ghibelline' positions, a political ideology that led to serious conflicts between rival families and cities beginning in the last decades of the thirteenth century. Nevertheless it is an oversimplification to classify the convictions of fourteenth-century Italian intellectuals according to a rigid 'pro-imperial, pro-papal' opposition. When we look at the complex interchange between politics and the law during that particular period of communal history, such categories appear inadequate and dated (see Chapters 1 and 4).

## Politics and public law between the twelfth and fourteenth centuries

Dante's placing of Gratian in contrast to the Decretalists – an opposition which he saw as that between time-honoured and authoritative canon law learning and recent opportunistic forms of the same – highlights the important position that medieval juridical categories had not merely in the poet's thought but also right across the late-communal political world. In this regard, until Aristotle's *Politics* was translated from Greek into Latin by William of Moerbeke (*c.*1215–86) during the second half of the thirteenth century, no tradition of specifically political writing had emerged in the medieval Latin West. Obviously this does not mean that politics were not the subject of intense reflection, but rather that late medieval political ideas tended not to circulate independently, but rather were subsumed into theological and juridical doctrines. In this light, the question of whether or not Dante may have studied law is less important than the fact that, in his political reflections, the poet employed juridical categories, which he was able to do thanks to his familiarity with the law, an essential component of a fourteenth-century intellectual's doctrinal make-up.

*Law* 53

Public law was a significant area in which politics and the law met. However, historiography has long neglected this branch of medieval juridical thought and, up to a few decades ago, public law was thought to have been almost non-existent well into the fourteenth century. Communal jurists were deemed to be largely disinterested in political and juridical questions about the functioning of the State, an attitude that seemed to be a natural corollary of the political fragmentation of northern and central Italy. The view that there was little interest in the functioning of the State seemed to be confirmed by the legal doctrine produced in Italian cities. It had long been argued that such doctrine was entirely concerned with the private sector and ignored, as jurists undertook the massive task of reviving ancient Roman law, those sections dedicated to the State. However, it now appears that public law was of more central concern than had previously been thought; and this was the case not just in Italy, but also in all schools of civil law from the middle of the twelfth century onwards. Thus, while the Bolognese school of Irnerius was largely focused on private law, the situation was quite different elsewhere. In informal circles of study in Piacenza, Modena, and Tuscany, as well as in southern France, there was an early and lively interest in the last three volumes of the *Code*, those in which, boldly combining past and contemporary Roman law, Justinian had outlined the model of an ideal state, one in fact very distant from the reality of the Byzantine Empire in the sixth century.

If the many constitutions governing imperial administration could not but seem remote and exotic during the early Middle Ages, these became of great interest during Frederick Barbarossa's (b. *c.*1123; Holy Roman Emperor 1152–90) time, when the revival of imperial authority clashed with the communal governments and their ambitions to present themselves as embodiments of public political power. The old idea that the conflict inspired civil jurists to a new militancy on behalf of Frederick I appears untenable. What it actually inspired was a deep reflection on the empire as an abstract model and on its public aims and consequences. The empire was thus not viewed as antithetical to urban freedoms, but as a legitimating framework, the 'common homeland' (*communis patria*) uniting the new forms of public power, the communes, whose institutions drew vital force from their contacts with the abstract imperial model. Supporting the empire thus expressed a sentiment that was not really equivalent to backing one particular political faction. It was instead the result of a deep appreciation of the public function of imperial government, from which the city, irrespective of its concrete realities, could draw both inspiration and legitimation by appropriating a model of civic cohabitation.

The empire thus became a legal institution, an archetype to serve as the point of reference for the creation of concrete political systems in the late Middle Ages, beginning with those of the city. This was the idea of empire that communal jurists extrapolated from their rediscovery of Roman law, and which they projected on to the flesh-and-blood Emperors who appeared on the Italian political scene, although without ever completely recognizing the latters' authority and prerogatives. This is evident in the widespread condemnation expressed in civil legal circles of the notion – supported by pro-imperial teaching beginning with the religious reformer and critic of ecclesiastical wealth, Arnald of Brescia (*c.*1100–55) – that the emperor could freely dispose of all the goods in the world, even those belonging to his subjects. What prevailed was a narrow interpretation of those passages in the *Corpus iuris* to which historians have traditionally linked the debate on late medieval sovereignty. If the expression 'Lord of the world' (*mundi dominus*) found in the *Digest* (14. 2. 9)[3] most probably did not circulate for most of the twelfth century, the assertion that 'everything is understood to belong to the Emperor' (*omnia principis esse intelligatur*) present in the *Code* (7. 37. 3. 1a)[4] was quickly the object of extensive legal opinion and restriction.

## Civil legal schools in the late Middle Ages: 'minor schools', Bologna, Orléans

The second half of the twelfth century was the founding ideological moment of urban public power. It was at this time that juridical thought developed the theoretical structures to which fourteenth-century intellectuals consciously looked back when they sought to arrest the decline of municipal institutions brought about by factional infighting and by the ambitions of the new *signorie* (lordships). It was not in Bologna, as might have been expected, given the importance of the law faculty at the university, that such ideas were most vigorously pursued; or to be more precise, they were not part of what is considered mainstream Bolognese legal thought in the thirteenth century. Such thought finds its principal expression in the *Magna Glossa* (Great Gloss), compiled by Accursius (*c.*1182–*c.*1262) around the middle of the century, which served as the principal means through which the manuscripts of Justinian's *Corpus iuris* circulated in the late Middle Ages, and indeed until the invention of printing and beyond. The influence of Accursius and his sons – three of whom were jurists – on the teaching of law, thanks to their position as professors at the *studium* of Bologna and at those of other European cities, and on the production of legal texts, thanks to their prosperous manuscript-selling business in Bologna, meant that the *Magna Glossa* took on the status of an official text.

If Accursius' compilation had the merit of including the thousands of annotations that the Bolognese glossators, beginning with Irnerius, had produced on Roman law, it was nevertheless vulnerable to two major criticisms: first, that it had ossified a genre, the gloss, which had previously been relatively fluid and open; and second, that the popularity of the *Magna Glossa* ensured that Accursian ideas dominated legal thought in Bologna, thereby making it difficult to express dissenting opinion. While it would be wrong to see Dante's damning of Accursius' oldest son Franciscus (1225–93) to Hell (*Inf.* XV, 106–10) as a wholesale condemnation of the *Magna Glossa*, it is nevertheless likely that the poet saw Franciscus as an example of those Bolognese jurists who relied heavily on their earnings from the law and from usury, an activity that was widely practised by *doctores legum* in Bologna and elsewhere. At the same time, it is also the case that, as we will see, Dante did express opinions that diverged sharply from the *Magna Glossa*, and this on matters that were anything but secondary.

The changed intellectual climate in Bologna helped other centres that were exploring alternative legal approaches to flourish. The most distinguished of these was that at Orléans, which was in open disagreement with Accursius' brand of Bolognese law, considering the latter stifling and old-fashioned. It was in this more open intellectual environment that, between the thirteenth and fourteenth centuries, part of the civil law tradition excluded in Bologna – or considered minor – migrated. 'Minor' in fact is the term that historians have unfairly applied to the work of those schools that developed during the twelfth century in northern Italy and in southern France, and that were frequently informal in character. The technique of commentary that later emerged in the different environment of Orléans, in north-central France, was powerfully shaped by the ideas of these so-called 'minor schools'. In these, although a conscious shift from the words (*verba*) to the *ratio* (reason) of the law had not yet happened, as would occur in mid-thirteenth-century Orléans, scholars had begun to reflect deeply on the philosophical-juridical concept of *causa* (cause). Greater links with the liberal arts, and a consequent openness to non-juridical culture, meant that jurists such as Joannes Bassianus (d. end of the twelfth century) at Mantua became interested in the new

Aristotelian translations prepared by James of Venice (*fl.* mid twelfth century), including the Latin version of the second book of the *Physics* that restored Aristotle's detailed explanation of the four *causae* to scholars in the West. The transition from an interest in the *causa* of a contract, as explored by Joannes Bassianus, to that of the *causa* or *ratio* of the law, as developed in Orléans in the second half of the thirteenth century, is a key sign of the willingness, a century later, on the part of the new French civil jurists to dialogue with ideas that had first emerged in the Italian 'minor schools'. Other signs of that dialogue can be found in debates on sovereignty and the empire – debates that perhaps were known to Dante via Cino da Pistoia, the Italian jurist who first embraced the ideas and methods of Orléans, and who served as a conduit for the spread of French legal ideas in Italy.

The masters at Orléans, despite the fact that they were churchmen, enjoyed close ties to the French crown. As a result, their approach was anything but hierocratic, which meant that they gave short shrift to the views of the Decretalists. They thus rejected Boniface VIII's extreme positions, especially as they were the first to start to consider the notion of national sovereignty. One of the leading voices in the school, Pierre de Belleperche (*c.*1230–1308), joined the court of Philip the Fair (1268–1314) in 1296 and quickly became one of his most trusted advisors. Belleperche opposed spiritual interference in secular jurisdiction, arguing that the sphere of ecclesiastical justice should not extend beyond matters of faith. The views of Jean de Monchy (active mid thirteenth century), the first to posit imperial power as an abstract quantity, were transmitted by his better-known pupil Jacques de Revigny (*c.*1230–96), who insisted that the empire had a jurisdictional function. In support of his position he cited a century-old constitution of Frederick I, still in circulation in feudal law; in addition, he drew on notions not unlike those developed in the twelfth century by those 'minor-school' authors who had focused on public law. Much of this material made its way, perhaps via Cino, into Dante's *Monarchia*, where the empire, following Frederician law, was defined as 'jurisdiction which embraces within its scope every other temporal jurisdiction' (III, x, 10).

Influenced by French thinkers, Cino firmly denounced as erroneous a gloss in the *Magna Glossa* claiming that the empire, rather than having been established by God, had come about as consequence of fortune. The origin of the empire was one of the most controversial ideological issues of the early fourteenth century. Anti-papal intellectuals strongly opposed the claim that the empire derived its authority from the Church, an idea that

*Law* 57

Decretalists sought to impose in place of the older view that both powers were of divine origin. It may well have been that particular gloss that aroused Dante's ire against jurists in the *Monarchia*, an attack that, rather than of a general nature, was most likely a repudiation of what he deemed to be the mistaken interpretation of Bolognese glossators.

In the juridical thinking of fourteenth-century Italy, ideas from Orléans were sometimes received together with those of that earlier civil tradition that had flourished largely separate from the *Magna Glossa*. An interesting expression of this intellectual current, dating back to the end of the twelfth century, was the idea of an abstract imperial power that did not concurrently involve anti-papal sentiment. It was from this perspective that the Peace of Constance (1183), by which Frederick Barbarossa, while ostensibly safeguarding imperial administrative rights, was actually forced to grant Lombard cities communal liberties and jurisdiction, took on a new significance in fourteenth-century legal thought. A striking example is that of Albericus de Rosciate (*c.*1290–1360), a jurist actively involved in Lombard politics, and who began to reflect on Frederick I's concessions and to study Rolandus of Lucca's *Summa Trium Librorum* (*c.*1145–*c.*1234; Summa of Three Books), the most extensive commentary on Roman public law written in an environment far from Bologna. The ease with which Albericus combined elements taken from the earlier tradition with passages from Cino, from French jurists, and from the authors of late-thirteenth-century Bolognese *quaestiones* (questions) suggests that various currents of European political-legal culture that have mostly been treated separately ought in fact be considered together. Furthermore, Albericus' frequent references to Dante should encourage us to pull down the walls that have traditionally been erected around medieval juridical culture. Its high level of technical expertise did not prevent communication with ideas coming from beyond the universe of legal thought. Albericus' admiration for Dante led him to translate into Latin Iacopo della Lana's (*c.*1278–*c.*1358) commentary on the *Commedia*. Bartolo da Sassoferrato (1313–57), who taught law in both Pisa and Perugia, consulted the *Monarchia* and accepted its basic political message. He even found the poet's literary arguments worthy of doctrinal consideration, including, in a commentary on the Justinian *Code*, a learned refutation of the idea of nobility that Dante had presented in the *canzone* 'The sweet rhymes of love'. Equally important is to recognize that such intellectual curiosity was reciprocal. Thus, if Dante's ideas on the Church and empire grew out of an intense dialogue with the most advanced

58 Sara Menzinger

currents of learned legal thought, in their turn Italian jurists of the fourteenth century read and reflected on Dante's work with considerable acumen.

## Notes

1 *Decretum Magistri Gratiani*, ed. E. Friedberg, 2nd edn (Leipzig: Tauchnitz, 1879).
2 See especially the *Novella* 'Quomodo oporteat episcopos' (Nov. 6 = Auth. coll. I. 6), *praef.*, in *Novellae*, ed. R. Schoel and W. Kroll (Berlin: Weidmann, 1912).
3 *Omnia Digesta seu Pandectarum*, ed. T. Mommsen and P. Krueger (Berlin: Weidmann, 1899).
4 *Codex Iustinianus*, ed. P. Krueger (Berlin: Weidmann, 1954).

CHAPTER 4

# *Justice*

*Giuliano Milani*

*Translated by James Cotton*

Justice, in both its meanings of virtue and of political function, plays a central role in Dante's work. The *Commedia* is not only a great judicial machine, but also the result of a meditation that began with the lyric poetry, written in exile, and that culminated in the *Monarchia*. In the course of this analysis, Dante begins by identifying the triumph of injustice as the determining sign of the political crisis of his time, and concludes by finding a solution to the crisis in the idea of a universal empire, which, as the supreme political authority, would be able to restore justice and peace to the world. Dante's identification of the exercise of justice with political power along with his interpretation of the political crisis as a judicial crisis find their roots and explanation in the contemporary context.

## Justice as social experience

In medieval Italian communes, citizens actively frequented the law courts. In Bologna, whose population reached around 50,000 in the last decade of the thirteenth century, the *podestà*'s criminal court, where felonies were tried, alone held between 1,400 and 3,000 trials a year (the *podestà* was the official in charge of maintaining peace and justice in a city). Fifty years earlier, in Perugia, a city half the size of Bologna, the criminal courts hosted less than half this number of trials. It is thus likely that, during Dante's age, the number of trials, already high from the outset, continued to increase. Moreover, as research on Perugia has demonstrated, these trials came to involve in one role or another (accuser, accused, witness, and guarantor) around a quarter of the entire urban population, women and children included. The surviving evidence does not allow for similar estimates for Florence; however, it is safe to surmise that participation in the judicial system was equally, if not even more intense. From the time of

Dante's great-great-grandfather Cacciaguida (*c*.1091–*c*.1148) to the poet's own, the number of courts consistently increased.

In Florence at the beginning of the twelfth century, the magistrates who dispensed justice were the consuls, the same who signed agreements with other cities, lords, and villages on behalf of the commune. They did so in a tribunal located near Orsanmichele, and they behaved almost like arbiters tasked in each case by the parties to find an agreement and settle the dispute. After the middle of the century, though their role as arbiters remained unchanged, the judges of the consular tribunals would mete out punishment to those who had failed to appear in court, ruling in favour of the party present and issuing sentences that, unlike arbitration, could not be rejected. For instance, in 1189 the Florentine consuls ruled in favour of the priest of the Church of San Martino del Vescovo who had brought a suit against various families for refusing to cut back the fig trees that grew on their properties adjoining the church and damaged its walls. Since his neighbours failed to appear in court to defend themselves, the consuls ruled that the fig trees should pass to the priest, who could then cut them down. Among the losers who had to act on the consuls' judgment were Cacciaguida's two sons, Preitenitto and Alighiero, Dante's great-grandfather.

Litigants went to the tribunal in the hope that the judge would recognize the validity of their case and rule accordingly. In twelfth-century Italy many of the authorities that had exercised justice in previous centuries (counts, marquises, and bishops) were ceasing to do this, choosing instead to increase their wealth through other means, such as war, the imposition of taxes, and from land holdings. In the resulting power vacuum, the widespread demand for justice, which economic expansion had further increased, was satisfied by the communes. After an initial period of uncertainty, which coincided with the coming into being of the communes and for which little documentary evidence has survived, the city tribunals appear to have been quickly granted the public power of *iurisdictio* (jurisdiction), which consisted in passing judgments, assigning assets, and providing titles that recognized the claims of the plaintiffs. Rather than delegated by a higher authority such as the empire, which would sometimes recognize the city tribunals after the fact, the communes were granted judicial power, on the one hand by the litigants themselves, since it was they who entrusted their disputes to the communes, and therefore accepted their rules, and on the other by the legal experts who maintained and replicated the system as judges, lawyers, and guarantors.

# Justice

At the beginning of the Duecento an important change occurred. The city consuls were replaced by the *podestà*, the foreign magistrate chosen from one of the allied cities to govern the commune for a year, presiding over the tribunals and councils, and leading the army. With the coming of the *podestà*, the number of tribunals increased. For instance, in Florence, the *curia forensium* (foreigners' court) was established to handle legal disputes that involved the inhabitants of the surrounding countryside, who were dependents of local noblemen or of religious institutions. Formerly, these kinds of cases were mostly handled in the bishop's tribunal, which nevertheless continued to operate. The result was a multiplication of different types of court. Furthermore, foreign judges, whom the *podestà* brought in from the outside together with notaries and armed guards, began to play an influential role. The non-Florentine judges dealt with the same kinds of cases that had previously been debated in the city's other tribunals, thereby offering citizens an additional means of legal judgment, and quickly became the only tribunal for cases of *maleficia*, namely of criminal trials. The foreign judges were impartial by contract if not by vocation, given that, at the end of their mandate, the *podestà* were subject to the *sindacato*, the administrative proceedings that oversaw the correctness of their actions during their time in power. On the occasion of the *sindacato*, citizens could denounce magistrates who, if found guilty, would not be paid by the commune. In addition, by exercising justice in a different city every six months, the magistrates knew the rules that worked best and tried to adapt them to different situations on the basis of the shared procedures that jurists elaborated and set down in the *ordines iudiciarii* (procedural handbooks). These were indispensable tools because, from the middle of the twelfth century in Italy's communal courts, as a result of the growing influence of civil lawyers and canonists, the ancient procedural rules of Roman law began to be practised again. Throughout the century the number of courts continued to grow. In line with reforms that sought to tidy up the administration of justice, cases instigated by the residents of a particular administrative area were entrusted to the existing courts. As a result, individual tribunals that had once adjudicated cases for three city districts (*sestieri*), later adjudicated for two, and finally for just one. The new foreign magistrates, who were established alongside the *podestà*, namely the Capitano del Popolo (Captain of the People) and then the Esecutore degli Ordinamenti di Giustizia (Executor of the Ordinances of Justice), presided over the new courts. The tribunals of the individual guilds, the cooperative societies that brought together practitioners of the same trade, continued to deal with disputes among their own members.

In 1308 some of the guild courts became confederated, forming the tribunal of the Mercanzia (Merchant Guild), whose expertise lay in cases of retaliatory action and commercial debt. Between city and guild, secular and ecclesiastical, civil and criminal courts, the Florence of Dante's time had no less than thirty-eight tribunals.

To explain these developments, it is important to remember that, as the Duecento went on, Florence's population not only increased, but also had ever more important economic and political interests to defend. As a result, people turned to the courts seeking to gain advantage in private disputes, which furthermore, before and after the trial, were continued outside the courtroom. Petitioning a judge was in fact only part of a larger campaign that was fought by means of notarial contracts, compromises, private peace accords in which the disputants promised to comply with the terms of the settlement, or vendettas that involved the regulated use of violence. These practices, which were considered legitimate within the communes, and which were undertaken at various social levels, were embroiled in different ways with the legal process. Citizens, then, used public justice as an important means to reach their own objectives; whether directly or through their representatives, they were familiar with legal rules and procedures.

The *ordines iudiciarii* reveal, and this is confirmed by the court documents of the period, that a lawsuit would begin with the filing of a *libello*, a written document where the plaintiff asked for the award of the matter under dispute, and which followed a precise and complex form based on canon and Roman law. The judge would summon the defendant to appear within a given period of time. If the defendant did not reply, s/he was declared in default, and the judge, as we have seen, immediately ruled in the plaintiff's favour. If the defendant did appear in court, s/he, like the plaintiff, had to take an oath against slandering the other party. Then the assessment of the evidence would begin. Typically, this took the form of documents (notarial acts, account books, and public registers) or witnesses, who were questioned by the judge on the petition of the parties, with the possible introduction of objections. Finally, often after having sought the advice of a jurist, the judge would pass sentence. This could involve the transfer of ownership of the disputed good; the obligation to pay legal fees; and, to this end, the possible seizure of property or, in cases of insufficient goods, arrest followed by imprisonment.

Beginning a civil case, the plaintiff tried to bring pressure to bear on someone to discharge an obligation – pay a loan, accept the division of an inheritance, or fulfil a business contract. Turning to a judge charged

# Justice 63

with handling *maleficia*, namely crimes, one sought rather to reinterpret to one's own advantage the legislative rules that defined what qualified as criminal conduct. In Dante's time, the goal of pursuing a civil case was thus to obtain something, while the goal of pursuing a criminal case was to obtain someone's punishment. In criminal cases, the *libello* presented to the judge had to refer to a crime defined as such in the statutes, namely murder, bodily injury, theft, armed robbery, usurpation, forgery, and so on, that the accuser would affirm had occurred, often employing the very same words as those written in the statute. Both parties had to swear to tell the truth. If the accused did not show up in court, the judge would issue a ban. The ban was the city's response to a failure to follow an order of the court, and it deprived the *bandito*, the person receiving the ban, of the chance to denounce in court anyone who attacked their property or even their person. The *bandito* was thus denied the protection the court normally guaranteed citizens, so that anyone could offend them, even kill them, without having to face the consequences. Usually, the ban could be revoked. By presenting themselves in court and paying a fine, *banditi* would regain their rights, including the right to denounce whoever had offended them. However, in cases where the offence was particularly grave, such as rebellion, forgery, or treason, the judge would issue a 'perpetual' ban, one that in theory could not be revoked.

If instead the accused showed up in court and the trial proceeded, both documentary evidence and that of witnesses was presented, sometimes through the use of *intentiones*, the lists of questions written by the opposing party. The ruling would be preceded by possible objections and the frequent recourse to the opinion of experts. If the accused was found guilty, a punishment was decreed, most often financial, and perhaps accompanied by restrictive measures, such as exclusion from office. Less often, the punishment was physical, such as the pillory or the stocks, flogging or the *secchiate d'acqua* (a form of public humiliation), or mutilation of the hand or tongue. In cases of capital punishment, various means were available, such as hanging, burning at the stake, or quartering by horses, all depending on the type of crime committed and the social class of the criminal.

However, even bringing an accusation before a judge *ad maleficia* was more a way to obtain an advantage than an effort to punish an enemy effectively. This is proven by the fact that the overwhelming majority of accusatory trials for which we have information ended in acquittal. More often than not, proceedings would stop at the very first stages, sometimes as a result of the stipulation to arrive at a 'private' peace. This points to the fact that simply presenting the accusation could be sufficient to put pressure on an adversary and to achieve one's objective. Proceeding with the trial until its conclusion would only happen as a last resort, when all other possibilities for arriving at an agreement had failed. The aim of the accuser was therefore to reach a favourable settlement, one that could not be reached without the intervention of an independent legally sanctioned third party, who was able publicly to redefine the conflict in new terms.

Beginning in the twelfth century, Italian city records document the principle that 'it is not in the public interest for crimes to go unpunished'. However, it was only in the following century, that this norm was invoked to conduct a new kind of trial, the inquisitorial. As we have seen thus far, in accusatory trials justice was a function of private initiative, where the accuser had to provide the evidence to support their claims. Conversely, the inquisitorial trial began with the public initiative of the judge, and the accused had to defend themselves to prove their innocence. This system was introduced by the Church to counter and control deviant behaviour and was codified in the decretals of Pope Innocent III (b. 1160/61; papacy 1198–1216) around the time of the Fourth Lateran Council (1215). In the decades that followed this system was also employed by the tribunals of the Italian cities. The city-states promoted inquisitions both for repressing heresy and for other crimes considered especially detrimental to civic peace. These included political crimes (such as rebellion) or crimes, such as forging documents or counterfeiting money, that undermined the commune's right to exercise control over activities that it deemed its own exclusive prerogative. The inquisitorial trial could come about through an *inquisitio generalis*, or general inquest, promoted by the local city authorities, namely those in charge of parishes; or as a result of *clamor* or *rumor* (news or gossip) that reached the ears of the judge via an anonymous accusation or as a result of someone's poor reputation; or yet again as a consequence of private reporting, at times incentivized by the promise of a reward decreed in emergency legislation. After criminal conduct had been recognized, summons would be issued against the accused. If the accused failed to respond, a ban was once again imposed. If the accused appeared in court, they would be interrogated, possibly under torture, which was considered a means of obtaining information and not a punishment in itself, and which, with the exception of some political trials, was used primarily on foreigners and 'persons of ill repute'. The summons and interrogation of witnesses would follow on the basis of questions prepared by the judge, who in this way would try to reconstruct the truth of the matter and establish the suspect's reputation, in this instance after also having consulted experts and weighed the objections of lawyers, in order to arrive at a verdict and the possible meting out of punishment.

Conducted much less frequently than accusatory trials, inquisitorial trials, once they had become part of a city's judicial system, began to be another weapon citizens could employ to continue their private battles. At the same time, having to defend themselves, citizens and their lawyers challenged the most repressive aspects of the inquisitorial trial on the basis of testimony, procedural exceptions, and legal arguments. Generally speaking, the spread of the inquisitorial trial further served to increase citizens' participation in the judicial system, as well as their knowledge of its inner workings, its structures, and the language of the law.

## Justice as political conflict

By conducting inquisitorial trials, the city-states, just as the monarchies, the Church, and the papacy were doing, did not limit themselves to placing at their citizens' disposal a new system that could address their requests for justice and offer them the possibility of recompense, but also affirmed the autonomous right of those in power to seek out anyone who had offended the community, to make them confess, and to punish them. As we have seen, the commune was born essentially as a tribunal, and had developed by extending its control over conflicts and over the procedures for resolving these. Acquiring the ability to launch judicial proceedings, the commune extended its control over one of the key means by which political power was exercised. Precisely because justice was such an important function of government, from the very beginning the commune found itself in conflict with other authorities over matters of jurisdiction, so that its ability to exercise justice was a source of debate and conflict. During the first half of the Duecento, for example, the commune of Florence challenged the emperor in order to be allowed the right of appeal to annul the verdicts of other courts. The commune only managed to exercise this right when imperial control was weak, since emperors, as the traditional source of all political power, and thereby occupying the highest rung of the judicial hierarchy, were the only ones who could claim the right of annulment. As soon as they were able, emperors reclaimed the power for themselves, first with Otto IV (1175–1218) in 1214, and later with Frederick of Antioch (c.1223–55/56), Frederick II's (1194–1250) legate in 1246.

Another significant jurisdictional clash occurred between the commune and the Bishop of Florence. Beginning in the Duecento, the opening of the communal court for foreigners extended the commune's control over the inhabitants of the surrounding countryside who lived on the properties of the bishop and of other lords, and who therefore were subject to their judicial authority. At first, when summoned to the new court, some of the inhabitants of the countryside protested that they were only legally bound to the jurisdiction of the bishop's tribunal, but in time the commune prevailed. The bishop retained jurisdiction over the clergy and, in a few instances, over the laity: specifically for marital conflicts, usury, and later blasphemy. At the same time, the commune handled marital conflicts regarding a spouse's assets.

From the end of the twelfth century, the bishop exercised inquisitorial and judicial power in controlling heresy, while the commune continued to implement the verdicts against heretics and to punish them. An important change occurred around 1230, when new papal regulations delegated an inquiry's preliminary stages, such as the gathering of facts, to the communes. In Florence as elsewhere, this new state of affairs created tensions between the inquisition, then under Dominican control, and the commune. Only when Pope Innocent IV (b. *c.*1195; papacy 1243–54) issued the Bull *Ad exstirpanda* (For the Extirpation) in 1254, which deprived the commune of inquisitorial responsibilities, were the tensions finally eased. Despite this, and despite assigning the persecution of heretics to the friars minor (1251), the commune continued to interfere in the courts of the inquisition. In subsequent decades it would claim a share of heretics' confiscated goods, seek and obtain the repeal of some verdicts, and appoint its own lay representatives.

As we have seen, precisely because justice was a shared experience present in every citizen's life, the commune's jurisdictional battles with the emperor, the bishop, the mendicant inquisitors, and through them the pope, created deep divisions in the citizenry, especially as these clashes became entangled with conflicts between organized aristocratic factions, just then beginning to be termed Guelfs and Ghibellines, and with the social tensions between the traditional elite and the *popolo*, namely, the members of the guilds.

In their turn, these internal tensions found a focal point in the execution of justice, allowing different groups to pursue their interests. As in the rest of Italy, in the second half of the Duecento, when the *popolo* managed to assume the government of the city, it promulgated a 'legalist' ideology, which led to an increase in the number of actions considered criminal and to the prescription of more severe punishments for crimes. It was based on a moralizing programme meant to define as 'good citizens'

## Justice

those who supported themselves through work, were members of a guild, participated in council meetings, and stayed clear of gambling houses and brothels. The legalist programme carried out significant reforms that concentrated penal justice in the courts of the *podestà*, and reduced the role of non-professional figures (consuls of justice and temporaries, who still presided over some civil courts), to the benefit of judges, who constituted the hegemonic block and intellectual bulwark of the first government of the *popolo*, the so-called *primo popolo* (1250–60).

After a brief period of Ghibelline rule following the *primo popolo*, the Guelf regime in Florence, which came to power in 1267, was the one under which Dante grew up. The regime was heir to different preceding political experiences: that of the commune of the *podestà*, whose courts, from the beginning of the Duecento, had become increasingly powerful and autonomous; that of the repression of heretics, begun thirty years earlier and then renewed on various occasions despite tensions with Rome and the friars minor; and that of the legalist ideology of the *primo popolo*, with its programme of morally edifying punishment, which retained ties to the new Guelf government through key figures such as Brunetto Latini (*c.*1220–93). To all this was added the anti-Ghibelline politics of Charles of Anjou (1226–85), who, after conquering the Kingdom of Sicily and defeating the Hohenstaufen, was nominated *podestà* of Florence in 1267. Taken together, these represented divergent political experiences, whose clash would give rise to moments of political tension in the decades to follow. However, they also constituted experiences that converged in their aim to reinforce public institutions' control over conflicts, behaviour, and ideas. From the last quarter of the Duecento onwards, even as shifts occurred in the balance of power, administrative justice in Florence was characterized by the ever-escalating use of policing strategies, of preventive measures, and of punishments, as well as by the expansion of what was defined as constituting criminal behaviour.

The first significant change involved the Ghibellines. After the arrival of Charles of Anjou's troops in Florence, the authorities did not stop, as they had done previously, at banishing the rebellious citizens (in this case the Ghibellines), who had left Florence and regrouped to continue to fight the city from the outside. Instead, they took a census of all the Ghibellines' potential allies (who turned out to be several thousand), listed their names, and divided them into different classes of *confinati*, people expelled from the city and required to reside in specified locations outside the city. The more dangerous they were judged to be, the further away they were sent. The *confinati* were also subjected to periodic checks.

Examining the lists of people sentenced to confinement written at different times reveals that in cases when *confinati* were not present in their place of internment, they could be transferred to a more distant location or be banned, thereby losing their rights and protections under the law.

The new anti-Ghibelline measures were not established by judges in courts of law on the basis of trials, but by exceptional political institutions controlled by the Guelfs. Nevertheless, the new repression of the Ghibellines became part of the city's judicial system because it introduced new offences. Thus, in the tribunals, one could be denounced for breaking confinement, for harbouring banned persons, or for plotting against the Guelfs. This system lasted until the peace of 1280 brokered by Cardinal Latino (d. 1294), which initiated a period when the *popolo* made advances over the Guelfs, although without loyalty to Charles of Anjou being compromised. During the *popolo*'s second government, there was a return to the legalistic and penal programme that had characterized the first. Between 1281 and 1292 its ever more radical politics sought to maintain public order by preparing lists of magnates who were considered potentially dangerous because of their power, their belonging to elite families, and their propensity for violence. The magnates were expected to provide the commune with the so-called *sodamenti*, financial guarantees to ensure that they did no harm. Furthermore, from 1286 every male relative of a magnate was held liable for any infraction of the guarantee. In 1293, in the context of worsening tensions between the minor and major guilds encouraged by the aristocratic, pro-*popolo* merchant Giano della Bella (*c.*1240–*c.*1305), the Ordinances of Justice were approved. Among other things, the Ordinances set particularly severe punishments for magnates who offended members of the *popolo*. Despite the successive 'temperings' of 1295, which toned down some aspects of these rules (and which were supported by Dante), the Ordinances remained in force, and with them the principle in Florentine legislation that stipulated that anyone identified a priori as dangerous or suspicious would receive different treatment in the courts.

In keeping with this principle, other changes along the same lines followed: systematic inquiries in the parishes aimed at suppressing deviant behaviour; an increase in the severity of punishments, with the introduction of the death penalty for murder; and more frequent recourse than had been the case in the past to imprisonment or confinement to suppress crimes considered as especially serious. As a result, justice in Florence in the last years of the Duecento – the years when Dante was involved in the highest levels of government – could avail itself of new and radical

# Justice

means of repression. Not surprisingly, justice was employed regularly as a weapon in political conflict. Indeed, as the conflict intensified, it assumed ever more violent forms.

Events in Florence at the end of the thirteenth century reveal an unbroken chain of judicial scandals and of political battles fought out in the courts. In 1296 Corso Donati (d. 1308) married Tessa degli Ubertini, the rich heiress of the nobleman Ubertino da Gaville, with the understanding that she would bring with her a dowry of 6,000 florins. Soon after, however, the bride's widowed mother Giovanna, with ties to the Cerchi bank, refused to pay the dowry, which led to a civil suit during the course of which even the pope became involved. First, Boniface VIII (b. c.1235; papacy 1294–1303) issued a brief that annulled the marriage on the basis of canon law. However, changing sides, he then issued an opinion that declared the marriage valid, justifying his about-face with the need to avoid further scandal. In 1298, in the very same bishop's tribunal, the case between several canons and the jurist Giovanni di Angiolino di Boninsegna dei Machiavelli (c.1250–1330) began. Machiavelli, the treasurer of the *capitolo fiorentino* (College of Canons), had been accused of rape, sodomy, gambling, usury, and of having an innocent man condemned to death. That same year, the captain of the *popolo* was granted the *arbitrium*, or the special power, justified in terms of the commune's good, to sue witnesses who had given false testimony in the previous two trials. In 1299 the *podestà*, Monfiorito da Coderta (d. after 1330), promoted extraordinary new inquiries. One of these, the case against Giovanna, Corso Donati's mother-in-law, condemned her for having begun the conflict that had caused division in the city, and thus for having harmed the public good. Subsequently, however, Monfiorito himself was investigated for improper exercise of justice. The condemnation of the *podestà* for corruption, after he confessed under torture, triggered a new inquisition against 'all corrupters of the regime, rectors and officials',[1] which, after resulting in the ban against Corso Donati, lasted for nine months. The following year, in 1300, the new *podestà* too was condemned for having made errors during an investigation. Also in that year, a new trial began against several bankers close to the papal curia. It concluded with a guilty verdict that would weigh heavily on relations between Florence and Boniface VIII.

In this atmosphere of granting of special powers, of inquests motivated by political emergencies, and of harsh and contested sentences, the most acute phase of the conflict between Black and White Guelfs began (see Chapter 1), including the establishment in 1301 of the inquiry that, the following year, led to Dante's ban. The political and judicial escalation that marked Dante's years as a politician had become a vicious circle. On the one hand, recourse was habitually made to the courts to eliminate adversaries; on the other, those condemned always attempted to counter-attack using the same weapons, defending themselves in court and responding with new inquiries. The overall result was that everyone contributed both to bolstering the law's repressive aspects and to making justice ever more politicized.

## Conclusion: beyond Florence

In the years immediately following these events, a similar escalation occurred beyond the borders of the Italian city-states. As a result, trials became a form of governing. The age of the big political trials had begun, first with Philip the Fair, the King of France (1268–1314), bringing post-mortem proceedings against Pope Boniface VIII (1303–13) and against the Templars (1308–12), and then with Pope John XXII's (b. 1244; papacy 1316–34) inquisitions against the Italian Ghibellines, when political enemies were accused of 'unspeakable' crimes such as sodomy and witchcraft. As had already happened in the Italian communes of the Duecento, accusations of heresy were also used to invoke an eternal, divine justice that assured the accused punishment in the afterlife. Yet even in these grandiose, high-flown trials, as had been typical of communal justice, the same respect for formal procedures was maintained, and the court was treated as a source of legitimation, as well as a weapon, in personal battles.

In the years when Dante started to think about composing the *Commedia*, in Italy as elsewhere – from the city-states to the monarchies and the papacy – the exercise of justice had reached a stage of development that made evident some of its fundamental underlying contradictions. Justice no longer seemed solely the means whereby anyone might obtain restitution, but was also the instrument with which to legitimize private interests and political goals. Precisely because justice had returned to being a powerful political tool, people became disillusioned with the legal process. New clashes began over what was legally appropriate and over how justice should be pursued, with both those who used the system to their own advantage and those who suffered its effects being pushed towards redefining it in radically new ways.

## Note

1 R. Davidsohn, *Forschungen zur Geschichte von Florenz* (Berlin: Mittler, 1901), vol. III, p. 268.

CHAPTER 5

# Men and women

*Holly Hurlburt*

At roughly the same time that Dante Alighieri was composing his *Commedia*, his fellow Florentine poet, Francesco da Barberino (1264–1338) was writing a rather different type of book. His *Reggimento e costumi di donna* (Conduct and Customs of Women, *c.*1318–20), written partly in verse and partly in prose, imagined dialogues between real women at various stages in their life cycles, interspersed with advice from allegorical virtues such as Patience and Chastity. Francesco classified women according to their marital and religious identity: maiden, wife, widow, nun, hermit, or servant. Within each of these categories he subdivided according to social class, expending the least energy on working and working-class women. By inscribing the female life cycle according to marital status, he embraced the standard medieval ideology, following the patriarchy of Aristotle's *Politics* and the pseudo-Aristotelian *Economics* among others, which dictated that, given the female's inherent weaknesses, the best place for women was the home, under the close tutelage and guardianship of fathers and husbands.

In many ways law statutes promulgated in the emergent communes of the twelfth and thirteenth centuries in northern and central Italy reflected this familial patriarchy. Women were not defined as citizens, suggesting that they played no defined role in political life. Only in feudal Naples did the fourteenth century witness female rule, in the much-maligned person of Giovanna I of Anjou (1325–82; reign 1343–81). Inheritance laws in most city-states limited a woman's inheritance to her dowry portion, demonstrating that money, like politics, was best left in the hands of men. Furthermore, in many places a woman required male oversight to enter into legal agreements. Francesco da Barberino's text, directed at a female audience, presents an idealized summation of the gendered separate sphere ideal that situated men as leaders in both the State and the home, while constraining women's public and private lives. Nonetheless, in the fourteenth century the vicissitudes of daily life meant that some women

71

fulfilled the roles Francesco ascribed to them while engaging in activities well beyond the gendered expectations of prescriptive literature.

Treatises such as Francesco da Barberino's combined advice on how women should fulfil their limited sphere of activities with moral instruction. A well-off wife's duties, beyond swearing to love and be loyal and faithful to her spouse, and possessing unimpeachable virtue, included regulating the house and servants, and maintaining her husband's belongings. The nature of the proto-capitalist merchant economy of fourteenth-century Italy often meant that the reality of household management for women entailed considerably more than what prescriptive literature described. For example, merchant Francesco Datini's (1335–1410) business dealings often took him far from his homes in Prato and Florence. His wife Margherita Bandini (*c*.1360–1423) engaged in frugal day-to-day management of the household, and in his absence her managerial skills extended to providing provisions for him, overseeing his various properties, and writing or dictating detailed letters to him concerning all aspects of the household entrusted to her. Very few medieval Italian women left behind such an invaluable record; however, many whose husbands were merchants, sailors, soldiers, or guild masters engaged in similar practices. These examples suggest that a combination of personal feelings and necessity prompted men to entrust the well-being of family and business to their wives, despite whatever failings prevailing ideology attributed to the latter's sex.

In addition to her tangible activities overseeing servants, provisioning the house, and managing her spouse's business concerns, a wife was expected to conform to strict moral expectations of modesty and chastity – assets which reflected and enhanced the honour of her spouse and family. Such virtues qualified queen consorts and other rulers' wives to provide their spouses with moral counsel when necessary, according to Francesco da Barberino. On the other hand, prescriptive literature abounded with examples of the dire personal suffering and familial dishonour resulting from the absence of these virtues in women, as in the case of Francesca da Rimini, an adulterer encountered by Dante among the lustful in the second circle of Hell (*Inf.* V, 79–142). That Dante's circle of the lustful contains the largest group of women to be found in his Hell is emblematic of contemporary concerns about women's alleged propensity to sexual sin. Modesty and chastity, crucial both in the process of attracting a husband and as evidence of loyalty, love, and obedience to him thereafter, defined a woman's moral existence. Behaviour trumped beauty in Francesco da Barberino's story of Messer Corrado, who chose

*Men and women* · 73

the well-mannered Gioietta over the glamorous Princess Anna. Francesco urged women to speak, walk, and even eat modestly, and cautioned them about public appearances, but noted that there were occasions where ornament and behaviour functioned to enhance family honour and to indicate power and status. Yet women constantly trod a thin line between honour and vainglorious shame. Their alleged tendency to sensuality accompanied by a ceaseless desire for luxury consumption was increasingly thought to endanger husbands' pocketbooks and society as a whole, as is suggested by Dante's progenitor Cacciaguida (*c.*1091–*c.*1148), who recalled nostalgically the city of Florence, gendered female, of his own time: 'She had no bracelet, no tiara, no embroidered gown, no girdle that should be seen more than the wearer' (*Par.* XV, 100–2). Such concerns, pointed at women guilty of ruinous spending, also punctuated the language and restrictions of fourteenth-century sumptuary law, which Dante's interlocutor Forese Donati (d. 1296) called for in order to reign in 'the brazen women of Florence', who, in contrast to Saracens and other non-Christian women, require 'spiritual disciplines' in order to 'make them go covered' (*Purg.* XXIII, 101–5). And at least in Florence, such anxieties, real or imagined, prompted the creation of the *Ufficiale delle donne, degli ornamenti e delle vesti* (Office for Women, Ornaments, and Clothes; 1330) for enforcement of sumptuary laws. The very title of this magistracy indicated that there, as elsewhere in Italy, women's consumerism, like their sexuality, was perceived to be in dire need of restraint, even in girls as young as ten.

It must have been a source of great anguish to Margherita Bandini, and many other women, not to fulfil the other main expectation of medieval wives: reproduction and motherhood, or in Dante's approving terms, keeping 'watch, tending the cradle' (*Par.* XV, 121). Children were tremendously important to late medieval men and women, for emotional reasons, to be sure, but also as sources of family continuity, honour, fame, and social networks for the elite and up and coming, and as a source of labour and income in the family economy for the less well off. Perhaps it was the pressure of maternal expectations that prompted Margherita Bandini to agree to care for her husband's illegitimate child. Many advice manuals, including Francesco da Barberino's, contained instructions on what to do in case of infertility. Moderation in food and behaviour was likewise his counsel to pregnant women: no doubt reasonable advice at a time when mother and infant mortality rates were high. On the other hand, he had little to say about actual mothering practices. Like many of his time he had an ambiguous attitude towards nursing – he urged women to breastfeed for the sake of their children and to please God, but, acknowledging the ubiquity of wet nurses, offered advice both to supervising mothers and to women who cared for the children of others. Francesco da Barberino did not dedicate a separate chapter in his treatise to motherhood; perhaps he regarded child-rearing as the work of the father (certainly the case for sons), or perhaps he took motherhood for granted as an innate element of womanhood. When he did discuss mothers' roles, it was mostly in terms of careful gate-keeping and of the moral education of their daughters in preparation for marriage, which for most women took place in their mid-to-late teens.

Mothers and fathers shared in the educating of their children, with the former caring for and imparting basic practical and religious teaching to girls and boys, and the latter increasingly called upon to provide moral education, especially to boys (some elite women received rudimentary schooling from tutors, fathers, or convents). Mothers taught their daughters how to be wives, sometimes participated in the selection of a spouse, and used their personal wealth to contribute to their daughters' dowry, the money provided by a father for the upkeep of his daughter and her children upon leaving the natal family. The dowry system, inherited from Roman times, had co-existed with other, Germanic forms of marital exchange in the Middle Ages, but re-emerged in force in Italy in the thirteenth century as a marker of status and as a crucial source of revenue in an age of commercial development. Marriage was thus a financial exchange, though for many in fourteenth-century Italy it was also a crucial facilitator of social networks. In merchant and elite classes, marriage cemented and symbolized social, political, and business alliances between families: Francesco Datini selected Margherita Bandini on account of her kin, well-established in the important merchant entrepôt of Florence, despite her lack of dowry.

The late Middle Ages did witness the development of a cult of motherhood relating to perceptions of the Virgin Mary. The Virgin was a woman of great significance to many medieval Christians, including Dante, who wrote rapturously of his encounter with the Queen of Heaven in the final pages of the *Commedia*: 'and if I were as rich in speech words as in imagining, I should not dare attempt the least part of her delights' (*Par.* XXXI, 136–8). The idea of the Virgin as patron for authors and intercessor not just for women, but for individuals of both genders, corporate groups, and cities was a powerful one in this time period of war, disease, economic instability, and inconsistent spiritual leadership. The city of Siena was one of many Italian and European cities that adopted the Virgin as its patron, after an unexpected victory over the neighbouring city of Florence in

## Men and women

1260. Her metaphorical succouring of humanity featured prominently in the fine arts of the time in several ways – Dante was only one among dozens of poets who transferred their literary devotion from the unattainable court lady of chivalric literature to the Virgin. Contrasting her constancy with the fickleness of love between humans, monk and poet Gautier of Coincy (1177–1236) wrote: 'Let us leave off the mad practice of love ... let us love the one who is beautiful and good, sweet and quiet'.[1] The idea of the Virgin as protectrix was expressed visually in votive images of the *Madonna della Misericordia* (Madonna of Mercy), who literally embraced followers (citizens, guild and confraternity members) in a protective voluminous cloak. In the visual arts, the Virgin became more human, depicted as simple, humble, and beautiful, often literally in the act of helping her infant nurse: by feeding him, she fed all Christians. John of Garland wrote in the thirteenth century that 'her milk is truly virginal, the nectar of spiritual life, through which death meets its defeat', words especially resonant in a time of famine, war, and plague.[2] With such imagery the Virgin became the ideal good mother – a reflection of all fourteenth-century women who bore, raised, nourished, and interceded on behalf of their children. The Virgin provided an ideal model for femininity, but at the same time she reminded women that they fell short of her perfection.

The less than perfect nature of earthly women became a hotly debated literary topic during Dante's life and in the decades following his death. The ideas of Aristotle on women's innate physical and moral inferiority, echoed by Thomas Aquinas (1225–74), found their way into the literary works of the period, especially Jean de Meun's (*c.*1240–*c.*1305) section of the allegorical poem the *Roman de la Rose* (Romance of the Rose, *c.*1285). Intellectual figures from all over Europe responded to Jean's claims, many agreeing with the idea that women were deceptive and prone to vice. Although Dante did not participate in this debate explicitly, Giovanni Boccaccio did in his *De mulieribus claris* (On Famous Women; 136–62), a compendium of *exempla* of good and bad female behaviour past and present, both real and mythological. Some of Boccaccio's examples echo the many and diverse charges of female inferiority found in *Roman de la rose* and other works of what would come to be called the *querelle des femmes* (debate on women), as well as in his own starkly misogynistic *Corbaccio*. Nonetheless, in *De mulieribus claris*, dedicated to a lady-in-waiting at the court of Queen Giovanna of Naples, he prudently applauded feminine courage and intellect on certain occasions, praising the learned creativity of the Greek poet Sappho, and assessing positively the governance skills of Irene of Constantinople (*c.*752–803) and of Queen Giovanna as being equal to or even surpassing those of men, in contrast to Dante, who trenchantly recounted the licentious flaws of ruling women such as Semiramis, Dido, and Cleopatra in the circle of the lustful (*Inf.* V, 52–63). A movement of female scholars that began in the late fourteenth century with the Paduan humanist Maddalena Scrovegni (1356–1429) and the Venetian-born widow Christine de Pisan (1363–1430), author of the first defence of women to be penned by a woman, followed in Boccaccio's footsteps by praising elite women and their learning.

Like Christine de Pisan, Maddalena Scrovegni, and Margherita Bandini, many married women faced widowhood because they tended to be younger than their husbands and because their lives, outside the travails of pregnancy, were better protected and less perilous. Francesco da Barberino acknowledged at the outset of his treatment of widowhood the variety and difficulty of questions it raised: depending on whether the widow was old, middle-aged, or young, and whether she had children or not. Should she retain her husband's belongings, 'take the habit or clothes of religion', or remarry?[3] Widowhood was theoretically the only time in a woman's life when she might be freed from the legal guardianship of father or husband; however, laws and circumstances often rendered such freedom largely meaningless for most save the wealthiest women. If they could support themselves and their children with their dowries, investments, or other inheritance, they might have some choice between marrying again, entering a convent, or embracing the ideal of chaste, pious widowhood while remaining uncloistered. As Dante noted, dowry prices were on the rise in the fourteenth century (*Par.* XV, 103–5), an inflation from which, paradoxically, some widows benefitted. Lucia Falier (d. 1387), the childless former dogaressa of Venice, came from a wealthy family and possessed a substantial dowry, so she sustained herself comfortably for some thirty-two years of widowhood, hiring an agent to manage her investments, and making generous bequests to her kin in testaments. Significant dowries and children also meant that the future of a widow would likely be of interest to her natal and marital families, who sought control of funds and heirs. Widowed wives of guild masters were in some cases allowed to assume control of the shop, but often encouraged to remarry so that business would remain in masculine hands. For the poorest widows, remarriage was often the best option for financial and physical protection; while for widows with children, remarriage often meant leaving their offspring with relatives of their deceased spouses. Elderly and impoverished widows relied on the charity of their families or society, and were often marginalized.

# Men and women

As noted above, the prevailing system of patriarchy situated men as superior to women, and thus entrusted to them full responsibility as the governors of family, business, state, and Church. Male behaviour nonetheless had rules: Francesco da Barberino began the *Reggimento* by observing that many books had been written about male customs: here he probably refers to his own previous work, *Documenti d'amore* (Teachings of Love), a manual of masculine virtues, etiquette, and the 'rules of love'. Indeed, many other genres of late medieval literature, from sermons to educational tracts to biographies of famous men, addressed issues of masculinity, suggesting concern with ideal male behaviour. Relations with women encapsulated in marriage and parenting went a long way towards defining late medieval masculinity and adulthood. That marriage and the birth of heirs were crucial turning points in the lives of men is likewise indicated in the dozens of *ricordanze*, diaries kept by Italian merchants, especially in Florence. Alongside meticulous records of business dealings, these diaries recorded genealogy (paternal) and births and deaths of, in particular, male children who would inherit and enhance the patriline.

As curious blends of family history and accounting, many *ricordanze* document the processes of male upbringing. Whereas such texts contain little or nothing about girls until they are of marriageable age, in his own account, fourteenth-century merchant Goro Dati (1362–1435) wrote that 'when I had learned enough arithmetic, I went to work in the silk merchant's shop ... I was thirteen'.[4] Such experiences were common for adolescent boys, whose schooling and vocational training depended on their social class. The chronicler Giovanni Villani (*c.*1275–1348) suggested that many boys (and perhaps some girls) attended rudimentary grammar schools in Florence before or in conjunction with mathematical training for sons of merchants (see Chapter 16). Like Dati, many were apprenticed to a shop, or as with Francesco Datini, learned the family trade from their fathers or other men in the family. They largely left behind mothers and younger or female siblings until training was complete (in the case of craft guilds), or young men were wealthy enough to support a wife and family. Unlike female adolescence, which ended for elite women in their teens and perhaps a little later for lower-class women, male adolescence provided a long period of relative sexual freedom. Datini was one among many men who fathered at least one child before marriage, a practice frowned upon but tolerated by society, and one which in part explains the prevailing concerns with protecting female chastity found in Francesco da Barberino and elsewhere.

If the procreation and rearing of male heirs was a crucial element of medieval male identity, so too was the legitimacy and stature provided by office-holding and civic duty. Many medieval thinkers followed Aristotle in seeing the family as a microcosm of government: Fra Paolino Minorita (d. 1344) made this connection explicit in his *De regimine rectoris* (Treatise on Rules for Governors; 1315), dividing the work into sections on how to rule self, family, and state. Not surprisingly, newly emergent Italian communes limited governance and its responsibilities to men, and in many cases, to elite men. In new and wealthy urban spaces, competition for office became a meaningful factor in persistent factionalism, as Florentine chronicler Dino Compagni (1255–1324) observed of his compatriots: 'by their pride and ill will and competition for office, they have undone so noble a city', a concern echoed by Compagni's contemporary and compatriot Dante several times in the *Commedia*.[5] Such offices provided an urban alternative for the ethos of knightly competition popularized by chivalric romances and courtly culture. Goro Dati noted with pride that at the time of his father's death, Stagio Dati (1317–74) was 'Consul of the Wool Guild and Treasurer of the Commission on the Salt Tax'.[6] Dati echoed an emerging humanist ideology that, following Cicero, urged men to engage in public life and government in order to achieve their most refined identity. As Dati indicates, competition for office and display of masculinity existed elsewhere as well, in mostly or all-male organizations such as guilds, confraternities, and universities, whose myriad of public rituals displayed the parameters of maleness across the lines of social class. Some cities required men seeking office to be members of guilds, and in most places, like Florence, membership in certain elite guilds (banking, international trade) offered both the most prestige and easiest access to office.

Like communal government, the institutional Church was a male-dominated body. Some elite younger sons, such as Cardinal Giovanni Visconti (d. 1354), son of Matteo, the Lord of Milan, were destined for careers of considerable power within the hierarchy of the Church, and as in politics, they sought prestigious and wealthy Church benefices. The Church was one of the biggest employers in the Middle Ages, offering employment to elite sons, but also secular notaries, scribes, and scholars such as Francesco Petrarca. While some men entered ecclesiastical careers in order to further family ambition, others became monks or priests from vocation and, following the canonical model of the recently canonized St Francis (1228), pledged to renounce family and sexuality, wealth, and politics, precisely the things that defined men in the secular world. This alternate model of masculinity prized rhetorical skill, study, and moral discipline.

*Men and women*                                                                          79

Church structure also allowed churchmen to define themselves through authority over their spiritual sisters. For centuries, the once-significant powers of abbesses had been reduced by the Church: they no longer controlled double monasteries, leading communities of men and women as they had in previous centuries. The papal bull *Periculoso* (Dangerous; 1298) called for all women religious to be, in theory, strictly cloistered; earlier Church doctrine had decreed that all religious must live under a series of regulations called a rule. Francesco da Barberino supported such strict enclosure for women's own safety, urging abbesses to guard closely the doors of the convent, allowing letters and visitors only occasionally. However, he reflected his times in acknowledging, grudgingly, the presence of spiritual women beyond the confines of the convent, dedicating two (largely critical) chapters to women who either lived lives of quiet piety in isolation (hermits or anchoresses) or resided at home, having been married, elderly, or in possession of an unusually 'great gift from God'.[7] One in possession of such a gift was Margaret of Città di Castello (1287–1320) who, born blind, was abandoned by her parents, and found convent life too lax. She became a Dominican tertiary, taking vows but continuing to reside outside the convent, and engaged in lifelong charity and prayer for her community. Margaret followed a long tradition of women whose spirituality called for them to stay or work within the secular world, emanating in part from St Clare of Assisi (1194–1253), a prominent female follower of St Francis (1181/82–1226), whose rule for nuns included secular manual labour and complete poverty. Clare's vision was tempered by Francis and Church authorities conforming to *Periculoso*, but some of her spiritual heirs, like Chiara of Montefalco (*c.*1268–1308) and her sister Giovanna (1251–91), founded convents, while others – individual women and organizations such as the *Umiliate* and tertiary groups like that founded by Angela of Foligno (1248–1309) – operated beyond cloistered walls.

For some women, the Church allowed for a greater range of activities beyond the confines of family. Women became nuns for many reasons: a calling, to escape from bad marriages or fear of the perils of pregnancy, and because their parents could not afford a full dowry or had already married off many children. Nonetheless, some women, like men, found spiritual and intellectual reward in the monastic world. The convent, along with certain elite homes, provided the few possibilities for formal education to women in the late Middle Ages, where many (including some elite laywomen) could learn to read if not write. Convents allowed women to participate in rudimentary governance, and elected abbesses could have considerable authority, often marshalling convent resources in the form of property and cash donated by wealthy male and female citizens. The influence of individual abbesses and their convents often extended well beyond the cloister. A few of Venice's older convents played important roles in the city's history – donating land and other gifts to the city's ruler, the doge – largesse which was repaid with significant participation in the city's rich ritual calendar, as well as ducal patronage. The doge annually visited the nuns of San Zaccaria at Easter, and participated in the confirmation of newly elected abbesses at the convent of Santa Maria delle Vergini. Despite their claustration, nuns played various roles in the civic life of late medieval cities, including nursing, educating, praying, and participating in religious rituals.

In addition to public activities for which they were praised, some spiritual women of the thirteenth and fourteenth centuries, like Chiara of Montefalco, found a voice through the experience and expression of contemplative visions in which they communicated directly with Christ. The visions were also sometimes expressed in language and metaphors involving food or the rejection of it: Angela of Foligno described the host as having 'the savor of meat with a completely different taste ... had I not heard it said that a person ought to swallow quickly I would have held it in my mouth'.[8] Although many female contemplatives could not write, male confessors legitimated, popularized, and published their words and authority, as was the case for Angela of Foligno's contemplative *Book of Divine Consolation* (1298). The authority – secular and sacred – wielded by female nuns and contemplatives would culminate in the fourteenth century with the political activities of St Catherine of Siena (1347–80), whose visions and spirituality emboldened her to enter into correspondence with influential men and women including the mercenary soldier John Hawkwood (*c.*1320–94), the Queen of Naples Giovanna I, and Pope Gregory XI (b. *c.*1329; papacy 1370–78). In particular, her letters to successive popes played a significant role in persuading the papacy to return to Rome from Avignon.

As we have seen, one of the ways in which male identity was defined was through social class and profession. Women were rarely identified in such a way, because they did not work in skilled trades requiring formal training. Nonetheless, most medieval women worked in one way or another to supplement family income, earn dowry money, or to support themselves, their children, and their families. Scholarship suggests a decline in female employment options in the fourteenth century caused by a saturation of workers in the early part of the century, and not

## Men and women

ameliorated by the loss of workers to the plague. Francesco da Barberino was unusual in his addressing the reality of women's employment, even if his interest mostly lay in women's work within the home as servants, being generally dismissive of women's labour outside the home, warning that female workers were more inclined to cheat and sin. He cautioned fruit vendors not to attach duplicitously green leaves to stale fruit, and inn and tavern keepers to 'sell things but not your person'.[9] Later treatises on women and the family may have failed to acknowledge women's work altogether because, like Francesco da Barberino, their primary audience were elites whose wives and daughters did not work beyond household confines. But Dante's 'ladies busy with their spindles and their flax' (*Par.* XV, 117) did more than keep their idle hands occupied: the constant sewing urged upon them may well have contributed to their own trousseaux, if not the family economy, in the same way that delicate lacework and other textile work provided income for many convents. In addition, many non-elite women engaged in work outside the home, especially in the textile industry, but also, according to Francesco da Barberino's catalogue of female workers, as barbers, bakers, food vendors, mercers, inn and tavern keepers, and beggars. In these pursuits and others, women both assisted male family members, as did Margherita Bandini, and worked independently, as did Fiore, an elderly and probably widowed vendor of rags and old clothes in Bologna.[10] Although some trades were commonly practised by women, Italy seems to have had no all-female guilds, unlike elsewhere in Europe. Although some women worked in trades regulated by guilds, they were generally not extended full membership – those few women listed as members were likely widows of masters, who were permitted limited rights. Much of women's textile work was in weaving or combing, which could be done at home and was thus excluded from guild membership, as indeed were other elements of textile trade.

Other women worked in trades dominated by women but not recognized in the guild system, as midwives and wet nurses, or as prostitutes, either in recently opened city-run bordellos such as that in Venice (1360), or independently. Prostitution was the largest documented female profession according to a late-fourteenth-century census in Bologna. Following the teachings of Church Fathers such as St Augustine (354–430), Italian medieval communes sanctioned prostitution, considering it to provide a more tolerable outlet for male sexuality during the long period of male adolescence than homosexuality. Most frequently called sodomy, homosocial relations between men were criminalized and regarded by the Church as one of the most heinous sins, a sentiment echoed in

Dante's *Inferno* where sodomites (including the poet's mentor, Brunetto Latini, *c.*1220–93) are punished under a relentless rain of fire (canto XV). Although prostitutes were castigated by the likes of da Barberino and forced to wear distinguishing items of clothing, urban laws protected them and their profession.

Men and women of late medieval Italy were subject to a number of hierarchies and idealized notions. These structures stressed rich over poor, male over female, masculine over effeminate. Historical developments such as the emergence of a proto-capitalist economy and communal-style government provided a masculine identity for some men and occasional investment and managerial opportunities for their wives, while driving other women from the marketplace. The Church also provided prospects for some and restriction for others. Yet the structure of patriarchy and its ideals did not universally empower all men or subjugate all women. The realities of medieval life, which left men often absent, allowed some women negotiated gendered positions considerably more flexible than manuals such as the *Reggimento*, patriarchal laws, or traditions such as enclosure would suggest.

### Notes

1 Gautier of Coincy, *Les Miracles de Nostre-Dame*, quoted in M. Warner, *Alone of All Her Sex: The Myth and Cult of the Virgin Mary* (New York: Vintage Books, 1976), p. 154.
2 John of Garland, *Stella Maris*, quoted in Warner, *Alone of All Her Sex*, p. 198.
3 Francesco da Barberino, *Reggimento e costume di donna*, ed. G. Sansone (Rome: Zauli, 1995), p. 95.
4 G. Dati, 'The Diary of Gregorio Dati' in G. Brucker (ed.), J. Martines (trans.), *Two Memoirs of Renaissance Florence* (Prospect Heights: Waveland Press, 1991), p. 108.
5 D. Compagni, *Chronicle of Florence*, trans. D. Bornstein (Philadelphia: University of Pennsylvania Press, 1986), p. 6.
6 Dati, 'The Diary of Gregorio Dati', p. 108.
7 Da Barberino, *Reggimento*, p. 121.
8 As quoted in C. Walker Bynum, *Holy Feast, Holy Fast: The Religious Significance of Food to Women* (Berkeley: University of California Press, 1988), p. 141.
9 Da Barberino, *Reggimento*, p. 171.
10 D. Herlihy, *Opera Muliebria: Women and Work in Medieval Europe* (New York: McGraw Hill, 1990), p. 87.

CHAPTER 6

# *Church and orthodoxy*

## *George Dameron*

Nestled within the densely packed warren of narrow medieval streets north of the present-day Piazza della Signoria are the Piazza San Martino and the tiny Church of San Martino del Vescovo. Originally founded in the tenth century, the oratorio of San Martino is named after the Compagnia dei Buonomini, but the church still seems to be known as San Martino del Vescovo. It is the fifteenth-century incarnation of the church that was once Dante's neighbourhood parish church. During Dante's lifetime the local priest of this small, simple church probably lived and worked precisely as his predecessors had done for two centuries: he administered the sacraments, heard confessions, married his parishioners, presided over their funeral masses, witnessed important agreements involving locals, and probably recited the divine office in private as often as possible. In the course of Dante's lifetime in Florence – from his boyhood in the 1260s and 1270s to his exile in 1302 – the routines and traditions of this neighbourhood church probably changed very little. However, this was not the case with regard to the Florentine Church as a whole, particularly its institutions. Indeed, they were undergoing significant and far-reaching transformations.

From the middle of the thirteenth to the beginning of the fourteenth century, Florence emerged as the dominant economic, political, and military power in Tuscany. Its new hegemony was dramatic, since for centuries Dante's native city had been overshadowed by its neighbours, Lucca and Pisa, and challenged by its rival, Siena. In the spring of 1267 the standard-bearer of the pro-papal, Angevin alliance, Charles of Anjou (1226–85), marched into the city with his army and brought a formal end to seven years of Ghibelline rule. Thenceforth, for the next seventy years Florence became the principal Tuscan ally of the papacy, the house of Anjou, and the kingdom of Naples. In 1282 the most prosperous, non-noble men in the guilds of the city (the *popolo*) consolidated their political control through the institution of the magistracy of the priorate,

83

and by 1295 they had deepened their power and influence through the passage of the Ordinances of Justice. At the same time, Florentine urban population was growing exponentially, fuelled by rural immigration, and by 1300 it had exceeded 100,000. The rural population of its territory (*contado*) was around 245,000.

Accompanying these changes was a significant alteration in the physical landscape of the city. The Ghibelline-dominated district just south of Dante's local neighbourhood around San Martino was being cleared of its towers to make way for a new public square, the Piazza della Signoria. Construction of a new circle of walls had commenced in 1284 to enclose the expanding suburbs in a new defensive shield, and construction for the new palace for the priors (the Palazzo della Signoria) began in 1299. An alliance of communal and ecclesiastical officials was presiding in 1296 over the construction of a new cathedral to replace the former church (Santa Reparata), which it dedicated to the Virgin Mary. To the west and east of the cathedral–baptistery complex, at opposite ends of the city, were the two major friaries of the Dominicans and Franciscans: Santa Maria Novella and Santa Croce, respectively. In 1300 both were major construction sites, with the wealthiest families endowing new chapels and engaging the best artists of the day. All in all, the political and ecclesiastical world in Florence was in a state of agitation and transformation (see Chapter 25).

Changes in the Florentine Church were equally rapid at this time. Four major points are worth noting. First, the ecclesiastical landscape of Florence was in an energetic state of becoming, with new construction and growth everywhere. From the second half of the twelfth century, the quest on the part of many Europeans to imitate Christ by embracing the apostolic life and pursuing evangelical poverty led to the formation of new forms of spiritual communities and the creation of new religious orders. In the thirteenth century, especially the second half, many of those new orders and communities were establishing footholds in Florence, and their communities were expanding physically and demographically. Second, these institutions were increasingly prominent in the political, economic, and cultural affairs of the city. This was not unique to Florence, but the tension between the scriptural ideal of the imitation of Christ and the reality of what the Church represented in the world troubled many Florentine intellectuals. Third, the Florentine Church, like ecclesiastical institutions elsewhere in the largest cities of Europe, was the arena in which major conflicts occurred, careers were made, and the political and economic ambitions of both the elite and non-elite were realized. The conflicts that emerged from clashing ambitions confused jurisdictional boundaries, and differing

## Church and orthodoxy

political agendas of the powerful contributed to and exacerbated the many factional disputes that were profoundly dividing the Florence of Dante. However, not all such clashes were signs of institutional instability and dysfunction. Indeed, they often served to resolve disputes and clarify previously ambiguous jurisdictional boundaries.

A fourth and final observation is that the papacy was becoming increasingly active and interventionist in communal and ecclesiastical affairs at this time, especially after the mid thirteenth century. This was also not necessarily a negative development. The papal court served as an important arbiter for some of the most serious ecclesiastical disputes, and the papacy in Rome was one of the primary clients of Florentine bankers and their families (such as the Frescobaldi, Bardi, and Mozzi). Nevertheless, papal interests in Florentine affairs were dividing the commune, especially after 1300 when the Florentine elite split into the pro-papal Black Guelfs and the pro-imperial White Guelfs. As a Florentine, whether you thought papal involvement in the city was healthy and constructive or dangerous and divisive helped to define where you stood in the increasingly violent factional struggles in the early fourteenth century. Dante's own hostility to the secular power of the papacy and of the upper Church hierarchy put him at odds with the Guelf faction of the Blacks in 1300, and it contributed to his and his sons' exile in 1302. Politics and religious ideas were inextricably intertwined in Dante's Florence.

Many Christians in early fourteenth-century Florence, like Dante, were concerned about the tension between the ideals set forth in the New Testament and the actual reality of the temporal Church. All agreed, however, that its mission, as the institutional vehicle of the Holy Spirit, was to glorify God and facilitate the pursuit of salvation. Orthodoxy emerged primarily from the rulings and decisions of the major councils. The most influential of these were the Fourth Lateran Council (1215), the First Council of Lyons (1245), the Second Council of Lyons (1274), and the Council of Vienne (1311–12). Men and women were considered fallen and deeply imperfect creatures who repeatedly sinned and disobeyed God, inheriting the stain of original sin. Salvation was possible only through the reception of God's healing grace, made accessible through the sacraments, which were administered by the clergy. By the thirteenth century theologians agreed that there were seven sacraments. These were the inward and outward signs of God's healing power (grace), administered to men and women to enable them to turn away from sin, embrace goodness, love God, and achieve salvation. Baptism wiped out the original sin of Adam and Eve and conferred the forgiveness of sins up to the moment of its administration. Confirmation by the bishop admitted the baptized individual into the community of the Church and bestowed the seven gifts of the Holy Spirit. The sacrament of penance was necessary for the remission of all sins committed since baptism. The faithful were supposed to confess to a priest at least once a year (as stipulated by the Fourth Lateran Council), and this sacrament consisted of three phases: contrition, repentance, and penance. It was the role of the clergy to hear confession and assign penance. Ordination marked the receipt by an individual (always male) of the minor or major orders of the clergy.

The Eucharist or the mass was the central worship service of the Church, and it commemorated the sacrifice of Jesus Christ for human salvation through the transubstantiation of the bread and wine into the body and blood of Christ (transubstantiation became official doctrine at the Fourth Lateran Council). Its importance is attested by the fact that there were many testaments in Florence after 1250 that provided material objects for the mass: altar cloths, chalices, painted images of the Virgin or Passion, candles, and vestments. On major feast days – Pentecost, Easter, Christmas – there was communion for all. At other times, generally, only the priest took communion. The final two sacraments of medieval Christianity were marriage and extreme unction. Neither was considered to be necessary for salvation. Regarding the latter, prior to death the priest anointed the dying person with oil following the sacrament of penance but before the reception of the Eucharist.

The fear of death and eternal damnation was a principal concern of all. However, for those who had confessed their sins to a priest before death, belief in Purgatory offered hope. It was a post-mortem opportunity for penance. Few ideas were more central to Florentine piety than belief in Purgatory. Though rooted deep in the Christian past (1 Cor. III, 15), the idea of Purgatory had only recently become official Church doctrine at the Second Council of Lyons. In the most prosperous regions of Europe – in Tuscany, Provence, southern England – its dissemination was widespread. Purgatory was where, before ascending to Heaven, confessed sinners were cleansed of their sins. Within a religious tradition that stigmatized wealth as an impediment to salvation, it offered hope to those who were responsible for the economic prosperity of the High Middle Ages but were deeply troubled by their money-making. They were the merchants, the bankers, the manufacturers, the lords of major estates, and the petty lenders of loans – anyone who had created great wealth but feared that it was a threat to their eternal salvation. The rapid rise of Florence to economic prosperity, made possible by usury, had carried with

*Church and orthodoxy* 87

it terrible spiritual perils. Giordano da Pisa (*c.*1260–1310), the Dominican preacher in Florence and Tuscany, condemned usury consistently and severely. He was not alone among Florentine preachers to do so. Remigio dei Girolami (*c.*1235–1319) did as well. To shorten time spent in Purgatory, Florentines directed their testamentary legacies to clergy and ecclesiastical institutions so that masses would be celebrated, chapels endowed and embellished with frescoes, suffrages (perpetual prayers for the soul) said, altar cloths and chasubles purchased, the Divine Office recited, and charity given to the needy. All such gestures gained merit and shortened time spent in Purgatory.

Orthodoxy therefore constituted those beliefs declared as right and true by the principal councils. In contrast, heterodoxy, or heresy, constituted those ideas 'chosen by human perception, contrary to Holy Scripture, publicly avowed and obstinately defended'.[1] In Florence and Fiesole, the threat to orthodoxy posed by the Cathars – which had been serious before 1250 – was receding, especially after the exile of the Ghibellines in 1267. And even contemporaries such as Giordano da Pisa and Giovanni Villani (*c.*1275–1348) did not consider heresy to be a significant cause for concern in the late thirteenth and first half of the fourteenth century. Nevertheless, the office of the inquisition seated at the Franciscan convent of Santa Croce remained active throughout this period. It pursued isolated cases associated with vestiges of Catharism, a belief tradition that, among its many tenets, denied the existence of Purgatory. Many of the cases that came before it had strong political overtones. By linking Catharism to Florentine Ghibellines, the office of the inquisition sought to shore up the political legitimacy of the new Guelf regime. A good case in point is the posthumous condemnation of the Ghibelline Farinata degli Uberti (d. 1264), whom Dante placed among the heretics in the sixth circle of Hell (*Inf.* X). A more serious challenge to the ecclesiastical hierarchy in the early fourteenth century, however, came from the Spiritual Franciscans and from the followers of Fra Dolcino (*c.*1250–1307). But even here the numbers were small and the challenges to orthodox thinking were probably slight. There were only two alleged followers of Fra Dolcino in the prison of the office of the inquisition at Santa Croce in 1310. For a Florentine intellectual such as Dante, Fra Dolcino was more of a political than an ideological threat. After all, in *Inferno* XXVIII he is situated not among the heretics but among the sowers of discord (see Chapter 7).

The secular clergy, like their counterparts elsewhere in Europe, were those members of the clergy who were in day-to-day contact with the laity. They did not live according to a rule or set of religious regulations, as

88 George Dameron

did the friars, regular canons, and monks. Dwelling in the world and not in a monastery, they were those members of the clergy most responsible for the care of souls. They usually either lived alone among the laity in a single parish church or in a community or chapter associated with collegiate churches or cathedrals. The secular clergy was organized hierarchically into minor and major orders, of which there were eight ranks. In ascending order, minor orders included door-keepers, exorcists, lectors, and acolytes. Major orders were sub-deacons, deacons, priests or presbyters, and bishops. Only clergy in major orders were required by Church (canon) law to be celibate. Presiding over the secular clergy in each diocese was the bishop, and only he was able to ordain new clergy.

The secular clergy was also expected to perform important functions, both temporal and spiritual, in Florentine life. Priests were ideally supposed to recite in private the Divine Office, a principal worship service of the Christian tradition that originated in the monasteries of the early Middle Ages. There were eight services in a twenty-four hour period (seven during the day, one at night). They normally consisted of scriptural readings and hymns: Matins (the night office), Lauds (before dawn), Prime (dawn), Terce (third hour of day), Sext (sixth hour), Nones (ninth hour), Vespers (sunset), and Compline (evening before bed). The importance of the Divine Office is attested by the fact that many prosperous Florentines included numerous legacies in their testaments to facilitate its practice in specific churches and chapels. In addition, because members of the secular clergy lived in close contact with the laity, they were involved in the daily life of their parishioners. They were important spiritual advisors. They were also significant leaders in their own communities, serving as witnesses in significant transactions such as marriage pacts or sales of property. They occasionally served as representatives of their communities before urban authorities, and they were often key orchestrators of peace pacts. Parish priests, especially in the countryside, could also be important landlords, renting the holdings (endowment) of their churches to local residents (often for very favourable if not extremely low rents). All in all, the secular clergy were deeply embedded in the religious, social, economic, and cultural life of their parishioners. For that reason, as we can see from the many bequests made to them in surviving testaments, they were much valued by many of their parishioners.

From at least the twelfth century, the basic unit of ecclesiastical organization in medieval Tuscany was the baptismal church district (*plebatus* in Latin, *piviere* in Italian). Each *plebs* (or *pieve*), baptismal church, was equipped with a baptismal fount and was collegiate in nature. The

*Church and orthodoxy* 89

principal priest of the *plebs* was the archpriest (*plebanus*, or *pievano* in Italian). In descending order, the next administrative unit of organization within each *plebs* were the individual parishes or oratories (the *ecclesiae* or *cappellae* or *parrochiae*), each of which was staffed by a local parish priest (*rector*, identified usually as a priest or presbyter). These parishes did not have baptismal founts. The *plebes* and the *parrochiae* functioned as parish churches in their respective districts. For Florence there was only one urban *plebs*, the *pieve* of San Giovanni, located within the pre-1284 walls of the city. In the countryside in the diocese of Florence in 1302, there were fifty-nine *plebes*, compared to the thirty-five for Fiesole. Two types of communities existed among the parish churches of the secular clergy: collegiate and non-collegiate. In the city and suburbs of Florence there were fifteen collegiate churches (excluding the *plebes*), including San Lorenzo and Santa Maria Maggiore. The most important collegiate church of the secular clergy was, of course, the cathedral chapter. In the countryside there were twenty-seven collegiate churches. Regarding non-collegiate churches, there were 55 in the city and 513 in the countryside in 1302. In the diocese of Fiesole, for 1302, there were 285 non-collegiate churches (not counting the *plebes*).

The appointments or elections of archpriests and rectors to the baptismal churches and their dependent parishes functioned in Florence and Fiesole as they did elsewhere in Italy. By canon law, the patrons of the church had the right to select them. This privilege of election depended on the possession of the patronage rights in that church. According to Church law, confirmed in Gratian's (*c*.1090–*c*.1150) *Decretum* (Decree, *c*.1140) and developed further by the Decretists in the twelfth and thirteenth centuries, the right of election of an archpriest or rector by a patron or patrons was normally subject to the approval of the bishop (in the case of the archpriest) and the archpriest (in the case of the rector). Patrons of churches of the secular clergy could be families, monasteries, bishops, the parishioners themselves, or a combination of any of these groups. Contested elections or arguments over patronage rights were few and uncommon, but they could also be extremely divisive, long-lasting, and significant in their effects. Perhaps the best-known conflict over ecclesiastical patronage rights in the early fourteenth century was the clash between the Bardi and Buondelmonti families over the patronage rights in Santa Maria Impruneta (1322–32). Disputes like these were first adjudicated in the episcopal court, and the loser had the right to appeal to the papal court in Rome.

The income of a member of the secular clergy varied greatly, depending on rank (archpriest or presbyter), order (major or minor), location, and wealth of the church in which he served. Sources of income included rents (for property in the parish endowment), tithes, burial fees, prebends (for cathedral and collegiate canons), and testamentary legacies. The third and fourth decades of the fourteenth century constituted a watershed in terms of the economic well-being of the average Tuscan priest, whether he served near Florence or Cortona. In the Florentine countryside alone, 60 per cent of parish priests around the year 1330 were better off economically than a mason. This was certainly not the case a decade later. The economic fortunes of the average parish priest during the lifetime of Dante were certainly better in the first third of the fourteenth century than in the second.

Among the fifteen collegiate churches of the secular clergy in the city and its suburbs, one of the two most important and largest was San Lorenzo. Founded in 393 and before 1000 the principal church in the city, it became one of the fastest growing and important parishes in Florence during Dante's lifetime. Located just inside the old walls, it supported a community or chapter of canons. In 1300 the building was about 150 years old, as the original basilica had been rebuilt in the middle of the eleventh century. In 1287 the governing set of constitutions or internal regulations set the number of canons at nine, plus a prior. Like all the other ecclesiastical institutions of the city, San Lorenzo was benefitting from the growing wealth of the city. Principal families of Florence were establishing chapels in the church, dedicated to specific saints, and each was staffed by at least one chaplain. One such chapel in San Lorenzo, for example, founded by Durante degli Anchioni in 1297, supported one chaplain with income from a testamentary legacy of 600 *lire*. The establishments of other chapels are documented for a variety of years, including 1295, 1320, 1325, 1326, 1338, and 1346, and they were dedicated to several saints, including Matthew, Peter, and Paul. Most of the day-to-day pastoral duties at San Lorenzo seem to have been handled by the chaplains, not the canons.

The chapter of San Lorenzo was nevertheless the centre of numerous controversies and conflicts that involved internal factional disputes, disagreements with parishioners, and arguments with rival ecclesiastical institutions over parish boundaries and pastoral rights. Increased papal involvement in the chapter, specifically a papal appointment in 1250, led to a serious clash within the community that resulted in two bloody confrontations between canons in the cloister in 1258 and 1260. Efforts on the part of the collegiate church to protect its properties in the parish also led to a serious dispute with the Chiarissimi family over ownership of a house, and the protracted legal struggle lasted over four decades (from

## Church and orthodoxy 91

1244 to 1289). The indeterminacy of parish lines in this increasingly populated area of Florence led to clashes with other ecclesiastical institutions over pastoral rights. For example, San Lorenzo and San Giovanni Battista dell'Ordine dei Cavalieri di Gerusalemme were in dispute over burial fees and confessions between 1272 and 1276. It is tempting to conclude from a survey of these controversies that San Lorenzo was neglecting its spiritual mission, but such a conclusion would be unwarranted. The number of testamentary legacies it received, the growth in the number of its chapels, and the large number of parishioners choosing to be buried in the parish suggest that the local population valued the quality of its pastoral care.

The most important community of secular clergy in Florence was the cathedral chapter, and by far the single most significant building programme after 1296 was the construction of the new cathedral, Santa Maria del Fiore. Preparation work for the new cathedral began in 1289, but the actual construction of Santa Maria del Fiore did not commence until 1296. The canons of the cathedral chapter, whose residences were adjacent to the cathedral, had several important pastoral as well as temporal responsibilities and roles. In 1310 the community consisted of twelve canons, plus one head of the chapter (the *prepositus*). Each canon was supported by a prebend, a portion of the overall endowment of the community. Also part of the community were a treasurer (*camerarius*), an archpresbyter or archpriest of the single urban *pieve* of San Giovanni, an archdeacon, and several chaplains associated with various chapels.

The tasks of the cathedral canons were numerous. They were primarily responsible for the pastoral care of their own parish and for the sacramental and ceremonial duties of a major city cathedral. These included the administration of the sacraments, recitation of the Divine Office, supervision of the liturgy of the cathedral, preaching to the laity, the appointment and supervision of the archpriest of the *plebs* and the various chaplains of its numerous chapels, the promotion of the cults of the principal patron saints of the chapter (St Zenobius), *plebs* and Commune (St John), and cathedral (the Virgin Mary), and the orchestration of the processions of the clergy on major feast days. In the twelfth and early thirteenth centuries there were eighty to one hundred processions by the canons through the streets, and there is no reason to think there were any fewer during Dante's lifetime. The cathedral canons also safeguarded the principal relics of the city, preserved in Santa Reparata and later in its successor, Santa Maria del Fiore. These included the head (in a silver reliquary) and body of St Zenobius, the remains of St Eugenius and St Crescentius, and the arm of St Philip. There was no relic of St Reparata until the early seventeenth century. Among their many temporal concerns were the following: the management of the chapter's extensive rural and urban estates and properties, the exercise of its many patronage rights in churches, the election of new bishops, and the administration of the vacant bishopric until an election occurred. Like the chapter of San Lorenzo, the cathedral chapter depended on its chaplains to handle many of its daily liturgical and sacramental duties. On the north side of the cathedral *piazza* was a diocesan school (documented in 1285 and 1301), but it was one of the structures eventually demolished to make room for the new cathedral of Santa Maria del Fiore.

The many responsibilities and duties of the cathedral chapter, as set forth in canon law, often made controversies and conflicts unavoidable. Competing factions within the chapter coalesced around rival families whenever a new bishop was elected, causing deadlocks and prolonging episcopal vacancies. Although the chapter was responsible for administering the diocese when the bishopric was vacant, the family alliance of the Visdomini, Tosinghi, and Aliotti lineages managed the episcopal estate. The lines between them were not clear, and clashes were inevitable. Dante himself was aware of the dangers of such a privilege, and in *Paradiso* XVI he condemned the Visdomini for enriching themselves during such vacancies. In addition, clashes with the bishop were not uncommon. For example, the appointment as cathedral canon in 1292 of the nephew of Bishop Andrea Mozzi (tenure 1286–95), Aldobrandino dei Cavalcanti, provoked resistance on the part of many within the chapter and elicited an excommunication and interdict of the chapter by the bishop. Papal provisions such as those of the Frenchman, Stefano de Broy, to the cathedral chapter in 1291, and of Giovanni di Angiolini dei Machiavelli to the post of cathedral treasurer in 1297, encountered initial resistance on the part of many of the canons. Such appointments caused consternation within the institution, but they also significantly extended the reach of the papal curia into the highest levels of the Florentine Church and consolidated the ties between Rome and the major families of the city.

Presiding over the diocese as its administrative and spiritual authority was the bishop. He was the principal officer of the secular clergy, held the highest rank in holy orders, and managed one of the most extensive estates in northern Tuscany. Furthermore, he was primarily responsible for the care of the souls of all those baptized within his diocese. Because of its high status and possibilities for further advancement, the bishopric of Florence was a post eagerly sought after by members of the major families. Because some bishops also harboured secular ambitions for themselves

# Church and orthodoxy

and members of their families, they were often not well suited for the responsibilities that canon law stipulated. Among them was Andrea Mozzi, whose efforts to promote his nephew to high posts elicited significant controversy and resulted in his transfer by the papacy.

Among the many duties of the bishop were the following: he confirmed clergy in clerical orders, celebrated mass on solemn occasions, presided over the episcopal court (adjudicating, in particular, cases involving ecclesiastical disputes, marriage, usury, and adultery), celebrated the cults of the principal saints of the commune (Zenobius, John, the Virgin Mary), supervised and orchestrated the public liturgy of the commune, conducted periodic visitations of the clergy in his diocese, and presided over infrequent synods (formal meetings of the diocesan clergy called by the bishop) to handle official business. The bishop called and presided over two separate and formative synods in 1310 and 1327. They produced two constitutions of the clergy. The 1310 synod, presided over by Bishop Antonio degli Orsi (d. 1321), was especially important with regard to the organization of the liturgy and to the promotion of the principal saints of the commune. For the first time in 1310 the bishop required his clergy to celebrate annually the feast day of St Zenobius. Visitations were rare in the diocese of Florence before 1330, but they began as early as 1275 in the diocese of Fiesole and continued during the tenure of the Franciscan Bishop Filippo da Perugia (1282–98). The Second Council of Lyons conferred on the bishop the right to assess the amount of ill-gotten (usurious) gains from which the usurer was required to make restitution. He had the right to impose interdicts (suspension of all religious services in a locality) and issue excommunications (the severing of an individual or individuals from access to the sacraments). There were perhaps as many as eight episcopal or papal interdicts in the thirteenth century and eight between 1300 and 1375. The Bishop of Florence also routinely approved the election of archpriests in his diocese, issued dispensations and indulgences, represented the clergy in its relations with the commune, supervised clerical discipline, served as executor of testamentary legacies bequeathed to him, and presided over the major ceremonial processions and rituals on major feast days.

The role of the bishop in the public liturgy of the Church, ritual processions, and major feast days was extremely important. The liturgy of the Church constituted its principal public rituals, prayers, and readings. The bishop presided over the major feast days of both the Christian calendar (Christmas, Easter, and Pentecost) and the principal saints of the city: St John (24 June), St Zenobius (25 May), and the Virgin Mary (15 August).

He also presided over special events such as the exhumation of the body of St Zenobius from under the cathedral altar in 1331, the subsequent encasing of that saint's skull for future processions, and his re-inhumation. This exhumation, during which the Bishop of Florence was accompanied by other prelates, boosted funding for the new cathedral and added impetus to the public veneration of St Zenobius. One of the most important of the ceremonial processions was the new bishop's ritual 'entry' into the city to assume this bishopric. This tradition, which had begun no later than 1286, involved a ritual marriage of the bishop with the abbess of the urban convent of San Pier Maggiore – an event that commemorated symbolically the marriage of the bishop with his diocese. Like the cathedral canons, the bishops also had significant worldly concerns, in which they were assisted by vicars, treasurers, syndics, notaries, and procurators. The bishops also exercised patronage rights in various ecclesiastical institutions and saw themselves as the primary guardians of the poor. From the last decade of the thirteenth century, in addition to their regular duties, the construction of the new cathedral required significant attention, and it was probably through Bishop Francesco Monaldeschi (tenure 1295–1301) that papal interests regarding the new cathedral were communicated to Florence. A close associate of Boniface VIII (b. *c.*1235; papacy 1294–1303), he had previously served as Bishop of Orvieto (1280–95) when the new cathedral of that city was also taking shape.

The regular clergy included friars, monks, nuns, regular canons, and other members of the clergy who sought to imitate the life of Christ by living according to a set of provisions or regulations set forth in a rule. Canons in cathedrals or collegiate churches usually followed the Rule of St Augustine. Members of the mendicant orders were friars and lived in convents. Monks lived in monasteries, and most did so in accordance to the Rule of St Benedict. In contrast to the secular clergy, monks, nuns, and hermits withdrew from the world to imitate Christ, embracing the contemplative life, and taking vows of poverty, chastity, and obedience. Depending on the privileges granted to them by the papacy, members of religious orders exercised full or limited pastoral rights, which often placed them in conflict with the seculars. There were about fifty-nine rural monasteries in the two dioceses: thirty in Florence and twenty-nine in Fiesole. In the city of Florence, however, there were as many as ninety-seven of such communities, which varied greatly in size. Many of these were the houses for women, located between the second and third circle of walls of the city. Monasteries in general could vary in size from small (a handful of monks or nuns) to large (eighty to one hundred).

# Church and orthodoxy                                                     95

The largest orders of the regular clergy in Florence were those of the mendicant friars. By far the most important of these were the Franciscans and Dominicans. Other mendicant orders in Florence included the friars of the Sack, the Carmelites, and the Augustinian or Austin friars. At Siena, which was considerably smaller in size, there were a total of eight mendicant communities in 1262. There were considerably more in Florence. The mendicants emerged in the early thirteenth century as part of the general movement to embrace the apostolic life. Embracing evangelical poverty, the mendicants sought to imitate Christ, not by withdrawing from the world into a monastery, but by remaining engaged with the world. The Franciscans followed the papally approved Second Rule of St Francis (1223), and the papacy subjected the Dominicans to the Rule of St Augustine with the addition of constitutions specific to their order. Both orders were governed by chapters general, and the principal officers of the orders were the Minister-General (Franciscans) and the Master-General (Dominicans). By the middle of the thirteenth century the Franciscans and Dominicans throughout Europe had received from the papacy various privileges associated with pastoral care, including the right to preach, hear confessions, use portable altars for the office, and bury members of the laity. This caused occasional jurisdictional conflicts over pastoral rights with the secular clergy.

Consistent with their pastoral mission to serve where growth and settlement were most intense, the two major mendicant orders in Florence in the early thirteenth century established their houses at opposite ends of the city on the north bank of the Arno River. The third and fourth most important orders of friars, the Austin and Carmelite friars, established themselves in the Oltrarno (south bank of the river). Seeking areas where there was intensive demographic growth and new settlement, the Franciscans located themselves in the eastern zone of the city at Santa Croce (from 1228). The Dominicans established themselves in the west of the city at the Church of Santa Maria Novella (from about 1219 or 1221), and a Dominican house for women was established nearby in 1229 at San Jacopo di Ripoli. In the countryside before 1340 there were at least eight to ten small Franciscan and three Augustinian convents. The two urban friaries of the Franciscans and Dominicans were among the largest in Europe. Each had over a hundred friars, and both were undergoing significant expansion at the end of the thirteenth and beginning of the fourteenth centuries. The extensive programme of construction at Santa Croce had been underway from about 1294. It was designed to enlarge and embellish a structure that was the second building (from 1252) of the

96 George Dameron

original structure (1225) housing a Franciscan community at that location. Brothers Giles (c.1190–1262) and Bernard (d. 1241) had first come to the city in 1208 or 1209, and St Francis himself had visited Florence in 1211 and 1217. Work on the Dominican friary of Santa Maria Novella began most likely in 1279, a generation after the Dominicans had first established a community there (1221). The mendicant convents that we recognize today, with their wide public squares that accommodated large crowds that came to hear sermons preached by friars such as Giordano da Pisa, date from the late thirteenth and early decades of the fourteenth century. Living next to these convents in private homes from at least the middle of the thirteenth century were large numbers of lay female tertiaries. They sought to imitate Christ by living lives of penance, charity, poverty, prayer, and austerity.

The two convents of the major mendicant orders were also the primary centres of education and inquisition in Dante's Florence. By 1281 Santa Maria Novella had a school of theology for the Dominican province associated with Florence, and by no later than 1311 this school had become a prestigious general institution of theological studies (*studium generale*). Among its masters of theology was Remigio dei Girolami (d. 1319), who helped to develop it into a centre of scholastic learning that privileged the study of Aristotle and Aquinas. At Santa Croce there was also a theological school by 1281, and among those who taught there were Pietro di Giovanni Olivi (1248–98; taught 1287–89) and Ubertino da Casale (1259–c.1330; taught 1285–89). The two institutions undoubtedly had an impact on Dante's intellectual formation; however, the nature and extent of this remains unclear. As centres of learning and education, the mendicant friaries were also guardians of orthodoxy. During Dante's lifetime Santa Croce hosted the office of the inquisition against heresy. It had originally been staffed by the Dominicans at the command of the papacy, but in 1254 Rome shifted those responsibilities to the Franciscans at Santa Croce.

Four remaining orders of friars settled in the city in the thirteenth century, and at least two of them constructed large friaries and public squares. These were the Austin friars, the Carmelites, the Servites, and the Friars of the Sack. The Austin Friars, or Order of Friars Hermits of St Augustine, were organized into an order by the papacy in 1256. Like regular canons and the Dominicans, they were subject to the Rule of St Augustine. They had at least three convents in the countryside and one major friary in the Oltrarno at Santo Spirito. By 1287 Santo Spirito also hosted a major school of theology, which made it the second oldest in the city. The Augustinian

## Church and orthodoxy

friary at Santo Spirito was also undergoing significant expansion in the second half of the thirteenth century, so that by 1317 the friars were presiding over a convent with family chapels and seven altars, serving a growing community of Florentines between the second and third circle of walls.

Also in the Oltrarno were the Brothers of the Blessed Virgin of Mount Carmel, the Carmelites. By 1268 they had established a house at Santa Maria del Carmine (outside the older set of walls). Like the Augustinian friars, they were eremitical in origin. Founded in the early thirteenth century in the Middle East, they first arrived in Tuscany at Pisa in 1249 and were granted privileges to exercise pastoral rights there by the archbishop in 1261. Although they always retained a connection to their original mission as hermits, they were also involved in the pastoral care of those living in their vicinity. At Santa Maria del Carmine they were associated with several confraternities from at least the end of the thirteenth century. The friars also had their own school by 1324 at Santa Maria del Carmine, and like the two major mendicant orders, had attracted a group of female tertiaries to their neighbourhood. During Dante's lifetime the commune enlisted two Carmelites to serve as treasurers.

At the opposite end of the city, across the river, were the Servites of Santa Maria. From their original refuge on Monte Senario north of the city, they moved in 1250 into the area north of the second circle of city walls, the Cafaggio. There they began building their own friary, Santissima Annunziata. Recognized for accounting talents and respected for their integrity, the Servites served the commune as treasurers of the massive wall building project that began in 1284. Two were appointed for six-month terms. The third minor order of friars that settled in Florence was the Friars of the Penitence of Jesus Christ (or friars of the Sack). Emerging as an organized group in the 1240s, they were placed by the papacy in 1255 under the Rule of St Augustine. By 1259 they resided in the small Church of Sant'Egidio. However, by the end of the century they had virtually disappeared from Florence (and from Europe). In 1274, at the Second Council of Lyons, their order was disbanded, consistent with the rule that no orders founded before 1215 should continue. Nevertheless, some friars of the Sack were still present in Florence a decade later. In 1286 they were involved with Folco Portinari (d. 1289), the father of Dante's Beatrice, in a property transaction connected to the building of his hospital of Santa Maria Nuova.

Among the largest of the ninety-seven monastic communities in Florence were five institutions with more than eighty monks. The rule governing most of these monastic institutions in the two dioceses of

Florence and Fiesole was the sixth-century Rule of St Benedict. One of the oldest Benedictine monasteries within the circuit of walls was the Badia, founded in the tenth century by the Tuscan marquis, Hugo (953/54–1001), and his mother, Willa (911/12–70). On the ridge on the south side of the Arno overlooking the city was the Benedictine monastery of San Miniato al Monte. A stunningly beautiful Romanesque church dating from the early eleventh century, it was the proprietary monastery of the bishopric. It was founded in 1018 as a final resting place for the relics of Minias, the first martyr of Florence. The first monastery established by the Cistercians in Tuscany was at San Galgano in 1201 in the diocese of Volterra. A generation later, in 1236, the Cistercians located their house in Florence just outside the city at San Salvatore di Settimo. Manual work at this and other monasteries was performed by lay brothers or *conversi*. Cistercian nuns established a community in 1259 at San Donato, a Torri outside Florence in the convent of the Humiliati. The commune called upon the Cistercians at Settimo to serve as treasurers of the city as early as 1257, and they continued to act as trusted public officials well into the fourteenth century. Though ostensibly withdrawn from the world, the major monastic orders of the city were in reality deeply involved in public (especially financial) affairs.

The Humiliati first emerged in the Po valley at the end of the twelfth century as part of that broad penitential movement of both women and men dedicated to the pursuit of the apostolic life. They were originally condemned in 1184 as heretics, but became a religious order in the early thirteenth century when the papacy accepted them in 1201. A rule was broadly disseminated within the order only by 1227. In Florence in 1236 Bishop Ardingo granted them the Church of San Donato a Torri. In 1250 they were transferred to another, larger Church at Santa Lucia, located near the intersection of the Arno and the Mugnone Rivers (at this point the Humiliati nuns disappear from the record). At Santa Lucia, they began building a larger facility for themselves, Ognissanti. It was completed around 1300. Well known for their manufacture of medium-quality cloth at Ognissanti until production stopped around 1277, from 1256 the Humiliati were also enlisted by the commune as treasurers. Giotto's (1266–1337) *Ognissanti Madonna*, completed in the second decade of the fourteenth century, was originally placed on the high altar of their church.

In the countryside, many of the monasteries and convents were associated with the Vallombrosan, Camaldolensian, and Benedictine orders. The two rural monasteries of Camaldoli, founded by Romuald (d. 1027), and Vallombrosa, established by Giovanni Gualberti (d. 1073), were located in

## Church and orthodoxy

isolated, wooded, and mountainous areas of the diocese of Fiesole. Both sought to follow a strict interpretation of the Benedictine Rule, and both inspired monastic orders. Whereas the former created a loose society of hermits living in a community, the latter emphasized silence, contemplation (no work), prayer, and enclosure. The Camaldolensian order counted eleven houses for women and two for men, all within Florentine territory. At Vallombrosa, as at Settimo, lay brothers performed manual labour. Dependent on the Vallombrosan Order in the Florentine *contado* were twelve monasteries for men and four convents for women, including one of the wealthiest and most powerful monasteries for males in the area: San Michele di Passignano. Founded in the Pesa River valley south of the city at the end of the ninth century, it was a commanding presence in this part of the countryside. Consisting of at least six monks (including the abbot) and several *conversi* in the early fourteenth century, Passignano was the principal landlord of the region and possessed considerable patronage rights to local churches. In the late thirteenth and early fourteenth centuries it was often in conflict with the local population over the governance of the local community. The Benedictine order, unlike the Camaldolensian and Vallombrosan Orders, had a presence throughout Europe and was represented locally by its eleven monasteries for men and eight convents for women. In both countryside and city, hospitals were commonly associated with the monasteries.

In the city and its suburbs, there were more than fifty women's monastic communities of various types and sizes. Most were quite small. Especially numerous were the establishments outside the older circle of walls and situated along the major roads linking central Florence with the northern and southern suburbs (along Borgo San Lorenzo, Borgo Pinti, the Via Romana). Among the most important were San Pier Maggiore, Sant'Andrea, Sant'Ambrogio, and Santa Felicita. Women's communities around 1300 ranged in age from the two-hundred-year-old Benedictine convent of San Pier Maggiore in the centre of the city to the post-1250 and loosely organized groups of Franciscan and Dominican tertiaries living in houses adjacent to the two major friaries at opposite ends of the city. San Pier Maggiore also played an important role in the ceremonial entries of new bishops into the city from at least the last quarter of the thirteenth century. The Franciscans had a convent at Monticelli in the southern suburbs of the city, founded by the sister of St Clare (1194–1253), St Agnes (1197–1253). It was located outside the southern gate of the post-1284 circle of walls, the Porta Romana. There were also communities of lay women dedicated to the sick and the poor in the major hospitals such as San Paolo and San Gallo.

In addition to these communities, many single women lived secluded lives as *recluse*, including Umiliana dei Cerchi (d. 1249). They lived enclosed in their family towers, in small oratories, or in public places such as bridges. The widow Umiliana, deeply influenced by Franciscan piety, devoted her life to charity and penitence. After the death of her husband, she lived in her family tower near San Martino del Vescovo until her own death. Shortly after her passing the friars of Santa Croce promoted her cult as a model of female piety. Women left numerous testamentary legacies to mendicant friaries, female monasteries, hospitals, and members of the secular clergy. Painted altar panels also served as important and valuable objects of veneration and prayer for women.

From the second half of the thirteenth and well into the fourteenth century, three major trends are evident. Many women's religious communities in the countryside, informal organizations that had originally begun as rural hospitals, were increasingly moving into the city to escape the instability caused by war, lack of economic resources, and the loss of protective patrons. At the same time, ecclesiastical authorities, especially the papacy and the bishops of Florence and Fiesole, made concerted efforts to bring these communities under the norms of episcopal control and discipline. This occasionally led to cleavages between the commune and the papacy or between the bishop and the commune. New institutions also continued to emerge in the city during this period. Several examples are typical. Umiltà da Faenza (*c*.1226–1310) moved her community into Florence and founded the convent of San Giovanni Evangelista on the Mugnone, north of the second circle of walls. The convent dedicated to Sant'Orsola was established in 1309 in the parish of San Lorenzo.

Like other Florentine ecclesiastical institutions, hospitals and confraternities were growing in number in the course of the thirteenth and early fourteenth centuries. The medieval hospital served a variety of purposes: they assisted travellers, the sick, the poor, orphans, and immigrants. A person travelling through the city and countryside in 1300 would have encountered over a hundred hospitals in the *contado* and about a third of that number in the city. The historian Charles-Marie de La Roncière counted at least 136 hospitals in the countryside for the decades between 1280 and 1350. These were usually very small structures with only a few beds. The fourteenth-century chronicler Giovanni Villani estimated that the city had 30 hospitals in 1338 and 1,000 beds. At least 24 of these institutions were founded in the thirteenth century, with a majority of them still in existence around 1340. They were at least partially supported by testamentary legacies left by prosperous Florentines. Chief among these

## Church and orthodoxy

institutions was the Domus Dei (House of God) for members of the clergy, located in the parish of San Lorenzo and dating from at least 1311. San Gallo, one of the largest hospitals of the city, was well known for its care of the seriously ill, and from 1316 Santa Maria della Scala focused on homeless children. In the early fourteenth century San Paolo was recognized for the generosity of its alms to the poor and the sick. Its charity occasionally included grain distributions. Most of the institutions established at the end of the thirteenth and beginning of the fourteenth centuries developed between the older and post-1284 sets of walls. This was where space was available, and it mirrored the settlement pattern followed earlier by the new mendicant convents and female monastic communities. Especially popular as a location for hospitals were two arteries, Via San Gallo and Via Romana, as they were commonly used by travellers and pilgrims entering the city from both the north and south, respectively.

There were at least thirty-nine confraternities, or religious lay brotherhoods, in the city between 1277 and 1330, with as many as forty-five for the period between 1250 and 1349. Emerging out of the lay penitential movement and the struggle against heresy in the thirteenth century, confraternities were closely associated with the friars, especially the Franciscans and Dominicans, and with the secular clergy. There were five types of confraternities in Florence: charitable, flagellant (*disciplinati*), hymn-singing associations (*laudesi*) frequently dedicated to the Virgin Mary, societies for children (*fanciulli*), and artisanal fraternities. They all brought together a variety of Florentine laity who met at least once or twice a month in chapels of the major ecclesiastical institutions of the city. In both city and countryside these associations were important sources of support and sociability in addition to their original religious purposes. There was at least one association for women before 1350 (created in 1303 at San Lorenzo), and fourteen rural confraternities existed in various communities during Dante's lifetime. Each was normally associated with a rural parish.

One of the most important locations of a charitable confraternity was at the open-air *loggia* of Orsanmichele, which also served as the public grain market. This confraternity had originally begun as a *laudesi* brotherhood about 1291. After an image of the Virgin on one of its pillars was linked to a series of curative miracles in 1292, the association developed into one of the most important charitable confraternities in the city. Along with the Bigallo (from the 1240s) and the Misericordia, Orsanmichele served as a source of aid to the poor. Also among the most important *laudesi* confraternities in the city was that of San Pier Martire e Laude della Vergine Maria, founded in 1244 in the Dominican friary of Santa Maria Novella.

This particular confraternity was responsible for the commissioning of Duccio's (*c.*1255/60–*c.*1318/19) magnificent *Rucellai Madonna* (1285).

The ecclesiastical institutions of Florence were deeply embedded in the economy of the city and its surrounding countryside. This could hardly be otherwise. New churches and convents had to be built to accommodate a growing population; sacraments needed to be administered and masses celebrated; the clergy supported with food and housing; taxes paid to bishops, popes, and the commune; lawsuits adjudicated; and charity distributed to the poor. The economic contributions of ecclesiastical institutions to the urban economy cannot be measured with precision, but they should also not be underestimated. The extensive estates of the bishopric and cathedral chapter in the major river valleys of the Elsa, Pesa, Arno, and Sieve rivers, for example, helped to produce food for a growing population. Hospitals sheltered the poor and sick and provided places where travellers could stay. The construction and embellishment of parish churches, new chapels, and the cathedral (after 1296) provided employment, stimulated economic demand, and led to the commissioning of innovative artistic and architectural projects. Among the most outstanding examples are the frescoes of the Bardi, Baroncelli, and Peruzzi Chapels at Santa Croce (completed between 1310–30), the cathedral project, Giotto's *Ognissanti Madonna*, and the *Rucellai Madonna* of Duccio. In the second half of the thirteenth century the bishopric and cathedral chapter began to develop their properties in the northern suburbs of the city (the Cafaggio) into rental properties, shops, and houses to meet the economic demands of an increasingly prosperous city. This provided a valuable and growing source of income. Aside from urban monetary rents, the most important source of income for the largest institutions was grain rents from landed properties. Other sources of income for ecclesiastical institutions of the secular and regular clergy included testamentary legacies (for chapels, suffrages, and recitations of the Divine Office), altar offerings, tithes, and mortuary income (burial fees).

If ecclesiastical income was growing at the end of the thirteenth and beginning of the fourteenth centuries, so were expenses and debts. Again, it could hardly have been otherwise. Passignano, for example, had properties to purchase, parcels to consolidate, estate agents and *conversi* to pay, lawsuits to adjudicate, and grain to transport to market. Office-holders such as the bishop had households to support, and some of them could be quite large. For example, the household of Bishop Antonio degli Orsi

## Church and orthodoxy

(d. 1321), which travelled with him from residence to residence throughout the diocese, included as many as thirty-five people. Institutions large and small had to spend money on candles, paper or parchment, maintenance of buildings, notarial services, and poor relief. Above all, at the end of the thirteenth and beginning of the fourteenth centuries, an ever-larger portion of ecclesiastical income was going to the papacy, to the bishop, and to the commune in the form of the papal tenth, special subsidies, and indirect taxes (*gabelle*). Regarding the papal tenth, all but exempt ecclesiastical institutions were assessed for payments by the papal collector (exempt institutions were usually those within the *collatio* or control of the papacy). Payments also included levies imposed by the bishop for the new cathedral (in 1299 and 1318) and for the ceremonial entries of new prelates.

The burdens on ecclesiastical institutions imposed by the commune, with papal acquiescence, were the most onerous, however. According to the Fourth Lateran Council (1215), lay taxation of the clergy was forbidden, and Boniface VIII's bull, *Clericis laicos* (The Laity to the Clergy, 1296), stipulated that papal consent was necessary for any clerical taxation at all. Nevertheless, although they went under other names (*imposte, donativi*), the money transferred by the ecclesiastical institutions to the commune was still taxes. They included special levies as well as indirect communal taxes (*gabelle*), and they supported a variety of purposes. In 1299 there was the new cathedral, in 1307 there was the war with Arezzo, in 1318 the new cathedral again, in 1323 the new walls, in 1326 the *gabelle* for the war against Lucca, and in 1328 there was the war against Lucca and Castruccio Castracani (1281–1328). Such payments were common elsewhere in Tuscany. At Siena, for example, significant subsidies levied by the commune took the form of voluntary loans, a ruse that performed the same role as the Florentine payments: they circumvented the prohibition of clerical taxation. Acting on behalf of the clergy of the diocese of Florence in 1326, the procurator of the clergy complained before the vicar of the bishop about the burden of the *gabelle* on the secular clergy. The demands of war and the cathedral were pressing increasingly on ecclesiastical finances. Indeed, the fiscal pressures of 1307 had already contributed to the financial ruin of the monastery of Santa Maria di Firenze (the Badia). In 1323 and 1329, however, even as there was an understanding on the part of the papacy that the levels of the payments were to be moderated, these levies constituted significant contributions to the welfare of Florence.

Common interests between the commune and the papacy had overridden the traditional policies of the bishop and the pope to protect the fiscal liberty of the clergy.

At the institutional apex of the ecclesiastical hierarchy in Florence (as elsewhere) was the papacy. During the pontificate of Boniface VIII, papal influence over the direction of Florentine political and economic affairs reached a high level of intensity. Although the bishop was primarily responsible for the administration of the diocese and the care of souls, he was always circumscribed by the power of the papacy. After all, the papacy increasingly took a direct hand in the selection of new bishops, especially after 1286. Papal influence in Florence was not absolute, however. After all, the papacy, as well as all other institutions of the Church, was subject to the rules and regulations of canon (or Church) law. Nevertheless, popes exerted significant influence in Florentine affairs. They did so by dispatching papal legates such as Cardinal Malabranca Latino (d. 1294) to resolve the serious factional disputes in 1279. They also did so through the rulings of the papal court. The papacy could also appoint local judges delegate to decide cases that had been appealed. In addition, the pope had influence in Florence through the exercise of ecclesiastical patronage rights, his right to impose interdicts and issue excommunications, and his power to require payments of the papal tenth in 1275, 1297, and 1302–03. The pope could also impose payments for subsidies or reimbursements for his visiting legates (as he did in 1304 and 1306 for the loss of property and for various other expenses). Through papal provisions, Rome controlled many of the key positions within the cathedral chapter and other major institutions.

The reach of the papacy in Florentine ecclesiastical affairs was formidable. It is therefore easy to understand why some Florentines such as Dante resented the presence of the papacy in Florentine affairs. For them, it was simply the starkest manifestation of an excessively materialistic, carnal Church. There were certainly many within the Florentine Church who would have agreed with him. But there were also many others such as the cathedral canon, Stefano de Broy, who would have argued that the mission of the Church required profound engagement with the world. This unresolved tension between Christian ideal and reality is not only at the heart of Dante's work, but is also present in the development of medieval Christianity itself.[2]

## Notes

1 The definition of heresy is from Gratian's *Decretum* C. 24 q. 3 cc. 27–31, quoted and cited in R. Moore, *The Formation of a Persecuting Society*, 2nd edn (Malden, MA and Oxford: Blackwell, 2007), p. 64.

2 I wish to express my gratitude to the Harvard Center for Italian Renaissance Studies at the Villa I Tatti and to its former director, Joseph Connors, and his wife, Françoise Connors, for their hospitality as I completed the first draft of this essay. I also wish to thank Daniel Bornstein for his comments on that earlier draft.

CHAPTER 7

# Heresy and dissidence

*David Burr*

Dante's age was notable both for the sheer variety of heresies and hetero-doxies identified by contemporaries and for the vigour with which the institutional Church attacked them. By 1300 papal inquisitors, follow-ing established procedures and normally able to rely on substantial force, worked in collaboration with local bishops to enforce orthodoxy.

It was a struggle. The thirteenth century had been a period of spiritual and theological creativity. To recognize this much we need only look at the Dominicans and Franciscans. Both orders appeared early in the century and soon proved their value as a response to the needs of an expanding urban culture with a religiously enthusiastic, increasingly well-educated laity. Both orders also threw themselves into the world of scholastic thought and developed it rapidly. On both the institutional and intellec-tual levels, the new mendicant orders gave Europe a sense of direction as it negotiated an important period of western history; yet the nature and wisdom of that direction was open to serious debate. The new orders were seen as interlopers by a number of university masters and secular clergy; Dominicans and Franciscans often resented one another's presence; and, among the Franciscans themselves, factions differed as to what the order should be doing.

Such tensions might have been easier to deal with had they not inter-acted with a strong tendency on the part of the laity and lower clergy to develop new patterns of religious life. By 1300 Church leaders had long since decided it was necessary to rein in further novelty and contain exuberance within stable, controllable, orthodox channels. The mendi-cant orders were potentially useful for that purpose, and for more reasons than that they made excellent inquisitors (although they did). It seemed possible to limit dangerous experimentation by enticing pious Christians into existing religious structures tied especially to the Franciscans. But if the Franciscans themselves were at odds over who they were, that strategy could have its dangers.

106

## Heresy and dissidence

In the dynamic religious world of the early fourteenth century it was often hard to decide precisely where the boundary lay between official and unofficial Church, or who should be identified as heterodox and who orthodox. There were, to be sure, old heresies that continued into the fourteenth century as unfinished business, Catharism and Waldensianism being the major examples. Both were very much going concerns in Dante's day, and those within the Church were confident that they were indeed heresies, and inquisitors were still combatting them (as we see from Emmanuel Le Roy Ladurie's 1975 classic, *Montaillou*, which analyses the campaign against Catharism in a single French village); yet neither interested Dante all that much. He does allude to Catharism throughout *Paradiso* XII, but without actually naming it. *Inferno* X, the canto we usually identify with heresy, features Farinata degli Uberti (d. 1264), who was indeed accused of Catharism; but Dante treats him in a way that has nothing to do with his being a Cathar, choosing instead to present Farinata and three others as Epicureans whom he saw as heretical in denying the immortality of the soul, either explicitly or in their way of life. In *Inf.* XI, 3–6, a short coda to the heresy circle, we finally arrive at something besides Epicureanism, but in the form of Pope Anastasius II (papacy 496–98), an obscure late-fifth-century pope identified with the equally obscure Acacian heresy, which rejected Christ's human nature.

Some newer movements were generally recognized to be heretical in Dante's day, but they too go virtually unnoticed in the *Commedia*. The Gugliemites at Milan developed from a cult that grew up around Guglielma of Bohemia after her death in 1281. Adherents identified Guglielma with the Holy Spirit, expecting her to inaugurate a third age of history when women would become priests, cardinals, and even popes. This new age was anticipated to some extent in the Humiliate Sister Maifreda, a relative of the Visconti family, who would be Guiglielma's first earthly vicar. The result was an inquisition in 1300 that led, in the same year, to the burning of three people including Maifreda.

If Dante makes no mention of this drama, he does acknowledge another, but only in passing. In *Inferno* XXVIII, 55–60 he has Mohammed refer to Fra Dolcino (*c.*1250–1307). According to the logic of the *Commedia*, Mohammed is speaking in 1300, prophesying a military victory that would occur in 1307, when a crusading army defeated Fra Dolcino and the heretical sect of Apostles, or at least those Apostles who were with Dolcino.

By 1307 the Apostles had gone through a striking evolution. They came into being in 1260 when Gerardo Segarelli (*c.*1240–1300), an admirer of St Francis (1181/82–1226), was rejected by the Franciscan order and decided to imitate Francis on his own. He eventually attracted a following, but by that time the Church, sensitized to the dangers of uncontrolled innovation, had become cautious about recognizing new groups. Gerardo found himself presiding over an unapproved order. In 1300 he was burned at the stake, and eventually leadership of the group was assumed by Dolcino, under whom it turned violent. That is perhaps why Dante alludes to the story at all in the *Commedia*. Rather than appearing in *Inferno* X, where the emphasis is on denial of immortality, Mohammed and indirectly Fra Dolcino are presented as sowers of religious discord.

A third movement – or perhaps better, a tendency – went unmentioned by Dante: the so-called *spiritus libertatis*, or what is now referred to as the heresy of the free spirit. Churchmen worried a great deal about it in the early fourteenth century. Some scholars have argued that it was, on the whole, a figment of the clerics' imaginations; yet in Italy we find enough evidence in sources such as Angelo Clareno's (1247–1337) chronicle or the canonization process for Clare of Montefalco (*c.*1268–1308) to identify a set of behaviours identified with *spiritus libertatis* and widely considered to be heretical. Even there, what we find is not a substantial heretical Church like the Cathars or a small heretical sect like the Gugliemites or Apostles, but rather what one would be tempted to describe as the extension to dangerous extremes of an adventurous mystical piety found not only in Marguerite Porete (burned at the stake in 1310), Na Prous Boneta (burned in 1328), and Meister Eckhardt (condemned posthumously in 1329; 1260–1328), but also in mystics like Angela of Foligno (1248–1309) and Jacopone da Todi (*c.*1236–1306), both of whom escaped condemnation entirely. (Jacopone was imprisoned, but for different reasons. He sided with the Colonna family, enemies of Pope Boniface VIII.)

So far we have dealt with beliefs or behaviours that were generally considered to be heretical but excited no great interest on Dante's part; yet there are common features in the Manfreda and Dolcino stories that bear on what Dante *was* interested in exploring. First, Dolcino, like Manfreda, may have been connected with the Visconti. Second, the Gugliemites, Apostles, and *spiritus libertatis* all had an apocalyptic dimension. Third, the apocalyptic expectations included ecclesiastical reform involving genuine institutional change. These three elements interacted in various ways during the period when Dante was writing, and they also interact within the *Commedia*.

The point here is a simple one. In Dante's time certain beliefs and/ or behaviours struck most people as incontestably heretical. The Cathars themselves might have argued that they were not in fact heretical, but

*Heresy and dissidence* 109

few educated Catholics would have agreed. On the whole, Dante pays little attention to heresies of this sort. One might object that he devotes an entire canto to denial of immortality, which certainly would have been recognized as a heresy; yet even here his two major case histories, Cavalcante (*c.*1220–*c.*1280) and Farinata, are presented, not as explicitly denying immortality, but as concentrating on earthly matters so single-mindedly as to suggest that the fate of their immortal souls was unimportant to them.

On the other hand, there were beliefs and/or behaviours that were open to lively debate in which the accusation of heresy might travel in several directions. This was the kind of issue that attracted Dante, and here we return to the matter of the Visconti, who established a Ghibelline centre of power in northern Italy. In an age when the papacy made increasingly ambitious claims involving both political power and religious authority, pontiffs were often tempted to accuse their political enemies of heresy. They did so in the thirteenth-century battle with Frederick II; in the prolonged battle between Pope Boniface VIII (b. *c.*1235; papacy 1294–1303) and King Philip IV (1268–1314) of France toward the end of the century; and yet again in the 1320s during the contest between Pope John XXII (b. 1244; papacy 1316–34) and Emperor Ludwig of Bavaria (1282–1347). (In between, there was trouble between Pope Clement V (b. *c.*1264; papacy 1305–14) and Emperor Henry VII (*c.*1275–1313), but it was less dramatic than the other battles.)

During these years popes were interested in suggesting that the temporal ruler was disobeying God by disobeying the pope; but secular rulers were equally enthusiastic about claiming that it was the popes, not they, who were heretics (see Chapters 1 and 3). Philip drove his point home by sending a military expedition to capture Boniface and presumably bring him back to France for condemnation. Even after Boniface died, Philip continued to insist that he be tried for heresy. In the later John–Ludwig struggle, John remained in Avignon well out of Ludwig's reach, but that did not prevent Ludwig from declaring John a heretic and sentencing him to death. In these battles it was not always easy to judge who represented the official Church and who did not, since respectable churchmen lined up on both sides.

Even apart from Church–State disputes, we see a Church that was hardly monolithic. The case of Angelo Clareno's group is instructive in this respect. In 1294, after two decades of dispute with their Franciscan leaders in the province of Ancona concerning the degree of poverty demanded by the rule, the group managed to get Pope Celestine V's (1215–96; papacy

1294) permission to form a separate order called the Poor Hermits of Pope Celestine, which would observe the Franciscan rule. Once Celestine resigned and Boniface VIII succeeded him, that permission vanished and Angelo's group retreated to Greece, pursued by a papal excommunication. During the subsequent reign of Clement V, the group returned to Italy and occupied a number of hermitages in central Italy, while Angelo went to Avignon and, aided by supportive cardinals, tried to get the Poor Hermits officially recognized. Had Clement not died, he might have succeeded. When, under John XXII, it became obvious that such recognition was out of the question, Angelo returned to Italy where he was protected at Subiaco by a friendly Benedictine abbot. From that point on, he and his group survived largely by staying out of the way and not offending local authorities.

In short, even in the papal court a renegade group like Angelo's might find supporters within the Church hierarchy, and in the remote, mountainous areas of central Italy, at a time when the papacy had absconded to Avignon, the official Church that mattered most to such a group was likely to be a supportive bishop or abbot, not the pope. That level of support or at least tolerance allowed the group to weather the fourteenth century and to emerge in the fifteenth as the Clareni, whose legitimacy as an order was taken for granted by some episcopal documents and by at least one papal document.

Dante was quite aware that in matters of this sort the 'official Church' spoke in a series of conflicting voices, and he was equally aware that its leaders were often great sinners. He thought little enough of Boniface VIII to place him in Hell for simony along with Nicholas III (b. *c.*1216; papacy 1277–80) and Clement V (*Inf.* XIX, 49–81). At *Inferno* XXVII, 82–7 he has Guido da Montefeltro (1223–98) refer to Boniface as leader of the modern pharisees and roundly condemn his siege of Palestrina, the stronghold of the rival Colonna family. At *Paradiso* IX, 127–38 he suggests that love of money has corrupted Boniface, turning the shepherd into one of the wolves. At *Paradiso* XXVII, 22, St Peter says Boniface has usurped his place and turned his sepulchre into a sewer of blood and filth. At *Paradiso* XVII, 49–51, Cacciaguida informs Dante that in Rome, 'where Christ is sold daily', Dante's own exile is already being plotted 'by him who seeks it', presumably Boniface. Yet none of this leads to a full-throated cry of support for Boniface's nemesis Philip IV. At *Purgatorio* XX, 85–93, Hugh Capet (938–96) rounds out his litany of French royal sins by predicting the 1303 capture of Boniface at Anagni by Philip's agents, a crime Hugh indignantly describes as Christ being taken captive in the person of his vicar. He labels Philip 'the modern Pilate'.

## Heresy and dissidence

Dante censures other popes of his time, though less emphatically. In addition to the criticism of Clement V and Nicholas III just cited, at *Paradiso* XXX, 133–44 Beatrice criticizes Clement for his opposition to Emperor Henry VII, and at *Paradiso* XXVII, 58–9 Peter, in the process of criticizing his papal successors, explicitly mentions 'Gascons and Cahorsines [who] come to drink our blood', an obvious allusion to Clement V and John XXII, both of whom opposed imperial ambitions.

In the area of imperial–papal relations, and in others as well, popes from Boniface VIII to John XXII were increasingly inclined to see opposition to the pope as itself a form of heresy. John XXII was willing to base a whole series of heresy accusations on that assumption. In 1318, for example, four spiritual Franciscans of Languedoc were burned at the stake for refusing the pope's order that they submit to their leaders' sense of what Franciscan poverty should be. The rationale underlying this condemnation was that, once the pope had decided the matter, refusing to accord with his decision represented a heretical denial of that part of the creed that affirms that there is one Church. The pope was, in effect, the visible symbol of Church unity. The same logic was used in levelling heresy charges against Ghibellines who challenged the pope's notion of where he fitted in the political order. It was even used to attack those who claimed the papacy should be in Rome, not Avignon, which is exactly what Dante seems to suggest in *Purgatorio* XXXII, 148–61, and in fact what any number of Italian reformers and mystics suggested.

Dante's *Monarchia*, written in support of the claim that the emperor derived his authority directly from God, placed him within a small group of early-fourteenth-century polemicists such as John of Paris (*c.*1255–1306), Marsiglio of Padua (*c.*1280–*c.*1343), and William of Ockham (*c.*1285–1347/49) who rejected the claim of papal *plenitudo potestatis*, namely, absolute power. Each of their works was informed by a slightly different context. Although scholars differ on this matter, one highly defensible view is that the *Monarchia* was written around 1318 as a response to the fact that, shortly after becoming pope in 1316, John XXII had promulgated the bull *Si fratrum* (If of our Brothers) attacking certain northern Italian lords for retaining the title of imperial vicar after the death of the Emperor Henry VII, despite the fact that by papal logic their appointments had been cancelled by Henry's death. It was now up to the pope to select interim vicars, since imperial power had shifted to him until he approved the election of a new emperor. John sent papal legate Bertrand du Poujet (1280–1352) to oversee the excommunication of the disobedient lords and, if necessary, organize a crusade against them. One of the lords was Dante's patron Cangrande della Scala (1291–1329). Another was Matteo Visconti (1250–1322).

Dante's treatise was inspired by more than personal loyalty, although that element is apparent in the Letter to Cangrande. The *Monarchia* was also a statement of his political credo, and he paid a price for it. The work seems to have attracted little attention until, a few years after Dante's death, it was used by Ludwig in his polemical campaign against John. It was then condemned by Bertrand du Poujet and burned, although, thanks to the personal intervention of other powerful lords, Dante himself was not condemned as a heretic.

The other two elements mentioned earlier, apocalyptic expectation and the call for ecclesiastical reform, often travelled together in this period. Historians tend to speak of the apocalyptic element as Joachite, and correctly so if what is meant is that, rather than reproducing Joachim of Fiore's (1130/35–1202) thought, apocalyptic thinkers developed elements within it in such a way as to create scenarios different from Joachim's. (In fact, it is hard to speak of Joachim's thought itself as a coherent entity. Recent scholarship suggests that throughout his life it remained very much a work in progress.)

In the thirteenth century elements within the Franciscan order were especially enthusiastic about both Joachim's authentic works and the pseudo-Joachite writings produced after his death. Like the order itself, Joachism serves as an apt symbol of the dynamism that characterized the period. Salimbene de Adam's (1221–88) chronicle gives us a sense of how the excitement grew, then received a serious check when the Franciscan Gerard of Borgo San Donnino (d. 1276) published Joachim's major works along with an introduction in which he presented the works as the new gospel of a dawning third age. The resulting scandal proved useful to enemies of the new mendicant orders and meant not only imprisonment for Gerard, but removal of the Franciscan minister general John of Parma (1209–89), himself an enthusiastic Joachite.

After Gerard, Joachism was regarded with increased suspicion by many, yet a strong Joachite current continued in the Franciscan order. Toward the end of the thirteenth century a Franciscan scholar in Languedoc, Peter John Olivi (1248–98), who taught in Florence between 1287–89, produced several works that combined Joachite apocalyptic with the notion that Francis inaugurated a third age of world history, an age of reform, peace, and enlightenment in which the carnal Church of that era was to be replaced with an *ecclesia spiritualis* (spiritual Church). Leadership would be more charismatic than juridical, with a holy pope presiding over a Church in which people obeyed because they wanted to do so.

# Heresy and dissidence

Olivi's sense of this third age was sketched only provisionally, but his view of the corrupt Church to be replaced by it was rendered in bold strokes. He saw the period from Charlemagne (*c.*747–814) to his own time as one in which the Church grew in numbers while declining in virtue. The third age had begun with Joachim and Francis, and had been opposed ever since by an entrenched carnal element. In the near future, that carnal element would gain control of the institutional Church and the mystical Antichrist would reign. Olivi was partial though not entirely committed to the notion that the mystical Antichrist would be a Franciscan who became pope. In any case, the true children of the dawning third age would be persecuted until the entire carnal Church was destroyed by an invading non-Christian army, which would think it was attacking Christianity but would merely succeed in destroying the carnal Church. Then the reign of the true Antichrist would begin. During the resultant persecution, true disciples of St Francis, forced to escape, would continue the programme of evangelization already foreshadowed by Francis' journeys east. They would receive a better hearing among non-Christians than among Christians, and a better one among simple laity than among learned clergy. Once the Antichrist was destroyed by Christ himself, the third age of peace and contemplative knowledge would develop fully.

Olivi's scenario was concerned with decay and reform on two levels: within the Franciscan order and within the Church as a whole. The two were intimately related because he saw the order as playing a major role in the transition to the third age. The same thing could be said about other Franciscan reformers in Dante's time, but with important distinctions. Olivi and Angelo Clareno are now described as 'spiritual Franciscans' at odds with the direction the order had taken, and both were apocalyptic thinkers who saw Francis as ushering in a new age; yet their aims differed sharply. Olivi accepted most of the developments that had transformed the order by his time, including heavy scholarly involvement in the universities and a pastoral role in the cities. His notion of Franciscan poverty was nuanced and entirely fitting for such a role. Angelo, on the other hand, saw the original Franciscan life as an essentially eremitical existence. Shortly after its inception, according to Angelo, the order, seduced into measuring success by worldly standards, had established itself in the towns, where it constructed elaborate buildings, involved itself in parish life, and pursued academic honours. In his own time it was almost inextricably enmeshed in this life. One can see why Angelo spent his time seeking not reform of the Franciscan order in an institutional sense, but a separate group that, whatever it might be called, would live the Franciscan life as Francis himself envisaged it.

Nor were these the only alternatives. In the 1290s Olivi found himself writing against a group of Italian Franciscans who refused to recognize the legitimacy of Boniface VIII's election as pope. During roughly the same period he had to defend his own orthodoxy when the pope ordered inquisitors to proceed against zealots in southern France who apparently stood well to Olivi's left. Later, when a group of Tuscan Franciscans forcibly took over their houses and elected their own minister general, Angelo thundered against them. And then there were the quiet rebels, who avoided open defiance but studied and disseminated works like the series of papal prophecies, *ex eventu* 'predictions' of papal history from the later thirteenth century on, which passed negative judgement on every pope except Celestine V and the angelic popes to come. The 'spiritual Franciscans' were a heterogeneous lot.

Most of them did have one thing in common: persecution by popes and by leaders of the order. Angelo and his group of Anconan zealots spent much of their lives either in prison or staying out of sight. Olivi was apparently able to live out his final years in relative peace, but immediately after his death in 1298 zealots in his province were subjected to several years of persecution by both the pope and the Franciscan order until Pope Clement V intervened. In 1312, at the council of Vienne, Clement acknowledged that many of their complaints were justified and, in the wake of the council, he tried to allow the zealots specific houses where they could observe the rule as they thought fit. That arrangement died with Clement in 1314. Finding themselves again persecuted by superiors who had little sympathy for their aims, the zealots eventually chased them out and, protected by lay supporters, turned the houses at Narbonne and Béziers into spiritual Franciscan strongholds.

Their project was aided by a two-year papal interregnum. Once John XXII was elected in 1316, the writing on the wall was clear; but by the time he managed to summon the zealots to Avignon, imprison them and demand their submission in 1317, the zealots had prepared the laity for what was about to happen, explaining it in terms of Olivian apocalyptic. Olivi himself had shown the way by writing for the laity in the vernacular. After his death other works, notably his Apocalypse commentary, had been translated into the vernacular. Thus when, in 1318, four zealots who refused to submit were burned at the stake and inquisitors began to arrest others, their regional supporters (secular priests and laity, male and female, some third-order Franciscans and some not, all whom we now label 'beguins') concluded that John XXII was the mystical Antichrist and began a non-violent but effective resistance, smuggling fugitive zealots out

## Heresy and dissidence

of France to Majorca and then to Sicily. Inquisitors soon expanded their attention to the beguins and were burning them at the stake from 1319 on. This nexus between spiritual Franciscans and the laity is also seen in Italy during the same period. For example, Ubertino da Casale's (1259–*c*.1330) 1304 *Arbor vitae* (Tree of Life) is a *Who's Who* of contemporary Italian lay mystics, most of them women; and the fascinating thing about his references to them is that Ubertino, a Paris-trained Franciscan cleric, is less interested in what he taught these lay contemplatives than in what *they* taught *him*.

Granting that Dante represented this new laity in one of its more intellectually challenging forms, we might expect him to appreciate the lay–zealot alliance just suggested; yet what we get from him is more enigmatic. In *Paradiso* XII, Dante offers a brief comment on the Franciscan poverty controversy and perhaps its apocalyptic dimension as well. In *Paradiso* XI, Thomas Aquinas (1225–74) presents a generous homage to Francis of Assisi and follows it with criticism of laxity within his own Dominican order. In *Paradiso* XII, St Bonaventure (1221–74) offers a parallel testimony to Dominic coupled with reference to current slippage among the Franciscans, who are described as moving in the wrong direction and due for a reckoning. You will still find some people in the order who retain the old standards, he says, but not at Casale or Aquasparta, 'where they come to the rule in such a way that one flees it and the other coerces it' (*Par.* XII, 125–6). This has been read in various ways, but certainly the reference is to Ubertino da Casale and Matthew of Aquasparta (1240–1302). Matthew was a Franciscan minister general and then a cardinal who had represented Boniface VIII's interests in Florence. Dante had good reason to see both him and Boniface as instrumental in the political intrigue that led to the exile of the White Guelfs, including Dante. Here, though, he criticizes Matthew and those like him for laxity in observing the Franciscan rule.

Ubertino da Casale is presented as the opposite extreme, and here the problem begins. Ubertino was at Santa Croce in 1287 when Olivi began his two years there as a lector, a period when Dante would have been likely to know one or both of them at least by reputation and perhaps personally. Presumably in this passage Ubertino is being criticized by Dante for interpreting the rule in a manner that distorts it by making it too harsh. The passage is puzzling because over the years so much scholarly effort has been put into interpreting Dante in the light of Ubertino or Olivi or both. The effort has extended to his criticism of the Church and, by extension, to his apocalyptic thought. Putting apocalyptic aside for a moment, we can certainly say that Dante's vision of a Franciscan order living poorly and without possessions – which he seems to extend unwarrantedly to the Dominicans – locates him closer to Casale than to Aquasparta. In fact, Dante goes well beyond Casale by wishing such poverty on the entire clergy.

Some historians have suggested that, in rejecting both Aquasparta and Casale, Dante is simply being diplomatic; yet *Paradiso* XII seems an odd moment for him to begin pulling his punches. More likely, here as elsewhere, he means what he says. Perhaps what he does mean is related to the fact that at Florence he had more than just Aquasparta and Casale to choose from. Olivi was also there, and what he represented was a position that rejected less of what the order had become by the end of the century. He was more comfortable with the Franciscan educational programme and with Franciscan involvement in the cities. That made him a different kind of reformer than Ubertino da Casale.

As for Dante's apocalyptic proclivities, that brings us to a second element in Bonaventure's presentation: his kind words concerning Joachim of Fiore, who stands next to him in the circle of intellectual luminaries introduced in *Paradiso* XII. Bonaventure describes him as gifted with the prophetic spirit, which accords not only with the view of Joachim held by Franciscan apocalyptic thinkers such as Gerard of Borgo San Donnino, Angelo Clareno, and Olivi, but also to some extent with Joachim's view of himself. With these words, Dante not only endorses that estimate but makes a valid historical point: Bonaventure himself was in some important ways a creative adapter of Joachim's apocalyptic scenario.

It is somewhat harder to say the same of Dante. He was certainly an apocalyptic writer, but his imagery (e.g., the greyhound in *Inferno* I, 101–11, the monstrous procession in *Purgatorio* XXXII, and the DXV prophecy in *Purgatorio* XXXIII, 37–45) was very much his own. He expected the decline of the Church to be reversed in the near future (e.g., Beatrice's prophecy in *Paradiso* XXVII, 148), but the collapse of his hopes regarding Emperor Henry VII, who died in 1313, left him with no obvious name to connect with his expectation.

If *Paradiso* XII presents us with a problem concerning Dante's view of the Franciscan poverty controversy, *Paradiso* X offers a parallel problem concerning his view of scholastic thought. The thirteenth century saw a genuine revolution in both the form and content of university instruction, and one of the most important changes in content was precipitated by the translation of Aristotle into Latin. Study of the Aristotelian corpus led to his being venerated by many as 'the philosopher', the voice of reason,

*Heresy and dissidence* 117

and thus the purveyor of what the mind would inescapably conclude on the basis of reason unaided by revelation. That entailed problems, because some of what Aristotle contended contradicted Christian doctrine. The problem was intensified as the writings of earlier Islamic commentaries on Aristotle became available in Latin. Ibn Rushd (1126–98), known in the Latin world as Averroes, was especially problematic because his reading of Aristotle was opposed to Christianity yet particularly attractive to some Parisian philosophy teachers. In the course of the thirteenth century, ecclesiastics attempted to solve this problem through a series of edicts. The most important came in 1277, when Etienne Tempier (d. 1279), the Bishop of Paris, condemned 219 propositions. Much of this censure was implicitly aimed at Siger of Brabant (*c.*1240–81/84), a teacher of philosophy at Paris and possibly an Averroist, but some of the propositions also seemed to indict Thomas Aquinas as well.

What happened next is unclear. The popular notion that Siger, cited to answer heresy charges, fled to Italy with the intention of appealing to the pope but was killed there by an insane secretary, has been challenged in recent research by a less dramatic narrative according to which he was cleared of heresy charges, then went back to Liège and relative obscurity. In any case, the 1277 condemnation is considered particularly important by historians because it encouraged a more critical reading of Aristotle. By doing so, it facilitated the development of modern science on the one hand and, on the other, a new emphasis in theology on divine omnipotence. Initially, however, it contributed to a great deal of flailing around as organizations such as universities and religious orders attempted to protect themselves from the charge of heresy. Olivi became a victim of this process when, in 1283, a committee of Franciscan scholars censured a miscellaneous grab-bag of propositions taken from his works. Others fared equally poorly, though, in most cases, the scholar could eventually regain his status by a timely recantation or even, as in Olivi's case, a grudging one.

Siger of Brabant makes an intriguing appearance in *Paradiso* X when Aquinas introduces him. The relationship between Aquinas and Siger, like the total context, parallels the one found in *Paradiso* XII when Bonaventure, the most eminent intellectual in the Franciscan order, appears as part of a circle of luminaries, praises the founder of the Dominican order, criticizes his own order, and introduces the other luminaries in the circle, ending with Joachim the luminary, a controversial figure whose thought was both employed and corrected by Bonaventure himself, immediately on his right. In *Paradiso* X, Aquinas, the most eminent Dominican intellectual, lavishes praise on Francis, criticizes his own order, and introduces his own circle of luminaries, with Siger, whose affection for Aristotle Aquinas concurred with even as he rejected Siger's Averroist interpretation of the philosopher, ending on his right. Whatever fault Bonaventure might have found with his thought, Joachim was 'endowed with the prophetic spirit' (*Par.* X, 141). Whatever errors Aquinas saw in his work, Siger 'syllogized truths that earned him envy' (*Par.* X, 138) in Paris. Heaven is apparently big enough to contain all four, though not big enough to contain Aristotle and Averroes, two genuine unbelievers, who are in Hell, albeit in the least unpleasant part of it, the noble citadel of *Inferno* IV inhabited by those who realized the highest possibilities available to non-Christians. (To what extent Dante himself may have drawn on Averroist positions remains a question on which scholars differ.)

We might conclude that Dante's *Commedia* actually reflects the haziness of any line one might be tempted to draw between orthodoxy and heresy in the early fourteenth century. Obvious heresies, especially long-term ones such as Catharism, were clearly beyond the pale, so much so that they apparently did not interest Dante all that much. What did interest him were those phenomena that lay along the borderline, such as apocalypticism, its fellow-traveller the Franciscan poverty controversy, the recondite conflicts waged within scholastic thought, and, above all, the various ways in which authority was contested not only by Church and State but within the Church itself. This contestation is of upmost importance, because Dante's recognition of it encouraged him to believe that, as an intelligent layman, he had the right to explore and form his own opinion on disputed issues, whatever the pope might tell him to conclude about them.

CHAPTER 8

# *Daily life*

## *Edward D. English*

Dante's lifetime spanned an era of great change in most aspects of daily life in Florence and northern Italy, where he spent his nineteen-year exile. There is a vast secondary literature on daily life, especially food, housing, dress, work, health, and pastimes. Each topic could be a book in itself and many already are. However, the more detailed scholarship treats the period after Dante's death, the era that began with the financial crises and the first visitation of the Black Death in the 1340s. This reflects not just scholarly interest but also the huge growth in literary and archival sources for the history of Florence. Sources for Florentine history and daily life do survive from the 1280s on, especially records for political and civic institutional history, along with the famed chronicles of Dino Compagni (*c*.1255–1324) and Giovanni Villani (*c*.1276–1348). This era also saw the great growth and increased survival of notarial material in the form of individual parchments and cartularies. These documents also become more detailed and sophisticated in terms of the information they provide on daily life. The late thirteenth century is also the era of the development of account books and records for business and building activities, both for lay or communal and clerical organizations. These become a flood of documentation for material life and culture after Dante's death. The politics of the period 1280 to 1302, the decades leading up to Dante's exile, have been well studied. As we shall see, there are adequate, if not good summaries on the details and practices of everyday life until 1321, but much more could be done using archival sources. The period after 1340 also has the benefit of the distinctive Florentine production of memoir and account books by various merchants and heads of families. All of these later sources contain much information on food, housing, dress, health, work, and pastimes, and have been more mined by scholars of the fourteenth and fifteenth centuries. There do survive the stories of writers such as Giovanni Boccaccio (1313–75), Franco Sacchetti (*c*.1330–1400),

Giovanni Sercambi (1348–1424), and Gentile Sermini (*fl.* 1424) among others who relate stories involving everyday life around 1300, including some that refer to Dante. But whether these are true representations of the earlier period is another issue. There can be little doubt that the study of material life from the earlier era does offer opportunities for research and study.

It is important to remember that during Dante's years in Florence, from 1290 on many of the great monuments of civic and religious life were under construction. The city was a massive building site, including the newest walls, the new cathedral, the town hall, major paved streets and *piazze*, the great mendicant churches, and family palaces. Florence, although then a city of perhaps 100,000 inhabitants, remained a face-to-face society where politics and daily life were often carried out in the streets. The period also saw great economic growth and the huge enrichment of mercantile and banking elites. Many new rich families displayed their wealth in palaces and style of life. Other families declined in relative wealth, which fostered tensions over displays of food, clothing, and ritual practices.

## Housing

Housing in Florence before Dante's exile was very much divided according to class, both within the city and in the surrounding countryside. Peasants and most rural inhabitants occupied simple shelters, some of stone. Inside the city the working poor crowed into overflowing neighbourhoods consisting of ramshackle more-or-less temporary structures, often shared among migrants from the same places in the countryside. We know little of these humble buildings made from wood or rubble, home to skilled artisans as well as the poor. They were quite vulnerable to fire, and burned not only by accident but also during factional conflicts. Some may have been similar to the *insulae* apartment buildings of ancient Rome, often occupied by numerous families over several floors with shared access to water and simple cooking facilities. Other houses were single-storey affairs, so that families lived right at street level, in spaces open to the streets. As the commune cut roads and squares through the fast-growing city, most of these houses were torn down and replaced time and again through the later Middle Ages and early Renaissance. There were some efforts during the later thirteenth century to control waste by building drainage systems, imposing fines for dumping trash and dead animals on the streets, and erecting fountains distributing better water.

*Daily life* 121

Rural and urban elites enjoyed much more sturdy structures. Elites, like the peasantry, tended to move from the countryside into the city. Dante particularly blamed these immigrants, rich and poor, for the changes in Florentine society and politics during his lifetime. The wealthier migrants from the countryside were often related to the old noble families who owned castles in the rural jurisdiction of the city, termed the *contado*. In town, the older established families lived in tower-houses that had been built from the twelfth century. Some survive, including those of the Marsili, Amidei, Alberti, Ghiberti or delle Vedove, and that of the Corbizi or Donati. After 1250, many of these buildings were torn down or suffered decapitation in factional conflicts. By the 1280s families began to replace them with larger structures of a much less defensive nature, such as those of the Mozzi, Feroni-Spini, and Gianfigliazzi. These are the predecessors of the palaces of the later fourteenth and fifteen centuries, including the Davanzati, Acciaioli, Canigiani, and eventually those of the Medici, Pazzi, Rucellai, and Antinori. These buildings were much more suited to a comfortable domestic life than fortified towers, but still had impressive and intimidating facades.

Elite families sought to create what amounted to fortified compounds within the city, including towers where the family could retreat in case of fighting. These compounds were built around small squares difficult to access from the surrounding streets. They contained the tower, the family parish church, a residence for the head of the family, apartments for family members and clients, as well as storehouses, workshops, and shops. One of the few surviving examples, although much disguised by later changes, is that of the Peruzzi. Nearby Siena is more like a museum than Florence, and many buildings retain their fourteenth-century appearances. Medieval Sienese compounds were called *castellari*. They were jointly owned by members of the family and divided into shares that devolved over generations, so that by the 1340s a clan member's share could be as small as a 140th part. These structures and their constituent buildings were considered the core of the family's wealth and prestige, a way to represent the family's social, political, and economic power. For Dante, they were also symbols of overly ambitious elite lineages that were not civic-minded.

Domestic possessions within these houses included beds, bedding, mattresses, combs, oil lamps, pottery, ceramics, glassware, curtains, hangings, jewellery, arms, armour, implements for trade such as scales, and cooking utensils. Few actual physical examples have survived, but these goods were frequently described in dowry and trousseau agreements and wills or last testaments from the late thirteenth century, as well as confiscations for debt. Domestic goods became more common and elaborate from the better-documented mid fourteenth century.

We know little of internal arrangements during the earlier period: was there an ideology of domesticity, with living quarters divided neatly into areas with separate functions? Clearly, security was important. What about privacy? Elite domestic arrangements such as household structure and living and work space are better documented over the course of the fourteenth century. Fiscal records are major sources.

Another aspect of the building boom after 1280 was the construction of charitable establishments for the poor, ill, and pilgrims such as San Pier Maggiore and San Gallo. For the large number of clergy living in and around the city, the various mendicant convents and monastic establishments expanded their dormitories and other facilities during the years Dante spent in Florence.

## Food

The production, distribution, and consumption of food is central to culture and society. Food had medical and scientific aspects resulting in ideas about proper and ethical food regimes or menus. The fasts of the Church calendar were an important aspect of the influence of the Church in everyday life, both for the laity and the clergy. The provisioning of an adequate food supply was a major concern for communal governments, since famine could provoke violent uprisings. During conflicts, enemies both external and internal might try to cut off supplies of food to the city. Transport could be blocked, crippling markets.

Despite ideological and ethical guidelines, elites enjoyed banquets and prestigious conspicuous consumption, while the urban and rural poor were too often unsure of their next meal. Manuals that we might consider cookbooks came into existence only at the very end of Dante's life, though recipe collections written in pharmacological terms were common. They rarely contain instructions on actual preparation. Sumptuary laws were devised to regulate display, such as lavish feasts at weddings and funerals. In nutritional terms, the consumption of certain socially defined dangerous foods was forbidden according to class. The poor suffered illness in digestion if they ate above their station. Sight, colour, and taste were more important than smell. Sweeteners were employed on a wide scale, although sour flavours were common at sophisticated tables. Pepper, saffron, and garlic were among the most used spices. Impressively exotic and rare spices from far away included nutmeg, cinnamon, cloves, ginger, and supposed ground Egyptian mummy. Many spices had explicit medical uses and served to complement one another on the palate.

Again, most of the scholarship on food and society treats the period after the death of Dante, as sources such as the account books of priors of the city and records of institutional buying become available. Even these documents need to be used with care to establish what people actually ate. Vegetables and fruit and many other foodstuffs were not listed when they came from the properties of the institution itself and were not purchased. Much work remains to be done on eating, cooking, preservation, and etiquette with spoons and forks along with the rules for drinking for the late thirteenth century. It is clear that diners expected proper, civil, and conventional table manners and comportment, as well as ordered serving and seating.

Dante and later-fourteenth-century lay and clerical authors wrote of a clear moral danger involved in the consumption of food. Spices could instigate wickedness, including the sexual. For Dante over-indulgence in spending on rich foods was regrettable if not a sin, as when he makes caustic remarks about the prodigal 'Spendthrifts' Brigade', the *Brigata spendereccia*, from foolish and vain Siena (*Inf.* XXIX, 130–2). These were members of the noble, banking, and commercial elite in the city who formed a crew and vied with one another to squander in a self-destructive manner their fortunes on extravagant dining and drink. They even lavished large sums to introduce imported cloves to their menus (*Inf.* XXIX, 127–9). Dante followed contemporary moral guidelines on the sin of gluttony, one of the seven capital vices, linking it to Ciacco, the first Florentine he meets in Hell and whose name is probably meant to suggest his hog-like nature. The poet described the effects of hunger on the appearance of the penitent gluttonous in Purgatory.

Late medieval society reveals many anxieties about food, including the moral implications of a sinful lack of self-discipline compounded by fears of deprivation and starvation. Moreover, poisoning, both intentional and accidental, was a recognized fact of life.

## Dress

In his diatribe in *Paradiso* against luxuries corrupting Florence, Dante's great-great-grandfather Cacciaguida (*c.*1091–*c.*1148) mentions that in the more modest and sober city of his time, 150 years earlier, women did not indulge in a passion for gold chains, embroidered gowns, or elaborate belts. Houses were still simple structures and not the ornate buildings going up in the late thirteenth century. Fathers were not terrified that the wealth of the family would be destroyed by huge dowries, used in part to buy fashionable clothes to show off the riches of the families of the bride and groom (*Par.* XV, 97–129). We know from other sources that families could be intimidated by such expenditure to delay marrying off their daughters. Responding to a growing consumer society during Dante's lifetime, industries began to produce high-quality goods to feed an expanding market for elegant dress. Florentines enriched by banking and trade had more resources to pay for fashion. Again, the sources documenting these developments begin primarily a decade or two after Dante's death. They include images in wall paintings and manuscript illuminations, references to fashionable clothing in authors such as Boccaccio and Sacchetti, sumptuary legislation, thorough records of marriage agreements and trousseaux, detailed wills and last testaments, as well as in-depth documentation relating to the guilds and trading companies such as the Peruzzi and others.

Original clothing rarely survives. Fabric is fragile, and clothes were usually worn until they were worn out, particularly everyday clothing. Burial clothes provide some indication of luxury clothing. Cangrande della Scala (1291–1329), the patron in Verona of the exiled Dante, was buried in luxurious Mongol silks. Worn-out cotton could be used to make paper. There was a very active market in used clothing, and fabrics were often reworked. Some valuable articles of clothing and jewellery were worn only on special occasions and passed down over generations in testaments. People often pawned clothes and even gambled with them. It was literally possible to gamble away your trousers.

The fabrics available to Dante and his contemporaries were wool, linen, hemp, cotton, and silk. Florence had an industry for each of these fabrics, producing them for local consumption and for export. Because only organic dyes were available, colours were limited; some shades were very expensive. Not everyone wore drab clothing, however; brighter colours were a form of display of social status and wealth. Studies have shown that during the fourteenth and fifteenth centuries people became increasingly convinced that colours were a reflection of the wearer's character. The fashion industry grew, and both men and women paid considerable attention to style. There is less research on the early period, including the use of colour by artists such as Duccio (*c.*1255/60–*c.*1318/19) and Giotto (1266–1337). The colour of one's clothing could be imaginatively interpreted as ascetic, aristocratic, or even demonic. Clothing highlighted distinctions between the laity, as well as among the clergy, including prelates, priests, nuns,

*Daily life* 125

friars, and monks. People actively debated whether clerical dress should be luxurious or even comfortable. Occupations such as physicians, academics, and notaries wore distinctive garb. City officials were expected to dress the part. Those doing hard labour on farms or labouring at a trade wore clothing appropriate to the season but were often constrained by what they could afford or acquire. Some professions, such as butchers, bakers, smiths, or those riding horses, wore protective clothing. These included aprons, boots, and hoods. Military activity required armour and protective linings. From 1215 the Church required people on the fringes of society, including heretics who had returned to the faith and Jews, to wear distinctive garb that made them easily identifiable. Prostitutes were sometimes also marked by their clothes, as were lepers.

Before 1350 styles of fashionable dress probably changed only slowly. Images do show what men, women, the clergy, and children wore. This might include undershorts, undershirts, chemises, stockings, and hose. Outerwear included tunics, doublets, surcoats, capes, cloaks, dresses, and gowns. Both sexes wore brimmed hats, and perhaps berets or headdresses of various levels of elaboration. Around 1300 those who could afford furs turned them inside out for more warmth and less ostentatious display. Other fashionable items were pockets, bags, purses, gloves, mittens, buttons, brooches, pins, buckles, belts, ribbons, fasteners, jewellery, and of course shoes. Children were often portrayed dressed as adults. Images of all these items of clothing exist from Dante's time; and these became more elaborate a few decades after his death. One example is the elaborate portrayal of clothing by Ambrogio Lorenzetti (*c.*1290–1348) in the Good Government frescoes in the town hall of Siena from the 1340s.

During Dante's lifetime, town governments made efforts to regulate luxurious clothes, as well as weddings and funerals. Part of the motivation would have been congenial to Dante: these were attempts to enforce public morals, limit competitive displays by elites, and encourage thrift. The commune of Florence issued sumptuary laws from at least 1281. While a town government might want to promote the businesses of its members, it also felt that there had to be limits on display, especially if this involved obtaining materials from outside its jurisdiction and local economy. The laws were also efforts to reinforce social hierarchy: people should not dress above their rank. A merchant or his family, though they might be able to afford it, should not ape the style of a noble. These laws were efforts to define and tag people, and to control the display of pearls, jewellery, gold, silver, and exotic furs according to social class. Clothes were registered as permissible, although the laws were not in force to permit more explicit celebration of special feast days. Specific regulations permitted or banned certain styles of apparel. On feast days, these banned styles were sometimes permitted or overlooked to allow personal displays of celebration. When foreign entourages visited the city, especially princes like Charles of Anjou (1227–85), they might put on a show of fashion. Some locals chose to imitate them, to Dante's disapproval, affecting sleeves stretching over their hands or long trains dragging behind them.

Scholars have claimed that laws relating to clothing were aimed primarily at the clothing of women to limit their sensual display and to protect the familial wealth of their husbands or fathers. But other scholars have questioned that motivation, suggesting other factors such as social control of both men and women by demonstrating that the statutes were enforced against both sexes.

It became a great game to keep one step ahead of the rules as notaries wandered the streets ogling men and women searching for sartorial offences. They might even pursue suspects home. In one case from Bologna, a woman with an illegally long train escaped the notary and slipped into her father's house. Her husband was summoned by the court the next day, where he produced the dress, which had become the legal length. The language of the statutes could open up loopholes. People challenged the definitions of banned clothing, and usually did not expect the statutes to be enforced. Scholars have suggested that these became formalities that required people to pay for licences in order to flaunt the rules that they did not wish to respect. However, recent research on Bologna and Florence has demonstrated that there was serious – if erratic – enforcement. Over time, cities became more tolerant, although they imposed fines or luxury taxes that permitted the wearing of certain items of clothing, such as elaborate and long trains.

## Health

Studies of health in this period explore ideas about disease and its treatment, efforts to protect public health and hygiene, hospitals and care, and also what activities and experiences were to be expected at different stages of life. Contrary to the popular view of medieval cities, there were efforts at public health and personal hygiene. This was an inescapable task of civic governments, especially in cities such as Florence where the population grew rapidly. Diseases such as dysentery that are associated with crowded conditions were common, but chroniclers tended to mention them only when a city was under siege, its populace trapped inside the walls and

# Daily life

struggling with refuse and human waste, and probably hunger as well. Towns took great care to provide water that would not kill people; during Dante's lifetime many hill towns built massive aqueducts. Outbuildings were placed away from habitations. Communal governments tried to promote street cleaning, sewers and cesspits. Despite the lack of knowledge of pathogens, there was an understanding that certain conditions were dangerous. In both punitive and preventive terms, communal governments regulated trades that produced waste, such as tanning or butchering, and how offal was to be handled and tainted meat avoided.

Bathing was considered an enjoyable pastime and healthy activity, although public baths could also endanger a person's morals. People probably washed their heads, faces, and feet more frequently than they took full baths, and they did clean their teeth. Sugar used in cooking was expensive but was popular and available at least to the well off. Civic and private laundry facilities existed, as did dry cleaning, which was done with urine. Lye soap (alkaline potash) was used to wash wool and also for personal needs, although gentler soaps based on olive oil were probably preferred. Linen and cotton underwear was available, but it is not clear how commonly it was worn. It is important to remember that documentation on hygiene is sparse at best.

The thirteenth century saw the appearance of university-trained physicians (see Chapter 12). Medicine remained shaped by assumptions about miasmas in the air and classical ideas on medical ethics and the humours derived from Hippocrates of Cos (c.460–c.370 BCE) and especially Galen of Pergamum (129–c.216). However, while recently translated Arabic medical texts had begun to encourage a more scientific attitude towards disease, the idea that illness was God's punishment for wrongdoing did persist. Illness could even be tied to a single sin. Theorists continued to explain the transmission of disease as a righteous punishment for sin, as the malign intervention of Satan, or as an unfortunate astrological configuration. But by the late thirteenth century physicians also believed that human beings could address health problems with rational treatments that might ameliorate or even cure them. Depending on their wealth and social class, people might have access to university-trained and licensed physicians, surgeons, barbers, empirical practitioners of traditional medicine, and home remedies. Some treatments did work, but many now sound absurd at best.

Often modern scholars do not know whether the diseases and medical conditions that could have affected Dante still exist today. We frequently lack adequate diagnoses and archaeological studies on remains that might indicate whether they are really the same diseases. Bacteria and especially viruses can mutate. Environmental factors are complex: while sanitation and hygiene could be awful, chemical factors were simpler and less artificial. Then as now, disease was spread by bodily fluids, contaminated food and water, and insect vectors. The thriving travel and trade of the period contributed to the spread of sickness.

Many diseases were endemic and are described reliably in surviving sources. Conditions caused by bacteria were pneumonia, anthrax, tuberculosis, scarlet fever, typhoid fever, and dysentery, among many others. Viral infections had a greater morbidity and included smallpox, measles, influenza, and mumps. Insect vectors spread typhus and malaria. The latter was especially common in low-lying lands with standing water, such as the Maremma and the Val di Chiana. Other serious and recognized diseases included cancer, epilepsy, arthritis, and gout. Dietary deficiencies were present in the countryside and in the city, as most people did not eat what we might consider a balanced diet, and led to widespread problems such as anemia. Crowded housing was conducive to the spread of disease.

Dental care was primitive with extraction without anaesthesia the last resort. Childbirth was dangerous to both the mother and child, and puerperal fever was not unusual. Midwives attended most births, although professional physicians who had far less experience were already trying to oust them. Surgeons did perform caesarean births. We know little about the actual obstetrical practice of these caregivers. Child neglect was present, but was more likely caused by working conditions rather than an emotional lack of concern for offspring, as was once proposed by scholars.

Prevention and cure could be elusive. Even before the great plagues after 1347, communities attempted to impose quarantines, but success was uncertain. One could obtain alleviating medicines – some even effective on symptoms – from apothecaries or providers of herbal remedies. Physicians did prescribe dietary regimens and other vehicles to manipulate humours that were out of balance. Medicines were made by compounding plants, using spices, vegetables, oils, seeds, herbs, and minerals. Many were harmful. If not, they likely helped the patient mostly because of belief in their effectiveness. These cures were all of dubious effectiveness on mortality and the alleviation of suffering.

Magic and prayer may also have been of some solace to the sick. Miraculous cures were collected as evidence of sainthood. The agents of the Church generally took mental illness and emotional problems out of the hands of medical practitioners, and sought divine aid instead, at times assuming demonic causes. The wealthy could afford care for those

# Daily life

suffering mental or emotional problems, although families might abandon sufferers and leave them to beg in the streets with other disabled people.

This was an era of the founding of hospitals in Florence that evolved from earlier almshouses and hospices and care offered by parishes. The hospitals were primarily established for sick pilgrims, although care and services were given to others by monks and nuns. Some hospitals specialized in the care of lepers. Others looked after unwed mothers and orphans. These institutions became major establishments after the time of Dante and have been studied in greater detail than those contemporary with his life.

Health conditions affected the life cycle and expectancies. Everyday life in Dante's Florence revolved around the experiences of courting, marriage, sexuality, birth, baptism, parenting, illness, death, funerals, and inheritance. Everyone was profoundly affected by gender, social and personal status, and urban and rural conditions. Expectations varied by age. Children were innocent. Male youths were violent, lacked reason and sexual self-control, and were therefore excluded from public office. Adulthood, according to Dante (*Par.* VII, 58–60), was when one attained and practised self-control and discretion, and had sufficient self-knowledge to lead a virtuous life. The elderly were to accept that they were coming into the calm harbour of approaching death.

Marriage had to have a public aspect, so that the community might witness and recognize a binding union. The practice of marriage was affected by demographic conditions, the dowry system, and economic opportunity. Once again, the sources for these demographic realities are much richer for the later period, the 150 years after Dante's death. In general, women were married young to much older husbands, although the gap in age varied over the next two centuries. Elites and merchants played in a competitive marriage market that was very much affected by dowry inflation. An increasingly high proportion of lifetime bachelors meant a lower birth rate, and so a decline in the population so essential for a healthy commune. Elite marriages also required expensive ritual celebrations, which regularly provided entertainment to the community. Expensive celebrations such as those for espousals, baptism, funerals, and godparenting were also common.

The urban lower classes and peasantry married or had informal long-term relationships, forming household and work partnerships. The very poor more likely did not bother with legal marriage, since there was little or no wealth involved. A sex industry existed for both men and women in Florence, though it is little documented until later in the century.

## Work

Dante lived during a period when the Florentine economy took off. A person's work was determined by class, gender, economic status, clerical or lay identity, and residence in the countryside or the city. Most people did physical labour, though some performed managerial tasks. This period saw the highest population densities in Tuscany until modern times. Lots of people needed to work and to eat. Again, a serious market for luxury items was developing and had to be paid for, a fact much lamented by Dante. The manufacturing sector responded to the rising demand for luxury and taste for new clothes and fabrics, thereby providing much low-paying and irregular employment. The sources for wages and standards of living are not good for this early period compared to the period after the 1340s.

For priests, friars, monks, and nuns, prayer was an important part of their existence. Those in higher positions in the hierarchy of the Church carried administrative burdens. Friars preached and provided pastoral care. Monks and nuns did physical labour or ministered to pilgrims or to the ill, although servants attached to a monastic or charitable institution did the hard work.

For the elite or even the nobles, work could mean managing estates or military practice, sometimes even service on behalf of the commune or as independent entrepreneurs or mercenaries. There were manuals for managing farming enterprises or managing peasant workforces. Elites did practise skills useful in war, such as horsemanship, archery, and sword-fighting from a young age. Again the sources for this are sparse and indirect, such as denunciations for 'accidently' shooting a passer by. This was the beginning of the great era of Florentine banking and capitalism, so some merchant bankers travelled as agents to markets or fairs outside Florence and even over the Alps to Champagne, where they traded in wool or money and sent the proceeds back to Florence. Some attended royal and papal courts, lending money or facilitating exchanges among the complex currencies and coinages of western Europe and the Mediterranean. The dangers of travel, the marginal liquidity behind these businesses, and the risky and fickle powerful clientele meant that this work had its ups and downs. It could sometimes be quite lucrative, but then could suddenly become dangerous with flight or imprisonment definite possibilities. For their work as partners or factors, merchant bankers had to conduct commercial or banking correspondence, do the accounting, and understand the market for money and commodities. Dante lamented their absence from the city

*Daily life* 131

and their families as having a deleterious effect on Florence's social fabric. Some members of the elite and educated classes worked as administrators for communal governments across northern Italy as *podestà*, judges, and soldiers. They left their families and households in Florence, usually in the hands of their wives, who raised the children and ran the family properties, working with the help, often very limited, of their husband's male relatives.

In the countryside, a few men worked as estate managers. Most people were farm labourers under various forms of tenure or obligation. Genuine serfdom had withered away by the late thirteenth century, although peasants still had serious obligations, often violently disputed, towards the owners of the farms on which they worked. Monasteries owned large estates in the countryside and had the reputation for being hard and aggressive taskmasters. The *mezzadria* or share-cropping system, in which peasants were formally obligated to pay their landlords specific amounts of their produce, was just taking form. That system became the common land tenure system for centuries, as landlords tried to cope with a changing labour market and further monetization of the economy.

Actual labour was tied to the geographical economy of the estate. It might involve animal maintenance and the pasturing of sheep and cattle, as well as hard manual labour over the seasons in the fields, orchards, vineyards, and forests. Some produced foods such as cheese for local consumption and sometimes sale at markets. Others transported produce. People from the city often had properties close to the walls where they maintained gardens for their own use or sold the produce in the city.

The city of Florence in the 1290s encompassed seven major guilds and fourteen minor guilds. They reflect a hierarchy and segregation of economic activity and work, but were primarily the basis for political organization and participation. They did influence entry into a trade and business practice, and tried to protect the interests of their members. Eighteen guilds included artisans and shopkeepers, although three had no artisan members (*Cambio*, local bankers; *Calimala*, cloth importers; and *Giudici e notai*, judges and notaries). Whatever roles guilds played in communal life, the economic lives of their members were not deeply affected by institutional relations linked to guild membership. This was a much less-restricted world than elsewhere. Artisans functioned without much protection by restriction. Some industries drew workers from several different guilds, actively working together in sectors such as the booming construction industry. Dominated by masters, the more skilled trades required apprenticeships but had minimal entry requirements. People were quick to migrate from the countryside in the late thirteenth century, so for industries such as the finishing of wool there was an ample population willing to endure hard conditions. Some work, such as spinning, was shipped out to cottage industries in the countryside. Other work was done in small shops, often for the trade in luxury items such as gold work. Women worked in some industries in various capacities but are barely reflected in the sources or literature. Later in the fourteenth century, and likely in the late thirteenth century, in Florence hundreds, if not thousands, of women and children were doing piece-work spinning for the manufacture of cloth.

Wage patterns and the price of labour are difficult to compute for this period. Vulnerable to currency manipulation, especially for silver, trends in prices are likewise unclear in comparison to the period after 1330. It seems unlikely that wages for most workers, especially day labourers, were at more than subsistence level, with misery compounded by debt. Foreigners with mobile occupations such as carpenters or masons were recruited. Slaves certainly existed in Florence, but were mostly women bought as household staff, and were a status symbol for their owners. Low wages for the free but marginally skilled made slaves too expensive for most industrial or artisan work. Masters owned their own shops and could take in apprentices and employees. The rhythm of work must have followed the daylight hours and the cathedral's bells. Later in the fourteenth century, clocks and more secular bells gave employers a greater ability to impose structure to the working day.

### Pastimes

The Florentines of Dante's time enjoyed a long list of amusements. If a contemporary of Dante's walked around the city, he or she would come across the infamous *pitture infamanti* (defamatory paintings) intended to humiliate offenders and painted on the walls of buildings near the town hall, or insulting outbursts against rivals of political figures such as Corso Donati. Citizens might attend and participate in street dancing, though such festivals could lead to violent confrontations between factions, and soon were banned as threats to public order and morality.

The opportunities for people to participate in pastimes were determined by their economic and social status, though some were open to everyone. Some sports or training exercises required physical strength and long practice, while games such as chess were based on intellectual faculties. For others, luck was the key. Pastimes could be open to spectators, or

*Daily life* 133

restricted and even clandestine, open daily or at irregular intervals. The commune and religious authorities sponsored events and pageants, and tried to control other pastimes. The actual activities and rules of medieval pastimes are often obscure, being rarely documented or illustrated.

Popular public sports might mimic warfare such as battles on bridges and dangerous brawls (*battagliole*). Participants representing various areas in the city used clubs and fists, or threw stones, sometimes killing opponents. In Siena, for example, the commune tried to regulate these battles, fearing they might become attacks on the regime in power. Such battles took place on the *Campo* or square before the town hall.

Ball games were probably more like rugby than modern football. Horse and foot races took place in city streets and around the outside of city walls. There was a horse race in Florence on 24 June in honour of the city's patron saint, John the Baptist. Besiegers surrounding a city might insult it by means of organized races near the walls, taunting the people inside. Noble families put on tournaments and knighting ceremonies, impressing or perhaps intimidating their neighbours with great pomp and even with costly distributions of food to spectators. Communal or ecclesiastical ritual processions competed with these events, though crowds more likely found battles more entertaining than processions or parades of sumptuously attired government male officials and clerics.

Excursions into the countryside were common, perhaps to bathing resorts that were also known for gambling, and perhaps for wrestling contests, hunting, falconry, and fishing. Elites did put on feasts with varying numbers of invitees, entertaining guests with musicians, singers, storytellers, and jugglers. There were displays of trained animals along with the torture of bears or bulls and dog and cock fights.

The best-documented pastime from Dante's lifetime is the game of *zara* or *azzardo*, a name that might derive form the Arabic word *zahr* or *zahar* for 'die'. It came into English as 'hazard'. Another popular gambling game was *tavole*, something like backgammon. However, it was *zara* that aroused the most concern or regulation, and it is mentioned in most of the collections of statutes from this era. It involved three dice and two players who called out numbers. The rules were vague and debatable. *Zara* was clearly regarded as a high-risk pastime that depended on luck. Dante mentioned *zara*, depicting a winner whose friends beg him for money (*Purg.* VI, 1–9). Dante's account of the 'Spendthrifts Brigade' linked it with self-destructiveness. *Zara* was different: absorption in the game could become an uncontrollable passion, leading to the impoverishment of the players and their families. Gambling obsessions were a sin against fate or an attempt at divination, close to a mental illness. For communal regimes, it was an immoral threat to public order often leading to violence and drunkenness. We do know that the commune of Siena tried to ban or regulate gambling, restricting it to feast days and permitting it only in certain areas of the city. Despite these efforts, gangs preyed on people, especially students, to draw them into rigged games in which they lost heavily.

Scholastic theologians in the thirteenth century and into the fourteenth century called the proceeds from gambling *turpe lucrum* or *male ablata*, ill-gotten gains, whose restoration was necessary for true penance and contrition. Although *zara* involved a contract and obligations between players, at its core was reckless disregard for risk. Such views on the manipulation or avoidance of risk came to be linked to the rationalizing of business ethics and practices. Over the course of the fourteenth century, the rationalization and justification of usury, the collection of interest, and the practice of insurance agreements became more tolerated because of the risks involved in moving money and goods around. One could earn a return for taking such chances. It is unclear how many of these scholastic ideas or warnings were known to Dante and his contemporaries. As with other ethical topics of this period, more research needs to be done on pastoral care and preaching about the evils of games of chance and the handling of risk. As part of the rules for partnership or active participation in establishing a commercial or banking company or business partnership, there was often a clear ban on members or employees gambling.

Daily life in the time of Dante was changing. Besides being appalled by the factionalism and conflicts of his contemporaries, Dante, typically brimming with moral rectitude, was also disgusted with many of the changes in daily life. He scorned the pretentions of his contemporaries and felt much nostalgia for an imagined simpler lost world of Florence of the twelfth century, the 'good old time' evoked in *Paradiso* XV–XVI. His city was becoming richer, but was also enveloped in much competition and factionalism. Unfortunately for Dante, he was not a participant in the daily life of Florence for the last twenty years of his life. However, it was hardly absent from his writing.

# PART II

## *Intellectual traditions*

CHAPTER 9

# *Philosophy and theology*

## *Andrea A. Robiglio*

### *Philosophia* and *theologia*

To understand the role of theology and philosophy in Dante, it is important to remember that, in the Middle Ages, the symbiosis between knowledge and religious faith was universally accepted. The Bible constituted the culture's key and determining authoritative text, which in practice meant constant reference to the Christian idea of the divine based on scriptural revelation, namely the Trinity, creation from nothing, the Incarnation, and the resurrection of the dead.

In order to grasp the key features of this synthesis, it is useful to stress four elements: one terminological, the other three historical. Let us begin by examining the meanings and values of the two terms that circumscribe this chapter: philosophy and theology. During the long Latin Middle Ages, from Augustine (354–430) and Boethius (*c.*475–*c.*526) until the time of Bonaventure (1221–74) and Thomas Aquinas (1225–74), the terms *philosophia* and *theologia* were far from semantically stable. A rapid glance at the late-antique and high-medieval tradition brings to the fore the terms' distinct principal meanings – meanings that persist up to Dante's time.

*Philosophia* covered a wider semantic area than *theologia*: 'it embraces all knowledge, all education, even rhetoric and poetry'.[1] In general terms, however, it is possible to distinguish two fields, a general and a particular one. In its general meaning, *philosophia* refers to wisdom (*sapientia*), namely the highest and most fundamental form of knowledge, as well as the perfect way of life for a rational entity such as a human being. This did not mean simply a notion of wisdom as a superior organizing and hierarchizing activity, which pagan thinkers such as Aristotle had already theorized, but also a proper way of living based on Christ's teachings and Christian values. When such a meaning of wisdom was associated with religious monastic life, for instance, 'philosophy' could become

137

synonymous with 'monastic rule'. The ethical dimension of such a perspective is both implicit and essential: in negative terms, it contributes to defining that which is not useful for achieving salvation. Consequently, 'true philosophy' cannot be considered in its essence without also thinking about what stands against it, what prevents humanity from receiving the gift of divine grace. This is not merely an error of knowledge, but an actual sin, a 'heresy'. The implications of the effects of the notion of 'heresy' on that of philosophy, as will be discussed below, were especially weighty in the thirteenth and fourteenth centuries.

Alongside *philosophia*'s general value, the notion also had quite specific meanings. According to these, *philosophia* was associated with the idea of a 'particular sphere of knowledge', a rational form of cognition based on a shared method of conceptual analysis and applied to a particular category of objects. The term is thus used to refer to linguistic (logic) and natural (physics, astronomy, zoology) sciences, to medicine, to law, and even to engineering. Preceded by the epithet *moralis*, *philosophia* coincided with ethics (see Chapter 10).

*Theologia*, on the other hand, in antiquity and in the High Middle Ages, was a term that was not commonly employed. The Church Fathers, including Augustine, used it rarely, and only Boethius had recourse to it on a regular basis in his theological works. Some of these, such as the *De trinitate* (On the Trinity), were glossed in twelfth-century schools, for instance, by Gilbert de la Porrée (1070–1154), teacher at Chartres and in Paris, as well as in the universities of the next century, a notable example being Thomas Aquinas. *Theologia* too had a range of meanings, which once again can be divided into two groups. On the one hand, *theologia* signified the study of the Bible whose aim was a 'useful' understanding of God. Used in this sense, the term coincided with *sacra doctrina* (sacred doctrine). In a more specific sense, however, and in keeping with Boethius' use, for instance in his *In Isagogen Porphyrii Commenta* I, 3, *theologia* indicated a particular science: that part of 'true philosophy' that deals with God, with the incorporeal substances, and with the human soul, itself also incorporeal and immortal. For Boethius, furthermore, the Christian model based on creation, fall, redemption, and final restoration is reconciled with Neoplatonism, namely, with the interpretation of Plato's metaphysics and cosmology as elaborated at the end of antiquity by thinkers such as Plotinus (204/05–70) and Proclus (412–85), as is evident in the structure of the *Consolation of Philosophy*, a text that was glossed in the twelfth century, and that became increasingly popular towards the end of the following century.

*Philosophy and theology*

In addition, beginning in the twelfth century, *theologia* takes on a third meaning, namely an institutional one. Alan of Lille (*c.*1116/17–1202/03), around 1160, was among the earliest authors to speak of a 'theological faculty'. He was referring to that body of knowledge on God and humanity present in the Bible, which, integrated with the teachings of the Fathers and presented in a manner that minimized or neutralized contradictions between contrasting interpretations, could be made the subject of teaching. A compilation such as Peter Abelard's (1079–1142) *Sic et Non* (For and Against) presents a good example of the effort made to arrive at ideological harmony. In order to present the tenets of faith as a unified and shared truth, 'theologians' drew on the example of canon law, which had developed at the close of the previous century, and which in Gratian's (d. *c.*1145) hugely influential *Decretum* (Decree) had found its summation. The *Decretum Gratiani* employs an approach that the theologians, namely the masters of the *facultas theologica*, quickly imitated. Thus, Peter Lombard's (*c.*1096–1160) *Book of Sentences* (*c.*1140) is a work of 'concord of discordant views', that 'consisted of four books of theological passages culled from the Fathers with discussions and explanations, arranged according to the Augustinian model (found in *De doctrina christiana*; On Christian Teaching) of the difference between things and signs and between use (*uti*) and enjoyment (*frui*)'.[2] Beginning in the third decade of the thirteenth century, the *Sentences* became the leading theological textbook, and would continue to enjoy this status for more than another two centuries. Nonetheless, it was not simply a case of taking advantage of dialectics to resolve contradictions between different authorities on matters relating to faith. The *Decretum*, in fact, contributed to defining heresy in terms that permitted establishing rigorous legal procedures: the 'heretic' was a follower of false opinion, who had recourse to his own judgement rather than conforming to the lessons of Scripture, and who led others into error by having recourse to dialectics, thereby introducing division into the community of Christian believers.

When Dante, in mid-1315 after more than ten years of exile, reminisced about his native city while writing to an older Florentine friend, and proclaimed himself the honourable 'servant of Philosophy' (*Ep.* XII, 5–6), he was clearly referring to the general, inclusive meaning of the term. When Giovanni del Virgilio (late thirteenth century–*c.*1327) – Latin poet and professor of Latin literature at the University of Bologna – penned an epitaph intended for Dante's tomb, which begins: 'Dante, a theologian, lacking no doctrine which philosophy may cherish in her illustrious breast',[3] he was again alluding to learning in general, while suggesting the multiplicity of knowledge and disciplines that philosophy might embrace. A half century later, at the beginning of his *Life of Dante*, Giovanni Boccaccio (1313–75) amplified Giovanni's observations, declaring that, as soon as Dante had discovered the seductions of philosophy, 'he completely abandoned all the cares of this world, and devoted himself entirely to this; and in order that no part of philosophy should be left unscrutinized by him, he plunged with keen intellect into the profoundest depths of theology'.[4] In the Trecento, 'theology' was considered the deepest part, but still a part, of philosophy. On the other hand, any 'philosophy' unwilling to include 'theology' would turn out to be irrelevant or, even worse, false and 'heretical'.

## Mendicant orders, universities, and church reform

As well as matters of terminology, three historical factors need to be kept in mind when considering the status of philosophy and theology in the late Middle Ages. The first relates to the establishment of the mendicant orders, specifically the Franciscans and the Dominicans, during the first decades of the thirteenth century. Depending directly on the pope and the Roman curia, and hence important elements in the increasing disciplinary centralization of the period, these new orders grew rapidly during the thirteenth century. Indeed, by the end of the century they exercised almost total control over religious education in the cities of northern Italy, including Florence. During Dante's time in his native city, there were three schools: the Dominican *studium* at Santa Maria Novella, the Franciscan at Santa Croce, and the Austin Friars at Santo Spirito. Equally, Bonaventure and Thomas, the two most important masters at the most significant *facultas theologica* of the thirteenth century, that of the University of Paris, were mendicant friars.

The second factor, which was already apparent in the previous century, concerns the development of higher education, and especially the birth of the universities, which quickly supplanted the episcopal schools of the Rhineland (Cologne) and especially of northern France (Laon, Chartres, and Paris). The University of Paris had its roots in the city's episcopal school, while a highly prestigious monastic school had also flourished at the abbey of St Victor. During the twelfth century the episcopal schools had undergone a veritable pedagogical renaissance, which was centred on the widespread circulation of recently translated philosophical texts from Arabic and Greek, most notably Aristotle's hitherto largely inaccessible texts: the logical writings, such as the *Prior* and *Posterior Analytics*, *Topics*, and *Sophistic Refutations*; the *Physics*, *On the Soul*, parts of the *Metaphysics*; the *Nicomachean Ethics*; and the *Rhetoric*. The remaining works, such as the *Politics*, *Poetics*, *Problems*, and *On the Universe*, would be translated during the following century. Furthermore, a vital contribution was made by the Flemish Dominican William of Moerbeke (*c*.1215–86) who, besides translating and revising part of the *corpus aristotelicum*, made available several texts of the Neoplatonist Proclus, which may have circulated among Florentine Dominicans.

During the twelfth century, at Chartres, before the arrival of Aristotle's *Physics*, the study of the Platonic tradition, based on Plato's *Timaeus* accompanied by the commentary of the Christian Roman philosopher Calcidius (fourth century), was accompanied by a renewed appreciation of the concept of 'nature'. Thus the order of created causes (*causae secundae*) began to be considered as a sphere of knowledge that could be studied on its own terms, thereby restricting the Bible's influence on an understanding of the natural world. William of Conches (*c*.1080–*c*.1154), a key representative of the school of Chartres, is a noteworthy example of these new 'scientific' interests. In the dialogue *The Plaint of Nature* (late 1160s), Alan of Lille imitated Boethius' *Consolation*, adopting its prosimetrical form, a mix of prose and poetry, and substituted *Natura* for Boethius' personification of *Philosophia*. Alan's Nature is essentially a self-sufficient power regulating created life and offering a norm for social and moral order. Hugh of St Victor (*c*.1096–1141) was the author of an influential pedagogical manual, the *Didascalicon*, and of a comprehensive theological summa, *De sacramentis christianae fidei* (On the Mysteries of the Christian Faith). In his work, Hugh presents theology as the highest part of philosophy, and, in addition, distinguishes between a theology ignorant of Revelation (*theologia mundana*) and *theologia christiana* that holds as true the tenets of the faith. The teaching of theology in the universities had its point of departure in such premises, most notably 'nature' as an independent sphere of knowledge and the distinction between logical–dialectical methods to arrive at definitions and the absolute status of the tenets of faith. The school system, however, introduced a specific form and particular techniques of analysis, dissemination, and argumentation: the *quaestio* as a means of presenting and organizing knowledge (see below); the growing and systematic recourse to the new body of translations, with Aristotle at their head; and the commitment to ensure that theology constituted an organic subject-matter that could be taught, namely, a 'doctrine'.

The third factor, at first sight less evident, but in no way less significant because of this than the other two, has its origins in the mid-to-late eleventh century and in the reforms of the Church known as the Gregorian Reform after their driving force, Pope Gregory VII (b. 1020/25; papacy 1073–85). Out of these emerged the imperative to exercise greater control over the behaviour of the clergy and the desire to bring about a religious cultural renewal. An excellent example of these tendencies may be found in the work of the Benedictine monk Peter Damian (*c.*1007–72), who was also among the first to show an interest in reviving Roman law. Some of the epistles in his rich collection of letters constitute actual philosophical treatises. They transmit to the later Middle Ages key themes such as the question of 'God's power', introducing the weighty distinction between unbounded omnipotence in itself (*potentia absoluta*) and omnipotence that is made evident in history, namely in relation to those natural principles established by the Creator Himself. In addition, the Gregorian Reform clarified and sharpened the distinctions between the clergy and the laity, a separation that would have a major impact on society, as well as on the organization of knowledge two centuries later.

The very structure of academic learning, with the separation of the university Faculty of Theology from a lower (introductory) Faculty of Arts, steadily transformed a simple institutional subdivision into a source of potential ideological conflict. Through their application of rational principles and their pursuit of strictly philosophical goals, Arts masters were constantly in danger of falling under suspicion that their views ran contrary to the tenets of the faith. A noteworthy case in point is that of the Parisian Master of Arts Siger of Brabant (*c.*1240–*c.*1284), who was condemned for purportedly asserting the independence of philosophical 'truth' from the 'truth' of faith. This supposed distinction has come to be known as the doctrine of the 'double truth'. It is important to stress, however, that no direct documentary evidence for the existence of such doctrine in the Middle Ages exists. At the same time, it is the case that at least some masters of Arts did claim autonomy for their philosophical inquiries. Furthermore, the distinction between clerics and laymen complicated matters further, since laymen, once they had completed their course in the Arts Faculty, could proceed to the study of medicine or law, but were not allowed to enter the Faculty of Theology.

## Clerics and laymen, and disputed questions

Dante has routinely been depicted as a man of considerable learning, both a philosopher and a theologian. Dante's philosophical and theological background is thus vital for an appropriate understanding of

*Philosophy and theology* 143

the poet and his works; and the extent to which this is the case greatly exceeds that of other medieval authors, including Petrarch. At the same time, the question arises as to how precisely one might define Dante's 'intellectual context'. Giovanni da Serravalle (*c*.1350–1445) was one of several fifteenth-century commentators of the *Commedia* who characterized the poet as a scholar of unquestionable academic pedigree. The image of Dante that, from the fourteenth century onwards, increasingly emerged was that of an accomplished, well-educated scholar with access to important book collections, who regularly communicated with other intellectuals. Although this image is now increasingly called into question, some elements of it stubbornly persist in current approaches to Dante and his writings. For instance, Dante the thinker is portrayed without adequate attention being paid to the fact that, in spite of some intense though brief and intermittent contacts with the Florentine schools of the mendicant friars, he was fundamentally self-taught; and that he would have had, at best, very restricted access to institutional libraries, which, in any case, had relatively limited holdings. Moreover, although, especially in the *Commedia*, Dante spoke of theological matters authoritatively, namely in a scholarly acceptable manner, as a layman he could not formally exercise such a role. To put it simply, Dante, when it came to matters theological, was an autodidact and, in institutional terms, an 'outsider'. A survey of scholastic theological learning in northern and central Italy at the end of the thirteenth century cannot thus be presented as the exclusive 'context' for Dante's intellectual formation. Rather the impact of mediating factors and of extra-academic intellectual traditions need to be recognized.

Preaching, for instance, was a major means of mass communication in late medieval urban environments, which not only offered indirect access to theological debates and doctrines, but also made reference to key questions of the day, such as ethics, emotional life, virtues and vices, the condition of the human soul after death, the role of the sacraments, and so on. The more complex scholastic debates, such as that on the ontological status of the universals or on the question of the immortality of the soul, albeit hotly debated in the *studia* – the schools founded by the religious orders in their administrative districts or *provinciae* where future preachers were educated (only the most able were sent to a *studium generale*, to study for the title of 'master of Theology') – were not especially popular in general theological discussions. They were probably considered too doctrinally sensitive, and too removed from the concerns of pastoral care. At any rate, they were not examined in any detail in sermons, but rather were quickly curtailed with reference to doctrinal and scriptural authorities (an echo of this approach may possibly be heard in *Convivio* II, viii, 8).

Theological education in northern Italy developed under the direction of the 'new' doctrinal standards promoted by the Fourth Lateran Council (1215), which emphasized techniques of ideological control, in particular individual confession, and the need to forestall heresy. The latter involved the definition of 'heresy'. Consequently, an explicit ideological agenda underpinned theological teaching, especially among the new mendicant orders. Indeed, the Church's cultural project coalesced with the new pedagogical techniques employed in the recently founded universities. At the lower, secular end of the educational system, primary teaching (reading and writing) was well established in cities. Students could subsequently choose between two types of 'secondary' institution, either commercial schools, which taught the abacus, or grammar schools, which taught Latin and the 'authoritative' Latin authors, as well as rhetoric (see Chapter 16). However, prior to entering a university Arts Faculty, it was most unlikely for students to receive a systematic introduction to philosophy. If a student did become acquainted with philosophy, it was mostly by chance, either through the allegorical reading of classical texts such as Virgil's *Aeneid* in school or by hearing the technical philosophical and theological vocabulary employed by Franciscan and Dominican friars in their sermons. Furthermore, rhetorical education did not remain unaffected by philosophical notions. Thus the definition of 'philosophy' given by Dante in *Convivio* III, xi, 5–6 is taken from Brunetto Latini's (*c.*1220–93) *Rettorica*.

Around the age of fourteen, students could enrol for courses in a university Faculty of Arts. The curriculum largely consisted of an introduction to Aristotle's logical writings – the *Categories*, *On Interpretation*, and the above-mentioned texts of the 'New Logic' – with special prominence given to dialectics, and to his metaphysical and natural writings: *Metaphysics*, *Physics*, *Meteorology*, *On Generation and Corruption*, *On the Soul*, *On Animals*. As regards logic, the twelve treatises of Peter of Spain's (thirteenth century) *Summulae logicales* (Collection of Logical Matters, *c.*1240) constituted a popular handbook. In the last decades of the thirteenth and in the first half of the fourteenth century, moreover, new developments emerged in the theory of both argumentation and semantics. The latter was commonly termed 'speculative grammar', to signify that language reflects the external world's underlying reality, and speculative grammarians were those who endeavoured to establish a universal grammar applicable to any language. It is unlikely that Dante would have been aware of such recent intellectual acquisitions.

# Philosophy and theology

In the second half of the thirteenth century and the first half of the fourteenth, the *studia* of the religious orders rapidly spread throughout Italian cities. The teaching they offered, though abridged and centred on theology, included two years of preparatory philosophical learning, largely based on Aristotle's writings, moving from logic to metaphysics, and passing through natural philosophy and ethics. The fundamental texts in the curriculum of the *studia*, however, were the Bible – accompanied by its standard commentary, the so-called *Ordinary Gloss* – the *Sentences* of Peter Lombard, and compilations on moral casuistry (the second part of Aquinas' *Summa theologica* was a popular text). The standard courses were available only to friars, and were not open to the public, although there may have been exceptions to this rule. Courses on the Bible, on the other hand, were possibly accessible to a larger audience and, as is evident from scholastic commentaries to the books of the Bible, these courses could include a generous amount of logic and natural philosophy. The laity could certainly attend and probably even contribute to the so-called disputed *quaestiones de quolibet*, public events where masters and pupils would debate various aspects of a problem (*quaestio*) chosen at random (*de quolibet*); these were biannual events – taking place both during Advent and Lent – when various issues, both theological and philosophical, were discussed according to well-defined procedures, based on the debates held at the Parisian *studium generale*: formulation of a specific question, presentation of arguments for and against, magisterial resolution (*determinatio*), responses to objections, and finally, the possible introduction of a related sub-question. In theological quodlibetal debates, the topics under discussion could include matters of local politics, religious practice, customs, and scriptural exegesis. Furthermore, given the nature of the exercise, dialectical reasoning, shaped by Cicero's rhetorical writings and Aristotle's *Topics*, held pride of place. Finally, problems relating to language and meaning emerged in discussions of biblical passages that seemed to contradict each other.

The fascination with Aristotle, although with differing emphases, was common to both secular and religious institutions of higher learning. The Aristotelian model, especially through the reception of the *Posterior Analytics*, had imposed a particular conception of 'science', which, during the last decades of the thirteenth century, had also increasingly become the paradigm for theology. The scholastic notion of science does not correspond to what we are likely to think of as 'science' today. Science was understood in the Aristotelian sense, as the knowledge of syllogistically – deductively justifiable – demonstrated conclusions; or, more precisely, science was the intellectual habit by which the mind is disposed to assent to conclusions that are true and certain, because they are derived syllogistically by demonstration from principles and causes within a given domain of real entities. Of course, the syllogism – a deductive reasoning consisting of two premises, linked each to the other by a middle term, and a conclusion made possible by the middle term, which does not reappear – was not the only mode of argumentation: exegetical, inductive, analogical, and rhetorical argumentation was in fact paramount. Nonetheless, the syllogistic form enjoyed the prestige of representing the most effective way of organizing an argument.

The principles, or 'foundations', of any given science correspond to the conclusions of a higher science (for instance, the conclusions of metaphysics may serve as the principles of physics). The sciences are ordered according to degrees of excellence, and the problem of subordination among distinct disciplines acquires a place of honour in scholastic debates. At the top of the hierarchy, theology stands as the highest demonstrative science, the assumed premises of which are not conclusions of any further science, since they are derived from God through revelation (namely, through Scripture). In this life they have to be taken for granted and believed, since the understanding of the first truth is possible only in the afterlife. Each science does not demonstrate its own principles or axioms. Metaphysics, moreover, deals with the eternal and unchangeable – the 'separated substances' and the realities that exist beyond the orbit of the moon – while the other sciences deal with the sub-lunar world that embraces 'temporal' things subject to motion and change, generation and corruption. As a consequence, the sciences of the human world cannot be absolutely 'certain' and must take into account chance and probability, although their formal, syllogistic structure is nevertheless maintained. Still, the hierarchy of perfection is inversely proportional to the order of learning, in that the latter proceeds 'from effects to their causes', from sensible to intellectual knowledge. Averroes (Ibn Rushd, 1126–98), in his commentary to Aristotle's *Physics*,[5] suggested that, mathematics aside, neither physics nor metaphysics could be genuinely deductive sciences, since both presuppose an argumentative procedure, *quia*, whereby in each domain of entities the movement is from the effects to the causes, *a via inducens* (the causes in the domain of moveable and changeable entities being the effects in the upper domain of 'unchangeable entities', etc.). The deductive use of principles thus presupposes their prior inductive discovery. Dante employed this approach when arguing philosophically in his late *Questio de aqua et terra* (e.g., paragraphs 60–61).

## Theological traditions beyond scholasticism

What has been said so far should not blur 'the rebellious multiplicity' (to use Paul Vignaux's expression[6]) of medieval theological paradigms. The 'scientific' paradigm, though prevailing in the schools, coexisted with older forms of theological reflection, such as 'figural theology', which had its foremost representative in the twelfth-century abbot Joachim of Fiore (1130/35–1202), who attempted to 'make concrete' the rational understanding of the divine in a series of *figurae*, in which pagan or philosophical authorities had no place. The diagrams are meant to reveal the hidden pattern of reality, the relationship between God and His creation, and the intimate coherence (*concordia*) of Scripture, while standing as the 'figures' guiding hermeneutical principles. Despite attempts to marginalize this kind of theological enquiry at the Fourth Lateran Council, the whole of the thirteenth century bears witness to the lasting appeal of Joachimite thought, significant aspects of which resurfaced among the new mendicant orders. In particular, the Franciscans deemed that they had been described in Joachim's eschatological visions, and took over his message concerning the advent of the Antichrist, represented by the famous image of the seven-headed dragon. The Franciscan theologian John Peter Olivi (1248–98) used Joachim and Richard of St Victor (d. 1173) as key sources for his influential *Commentary on the Apocalypse*, which Dante may have known. It should also be noted that Joachimite thought considered history as the 'unfolding' and mirroring of the Trinity (see Chapter 7). Theology was thus a means to interpret history, something which was inconceivable according to Aristotle's account of the first philosophy or metaphysics as theology in *Metaphysics* VI, 1, since this dealt exclusively with 'atemporal' and unchangeable entities – a view that was reinforced by the influential Arabic compilation known as *Book of Causes*, that was often read as the completion of the account of the divine found in Aristotle's *Metaphysics*, Book XII.

Despite the success of scholastic theology, so-called monastic theology also continued to maintain a strong appeal, particularly in thinkers such as the Franciscan master Bonaventure of Bagnoregio, theologian in Paris in the 1250s, who knew Aristotle's works well and used him extensively in his writings; at the same time, his appreciation of the great Cistercian reformer, contemplative, and exegete Bernard of Clairvaux (1090–1153) was even greater. Bonaventure ended his university career to become master general of the Franciscan order and, lecturing in such a capacity at the Franciscan convent in Paris, he defended a conception of theology as

148         Andrea A. Robiglio

*sapientia* (wisdom) rather than as *scientia*, whereby knowledge of the divine was 'affective', not so much established through syllogisms but experienced and 'tasted': 'only faith can discriminate light from the darkness of heresy' (*Collationes in Hexaemeron*, IV, 13).[7] The extensive presence of this tradition in Dante's writings may be taken as evidence of its enduring influence.

Since the twelfth century there flourished in the monasteries a type of reflection that was distinct from the intellectual approach that would come to predominate in the schools a century later. Although the study of the Bible was at the centre of both theological traditions, their differences are profound, since they were predicated on distinct intellectual approaches. In the schools the Bible was broken down into single syntactic textual units, and their analysis was conducted employing philosophical authorities, dialectical commonplaces, and logical devices – in a manner close to that employed by Dante when analysing his *canzone* 'The sweet love-poetry', in the fourth book of the *Convivio*. The monastic 'reading', on the other hand, privileged patient reading and continuous meditation. The monastic engagement with the Bible was not strictly speaking an academic activity; rather it was the fraternal conversation between master and pupil that taught how to choose between various existential options. Theology, most important of all, was a part of everyday experience. In the monasteries there were neither degrees to be awarded nor academic titles to be bestowed. The only relevant examination was that of a 'life examined', the opening of the 'heart' of the monk to Christ. In this context, scholastic instruments and forms of argumentation were superfluous, if not actually dangerous. The process toward spiritual perfection – from *being*, through *good being*, to *best being* – moved along an anagogical rather than an ontological scale. Although Neoplatonic elements are discernible in this approach – as they were in Boethius' *Consolation* – they serve as metaphors for a reality that lies beyond the grasp of human reason; they do not aim to build up a coherent doctrine, since what really matters cannot be 'taught'. Meditation on Scripture and on *The Lives of the Fathers* (a popular collection of ancient hagiographies); the symbiosis of prayer and reflection; the emphasis on the affective dimensions of faith, on conversion, and on spiritual discrimination (*discretio*), these are the key elements of 'monastic theology'.

Twelfth-century theological pluralism had been both institutional (abbeys and episcopal schools or university) and doctrinal (monastic theology and scholastic theology). In Dante's age, in the aftermath of Boniface VIII's pontificate (b. *c.*1235; papacy 1294–1303), institutional diversity

## Philosophy and theology

tended to disappear, since, with the rise of urban society, academic culture rapidly achieved institutional monopoly as regards learning, although doctrinal pluralism, now within the schools, was still a reality. Although attempts were made to condemn diversity as 'heresy', Dante lived during a period of considerable intellectual ferment and freedom, especially, but not exclusively, beyond the boundaries of the universities. A follower of Aristotle and a champion of 'intellectualism' (the doctrine according to which good ethical conduct depends on the correct knowledge of what is 'good'), the theologian Godfrey of Fontaines (before 1250–*c*.1306), master of Theology in Paris (1285–99, and again in 1303–04), read sympathetically the anti-intellectualist *Mirror of Simple Souls* by Marguerite Porete (d. 1310, burned for heresy in Paris) and found himself 'approving' of its doctrine. Marguerite was no scholastic theologian; rather she was a representative of so-called 'vernacular theology', a third type of theology accessible to the laity (women included) and nourished by attendance at sermons and the reading of vernacular works: not only devotional treatises, but also courtly literature and adaptations of popular Latin works such as Jean de Meun's (*c*. 1240–before 1305) reworking of Boethius, *Li livres de Confort de Philosophie* (The Books of the Consolation of Philosophy), and Bono Giamboni's (*c*.1240–92?) *Della miseria dell'uomo* (Man's Misery), which 'vernacularized' the *De contemptu mundi* (On the Contempt of the World) by Lotharius, later Pope Innocent III (b. 1160/61; papacy 1198–1216). 'Vernacular theology' often flirted with ideals of social reform and forms of mysticism. Scholastic culture, despite the pre-eminence of Aristotelian arguments and models, was far from monolithic.

It is thus not surprising that, in an environment of intellectual pluralism, Dante should have drawn on a broad swathe of sources and made original contributions in a number of areas. In the *Monarchia*, for instance, he presents a cosmopolitan notion of 'human community' (*humana civilitas*), that embraced families, city-states, and kingdoms, that was unparalleled in late medieval political thought, while drawing on ideas taken from Aristotle's *Politics* recently made available and glossed by masters of Theology such as Aquinas and Peter of Auvergne (d. 1304). Dante provided a personal account of the relationship between the soul and the body, yet remained close to scholastic arguments on the subject; he provided an anthropological interpretation of cosmological categories, which was not uncommon in some mystical traditions, namely interpreting the cosmological 'noble soul' mentioned in the third 'axiom' of the *Book of Causes* as if it were the virtuous 'human' soul of special distinction (*Conv.* IV, xxi, 9 and xxviii, 5).

Even when Dante seems to be making an original and radical proposal, he was in fact selecting between alternative ideas and concepts that were available in his intellectual context. Dante reveals how a medieval intellectual could negotiate between different and contrasting suggestions. A good example of this is his conception of the order of wisdom (*sapientia*). In the *Convivio*, Dante elaborated the system of the sciences discussed above, introducing an unexpected reversal, asserting the primacy of moral philosophy over metaphysics (II, xiii, 8). The great historian of ideas Étienne Gilson claimed that Dante's position was unique in the Middle Ages.[8] Given, as we have seen, that the degree of perfection of each science is predicated on the perfection of its subject-matter, metaphysics is necessarily higher than ethics, since the latter deals with human actions, which are historical and far from unchangeable and eternal entities.

However, Bruno Nardi established that Dante's presentation was not exceptional, but rather that he was following a minority position.[9] Thus, Al-Fārābi (*c.*870–950) was a proponent of this view in his *Liber de scientiis* (Book of the Sciences), which had been translated into Latin by Gerard of Cremona (*c.*1114–87), where he placed ethics (*scientia civilis*) above metaphysics in the hierarchy of knowledge. The same view could also be found in early commentaries on Aristotle's *Ethics* (before 1250), as well as in civic thinkers such as Brunetto Latini. Even when Dante departed more explicitly from scholastic models, he nonetheless maintained links with established medieval learning. His unconventional association of physics with metaphysics, since both resemble the Starry Heaven, recalls an aspect of natural philosophy that was taught in the Dominican *studia*, having a possible motivation in Aquinas' prologue to his commentary on Aristotle's *Ethics*.

For Dante ethics was the highest science that human beings could attain through the judicious use of reason (*Conv.* II, xiv, 14). Theology lies beyond the Crystalline Heaven – that is to say, beyond the powers of human intellection (*Conv.* II, xiv, 19). What is striking about this section of Dante's cosmological discussion is that it includes the sole use of the term 'teologia' (*Conv.* II, xiii, 8) in his *oeuvre*. Dante's solution might very well represent 'the dismissal of reason from the realm of theology',[10] even if it probably in part also re-echoes an old Augustinian sceptical motive: in this life, after the Fall, human reason cannot be relied upon; only the testimony of God is fully trustworthy – or, as Aquinas would put it, 'the argument based on divine revelation is the strongest of all' (*Summa theologica* I, q. 1, a. 8 ad 2m).[11]

On the other hand, the majority of masters of Theology, albeit with different emphases, supported the vast scholastic project of the thirteenth

*Philosophy and theology* 151

century that was heavily reliant on human reason (namely, logic and metaphysics) in the construction of 'theology as science'. Thus, Aquinas at times seems to have believed in the possibility of such a 'scientific' enterprise, and his *Summa contra Gentiles* (Summa against Unbelievers), which Dante almost certainly knew, is a noteworthy example of this perspective. Dante clearly did not share in this belief; and his view of the potential of human reason was less optimistic. For the poet, theology had to lie beyond the controversies of human reason. Just as the contemplatives in the Heaven of Saturn (*Par.* XXI–XXII) have a greater 'measure of sight' than the theologians and philosophers present in the Heaven of the Sun (*Par.* X–XIII), so Dante's idea of theology was different to that of most scholastics. It was in fact closer to the thought of monastic theologians such as Richard of St Victor for whom theology – as his *On Trinity* attests – is fundamentally a discipline of prayer aimed to purify the living and dispose them to obtain from God the grace of mystical contemplation.

In any case, as discussed earlier, the 'theology as science' paradigm only emerged in the mid thirteenth century. In fact, Thomas Aquinas was the first to introduce Aristotelian logic into the structure of the prologue to his *Commentary on the Sentences*, which dates back to a decade before Dante's birth. Dante appears to have preferred the theological approach of older authorities, such as Bernard of Clairvaux's, to that of his contemporaries. As the poet makes clear in the upper reaches of Paradise, his understanding of the divine is the result of 'vision' and inspiration rather than of intellectual prowess (*Par.* XI, 2), whose limitations are made clear during the ascent of Purgatory: 'Rest content, race of men, with the *quia*; for if you had been able to see all there was no need for Mary to give birth' (*Purg.* III, 37–9).

### Vernacular theology, humility, and the motive of the quest

The non-scholastic dimension of thirteenth- and early fourteenth-century theology that we have begun to explore, and that we have tagged as 'vernacular theology', is effectively captured in the early-fifteenth-century devotional text *The Imitation of Christ* (1418), in which we find the following question: 'What does it avail thee to dispute profoundly of the Trinity, if thou be void of humility, and thereby displeasing to the Trinity?' (I, 2).[12] This view was far from unpopular in Dante's age and returned regularly in the sermons of the mendicant orders. It was consonant with the Augustinian condemnation of curiosity, such as Bernard of Claivaux's reference to 'foul curiosity' – that curiosity which, by their opponents, was

deemed to characterize philosophical disputes and the theological endeav-
ours of the 'professional' thinkers working in the universities. The focus
was not so much on the theological content but on the proper way to
approach such content. How should we know God? How can we hope to
understand God's teachings? Such questions were accompanied by consideration of the role of humility and of the dignity of the investigator
who, in keeping with the scriptural warning – 'O the depth of the riches
of the wisdom and of the knowledge of God! How incomprehensible are
his judgments, and how unsearchable his ways!' (Rom. 11, 33), a commonplace that Dante repeated (*Conv.* IV, xxi, 6; *Questio*, 77) – was keen not to
offend and challenge God.

The restrictions of human reason were evident in the divisions, arguments, and relentless disputations of the 'philosophers', since, where division reigns, truth cannot be present, as Gratian's *Decretum* had made clear.
Recognizing the limits of our knowledge, our finitude, and our lack of
self-sufficiency was a philosophically justifiable response to the challenges
of 'scientific' certainty. Furthermore, philosophy was a meagre resource in
ensuring salvation. The nature of God, the motives and nature of creation,
the first causes of fundamental effects, the demonstration of the basic
principles on which human certainty depends cannot be understood, at
least not fully, through the exercise of reason alone. Dante's example of a
metaphysical problem which human argumentation cannot comprehend
concerns 'prime matter' (the lowest ebb of being, the pure potentiality
to be without being anything yet): specifically, whether 'prime matter' is
intelligible in itself or not. The problem was one of those fundamental
questions that required the full appreciation of the notion of creation in
order to arrive at its Christian understanding; and yet the role of divine
creation was something that intrinsically transcended the possibilities of
the created intellect. Human reason – Dante and others maintained –
should thus recognize its limits rather than strive toward the impossible
task of overcoming its boundaries.

As several texts of vernacular theology stressed, the key issue was less
knowledge than the knower's moral purification. The latter required, to
some extent, self-knowledge, as well as the decision to eradicate any form
of narcissism from the self. Such a 'therapeutic' process needed to pre-
cede the study of both metaphysics and 'divine science'. Remembering
the quotation from the *Imitation of Christ*, the thinker, first of all, must be
virtuously worthy, hence Dante's privileging of moral philosophy in the
*Convivio*. Philosophical research, in other words, had to mark out a viable
path before attempting to reach its final aim. This raised serious problems.

*Philosophy and theology*   153

Knowledge of basic realities was perceivable and seemingly certain, while knowledge about our moral, civic, and spiritual life was less tangible and at most probable. Finally, knowledge of the First Cause, 'prime matter', and 'creation' could not be established by the use of human reason. These difficulties, of course, emerged as a result of the process of philosophical inquiry, and thus did not imply the dismissal of reason. Indeed, it was in its awareness of its own limitations that human 'dialectical' thought demonstrated its full power and effectiveness. This dimension of Christian scepticism, which was already present in the English scholastic philosopher and diplomat John of Salisbury (*c.*1115–76), had close ties with the basic tenets of vernacular theology. The stress, as is apparent from John of Salisbury's *Metalogicon* (III, 5–10), falls on dialectical, namely probable, thinking, rather than on deduction and syllogism. This perspective is especially evident in literary texts and courtly writings, written largely in the vernacular rather than in Latin. Even though some connection with the world of the schools and universities is still visible – for instance, John was the first writer who knew and used Aristotle's new logic, namely the *Posterior Analytics*, which Peter Abelard had not known, the logic of vernacular texts, both theological and secular, is the logic of the *Topics* and of legal reasoning rather than that of the *Analytics*.

The trope of the 'quest', which is developed in so many medieval narratives, and in particular in accounts of journeys to the afterlife (see Chapter 20), might very well take us away from the world of the universities, though not that far away from much of the philosophy and theology characteristic of the time. Keeping this in mind – the pursuit to understand oneself and one's relationship to God, rather than knowledge as an end in itself – will allow us to appreciate better not only the literary but also the theological models that Dante would have sought out and come across. Outside the universities, in the urban lay culture, vernacular theology took on different textual guises. The popularization of science was on the rise, ranging from schematic compilations, such as Ristoro d'Arezzo's *The Composition of the World* (*c.*1282), to more sophisticated encyclopaedic works such as Brunetto Latini's *Tresor* (Treasure). However, as we noted earlier, there were also old 'classics', most notable among these, as Dante himself remarked (*Conv.* II, xii, 2), was Boethius' *Consolation of Philosophy*. In the *Consolation*, philosophy is therapy: it is not only a discipline or a set of conclusions, but a lady; her techniques provide 'medicine' for the soul, fortifying the spirit, purifying the mind, and ennobling character. Questions relatively overlooked in the theological *summae*, such as discriminating between true and false nobility, become central in this regard.

## Contemplation, love, and grace

Lacking the vision that only divine grace can grant, a human being can only develop limited theories that are speculative in nature. The most sophisticated form of human reasoning cannot be exercised except after a sort of intellectual and moral purification. Purification is a condition required to obtain divine grace, even though grace does not respond to any human merit or attempt. With regard to the bliss of contemplation, Dante explains in Book IV of the *Convivio* that 'God is always in advance of our contemplation, and that here below we can never reach him who is our supreme blessedness' (*Conv.* IV, xxii, 17). At best, intellectual happiness can be 'almost' perfect (*Conv.* IV, xxii, 18). The scholastic discussion of 'imperfect happiness' (*beatitudo imperfecta*) may in part lie behind this declaration. However, the main thrust of Dante's argument is to be sought elsewhere: philosophy is valuable not so much because it offers a degree of knowledge of God, but because of the lucidity of its judgements, judgements that allow it to recognize failure and to envision a new outcome. As Virgil says at the start of the otherworldly journey, 'you must take another road' (*Inf.* I, 91). This lucid recognition of the limits of human knowledge is symbolized too in Ulysses' shipwreck in *Inferno* XXVI. Drawing on both scholastic and non-scholastic sources, Dante clearly illustrates how a very intelligent man can lose his way if he refuses to accept, or to recognize, his own limits. Our faculty of judgement, in other words, must be reformed on an ongoing basis, at both the individual and the social level; and this is because there is a constant reciprocity between man – Aristotle's 'civic animal' – and the society of which he is a part. Indeed, truth cannot be attained by someone who relies exclusively on their own intellectual and moral powers. Divine vision cannot be attained by the force of human intelligence; it can only be 'received' once human reason has abandoned its hubris and overcome its blindness. The state of purification necessary to contemplate divine truth, therefore, is possible only thanks to a radical conception of love, which, as Richard of St Victor revealed in *On the Four Degrees of Violent Love* (c.1170), and as Dante remarked in *Paradiso* XX, 94–6, overcomes the antinomies between passion and reason, and between passion-love and charity. Vision is granted to one who is recognized, namely loved and 'chosen' by God. In brief, reason is elected to contemplation as an honour bestowed upon it. As Bernard of Clairvaux wrote in his *On Consideration* (V, ii, 3):

# Philosophy and theology

> He is no less great who makes steps of the sensible things to climb up to invisible things by philosophy (*philosophando*). But the greatest of all is he who, scorning the use of sensible things, so far as human frailty permits, has accustomed himself, not by gradual steps, but by sudden ecstatic flights to soar aloft to the glorious things on high ... Consideration is speculative when it retires within itself, and so far as Divine help is given, detaches itself from human affairs in order to contemplate God'.[13]

Since humans cannot achieve perfect contemplation through their own efforts, they must create the conditions whereby such contemplation becomes a possibility. Their happiness absolutely depends on this. In other words, a human being must do whatever it takes to make herself worthy to receive God's gift, even though she is unable to demand it. Spiritual purification is vital, as the poet-pilgrim demonstrates during the course of his climb up the steep slopes of Purgatory before crossing the threshold into Paradise, which one cannot enter unless invited to do so. From this perspective, philosophical inquiry thus presupposes an act of repentance that permits one to hope for a direct encounter with God. While on the journey of this life, the wayfarer must first find herself and make herself worthy of the encounter. She needs to guard herself and watch over the society in which she lives – behaving morally and accepting her limitations. Philosophical problems, such as 'being', 'prime matter', and the First Cause, can thus only be tackled after the preliminary ethical questions concerning personal dignity and love have been resolved. Human excellence depends on a divine gift: such an insight lies at the core of Porete's *Mirror of Simple Souls*.

At the dawn of the fourteenth century the theological understanding of human nobility as divine election conflicted with competing notions, whether social (nobility as social pre-eminence, as evidenced in texts like Jean de Joinville's (*c.*1224–1317) *History of Saint Louis*) or juridical (nobility as a legally recognized political privilege, as in Bartolo da Sassoferrato's (1313–57) commentary on Justinian's *Body of Civil Law*). A close interplay between social and theological notions of nobility, defined against the juridical one, furthermore coalesced in a late-twelfth-century text such as Andreas Capellanus' *On Love*, which, significantly, was condemned by the Bishop of Paris in 1277 as a dangerous manifesto of 'free love'. In such courtly writing, the link between nobility (*nobilitas*, hereafter 'N') and moral virtue (*virtus*, *probitas*, hereafter 'V') on the one hand, and nobility and love (*amor*, hereafter 'A') on the other, provided the two premises on which a syllogistic argumentation intended to establish the link between virtue and love was based. If nobility implied virtue, and love implied nobility, then love implied virtue. The following outline may help to visualize the structure of such an argument:

$$N - V$$
$$A - N$$
$$\overline{A - V}$$

In his turn, Dante adopted the same categories and principles, but he did so only to subvert them. Specifically, love was no longer a term of the demonstration. It became the new middle term, the *medium*, namely the concept present in both premises but not in the conclusion. It is the concept that brings about the conclusion:

$$N - A$$
$$A - V$$
$$\overline{N - V}$$

For this demonstration to work, the middle term cannot have multiple, disparate meanings. If this were the case, it would introduce a logical failure into the argumentation, known as the 'fallacy of four terms'. As a consequence, love as an emotion (*amor ut passio*) and love as a spiritual sentiment (*dilectio, caritas*) must merge and cannot remain reciprocally exclusive. A cosmic force, love can be both corporeal and spiritual, without contradiction. While the scholastic tradition before Aquinas and medical science as filtered through poets such as Guido Cavalcanti (1250/59–1300) had resisted the merging of passion and sentiment, Boethius had in fact already powerfully expressed in his *Consolation* the unitary conception of a single world-governing *Amor*: 'If the love that rules the stars / May also rule your hearts!' (II, 8v, 29–30).[14]

Once more, Dante had not invented something totally new when making a vital and original contribution to one of the fundamental debates in late medieval thought. The burden of proof, for Dante, rested on the claim concerning human excellence, namely human 'purification', and not on that concerning love, which, for him, assumed the role of unquestioned *medium* in the demonstration. The link between love and virtue was guaranteed by the New Testament and the monastic theological tradition dependent on Christ's word. Conversely, the link between love and nobility was a 'courtly' assumption, frequently expressed by vernacular poets with whom Dante had been familiar, and was accepted by him in the *Vita nova*. These two associative systems, the scriptural (and also

## Philosophy and theology

monastic) and the 'poetic' (vernacular, non-scholastic), forged the premises for the poet's new insight, whose aim was to establish the kinship between virtue and nobility.

In conclusion, it is important to stress that, in order to understand Dante's intellectual formation and interests, it is necessary to consider the whole of his cultural context. His philosophical background, on account of his limited education and varied cultural experiences, cannot be assessed only against medieval scholastic thought. His conventional treatment of traditional philosophical issues, as in the late *Questio de aqua et terra*, was in part meant to affirm and consolidate his intellectual reputation. In general, he dealt with the doctrinal issues of his day in a multifaceted, synthetic, and personal manner. More than standard scholastic works, Dante's writings define themselves in opposition to what had already been taught, so that they cannot simply be reduced to their 'sources', no matter how authoritative those sources may have been. While fully endorsing the Christian tenets of the faith, the poet's primary emphasis was on the quest for truth, which he intimately associated with the 'vision of God'. His profound intellectual drive had a discernible existentialist character. Its subjectivity sharply distinguished it from the approaches and ideas of other scholastic writers. Finally, and this is of no little consequence, Dante's writings reveal a more complex vision of the theological and philosophical landscape at the dawn of the fourteenth century than historians of medieval thought are normally willing to recognize.

### Notes

1 E. R. Curtius, *European Literature and the Latin Middle Ages* (Princeton University Press, 2013), p. 529; for a catalogue of distinct meanings of 'philosophy', see pp. 207–8, and for the meanings of 'theology' in relation to literary learning, see pp. 214–27.

2 B. McGinn, *Thomas Aquinas's 'Summa theologiae': A Biography* (Princeton University Press, 2014), p. 15.

3 P. H. Wicksteed and E. G. Gardner, *Dante and Giovanni del Virgilio* (Westminster: Constable, 1902), p. 174.

4 G. Boccaccio, *Life of Dante*, trans. P. Wicksteed (Richmond: Oneworld Classics, 2009), p. 10.

5 Averroes, *In Aristotelis Physicorum libros. I. Commentum* 2 (Venice: apud Junctas, 1562), pp. 6–7.

6 P. Vignaux, *Pensée au Moyen Âge – Précédé d'une Introduction nouvelle et suivi de 'Lire Duns Scot Aujourd'hui'* (Albeuve: Castella, 1987), p. 64.

7 Bonaventure of Bagnoregio, *Collations on the Six Days*, trans. J. de Vinck (Paterson St Anthony Guild, 1970), p. 116 (slightly revised).

8 É. Gilson, *Dante et la philosophie* (Paris: Vrin, 1953), p. 107.

9 B. Nardi, *Nel mondo di Dante* (Rome: Edizioni di Storia e Letteratura, 1944), pp. 213–4.

10 K. Foster, 'Teologia', in *Enciclopedia Dantesca* (Rome: Istituto della Enciclopedia Italiana, 1976), vol. V, p. 565.

11 The translation is my own.

12 Thomas à Kempis, *The Imitation of Christ or the Ecclesiastical Music*, trans. J. Payne (Cambridge University Press, 1908), p. 2.

13 St Bernard, *Treatise on Consideration*, trans. anon. (Dublin: Browne and Nolan, 1921), pp. 148–50.

14 Boethius, *The Theological Tractates and The Consolation of Theology*, trans. S. J. Tester (London: Heinemann, 1973), p. 227.

CHAPTER 10

# *Moral philosophy*

### Luca Bianchi

Dante terms 'moral philosophy', 'moral science', and 'moral doctrine' the 'part' of 'wisdom' (*Conv.* III, xv, 14) that establishes what is good, how human beings should act, and which kind of life is best for them. When he speaks of *ethica* (in Latin) and *etica* (in Italian), he instead generally refers to a clearly identified text, namely the *Nicomachean Ethics*, the only Aristotelian work devoted to this branch of learning that was known during the Middle Ages, apart from a compilation of short passages from the *Magna moralia* (Great Ethics) and the *Eudemian Ethics* called *Liber de bona fortuna* (Book of Good Fortune). Dante's terminological precision is significant, but should not be overstated. Of course, one cannot approach the treatment of 'ethics' in his times without bearing in mind that a variety of sources for discussing moral problems were available, and that there existed a plurality of paradigms of moral philosophy and theology. This means that Dante's own views on ethical issues cannot be properly understood without recognizing that he was influenced – directly or indirectly – by Latin moral thought, in particular Cicero (106–43 BCE) and Seneca (*c.*1 BCE–CE 65; called 'moral Seneca' in *Inf.* IV, 141); by the Roman juridical tradition; by the Bible and the Church Fathers, beginning with Augustine (354–430); by Boethius' (*c.*475/77–526?) *Consolatio philosophiae* (Consolation of Philosophy, *c.*524); by Christian moral compilations such as the *Formula vitae honestae* (Form of Honest Living) composed by Martin of Braga (*c.*520–80) between 570 and 579; by the classifications of sins elaborated by Cassianus (*c.*360–435) and Gregory the Great (*c.*540–604) and developed in compendia for preachers and in treatises on vices and virtues; by Giles of Rome's (*c.*1243–1316) *De regimine principum* (On the Government of Rulers, 1277–81), quickly translated into Italian; and by the moral sections of theological *summae*. Nevertheless, the fact remains that for Dante, as well as for his contemporaries, the study of a discipline meant in the first place the study of the book that had laid its foundations. And as we shall see, from the thirteenth century onwards all agreed that the *Nicomachean Ethics* was *the* 'handbook' for teaching moral philosophy.

What is more, the *Nicomachean Ethics* – 'your Ethics', as Virgil says to Dante in *Inferno* XI, 80 – was one of Dante's *livres de chevet*. He almost certainly owned a personal copy, since he quotes it more than sixty times explicitly and often extensively, and uses it frequently in all his major works. He was acquainted with its different translations and with the *Summa Alexandrinorum*, a compendium of Aristotle's text translated from Arabic into Latin by Hermannus Alemannus (d. 1272) in 1243–44, and retranslated into Italian by Taddeo Alderotti (*c.*1210–95) and into French as a part of Brunetto Latini's (*c.*1220–93) *Tresor* (Treasure; 1262–6). And even if claims that Dante borrowed significantly from Albert the Great's (*c.*1200–80) *Quaestiones super Ethicam* (Questions on the Nicomachean Ethics) should be treated with caution, it is certain that he knew Thomas Aquinas' (1225–74) *Sentencia libri Ethicorum* (Commentary on the Nicomachean Ethics, 1271–72). It is therefore easy to understand why, given the lack of reliable information about Dante's 'library' and the tremendous complexity of the problem of his sources, scholars should have systematically used the *Nicomachean Ethics* and its exegetical tradition as an interpretive key to understanding not only the *Convivio* and the *Monarchia* – where the presence of Aristotle's moral doctrines is substantial – but also the *Commedia*.

It is useful to recall that the *Nicomachean Ethics* – translated before 1150 by Burgundio of Pisa (d. 1193) – had a unique and in a certain sense ambiguous position among Aristotle's writings made available to Latin readers between the twelfth and thirteenth centuries thanks to translations from Greek and Arabic. The first surviving statute of the University of Paris, promulgated in 1215 by the papal legate Robert of Courçon (d. 1218), confirmed the centrality of logical training based on Aristotle's *Organon*, allowed optional and feast days lectures on his *Ethica*, or rather on the part of Burgundio's translation in circulation, namely, the *Ethica vetus* (Old) – Books II and III – and the *Ethica nova* (New) – Book I – and forbade the teaching of his natural philosophy and metaphysics. The *Ethics* was therefore Aristotle's only non-logical work whose classroom 'reading' was permitted, though it had a marginal role in the curriculum. About 1246–47, Robert Grosseteste (*c.*1168–1253) retranslated it in full, and his version was well received: yet only its first four books were included among the regular subjects according to the new statutes of 1255, when almost all of Aristotle's writings were adopted as textbooks for the Arts Faculty. It is true that from the 1250s onwards, Aristotle's *Nicomachean Ethics* was studied more

# Moral philosophy 161

intensively, and often in its entirety, but it continued to receive less attention than his logical treatises and his newly authorized works on natural philosophy and metaphysics. Despite the early interest on the part of several professors of medicine and law, courses on the *Ethics* had a minor place also in Italian universities. Aristotle's text instead aroused the growing attention of Dominican friars: the influence of Albert the Great's and Thomas Aquinas' commentaries and the deep assimilation of Aristotelian moral doctrines into the *Secunda secundae* (Second Part of the Second Part, 1271–72) of the latter's *Summa theologica* (Sum of Theology) spurred Dominicans to consider the study of these doctrines as a preparation for the study of theological ethics, which explains their decision in 1314 to incorporate 'moral studies' into the curriculum of their schools.

So ethics – whose independence from religious teachings and whose place among the liberal arts had been the subject of lively discussion during the twelfth century – became in the universities, in the Dominican schools, and later in the schools of the other religious orders, one of the disciplines to be studied that had its basis in philosophical rather than Christian sources. This represented a turning point in the history of medieval moral thought: it granted philosophical ethics the status of an autonomous field of research that could be explored rationally without recourse to theological principles; and it also sanctioned the supremacy of Aristotle in this field, where his authority, far from being uncontested as in logic, physics, and cosmology, might have been seriously challenged by classical and Christian authors such as Cicero, Seneca, Augustine, and Boethius.

The earliest Latin commentators of the *Nicomachean Ethics* tended to read it in a Christian light and, knowing only the first three books, they misinterpreted important doctrines, such as the fundamental distinction between moral and intellectual virtues. Being acquainted with the short passage at the end of the first book where Aristotle introduces this distinction (I, 13, 1103a 4–10), but ignoring his further explanations, and in particular his treatment of 'practical wisdom' or *phronesis*, they often considered the latter a form of knowledge and love of the highest good, identified with the First Cause. Grosseteste made available not only the whole text of Aristotle's *Ethics*, but also a huge compilation of Greek commentaries, generally attributed to 'Eustratius', although actually authored by a plurality of thinkers. Some of them are unknown, but among those whose identity is known, there is only one, Aspasius, interpreter of Book VIII, who lived in the second century CE, while the other two, Eustratius of Nicaea (*c.*1050/60–*c.*1120), interpreter of Books I and VI, and Michael of Ephesus (*fl.* early or mid 1100s), interpreter of Books V, IX, and X, worked in twelfth-century Byzantium and gave a markedly Neoplatonic and Christian colouring to Aristotle's moral philosophy, praising it as a preparatory step to heavenly beatitude.

This perspective influenced all Latin commentators, including the two great Dominican interpreters of the *Ethics*, namely Albert the Great and Thomas Aquinas. Albert expounded the text twice: first in the Dominican convent of Cologne between 1250 and 1252, and then in a later paraphrase, probably redacted between 1262 and 1265. Despite their different format, both commentaries attempt to show the harmony between Aristotle's teachings and Christian ethics – a goal that was often achieved, however, by means of an interpretive strategy deeply different from that of 'Eustratius', who remained one of Albert's main sources. Albert pointed out the differences of method and object between theological and philosophical ethics. He claimed that Aristotle examined only the natural causes of earthly happiness, without taking into account the supernatural dimension of human life, and that he dismissed troubling questions, such as the state of human souls after death, or the role played by divine influence in the generation of virtue, as belonging to theology. Although some scholars believe that Thomas Aquinas composed his commentary on the *Ethics* for private purposes, namely to prepare himself to write the moral sections of his *Summa theologica* it is also the case that he conceived it as an exegetical work, aiming first of all at a faithful presentation of Aristotle's doctrines. Throughout this work, however, Thomas defended Christian beliefs, such as divine providence and the necessity of personal immortality as a condition for attaining perfect happiness (judged unachievable in this life), and at times he attributed such views to Aristotle. In agreement with his teacher Albert, Thomas conceived of moral philosophy as a limited but valuable discipline; unlike Albert, however, he seems less concerned with its autonomy than with its complementarity to theology.

Despite Thomas' efforts, it became increasingly difficult to avoid the conflict between religious morality, founded on divine law and aimed at directing humanity to a supernatural end, and philosophical ethics taught in university classrooms. Several Arts masters, especially in Paris, extended into this area their hermeneutic approach to the *Corpus Aristotelicum*, and dealt with the problem by basing themselves both on the distinction between 'expounding' Aristotle's ideas and 'asserting' them, and on the variance between the point of view of the philosopher and that of the believer. In so doing, they were following the methodological principle, borrowed from Albert the Great, that every specialist of a 'science' – or, to

## Moral philosophy 163

use their own terminology, every *artifex* – must keep within the boundaries set by the principles of that 'science'. As they treated physical and cosmological problems 'naturally speaking', trying to explain phenomena as they normally occur without taking into consideration the possible intervention of supernatural causes, so they discussed moral matters 'morally speaking', without adapting the results of their philosophical analysis to the requirements of Christian doctrine. It is significant to find this approach in the works of Boethius of Dacia (d. after 1277), one of the most outstanding figures of the Parisian Faculty of Arts in the 1270s.[1] In his *De aeternitate mundi* (On the Eternity of the World, p. 349) Boethius justifies Aristotle's doctrine of the eternity of the world by emphasizing that he was 'speaking as a natural philosopher', and therefore had to deny a natural beginning to the universe. Equally, in his discussions of ethical problems, Boethius assumes that, 'morally speaking', bad acts depend on choices contrary to right reason, and praises the philosophers because, 'morally speaking', they provide a paradigm of the virtuous life (*Quaestiones super librum Topicorum* (Questions on the Topics), IV, 20, p. 249; *De summo bono* (On the Supreme Good), p. 374).

Such an attitude, while methodologically acute, left little room for readings of Aristotle's ethics in harmony with Christian doctrine on major issues such as the nature and origin of human happiness, the preconditions for a good life, free will, sexual morality, and the Christian virtues, since some of these seemed incompatible with Aristotle's thesis that every virtue is a state that lies between two vices, one of excess and the other of deficiency. It should not come as a surprise, therefore, that many ethical theses were targeted in the great condemnation issued on 7 March 1277 by the Bishop of Paris Etienne Tempier (d. 1279).[2] Indeed, several prohibited articles, allegedly disseminated by the members of the Parisian Faculty of Arts, called into question human freedom by presenting the will as a passive power determined by the heavenly bodies, by reason, or by passions (articles 129, 132–3, 135–6, 158–9, 161–5, 173, 194, 208, 209). Other articles claim that 'simple fornication' (i.e. between unmarried partners) is not a sin and that 'abuse in intercourse, although it is against the nature of the species, is not against the nature of the individual' (183, 166). Other articles denied that continence (168) and humility (171) are virtues, while others stated that 'chastity is not a greater good than perfect abstinence' (181), that the latter 'corrupts both virtue and the species' (169), and that 'a poor person lacking the goods of fortune cannot act well in moral matters' (170).

Moreover, the fact that the bishop and his advisors also censured articles claiming 'that there is no state more excellent than to devote oneself to philosophy' (40), 'that the wise men of the world are the philosophers alone' (154), 'that God cannot infuse happiness directly' (22), and 'that happiness is to be had in this life and not in another' (176) reminds us that the diffusion in Christian Europe of the *Nicomachean Ethics* – furthered, ironically, by a papal legate – could turn out to be quite subversive. Medieval Christendom was faced with a pagan thinker who was not only presenting a theory of virtue that was able to challenge the traditional system of values, and that therefore had to be carefully revised and put at the service of theological ethics. He also provided philosophers with new conceptual tools for discussing the problem of the ultimate end of human life; and he encouraged them to focus on a strictly human end, depending only on human effort and first of all on the exercise of human virtues.

It is well known that in Book I of his *Nicomachean Ethics* Aristotle claims that the highest good for humans is happiness, which is desirable in itself and not for the sake of some other good. He argues that happiness does not consist in a certain state or condition, but in virtuous activity that may be identified by discovering men's proper 'function' (I, 7, 1097b 24–5). Aristotle assumes that what distinguishes human beings from other forms of life is that, although they share lower capacities dependent on the vegetative and the sensitive part of their soul, they also have the higher capacities of the rational part of their soul. He then concludes that happiness resides in the full development of the properly human function, namely in the virtuous activity of the rational part of the soul. After a detailed study of moral and intellectual virtues, at the end of Book X, Aristotle turns again to the problem of happiness, and in chapters 7–8 argues that the happiest kind of life for humans is the one that realizes the highest form of human perfection: the life of someone who, using reason effectively, has achieved theoretical wisdom and enjoys a full understanding of the basic principles that regulate the cosmos. The life of such a person – Aristotle emphasizes – is pleasant because it actualizes in the best possible way human intellectual potentialities and, at the same time, it resembles the life of a god: as a god eternally enjoys the 'single and simple pleasure' of pure thought (VII, 14, 1154b 26), by contemplating the truth, the philosopher experiences 'pleasures marvellous for their purity and their stability' (X, 7, 1177a 25–6).

If Aristotle insists on the superiority of the *bios theoreticos*, however, he does not deny that life committed to practical thought and ethical virtue may be happy 'in a secondary degree' (X, 8, 1178a 9) and emphasizes that the welfare of human communities is predicated on the fact that some are willing to lead this kind of life, studying and practising the

# Moral philosophy

art of politics. One of the most remarkable features of many medieval interpretations of the *Nicomachean Ethics* – in the Arabic, the Byzantine, and the Latin world – is that they devalue political life, considering it not as a second-best choice, but as a form of existence inferior to one totally oriented towards philosophical life. In some authors – for instance in Thomas Aquinas – this derives mainly from the assumption that the 'unity of human nature' implies that there must be only 'one ultimate end for man' (*Sentencia libri Ethicorum*, I, 9). In other cases, this is the predictable outcome of a decidedly intellectualistic version of Aristotle's thought, based on a peculiar reading of his claim that man is intellect 'more than anything else' – 'maxime' in the medieval Latin translation (*Nicomachean Ethics*, IX, 8, 1169a 1–3; X, 8, 1178a 7–8). Accurately glossed by Aquinas, this claim had been slightly transformed by Albert the Great, who frequently went so far as to say that man is 'only (*solum, tantum, simpliciter*) intellect' (see *De anima* (On the Soul), I, 1, 1, p. 2; *Super Ethica*, IX, 10, p. 689; *Metaphysica* (Metaphysics), I, 2, 9, p. 26).[3]

Like many Dominican and Franciscan theologians, Albert criticized Averroes' (Ibn Rushd, 1126–98) interpretation of Aristotle's distinction between the agent and the potential intellect. In order to explain intellective cognition, in a highly controversial passage of the third book of his *De anima*, Aristotle introduced the distinction between an active power (later called agent intellect), which abstracts intelligible forms from sensible images, and a passive power (later called potential or possible intellect), capable of receiving them. Albert rejected Averroes' suggestion that there is only one separate potential intellect for all mankind – which challenged Christian belief in the immortality of man's individual soul – and claimed that each human being has his own individual agent and potential intellect. Yet Albert openly declared his proximity to Averroes, who maintained that the ultimate goal of human life consists in the 'conjunction' with the separate substances, namely the celestial intelligences. As a matter of fact, Averroes argued that Aristotle considered the human knowledge of these substances difficult, but not 'impossible' (*In Metaphysicorum libri* (Commentary on the Metaphysics), II, 1, fol. 29C); he believed that the celebrated first sentence of the *Metaphysics*, claiming that 'all men by nature desire to know' (I, 1, 980a 1), entails that they also desire to know 'what God thinks' (*In Metaphysicorum libri*, XII, 51, fol. 335rD); and he described intellectual felicity as a state in which 'man is made similar to God in that he knows all things somehow and is them somehow' (*In Aristotelis de Anima libros* (On Aristotle's On the Soul), III, 36, p. 501).[4] Strongly influenced by this position, as well as by other

166 Luca Bianchi

Islamic and Byzantine Neoplatonizing 'Peripateticians', Albert assumed that the highest human happiness attainable in this life is the cognition of the most noble and divine intelligible objects, that is the immaterial substances and God. Borrowing an expression introduced by al-Farabi (Abu Nasr al-Farabi, *c.*870–*c.*950), Albert stated in his commentary on the *De anima* that the 'confidence of the philosopher' is precisely to experience this happiness through the 'conjunction' of his individual intellect with the separate agent intellect. He explained in detail the complex process through which the philosopher achieves the knowledge of all speculative intelligibles and joins his potential intellect to the agent intellect, which therefore becomes not only the cause of such intelligibles, but also the form of the potential intellect. Through the 'acquisition' (*adeptio*) of the agent intellect, the potential intellect is disposed to 'grasp in thought the separate substances', and such a cognition allows man to reach his most perfect 'state' (*status*): once he has attained this 'wonderful and best' condition, 'man becomes in a certain way like God' and is able to 'bestow on himself and others divine understandings and in a certain way receive everything that is understood' (*De anima*, III, 3, 11, pp. 221–3).

From the 1260s onwards confident assertions concerning the perfection of the intellectual life became a commonplace in the introductions to Aristotelian commentaries, in orations celebrating the study of philosophy, and in treatises or disputations about the supreme good and happiness, such as Boethius of Dacia's *De summo bono* – the most famous medieval treatise in praise of philosophy, written around 1270 – and the *Quaestio de felicitate* (Question on Happiness) authored about twenty years later by the Italian master James of Pistoia (*fl.* end of the thirteenth/beginning of the fourteenth century) and dedicated to Dante's friend, Guido Cavalcanti (1250/59–1300). Both authors present philosophy as the activity that allows man to realize himself as a rational being; and if Boethius relates man's supreme good not only to the speculative but also to the practical intellect, they both agree that happiness cannot be achieved without cultivating all moral virtues. Like most of their contemporaries Boethius and James believed that passions and inordinate desires distract most people from the contemplation of truth and, developing an Aristotelian remark (*Nicomachean Ethics*, I, 3, 1095b 14–22), claimed – as Dante would do in *Convivio* II, vii, 4 – that anyone who pursues bodily pleasures lives like a 'beast'. Boethius went even further and argued that the philosopher lives 'according to the right order of nature', while 'whoever does not lead such a life does not live rightly' (*De summo bono*, p. 377). This means that only philosophers are men in the fullest sense of the term, whereas the illiterate 'laymen' who lack the 'perfection bestowed by theoretical sciences' are 'quasi-human' – as Boethius says in his *Quaestiones super librum Topicorum* (I, 5, p. 23), a text available at Bologna as early as 1286. Several of his colleagues shared this provocative view. Siger of Brabant (*c.*1240–1281/84) – extolled by Dante in *Paradiso* X, 133–8 – repeated Seneca's saying that a life 'without study is death' (*De anima intellectiva*, 9, p. 112). Others affirmed that ignorant people are men only 'potentially' or – according to the shocking formula introduced by Averroes – 'equivocally'.[5]

If today we find such blatant elitism disturbing, in the thirteenth century Boethius' treatise worried theologians and Church authorities for other reasons. Far from denying the beatitude expected after death – as the above-quoted article 176 of the 1277 condemnation maintained – Boethius explicitly mentioned it. Yet he insisted that men can acquire true happiness during their earthly life by purely natural means, practising moral virtues and using their rational powers at their best to ascend the various degrees of knowledge culminating in metaphysical speculation. Besides neglecting the essential Christian theme of the inability of human beings, burdened by original sin, to reach moral perfection without the help of divine grace, such an approach implied that when someone performs the operations of the intellective powers, 'he enjoys the highest state possible for man' (*De summo bono*, p. 374). This left little room for other experiences and ways of life that the Christian tradition had always considered as pre-eminent and blessed: those of the saints, of the contemplatives, of the theologians, and of the simple but faithful believers.

Nonetheless, the ideal of philosophical life was not perceived as necessarily in opposition to religious orthodoxy, and attracted many thinkers even outside the milieu of the Arts masters. Emblematic in this respect is Remigio de' Girolami (*c.*1247–1319), the famous Dominican friar who, after studying in Paris with Thomas Aquinas, taught in the Florentine *studium* of Santa Maria Novella in the last decades of the thirteenth century. In the prologue to his commentary on the *Ethics*,[6] Remigio developed at length Aristotle's remarks on philosophical 'delights', claiming that they are 'the greatest (*maxime*)' and 'the best'; that they are 'marvellous' especially because they are 'unusual' in respect of sensual pleasures generally pursued by human beings; and that they are 'pure' and 'stable' because they deal with eternal things. Although the hypothesis that Dante may have attended his lectures and disputations is now considered unlikely, Remigio's intellectualistic eudemonism, namely his evaluation of actions in terms of their capacity to produce happiness – grounded on the

168                                    Luca Bianchi

assumption that 'man is man and possesses his human nature through his intellect' – reveals that not only the so-called 'radical Aristotelians' (the masters of Arts teaching at the Universities of Paris, Padua, and Bologna who emphasized the autonomy of rational philosophical inquiry), but also some theologians contributed to the cultural climate that nourished Dante's love for philosophy. Such love is voiced, in particular, in the *Convivio*, which emphasizes the necessity to promote the study of philosophy in the conviction that 'life for a human being is the use of reason', so that 'to renounce the use of reason is to renounce being, and is thus the same as being dead' (*Conv.* IV, vii, 11–12; and see II, vii, 3).

Even Albert the Great's idea that man's ultimate end is the knowledge of – and a sort of intellectual union with – the most divine things was well received from the 1270s onwards, but was interpreted differently by Parisian and Italian Arts masters, and later by German Dominicans such as Dietrich of Freiberg (*c.*1250–1318/20) and Eckhart (1260–1328). In his *De summo bono* Boethius of Dacia argued that the life of the philosopher is as *voluptuosa* as God's life. The choice of this adjective, which in medieval culture was generally associated with bodily pleasures and had a negative connotation, is unusual, but, being most likely inspired by the Latin translation of Averroes' *Metaphysics*, its significance should not be exaggerated, as has been done by those who have surmised that Boethius was here departing from the Aristotelian tradition and moving towards Epicureanism. Two points are actually relevant. First, although he was ready to adopt Averroes' terminology, Boethius completely disregarded his doctrine of philosophical felicity: he never hints at the 'conjunction' with the agent intellect, but instead describes the steps leading the philosopher to 'know', to 'admire', and to 'love' the First Principle, openly identified with 'the glorious and most high God, who is blessed forever and ever'. Second, if Boethius claims that 'the desire to know will never be satisfied until the uncreated being is known' and insists that in contemplating God 'the philosopher leads a life productive of intense pleasure (*valde voluptuosam*)', he never mentions a knowledge of His essence (*De summo bono*, pp. 370–1, 375–6). This is a telling silence, given that the possibility of understanding the separate substances' and even God's essence in earthly life was a very controversial matter. Harshly criticized by Thomas Aquinas, Averroes' position on this point was nevertheless defended by several Arts masters. If we can trust the Renaissance philosophers Agostino Nifo (1473–after 1538) and Alessandro Achillini (1463–1512), at the beginning of the 1270s, Siger of Brabant argued in his lost treatises *De intellectu* (On the Intellect) and *De felicitate* (On

*Moral philosophy* 169

Happiness) that happiness is formally identical with God, and that only by knowing Him can both human and separate intellects be made blessed. Although scholars disagree about the reliability of these late witnesses, it is certain that in his lectures on the *Metaphysics* (III, 1, p. 90) Siger taught that by reasoning from what is caused by the First Cause, 'a man very skilled in philosophy' might come to understand its essence. This sparked the reaction of the Church authorities, worried by a conception of philosophy that announced that the same goal that religion envisaged for the afterlife – a full contemplation of the divine – might be attained in this world by purely natural means. It is therefore easy to comprehend why one of the articles condemned in 1277 by Bishop Tempier, namely article 36, was prohibited since it taught 'that in this mortal life we can understand God in his essence'.

The bishop's intervention did not stop the dissemination of this view, repeated around the end of the thirteenth century by some anonymous commentators and painstakingly defended around 1320, in open polemic against Thomas Aquinas, by the 'Averroist' John of Jandun (*c*.1285/89–1328). The majority of Dante's contemporaries, however, expressed more prudent views about the scope of the philosophical life, searching for a 'third way' between that of Averroes and Albert the Great and that of Thomas Aquinas. As is well known, Thomas spoke repeatedly about a twofold human happiness and, following an established theological tradition, distinguished the 'perfect beatitude' of the life to come from the 'imperfect beatitude' of the present life. In his view, if one assumes first that happiness requires the complete satisfaction of men's desires and, second, that the 'perfection' of the intellect entails the knowledge of the essence of things, there follows that perfect happiness can be reached only when the intellect attains the essence of God. Aquinas therefore concludes that man by nature desires an end that he cannot naturally achieve and that he will completely satisfy only in Paradise, when he will continuously, immediately, and eternally contemplate God as He is (see *Par.* XXII, 61–5). Although Thomas emphasizes that the felicity man tries to achieve on earth through philosophy is already a participation in and an anticipation of the heavenly beatific vision, he judges it from a theological viewpoint: he thus labels it as *beatitudo* or *felicitas imperfecta* and, even in his commentary on the *Ethics* (see for instance I, 16, p. 60 and X, 13, p. 595), he suggests that Aristotle himself agreed that such happiness is merely human and incomplete.

Some Arts masters criticized Thomas' position, defending worldly beatitude and arguing that it may reasonably be called perfect, because it perfectly actualizes human intellectual potentialities. But they also acknowledged that such potentialities are limited, and that Averroes' and Albert the Great's conviction that man can 'deify' himself by coming into 'conjunction' with the separate substances was too optimistic. Their emphasis on the limits of philosophical happiness is extremely significant in the perspective of a correct appreciation of the intellectual background of the *Convivio*. Here Dante repeatedly insists that the human intellect can know the first matter, the immaterial substances, and God only from their effects (see *Conv.* III, viii, 15 and IV, xxii, 13). Furthermore, in a famous and controversial passage (*Conv.* III, xv, 7–11), he also maintains that the restrictions of human knowledge do not inhibit intellectual felicity because our desire for knowledge is 'measured in this life in accordance with that knowledge which can be gained here', and since 'it is impossible for our nature to know of God what he is ... this is not something which we naturally desire to know'. This statement provides decisive evidence against the 'legend' of Dante's Thomism, since it is clearly at odds with the basic tenets of Aquinas' ethics and anthropology. As recent scholarship has shown, however, one should not exaggerate the originality of Dante's position, which is close to views already circulating among Arts masters from the 1270s onwards. In particular, scholars have called attention to a passage in Peter of Auvergne's (1240s–1304) questions on the *Nicomachean Ethics* where he claims that if man, once he has achieved 'in this life' a limited knowledge of the separate substances and of the First Cause, wished a 'further cognition' – that is the cognition of their essence – his desire would be irrational, because 'reason does not assert that one should desire what cannot be had'.[7]

A final remark. I have highlighted the elitism of professional philosophers. When they routinely repeat Aristotle's saying that 'all men by nature desire to know', they seem little worried by the fact that most humans cannot fulfil this desire. They show no qualms in acknowledging that philosophical life is for the happy few able to master all the theoretical sciences; and they limit themselves to explaining that most people are removed from this perfectly delightful life because of several 'impediments': a bad disposition of the bodily organs, extreme poverty, and the passions of the soul, such as anger, lust, and greed. There is no need to recall that Dante completely broke with this attitude, and that he wrote the *Convivio* with the purpose of initiating a multitude of morally noble yet illiterate men and women to the study of wisdom, departing from his predecessors precisely because, from the very beginning of the first book (*Conv.* I, i, 2–7), he insisted on the need to remove

*Moral philosophy* 171

'impediments'. In the fourth book (*Conv.* IV, iv, 3–4) Dante presents 'wars' as one of the hindrances making it impossible 'to attain happiness' and argued that only 'monarchy' can ensure 'peace'. In the *Monarchia* this becomes, as is well known, the first premise of a long line of reasoning that aims to show that a single world-ruler or emperor is necessary for the well-being of humanity. Dante claims first (*Mon.* I, iii) that the complete actualization of human intellectual potentialities is not the task of the individuals but of the whole of humanity – as John of Jandun would also teach a few years later in Paris. Dante then makes clear that mankind can 'most freely and readily' attend to its 'almost divine' intellectual activity 'in the calm and tranquillity of peace', under the guidance of the Emperor (*Mon.* I, iv, 2).

Scholars have drawn attention to Remigio de Girolami's *De bono pacis* (On the Good of Peace, 1303–04), where the importance of civic unity and peace – conceived in Augustinian terms as *tranquillitas ordinis* (calm of order), the expression of divine charity – is combined with the Aristotelian thesis that man is a 'political animal' whose individual welfare ought to be subordinated to communal welfare. It is nevertheless worth noting that, in his commentary on the *Nicomachean Ethics*, Thomas Aquinas stated (X, 11, p. 587) that 'the whole of political life' is directed towards 'speculative happiness', because it 'establishes and preserves peace, giving men the opportunity of contemplating truth'; and that Boethius of Dacia in his *De summo bono* (p. 371) argued that 'the art of war is prescribed in the city by the lawmaker for this reason, that when the enemies have been expelled, citizens may devote themselves to intellectual virtues in contemplating the true, and to moral virtues in doing good, and thus live a happy life'. Needless to say, while Thomas simply hints at peace and Boethius calls attention to the risk of local conflicts, Dante insists on the need for universal peace, guaranteed by a universal power. Still his conviction that there are not only moral, but also political preconditions for the achievement of intellectual happiness clearly rests on the original version of Aristotle's eudemonism proposed by late-thirteenth-century thinkers. Many of them, as we have seen, considered all aspects of social life as totally functional to speculative life, so that even peace might be conceived not as an end in itself, but as a means that enables human beings to realize their proper end, namely to satisfy in full their natural desire for knowledge. This means that not only Dante's moral thought, but also relevant aspects of his political thought cannot be properly understood unless they are placed against the background of the interpretive tradition of the *Nicomachean Ethics*.

# Luca Bianchi

## Notes

1 I quote Boethius of Dacia's works from the critical edition in the *Corpus Philosophorum Danicorum Medii Aevi* (The Hague: Gad, 1969–). All translations in this chapter are my own.

2 The 1277 articles can be found in D. Piché, *La Condamnation parisienne de 1277* (Paris: Vrin, 1999).

3 Thomas Aquinas' works are quoted from the Leonine edition (Rome: Typographia Polyglotta, 1882–); Albert the Great's works from *Opera omnia* (Monasterii Westfalorum, Aschendorff, 1951–).

4 Averroes' commentary on Aristotle's *Metaphysics* is quoted from the facsimile reproduction of the Giunta edition (1562–74) of *Aristotelis Opera cum Averrois Commentariis* (Frankfurt: Minerva, 1962); Averroes' commentary on the *De anima* is from the critical edition by S. Stuart Crawford (Cambridge, MA: The Mediaeval Academy of America, 1953).

5 Relevant texts are quoted and discussed in L. Bianchi, *Studi sull'aristotelismo del Rinascimento* (Padua: Il Poligrafo, 2003), pp. 41–61. Siger's *De anima intellectiva* is quoted from B. C. Bazán's edition (Louvain and Paris: Publications Universitaires and Béatrice-Nauwelaerts, 1972).

6 The text of the prologue is published in E. Panella, 'Un'introduzione alla filosofia in uno *studium* dei frati predicatori del XIII secolo. *Divisio scientie* di Remigio dei Girolami', *Memorie domenicane*, 12 (1981), 27–126, at 122–4.

7 Peter of Auvergne's text is cited from A. J. Celano, 'Peter of Auvergne's questions on Books I and II of the *Ethica Nicomachea*. A study and critical edition', *Medieval Studies*, 48 (1986), 1–110, at 80–1.

CHAPTER II

# *Natural philosophy*

## Edward Grant

In the evolution of physics, or 'natural philosophy', as it was more popularly known, the period 1250 to 1350 was of crucial importance. By 1250, dramatic changes had transformed the intellectual life of western Europe. By the latter half of the twelfth century, Aristotle's (384–322 BCE) natural philosophy, which had been virtually unknown in western Europe since the sixth century CE, was turned into Latin by a number of translators, most notably Gerard of Cremona (c.1114–87), who translated Aristotle's natural philosophy from Arabic; also noteworthy is Michael Scot (1175–1232) who around 1220 translated, from Arabic to Latin, a number of commentaries on Aristotle's treatises on natural philosophy by the famous Islamic scholar Averroes (Ibn Rushd, 1126–98).

Because Latin and Greek are cognate languages, translations from Aristotle's Greek texts were normally more faithful to the originals than were those from Arabic. For this reason, the translations of Aristotle's natural philosophy from Greek by William of Moerbeke (c.1215–c.1286) in the 1260s were of great importance. Moerbeke also translated a few Greek commentaries on Aristotle's works by such ancient Greek commentators as John Philoponus (c.490–c.570), Simplicius (c.490–c.560), and Themistius (317–c.387). Thomas Aquinas (1225–74) was one of the first to use Moerbeke's translations. By the last quarter of the thirteenth century in western Europe virtually all of Aristotle's treatises on natural philosophy were available in Latin.

Indeed, as early as 1200 Aristotle's treatises on natural philosophy were readily available and sufficiently well known to form the basis of the curriculum in the Faculties of Arts in the two great new universities of Paris and Oxford (the University of Bologna, which may have preceded Paris and Oxford by a few years, emphasized law rather than arts). Within the university context, natural philosophy, or the less often used equivalent natural science, was taught in the Faculty of Arts, in which all students were required to enrol and study for the Bachelor of Arts degree and, if

173

they continued on, a Master of Arts degree. Degrees in the Arts Faculties were required before students could go on to study in the graduate disciplines of theology, law, and medicine. Because all university students across Europe were required to study natural philosophy, it is no exaggeration to claim that knowledge about the physical world and its operations was widespread and deeply embedded in European intellectual life, a phenomenon unique to western Europe.

During the period 1250 to 1350, natural philosophy was not significantly different from what it would be in 1500; nor was it taught differently. But the attitude of some Church officials and a number of theologians toward natural philosophy was destined to change from what it was at the beginning of the thirteenth century to what it would become at the end of that century, when it changed dramatically from rejection to near full acceptance.

Controversy greeted the introduction of Aristotle's natural philosophy in the region of Paris, primarily because of the recently established University of Paris. In 1210 the provincial synod of Sens decreed that Aristotle's books, and commentaries thereon, were not to be read in Paris in public or private. The decree was repeated in 1215 with the University of Paris specifically mentioned. In 1231 Pope Gregory IX (b. *c.*1145; papacy 1227–41) ordered the deletion of all errors from Aristotle's offensive works, a task that was apparently never performed, although the directive indicates that the Church had come to realize the overall value of Aristotle's works, and was prepared to allow their use, provided that parts offensive to Christian belief were deleted. Yet sometime in the 1230s, shortly after Pope Gregory's edict, Richard Rufus of Cornwall (d. *c.*1260) presented lectures at the University of Paris on Aristotle's *Physics* and *On Generation and Corruption*, and in the 1240s Roger Bacon (*c.*1220–92) also lectured at the University of Paris on Aristotle's natural philosophy. In the 1260s and 1270s Church authorities altered their strategy. Instead of banning Aristotle's books, they chose to condemn ideas in his works deemed contrary to the faith. After an initial condemnation of 13 articles in 1270, the Bishop of Paris, Etienne Tempier (d. 1279), issued a condemnation of 219 articles in 1277. Some of the condemned articles were drawn from the works of Aristotle and his Islamic commentator Averroes. Indeed, some of the condemned articles may not have been written, but probably circulated orally among the teachers and students at the University of Paris, as we may infer from condemned articles 150–154 cited below.

The course of events just described reveals that in the thirteenth century theologians and natural philosophers at the University of Paris sought to reach a resolution of the outstanding conflicts between reason and

*Natural philosophy* 175

revelation. Although it was drawn up in haste, the Condemnation of 1277 is of great historical significance, because by means of it the Bishop of Paris, and the Church in general, sought to compel teachers and students at the University of Paris to acknowledge that Aristotle was in error about matters vital to the Catholic faith, and therefore had to be corrected. Aristotle's reasoned arguments had to yield to the revelations of faith.

The most significant condemned articles were those directly relevant to Aristotle's natural philosophy. A number of Aristotle's ideas were regarded as unacceptable, but the most offensive was his insistence that the world is eternal. As a measure of how dangerous this view was regarded, approximately 27 of the 219 condemned articles were directed against it. The articles assumed various forms, as can be seen by the following examples (the number preceding each article represents its place among the 219 articles):[1]

> 9. That there was no first man, nor will there be a last; on the contrary, there always was and always will be the generation of man from man.
>
> 98. That the world is eternal because that which has a nature by [means of] which it could exist through the whole future [surely] has a nature by [means of] which it could have existed through the whole past.
>
> 107. That the elements are eternal. However, they have been made [or created] anew in the relationship which they now have.

The condemned articles also had a significant impact on the development of natural philosophy. One important indirect consequence of the Condemnation of 1277 was an unusual emphasis on God's absolute power to do anything whatever as long as it did not involve a contradiction. This came about largely because of claims in Aristotle's natural philosophy that certain actions were naturally impossible, implying that not even God could perform those actions. Such claims were regarded as contrary to faith, and a number of the condemned articles were intended to show that by His supernatural power God could indeed perform acts that Aristotle regarded as naturally impossible. Some of these articles will be considered below.

A number of the condemned articles reveal tensions that existed between the Faculties of Arts and Theology. One can readily see why theologians would have been incensed at the following articles:[2]

> 150. That on any question, a man ought not to be satisfied with certitude based on authority.
>
> 152. That theological discussions are based on fables.
>
> 153. That nothing is known better because of knowing theology.
>
> 154. That the only wise men of the world are philosophers.

176                                Edward Grant

If these views were actually expressed, they probably circulated orally among arts masters and were not written down – at least none has been found in any treatise known to modern scholars. Despite these alleged denigrations of theologians by natural philosophers, the relationship between theologians and the discipline of natural philosophy was of great importance, as shall be shown below.

## The essence of natural philosophy, 1250–1350

Many of the greatest medieval natural philosophers lived during the period 1250 to 1350, including Robert Kilwardby (*c*.1215–79), Roger Bacon, Albertus Magnus (Albert the Great) (*c*.1200–80), Thomas Aquinas, Cecco d'Ascoli (1269–1327), William of Ockham (1287–1347), Thomas Bradwardine (*c*.1290–1349), John of Jandun (*c*.1285/89–1328), John Buridan (*c*.1300–after 1358), Nicole Oresme (*c*.1320–82), and Nicholas of Autrecourt (*c*.1300–after 1350). We learn of their contributions to natural philosophy in the commentaries they wrote on what was known as Aristotle's 'natural books', comprising Aristotle's *Physics*, *On the Heavens*, *On the Soul*, *On Generation and Corruption*, and *Meteorology*. Alongside these commentaries, there existed a considerable body of literature encompassing commentaries made by theologians on the *Four Books of Sentences* of Peter Lombard (*c*.1096–1164), a theological treatise composed between 1155 and 1158 that became the basic textbook in schools of theology until the end of the seventeenth century. Of the four books, the questions proposed in book two of the *Sentences* were the most relevant, because the second book was concerned with questions about creation and angels that invariably involved an extensive use of natural philosophy. To these basic sources of natural philosophy we must add thematic works usually known as tractates, or treatises, where natural philosophers pursued particular themes, as, for example, Nicole Oresme did in his *Treatise on the Commensurability or Incommensurability of the Celestial Motions*.

From approximately 1200 to 1500 more than four hundred questions were discussed in the commentaries on Aristotle's natural books. Many of them could be appropriately assigned to one or another of our modern sciences, while others were peculiar to the Middle Ages. Here is a sample of questions that can be assigned to particular sciences:

**Physics**

Whether the existence of a vacuum is possible.
Whether if a vacuum did exist, a heavy body could move in it.

*Natural philosophy* 177

We inquire what it is that moves a projected body upwards after separation from what has projected it.

On the supposition that a rainbow can occur by reflection of rays, we inquire whether such reflection occurs in a cloud or whether it occurs in tiny dewdrops or raindrops.

### Geology

Whether the whole earth is habitable.

Whether the waters of springs and rivers are generated in the concavities of the earth.

### Chemistry

Whether elements remain [or persist] formally in a compound [or mixed] body.

Whether a compound is possible.

### Meteorology

Whether the middle region of air is the place where rain is generated.

Whether hail occurs more in spring and autumn.

Whether a typhoon and a hurricane are made from a hot and dry exhalation.

Although biology was a part of natural philosophy, no biological questions were included because commentaries on Aristotle's biological works were virtually non-existent.

### The relations between natural philosophy and theology

In his *Commentary on the Sentences*, Thomas Aquinas argued that theology was a science, but gave his more detailed arguments in his great *Summa of Theology*. Some sciences, Thomas argues, derive from principles of a higher science, just as:

> the science of optics proceeds from principles established by geometry, and music from principles established by arithmetic. So it is that sacred doctrine is a science because it proceeds from principles made known by the light of a higher science, namely the science of God and the blessed. Hence, just as music accepts on authority the principles taught by the arithmetician, so sacred science accepts the principles revealed by God.[3]

Because it derived its first principles from God, Thomas Aquinas regarded theology as the most important of all the sciences – more important than mathematics, logic, astronomy, optics, and natural philosophy. During the late Middle Ages almost all theologians agreed with Aquinas. As a subordinate discipline to theology, theologians could use natural philosophy to elucidate theology.

But the converse was not acceptable: those natural philosophers who were not also theologians could not use theology to explicate natural philosophy. Indeed, beginning in 1272 all Arts masters in the Arts Faculty of the University of Paris were required to take an oath, swearing that they would not introduce theology into their natural philosophy. If, however, it was unavoidable, they further swore that they would resolve all issues in favour of the faith. In his *Questions on the Physics* (VIII, q. 12), John Buridan suggested that instead of moving the celestial orbs by external agents, God, when He created the world, might have chosen to move them by impressing a force, or impetus, into each orb, thus enabling it to move by its own power. In the absence of resistance to celestial motions, the impetus would be permanent. Fearing that he might have gone too far in suggesting what God might or might not have done, Buridan declares: 'But this I do not say assertively, but [rather tentatively] so that I might seek from the theological masters what they might teach me in these matters as to how these things take place.'[4] Elsewhere Buridan declares: 'I say that there is no body beyond the heaven or world, namely beyond the outermost heaven; and Aristotle assumes this as obvious. But you ought to have recourse to the theologians [in order to learn] what must be said about this according to the truth of faith or constancy.'[5]

And so it was that natural philosophy and theology became separate, but unequal, disciplines: theology could – and did – use natural philosophy extensively; but natural philosophy rarely used theology. By making theology an independent science, Thomas Aquinas also – inadvertently – made natural philosophy an independent science. Natural philosophers who were not also professional theologians kept natural philosophy distinct from theology and religion, as indeed did Dante himself.

### Natural philosophy in theological treatises

Natural philosophy was most often integrated into theology when theologians commented on the second book of Peter Lombard's *Sentences*, which was concerned with the creation and angels. The questions considered

## Natural philosopy

were usually about aspects of creation, which only theologians were qualified to discuss. The following questions were typical:

Whether light was created on the first day.

Whether the crystalline heaven is moved.

Whether the firmament has the nature of fire.

Whether the empyrean heaven has stars.

Certain questions were posed about angels and answered by invoking natural philosophy. In Question 52 of his *Summa of Theology*, Thomas Aquinas inquired about the relationship of angels to places and divided the question into three articles:

Does an angel exist in a place?

Can an angel be in several places at once?

Can several angels be in the same place at once?

In Question 53 Thomas posed the following three questions:

Can an angel move from place to place?

Does an angel, moving locally, pass through an intermediate place?

Whether an angel's motion occurs in time or in an instant.

Because the concepts of 'place' and 'motion' are fundamental to material bodies in natural philosophy, those concepts were applied to immaterial angels, taking into account the differences between material and immaterial entities.

A fair number of virtually identical questions appear in treatises on natural philosophy and also in treatises on theology. Examples of this category of questions are:

Whether the heaven is composed of matter and form.

On the number of spheres, whether there are eight or nine, or more, or less.

Whether the heaven is spherical in shape.

Whether the stars are self-moved or are moved only by the motions of their orbs.

Natural philosophy had penetrated theology so pervasively that some purportedly theological treatises were virtually transformed into natural philosophical treatises, as, for example, treatises by Peter John Olivi (1248–98) and Gregory of Rimini (d. 1358).

## The structural organization of a typical question in natural philosophy

Authors who wrote treatises involving numerous questions on various aspects of natural philosophy usually followed an outline based on six steps, which were derived from oral disputations in the classrooms of universities:

Statement of the question.

Arguments opposed to the author's position, usually referred to as the 'principal arguments' (*rationes principales*).

Assertion of one or more opinions opposed to the 'principal arguments', often accompanied by an appeal to a major authority, usually Aristotle.

Clarification about the meaning of the question or any of its terms; an optional step.

Author's main arguments, which were presented in a variety of ways. Sometimes the arguments were given as ordinally numbered conclusions (*conclusiones*); or they were not identified as conclusions, but were numbered ordinally; or they were left unnumbered, but presented one after the other.

Brief refutation of each of the principal arguments presented in the second step.

All of the great variety of themes and topics in Aristotle's 'natural books' were treated in the format of questions, as just described. One important consequence was that each question was basically independent of all others. No effort was made to integrate the content of these disparate questions. Moreover, rarely were there any references from one question to another.

## Aristotle's cosmos: the foundation of medieval natural philosophy

With the exception of ideas that conflicted with the tenets of faith, medieval natural philosophers adopted almost all of Aristotle's basic ideas about the cosmos and its operations as he expounded them in his 'natural books'. One of Aristotle's unacceptable ideas was, as has been noted, his belief in an eternal, uncreated world that would never end. Although he did not believe in a creator God, Aristotle did, however, believe in a God, albeit a strange one who is unaware of the world's existence and who only

# Natural philosophy

thinks about himself, because he is the only existent entity worthy of his thoughts.

Most of his other opinions, however, were acceptable. Aristotle regarded the cosmos as a very large finite sphere filled everywhere with different kinds of matter, thus eliminating the possibility of void spaces. Aristotle emphatically denied that anything could exist beyond our world – not matter, places, void spaces, or time. The world itself comprises a series of concentric spheres, ranging from the outermost sphere of the fixed stars all the way down to our spherical earth lying immobile at the geometric centre of the world. He believed our world was divided into two radically different parts: terrestrial and celestial. The dividing line between the two regions was the concave surface of the lunar sphere. The terrestrial region, below the concave surface of the moon, was a place of continual change. It consisted of four elements: earth, water, air, and fire. If these elements were to cease their motions, they would form four immobile, concentric circles in the ascending order of earth, water, air, and fire. But this cannot occur because the four elements are in constant motion, entering into combinations to form compounds that constitute the visible, physical bodies of our terrestrial world. Aristotle assumed that all compound bodies were composed of two or more elements. The compound bodies were always in a process of change as the elements of which they were composed disassociated and entered into different combinations to form new compound bodies.

The celestial region was radically different. It was filled with a material ether that left no void spaces. This ether was an incorruptible substance that functioned as a fifth element that moved naturally with an eternal, uniform, circular motion. The only change it endured was change of place, as was obvious because the visible planets and stars, which were composed of this ether, were observed to move with uniform, circular motion. Because they did not move with circular motion, comets, shooting stars, and similar occurrences, were not regarded as celestial phenomena, but were rather assumed to move in the uppermost reaches of the terrestrial region. Aristotle presumed that the celestial ether existed in the form of fifty-five concentric spheres within which all the stars and planets were embedded and carried round in eternal, uniform circular motion. There is much more to Aristotle's cosmos, including his fundamental attempt to explain natural phenomena by positing four kinds of causes and four kinds of changes. In his natural philosophy, Aristotle discussed many themes that lie beyond the scope of this chapter. But it will serve our purposes to discuss some of the major topics that scholastic natural philosophers considered in their treatises on Aristotle's natural philosophy. Among these were motion, place, void, time, the finitude of the cosmos, the infinite, and the status of the earth at the centre of the world. In their commentaries on Aristotle's natural philosophy, medieval natural philosophers posed questions on all of these topics.

## Terrestrial phenomena

Although medieval natural philosophers were generally faithful to Aristotle's interpretations of the cosmos and its operations, they did not hesitate to criticize Aristotle's opinions and to depart from them where they felt his arguments failed to account for the phenomena or his explanations were simply inadequate.

## Motion

One of the most important challenges to Aristotle derived from his explanation of what kept a body in motion after it lost contact with the motive force that initially set it in motion. Aristotle believed that air propelled a body forward after it lost contact with its initial mover. He assumed that the air gradually lost its power to move a body. When the air's capacity to move a body was exhausted, the body came to rest. In the sixth century John Philoponus, a Greek commentator on Aristotle's natural philosophy, rejected Aristotle's explanation on the grounds that if air were capable of moving a body, one should be able to set an immobile body into motion by simply agitating the air behind it. Instead of air, Philoponus assumed that an initial mover of a stone, for example, imparted an incorporeal motive force to that stone thus enabling it to continue its motion. Familiar with Philoponus' ideas on impressed force, Islamic natural philosophers such as Ibn Sina (Avicenna, as he was known in the Latin West, c.980–c.1037) and Abu'l Barakat (d. c.1164) added important new ideas to what they had learned from Philoponus: the former assuming the impressed force to be a permanent quality, while the latter contended that it was a non-permanent self-dissipating force.

After the translations made from Arabic to Latin in the thirteenth century, these ideas came to be known in the Latin West. In the fourteenth century John Buridan, in his *Questions on the Physics*, was probably the first to introduce the Latin term *impetus* to designate an incorporeal, impressed force. He observed that Aristotle had not dealt particularly well with the question of continuous motion. Buridan added much to the theory of

## Natural philosophy

impetus. He insisted that the greater the quantity of matter in a body, the more impetus it could absorb and retain. Bodies in motion eventually came to rest because external resistances caused the impressed force, or impetus, to dissipate and disappear. Buridan assumed that impetus in a body was only corrupted by external resistances, and clearly implied that if all resistances to a body in motion were removed, the impetus would remain constant. Under these circumstances, it followed that a body set in motion would move indefinitely in a straight line at a uniform speed. In the finite Aristotelian world that Buridan, and all medieval natural philosophers accepted, such a motion would be impossible. In a world assumed infinite, however, it would be possible.

Buridan also applied impetus to explain the acceleration of naturally falling bodies. He did this by assuming that not only did a body's heaviness cause it to fall, but that same heaviness also caused successive increments of impetus in the falling body, where each increment causes an increase in the body's speed. The successive increments of impetus cause the body continually to accelerate its downward motion. In his early discussions of motion, Galileo's (1564–1642) views about acceleration did not differ much from Buridan's. Indeed, Galileo probably derived direct benefit from another medieval contribution involving a sound definition of uniform motion and its application to a theorem involving uniformly accelerated motion. In the fourteenth century scholastic natural philosophers attempted to show how qualities could be increased or decreased by the addition or subtraction of identical parts. Although this is unfeasible, the process was known to scholastics as 'the intension and remission of qualities'. It was an attempt to quantify qualitative changes by the use of arithmetic and geometry. At Oxford University arithmetic was commonly used to represent variable qualities, while geometry was employed at the University of Paris. Since motion, or velocity, was regarded as a variable quality, Nicole Oresme, sometime around 1350, used geometric diagrams to formulate a proof that modern historians have called 'the mean speed theorem', namely, $s = (1/2)at^2$, where $s$ represents distance, $a$ acceleration, and $t$ is time. In the sixteenth century Oresme's proof, along with its accompanying diagram, was printed in numerous editions and probably influenced Galileo, who gives essentially the same geometric proof in the Third Day of his *Two New Sciences* (1638).

Aristotle insisted that the upward and downward motions of a single stone were not to be regarded as one continuous motion, but must be viewed as contrary, or opposite, motions, namely up and down. A stone that was hurled into the air and fell to earth was not a single, continuous motion, but was, rather, two opposite and independent motions. To avoid the possibility that the motions could be regarded as continuous, Aristotle assumed that a moment of rest intervened between the upward and downward motions, an opinion that medieval scholastics called the 'moment of rest' (*quies media*). It was an opinion that was rejected by most Aristotelian commentators, who repudiated Aristotle by invoking a number of imaginary counter-instances. The most popular involved a descending millstone that strikes an upward moving bean. Under these circumstances, it would be impossible for the bean to have a moment of rest before descending. In an early work titled *On Motion*, Galileo directed five arguments against Aristotle's moment of rest, the fourth of which is essentially the 'millstone–bean' argument.

## *The earth*

The earth was the focus of attention in a number of questions about its status. Aristotle had assumed a spherical earth, which he located at the geometric centre of a spherical cosmos. No one to my knowledge disagreed with Aristotle: all medieval natural philosophers assumed the earth was a sphere, contrary to the widely held modern belief that, in the Middle Ages, the earth was assumed to be flat. Aristotle's further belief that the earth is completely immobile was challenged in significant ways, but not by Dante. In the fourteenth century a few scholastic authors – notably John Buridan and Nicole Oresme – argued that the earth's daily rotation around its axis would be compatible with astronomical phenomena. On the assumption of the relativity of motion, Oresme formulated a series of powerful arguments to demonstrate the soundness of the hypothesis of the earth's daily rotation. In the heliocentric astronomical system that he advocated in his monumental *On the Revolutions of the Heavenly Orbs* (1543), Nicholas Copernicus (1473–1543) did not improve on Oresme's arguments in favour of a rotating earth. However, because Oresme could not conclusively demonstrate an actual daily axial rotation, he opted for the traditional opinion of an immobile earth, a judgement that he believed was confirmed by biblical passages.

Although he rejected an axial rotation of the earth, John Buridan, and others, did not believe in the earth's absolute immobility, thereby radically departing from Aristotle. Buridan was convinced that the earth was constantly making small rectilinear motions in order to bring its centre of gravity into perfect coincidence with the geometric centre of the cosmos. The earth's centre of gravity is constantly shifting because the earth is not a homogeneous body. Its parts are always in a process of change and therefore vary in density so that the earth's centre of gravity differs from its centre of

*Natural philosophy* 185

magnitude. Hence the earth is constantly making slight rectilinear movements to bring its centre of gravity into coincidence with the geometric centre of the world. Buridan observes that this ongoing process, by which the earth's magnitude is constantly altered, causes mountains and rocks to erode. As a consequence, rivers and streams carry small rocks and bits of earth from mountains to the oceans. As this process proceeds, previously submerged lands rise out of the oceans and eventually form new mountains.

### Possibilities beyond our world

Although medieval natural philosophers simplified Aristotle's celestial configurations, they did not propose much that actually departed from his view of the celestial region. They did, however, suggest possible alternative interpretations of the universe that Aristotle would undoubtedly have rejected. Indeed, most of these suggestions would have destroyed Aristotle's conception of the universe. They are counterfactual propositions that required the use of scientific imagination to produce hypothetical worlds of which Aristotle had never dreamt. Let me briefly describe a few of these medieval departures from Aristotle.

### Do other worlds exist?

Because an article condemned at Paris in 1277 declared that God could not make other worlds, medieval natural philosophers were compelled to admit that God could make as many other worlds as He pleased. They thus accepted what Aristotle had rejected as impossible, namely that more than one world could exist. Aristotle denied the possible existence of other worlds because he assumed that if a plurality of worlds existed, the earth of one world, or some part of the earth, would rise up in that world and somehow move to the centre of another world. Scholastics denied this Aristotelian consequence of a plurality of worlds, insisting that the earth of every world would remain in its own world. Although these hypothetical worlds were assumed to be identical, each was imagined as wholly self-contained and independent of every other world. Whether any kind of life existed on these other worlds was not discussed.

### Void spaces

In Aristotle's world, void space was naturally impossible. Indeed, as we saw, Aristotle denied the existence of anything whatever beyond our world. Medieval natural philosophers adopted a radically different approach. They were convinced that if another spherical world existed beyond ours, a void space would lie between them. A few believed that void space was not simply a hypothetical entity, but actually existed beyond our world. Robert Holkot (d. *c*.1349) argued that void space must exist beyond our world, because if God could create a world beyond ours, a vacuum must exist where God could create that other world. As Holkot expressed it: 'beyond [our] world there is a vacuum because where a body can exist but does not there we find a vacuum. Therefore a vacuum is [there] now.'[6] In his Old-French commentary on Aristotle's *On the Heavens*, Nicole Oresme insisted that the human mind believed naturally that beyond our world some kind of space existed. For Oresme that space was an infinite, indivisible void, which he regarded as God's infinite immensity.

An article condemned in 1277 played a significant role in discussions about void space. Article 49 condemned those who held that God could not move the world rectilinearly because a void space would be left in the space vacated by the world. On the assumption that there is only one world, Oresme imagined that God did indeed move our cosmos with a rectilinear motion and regarded that motion as an absolute motion because there is no other body to whose motion it could be related.

A major reason why Aristotle rejected void spaces within our world was his conviction that bodily motions in a void would be instantaneous, because there would be no medium to resist them. Scholastics rejected this argument and provided a number of counter-arguments to show that a body's motion in a void would not be instantaneous, but occur in time as the body successively traversed part after part of the void space. Aristotle also rejected void space because he was convinced that bodies of unequal weight would fall with the same speed in a void, which he regarded as absurd. In Aristotle's opinion, bodies fell in a plenum with speeds proportional to their weights: the greater the weight, the greater the speed, because a heavier body could cleave the medium more easily than a less heavy body. In a void, however, there is no medium and, therefore, no reason why a heavy body should fall more quickly than a less heavy body. But in the fourteenth century a new concept of internal resistance was applied to 'mixed', or compound, bodies that were homogeneous. In a rather complicated way, scholastics showed that two homogenous bodies of unequal weight would fall in a vacuum with the same speed, although they would fall at different speeds in a plenum. Thus what Aristotle judged absurd, medieval natural philosophers regarded as intelligible. In his *Two New Sciences*, Galileo too believed that bodies of equal weight fell

## Natural philosopy

with equal speeds in a void, but generalized beyond homogeneous bodies to include all bodies of whatever weight and composition.

### The legacy of medieval natural philosophy

The late Middle Ages, and especially the period 1250–1350, left a profound legacy to western Europe: it laid the foundations for the science that received its mature development from the likes of Galileo, Kepler (1571–1630), Isaac Newton (1643–1727), and many others, in the sixteenth and seventeenth centuries. It absorbed the natural philosophy it received from Graeco-Islamic sources and shaped it into a body of knowledge that eventually included the exact mathematical sciences, when natural philosophy became 'the Great Mother of the Sciences', a characterization that was first made by Francis Bacon (1561–1626) in his *New Organon* (1620).[7] Most of this was achieved by scholars who had been trained at the universities of Europe, which were founded initially around 1200 and have ever since been an integral part of western civilization. The development of natural philosophy and its solid foundation in the universities of western Europe would not have been possible if the Church had been hostile to the study of secular disciplines. The condemnation of the Copernican heliocentric system in 1616 and of Galileo in 1633 have falsely led many to believe that the Church was an enemy of science and natural philosophy. Aristotelian natural philosophy served as the intellectual base of a medieval university education and, except for a few restrictions involving the Christian faith, it was taught independently of theology and religion, although theologians applied it extensively and intensively to theological problems. The Church expected its theologians to have studied natural philosophy, a secular discipline that was expected to provide them with knowledge of the physical world.

The objective of medieval natural philosophy was nothing less than a rational, inquisitive investigation of the physical world. A spirit of free inquiry, a spirit of probing and poking around, emerged in the period from 1250 to 1350. This rational, inquisitive approach was manifested in the questions format used by medieval natural philosophers. The spirit of free inquiry has been brilliantly characterized by William of Ockham, who, in the 1330s, declared: 'Assertions ... concerning natural philosophy, which do not pertain to theology, should not be solemnly condemned or forbidden to anyone, since in such matters everyone should be free to say freely whatever he pleases.'[8] Without the major developments of natural philosophy in the thirteenth and fourteenth centuries, without the great emphasis on reason and analysis, without the university as an institution, and without a host of important questions first raised in the late Middle Ages, we might yet be awaiting the arrival of Galileo and Newton.

### Notes

1 The three articles below are drawn from Edward Grant, *A Source Book in Medieval Science* (Cambridge, MA: Harvard University Press, 1974), pp. 48–9.
2 *Ibid.*, pp. 49–50.
3 Anton C. Pegis (ed.), *Introduction to Saint Thomas Aquinas* (New York: Modern Library, 1948), p. 6.
4 See Edward Grant, *Science and Religion 400 B.C.–A.D. 1550: From Aristotle to Copernicus* (Westport: Greenwood Press, 2004), pp. 194–5.
5 *Questions on Aristotle's On the Heavens*, I, q. 20, in Grant, *Science and Religion*, p. 195.
6 The translation appears in Edward Grant, *Much Ado About Nothing: Theories of Space and Vacuum from the Middle Ages to the Scientific Revolution* (Cambridge University Press, 1981), p. 351, n. 130.
7 For Bacon's remark, see Edward Grant, *A History of Natural Philosophy* (Cambridge University Press: 2007), p. 305 and nn. 87–8.
8 Translated by M. M. McLaughlin, *Intellectual Freedom and Its Limitations in the University of Paris in the Thirteenth and Fourteenth Centuries* (New York: Arno Press, 1977), p. 96.

CHAPTER 12

# *Medicine*

## Michael R. McVaugh

In 1293 the Venetian councillors drew up a contract that they hoped would allow them to acquire the services of the famous Bolognese medical master Taddeo Alderotti (1223–95). They agreed to pay him 47 *lire di grossi* annually (an exceptionally large sum, surely the result of his academic distinction) if he would move to their city, although they imposed a few conditions on him: he could leave the city for only ten days a year without the permission of the council; he would bring with him two assistants who would serve the poor for free; he would be allowed to charge no more than 10 *soldi di grossi* for treating any illness except an abscessed liver, arthritis, leprosy, or dropsy; he would give free medical advice to Venetian nobles who sought him out at his home; and if an epidemic broke out in the city, he would publish information to the citizenry as to how to protect themselves from it. Taddeo seems to have decided against the move, dying in Bologna two years later.

Fourteen years later, in late 1307, the citizens of Castelló d'Empúries, a town of perhaps 3,000 people on the Mediterranean coast 90 miles north of Barcelona, decided that they wanted their former physician, Bernat de Berriac (d. after 1343), to return to care for them. Bernat was a student in the prestigious medical faculty at Montpellier who had taken time off to practise medicine in that Catalan town from 1303 to 1305 before leaving for another post at Vic, in the hills to the southwest; now Castelló was willing to make him a generous offer if he would come back, and in November Bernat signed a contract with the town. The consuls agreed that if he would make his residence in Castelló, they would pay him 300 sous every year in return for his promise to examine without charge the urines of everyone who came to him and to advise them generally on bloodletting, diet, and other features of a healthy regimen; but he was not obliged to visit the sick in their homes. He was not to leave Castelló without their permission, except that he was explicitly allowed to take three winters off, from All Saints' Day until Sexagesima (roughly November to

March), in order to return to Montpellier to complete his studies for the master's degree. On the same day that the contract with the town was signed, nine citizens of Castelló entered into individual contracts with Bernat: for yearly sums ranging from 10 to 20 sous, he promised to treat them and anyone in their household, as well as he could, for any illnesses requiring the art of medicine. Over the next 6 months, more than a dozen others entered into similar contracts with him, so that he could expect an income of nearly 800 sous a year. By November 1309 Bernat had been able to finish his studies, had become *magister in medicina* – and had deserted Castelló again, this time for the capital, Barcelona. Within a few years more he had passed into the service of the kings of Mallorca.

These brief vignettes can serve to introduce a number of themes that characterize medicine in the western Mediterranean world – northern Italy, southern France, Catalonia – around the beginning of the fourteenth century. A growing appreciation of academic medical learning was setting in motion a general process that we can think of as 'medicalization' in something of its contemporary sense, a process that led not only to increasing numbers of medical practitioners with some claim to academic learning in the subject, but to a social willingness to concede that the expertise of such physicians entitled them to exert authority over matters that had previously been left to individual decision or to municipal decree. At the heart of this movement was the recovery of the writings of Galen (129–*c.*216). Many of these had already been translated from Arabic or Greek in the twelfth century, but after 1250 they began to enjoy enormous intellectual prestige in the new European medical schools, largely supplanting as an object of study the literature of the school of Salerno, which had been the great creation of the previous century. There were already a few academic faculties of medicine established in the early 1200s – in Paris, Montpellier, Bologna, and Padua – but the reputation of their individual teachers (and students) began to grow only at the end of the century. One of Montpellier's leading figures was Bernard Gordon (d. after 1308), with whom Bernat de Berriac could have studied; his great *Lilium medicine* (Lily of Medicine), a survey arranged literally from head to toe, spread a general understanding of Galenic theory and practice throughout Europe. At Bologna, the greatest figure, Taddeo Alderotti, was Venice's target as their civic physician. He introduced a curriculum of Hippocratic and Galenic learning studied against an appreciation of Aristotelian natural philosophy, and his students continued this tradition in the next generation at Siena and at Paris, as well as at Bologna. At Padua, Pietro d'Abano (*c.*1257–*c.*1316) placed even more emphasis on the integration of medical with philosophical (and astrological) learning.

In 1300 there were still relatively few students of academic medicine, however. It was only just beginning to appear that medical study might be a route to a career, so that these schools may have had as few as a dozen students at any one time, at different levels in their course of study. Study was expensive, and most students, like Bernat, found it convenient to break the course of their studies so as to earn money from practice; the case of Castelló shows that while Mediterranean towns may have dreamed of having a *magister de medicina* in their employ, they were quite willing to bid for the services of someone who had had only a few years of training and could only claim the title of *baccalarius in medicina* (bachelor in medicine) – if that. Full-fledged graduates gravitated towards the wealthiest patrons and the biggest cities: Bernard Gordon's more famous colleague at Montpellier, Arnau de Vilanova (c.1238–1311), was called on insistently by Jaume II of Aragon (1267–1327) and Popes Boniface VIII (b. c.1235; papacy 1294–1303) and Clement V (b. c.1264; papacy 1305–14).

Cities and towns concerned for the public health were themselves becoming important employers of physicians and surgeons. Already in the early thirteenth century there is evidence of municipal doctors, *medici condotti*, contracting with the towns of northern Italy, renewing a classical tradition perhaps made known through the revival of Roman law. They are seen first in Bologna and Reggio, then by the century's end in Florence, Siena, and a number of smaller cities. Sometimes cities contracted with more than one practitioner. Venice had already hired a physician when it tried to attract Taddeo; by 1324 it was paying stipends to eleven physicians and seventeen surgeons and had begun to recognize the need to retrench. The much smaller Castelló d'Empúrias and other similar Catalan towns bent on hiring their own physicians are recognizably in this same pattern. What all these Italian or Catalan towns wanted was the constant presence in the town of someone who would give free learned advice on health to their citizens, and who would be available to offer knowledgeable treatment in case of illness – for a further sum beyond his civic salary, to be sure, but towns typically tried to regulate physicians' fees and to ensure that the poor would be treated without charge. Venice expected Taddeo to provide free treatment to the poor through his assistants; Milan in 1320 insisted that its civic physicians themselves treat the poor without charge.

At the level of individual patients, what was attractive about Galenic medical learning was the promise it held of giving them rational assurance about their health, whether they were healthy or ill; if they were healthy, how to stay that way, and if they were ill, what illness they had and what was causing it, what could be done about it, and how it would turn out. When Bernat de Berriac agreed to inspect the urines of Castelló's citizens free of charge, he was in effect promising to provide them with diagnoses of their state of health, for the standard medical texts explained in detail how the colour and substance of urine reflected the physiological and pathological processes going on within the body. If they were healthy, they hoped to stay that way, and here is where the rest of Bernat's responsibilities fell, in advising the citizenry about bloodletting, diet, and regimen generally: how to govern what learned medicine called the 'non-naturals' – air, food, sleep, exercise, excretions, and the emotions, sometimes including bathing and coitus too – so as to maintain the body in the state of balance or temperacy that corresponded to health. Physicians were much more confident in the preservation of health through regimen than in the correction of illness by medicines.

By the early fourteenth century academic physicians were not just privately advising their patients on regimen, they were beginning to write in a new genre, that of the *regimen sanitatis* (regimen of health). Such works might still be written for a particular patient, but they achieved an enormous popularity among the middle and upper levels of society, and physicians certainly responded to this interest. They laid out rules for maintaining one's health that were easy to follow and that anyone could adapt to their own condition. The *Regimen* that Arnau de Vilanova prepared around 1307 for Jaume II of Aragon, which touched on all the 'non-naturals', but like many similar *regimina* gave special attention to diet, survives today in more than seventy copies and was almost immediately translated into Catalan and Hebrew.

Inevitably, as this learned medical doctrine filtered down to the general public, the outer world became, not a neutral environment for life, but one loaded with implications for health. Categorized as 'non-naturals', the air we breathe, the food we eat, the exercise we take were increasingly perceived as having medical consequences – all of them were indeed becoming, in the modern sense of the word, 'medicalized'. Air that was perceived as heavy or stale was not just unpleasant, it was bad for the health; eating fruits of different kinds together might be pleasant, but harmed the digestion; and so forth. It was dangerous to live, thoughtlessly, an unexamined life. We find the same medicalization beginning to affect the spas or thermal baths that had been a cultural feature of Europe since antiquity. Whereas in earlier times it is not easy to be sure whether they were frequented for reasons of health or pleasure, by the middle of

*Medicine* 193

the fourteenth century hot springs were above all a medical agent, just like foodstuffs: physicians began to recommend them to their patients, and their treatises on the subject were rapidly translated into the vernacular. One might soak pleasantly in the Abano baths near Padua, but one now knew from Paduan physicians exactly how long to do so in order to make the most of their medicinal effect. There was a growing unconscious acceptance that learned medicine would be the best judge of what was healthy, and the most trustworthy authority on such matters.

As a natural counterpart, physicians were also being conceded a growing authority over illness: who is ill, and with what? To some extent of course they had always had this authority to pronounce on disease, but lay society had long kept leprosy in a separate category because it mattered so much. Its biblical overtones of sinfulness, the hideousness of its disfiguring progress, its perceived contagiousness, had made it a general danger that local communities had diagnosed for themselves, acting on public denunciations to identify and expel or shut away the leprous. Beginning in the second half of the thirteenth century, however, on both sides of the Tyrrhenian Sea, we find the courts responsible for judging leprosy beginning to make use of physicians in coming to their decision, whether asking them merely to offer their opinion (as in Castiglione del Lago, 1261) or swearing to a diagnosis under oath (Pistoia, 1288). Naturally it was not long before suspected lepers began to ask for a medical opinion as soon as they were accused. In 1333 a citizen of Vic was denounced as a leper before the vicar's court there, appealed to medical opinion, and was straightway examined by the episcopal physician, a *baccalarius in medicina*, who pronounced him free of the disease and therefore incapable of communicating it to anyone. The judge thereupon freed the accused, making it explicit that the conclusions of learned medicine had to override the opinions and fears of lay society: as he declared, 'a physician is to be believed as regards his art'.[1] Very much the same principle had been expressed in 1324 in a very different context, in the *Defensor pacis* (Defender of Peace) by Marsilio of Padua (1275/80–1342/43): there, in effect, Marsilio drew an analogy between the acknowledged authority of physicians to determine whether a diseased person had leprosy, and therefore needed to be separated from the community, and the authority of the priesthood to excommunicate an individual because of a 'disease of the soul'. Behind both these statements we can see the tacit acceptance that medical learning now conveys an authority over certain aspects of human life that, in its restricted realm, is as much to be respected as canon or civil law is in its wider application.

194 Michael R. McVaugh

The inhabitants of Castelló d'Empúries who contracted individually with Bernat de Berriac were not content with the advice on regimen and the determination of their state of health or illness that came to them gratis as citizens of the town; they believed that, in case they became ill, an academically trained physician could bring his learning to bear and could hope to cure them. What sort of tools could such a physician deploy? These fell into three groups, listed by Galen in order of increasing riskiness: diet, drugs, and surgery. Manipulation of a patient's diet was the safest course, really no more than an extension of the principles used to structure a healthful regimen, but the other two raised difficult problems. A vast pharmacological literature from Greek and Arabic sources laid out the expected physiological and medical properties of individual drugs, as well as other drugs compounded from simple ingredients, but their effects often proved unpredictable in an individual case, so that what was supposed to be a mild purge might end up killing the patient, and the giving of medicines thus had to be approached with great circumspection. Surgery was even more dangerous; the only invasive procedures that were normally practised were for cataract and hernia, and practitioners tried to talk their patients out of such operations. Nevertheless, patients hoped – indeed, expected – that their physician could do something to heal them, and physicians agreed that in principle they should be able to, if the unexpected did not occur.

Our best guides to how physicians approached the treatment of a patient are the written *consilia* that begin to appear late in the thirteenth century: among the first are those of Taddeo Alderotti and of his student, Guglielmo da Brescia (d. 1326), who moved from medicine into minor orders and ended as chaplain and medical advisor to the popes at Rome and Avignon, from Boniface VIII to John XXII (b. 1244; papacy 1316–34). These early examples already manifest the traits that will become more formalized later in the Middle Ages. An idealized *consilium* addresses the case of an individual patient that the author himself has undertaken, or that has been communicated to him by a colleague asking for his advice and amounting in effect to a consultation. It begins with a brief summary of the patient's history and condition, proceeds to lay out the regime he should follow in his illness (usually with special emphasis on diet), and concludes with an account of the medicines that the physician recommends for use in the particular case. Such *consilia* were often collected and reworked for publication by their authors – they could even turn into mini-treatises on a particular disease – and no doubt were a kind of self-promotion; but even so, they show us something of a physician's

*Medicine* 195

unmediated response to a real patient: open appeals to scholastic authority are comparatively scarce.

For reasons that have already been suggested, surgical treatment is not often mentioned in a physician's *consilia*. Yet though it was an approach of last resort, it was a highly developed subject. A particularly rich tradition of surgical writing had evolved in northern Italy in the later thirteenth century, one that had culminated in the great texts of Teodorico Borgognoni (d. 1298) and Lanfranc of Milan (d. after 1296). It was a tradition that gradually succeeded in fusing the practical knowledge of empiric surgeons with the somewhat abstract surveys of the subject presented in the works of Galen and Avicenna (Ibn Sina, *c*.980–*c*.1037), and as a result it elevated surgery to the level of a quasi-learned discipline, so that by the early fourteenth century many academic physicians were quite willing to believe that the new surgical writing might have something to contribute to their own practice. Teodorico's book was perhaps the most influential. He had observed the surgical practice of his father, Ugo da Lucca (d. after 1258), and his observations had directed his own surgical practice in Bologna, which he managed to combine with his membership in the Dominican order, and finally his position as (non-resident) bishop first of Bitonto and then of Cervia. Between the 1240s and the 1270s he produced four recensions of a broad handbook of general surgery that continually incorporated new diseases and new therapies into its plan. Surgery did not just concern itself with invasive procedures, of course; its principal focus was on illness as manifest on the surface of the body, on rashes, sores, ulcers, and swellings, and Teodorico was among the first surgeons to lay special emphasis on new chemical remedies to treat them. One indication of his influence is Taddeo Alderotti's adoption, in a *consilium* for a scrophulous patient, of a recipe from Teodorico's *Surgery* for that condition. Another is that work's rapid translation into vernacular languages – it had already been translated into Catalan by 1303, and partial translations are also known in Spanish, Italian, French, German, English, and Hebrew.

Teodorico Borgognoni the bishop and Guglielmo da Brescia the chaplain exemplify the diminishing clerical element in medicine in the years around 1300. This was not because of increased ecclesiastical restrictions on clerical involvement in medical study and practice, for canon law became if anything more tolerant of such involvement during the thirteenth century; rather, it seems to have been a consequence of the growing availability of secular physicians and surgeons. These were sometimes university-trained individuals, but more often they were not, for while at the beginning of the fourteenth century many communities and individuals were arriving at an ideal of the medical practitioner as someone possessing a degree of academic training, it was not an entirely practicable ideal. Surgeons such as Lanfranc ambitiously tried to associate themselves with the world of medical learning, and wrote contemptuously of the illiterate *vulgi* who claimed to be surgeons but lacked the necessary foundations to be competent; nevertheless, empiric *cirurgici* (surgeons) and self-professed *medici* (doctors), self-educated or taught by their parents, still made up by far the majority of medical practitioners – though they might try to impress their patients by imitating the language of the science they did not possess.

There was thus a kind of tension between the goals of municipal authorities and practical reality. Perhaps an academic training was *ipso facto* proof of a physician's competence to practise, but in a society where there were not enough such physicians to meet the needs of the public, should everyone else be allowed to offer healthcare without restriction? Increasingly, towns were saying 'no' to this: they were beginning to introduce measures of at least nominal control over medical practice through what amounted to licensing provisions. Initially it was often municipal government that took responsibility for testing the learning of potential practitioners. In 1299 and again in 1319, for example, the Catalan town of Valls declared that its council would judge who had mastered the *scientia de medicina*, and that only by passing such an examination would someone be permitted to practise; Cervera, near Lleida, had enacted something very similar in 1291. But in the bigger cities where there was already a pool of competent physicians, this responsibility could be given to physicians. In Valencia in 1329 the king ordained that two leading physicians of the city were to examine all who wanted to practise medicine there, and to give them permission to do so only if they were found competent *and* had studied medicine in a university for at least four years. In Venice it was the Maggior Consiglio (Major Council) that ordained, in 1321, that either a medical degree or an examination would be required for a would-be practitioner. In Florence, where a strong guild structure existed, it was the broadly based guild of 'Doctors, Apothecaries, and Grocers' (Dante himself was a member) that initiated comparable regulation. Its first surviving statute (of 1314) laid it down that no one who was not already an academic medical master would be admitted to practise medicine or surgery in the city without having first been examined by the guild's six consuls (only two of whom were physicians) in company with four mendicant friars; by 1349 the friars had disappeared from the examining board, which was now composed exclusively of physicians.

How far such rules could be enforced is of course another issue. But the practical difficulties of enforcement cannot prevent us from recognizing here a movement towards what we can identify as an emerging medical profession, in the sense of a group of practitioners empowered by society to control admission to that group, and to base that admission on the possession of specialized technical knowledge and ability as defined by the group. What it meant to be a (competent) physician had originally rested on the judgement of clients or of public authority; now the decision, and the authority, were being turned over to physicians themselves – another instance of the spreading medicalization of Mediterranean society.

A further instance of this medicalization, of the concession of social authority to medical authority, is again observable on both sides of the Tyrrhenian Sea in the years around 1300; this time it involves forensic judgement. From the second half of the thirteenth century, in cities and towns all around the western Mediterranean, physicians and surgeons were beginning to be called on to supply various types of information to public authority. In Venice, for example, physicians were expected as early as 1281 to report all wounds to authorities, and in the case of murders they were required to report the cause of death. In Catalonia and Provence, as well as northern Italy, they were regularly called on to provide expert testimony before a court, summoned by varying parties, all of whom clearly shared a belief in the power and authority of medical knowledge. In a case of homicide their judgement might be requested by a magistrate, for example, as to whose blow actually killed the victim. In a case of assault they might be summoned by the accused to testify that the victim should recover, since in that case, if the victim were later to die, it would be presumed that not the attacker but his own failure to protect his health, his faulty regimen, had killed him. Often several practitioners would share in a judgement; they would study the body or examine the victim, sometimes several times, describe their observations and prognoses, and swear to their conclusions before a notary. It is probably no coincidence that such post-mortem examinations, which could include dissection, were soon followed by formal anatomies introduced into medical and surgical education, perhaps first of all at Bologna: in 1316 one of that school's masters, Mondino de' Liuzzi (d. 1326; another student of Taddeo's), completed a written *Anatomia* (Anatomy) that was designed to accompany such an exercise and that had a long popularity.

It was not just any self-identified healer who could act in this legal capacity, however. In Bologna, by the statutes of 1288, the medical examiners were to be chosen by lot from practitioners established in the city for at least ten years, which naturally included many of its most famous academics; the earliest formal forensic report surviving there (1302) has as one of its two signatories Bartolomeo da Varignano (d. after 1321), once a student of Taddeo Alderotti and one of the leading figures in the medical faculty. In Valencia, a licence to practice might be qualified to prevent the licensee from giving his opinion to the court except when accompanied by someone 'fit and sufficient'. Some level of expertise was demanded to establish a practitioner as *probatus* or *expertus* (expert), at least in the larger towns where a spectrum of experience existed, but once so established, his formal judgement was taken as an authoritative fact that overrode the self-interested claims of the lay opponents in a suit, and that thus suited the court very well. It is perhaps no wonder that the incorporation of the new learned medicine into cases at law occurred so early and so generally across Mediterranean Europe.

This establishment of medical authority in the law courts should remind us of the medical judgements just beginning to govern popular accusations of leprosy, and indeed even of the assessments and advice being laid down for patients in the new *consilia*, for they are all of a piece. In a variety of contexts within this evolving society at the turn of the fourteenth century, physicians and surgeons are no longer merely the traditional agents of therapy; they are coming to have the authority to decide for society which individuals are to be treated as ill and which as healthy, what is normal and what is abnormal, with all the consequences that such decisions can have for social institutions and for public policy, as well as for individual behaviour. A final vignette can offer a particularly pointed example of such implications. About 1330 the famous jurist Cino da Pistoia (1270–1336/37) was asked to decide on the legitimacy of a seven-month-old baby; the putative father insisted that it could not be his, and that it must be his brother's child born at full term. Thereupon Cino formally consulted Gentile da Foligno (d. 1348), then a medical master at Siena, to learn whether a seven-month pregnancy was in fact a possibility. Gentile wrote back to Cino that it was indeed possible, basing his carefully reasoned conclusion on a close analysis of not only Hippocratic and Avicennan but Aristotelian texts, and he underlined the new authority of physicians when he summed up with the words, 'when lawyers debate such a matter, let them trust to expert physicians'.[2] We will remember that at almost exactly the same moment, a judge across the sea in Catalonia was acknowledging essentially the same authority in medicine: 'a physician is to be believed as regards his art'.

## Notes

1 M. R. McVaugh, *Medicine before the Plague: Practitioners and their Patients in the Crown of Aragon, 1285–1345* (Cambridge University Press, 1993), p. 221.

2 H. U. Kantorowicz, 'Cino da Pistoia ed il primo trattato di medicina legale', *Archivio storico italiano*, 37 (1906), 115–28 (p. 128).

CHAPTER 13

# Islamic and Jewish influences

### Luis M. Girón Negrón

Muslims and Jews loomed large in Dante's Italy between 1250 and 1350. It is possible, indeed, to speak of Jewish and Islamic traditions visibly present in late medieval Italian culture and to which Dante's literary *oeuvre* offers a significant witness. However, *Jewish* and *Islamic* are equivocal terms, as they denote not only two religious traditions, but also their cultural heritage. Any effort to ascertain what these religions meant to Dante's contemporaries must thus reckon both with their limited, mostly distorted theological understanding of Muslim and Jewish religiosity as living traditions of faith, and with their mediated textual access to the cultural archives of Islamic and Jewish intellectual life. This chapter aims at such a dual reconnaissance of Judaism and Islam in the Italo-Christian Middle Ages, with selective recourse to Dante's works as a privileged historical source.

Of course, it is not easy even to establish direct cross-cultural exchanges between Muslims, Christians, and Jews in late medieval Italy. No unequivocal evidence has been found, for example, of specific Muslims or Jews among Dante's known acquaintances, nor other direct contacts that could have inflected his personal views on their faith and culture. However, such personal contacts were more than just a possibility for an Italian Christian in Dante's time. Jews in Italy between the late thirteenth century and the early fourteenth century were concentrated in Sicily and the peninsular south (Apulia, Campania), but there were smaller clusters of Jewish families in Dante's Tuscany (Pisa, Lucca), a larger Jewish community in Rome, and, most relevant, a significant centre of Italo-Jewish intellectual life in Verona at the time of Dante's two visits as a political exile, first at the court of Bartolomeo della Scala (d. 1304) in 1303–04 and later, for a lengthier sojourn from 1312–18 under the patronage of Cangrande della Scala (1291–1329). Dante's putative friendship with the Hebrew poet Immanuel ben Solomon of Rome ('Manoello Giudeo', *c.*1261–*c.*1335), posited by nineteenth-century scholars, has been mostly discarded in the

## Islamic and Jewish influences

absence of unimpeachable proof. But Immanuel's genuine admiration for Dante, whom he eulogized in exchanged sonnets with Bosone da Gubbio (between 1260–90 and 1349–77) and whose *Commedia* he also emulated in his *Maḥberet ha-tofet ve-ha-eden* (The Treatise on Hell and Heaven), gave way to the imagined possibility of such an encounter against the historical backdrop of a contemporary Italo-Jewish Renaissance.

Direct encounters with Muslims in Italy were more difficult but, again, not implausible. The last Islamic enclave on Italian soil, a colony of Siculo-Muslim exiles relocated by Frederick II (1194–1250) to Lucera in the first half of the thirteenth century (*Lucera Saracenorum*), was still thriving in Dante's lifetime and only came to an abrupt end with its conquest by Charles II of Anjou (1254–1309) in 1300. Maritime commercial ties also brought Muslim traders to such peninsular ports as Genoa and Venice. Indirect means of contact with the Islamic world also included a number of individuals who could have intersected Dante's social sphere. Dante was six when Edward I of England (1239–1307) launched the last major crusade, and with the fall of Acre to the Egyptian Mamluks in 1291 the last vestiges of Christian rule in the Levant disappeared. However, some of the mendicant friars who embarked on missionary trips across the Middle East came back to Europe with first-hand knowledge of Muslim life and piety. That was the case with Riccoldo da Monte Croce (1242–1320), the Florentine Dominican and author of a widely read polemical treatise against Islam, *Contra legem saracenorum* (Against the Law of the Saracens).

Riccoldo's knowledge of Arabic and Islamic theology was acquired during a lengthy missionary sojourn in the Levant between 1288–89 and 1290–91, including a substantive stay in Baghdad to pursue Quranic studies, which brought him into close contact with Muslims and Arab Christians, as chronicled in both his *Liber peregrinationis* (The Book of Pilgrimage) and his letters on the fall of Acre. Riccoldo's religious life (he became a Dominican friar in 1267 at Santa Maria Novella) overlapped almost fully the entirety of Dante's life. There is no evidence that they met, but it is certainly within the realm of possibility.

Even in the absence of personal contact, the literary archives of the Islamic and Jewish religious and cultural heritage were partly available to Latin Christians of the thirteenth and fourteenth centuries as potential correctives against the ahistorical caricatures that defined Muslims and Jews in the premodern Christian imagination. Muslims had forged a brilliant civilization in Arabic – the sacred language of the Qur'ān – with both a rich literature in the Islamic religious sciences and virtuosic contributions to most evolving fields of medieval secular learning. Rabbinic

Jews also had their own classical religious literature in both Hebrew and Aramaic, while also steeped in the Arabo-Islamic civilizational heritage, whose archives they engrossed with their own towering achievements in Hebrew and Judaeo-Arabic (Arabic was the spoken and cultural *lingua franca* of most Jews anywhere around the Mediterranean basin between the ninth and the thirteenth centuries). Moreover, the sundry contributions of Muslims and Jews to every sphere of premodern science, culture, and thought – for example philosophy, medicine, jurisprudence, belles-lettres, historiography, astronomy/astrology, mathematics, music, rhetoric, architecture, philology, mysticism (Sufism and Kabbalah), and the religious sciences – played a formative role in selected domains of European intellectual history through both Latin and vernacular translations – mainly from Arabic – of their voluminous written record.

The centrality of these translations to gauge Dante's views on – and possible debts to – Islamic and Jewish traditions cannot be exaggerated. Dante knew neither Hebrew nor Arabic. He had no unmediated access to the classical religious texts or scientific and literary corpora of Muslims and Jews in either language. The few Hebraisms in the *Commedia* are all Latinate forms of Biblical Hebrew terms known from the Vulgate, liturgical usage, or other Christian theological sources (e.g. *Hosanna, sabaoth* (Heb. *tsevaʾot*, 'hosts') and *malacóth* (corrupted form of Jerome's *mamlacoth*, from the Heb. *mamlakhot* 'kingdoms') in Justinian's hymn, *Par.* VII, 1–3). The somewhat larger sample of Arabisms in Dante's work is on a par with the encyclopaedic range of his vernacular register. They are mostly reflective of Italian's broader lexicographic debts to particular domains of European life and culture where Arabo-Islamic civilization made singular contributions (e.g. scientific lexica from astronomy, chemistry, and mathematics, luxury items bought through trade, Eastern games, and other forms of entertainment, etc.), although some of his Arabic loanwords are suggestively deployed in significant contexts, such as the red gleaming *meschite* (*Inf.* VIII, 70, 'mosques') in the infernal city of Dis (the only Arabism in the *Commedia* referring to a concrete feature of Islamic religious life, from the Arabic etymon *masjid* via Spanish) or Muhammad's graphic depiction of the running throng of fellow schismatics as a *risma* (*Inf.* XXVIII, 38, 'heap' from the Arabic *rizma*).

However, Italian Christians in Dante's time were also the potential beneficiaries of translation and other multicultural efforts in two cultural contact zones between Muslims, Christians, and Jews in medieval Europe: Sicily and the Iberian Peninsula. Sicily was under Muslim rule for almost two centuries (tenth and eleventh), whereas the political history of

## Islamic and Jewish influences

Islamic rule in parts of the Iberian Peninsula spanned almost eight hundred years (711–1492). The Arabo-Islamic cultural legacy still reverberated in both regions by Dante's lifetime when all of Sicily and most of Spain were already under Christian rule. A year after Dante's birth, the active patronage in Christian Sicily of cross-cultural exchanges with Muslims and Jews, both under Norman (1091–1194) and Hohenstaufen rule (1198–1266), and especially in the Palermitan courts of Roger II (1095–1154) and Frederick II, had practically come to an end with the demise of Manfred (1232–66), the last Hohenstaufen king and Frederick's natural son (although the Angevin rulers would continue supporting Jewish translators at the Palermitan court, especially the dynasty's founder Charles I (1226–85) until his ouster from Sicily in 1282, and Robert of Anjou (1309–43) as King of Naples). Some of the fruits of these exchanges were reaped by the poet himself from the translation corpus. Dante's falcon imagery and symbolism, with such precise references to game-hawking techniques as the *ciliatio* (sewing shut) of the envious' eyelids in *Purgatorio* XIII, or the binding knot that kept Bonagiunta and fellow poets away from the 'sweet new style' in *Paradiso* XXIV, 55–7, for example, have been shown to reflect concrete knowledge of the Islamic arts of falconry introduced into Italian courtly culture by Frederick II's *De arte venandi cum avibus* (On the Art of Falconry). Dante's complex representation of Manfred of Sicily as an *exemplum* of the Christian repentant *in extremis* may also reverberate with indirect echoes of the Siculo-Arabic cultural legacy. A Ghibelline supporter excommunicated by three popes, accused by his detractors of being an 'Epicurean' and even a Saracen (Muslim allies from Lucera fought by his side against the papal armies and at the Battle of Benevento in 1266), Manfred was nonetheless redeemed in Dante's poem as a last-minute penitent in *Purgatorio* III. His reputation as an Islamophile or even a Muslim was perhaps poetically folded by Dante into the analogical juxtaposition of his wounds with Muhammad's cloven breast in *Inferno* XXVIII, whereas Dante's very notion of Manfred's belated repentance may have found support in Manfred's own prologue to the Latin translation of a pseudo-Aristotelian Arabic work now lost (*Kitāb attuffāḥ* (The Book of the Apple)), the *Liber de pomo sive de morte Aristotelis* (The Book of the Apple or of the Death of Aristotle) translated not from the Arabic original, but from a mid-thirteenth-century Hebrew version (*Sefer hatappuaḥ*) by Abraham ibn Hasdai of Barcelona (*fl.* 1230s). Having found spiritual solace in this treatise while at the brink of death from an unspecified illness in 1255, Manfred had it translated into Latin in gratitude for his own conversion and for the benefit of other Christians.

While Sicily was closer geographically, the lion's share of the Arabo-Islamic works that Dante's contemporaries might have known in translation entered the premodern European intellectual mainstream through the westernmost corner of the Islamic world: al-Andalus. Dante's lifetime overlaps the political ascendancy of Christian rule over most of the Iberian Peninsula with the defeat of the Almohads and the fall of every remaining Hispano-Muslim kingdom except for Granada. His adolescence also coincides with the comprehensive efforts of Alfonso X of Castile (1221–84) to build upon the twelfth-century Toledan translation movement by commissioning Castilian versions of Arabo-Andalusian scientific, philosophical, religious, and belletristic works, many of which were, in turn, poured into both Latin and other European vernaculars. European scholar-translators came to Toledo in active pursuit of Arabo-Islamic learning and spearheaded the efforts to disseminate its fruits on their way back across the Pyrenees. Their ranks included the likes of Robert of Ketton (*c.*1100–*c.*1160), Hermann the Carinthian (*c.*1100–*c.*1160), and Gerard of Cremona (*c.*1114–1187) in the twelfth century; Herman Alemannus (d. 1272) and Michael Scotus (1175–1232) a century later (Scotus' literary activity indeed straddled both Spain and Sicily, with his having begun his post-Toledan intellectual trajectory as a court translator for Frederick II).

Dante's indirect ties with the Alfonsine intellectual milieu were varied and significant. It is not clear, for example, whether he was aware of Scotus' sustained interest in Arabo-Islamic civilization when he condemned him to the fourth *bolgia* of the eighth circle as a magician and astrologer (*Inf.* XX, 115–7), but he clearly benefitted, directly or via the scholastics, from Scotus' Latin translations of Averroes' ('Abū l-Walīd Muḥammad bin 'Aḥmad bin Rušd; 1126–98) commentary on Aristotle's *De anima* (On the Soul), the *De substantia orbis* (On the Substance of the Celestial Sphere) also by Averroes, and the seminal *Kitāb fī-l-hayá'a* (The Book on Cosmology) by the late-twelfth-century Andalusian astronomer al-Biṭrūjī (d. 1204; Alpetragius' *De motibus coelorum* (The Movement of the Heavens) in the Latin version that Scotus made in 1217). Dante also had a more personal connection to the Alfonsine world in his teacher Brunetto Latini (*c.*1220–93), who visited the Castilian court in Seville in 1260 as a Florentine ambassador, and whose substantive immersion in Arabo-Andalusian intellectual life deeply marked both his literary output during his French exile (1260–65), as evidenced by *Li livres dou trésor* (The Book of the Treasure), and his cultural activity back in Italy during his final years. The Alfonsine court also played a pivotal role in the

# Islamic and Jewish influences

trans-Pyrenean dissemination of the Muslim eschatological traditions to be discussed at the end of this chapter.

These translated materials of Muslim and Jewish authorship were mostly pressed to service in two directions: polemics and scholarship. Christian polemical efforts to refute the Muslim faith dominated, on the one hand, much active recourse to translations of classical and other religious sources on Islam, such as the Latin versions of the Qur'ān by Robert of Ketton (1143) and Mark of Toledo (1210; *fl.* 1193–1216) – both made in Spain in pre-Alfonsine times, the former at the explicit behest of Peter the Venerable of Cluny (*c.*1092–1156) – and the other Islamic theological and devotional treatises whose translation was also commissioned by the Cluniac abbot during his 1142–43 visit to Spain. These twelfth-century translations jointly comprised, along with Peter's own contributions, the *Corpus Toletanum* (or *Corpus islamolatinum*), the first comprehensive basis for Christian study of Islam in the western Middle Ages. The thirteenth-century compilation of Latin extracts from the Talmud (*Extractiones de Talmud*), made in France but well attested in the Iberian peninsula, also served as a textual resource for mendicant preachers and scholastic theologians intent upon polemical disputations with – and the active conversion of – European Jews, building upon the new style of Christian–Jewish controversies anticipated in the *Dialogi contra iudaeos* (Dialogues Against the Jews) by Petrus Alfonsi (eleventh–twelfth centuries), the famous Hispano-Jewish convert to Christianity (his *Dialogi*, it should be noted, also had a chapter on Islam that was deeply influential in Christian anti-Muslim polemics, as illustrated by the abridged version that Vincent of Beauvais (*c.*1190–*c.*1264) included in his *Speculum historiale* (The Mirror of History), *c.*1250). These Latin translations also supplemented the scholarly missionary efforts of Christian apologists (especially Dominican friars) from the thirteenth and fourteenth centuries, including contemporaries of Dante with primary access to Arabic or Hebrew, who built upon this corpus and brought their own authoritative knowledge of Islamic or Jewish tradition to bear on original polemical and apologetic writings, such as the Catalan Dominican Raymond Martí (d. 1284) and the aforementioned Riccoldo da Monte Croce. On the other hand, as we saw, the translation of Muslim and Jewish works on philosophy and the exact sciences helped to create a foundational basis for the cultivation and development of 'secular' disciplines in late medieval Christian Europe. The Alfonsine cultural initiatives were built, for example, on the active collaboration of Jewish and Christian scholars to capacitate the Castilian vernacular for the systematic translation of the Arabo-Islamic scientific corpus. All of Dante's explicit references to Arabo-Islamic philosophers and astronomers are clearly reflective of an active scholarly engagement with Graeco-Arabic science in Latin translations.

This heuristic distinction between polemical recourse to religious sources and detached scientific interest in non-religious ones is, of course, artificial and limited. Many of the towering philosophers and theologians of the Middle Ages – Christian, Muslim, and Jewish – were actively interested in the secular sciences as part of broader synthetic efforts in their religious thought, the scholastic impetus to harmonize *fides et ratio* (faith and reason) – Dante's *Commedia* is a shimmering example. The Christian engagement with Muslim and Jewish religious traditions in the Middle Ages is not always reducible, on the other hand, to polemical uses of such sources in the literature of religious disputation. Even the Latin translations of the Qur'ān, which were clearly commissioned for anti-Muslim purposes, also reflected a proto-humanist scholarly interest in Arabic philological reading and textual interpretation. Premodern Christian approaches to Judaism and Islam may also reflect genuine intellectual curiosity, perceived affinities in mystical spirituality, or other complex cross-cultural dealings across religious boundaries. This is the case – to name just one figure whose long life almost fully subsumes Dante's – with the Majorcan Franciscan Ramon Llull (*c*.1232–*c*.1315/16). The Arabic-speaking Christian philosopher and Catalan writer parted ways with the militant tenor of his Dominican contemporaries in his own efforts to convert Muslims, not only adopting a more conciliatory tone in his missiological writings (e.g. his *Libre del gentil e los tres savis* (The Book of the Gentile and the Three Sages) originally written in Arabic or the *Liber de participatione Christianorum et Saracenorum* (Book of Participation between Christians and Saracens), written shortly before his 1313 trip to Sicily drawn by Frederick III's (1272–1337) reputation), but also incorporating with syncretistic abandon Jewish and Muslim religious traditions into his own philosophical *Weltanschauung* (e.g. the kabbalistic materials in the *ars luliana* or the *paraules d'amor e exemplis abreujats* (love sayings and brief exempla) explicitly derived from Sufi love mysticism in the *Llibre d'Amic e Amat* (Book of the Lover and the Beloved), the most famous section of his prose narrative *Blanquerna*). The question now remains: where to place the encounters of Dante and his fellow Christians with both the religious and 'secular' traditions of Judaism and Islam within a spectrum of possibilities that could include the conciliatory syncretism of a young Llull and the more targeted conversionary efforts of the Dominican polemists?

*Islamic and Jewish influences* 207

So let us go back to our initial queries. How are Islam and Judaism understood by most Christian theologians among Dante's contemporaries? Not, of course, as world-religions proper in the post-nineteenth-century sense famously dissembled by Wilfred Cantwell Smith in his 1962 classic *The Meaning and End of Religion*.[1] Islam and Judaism rather loomed in thirteenth-century Christian apologetics as two monotheistic religious laws separate from Christianity, each in a distinctive way, yet theologically redefined in tandem with respect to the Church's faith partly by their adherents' overlapping advocacy of Christological heresies. The Church's self-image as the new Israel and its supersessionistic repudiation of biblical Judaism (namely the abrogation of Mosaic law with the new covenant of Christ) were foundational themes of the early Christian *Heilsgeschichte*. Islam, on the other hand, had emerged six centuries later as a genuine theological enigma for early medieval Christianity. Jews and Christians shared a scriptural heritage, and the former played a formative role in the theological self-understanding of the latter, whereas Muslims did not have a scriptural common ground with Christians, nor were they entwined with the historical formation of a Christian religious identity. Nonetheless, Christian polemical literature in the late Middle Ages often targeted its constructed images of Muslims and Jews with comparable arguments and disputational strategies over their shared repudiation of Christian belief in the Trinity and the Incarnation.

Dante at times also mentions jointly *Giudei* and *Saracini*, not on theological grounds, but either as non-Christian vehicles to cast in relief the corrupt Christian targets of his moral denunciation (*Inf.* XXVII, 85–7; *Ep.* XI, 4), or else to showcase the universal outreach of autonomous philosophical verities (*Conv.* II, viii, 9). However, the poetic representations – or lack thereof – of Jews and Muslims as distinct religious entities impose limitations on what one can gauge about Dante's theological views on their respective faiths.

On the one hand, although Dante consistently distinguishes between the *Giudei/Iudei* from Jesus' time to his own and the biblical *Ebrei/ Hebraeos* of ancient Israel, there are no Rabbinic Jews depicted in Dante's *Commedia* against whom to probe his theological understanding of post-biblical Judaism. There are no overt disparaging allusions to Jews in Dante's *oeuvre*; no caricatures of the satanic Jew, laced with the stock platitudes of the *adversus Judaeos* (against the Jews) tradition, anywhere in the *Commedia*. There is a single reference to Jewish contentment at Jesus' death ('From one act, therefore, came diverse effects, for the same death was pleasing both to God and to the Jews': *Par.* VII, 46–7; but see also

*Par.* VI, 92–3), and a more complex invitation to Christians in Beatrice's lips not to yield to greed and make themselves susceptible to derision by the Jews (*Par.* V, 79–81). There is another suggestive reference to the solar eclipse at the crucifixion and how it concealed the light of the sun (also a figure for Christ) to the Spaniards and the Indians as well as to the Jews (*Par.* XXIX, 101–2). But no Jews are condemned as usurers to the seventh circle of Hell, nor are there any Jewish damned among the flatterers, hypocrites, fraudulent counsellors, and thieves in the pouches of Malebolge, a few of the more tenacious anti-Jewish types in the medieval Christian imagination.

By Dante's time, the insidious ahistorical caricature of Jews as recalcitrant Christ-killers, ever blind to the fulfilment of their Messianic hopes and stubbornly attached to Mosaic Law, was undergoing a substantive change with the Christian rediscovery of Rabbinic literature as the foundation of post-biblical Jewish observance and its scholastic redeployment in Christian anti-Jewish polemics in the twelfth and thirteenth centuries. The ripple effects of the first public burnings of the Talmud in 1240 Paris spread through Italy in the second half of the thirteenth century, as manifested in both an increase of conversionary pressure through forced sermons – for example Lombardy (1274) – and such paroxysms of anti-Jewish violence as the brutal decimation of the Jews of Trani under Angevin rule in the immediate aftermath of Charles II's blood libel. However, none of these developments in premodern Christian attitudes to Judaism left a single textual trace in Dante's literary *oeuvre*. A conspicuous absence of any avowed sympathies for such anti-Jewish caricatures seems to have facilitated the sophisticated appreciation of Dante's literary genius across religious borders professed by such late medieval Italo-Jewish encomiasts of his work as the aforementioned Immanuel of Rome in his *Ha-tofet ve-ha-eden* (Hell and Heaven) and in his sonnets, the fourteenth-century Judah ben Moses ben Daniel Roman (who produced a Judaeo-Italian version with Hebrew commentary of selected philosophical excursus from *Purgatorio* and *Paradiso*), the late-thirteenth-century Ahitub ben Isaac of Palermo (who composed his own allegorical journey to Paradise, *Maḥberet ha-ṭene* (The Basket)), and Moses ben Isaac Rieti (who died after 1460 and whose *Miqdash meʿaṭ* (The Little Sanctuary) also emulates Dante's *Paradiso*).

Western Christian responses to Islam, on the other hand, evolved largely from its early perception as a polemical caricature of pagan idolatry and barbaric practices into a theological target of apologetic engagement as a Christological heresy comparable to Arianism by Dante's time.

*Islamic and Jewish influences*                                         209

The polemical backdrop to such a theological construal of Islam, compounded by the broader sociopolitical context of the crusades' legacy in Italy, sharpened Dante's scattered, mostly negative but more complex allusions to Islam as a political force and a schismatic movement with a distinctive religious profile within Christian heresiology. The early medieval characterization of Muslims as pagans popularized in early crusader chronicles and Carolingian epic has no place in Dante's universe. None of his *Saracini* – his favoured term for Muslims – ever appear professing an idolatrous cult to a pagan parody of the Trinity as portrayed, most famously, in the *Chanson de Roland* (Song of Roland); indeed, the only Saracen character from the Old French *chansons de geste* who finds his way into the *Commedia* is the giant Renouard from the epic cycle on Guillaume d'Orange, celebrated in *Par.* XVIII, 46 precisely as a Christian convert. There are a few other sideline references to Saracens (e.g. Forese Donati's denunciation of the immodesty of Florentine *donne* compared to Muslim women in *Purgatorio* XXIII, 103–5, and Dante's singling out of Italy as an object of commiseration even in the eyes of Muslims in *Epistole* V, 5). St Francis' preaching in Damietta 'in the proud presence of the Sultan' – namely, in the presence of the Ayyūbid Sultan al-Malik al-Kāmil (1180–1238) in 1219 – is echoed in Aquinas' paean in *Paradiso* XI, 101–5, who interprets it as an expression of both Francis' thirst for martyrdom and fruitless effort at converting Muslims. Dante at the same time allows his great-great grandfather Cacciaguida (*c.*1091–*c.*1148), who had died fighting Muslim forces in the Holy Land during the Second Crusade, to decry with unmitigated disgust the religious law of 'that foul race', a schismatic antagonist whose very existence is fully blamed upon the Church's profound failings (*Par.* XV, 142–8). Cacciaguida's exaltation among the blessed in the heavenly company of other military heroes is predicated on his very martyrdom to the crusader cause against Muslim forces ('and came from martyrdom to this peace').

There are, moreover, five Muslim characters in Dante's *Commedia*. They are all placed in *Inferno* (cantos IV and XXVIII), but with a significant contrast in their posthumous fates, mostly also reflective of contrasting attitudes to Islamic religiosity versus Arabo-Islamic culture. The first three are strikingly depicted among his emblematic figures of the noble pagan, objects of admiration for their intellectual attainments or moral stature, yet inevitably confined to the benign punishment of the virtuous non-Christian souls in Limbo. A single tercet (*Inf.* IV, 142–4), closing off the roster of philosophers that look up to Aristotle, brings together two intellectual giants from the Islamic world: Avicenna (Abū ʿAlī al-Ḥusayn ibn 'Abd Allāh ibn Sīnā; c.980–1037), the Persian Muslim philosopher and scientist whom Dante honours here, along with Hippocrates and Galen, as a medical authority (a reputation based on Gerard of Cremona's twelfth-century translation of his *Qanūn fi-l-ṭibb*, the *Canon medicinae*); and Averroes, the towering Cordovan philosopher and jurist to whom Dante pays tribute in his repercussive role as the most revered commentator of the Aristotelian corpus in the Middle Ages ('Averroes, him who made the great Commentary', *Inf.* IV, 144). The Muslim roster in Limbo is completed with Saladin (1138–93, Ṣalāḥ ad-Dīn), the first Ayyūbid sultan of Egypt and Syria, whose proverbial munificence and nobility outshone his military efforts against the crusaders as a Muslim avatar of chivalric virtue in the Christian imagination.

The notorious placement – on the other hand – of Muhammad (570–632) and Ali (Alī ibn Abī Ṭālib, c.600–61) among the sowers of scandals and the schismatics in the ninth pouch of the eighth circle (*Inf.* XXVIII, 22–45) folds the theological construal of Islam as a Christian heresy onto the Islamic rejection of the Incarnation and Trinitarian dogmas as source of a schism, a sectarian split from the Church gruesomely re-enacted in the *contrapasso* punishment meted out in their grotesquely mutilated bodies, Ali's face split in half, the Prophet's entire torso sundered apart with hanging viscera. The Trecento and Quattrocento commentaries on *Inferno* (including those by Jacopo Alighieri (c.1289–1348), Guido da Pisa (thirteenth–fourteenth centuries), Pietro Alighieri (before 1300–64), Benvenuto da Imola (1320/30–1387/88), Johannis de Serravalle (c.1350–1445), and Cristoforo Landino (1425–98)) are engrossed with a diverse *florilegium* of colourful anti-Islamic legends about the 'historical' Muhammad as a lascivious renegade Christian and impostor, a trickster and pseudo-prophet who deceived his followers with sham miracles, an apostate cardinal with a frustrated ambition for the Papacy, and so on, whereas recent scholarship has further enlarged the interpretive context for these verses, including a perceptive re-examination of Muhammad's fate as an imaginative transposition of Christian legends on the death of Arius the heresiarch, and a very suggestive effort to discern in his graphic punishment a poetic inversion of an Islamic miracle story – *al-šarḥ*, the miraculous splitting of Muhammad's chest to purify his heart (see the popular and learned elaborations on Sura 94, *al-Inširāḥ*) – potentially accessible to Dante, for example, in the Latin translations of the Qur'ān. It is more surprising to find Ali, Muhammad's son-in-law, sharing in his posthumous fate, as he was a lesser-known figure in Christian anti-Muslim polemics, perhaps indicating an awareness of Ali's centrality to the

## Islamic and Jewish influences

intra-Islamic schism over the Prophet's immediate successor between Sunnis and Shi'ites. But again, their consignment to *Inferno* is not premised on a theological appreciation of Islam in its own terms, only on their supposedly disruptive impact within the ecclesial community. Their very inclusion among the schismatics excludes them *a fortiori* from the heretics in the flaming tombs of the sixth circle, perhaps an understandable exclusion since the quintessential heresy punished in *Inferno* X is not the classical Christological and Trinitarian heterodoxies of the patristic period – for example Sabellianism or Arianism (whose founders Aquinas alludes to in *Paradiso* XIII, 115) – but the 'Epicurean' denial of the soul's immortality, from which Dante, as we saw, clearly dissociated Muslims. At any rate, the allegorical interpretation of *Purgatorio* XXXII, 130–5 shared by most *Commedia* commentators – the violent rupture of the chariot's floor by the venomous tail of a dragon as a reference to the divisive impact of Islam on the Church's mystical body – seems to highlight a Christian indictment of Prophet Muhammad not as the founder of a new 'religion' but as a quintessential schismatic.

So Dante's Christian self-understanding may have clashed on theological grounds with the religious *Weltanschauung* of Muslims and Jews in the thirteenth and fourteenth centuries. But as was the case with fellow Christian scholars, it did not make him less receptive to the cultural and intellectual legacy of Arabo-Islamic civilization. The principled commitment of Aristotelian thinkers – Jewish, Christian, and Muslim – to the autonomous value of propositional truths that were compatible with divine revelation regardless of their origin – a rationalist tenet adumbrated, on the early Christian side, in the patristic motif of 'the spoils of Egypt' – had buttressed in the Latin West the systematic engagement of scholastic theologians (most notably Albert the Great (*c.*1200–80) and Aquinas (1225–74)) with Graeco-Arabic philosophy and science. The Graeco-Arabic traditions, whether directly reconnoitred or mediated by the scholastics, left discernible marks in Dante's literary *oeuvre*.

Six Arabo-Islamic authorities in Greek philosophy and science are explicitly adduced by Dante in scholarly discussions, mostly throughout the *Convivio*. Three of them are Muslim philosopher-polymaths: Averroes, Avicenna, and the Persian Al-Ghazali (Abū Ḥāmid Muḥammad ibn Muḥammad at-Tūsī al-Ghazālī, 1058–1111), the leading Muslim theologian and Sufi thinker of the eleventh century and penetrating critic of Aristotelian philosophy. The other three were all renowned Islamic astronomers: Alfraganus (the ninth-century Abū al-ʿAbbās Aḥmad ibn Muḥammad ibn Kathīr al-Farghānī), Albumasar (Abū Maʿšar Jaʿfar ibn

Muḥammad al-Balkhī, also from the ninth century (d. 888), remembered in the history of medieval science for the theory of astral motions that he introduced), and Alpetragius (Nūr ad-Dīn ibn Isḥaq al-Biṭrūjī, the twelfth-century Andalusian astronomer (d. 1204) whose single surviving treatise revived an ancient critique of Ptolemaic astronomy). The scattered allusions to all six broadly represent two intellectual preoccupations that garnered Dante's attention: the philosophical debates on the nature of the soul and the scientific understanding of the cosmological order, with its concomitant implications for his metaphysical views (see Chapter 14).

Dante, as already pointed out, had no direct access in the original language to the Arabic works by the authors adduced on these two issues, but they had all been translated into Latin and fully incorporated into the intellectual repertoire of Christian scholasticism. Most of Dante's explicit allusions to these authors seem to be second-hand, derived from excerpted passages and interpretive discussions in scholastic sources, especially Albert the Great (e.g. *De meteoris* (On Meteorology) as the source of Dante's single allusion to Abulmasar in *Convivio* II, xiv, 22 on the effects of Mars) and Thomas Aquinas. He seemed, however, to have perused the Latin translation of Averroes' commentary on *De anima* directly (see below). Another possible exception among the astronomers may be found, perhaps, in his two explicit references (*Conv.* II, v, 16 and II, xiii, 11) and other possible debts to Alfraganus' *Kitāb fi jawāmi 'ilm an-nujūm* (On the Elements of Astronomy), the most popular compendium of Arab astronomy in medieval Europe, first translated into Latin by John of Seville (1134), but most likely consulted by Dante in Gerard of Cremona's later version (before 1175). Dante adduces two astronomical facts on Alfraganus' authority as part of broader discussions (i.e. the three types of motions that govern the celestial spheres in an angelological excursus on Venus and the diameter of Mercury in a discussion on dialectics, the science correlated with this planet). Finally, Dante's reference to the Andalusian Alpetragius – *Convivio* III, ii, 5 on how the causal effect of a circular body has something circular about it – is most likely not a textual quote from *De motibus coelorum* in Scotus' translation but rather derived from the scholastic discussions of his astronomical doctrine (al-Biṭrūjī – it has also been argued – may even lie behind Dante's claim in *Convivio* II, iii, 5 that philosophy 'necessitated the simplest *primum mobile*').

Among the philosophers, al-Ghazali is mentioned twice in tandem with Avicenna, both times juxtaposed over convergent philosophical views (*Conv.* II, xiii, 5 on the causal impact of the heavenly motions on the generation of substance; *Conv.* IV, xxi, 2 on the different degrees of nobility

## Islamic and Jewish influences

in the human soul), but most likely derived from Albert the Great's *De somno et vigilia* (On Sleep and Sleeplessness) III, 6. Avicenna's name is invoked twice again, once on the right nomenclature for a philosophical phenomenology of light (*Conv.* III, xiv, 5, derived from Avicenna's *De anima*, but probably a second-hand reference) and also to explain the whiteness of the Milky Way (*Conv.* II, xiv, 7, coincident with Albert, *De meteoris* I, ii, 6, who like Dante invokes the joint authority of Avicenna, Aristotle, and Ptolemy on this issue).

At any rate, the most prominent Arabo-Islamic figure in this limited panoply is, of course, the Cordovan Ibn Rušd. Dante does not merely extol Averroes in Limbo among the learned scholars 'of great authority', but explicitly and critically engages some of the philosophical ideas associated with the venerable Arabo-Andalusian polymath in thirteenth-century scholasticism. In *Purgatorio* XXV, 62–6 on the divine creation of the rational soul, Dante famously rejects Averroes' unorthodox theory of the possible intellect – a signature theme of his rationalist epistemology (Averroes' *Commentary on 'De anima'* III, 5) – in favour of Aquinas' philosophical psychology and concomitant defence of the soul's immortality. Dante's repudiation harks back to other intra-Christian debates over the compatibility of Aristotelian naturalism with orthodox belief exemplified in Etienne Tempier's (d. 1279) 1277 denunciation of 219 philosophical propositions (a critical engagement with Latin Averroism provided a significant backdrop to Thomas' rehabilitation of Aristotle in his scholastic theology). Dante, however, had also called upon Averroes' authority to buttress some of his own philosophical excursus elsewhere, whether in defending the natural thirst for knowledge as a step towards attainment of our divine end in *Convivio* IV, xiii, 7–8, in reaffirming the centrality of the senses to Aristotelian epistemology in *Questio de aqua et de terra* 5, or, most famously, in articulating the Aristotelian ideal of human perfection consequent upon the intellect through the realization of its potential not individually but collectively in *Monarchia* I, iii, 9. All these excursus, of course, revolve around the same Averroistic source: his seminal commentary on Aristotle's *De anima* (a fifth and final reference is made to Averroes' *De substantia orbis* (On the Substance of the Orb) – also translated from the lost Arabic original by Michael Scotus – on how the forms found *in potentia* within matter are ideally found *in actu* in the motor of the heavens in *Questio de aqua et de terra* 18). Some scholars seem to discern a progression in Dante's thinking from the *Convivio*'s detached engagement with disparate philosophical theories on the soul to an orthodox apotheosis of the Christian position in *Paradiso*. But Dante's fundamental orthodoxy, as recently argued by Barański,[2] provides the most cogent intellectual frame for his selective appreciation of the philosophical tradition that Averroes represented and the pivotal role it played in the scholastic vindication of Aristotelianism. The much-debated placement of Thomas Aquinas in the Heaven of the Sun (*Par.* X, 133–8) side by side with Siger of Brabant (*c.*1240–1281/84) – the thirteenth-century Latin 'Averroist' at the University of Paris, summoned by the inquisitor of France in 1276 over his philosophical errors – may have more to do with their joint role as representatives of the harmony between theology and philosophy than with Dante's putative views on Siger's 'Averroism' (if he had any awareness of this). In sum, Dante's principled rejection of the more heterodox rationalistic ideas impressionistically linked to an Averroistic tradition went hand in hand with a deferential regard for the Muslim philosopher as an authoritative commentator of Aristotle shared with the scholastic movement at large.

Obviously, other Arabo-Islamic and Jewish contributions to medieval European culture deeply marked Dante's work, directly or indirectly, whether or not he was aware of their ultimate origin and not limited to such explicit mentions. Dante's re-elaboration of Neoplatonic ideas in both the *Convivio* and the *Commedia* was enriched with selective borrowings from a repercussive synthesis of Neoplatonic metaphysics and the erotico-mystical emanationism of Plotinus (204–70) and Proclus (412–85) that circulated in the Arabo-Islamic world under the authority of Aristotle (*Kitāb 'l-īdāḥ li-Arisṭūtālis fī-'l-khayri 'l-maḥd* (The Book of Aristotle's Explanation of the Pure Good)) – the Arabic summary of Proclus' *Elements of Theology* known to him in Gerard of Cremona's late-twelfth-century Latin translation as the *Liber de causis* (Book of Causes), an important source for the 'sweet-new-style' poets and of equal interest among Italian Jews in Dante's lifetime (there are three different Hebrew translations from Latin by the Italo-Jewish scholars Hillel of Verona (*c.*1220–*c.*1295), Zerahyah ben Shaltiel Hen (*fl.* 1270–90s), and Judah of Rome (*c.*1293–after 1330)). *Liber de causis* is not only cited often throughout his works (*Conv.* III, ii, 4 and 7; vi, 4 and 11; vii, 2; IV, xxi, 9; *Mon.* I, xi, 17; III, xvi, 3; *Ep.* XIII, 20 and 21), but Dante's metaphysics of light in *Paradiso* is also indebted to it, along perhaps with other philosophical discussions on the nature of light partly rooted in Arabo-Islamic thought (e.g. Bartolomeo da Bologna's (d. 1294) *Tractatus de luce* (Treatise on Light)). It has also been argued that, in the *Convivio*, Dante primarily engaged with the *Nicomachean Ethics* not in Robert Grosseteste's (*c.*1168–1253) translation of the Greek original, but in the *Translatio*

*Alexandrina*, the 1244 Latin version of the Arabo-Alexandrian compendium on the *Ethics* attributed to Herman Alemannus and to which he was possibly introduced by Brunetto Latini, who discovered it in Spain, drawing from it in his own *Trésor* (although he probably knew both). On a purely speculative ground, Dante's 1320 *Questio de aqua et terra* enjoys an intriguing precursor in a comparable effort to show why the earth is not covered by water, that is the treatise *Ma'amar yiqqavu hamayim* (Let the Waters Be Gathered) by the Franco-Jewish Maimonidean scholar and translator Samuel ibn Tibbon (*c.*1165–1232), the subsequent object of a sharp critique by the Catalan kabbalist Jacob ben Sheshet Gerondi (mid thirteenth century).

The analytic separation of religion and culture in our overview also becomes less clear in two sets of conjectural claims about the Italo-Christian engagement (especially Dante's) with (1) Jewish Kabbalah and (2) Muslim eschatology. On the Jewish side, critical attention has been devoted to the diverse medieval traditions of Jewish theosophical-theurgical mystical theology and ecstatic-prophetic religiosity encompassed by the term Kabbalah. Between 1270 and 1295 there was an intense flourishing of kabbalistic creativity in Spain and Italy that culminated with a voluminous output of classical, deeply original works in this mystical tradition. The Iberian protagonists of this kabbalistic renaissance included Abraham Abulafia (1240–after 1291), the Saragossan founder of the ecstatic kabbalistic tradition who first studied Maimonidean philosophy in Capua with Rabbi Hillel ben Samuel of Verona (1220–95) and, after a short stint back in his native Spain, returned to Italy where he wrote most of his kabbalistic works. Another important and even more repercussive expression of Castilian and Catalan Kabbalah also flourished in Italy in Dante's lifetime: the synthesis of kabbalistic theosophy and theurgy in Moses de León's (*c.*1240–1305) venerable *Sefer-ha Zohar* (Book of Splendour, which was written in Castile mostly between 1280 and 1286), the most revered classic of Jewish mystical spirituality, introduced in the Italian peninsula by Menahem ben Benjamin Recanati (1250–1310). Dante's plausible encounter with the Jews of Verona has invited, for example, suggestive speculations against this Italo-Jewish backdrop as to the kabbalistic parallels with his linguistic ideas: more specifically, whether his changing positions on Adam's vernacular and the nature of language may be indebted to the Italo-Jewish debates between kabbalistic and philosophical views on the metaphysical status of Hebrew. In *De vulgari eloquentia* I, vi, 5, Dante affirms that Adam's mother tongue was Hebrew, an unchanging and incorruptible language created by God and spoken universally since the time of Creation until the 'confusion of languages' at the Tower of Babel. But in *Paradiso* XXVI, 124–36, Adam instead tells the pilgrim that natural languages change and evolve; that although we have a natural propensity to communicate, the chosen signs for linguistic expression are conventional; and that his own vernacular was not Hebrew but a different language, already extinct at the time of Babel. Dante's change of view on the character of the first language has a suggestive parallel in a contemporary Italo-Jewish debate between Hillel of Verona and the Barcelonan philosopher-translator Zerahyah ben Sha'altiel Hen: that is whether a child reared by a mute nurse would develop, like Adam, his natural capacity for language and speak in Hebrew – Hillel's naturalist position – or rather 'bark as a dog' unable to speak – Zerahyah's stance (the story of the mute nurse, pondered as well by Abulafia, may reflect, in turn, oral lore about Frederick II's putative indulgence in such an infant experiment). Likewise, in *De vulgari eloquentia* Dante states that Adam's first uttered word was God's Hebrew name *El*, whereas in *Paradiso* XXVI, 133–5, Adam affirms that God was first named *I*, a claim as yet unsatisfactorily explained by commentators that may echo the singling out of the Hebrew *yod*, first letter of the Tetragrammaton, as a kabbalistic shorthand for the divine name. Finally, Dante's much-discussed concept of *forma locutionis* (form of speech) as the prelapsarian foundation of our linguistic capacity has been perceptively compared to Abulafia's *tsurat hadibbur* (form of speech) in his kabbalistic theory of language. The coincident terminology and conceptual parallels are certainly striking. There have been even more ambitious efforts to interpret in an Italo-kabbalistic key the broader Neoplatonic motifs in Dante's 'mystical journey' from *Vita nova* to the *Commedia*. But all of these speculative comparisons are, of course, primarily founded on the assumption of Dante's possible contact with the main Italian centres of Jewish intellectual life. Unlike the Arabo-Islamic philosophical works, there is no evidence as yet of either Latin or vernacular translations of any of these kabbalistic sources in Dante's lifetime.

Our efforts to disentangle the religious disposition of Dante's contemporaries towards Islam and Judaism from their cultural engagement with the Muslim and Jewish intellectual legacy finally come to a head in the most intensely scrutinized contribution to the 'Dante and Islam' scholarly debate. In 1919 the eminent Spanish Arabist Miguel Asín Palacios (1877–1944) first argued that Dante's visionary journey had a substantive literary debt, both in its overarching narrative structure and in a wealth of specific themes and imagery throughout the *Commedia*, to the most famous pericope about Muhammad's life in Islamic eschatological

*Islamic and Jewish influences* 217

literature: the hagiographic traditions on the Prophet's mysterious nightly journey to Jerusalem (*isrā*) and concomitant visionary ascent to God's presence up a supernal ladder through the seven heavens (*mi'rāj*), with accompanying sights of Paradise and Hell while escorted by the Angel Gabriel.[3]

His sustained comparison of the *Commedia* with the Arabic sources of the *mi'rāj* tradition and selective discussions of other European literary visions of the otherworld produced a disparate array of thematic and structural parallels, some deeply striking and perceptive, others rather impressionistic, unpersuasive, and overstated. At any rate, since Dante did not know Arabic, whether or not these parallels reflected direct intertextual borrowings, independent derivations of common sources, polygenetic developments, or purely superficial resemblances, Asín Palacios lacked at the time any historical basis to account for Dante's mediated access to the Arabic channels of transmission for the *mi'rāj* story.

The subsequent controversy was, however, significantly refocused by an important discovery – a plausible missing gun in Asín Palacios' thesis – that fittingly embodies most of the historical contexts for the possible knowledge of Islamic and Jewish traditions in late medieval Italian culture at large. In 1949 two scholars – Enrico Cerulli[4] and José Muñoz Sendino[5] – independently published Latin and Old French accounts of this eschatological narrative that were potentially accessible to Dante. First discovered by Ugo Monneret de Villard (1881–1954),[6] they had both been translated in the second half of the thirteenth century from a lost Castilian version of an Arabic recension, the *Kitāb al-mi'rāj* (Book of the Ascension). Alfonso X had commissioned the Old Spanish translation to the Hispano-Jewish physician, Abraham Alfaquim of Toledo. Bonaventure of Siena – a Tuscan Ghibelline who had visited the Sevillian court of Alfonso X in 1264, joining the Alfonsine team of Italian collaborators – was responsible, in turn, for both the Latin *Liber scale Machometi* (Book of Muhammad's Ladder) and the Old French *Livre de l'eschiele Mahomet*. Bonaventure had undertaken the translation, according to the extant prologue in the Old French version, at the explicit behest of the Castilian king, but also as a means to facilitate direct recourse to Muhammad's life and teachings for Christian polemical purposes. Alfonso's original commission of the Castilian text may have also responded to an active scholarly interest in the best range of Arabo-Islamic sources on the *mi'rāj* story, all on a par with his broader cultural project and built upon a pre-existent Hispano-Christian fascination with this eschatological tradition that extended back to the tenth-century Mozarabic Christians. Alfonso's first historiographic venture, the *Estoria de España* (The History of Spain), already included, for example, a short vernacular precis derived from Rodrigo Jiménez de Rada's (*c.*1170–1247) *Historia arabum* (History of the Arabs), a succinct retelling of Muhammad's vision whose immediate source differed significantly from the Arabic recension behind the Latin and Old French texts. The lost Castilian version, on the other hand, was probably the source of the lengthier retelling inserted into the Spanish *Sobre la seta mahometana* (On the Mohammedan Sect) attributed to the Valencian bishop of Mozarabic descent Pedro Pascual (*c.*1227–1300).

At any rate, the Andalusian *Kitāb al-mi'rāj* attained a much wider European readership with Bonaventure's two translations. The manuscript tradition already attests to their trans-Pyrenean diffusion in France and England. The two extant manuscripts with the Latin version were produced in Brittany and Provence (thirteenth and fourteenth centuries, respectively), whereas the Old French text is preserved in a thirteenth-century manuscript from England. Soon enough, Dante's Italy entered the European orbit of the *isrā'-mi'rāj* pericope with the latter's circulation in these and other versions. A synoptic overview of the *mi'rāj* (not derived from Bonaventure's *Liber*) appears in Riccoldo da Monte Croce's *Contra legem saracenorum*. But there is an explicit Italian reference to Muhammad's depiction of Paradise 'in his book that is titled *Ladder*' in Fazio degli Uberti's (*c.*1302–*c.*1367) *Dittamondo* (About the World) written between 1350 and 1360. The Tuscan poet places its exposition in Riccoldo's lips (his guide and interlocutor at this particular point in the poem), but degli Uberti clearly knew the *Liber scale Machometi*, which he could have stumbled upon either in Verona or in Lombardy through the court of Mastino II della Scala (1308–51). More than a century later, moving now to Southern Italy, the Franciscan preacher Roberto Caracciolo of Lecce (*c.*1425–95) also includes a lengthy exposition of Muhammad's eschatological vision, probably drawn from Bonaventure's Latin version, among the anti-Islamic sermons in his vernacular collection *Specchio della fede christiana* (The Mirror of the Christian Faith) – a homiletic cycle perhaps inspired by the Fall of Constantinople to the Ottomans in 1453 and the mass execution of the Otranto martyrs in 1480. The *mi'rāj* story circulated so widely that it quickly engrossed late medieval polemical sources on Islam. For example, the incomplete version of Bonaventure's *Liber* in the fourteenth-century manuscript from Provence (nowadays at the Vatican Library) was added as an appendix to a late recension of the twelfth-century *Corpus Toletanum*. So yes, it was more than

# Islamic and Jewish influences

possible in fourteenth-century Italy for Dante and fellow Christians to have known the *Liber scale Machometi* or some other Western European retelling of this Muslim narrative.

Can we posit, though, more than just intertextual analogies between the *Commedia* and the Christian European retellings of the *isrā'-mi'rāj* story? Historical plausibility and thematic or imagistic parallels, however suggestive, are not by themselves proof of a direct reminiscence. Indeed, Dante's scholars after Cerulli and Muñoz Sendino have continued to debate on better historical grounds and with less overreaching ambitions than Asín Palacios his possible debts to the Latin and vernacular *mi'rāj* narratives, albeit without consensus. A discriminating appraisal, along Cerulli's more cautious line, of plausible formal parallels between the European *mi'rāj* tradition and the *Commedia*, can still yield intriguing concomitances that give reason to pause.

But even if such intertextual debts were demonstrable, it would still be a trivialization of Dante's imaginative process as a poet and of the Italo-Christian receptivity to Muslim cultural traditions at large to posit a purely mechanical incorporation of thematic and narrative materials from the *Liber scale Machometi*. What seems more significant is that Dante's antagonistic portrayal of Islam as a schism through the lenses of Christian heresiology did not hinder his engagement with · the Arabo-Islamic cultural legacy, an intellectual receptivity that could be plausibly extended to the literary appropriation of selected images and motifs even from a Muslim religious narrative. In this important respect, the Tuscan poet stands out among fellow Christians in fourteenth-century Italy. Dante's theological engagement with Judaism and Islam was obviously a far cry from the syncretistic aspirations of a Ramon Llull. But the crucible of his imagination was more than hospitable to the cumulative impact of non-Christian learning on European intellectual life.

## Notes

1 W. Cantwell Smith, *The Meaning and End of Religion* (Minneapolis: Fortress Press, 1962).
2 Z. G. Barański, '(Un)orthodox Dante' in C. E. Honess and M. Treherne (eds.), *Reviewing Dante's Theology*, 2 vols. (Oxford: Peter Lang, 2013), vol. II, pp. 253–330.
3 M. Asín Palacios, *La escatología musulmana en 'La Divina Comedia': Historia y crítica de una polémica*, 4th edn (Madrid: Hiperión, 1984; 1st edn Madrid: RAE, 1919).

4 E. Cerulli, *Il 'Libro della scala' e la questione delle fonti arabo-spagnole della 'Divina Commedia'* (Vatican: BAV, 1949). See also his *Nuove ricerche sul 'Libro della Scala' e la conoscenza dell'Islam in Occidente* (Vatican: BAV, 1972).

5 J. Muñoz Sendino, *La Escala de Mahoma: Traducción del árabe al castellano, latín y francés, ordenada por Alfonso X el Sabio* (Madrid: Ministerio de Asuntos Exteriores, 1949).

6 U. Monneret de Villard, *Lo studio dell'Islam in Europa nel XII e nel XIII secolo* (Vatican: BAV, 1944).

CHAPTER 14

# Cosmology, geography, and cartography

*Theodore J. Cachey, Jr*

Cosmology is an anachronistic category when applied to the Middle Ages. The earliest attestations of the word in the modern sense of a theory or doctrine describing the natural order of the universe date from the early modern period. In the thirteenth and fourteenth centuries cosmological issues were discussed in relation to a wide array of subjects, ranging from angels to astrology, astronomy, the four elements (earth, water, air, fire), the Empyrean, the heavens, nature, the planets, and so on. The approach reflects the fragmented state of cosmological knowledge during the late medieval period. The extensive scholastic literature of the time regarding cosmological questions typically took the form of discontinuous and digressive commentaries on canonical texts, and was characterized by the absence of any cohesive integration of such questions. According to one authoritative historian of science, 'no genuine cosmological synthesis was developed during the late Middle Ages'.[1] Yet Dante's *Commedia* stands out in contrast to the disorganized cosmographical context of its time. The intellectual ferment and debate surrounding cosmological questions stimulated Dante to pursue through poetry a higher synthesis of the diverse elements that constituted the contemporary cosmological picture. To achieve a full understanding of the order of creation was for Dante tantamount to achieving knowledge of the Creator. In the poem he attempted to present as comprehensive and integrated a picture of the cosmos as possible, thereby compensating for the lack of such a vision in the doctrinal contributions of the theological and philosophical masters.

This is not to say that a general consensus about the structure of the cosmos did not exist during the late medieval period. For instance, the standard image of the universe is exquisitely represented in the 'Creation of the World' (*c.*1445), a tempera on panel painting by the Sienese Giovanni di Paolo (1398–1482), long believed to have been inspired by the cosmology of Dante's *Commedia* (Figure 14.1). As recent scholarship has demonstrated, however, the cosmology depicted in the painting dates from well

221

Figure 14.1 Giovanni di Paolo (Siena 1398–1482), *The Creation of the World and the Expulsion from Paradise*, 1445. Robert Lehman Collection.

before Dante, and reflects a consensus that had been canonized by the first decades of the thirteenth century, as epitomized by Ioannes de Sacrobosco (c.1195-c.1265) in the *Treatise on the Sphere* (c.1230), which served as the most used elementary textbook in astronomy and cosmography from the thirteenth to the seventeenth centuries; the *Sphere* was an introduction for students at the beginning of their university studies. Thus, while the *Sphere* did not reflect the most advanced state of contemporary inquiry and debate, it did represent the consensus understanding of the basic elements of the Ptolemaic geocentric universe that was undergoing an intense process of re-examination and revision during Dante's time.

Sacrobosco's *Sphere* begins with the division of the universe into ethereal and elementary regions, and by providing a succinct description of the four elements:

# Cosmology, geography, and cartography

The machine of the universe is divided into two, the ethereal and the elementary region. The elementary region, existing subject to continual alteration, is divided into four. For there is earth, placed, as it were, at the center in the middle of all, about which is water, about water air, about air fire, which is pure and not turbid there and reaches to the sphere of the moon, as Aristotle says in his book of *Meteorology*. For so God, the glorious and sublime, disposed. And these are called the 'four elements' which are in turn by themselves altered, corrupted and regenerated. The elements are also simple bodies which cannot be subdivided into parts of diverse forms and from whose commixture are produced various species of generated things. Three of them, in turn, surround the earth on all sides spherically, except in so far as the dry land stays the sea's tide to protect the life of animate beings.[2]

How it was possible for the heavier element of the dry land, to stay 'the sea's tide', that is, to rise above the lighter element of water, was a problem that vexed contemporary natural philosophers, and Dante himself in his *Questio de aqua et terra* (The Question of the Water and the Land, 1320). Giovanni di Paolo's 'Creation of the World', meanwhile, presented the inhabited world, according to Sacrobosco's scheme, situated at the centre of the universe, with the element of earth coloured brown on the surface of the sphere of the world. The second element, water, coloured green, initiates the series of the concentric spheres of the four elements by enclosing and penetrating the land. The delicate blue, nearly white, colour of the next circle denotes the element of air, which is bounded, in turn, by a bright red circle, the ring of fire, the fourth and highest element. Note that the map of the inhabited world of Giovanni's panel reflects late-fifteenth-century developments in geographical exploration and biblical exegesis, while Dante's cartographical points of reference, as will be discussed later in this chapter, corresponded to late medieval geographical and cartographical models. In any event, the basic cosmological picture regarding the four elements as presented by Giovanni matches that of Dante and his age.

Sacrobosco next outlined the structure of the heavens:

> Around the elementary region revolves with continuous circular motion the ethereal, which is lucid and immune from all variation in its immutable essence. And it is called 'Fifth Essence' by the philosophers. Of which there are nine spheres as we have just said: namely, of the Moon, Mercury, Venus, the Sun, Mars, Jupiter, Saturn, the fixed stars, and the last heaven. Each of these spheres encloses its inferior spherically.[3]

In the 'Creation of the World', the spheres of the seven planets appear between the ring of fire that demarcates the boundary of the elementary region and the zodiac, and these planetary spheres were usually identified as such by name or symbol in manuscripts and printed editions of the *Sphere*. Together with the Primum Mobile (First Mover) and the Empyrean, they constituted the ethereal region of the cosmos. The three blue planetary rings beyond the red circle of fire belong to the Moon, Mercury, and Venus. The white circle that follows belongs to the Sun. Those beyond the Sun belong to Mars, Jupiter, and Saturn. The sphere of Mars is coloured pink rather than blue, as it appeared pinkish to the naked eye. The last planetary sphere belongs to Saturn, which is followed by the stars of the zodiac. The narrow deep blue circle that encircles the zodiac represents the Primum Mobile, which regulated the motion of the spheres beneath it. Its placement as the ninth heaven corresponds both to Sacrobosco's and to Dante's cosmological model, although there was great controversy during Dante's time about the number and nature of the heavens located beyond the planetary spheres. Giovanni di Paolo's representation of God and the angels beyond the finite spheres of the universe suggests that he shared with Dante a conception of the Empyrean that placed it beyond the limits of time and space.

The placement of God the Creator, gesturing with pointed finger, above and beyond the finite sphere of the world, and between the zodiacal signs of Aries and Taurus, which rule late March and early April, portrays a vital element of the Christian cosmology – one that is consistent with Dante's view of the structure of the cosmos and of the story of creation. The cosmic setting of Giovanni di Paolo's panel painting alludes to the act of creation and to the Incarnation, as well as to the Easter setting of the *Commedia* (*Inf.* I, 37–9). Dante's poem, too, recapitulates the story of creation and of man's sin and redemption within the same cosmic framework as the panel.

Nonetheless, beyond the terms of the basic parameters outlined above, cosmological thought in Dante's time was in a phase of development and renewal that was without precedent in the Latin West. Dante's cosmological context was far from the neutral 'backcloth' that scholarship, until relatively recently, had maintained. Inquiry into the nature of the cosmos during the period was characterized by intense debates and controversies that put under extreme pressure traditional systems of knowledge, including the liberal arts curriculum and medieval encyclopaedism. The borders between Aristotelian natural philosophy and Christian theology were especially fraught. During the twelfth and thirteenth centuries, translations into Latin of the works of Aristotle from Arabic and Greek, and the commentary tradition associated with those works, principally

# Cosmology, geography, and cartography

Al-Farabi (Abu Al-Nasr, *c.*870–*c.*950), Avicenna (Ibn Sina, *c.*980–*c.*1037), Al-Ghazali (Abu Hamid, *c.*1050–1111), and Averroes (Ibn Rushd, 1126–98), had made available to the West a cosmology that challenged the foundations of Christian belief. From a Christian perspective, an understanding of the cosmos could not be pursued solely by the methods of reasoning and observation characteristic of Aristotelian natural philosophy. The new Aristotelian cosmology, therefore, had to be reconciled with the authority of the Bible and with Christian theology, whose cosmology had been formed by a diverse mix of authoritative texts, beginning with a genre initiated by Church Fathers on the six days of the creation that took the form of commentaries on Genesis I, and included works such as Basil of Cesarea's (*c.*329–79) *Hexaemeron*, Ambrose's (*c.*340–97) *Hexameron*, and Augustine's (354–430) *De Genesi ad litteram* (The Literal Meaning of Genesis, 401–15). This hexameral, 'six-days', literature was combined with an array of late-antique and early medieval Neoplatonic sources to form the foundations of a Christian picture of the cosmos. These included Plato's *Timaeus* in the partial fourth-century Latin translation-commentary of Calcidius (fourth century), as well as other Neoplatonic authorities such as Macrobius (early fifth century), pseudo-Dionysius Areopagite (fifth to sixth century), Boethius (*c.*480–524), Martianus Capella (fifth century), and a short but extremely influential treatise, the *Liber de Causis* (The Book of Causes), which was attributed to Aristotle but was eventually correctly recognized by Thomas Aquinas (1225–74) to be a synthesis of the Neoplatonist Proclus' (412–85) *Elements of Theology*.

A period of intense and uninterrupted study of the newly available Aristotelian corpus, especially the *De caelo* (On the Heavens), by late medieval theologians and natural philosophers, stretched from the beginning of the thirteenth century to the end of the fifteenth. The ideological tensions between Aristotelian natural philosophy and Christian theology inherent in this process of translation and acculturation eventually produced the epistemological crisis that, at the end of the medieval period, led to the emergence of modern science. The syllabus of 219 philosophical and theological theses censured by the Bishop of Paris, Etienne Tempier (d. 1279), in 1277 for their incompatibility with Christian orthodoxy was symptomatic of the tensions between natural philosophy and theology around Dante's time. Tempier's Condemnation was in response to rationalist Aristotelian currents at the University of Paris, and sought to counter the rise of philosophy as an autonomous discipline distinct from divine revelation and the authority of theology. A number of the condemned propositions involved important cosmological features of Aristotle's natural philosophy. Some historians of medieval science have argued that Tempier's insistence on God's absolute power actually freed Christian thought from the dogmatic acceptance of Aristotelianism, thereby leading to greater freedom and creativity in the field of cosmological speculation. Other scholars have challenged this view, pointing out the paradox of attributing a liberating function to an essentially oppressive measure, and the anachronism of portraying the Aristotelianism of the time as an obstacle to the development of science.

Whatever its ultimate significance for the history of science, the Condemnation of 1277 had the effect of signalling the need for further cosmological reflection and research, so that conceptions compatible with both universally accepted principles of natural philosophy and with Christian revelation might be established. This general re-elaboration of the medieval cosmological model engaged some of the most original philosophers of the later Middle Ages, who were contemporaries of Dante, including Roger Bacon (1214–94), Giles of Rome (*c.*1243–1316), Richard of Middleton (*c.*1249–*c.*1302), John Duns Scotus (1266–1308), William of Ockham (1287–1347), as well as thinkers of the generation that immediately followed, Jean Buridan (*c.*1300–after 1358) and Nicholas Oresme (*c.*1320/25–1382), two of the leading philosophers of the fourteenth century. Both the cosmological picture that Dante developed in his poetry and his attitude toward the project of developing it can be usefully situated against this background of renewed debate and inquiry. Indeed, the intensity of speculative energy and commitment that Dante exhibited throughout his writings as regards cosmological matters was inspired by a situation of active ferment in the culture of his time. Even near the end of his life, at the same time as he was composing the final cantos of *Paradiso*, Dante engaged directly with this intellectual milieu in a treatise addressing the question of the location and form of the water and the earth, the *Questio de aqua et terra*.

However, as early as his discussion of the order of the heavens in Book II of the *Convivio*, Dante had sought to establish himself as a cosmographical authority by evoking and engaging with the traditions of cosmological debate. There he noted that 'concerning the number and the position of the heavens many different opinions are held, although the truth has at last been discovered' (*Conv.* II, iii, 3); and began by pointing out Aristotle's errors. The Philosopher, in fact, had held that there were only eight heavens, 'and that beyond it there was no other', and his ordering of the planets was also faulty, for the Philosopher had held that the Sun came after the Moon and was second to Earth in the order of the

# Cosmology, geography, and cartography

planets. Indeed, since Venus and Mercury were always in the vicinity of the Sun, the order of these planets was uncertain. Most authorities, following Claudius Ptolemy's (*c*.90–168) arrangement in his *Almagest*, had the Sun, followed by Venus and Mercury, followed by the Moon, which was generally considered to be the closest planet to the earth.

Ptolemy had established the generally accepted order of the heavens, from bottom to top: Moon, Mercury, Venus, Sun, Mars, Jupiter, Saturn, Fixed Stars or Starry Heaven, and had added a ninth heaven, the Primum Mobile. This heaven was added by Ptolemy in order to account for two observed movements of the heavens. First, their daily motion east to west around the pole of the equator was attributed to what Ptolemy called the 'sphere that moved the sphere of the Fixed Stars' (the Primum Mobile). Ptolemy attributed the other, slow movement of the planets from west to east at the rate of 1° every hundred years around the pole of the ecliptic known as the precession of the equinoxes – first discovered by Hipparchus (190–*c*.120) – to the heaven of the Fixed Stars. Initially astronomers had supposed that the eighth sphere, that of the Fixed Stars, was affected by as many as three different motions, and on the principle that a single sphere must be assigned to each distinct celestial motion, additional spheres plus an immobile Empyrean were often added for a total of eleven spheres. (Figure 14.2). However, as Dante, who posited ten heavens, explained in *Convivio* II, iii, 5, the idea that the heaven of the Fixed Stars was subject to contrary movements was felt to be inconsistent with the symmetry and simplicity of nature: 'Ptolemy … constrained by the principles of philosophy', Dante writes, 'which necessitated the simplest *primum mobile*, supposed that another heaven existed beyond that of the Fixed Stars which made this revolution from east to west.' In fact, the reasons why Ptolemy added a ninth heaven were mathematical and astronomical, while the Neoplatonic philosophical motive Dante attributes to Ptolemy, that the many must be derived from the one, instead ultimately came from Alpetragius (Nur alDin alBitruji, d. 1204), whose *Kitāb al-Hay'ah* (The Book of Theoretical Astronomy) Dante accessed indirectly through the commentary on the *De caelo* by Albert the Great (*c*.1200–80).

Beginning in the thirteenth century, scholars had to confront authoritative works of astronomy that were in disagreement with each other. The Latin translation of Aristotle's *De caelo* had been followed by the translation of the *Almagest* of Ptolemy, by the commentaries of Averroes, and by the *Kitāb al-Hay'ah* of Alpetragius that had been translated as the *Liber de motibus celorum* (Book of the Movements of the Heavens) in 1217 in Toledo by Michael Scot (1175–1232). The elaborate system of homocentric

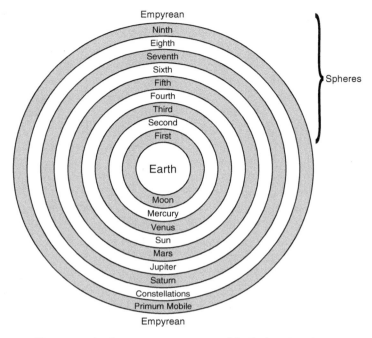

Figure 14.2 A schematic representation of the Ptolemaic universe.

spheres that Aristotle had developed to account for the irregularities of movement of the planets was substituted by Ptolemy's system of epicycles and eccentrics (referenced in *Convivio* II, iii, 16). Ptolemy's system was adopted by the Arab astronomers Alfraganus (Al-Farghānī, d. after 861) and Albatenius (Al Battānī, d. 929), but was challenged by Alpetragius and Averroes who reproposed versions of Aristotle's system.

Dantists have long held that Dante's chief direct astronomical source was the celebrated Arab astronomer of the ninth-century Alfraganus. His *Elementa Astronomica* (Elements of Astronomy, c.833) was a widely used epitome of Ptolemy's *Almagest* that had been translated into Latin in the twelfth century by Gerardus Cremomensis (*c*.1114–87), and again around 1142 by John of Seville (Johannes Hispalensis, *fl.* 1135–53). This latter version, which circulated under various titles, was in common use, and Dante cites it as the *Libro dell'aggregazione delle stelle* (The Book of the Gathering of the Stars) for its Ptolemaic account of the movement of the heavens in *Convivio* II, v, 16. Alfraganus's work, which has been identified as the source for numerous cosmological passages in the *Commedia* and

Dante's other works, offered a brief general sketch of some of the principal features of the Ptolemaic theories of the motions of the planets and served as an elementary introduction to Ptolemaic astronomy for students. It was the basis for a series of works that also served as textbooks used for the teaching of astronomy, including Sacrobosco's *Sphere*, which was followed by other treatises on the sphere, including works by the English scholastic philosopher and theologian Robert Grosseteste (*c*.1168–1253), and the Italian mathematician and astronomer Campanus of Novara (*c*.1220–96), whose *Theorica planetarum* (Theory of the Planets, 1261–64) contains the first-known Latin description of an *equatorium*, a mechanical device for computing the position of the planets. It is worth noting that *equatoria* made their first appearance in Europe outside Spain in the second half of the thirteenth century, and that the period witnessed a flood of astronomical reference works, including the first set of astronomical tables prepared in Christian Europe, the *Alfonsine Tables*, which enabled the calculation of eclipses and the positions of the planets for any given time.

Dante's first-hand observations of the heavens are referenced in the *Convivio* (III, ix, 15–6) and are exemplified throughout the *Commedia*. In keeping with the common tendency of medieval writers to cite classical and Arabic authorities yet rarely to refer to their Latin contemporaries by name, Dante mentions many, if not all, of the classical and Arabic cosmological authorities in the *Convivio*, while he never presents contemporary sources such as Sacrobosco or Campanus. For example, Dante mentions the ninth-century Arab astronomer and astrologer Albumasar (Abū Ma'shar, 787–886), who is remembered in the *Convivio* (II, xiii, 22) in connection with the 1301 appearance of Haley's comet. Yet Albert the Great's commentary on the *Liber de causis* has been identified as the likely source for information Dante attributes to Albumasar. This is just one example of the highly mediated character of Dante's cosmological knowledge. The works of Albert the Great, especially his commentaries on the *De caelo* and the *De meteoris*, are generally considered to be primary sources for much of Dante's cosmological knowledge.

Mention of Albumasar affords the opportunity to clarify the relationship between astrology and astronomy in the later Middle Ages. Dante uses one word, *astrologia*, to refer to what were increasingly perceived as two distinct categories of inquiry: astronomy and astrology. Astronomy concerned the motion of the stars and planets and sought to explain these using mathematics and geometry. Astrology, on the other hand, studied the influence of the stars on the sub-lunar world. Beginning in the thirteenth century, astrological questions were addressed in the context of moral philosophy or theology, including whether it was legitimate to predict the future or whether the influence of celestial bodies and motions of the heavens compromised free will – all issues that Dante addressed in the *Commedia*. The extent of the influence of astrology on Dante's poetry remains, moreover, an open question for Dante scholarship, particularly as regards *Paradiso*, where the disposition of the souls in the planetary spheres and the characterizations of the seven planetary heavens clearly reflect contemporary astrological lore.

Returning to the number and order of the heavens, a tenth, termed the Empyrean, was added to medieval Ptolemaic Aristotelian cosmology, and located above and beyond the other heavens, and had been 'put there by the Catholics', as Dante says in the *Convivio* (III, iii, 8). The concept had originated in scriptural exegesis and theological commentary on the distinction between the heaven that was created on the first day of creation (Gen. I, 1) and the firmament brought forth on the second (Gen. I, 6). The latter came to be designated as the visible heaven and the former was reserved as the abode of the angels and the place where they were created. The distinction first appeared in the Venerable Bede's (*c.*673–735) commentary on the book of Genesis, the *Libri quatuor in principium Genesis* (Four Books on the Beginning of Genesis), and later, in the *Glossa ordinaria* (Ordinary Gloss), the standard commentary on the Bible probably composed by Anselm of Laon (d. 1117), who used material attributable to Walafrid Strabo (*c.*808–49), in which the heaven of the first day was called the 'empyrean'. This gloss was quoted in the *Sentences* of Peter Lombard (*c.*1096–1164), a theological textbook that generated an extensive commentary tradition. It was in this way that the Empyrean secured a place in medieval cosmology. For example, both Robert Grosseteste and later Sacrobosco included discussion of the Empyrean in their astronomical treatises, while Michael Scot, in his commentary on Sacrobosco, gave careful consideration to the physical features of the Empyrean, developing some of the same arguments concerning its immobility that Dante would later use in his discussion of the heavens in the *Convivio* (II, viii–x). There Dante fashioned a kind of compromise between theological and astronomical perspectives on the Empyrean that was not untypical of his age, by combining Neoplatonic metaphysics of light (in calling it 'the luminous heaven') with Aristotelian physics of place (in describing it as 'motionless with respect to each of its parts').

Speculation about the physical and philosophical nature of the Empyrean had gained new impetus after the Condemnation of 1277, since the tenth heaven of the Christians seemed to offer a possible solution to

## Cosmology, geography, and cartography

the conundrum of the place of the world that had vexed the Aristotelians (see Chapter 11). Since, according to Aristotle's physics, the place of a body was defined as the motionless surface of the containing body, Aristotle had concluded that the last sphere, the heaven of the Fixed Stars, could not itself be in a place. This led to numerous discussions of whether the world is in a place, discussions that began in late antiquity (Themistius, 317–*c*.390) and continued among Arabic philosophers (Avicenna, Averroes, Avempace (Ibn Bājjah, *c*.1085–1138)) and among Christian theologians and philosophers during the late Middle Ages (Bacon, Albert the Great, Aquinas, Giles of Rome (*c*.1243–1316)). One opinion located the place of the outermost celestial sphere in an all-encompassing, immobile sphere that satisfied Aristotle's basic definition of place as a containing body. This immobile orb became identified with the theologically derived Empyrean, thereby canonizing the Empyrean's status. But while Dante's discussion of the tenth heaven in the *Convivio* offered a compromise between astronomical and non-astronomical perspectives, his conception of the Empyrean in the *Commedia* resolved any residual tension between astronomy and theology in terms of the metaphysical relationship between the Neoplatonic one and the many (*Par.* XXVII, 106–14). In the poem, Dante's Empyrean is immaterial and does not exist in space and time. Dante's identification of the Empyrean with the beatific vision was perhaps unique among theologians of his time. While the Catholic tradition held that the Empyrean was created together with the angels and matter, Dante did not include the Empyrean in his 'map' of the cosmos in *Paradiso* XXVIII, 13–39, nor did he list it among the first created things in *Paradiso* XXIX, 22–36.

No less than the problem of the number and the order of the heavens and of the Empyrean, the question of who moved the heavens was the subject of intense speculation and debate during Dante's time. In *Convivio* II, iv–v, Dante conveniently provides the context for his own proposals by offering a condensed history of different views about the matter, 'although the truth is now known' (*Conv.* II, iv, 2). They range from Aristotle's celestial movers, to Plato's Ideas, to the pagan gods and goddesses of the ancients, to the angels of the Bible, to the teaching of the Holy Church, which 'divides them into three hierarchies … each hierarchy itself having three orders … and affirms that there are nine orders of spiritual creatures' (*Conv.* II, v, 5). In a few paragraphs Dante managed to recapitulate a long process that over the centuries had brought into contact two originally distinct and unconnected sets of ideas relating to the celestial movers or separated substances of Aristotilean cosmology on the one hand, and those relating to the angels of the Judaeo-Christian tradition on the other.

A Greek Neoplatonic writer, known as the pseudo-Dionysius, or the Areopagite, who identified himself as the same Dionysius, a judge who was converted upon hearing St Paul's sermon delivered to the Areopagus, the Council of Athens (Acts XVII, 34), but who actually wrote between the end of the fifth and the beginning of the sixth century, had first brought together the intelligences of the pagan philosophers with the biblical angels, although nowhere in pseudo-Dionysius' Neoplatonic angelology is there the suggestion that the angelic intelligences have any physical cosmological role. (For Dante, as for other writers of the Middle Ages, the pseudo-Dionysius had authority nearly equal to that of Scripture.) It was only after the circulation of translations into Latin of Aristotle and the Arabic philosophers had aroused renewed interest in the question of how the physical heavens were moved that cosmological speculation began to intersect with Christian theological traditions regarding the angels, including the angelic hierarchy of pseudo-Dionysius.

Thomas Aquinas, for example, argued that an intellectual principle superior in nature to that of the material spheres must cause the movement of the heavens. By identifying that intelligence with the angels, Aquinas established a bond between cosmological and theological orders that prepared the way for Dante's *Paradiso*. Some theologians such as Robert Kilwardby (*c.*1215–79) shared Aquinas' willingness to equate the intelligences with angels, while other more conservative thinkers, such as Albert the Great, were wary of the use being made by Christian writers of the new Aristotelian learning and resisted efforts to reconcile philosophical and theological truths. Dante, for his part, supported the assimilation of Graeco-Arabic cosmology regarding separate substances into a Christian world-view, and went much further than Aquinas and any other philosophical or theological authority along this path. While Aquinas attributed the physical function of movers of the heavens only to the choir of Virtues, for Dante, each of the orders of the pseudo-Dionysian angelic hierarchy move one or the other of the nine heavens according to their position in the order.

Pseudo-Dionysius had set forth a clear system of three hierarchies of angels, each with three choirs in descending order: Seraphim, Cherubim, Thrones; Dominations, Virtues, Power; Principalities, Archangels, and finally, Angels. This arrangement was the most influential in the Middle Ages, although there was a great deal of discussion about the order and the characteristics of the hierarchies and their components among later writers, some of whom proposed different arrangements. In particular, Gregory the Great (*c.*540–604) proposed a different ordering in his *Moralia in Iob* (Moral Interpretation of the Book of Job, XXXII, xxiii, 48) in descending enumeration (Seraphim, Cherubim, Powers; Principalities, Virtues, Dominations; Thrones, Archangels, Angels), which Dante followed in the *Convivio* (II, v, 6), only to correct this ordering and replace it with that of pseudo-Dionysius in the *Commedia* (*Par.* XXVIII, 130–9). Theologians were well aware that the two leading authorities on the subject of angelology, Gregory the Great and pseudo-Dionysius, disagreed in their orderings of the hierarchy. While scholastics might cite one or the other, they appear to have felt little need to make a definitive choice between the two. Dante, on the other hand, makes a clear choice between the two options in the transition from the *Convivio* to the *Commedia*. In developing the architecture of *Paradiso*, he needed a sturdy cosmological account of the movers and he emphatically called attention to this structure at several points in the third canticle (*Par.* VIII, 34–7; IX, 61–3; XVIII, 28–30; XXVIII, 98–105).

Dante stands out against the background of contemporary cosmological thought for his remarkable powers of synthesis, as exemplified by his integration of Neoplatonic and Aristotelian strands in his conception of the heavens and their relationship to the angelic orders. The allegorical connections he further developed between the heavens, the angelic hierarchy, and the system of the liberal arts and sciences represented yet another groundbreaking fusion of cosmological ideas (*Conv.* II, xiii–xiv). A tradition linking the liberal arts to the heavens went back at least as far as Martianus Capella's *De nuptiis Philologiae et Mercurii* (The Marriage of Philology and Mercury), and the allegorical relationship between the heavens and the arts had later been featured in works ranging from Alain de Lille's (*c.*1116/17–1202/03) *Anticlaudianus* (Against Claudian, 1181–84) to Alexander Neckam's (1157–1217) *De naturis rerum* (On the Nature of Things, *c.*1180) to Ristoro d'Arezzo's *La composizione del mondo* (The Composition of the World, *c.*1282), to the ninth book of Boncompagno da Signa's (1170–1240) *Rhetorica novissima* (Newest Rhetoric, 1235), in which the list of the sciences is introduced as a cosmic 'vision' revealed to Boncompagno, the 'prophet'. However, as was noted at the outset, the traditional educational model of the liberal arts and the genre of the medieval encyclopaedia were both in crisis by Dante's time, having been put under increased pressure since the early thirteenth century by the revolutionary impact of the new currents of Aristotelian natural philosophy. Unlike other authors in this tradition, such as Martianus Capella, Dante did not actually use the order of the sciences to structure his own presentation. The allegorical construction of the relationship between the sciences and the heavens that he sketches in the *Convivio* would later become the subject of direct poetic representation in the cosmographical voyage of the poet-pilgrim through the heavens of *Paradiso*.

Dante's breakthrough in poetic cosmology was inspired by rich traditions of cosmographical literature associated with the so-called School of Chartres that merit brief mention here. Compared to the cosmological contexts of Ptolemaic–Aristotelian astronomy and of theological commentary regarding angelic intelligences, Dante scholarship has tended to undervalue the influence of Neoplatonic journeys through the heavens that provided an important cosmographical model for Dante. Authors associated in one way or another with the Chartrian 'School', such as Bernard of Chartres (d. before 1130), William of Conches (*c.*1100–54), Thierry of Chartres (d. before 1155), and John of Salisbury (1110–80), sought to reconcile Christian theology with a Platonist conception of the ordering of the world and a taste for natural science. Their primary source, aside from the information that they could gather from the Fathers (especially Augustine) and Boethius, was the *Timaeus* as translated and commented on by Calcidius. Another important source of Chartrian Platonism was Macrobius' commentary on Cicero's *Dream of Scipio*. The principal poets connected to the School of Chartres who developed Neoplatonic cosmological literature included Bernard Silvestris (1085–1178), author of the *Cosmographia* (Description of the Universe, between 1143 and 1148), a Latin philosophical allegorical prosimetron (mix of prose and verse) dealing with the creation of the universe; and Bernard's successor Alain de Lille, author of the *De planctu naturae* (The Lament of Nature, late 1160s) and the *Anticlaudianus*. Both the *Cosmographia* and the *Anticlaudianus* present suggestive similarities with the *Commedia*. The *Anticlaudianus*, for example, is an allegorical-philosophical epic in which the seven liberal arts construct a carriage that, guided by the five senses, conducts Phronesis, Reason, and Prudence through the seven spheres, a journey that features lengthy discussions of astronomy and astrology based on cosmographical authorities including Ptolemy and Albumasar, among others. The group encounters on their journey the goddess Theology and, subsequently, Faith. Only Phronesis in the end can gain access to the Empyrean. Dante's boldest innovation with respect to this tradition was to put himself, a historical individual, in the place of an allegorical figure on the journey through the spheres to the Empyrean.

To speak of cosmology in the late medieval period was to move between the poles of astronomy/astrology and of geography, that is, between the heavens and the earth. It is therefore time to return to the earth, as Dante

# Cosmology, geography, and cartography

did when he composed the *Questio de aqua et terra* around 1320, that is, at about the same time that he was rectifying, in the final cantos of *Paradiso*, the errors of the theologians as regards the order of the angels, and writing an account of creation and the fall of Lucifer. Recent Dante scholarship has argued for a fundamental continuity between the cosmology of the scholastic treatise and the *Commedia*. Indeed, the treatise explains that the reason why land emerges from the waters is a consequence of the providential design of creation, and specifically of the influence of the heaven of the Fixed Stars or Starry Heaven. Dante's participation in the contemporary debate on this question appears to have constituted an indirect *apologia* for the cosmology of the poem and a vindication of his authority as 'cosmographos' (*Questio* 53). Written on the cusp of the transition from the natural philosophy of the classical and medieval periods to the beginnings of observational and experimental science, the *Questio* offers an excellent example of the scholastic view of geography and geology. Dante's solution to the problem of the water and the land is in line with traditional cosmology, and is not in contradiction with principles of Aristotelian physics, even though his explanation for the emergence of the land cannot be deduced from physical principles.

In fact, the basic premises and the method of the *Questio* are characteristic of Dante's medieval context and derive from the same Ptolemaic–Aristotelian sources that were characteristic of his age. As far as his finalistic interpretation of the cause of the emergence of the land is concerned, Dante followed Michael Scot, Roger Bacon, Pietro d'Abano (*c.*1257–1316), Campanus of Novara, and Giles of Rome. In many details, Dante's explanation is similar to that of Ristoro d'Arezzo, for whom the stars caused the mountains by drawing them up into a topographical replica of the constellations by a kind of celestial magnetism. In terms of the history of science, Dante is not as bold as Jean Buridan, who, in the next generation, moved beyond Aristotle to develop his own cosmological theories, positing that the centre of the earth's magnitude did not coincide with its centre of gravity; that the two centres strove continuously to coincide; and that this process pushed previously immersed regions out of the oceans forming new mountains.

Dante had good reason to want to defend his status as 'cosmographos' in the *Questio* given the bold and unprecedented integration of Aristotelian cosmology and Christian theology that he presented in the *Commedia*. As with the heavens and the angels, Dante reserved for the poem his most original contributions in relation to contemporary cosmology, both in his account of Satan's fall and his 'discovery' (as a kind of Columbus *ante*

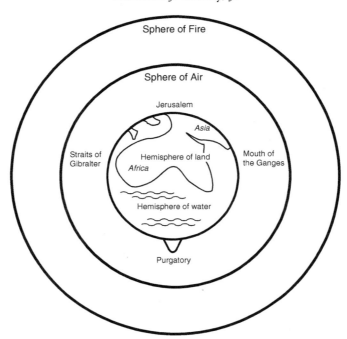

Figure 14.3 Map of the earth.

*litteram*) of the Earthly Paradise at the summit of Mount Purgatory, which he located at the antipodes from Jerusalem, the centre of the emerged lands and the site of Christ's redeeming sacrifice. Dante's highly original, not to say unprecedented location of the Earthly Paradise in the southern hemisphere (most authorities had placed it in the extreme East) was consistent with Aristotelian and Neoplatonic cosmological traditions that located the top of the world in the southern hemisphere (Figure 14.3).

Classical cosmologies had conceived of the world anthropomorphically, namely, according to the microcosm of the human body that projected onto the cosmos an organization of space according to three pairs of absolute orientations (high–low, right–left, front–back), so that high, right, and front represented the three principal spatial determinations. The top of the world was located in the southern hemisphere since, according to Aristotle, the proper orientation of man in the world (a prelapsarian orientation from a Christian point of view) was to have the heaven of the Fixed Stars rising in the East on the right and turning to the right (*De caelo* II, 2, 285b 16–19), which was also, according to Plato's *Timaeus*, the movement of identity

## Cosmology, geography, and cartography

and perfection and the visible form of eternity, as opposed to the retrograde movement of the planets along the zodiac from west to east, which was taken as the sign of generation and corruption. A body in space that realized these conditions could only be located in the southern hemisphere, as Dante made clear in describing the sunrise on the first day in Purgatory (*Purg.* I, 19–30). The northern hemisphere is the bottom of the world in Aristotelian cosmology, the 'widowed site' (*Purg.* I, 26) of man's exile from a Christian perspective. Fundamental to the *Commedia*'s cosmology and its poetic narrative, therefore, was the idea that the inhabited world is upside down with respect to the absolute orientation of the cosmos, a fact which, for Dante, assumed profound theological significance, and which he narrativized in his account of Lucifer's fall from Paradise, the preliminary event of salvation history (*Inf.* XXXIV, 121–6; *Par.* XXIX, 49–57).

Otherwise, Dante's geographical *imago mundi* was fundamentally the same as that of his medieval and late medieval contemporaries, as this was found in *mappaemundi* or world maps, both verbal mappings, such as the *descriptio orbis* at the beginning of Paulus Orosius' (*c.*375–418) *Historiarum Adversum Paganos Libri VII* (Histories against the Pagans in Seven Books, 416–7) or Brunetto Latini's (*c.*1220–93) *mappaemundi* in *Il tesoretto* (Little Treasure) and *Tresor* (Treasure, 1262–6), and in pictorial mappings, as found in illustrations of manuscripts of works of Sallust (*c.*86–*c.*35/34 BCE), Lucan (39–65), Macrobius, St Isidore (*c.*560–636), Beatus of Liébana (*c.*730–*c.*800), Hugh of St Victor (*c.*1096–1141), and Honorius Augustodunensis (*fl.* 1106–35), author of the *Imago mundi* (Image of the World). In addition, large-sheet maps and wall maps were produced, nearly all of which are lost. The lone complete survivor of a late medieval large-sheet world map is found in Hereford Cathedral (*c.*1300).

The so-called Beatus maps that accompanied the second book of Beatus Liébana's *Commentary on the Apocalypse* included a picture of Adam and Eve in the Earthly Paradise that was, according to some historians of cartography, the source of the genre of the encyclopaedic world map that developed in northern France and England, and that has often been associated with Dante's poetic encyclopaedic representation of the world. In fact, these maps, which were produced for display, for instruction, and for contemplation of God's world, placed within their geographical framework a great variety of information drawn from many sources including the Bible, accounts of the travels of Alexander the Great, bestiaries, and geographical works describing strange peoples in distant lands.

In general, the base form of these visual images of the world conformed to a common pattern, usually referred to as the T-O map. According to this model, the world was circular with the east and Asia at the top and the circle of the land surrounded by ocean. Africa and Europe were divided below by the Mediterranean, the stem of the T, which extended from the bottom of the map nearly to the centre. At the eastern end of the Mediterranean and at the top of the stem of the T, the Black Sea and the Don River to the left (north) and the Nile to the right (south), together extended horizontally to form the crossbar of the T, which marked the boundary of Asia. Jerusalem was located at or near to the map's centre. Dante integrated this basic pattern with his own innovative geographical concepts designed to support the Christian allegorical understanding of world geography in the poem. It has been suggested that Dante may have been inspired in his ordering of the poem's geographical structures by other current Christian geo-cosmological models of his time, such as the 'Great Circle' pilgrimage route from Rome to Egypt/Sinai to Jerusalem and back to Rome again for the plot structure of the three canticles, and by the medieval architectural mode of the Martyrium temple-tomb which marked a spiritual geographic centre that was related through earthly types and anti-types to Christ's tomb in Jerusalem.

The relative austerity of Dante's *mappaemundi*, however, when compared to examples of the encyclopaedic world map, such as the Hereford map, which were the product of cartographic traditions that had originated in England and France, may be related to Dante's Italo-centric point of view. During the thirteenth and fourteenth centuries, Italy and the Mediterranean witnessed the emergence of new, more empirically based forms of cartography. These portolan or nautical maps, of which some thirty survive from the fourteenth century, accurately represented for the first time the coasts and the ports of the Mediterranean and of the Black Sea, and also the Atlantic coasts of Europe, beyond the Straits of Cadiz. The earliest surviving example, the *Carte pisane* (Pisan Map), dates from the end of the thirteenth century, although the genre probably existed as long as a century before that. These were practical charts for use by navigators. They depict detailed coastal outlines and coastal towns are named. North is at the top of these maps and the magnetic compass, which came into use in the Mediterranean during this period, evidently played a part in their construction. At the same time, Palestine is the only area for which a significant number of regional maps survive from before the fifteenth century. Only two regional maps of Italy survive from Dante's time, both found in a single manuscript, a copy of Paolino Veneto's (*c*.1270–1344) *Chronologia magna* (Great Chronology, *c*.1323) produced in Naples during the 1330s. Dante integrated these newer forms of geo-cartographic representation with the traditional T-O pattern in the *Commedia*. Thus it is possible to find an analogy between Dante's representation of the inhabited world and the most advanced sectors of contemporary cartography. Dante's procedure brings together all three contemporary forms of mapping – the encyclopaedic *mappaemundi*, the nautical chart, and the regional map of Italy – and thus shows marked affinities to the contemporary cartography of the leading cartographer of his time, Pietro Vesconte (*fl.* 1310–30), who for the first time embedded the empirically based nautical chart of the Mediterranean within a *mappaemundi* scheme.

Yet the geographical setting of the poem presents a conservative, not to say somewhat outdated picture when considered in light of the contemporary travels by merchants and missionaries to the Far East, including those of Dante's contemporary Marco Polo (1254–1324), and the early explorations of the Atlantic in the west beyond the Pillars of Hercules, the Straits of Cadiz, that led to the rediscovery of the Canary Islands during the first decades of the fourteenth century. In order to achieve the cosmological synthesis in poetry that eluded his contemporaries, Dante had to exclude or suppress potentially disturbing or disruptive aspects that were appearing at the edges of the frame. Dante's cosmology in this sense, which he painstakingly began to assemble in the *Convivio* and brought to full expression in the *Commedia*, represented the over-determined swansong of a place-based Christian–Aristotelian conception of a world in which everything had its place and was in place. Dante conceived of the divinity located in the Empyrean outside of time and space, whereas philosophers and theologians of the next generation, such as Oresme, Buridan, and Bradwardine (*c.*1290–1349), would move in the direction of equating God with spatial infinity. The poet's unprecedented assignment of a rank of the angelic hierarchy as mover for each of the heavens (and his original addition of Fortune–Providence as an additional sublunary member of the celestial hierarchy; *Inf.* VII, 73–96), similarly sought to reinforce the metaphysical certainty of God's providential design for humanity, including Dante's role in salvation history. Dante's invention of the shipwreck of Ulysses, besides offering a foil for the poet's own successful Christian journey of return from exile, corresponds to the poet's over-determined picture of the heavens in so far as it represents a gesture of resistance to the new extra-Mediterranean Atlantic space that was emerging. In response to the impending pressures of modernity, Dante fashioned a coherent and harmonious cosmological synthesis in the poem that responded to and sought to overcome a lack of coherence characteristic of a cosmological context that was at odds with his faith in the ultimate harmony and coherence of the Creator's design.

## Notes

1 E. Grant, 'Cosmology' in D. C. Lindberg (ed.), *Science in the Middle Ages* (University of Chicago Press, 1978), pp. 265–302, at p. 265).
2 L. Thorndike, *The Sphere of Sacrobosco and its Commentators* (University of Chicago Press, 1949), p. 119.
3 Thorndike, *The Sphere of Sacrobosco*, p. 119.

# PART III
## *Linguistic and literary cultures*

CHAPTER 15

# Linguistic Italy

*Mirko Tavoni*

*Translated by James Cotton*

What language or languages were spoken and written in different social situations in Italy during Dante's time? 'Italian', namely a common language used across the whole peninsula, clearly did not exist, neither as the language spoken by the entire population, nor even as the language of culture shared by intellectuals coming from all of Italy's regions and used in written communication from the Alps to Sicily. Literary language was not standardized until the sixteenth century, between two and two and a half centuries after Dante had written the *Commedia*. From the Cinquecento onwards, Italian intellectuals throughout Italy wrote essentially in the same Italian language, while the uneducated, who were for the most part illiterate, continued to communicate orally – and exclusively – in their own dialects for all the practical needs of day-to-day life. It has been estimated that when Italy achieved political unification in 1861, only 10 per cent of its population spoke Italian, so that the language could only be considered national on the literary level. However, the presence of a unified state put social processes in motion that gradually led to Italian becoming the spoken language of all, or nearly all, Italians.

Indeed, it is justifiably asserted that Dante was 'the father of the Italian language', since Italian does not predate him. This fact inevitably raises the question in just what language did Dante write the *Commedia* and his other vernacular works. The correct response is that Dante wrote the poem in the Florentine vernacular, his mother tongue, which later was to become Italian through a process that would take more than two centuries. It would do so by imposing itself on the vernaculars of other Italian cities, thanks primarily to the prestige of the great Florentine writers of the Trecento, especially Dante himself, but also Petrarch (1304–74) and Boccaccio (1313–75). It can thus be claimed that Dante is 'the father of the Italian language' because, by writing his masterwork in the Florentine vernacular, he increased the expressive and communicative capacity of this language to such a degree that it was given a very powerful push towards

243

becoming the future hegemonic literary and national language of the entire country.

In Dante's time, Italy was a place of many vernaculars, among which Florentine was only one. To give a general idea of how many and what kinds of vernaculars there were, we can turn to the *Carta dei dialetti d'Italia* (Map of the Dialects of Italy), compiled by the dialectologist Giovan Battista Pellegrini.[1] We find that the dialects observable in the field in modern times essentially correspond to the spoken vernaculars of Dante's time. Over the centuries Italy's dialects have remained more or less stable. A well-defined linguistic boundary runs along the La Spezia–Rimini line and divides the northern from the central and southern dialects. To the north of this line lie the dialects of Emilia-Romagna, Liguria, Piedmont, and Lombardy. These dialects are termed 'Gallo-Italic' because they are influenced by the pre-Latin, Celtic peoples who once lived in the Po valley. In these regions, therefore, the spoken Latin, and later the vernaculars derived from Latin, developed a tone very similar to that of spoken French and Occitan, with a strong tendency to drop unaccented vowels (HOSPITALEM > *bsdèl*), to reduce intervocalic double consonants to single consonants (TERRA > *tèra*), to weaken voiceless intervocalic consonants (FRATELLUM > *fradèl*; CAPILLI > *cavéi*), and to use 'mixed' tonic vowels, as in French (ROTA > *röda*). In comparison with Tuscan, then, we observe a very different linguistic type. Although the dialects of the Veneto share certain characteristics with Gallo-Italic dialects, they do not belong to this group, so that they differ less from Tuscan.

South of the La Spezia–Rimini line, Tuscan has clearly defined characteristics. The differences between the spoken medieval vernaculars of Florence, Pistoia, Pisa, Lucca, Siena, and Arezzo are well known. For example, Florentine has *lingua* (tongue), *fungo* (mushroom), Sienese *lengua*, *fongo*; Florentine has *più* (more) and *piazza* (square), Pisan *pió* and *piassa*. However, what these vernaculars have in common clearly outweighs the few differences that distinguish them. The central dialects of the Marches, Umbria, and Lazio are rather similar to Tuscan. Extending roughly southeast of the Macerata–Latina line are the southern dialects of Abruzzo–Molise, Campania, Basilicata, northern Calabria, and northern Puglia. Still further south, the southern Calabrian and Apulian (Salentine) dialects belong to the Sicilian type, and constitute the 'far south' dialects, with a different vocalic system from the rest of Italy (as we will see below when discussing Sicilian poetry). Sardinian is a language in its own right, with its own vocalic system, different from those of both Sicilian and the other Italian vernaculars.

*Linguistic Italy* 245

Except for Sardinian, which like Catalan, Occitan, and so on, is a language, all of today's 'dialects' were 'vernaculars' in Dante's time.[2] For all practical purposes, there is no difference between 'vernaculars' and 'dialects'. The two are in fact the same. The medieval vernaculars, handed down from one generation to the next, form an unbroken chain with today's dialects. However, the word 'dialect' is used to refer specifically to vernaculars from the Cinquecento to modern times, the period during which the 'Italian language', namely, the country's common literary language, reduced the prestige of the country's other vernaculars. As 'dialects', they are viewed as tools for municipal communication, and as having only a local range and a low register. Spoken rather than written, they are considered ill-suited as vehicles to address cultural matters and for communicating with those who are not native speakers of a particular dialect (except in cases when a writer intentionally chooses dialect for her or his own expressive purposes to compose what is termed 'reflexive dialect literature').

In Dante's time, however, the vernaculars had not yet become dialects. The principal vernaculars, associated with major cities such as Genoa, Milan, Venice, Bologna, Rome, Naples, and Messina, were for all practical purposes languages. They were used for oral communication in day-to-day life, and for both utilitarian and, up to a point, cultural writing. Florentine was not yet the 'Italian language', and Milanese was not yet considered a dialect. Rather, the two functioned as equivalent, or nearly equivalent, vernaculars; and both were used in their own urban centres in a wide range of communicative situations. Speaking purely hypothetically, if Dante, Petrarch, and Boccaccio had written their greatest works in Milanese or in Sicilian, the Italian language would have taken another turn completely, and today would be based on a Milanese or Sicilian linguistic type rather than on Florentine.

This statement, however, should be qualified. Dante's *De vulgari eloquentia*, citing various compositions 'in derision' (I, xi, 4–5) of other people's speech, reveals that a Tuscan sense of superiority over other vernaculars, felt as somehow 'dialectal', already existed in the Middle Ages. Thus the otherwise unknown Florentine Castra, cited by Dante, could write a *canzone* in parody of the language of the Marches that begins, 'Una fermana scopai da Cascioli / cita cita se 'n gìa 'n grande aina' (I met a girl from Fermo, near Cascioli, who hurried off quickly quickly). Similarly, Cecco Angiolieri (*c*.1260–1312) wrote the sonnet 'Pelle chiabelle di Dio, no ci arvai' (By the nails of God's Cross, don't come back here) to parody both the Roman vernacular and unrefined Tuscan speech.

Naturally, all the vernaculars that we are discussing derived from Latin. In Dante's time, in its home territory, each vernacular was the living continuation of the Latin that had been spoken there a thousand years before. Thus the Bolognese of Dante's day was the continuation of the spoken Latin of the Gallic Boii, and it had that Celtic 'timbre' that even today continues to make the dialects of the Po valley sound similar to French. But a thousand years earlier, those communities had only spoken and written in Latin. In Dante's time, Latin and the vernacular coexisted, but with clearly defined roles and in a clearly defined hierarchical relationship. To Latin was granted the superior role of language of culture, of written language par excellence, even though it was also used orally. To the vernacular was given the lesser role of practical, day-to-day communication, of a language that was primarily spoken, even if it was also used in writing. Linguists call this coexistence of two languages with their hierarchical distinction of roles 'diglossia'.

Replacing Latin monolingualism, which had held sway for a thousand years, Latin–vernacular diglossia came on the heels of a long period of linguistic transformation. This change had involved the whole of Romania, namely all the territories of the Roman empire where Latin had taken root and replaced the indigenous languages. In late antiquity, with the break up of the empire's administrative and educational structures, the spoken Latin of the various regions of Romania increasingly departed from literary Latin, which continued to be studied by very few. Without the check of education, spoken Latin transformed itself freely, assuming different features in different regions. Gradually, as the actual distance between the spoken languages and scholastic Latin increased, the subjective perception of that distance also increased. This eventually led to the realization that the spoken language, even though it was made of the same lexical components as Latin, was nevertheless no longer that language.

This process of the vernacular's distancing itself from Latin happened faster and with more intensity in France than in the rest of Romania. It is thus in France, perhaps unsurprisingly, that the first two famous attestations of a distinct awareness of the vernacular's separate existence are recorded. At the Council of Tours in 813, the Church recommended that, rather than preaching in Latin, priests deliver their sermons in 'popular Roman language' in order to be understood by the faithful. Then, in 842, the armies of the brothers Ludwig the German (802/06–76) and Charles the Bald (823–77) confirmed their alliance in the famous Oaths of Strasbourg. While they made the same oath, one did so in the 'Roman language', a version of Old French, and the other in Rhenish Franconian,

# Linguistic Italy

a form of Old High German. The event marks the official birth of the two languages and of the two nations – on one and the other shore of the Rhine. In much more private circumstances, the *Placito capuano* of 961, a simple formulaic statement given before a notary regarding the possession of certain lands, records the earliest written attestation of an Italian vernacular, in this instance a distinctively Southern Italian one.

During the three centuries that go from the composition of the *Placito* to the end of the Duecento, the vernacular made great strides, such that by Dante's time most Italian vernaculars had instituted relatively stable written conventions, which found expression in the codification of practical writing, as well as in traditions of literary composition. Before considering the vernacular's written forms, attention must be paid to its various spoken uses. First and foremost, the problem arises of the precise character of the vernaculars spoken in different cities and regions. As has been noted, the map of Italy's medieval vernaculars was largely similar to today's dialect map. However, as the spoken language obviously did not leave behind any tangible records, we can only attempt to reconstruct it from the written records that have reached us.

A substantial amount of documentation survives on the Tuscan vernaculars, including texts dealing with practical matters and those of minor literary value. The authors of such texts were not expected to elevate their language rhetorically, thereby guaranteeing a good degree of fidelity to what must have been the vernacular's spoken forms. In particular, the Tuscan vernaculars have preserved more completely than others the Latin form of the word, and consequently Latin graphic conventions are almost perfectly able to render the sounds of the vernacular. Thanks to these written sources, then, we have strong evidence for what the spoken language of Tuscany must have been like. Systematic textual study of the written varieties of medieval Tuscan has produced accurate descriptions of the spoken varieties of the different Tuscan cities. The same may be said of Venetian and the Veneto region's other vernaculars, for which, like the Tuscan vernaculars, there exists a large amount of documentation, which scholars have systematically studied in detail.

For the Gallo-Italic dialects, as we have already seen, the integrity of the original Latin words had been highly compromised by strong phonetic transformations. As a result, the distance between the written form transmitted in texts and the presumed spoken forms of the spontaneous vernacular must be judged greater. Indeed, few texts survive that can be considered faithful transcriptions of the living, spoken vernacular of Milan, Mantua, Bergamo, or Forlì (some of the more faithful passages are discussed at the end of this chapter). Even when texts had a practical function or were of a modest literary value, two mediations intervened, as much in the author's mind as in the copyist's. The first was the tendency, perhaps unconscious, to minimize provincialisms and to drop traits that might have been felt as strictly local. The second was the influence of the memory of the written Latin word, which would have been familiar to anyone who had received even the most basic schooling, and which always conditioned the graphic form of a municipal vernacular text. Consequently, the written texts that have reached us are, to some degree, almost invariably Latinized in their graphic form. Similar observations can be made for southern texts, though these exist in considerably smaller numbers than northern texts. Thus, while almost all medieval texts reveal the characteristic features of their vernaculars, they do so in diluted form and only indirectly. They lack the fidelity of present-day transcriptions of original passages of spoken dialect into phonetic alphabet.

In some cases, there is no continuity between the old and modern forms of a city's spoken language. The most obvious case is that of *romanesco*, the Roman vernacular, which today is not a true dialect, but Italian with local features (the Roman variety of Italian is very well represented in the language of cinema, television, politics, etc.). In the thirteenth and fourteenth centuries, however, *romanesco* was a southern vernacular similar to Neapolitan. The change from medieval to modern *romanesco* was the result of two factors: first, the overwhelming Tuscanization brought about, in the first decades of the sixteenth century, by the Medici popes Leo X (1475–1521) and Clement VII (1478–1534), and second and more significantly, the repopulation of the city after the Sack of Rome in 1527 with immigrants transferred from central Italy.

But how did the different areas communicate verbally? The vernaculars of the Italian peninsula, as we noted, are very different from one another. It has even been maintained that there are as many linguistic varieties in the Italian peninsula as there are in the rest of Romania combined. The linguistic boundary of the La Spezia–Rimini line not only separates the northern Italian dialects from the central and southern ones, but also separates western Romance (the Gallo-Italic dialects belong to the same language group as the Gallo-Romance dialects of France) from eastern Romance (central and southern Italian dialects are akin rather to Rumanian). Given this state of affairs, how did speakers of different vernaculars understand each another?

Little evidence exists to help us answer these questions. Nonetheless, we can look at what merchants and preachers did, since these were the

*Linguistic Italy* 249

two main groups of speaker-writers involved in inter-regional communication. Merchants were a social class that produced a vast amount of writing. They needed to keep records of their business and commercial activities, and thus began to produce written texts very early. The oldest surviving Tuscan text is the *Conto navale pisano* (Pisan Naval Account), hailing from the end of the eleventh or the beginning of the twelfth century, a small piece of parchment that has miraculously survived and on which the costs of building a galley were set down. The oldest Florentine text is the account book of some bankers from 1211. Merchants, for reasons of professional need, all knew how to write and keep accounts, but only in the vernacular. They learned writing and arithmetic at the 'abacus schools', technical schools that exclusively taught in the vernacular. In contrast, grammar schools provided an introduction to a liberal education in Latin. Especially in Florence literacy rates of a technical and commercial rather than of a humanistic nature were very high (see Chapter 16).

Merchants, and along with them artisans, bankers, and all those involved in economic activity, produced copious quantities of particularly one type of writing: letters. There is a veritable explosion of letter-writing from the fourteenth century onwards; however, given the high levels of economic activity beginning in the thirteenth century (see Chapter 2), significant epistolary exchange must have been the norm for considerably longer. The archive of Francesco Datini (1335–1410), a merchant from Prato, with its tens of thousands of letters by more than four thousand writers, offers the most impressive evidence of this trend. A common feature of letter-writing was the spontaneous, reciprocal tendency of the writer to approach the language of the addressee. This occurred when the exchange took place both within Italian linguistic borders and within those of the Romance area in general. Tuscan writers addressed Sicilian, Apulian, Catalan, or Occitan colleagues in their own vernacular, but also included features of the recipient's vernacular, and vice versa. It does not appear that translators or interpreters were necessary within the Romance-language-speaking world. The case was different with English, German, or Arab merchants. German–Venetian exchanges of the fifteenth century bear witness to bilingual practices for trade beyond the Brenner Pass; but such exchanges were limited to the most common subjects of daily life and to standard business operations. Meantime, in the eastern Mediterranean, which was dominated by the naval and mercantile power of Venice, a form of the Venetian vernacular, the 'Venetian of across the sea', functioned as the lingua franca of trade with Greeks, Arabs, and Turks.

The ability to communicate within Romance-language-speaking Europe, as attested by the mercantile letters, must also, and especially, have held good for oral communication, which in addition would have been bolstered by pragmatic supports when the interlocutors came face to face. Equally, the merchant who traded by land across the Alps and by sea on the Mediterranean's southern and eastern shores must have developed similar skill through practical experience. The written documentation in support of this is largely of a later date; however, as trade was already highly developed between the thirteenth and fourteenth centuries, it is reasonable to assume that people were communicating with each other even before they left traces of this in the texts that have come down to us.

In the Middle Ages, preaching was an enormously important social practice, as well as the most significant, if not the only form of mass communication in a world where technology for such communication did not exist. As is clear from the resolution of the Council of Tours in 813, preaching had always been crucial in the life of the Church, and it had become even more important with the development of the Dominican and Franciscan mendicant orders in the middle of the thirteenth century. It is no accident that the Dominicans called themselves the *Ordo Fratrum Praedicatorum* (Order of Preaching Friars). With the mendicant orders, a new style of preaching, the *sermo modernus* (modern sermon), came into being (the former style was called *sermo antiquus*, or old). The *sermo modernus*, based on a rigorous, logical method of preaching, developed from the model of the university disputation, an unsurprising development given that the mendicants, besides being preachers, had also been the founders of universities. Their sermons were filled with *exempla*, moral anecdotes that recounted instances of good behaviour to imitate and of bad conduct to avoid.

Preaching was the primary means by which the Church stayed connected to the faithful, and thirteenth-century city planning has left proof of this (see Chapter 25). Spacious squares were built in front of big churches, where homilies could be given before a very large audience. Examples from Dante's Florence, which are still standing today, include the piazzas in front of the Dominican basilica, Santa Maria Novella, and the Franciscan Santa Croce. In a society where mass literacy did not normally exist, except for in a highly advanced environment such as Florence, preaching provided the people with fundamental education: moral instruction, naturally, which also functioned as a means of social control; however, it also served to bring about acculturation and offered a veritable 'language instruction'. In very general terms, the Franciscans were the

*Linguistic Italy* 251

more 'popular', and their sermons were more inclined to entertain, even resorting to theatrical and histrionic expedients as easy means of indoctrination. Conversely, the Dominicans were more didactic. They elucidated passages from the gospels, clarifying both the content and language, and were consciously focused on broadening the knowledge and vernacular lexical competence of their listeners. A contemporary of Dante, Giordano da Pisa (*c.*1260–1310), is the major example of the practice of giving 'language instruction' through preaching.

Often itinerant, preachers spoke all over Italy. We have very little direct evidence of how their sermons may have sounded. The preacher would normally map out the sermon in Latin, and its *reportationes*, the transcriptions of the spoken sermon prepared by listeners, were in their turn also often in Latin. Even when the sermons were copied in the vernacular, we cannot be sure how linguistically faithful they are to the actual, spoken sermons. And yet, despite this lack of conclusive evidence, the practice of itinerant preaching, like that of mercantile exchange, suggests an ability for communication between preachers and listeners, who were native speakers of different vernaculars, greater than we today consider possible. Nor can the possibility be dismissed that preachers employed Latin phrases during the delivery of their sermons, whether the lines of Scripture on which the sermon was focused, or passages of commentary that the preacher himself had written. A century later, from the mid Quattrocento onwards, we find the *sermoni mescidati*, sermons that mix Latin and vernacular, and which seem to be the model for macaronic poetry, comic verse from the end of the fifteenth century that Latinized the most rustic vernaculars of the Veneto and Piedmont and presented these in the high, courtly forms of the Virgilian hexameter. While macaronic poetry was undoubtedly parodic, and the *sermoni mescidati* were actual sermons of a serious nature, both were nonetheless made of the same linguistic mix. The problem arises of the reasons for the mingling of Latin and vernacular. While a fully satisfactory answer to this question is not possible, the evidence suggests that preachers in Dante's time began with an original text or an outline of a sermon written in Latin, but extemporized in the vernacular, yet without hesitating to deliver some parts in Latin. Furthermore, they were more or less able to modify a homily's vernacular according to the place and linguistic and cultural milieu in which they found themselves.

In general, communication within the Italian and Romance vernaculars must have been considerable. A continuum existed between geographically neighbouring vernaculars, whereby speakers must have been conscious of both what united and divided them linguistically, thereby facilitating communication. It would be the emergence of national languages and their grammatical formalization, running in tandem with the consolidation of the nation state in the sixteenth century, that would make the Romance languages much more obviously 'foreign' to each other in a manner that the ordinary speaker had never before been aware. Evidence that the linguistic zone of the Romance languages was perceived as unitary – Dante, in the *De vulgari eloquentia*, subsumed the three languages of *oc*, *oïl*, and *sì* under the designation *nostrum ydioma* (our language, I, x, 1; the languages are designated by their respective terms for 'yes': *oc* for Occitan, *oïl* for Old French, and *sì* for Italian) – is the fact that the two Gallo-Romance languages, Occitan and Old French, which had had an earlier literary development than Italian, were perceived rather than as the languages of other nations, as specialist languages suited for particular types of literary writing. Thus Occitan was deemed the most prestigious language for lyric poetry, while Old French stood out as the most prominent language for narrative and doctrinal prose. As a consequence, in the first half of the Duecento, numerous Italian lyric poets wrote in Occitan, as did the Genoese Lanfranco Cigala (d. before 1258), the Mantuan Sordello da Goito (1200/10–69?), and the Venetian Bartolomeo Zorzi (*c.*1260–*c.*1300). Then, in the second half of the thirteenth century, important Italian prose writers wrote in Old French, including the Venetian Martino da Canal (d. after 1275) in his *Les Estoires de Venise* (The Histories of Venice, 1267–75), and Rustichello da Pisa (d. after 1298), first in his compilation of Arthurian tales, and later, under Marco Polo's (1254–1324) dictation, *Le divisament dou monde* (The Description of the World; 1298) or *Il Milione* (this title may be based on Polo's nickname, possibly Emilione).

A kind of synergy must also have existed between Latin and the vernacular in oral communication in various social situations of day-to-day life. Latin was undoubtedly spoken among the *litterati*, those who had received a scholastic education based on the study of Latin. Thus, in the universities Latin was considered the requisite international language, given that teachers and students hailed from *nationes* (nations) as diverse as Spain and Hungary, as was the case at the University of Bologna, with which Dante had contacts. But Latin was also used among high clergymen, in legal disputes, and in the administrative offices of the State. The language also appeared in diverse social situations where *litterati* and *illiterati* interacted, alternating variously or intermingled with the vernacular. In the life of the Church, as we have seen, Latin passages were introduced into preaching. The liturgy was completely in Latin and, to some degree,

## Linguistic Italy

was understood by the faithful, who memorized Latin prayers and hymns. Merchants and artisans, who were *illiterati*, constantly interacted in the course of their commercial transactions with *litterati*, with notaries who employed a practical kind of Latin, quite different from literary Latin. In the statutes of the Commune of Bologna of 1246, notaries had to demonstrate that they were able to write, and that they were able to read what they wrote in the vernacular (*vulgariter*) and in Latin (*litteraliter*), as well as being able to speak or translate in Latin (*latinare*) and write letters in Latin (*dictare*). Notaries thus needed to show an aptitude, in both speaking and writing, for switching back and forth between Latin and vernacular – a skill similar to that expected of preachers.

The *volgarizzamenti*, the translations of Latin and Old French texts into the vernacular *di sì*, constituted an important development that occurred over the entire course of the Duecento. In essence, the *volgarizzamenti* effected a major transfer of Latin knowledge and literature to the language of *sì*. A similar process occurred with Old French, which, as we saw, had achieved pre-eminence over the other vernaculars as the language of prose. Only the first type of *volgarizzamenti* were vernacularizations in the strict sense of the word; that is to say, they were 'vertical' translations from Latin, the supreme language of culture, to a vernacular. The vernacularizations from Old French were 'horizontal' translations, moving from one vernacular (albeit a more prestigious one) to another. The *volgarizzamenti* of the Duecento enriched the language of *sì*, and they did so by expanding the lexicon and developing syntactic means able to support complex narrative structures and to express intricate subject-matter. They laid the linguistic foundations on which Dante, Petrarch, and Boccaccio would build their masterworks, which in turn would further elevate the vernacular to new heights of expressive and intellectual power.

In this environment of vernacularizing from Latin, beginning in the last decade of the Duecento, we find attested the first uses of the highly suggestive terminological opposition between *gramatica*, meaning Latin, and *volgare*, meaning the vernacular. Thus in Florence in 1292, in the *volgarizzamento* from the Latin of Paulus Orosius' (*c*.375–418) *Historie adversus paganos* (Histories against the Pagans), one reads: 'Here begins the first book of Paulus Orosius, teller of Histories, translated from "grammar" [Latin] into the vernacular [volgare] by Bono Giamboni.' Similarly, the *Statuti senesi* (Sienese Statutes) of 1305 state: 'The aforementioned constitutions must be written in "grammar" and in the vernacular, in a book of kid-goat or sheepskin leaves in "grammar"; and another book of similar leaves must be written in the vernacular.' The terminology reveals Latin to be identified with grammar, typical of medieval diglossia. The association is more than understandable: Latin had ceased to be anyone's mother tongue and had to be learned through the scholastic study of grammar, since, at the time, Latin was the only language whose grammar had been codified. The perception that the vernacular was a 'natural' language and Latin a scholastic one was a basic linguistic notion of the time. The idea finds its most rigorous theorized expression in Dante's *De vulgari eloquentia* (I, i, 2–4), which defined the 'vernacular language' as that language 'which we learn without formal instruction by imitating our nurses', and referred to the 'other language which is at one remove from us, and which the Romans termed *gramatica*' and in which 'few achieve complete fluency, since knowledge of its rules and theory can only be achieved by dedication to a long course of study', before concluding that the first 'is natural to us, while the other, in contrast, is artificial'.

Thus far we have concentrated on the spoken uses of language, the dynamics of linguistic communication in social contexts, and the perception of languages in the collective thinking of the period – all aspects regarding language that, in general, literary accounts tend to overlook. However, the time has now come to present, albeit briefly, the written and literary usages of the various vernaculars in Dante's Italy (the final section of this chapter ought to be read together with Chapters 21 and 22.).

The Florence of Dante's time, an exceptional economic powerhouse, was also at the heart of that part of Italy, as Villani would note, with the highest concentration of literacy and the greatest density of practical writing, especially mercantile and administrative. Generally speaking, the earliest and largest number of *volgarizzamenti* of city statutes and of various guilds come from Tuscany, as well as translations of scientific, historical, and moral writings, including sermons with substantial didactic aims. Furthermore, by 1282 the first encyclopedia in the vernacular, Ristoro d'Arezzo's *La composizione del mondo colle sue cascioni* (The Composition of the World and its Causes), had appeared. Taken together, the *volgarizzamenti* laid a very strong foundation of culture in the vernacular, one on which a strong literary tradition could arise, as it in fact did in both poetry and prose.

As regards poetry, lyric poems originally composed between 1230 and 1250 at the court of Emperor Frederick II (1194–1250) in refined Sicilian vernacular were copied in Tuscany and their original language was rendered in Tuscan forms. Around the middle of the century, this Tuscanized Sicilian poetry offered the stimulus for lyric production in imitation of Sicilian and Occitan models, hence its designation as 'Sicilian–Tuscan'

*Linguistic Italy* 255

(*siculo-toscano*), which found its undisputed master in Guittone d'Arezzo (*c.*1235–94). Beginning in the 1280s, Florentine and Pistoiese poets of the so-called *Stilnovo* (New Style) – Guido Cavalcanti (1250/59–1300), Dante, and Cino da Pistoia (1270–1336/37) – reacted against Guittone under the influence of the Bolognese Guido Guinizzelli (*c.*1235–76), who had been active between 1265 and 1276. As regards vernacular prose, the first example of a highly sophisticated moral prose was written in Tuscan, once again by Guittone in his letters. Furthermore, another instance of moral writing, the *Libro dei vizi e delle virtudi* (Book of Vices and Virtues) by Bono Giamboni (*c.*1240–92?), was composed in Florentine, as was the narrative prose of the *Novellino*, a Florentine collection of short stories that can be dated to the last two decades of the thirteenth century.

The total Tuscanization of the poetry of the Frederician court originally written in Sicilian is of considerable historical significance. This linguistic transformation is clearly evidenced in the language of the three surviving Tuscan lyric collections from the end of the Duecento: the Florentine MS Vat. Lat. 3793, the Pisan MS Laurenziano Redi 9, and the MS Banco Rari 217 of the Biblioteca Nazionale of Florence possibly originating from Pistoia. Except for a few fragments discovered centuries later, the Sicilian originals were destroyed. As the Sicilian vocalic system is different from that of Tuscan, the linguistic form after Tuscanization is markedly different from the original: tonic ĭ and ē in Sicilian become *i*, and not closed *e* as in Tuscan; while tonic ŭ and ō become *u*, and not closed *o* as in Tuscan. Taking an example from the Sicilian Guido delle Colonne (*c.*1210–*c.*1287) – 'Amor, che lungiamente m'ài menato / a freno stretto sanza riposanza, / alarga le tue redine in pietanza, / che soverchianza m'à vinto e stancato' (Love, you who has led me for a long time on a tight leash without repose, loosen your bridle in pity, because being overcome has defeated and fatigued me)[3] – it is obvious that, apart from the Occitanism in *–anza*, the entire phonetic system is Tuscan. Compare this to the quite different vocalism of one of the rare fragments to have survived in the original Sicilian, a *canzone* by Stefano Protonaro (*fl.* 1261), which begins: 'Pir meu cori allegrari / ki multu longiamenti / senza alligranza e ioi d'amuri è statu, / mi riturno in cantari' (In order to bring happiness to my soul that for a long time has been without happiness and joy of love, I return to sing). At the end of the Duecento in Tuscany, everyone, including Dante, read the Sicilian poets in their Tuscan form, and thus had no awareness that they had actually composed their verses in a different vernacular.

As evidenced by the influence exercised by Guido Guinizzelli on the stilnovist poets, Bologna and Florence enjoyed close ties. Indeed, Bologna too, and not far behind Florence, was at the vanguard of the literary use of the vernacular. The highly important Bolognese tradition of *ars dictaminis*, namely of rhetorical instruction in the composition of letters, was originally applied to Latin texts. Quite early on, however, at the beginning of the Duecento in fact, it was adapted to letter-writing and oratory in the vernacular by Guido Faba (*c.*1190–*c.*1243) in his *Gemma purpurea* (Purple Bud) and *Parlamenta et epistole* (Speeches and Letters), and subsequently, at the second half of the century, by the notary Matteo dei Libri (1214–75) in his *Arringhe* (Speeches).

A significant amount of literary activity in the vernacular also occurred on Tuscany's eastern border, in Umbria and the Marches, where a strong tradition of religious poetry developed, beginning with St Francis' (1182–1226) *Cantico delle creature* (Song of the Creatures), composed in 1224, and continuing with the *laudi* (lauds). Written for music, these poetic works emerge from the Benedictine tradition at Monte Cassino, and later are developed in Franciscan spiritual circles, whose major author was the friar Jacopone da Todi (*c.*1236–1306), active beginning in the 1280s.

Dante's literary-linguistic vernacular background is essentially Florentine and Tuscan, with a strong Bolognese influence and a degree of influence from the religious poetry of central Italy, though he does not appear to have been familiar with Jacopone's writings. The Sicilian poets are extremely important for him too, but Dante knew their poetry solely in its Tuscanized dress, never suspecting that its original linguistic form was Sicilian. He was also not acquainted with vernacular Roman texts, such as the *Storie de Troja et de Roma* (Histories of Troy and Rome) and the *Miracole de Roma* (Wonders of Rome), nor with texts from the north-west of Italy, from the Piedmontese *Sermoni subalpini* (Sub-Alpine Sermons) of the early Duecento ('E alò issì l'arma del corp, e li diavol l'enporterun el fo d'enfern'; And so the soul left the body, and the devils delivered it to the fires of Hell) to the verses of the Anonymous Genoese from the end of the thirteenth century ('Zenoa è citae pinna / de gente e de ogni ben fornia: / con so porto a ra marina / porta è de Lombardia'; Genoa is a city full of people and provided with every good: with its seaport it is the gate of Lombardy).[4]

Perhaps Dante was familiar with the moral-didactic poetry of Lombardy and the Veneto. There seems to be a suggestion of this familiarity, for instance, in a parodic line cited in the *De vulgari eloquentia* (I, xi, 5): 'Enter l'ora de vesper, ciò fu del mes d'ochiover' (Around the hour of vespers, that was in the month of October), given that the line is an alexandrine, the literary verse typical of this tradition that included the

*Linguistic Italy* 257

Milanese Bonvesin da la Riva (*c.*1240–*c.*1315), the Cremonese Uguccione da Lodi (d. after 1250) and Gerardo Patecchio, Giacomino da Verona, and the Venetian *Proverbia super natura feminarum* (Proverbs on the Nature of Women). To cite some examples that illustrate the linguistic character of this tradition:

> the Milanese grammar teacher Bonvesin da la Riva in his *Disputatio rosae cum viola*: 'Quilò se diffinissce la disputaïon / dra rosa e dra vïora, in le que fo grand tenzon' (Here the dispute between the rose and violet is resolved between whom there was great strife);
>
> Gerardo Patecchio's *Splanamento de li Proverbii de Salamone* (Explanation of the Proverbs of Solomon): 'Li savi no'm reprenda s'eu no dirai sì ben / com' se vorave dir, o s'eu dig plui o men, / q'eu no trovo per lor, … q'ig sa ben ço q'ig dé, / anz per comunal omini, / qu no san ogna le' (The wise should not rebuke me, if I fail to speak as well as I should speak, or if I say more or less, because I don't write for them, who well know what they should do, but for ordinary men, who don't know all the laws);
>
> the anonymous misogynistic *Proverbia super natura feminarum*: 'En prima començaa Eva enganà Adamo, / come fe' a Salamón la muier sot un ramo; / Elena cun Parìs se'n fuçì al re Prïamo; / quel que fe' al re Carlo, audito n'ai lo clamo' (First, Eve began to deceive Adam, as did Solomon's wife under a bough; Helen fled from Priam with Paris, and I've heard the clamour about what she did to King Charles);
>
> Giacomino da Verona's *De Babilonia civitate infernali* (On Babylon the Infernal City): 'Per meço ge corro aque entorbolae, / amare plui ke fel e de venen mesclae, / d'ortige e de spine tute circundae, / agute cum' cortegi e taient plu ke spae' (In the middle tumultuous waters run, more bitter than bile and mingled with poison, all surrounded by nettles and thorns as sharp as knives and more cutting than swords).

I have quoted these lines of Lombard–Venetian poetry to give an idea of their great distance from the Florentine phonetic system. Reading the *De vulgari eloquentia*, chapter I, xiv–xv, it becomes evident that during the first few years of his exile (1302–04), Dante must have become quite familiar with these northern Italian vernaculars. They left a lasting impression on him, making him keenly aware of the extreme dissonance and cacophony of the vernaculars that inhabited the 'forest' of Italian vernacular speech. And yet the texts written in these vernaculars had not interested him for their content. One cannot but note the cultural and artistic abyss that separates Giacomino da Verona's *De Babilonia*, a vision of Hell

(Giacomino also composed a vision of Paradise, the *De Ierusalem celesti* (On the Celestial Jerusalem)), from Dante's *Commedia*.

How did Dante address the linguistic context in which he found himself? As a linguist, in the *De vulgari eloquentia*, Dante reveals an acute and lucid level of cultural awareness and understanding of the salient structural aspects of his contemporary linguistic reality. First and foremost, as we have seen, Dante conceptualized the relationship between the vernacular and Latin as the relationship between *locutio naturalis* and *locutio artificialis*. He also appreciated the significant and inevitable change that the *locutio naturalis* underwent across space; and he brilliantly extended this concept to variety across time. Furthermore, he identified the Apennines as the clearly defined dividing line between the two linguistic halves of Italy. Although this intuition is in fact incorrect in absolute terms, it was perfectly reasonable in terms of the north-central part of Italy that Dante actually knew, given that the Apennines in Tuscany and Emilia-Romagna clearly mark the boundary between the northern and south-central vernaculars. Finally, in keeping with his personal political, linguistic, and cultural goals, Dante recognized and established a poetic tradition written in a supra-regional refined Italian vernacular that went from the Sicilian poets to Guinizzelli's Bolognese circle and reached its apex in the Tuscan stilnovist poets. He probably believed that these three lyric groupings had written in the same language: first, because he was unaware that the poets at Frederick II's court had written in Sicilian, and second, because Guinizzelli's refined Bolognese, on account of the cultural exchanges between the two cities, had come to resemble the Florentine vernacular.

Turning from Dante the linguist to Dante the writer: the vernacular literary culture that was key for Dante was essentially Tuscan and Bolognese, plus Tuscanized Sicilian poetry. Obviously Occitan and Old French literature were also important influences; but to restrict our attention to literary output in the language of *sì*, the vernacular culture that shaped Dante was not especially plurilingual, since it embraced a linguistic area of rather limited variation. Although it is the case that Dante drew part of this culture from north of the Tuscan–Emilian Apennines, and hence from a Gallo-Italic region, the poetic and rhetorical vernacular texts that he read in Bologna were written in a refined vernacular that transcended Bolognese, which Dante considered the least municipal of Italy's vernaculars. As he stated in the *De vulgari eloquentia* (I, xv, 5): 'it seems reasonable to suggest that their language [of the Bolognese], tempered by the combination of opposites mentioned above, should achieve a praiseworthy degree of elegance.'

During the first years of his exile, Dante was struck by the linguistic variation that he encountered during his travels; and this exercised some limited influence on the language of the *Commedia*. Although Dante enriched the language of his great poem with loanwords borrowed from all the cities in which he had spent time during his exile, these in no way diminished its essential Florentine phonology and morphology, which thus guaranteed the consistency of his vernacular. Rather, Dante's experience of multilingualism inspired him, albeit indirectly, to develop the *Commedia*'s plurilingual style that integrated different registers and genres, and which he masterfully transformed into a highly effective instrument with which to represent reality.

## Notes

1 Reissued by R. Simone (ed.), *Enciclopedia dell'italiano*, 2 vols. (Rome: Istituto della Enciclopedia Italiana, 2011), vol. II, pp. 1626–7.
2 Dialects are languages too, in the sense that they have their own complete and independent phono-morpho-syntactic structure and their own lexicon. The difference lies in the different geographical, social, and cultural context of use. A 'dialect' is a language used only locally and in informal and private situations, is spoken and normally unwritten, and is without grammatical encoding. A 'language' is a language that has spread over an area sufficiently large, typically an entire nation, has developed a written literary tradition, is grammatically encoded, and is used in formal and public situations.
3 Texts of the Sicilian poets are cited from *Poeti della corte di Federico II*, ed. C. Di Girolamo (Milan: Mondadori, 2008).
4 Lyric texts are quoted from *Poeti del Duecento*, ed. G. Contini, 2 vols. (Milan and Naples: Ricciardi, 1960).

CHAPTER 16

# Education

## Robert Black

Florentine society was highly literate in the later Middle Ages. Writing at the end of the 1330s, Giovanni Villani (*c.*1275–1348) provided the following statistics of children attending school in the city of Florence: 'We find that there are eight to ten thousand boys and girls at reading school; between a thousand and twelve hundred boys at six abacus schools; and five hundred and fifty to six hundred learning grammar and logic in four large schools.'[1] According to one interpretation, this estimate suggests that the male schooling rate in Florence was between 67 to 83 per cent. The accuracy of Villani's figures has been doubted, but in fact they tally with the picture of literacy disclosed by the Florentine tax records (*catasto*) of 1427.

Mass literacy, as suggested by Villani and confirmed by the Florentine *catasto*, was the product of a highly developed education system and syllabus. In later medieval Florence there were three types of schools for pre-university education. The first step was basic reading, taught in elementary schools by teachers normally called *doctores puerorum* (teachers of boys); this skill was always acquired through the medium of the Latin language. For pupils who continued in formal education, the next stage was the continued study of Latin at a grammar school (grammar was a synonym for Latin, and was normally used in that sense by Dante). An alternative syllabus focused on elementary arithmetic, known as *abaco* or *abbaco*, involving not the instrument for calculation now known as the abacus (by the beginning of the thirteenth century, *abacus* was a synonym for arithmetic), but rather consisting of a course, beginning with elementary arithmetic and culminating in basic commercial knowledge; the abacus was taught entirely in the vernacular. The first abacus teachers began to appear in Florence and Tuscany in the late 1270s; there is no evidence, however, that Dante attended an abacus school, and so this form of education will not be further considered here. Writing was taught after elementary reading by *doctores puerorum*, grammar masters, and abacus teachers.

# Education

## Elementary reading and writing

The first textbooks were usually called *tabula* or *carta*, *salterium*, and *donatus*. *Tabula* or *carta* was a sheet of parchment or paper that began with the alphabet and concluded with syllables to sound out; it was fixed on a wooden board and took its name either from the parchment or paper (*carta*) or from the board (*tabula*). The next stage was reading words and phrases, accomplished on the basis of the *salterium*, which, in later medieval Italian education, rarely meant the psalter, psalms having normally been replaced by common prayers and devotional texts. In medieval and Renaissance Europe the final stages of elementary education were presided over by Donatus (*fl.* 350). But it has long been recognized that in Italy during the high and late Middle Ages the principal textbook in elementary schools was not Aelius Donatus' *Ars minor* (Minor Art), but the manual spuriously attributed to Donatus that scholars have christened *Ianua* (Entrance) after the first word of its verse prologue, and that dominated the Italian manuscript tradition and early printing: all known Italian manuscripts and incunables identified as Donatus' treatise on the eight parts of speech are actually versions of *Ianua*. The latter is divided into eight sections, each treating a part of speech in the form of questions and answers. The core of each section is made up of an analysis of a particular example of one of the eight parts of speech, beginning with the question 'Poeta que pars est?' (Poet, what part of speech is it?) for the noun, and using *amo* (I love) for the verb and so on. For the four declinable parts of speech, extensive paradigms, declensions, and conjugations are given.

The techniques for learning to read were straightforward, if unfamiliar today. First, pupils mastered the names and sounds of the letters of the alphabet with the aid of an alphabet sheet (*tabula* or *carta*). Then the sounds of syllables were learned by reading already familiar prayers contained in the *psalter*. The final reading skills were attained through a two-stage process. Elementary texts such as *Ianua* were first read phonetically without understanding the contents. This was described in contemporary terminology as '*per lo testo*', '*a veduta*', '*testualiter*' or '*cum textu*'. The purpose here was to gain the skill of sounding out the syllables on the page phonetically (*compitare* in contemporary terminology). The second stage consisted of reading with understanding and memory. *Ianua* was read again, but now the emphasis was on meaning and particularly on memory: the text was actually learned by heart at this level. Here the contemporary terminology was '*per lo senno*', '*cum sensu*', '*sensualiter*', or '*per l'insenno*'. When Dante referred to 'Donato' who composed 'the first art'

(*Par.* XII, 137–8), he may have been alluding to his own use of *Ianua* as his first proper textbook.

A curious fact in the history of Italian pre-university education during the thirteenth, fourteenth, and fifteenth centuries is that the vernacular was not used at what must seem – given widespread literacy in the vernacular – the most obvious point (at least to us) in the curriculum: the elementary stages of learning to read. It may have been educationally problematic, if not impossible, to teach basic reading technique in a language without fixed orthography, such as the Italian vernacular before the sixteenth century. Indeed, in the Middle Ages Latin was regarded as an artificial, created, unchanging language, an *ars* (discipline) suitable for teaching, whereas the vulgar languages were considered changeable and unstable, regarded literally as forms of babble, learnt naturally but formally unteachable (Dante himself shared this view in *De vulgari eloquentia*); only with the triumph of the humanist view of Latin as itself a natural, historically changing language in the sixteenth century did it become conceivable to teach fundamental language skills in the vernacular. It is important to remember the close association, even identification, of *ars* and teaching in the Middle Ages; Latin was teachable precisely because it was considered an artificial language, whereas teaching the vernacular was inconceivable because it was natural, not artificial, not an *ars*.

The elementary curriculum was often extended to include a late-ancient school text: *Disticha Catonis* (Distichs of Cato, *c.*100 CE), a collection of moral aphorisms in verse couplets. This syllabus – beginning with *tabula/carta*, progressing to *salterium* and culminating in *Donatus* and *Cato* – was considered distinct from Latin (in contemporary parlance, *gramatica*). Its purpose was generic reading skill, whereas the grammar syllabus was intended to teach Latin composition and introduce pupils to Latin literature. The division between elementary and grammar education was made clear by a late fourteenth-century Aretine document: 'It seems and is useful and necessary to have in the city of Arezzo a teacher to instruct boys in their first letters and also to teach Donatus and Cato and other books before they are introduced to grammar [Latin]'.[2]

No concrete evidence survives regarding Dante's own elementary education. References to lay teachers multiply in thirteenth-century Tuscany, with increasing numbers of teachers identifiable as notaries, family men, citizens, and militia members. Siena – the Tuscan town best documented for education in the thirteenth century – had only one ecclesiastical teacher in the period. Florence alone shows comparatively more signs of vitality in its ecclesiastical schools during the thirteenth century.

*Education*  263

The cleric Bene da Firenze (d. *c*.1240), assuming a teaching post at the University of Bologna in 1218, swore the usual oath that he would teach only in Bologna, but reserved the right to teach clerical pupils (*clericos*) in Florence, if he were accorded an ecclesiastical office there; presumably, such teaching would have occurred at the Florentine cathedral school, called the school of St John the Baptist in a document of 1186. This chapter school evidently had a physical existence in the thirteenth century: in 1285, during a dispute between the cathedral and the baptistery, there was mention of a wall at the foot of the school. The mendicant orders also established schools in Florence during the thirteenth century. In 1231 a will was made in the Dominican convent of Santa Maria Novella at a school still operating in 1285. In 1274 the Augustinian hermits were operating a school at their convent in Santo Spirito. At the Badia a Settimo (about five miles west of Florence on the left bank of the Arno), a school was functioning in 1319. In the Florentine *contado*, at the Vallombrosan Badia a Passignano (about six miles northeast of Barberino Valdelsa), a 'master of pupils' was mentioned in 1316. There was thus some endeavour on the part of the Florentine mendicants to involve themselves in educational activities during the thirteenth century, perhaps in response to the lame educational efforts arising from the Florentine episcopate and cathedral chapter (at least in comparison with Arezzo and Siena). Nevertheless, Florentine friars were unable to rouse the bishop and canons of Florence to a more positive scholastic commitment: by 1301 the premises of the Florentine cathedral school had been demolished, and in the fourteenth century church schools in Florence had become so attenuated that it became necessary to pay for external teaching, for example, at Santa Maria del Carmine, Santa Trinita, and Santa Maria Novella. By contrast, lay *doctores puerorum* are documented in the city of Florence from the mid 1270s, in Siena from 1249, and San Gimignano from 1260; eight different *doctores puerorum* have been found teaching in Florence up to 1300, and they rapidly multiply in the early fourteenth century. Given the trend towards lay education in thirteenth-century Florence and Tuscany, it is likely that Dante went to a *doctor puerorum* to learn to read, although – given the survival of church schools in Florence in the later thirteenth century – it cannot be ruled out that he could have attended an ecclesiastical school as a secular pupil.

At his elementary school, Dante would have learned to read and write sufficiently well to cope with ordinary commercial and notarial Latin. The type of education provided by *doctores puerorum* is illustrated by a contract which Lippo Casini of the Florentine parish of San Lorenzo signed in 1304

264                 Robert Black

with 'Monna Clementia *doctrix puerorum*' of the parish of Santa Maria Maggiore, who, for the fee of 40 *soldi*, promised to teach and instruct Andrea, his brother, to read and write, so that he could competently read the psalter, Donatus (namely *Ianua*), notarial documents (*instrumenta*), as well as write, without any further fee.[3] Similarly, in 1313 Betto del fu Feduccio from the Florentine parish of San Donnino and Salimbene di Salto from the parish of San Mauro entered into a contract whereby the former would teach the latter's son Giovanni to read and write: he was meant to be able to read and to write written material and accounts, so that he would be equipped to work in an artisan's shop.

## Grammar school

The secondary grammar (Latin) curriculum in Italy was devoted, at the theoretical level, to learning to write in Latin (*lactinare* in contemporary terminology). In the earlier Middle Ages, Latin syntax had been taught by what foreign-language teachers now call 'total immersion'. Latin was spoken exclusively in the classroom; the texts to be read were all in Latin. Eventually pupils began spontaneously to be able to write Latin. This approach was acceptable as long as pupils and parents were in no hurry to finish secondary education. It was a method admirably suited to monastic and ecclesiastical schools, with their leisurely pace and long duration, prevalent in the earlier Middle Ages. However, with the rise of the Italian communes in the eleventh and twelfth centuries came greater pressure for rapid literacy. The burgeoning lay professional classes needed Latin to be able to pursue careers as lawyers, notaries, and physicians; merchants also needed Latin to be able to read simple legal and business documents; Latin was also necessary for the conduct of civic and public affairs. The pressure for rapid Latinity became even greater with the rise of the universities in the later twelfth and thirteenth centuries: Latin was a prerequisite for professional university courses in law and medicine.

The possibility of teaching Latin syntax rapidly and methodically was offered by developments in linguistic theory and logic that took place in French schools, and particularly in Paris, during the twelfth century. A philosophical and scientific approach to language was responsible for the emergence of a comprehensive theory of Latin composition. These philosophical and scientific concepts and methods, based on a logical approach to language, rapidly found their way into school-level grammar textbooks, beginning with Alexander of Villedieu's (*c.*1175–1240/50) *Doctrinale* (1199) and Everard of Béthune's (d. before 1212) *Graecismus*

*Education* 265

(*c*.1210), both extensively available in Italy, and soon into indigenous Italian manuals, such as Pietro da Isolella da Cremona's widely circulated *Summa* (1252).

The other major task of pre-university schools was teaching Latin literature. Here the syllabus had been divided since the twelfth century into two groups of authors: the *auctores minores* (minor authors), a cycle of late-ancient pagan, early Christian, and medieval texts (ranging from *Disticha Catonis* to poems by the likes of Prudentius (348–d. after 405), Theodulus (ninth or early tenth century), and Henry of Settimello (*fl. c*.1190)); and the *auctores maiores* (major authors), the Roman classics, mainly poetry (e.g. by Ovid, Lucan, Horace, and Virgil), but also some prose texts (e.g. Sallust or Cicero's shorter moral treatises). From the thirteenth century, there were strenuous attempts to make this formidable literary curriculum ever more accessible to pupils. Teachers began to offer vernacular synonyms for Latin words in literary texts to explain their meaning. This technique, now surviving in interlinear and marginal glosses written by pupils and teachers in manuscript schoolbooks, marked the first attempt to bring the vernacular into the Italian educational system, antedating its use as an aid to teach theoretical grammar by as much as a century.

The most radical change in the literary curriculum occurred between the twelfth and thirteenth century. Surviving manuscript schoolbooks from eleventh- and twelfth-century Italian schools show that the Latin classics continued to be read widely in the classroom. However, with the thirteenth century, the same kind of evidence indicates that there was a marked decline in school-level reading of the Latin classics. In place of the authors, there now burgeoned in thirteenth-century Italy indigenous Italian practical manuals for the study of secondary Latin (namely, at the post-elementary level, focusing on syntax), a genre that previously had hardly existed south of the Alps. The thirteenth century saw the first great flowering of Italian grammatical studies; this was also a period in which many copies were made in Italy of Alexander's *Doctrinale* and Everard's *Graecismus*. In some sense, the latter two works came to serve a dual purpose in thirteenth-century Italy: on the one hand, they reinforced previous grammatical knowledge, providing rules and lists in an easily memorized verse format; on the other, they offered a type of substitute for the study of the authors themselves, and were accordingly glossed repeatedly in the traditional school manner, as soon as they made their appearance in Italy. Another substitute for the classical authors was late-Latin literature, and in particular one text: Boethius's *Consolation of Philosophy*. This was considered a particularly suitable replacement for the more cumbersome Latin poets and prose writers, evidently because it provided a short and varied anthology of poetry and prose. This waning of the Roman pagan authors in the thirteenth century provoked a reaction by the beginning of the fourteenth century: in the fourteenth century surviving manuscript school books demonstrate that the Latin classics were once again being read in the pre-university classroom. With the reintroduction of the Latin classics to the schoolroom, a text such as Boethius's *Consolation* – with its convenient mixture of many different Latin metres alternating with prose passages – became a transitional text between the minor and major authors.

The grammar school curriculum in later medieval Italy was not limited to elementary reading, Latin grammar, and Latin literature. Towards the end of the syllabus, attention shifted to stylistics and rhetoric. The dominant textbook was Geoffrey of Vinsauf's (*fl.* 1200) *Poetria nova* (New Poetics, *c.*1208–13). *Poetria nova*'s treatment of stylistic composition begins with the distinction between natural and artificial word order: the former meant the logical order of the natural world (e.g. actor or subject coming before action or verb), as found in the vernacular languages; the latter signified the artful manipulation of word order to achieve literary effect. Although natural word order might have been thought appropriate for purely grammatical study, it was now considered sterile, and the artificial approach was regarded as more felicitous. It is clear from Geoffrey's text that the work at this new, rhetorical and stylistic level of school education involved exercises similar to those already encountered at the earlier secondary grammatical stage. The key term here is the theme, a grammatically correct but plain Latin passage to which the pupil must apply his art; the theme was given in natural Latin order and wording, and it had to be rendered elegant and artificial. Dante's own distinction in *De vulgari eloquentia* (I, i, 2–4) between *locutio vulgaris* (vernacular language) and *gramatica* (Latin), where the first is *naturalis* (natural) and the second *artificialis* (artificial), recalls Geoffrey of Vinsauf's scheme and terminology.

Dante recognized the fundamental importance of Latinity, calling grammar (Latin) 'the first art' and giving pride of place to Donatus. And yet his own formal grammar (Latin) education was minimal. When in *Convivio* II, xii he narrates the crisis he underwent after Beatrice's death in 1290, he says he turned to two Latin works renowned for their lessons in consolation: Boethius' *Consolation of Philosophy* and Cicero's *On Friendship* (*De amicitia*). 'Although it was difficult for me at first to enter into their meaning, finally I managed to enter into it', he wrote, adding crucially, 'with however much skill in Latin that I had'. Dante is suggesting here his limited formal preparation in Latin, going on to emphasize that he had to compensate with whatever 'a little of my intelligence' could do. The whole process was for him 'as though dreaming' (*Conv.* II, xii, 4): he seems to allude to the bewilderment and immaturity of a novice about to embark on a course of intense self-teaching in the classics. Cicero's *De amicitia* had been part of the Italian grammar school curriculum in the twelfth century, but had been dropped by Italian teachers in the thirteenth century as part of their turn away from the classics. Boethius' *Consolation*, by contrast, had become a central feature of the grammar school curriculum in thirteenth-century Italy; Dante's acknowledgement that he had not read this text before the age of twenty-five in 1290 might suggest that his education at grammar school had been minimal – perhaps not a great deal more extensive than that of the pupils of Monna Clementia in 1304 or Maestro Betto in 1313: enough to read basic texts such as *Ianua* and to decipher formulaic Latin notarial documents.

It has sometimes been suggested that Dante's turning to the classics and philosophy was an idealized, not a real occurrence, based on St Augustine's discovery of philosophy (*Confessions* III, iv, 7) after reading Cicero's dialogue *Hortensius* (now lost). Dante's new direction, however, might correspond to what is known of the chronology of his writings: there was a possible movement from the vernacular style characteristic of the early *Rime* to a somewhat more classicizing and philosophical approach, traces of which are first noticeable during the earlier 1290s in the *Vita nova*, where he cites not only Homer (albeit indirectly) (*Vn* II, 8), but also Virgil, Lucan, Horace, and Ovid (*Vn* XXV, 9, possibly at first hand). In the same work, he employs Aristotelian philosophical terminology (for instance, *Vn* XIX, 7, l. 17; XX), cites Ptolemy (*Vn* XXIX, 2), and in his comment on the last sonnet (*Vn* XLI, 6) explicitly refers to Aristotle's *Metaphysics*. If the text of *Vita nova* had been rewritten during the period of the *Commedia*, as a few scholars still maintain, one would have expected more literary and philosophical contamination; as it is, it provides a convincing picture of Dante's early turning to the classics – and collaterally, evidence of his earlier limited Latin education at grammar school.

At grammar school, Dante would have had instruction in basic Latin syntax and in writing simple Latin sentences. A remnant of such lessons appears in *De vulgari eloquentia*, when he cites the sentence 'Petrus amat multum dominam Bertam' (Peter really loves Bertha, II, vi, 4), offered as an example of the lowest stylistic level, 'insipidus, qui est rudium'. This has been translated as 'flavourless ... which is typical of the uncultured'.[4]

268                              Robert Black

A better rendering would be 'of the uneducated', because *rudes* is the technical term used in educational treatises to describe the pupils at a grammar school: for example, in Pietro da Isolella da Cremona's treatise, the author announces that he intends to offer his work as a compendium 'ad instructionem rudium' ('for the instruction of the uneducated', that is, of schoolboys, p. 28). The names *Petrus* and *Berta* recur constantly there[5] in invented examples of simple Latin phrases and sentences: for example 'ego Petrus lego' (I Peter read; p. 31) and 'Berta et mancipium sunt albi' (Bertha and the servant are white; p. 32); in the grammar treatise by Sponcius of Provence, which was one of Pietro's principal sources, there is even a sentence, like Dante's, combining the names *Petrus* and *Berta*: 'Petrus et Berta et hoc mancipium sunt albi' (Peter and Bertha and this servant are white).[6]

Remnants of Dante's imperfect Latin education may occasionally be evident in his mature writings, where intermittent basic comprehension errors are detectable. In *Aeneid* I, 664–5, Venus declares to Cupid, 'Son who are alone my strength, my mighty power – O son who scorn the highest father's Typhoean darts' ('nate, meae vires, mea magna potentia, solus, / nate, patris summi qui tela Typhoëa temnis'), but Dante translates in *Convivio* II, v, 14, 'Son, my virtue, son of the highest father, who do not heed the darts of Typhoeus' ('Figlio, vertù mia, figlio del sommo padre, che li dardi di Tifeo non curi'). Jupiter's darts are so called because with them he killed the Titan Typhoeus: Dante's rendering suggests that Typheous was still alive and not slain by Jupiter. In the *Ars poetica* 295–7, Horace wrote, 'Because Democritus believed talent a greater / blessing than poor old technique, and barred sane poets / from Helicon, a good few don't care to trim their nails, / or beards, haunting secluded spots, shunning the baths', but Dante in *Convivio* II, xiv, 8 wrote, 'Democritus, not caring about his own person, cut neither his beard nor his hair nor his nails', failing to distinguish, as did Horace, between Democritus, who prized talent over technique, and poets who did not bother about personal appearance. It might have been a medieval commonplace that Democritus did not care about how he looked, but Dante still failed to read Horace correctly.

Dante may have read some of the minor authors at grammar school. He refers to 'Aesop the poet' in *Convivio* IV, xxx, 4, suggesting that he was familiar with the Latin verse account of the fables made by Walter the Englishman in the late twelfth century, and not with the earlier Latin prose version, usually known as Romulus, upon which Walter based his elegiac couplets. Walter's poems were the texts read in Italian schools, and so Dante's reference may indicate a work with which he became familiar during his grammar school days. Dante specifically alludes to the fable of the mouse and the frog in *Inferno* XXIII 4–6 ('My thoughts were turned by the present brawl to Aesop's fable where he spoke of the frog and the mouse'). However, Dante's knowledge of the minor authors was limited. He seems to have been unfamiliar with *Ilias latina*, a Latin version of the *Iliad*, now thought to have been the work of Baebius Italicus in the first century CE, as is suggested in *Convivio* I, vii, 15, where he states that there was no Latin version of Homer. In fact, Dante's knowledge of the events of the Trojan War was restricted to what he could glean from indirect authorities such as Virgil, Ovid, Horace, and Statius, as well as vernacular sources. There is no indication that he profited from the more detailed account provided by *Ilias latina*, a work ubiquitous in medieval Italian grammar schools. Dante's limited acquaintance with the minor authors might suggest that the time he spent at grammar school in Florence was not extensive.

Grammar school seems to have been associated with sodomy for Dante. In *Inferno* XV, 109 Priscian is encountered by Dante and Virgil among the sodomites. Priscian (*fl.* 500), the most voluminous of all ancient Latin grammarians, was not tainted as a sodomite in the Middle Ages, and even the early commentators believed that Dante was speaking here generically: teacher meant sodomite. According to the Anonimo Fiorentino (late fourteenth century), 'the masters who teach grammar ... are tainted with this vice, perhaps because of convenient access to youths whom they commonly teach'; Benvenuto da Imola (1320/30–1387/88) declared: 'men learned in Latin tend to have more leisure and have a ready amount of material, namely a surfeit of boys'; but Boccaccio (1313–75) provided the fullest version of this interpretation:

> I have never read nor heard that he [Priscian] was a sinner in such a sin, but I think he [Dante] wanted to place him here, so that for him are understood those who teach this subject [i.e. grammar] ... because they have more young pupils, and because of their age the latter are more timid and obedient both to the improper as well as to the proper orders of their teachers; and because of this availability it is believed that they more often succumb to this vice.[7]

One might wonder whether Dante witnessed or even was a victim of sodomy at grammar school.

In *Convivio* II, xii, 2 Dante makes a perplexing remark, calling Boethius' *Consolation* 'that book not known by many'. He could not have meant that the *Consolation* was not yet widely read in Italian grammar schools: there are more than twenty surviving manuscripts of the text produced in Italy during the thirteenth century and annotated by pupils or teachers in that period, indicating use as schoolbooks in the Italian classroom. What Dante's comment could mean is that the *Consolation* was not much read in the city of Florence during the thirteenth century: there are only four school texts of the work now in Florentine libraries dating from the thirteenth century or earlier, and none has particular associations with Florence. Moreover, Nicholas Trevet (*c.*1257–*c.*1334), who wrote his commentary on the *Consolation* in Florence at the beginning of the fourteenth century, had to procure a copy of the text from outside the city. Such contrast between Florence and Italy as a whole points to Florence's weakness in grammar during Dante's youth. Florence was not a university city like Bologna and Padua; the leading thirteenth-century universities in Tuscany were at Siena and Arezzo. Florence lacked a Latinate culture that nurtured and was nurtured by a university. In the second half of the thirteenth century, grammatical study at Florence was meagre in comparison to Siena and Arezzo and compared unfavourably even to San Gimignano or Prato. Dante's weak preparation in grammar was not so much a personal shortcoming as a reflection of the weak Latinate culture of his native city.

## Rhetoric

Rhetoric was normally introduced at the end of the grammar curriculum, as is clear, for example, from Pietro da Isolella da Cremona's grammar textbook, which includes two chapters on *ars dictaminis*, the art of letter-writing, a popular medieval version of the subject. In the thirteenth century, students intending to pursue a career as a notary or chancellor for a commune, ecclesiastical prince, or ruler normally went on, after grammar school, to further study of rhetoric (*ars dictaminis*) at a university, sometimes enjoying the possibility of attending the lectures at the greatest seat of formal rhetorical learning in Italy – the University of Bologna – by famous professors of rhetoric such as Boncompagno da Signa (*c.*1170–*c.*1240), Bene da Firenze, and Guido Faba (*c.*1190–*c.*1243), and later Dante's contemporaries Pietro Boattieri (*c.*1260–after 1334), Guizzardo da Bologna (d. after 1323), and Giovanni del Virgilio (late thirteenth century–*c.*1327). There was, however, no possibility of advanced institutional study of rhetoric in thirteenth-century Florence, which lacked a university. It has often been asserted that Dante learned rhetoric from the notary and sometime Florentine chancellor Brunetto Latini (*c.*1220–93), whom he refers to as

*Education* 271

'my master' (*Inf.* XV, 97). The medieval Latin syllabus was progressive, moving from instruction in correct linguistic rules and usage (grammar) to ornate and embellished language (rhetoric). Dante's formal training in Latin grammar was limited: he had not even read a key minor authorial text such as *Ilias latina*, much less an intermediate work such as Boethius' *Consolation*. He had not completed enough formal grammatical study at school level to move on to formal Latin rhetorical study – even if that had been possible in Florence. He would have been prepared for rhetoric only after reaching a level of Latinity required by the mastery of texts such as the *Consolation* or *De amicitia*, which, by his own admission, he probably did not tackle until the age of twenty-five beginning in 1290. It is therefore unlikely that Dante could have been taught formal Latin rhetoric by Brunetto Latini while at the normal age of school or university study.

Nevertheless, the early commentators were insistent that Latini was Dante's teacher, Iacopo della Lana (*c.*1278–*c.*1358) categorically stating that Brunetto had been Dante's master. According to Boccaccio, Dante attended philosophy lectures by Latini. For the Ottimo commentary (1334), Dante had instruction in moral philosophy from Latini. According to Benvenuto da Imola, it was rhetoric that Latini taught not only to Dante but also to other young men in Florence. There is no evidence, however, that Latini was a teacher or professor of formal Latin rhetoric or *ars dictaminis*. All Latini's rhetorical works are in the vernacular, which was never the medium for academic instruction in Italy during the Middle Ages (or even the Renaissance). What Latini offered was informal guidance on a practical level in vernacular letter-writing and speaking to non-Latin speakers. More broadly and generally, Latini was an inspirational figure to the youth of Florence, offering training in civic culture and leadership, based on reading texts by classical authors such as Cicero and Sallust in vernacular translation (in the case of Cicero's *De inventione*, his own). It was in this sense that the commentators' allusions to Latini's 'teaching' of rhetoric, philosophy, and morals need to be understood. Giovanni Villani's account of Latini's activities in Dante's Florence – focusing on his vernacular writings – points to inspirational guidance in civic culture, based on the classics and rhetoric, not to formal lectures in the academic disciplines of rhetoric, philosophy, or moral philosophy. The tone of Dante's and Latini's imaginary encounter as recounted in *Inferno* XV suggests a warm and intimate relationship ('O my son', 'son', ll. 31 and 37), one typical of a teacher and pupil – Latini addresses Dante in the familiar second-person singular, while Dante uses the formal second-person plural. Dante explicitly refers to teaching, but it was occasional in nature ('from time to time you taught me', *Inf.* XV, 84–5) consonant with informal discussions rather than with regular formal Latin lectures; the content, insofar as explicitly revealed by Dante, concerned moral philosophy: 'how man wins immortality' (*Inf.* XV, 85). As a discipline, rhetoric was in fact frequently linked to moral philosophy. A less savoury side of Latini's relationship with Florentine youth comes with his damnation for sodomy: he was a charismatic figure with a youthful following, and noted by Villani as a 'mondano uomo' (a man tainted by the world; *Cronica* VIII, 10).

Dante's eventual rhetorical theory, as it emerged during the early years of the fourteenth century particularly in *De vulgari eloquentia*, is fully within the tradition of academic rhetoric and *ars dictaminis*. His fusion of poetry and prose; his tripartite division of style; his quest for ornate prose laden with rhetorical figures and techniques; his use of rhythmic prose (*cursus*) – these and numerous other features of his literary approach show the influence not only of classical rhetorical and poetic theory derived from the *Rhetorica ad Herennium* (Rhetoric to Herennius), Cicero's *De inventione*, and Horace's *Ars poetica* (Art of Poetry), but also from medieval poetics (by the likes of Matthew of Vendôme (second half of twelfth century), Geoffrey of Vinsauf, John of Garland (*c.*1185–1272)) and the Bolognese rhetorical school from Boncompagno da Signa to Bene da Firenze and Guido Faba. Dante spent up to six months in Bologna during 1287, but he was not yet prepared or equipped with enough Latin to attend or profit from university lectures there. Dante's absorption of and immersion in classical and medieval rhetoric came as part of his particular individual course of self-study and self-teaching, which, according to his own testimony, he initiated in 1290, continuing for the rest of the decade and into the next – a unique experience that would lead to a unique fusion of rhetorical and poetic theory in *De vulgari eloquentia*, probably written in the years 1303–05. Latini may have pointed Dante in the direction of rhetoric, but, as far as the academic discipline is concerned, he was self-taught.

## University

After his crisis of 1290, Dante says he discovered 'the words of authors and of the sciences and of books', which in turn led him to the conclusion that philosophy, as 'the mistress of these authors, of these sciences and these books, was the supreme thing' (*Conv.* II, xii, 5); the result was that philosophy now became his obsession ('I could hardly turn from it', *Conv.* II,

*Education* 273

xii, 6). What Dante is describing here is the traditional progression up the medieval ladder of knowledge, beginning with grammar and rhetoric and culminating in philosophy. Although Dante's more advanced educational experience with Latin language and literature was personal and outside an institutional context, the same was possibly not true of his philosophical studies. Although lacking a university in Dante's lifetime, Florence did have, attached to the city's various mendicant convents, advanced institutions of higher education called *studia* and *studia generalia*, where theology and its preparatory subjects such as logic and philosophy were taught. Dante describes how he now attended these religious *studia*: 'I began to go where it [philosophy] was explained in a true manner, that is, in the schools of the religious and at the disputations of philosophers' (*Conv.* II, xii, 7). However, it has been asserted that only the occasional quodlibetal disputations in the mendicant *studia* were open to lay auditors in Florence at which both philosophical and theological issues were discussed (medieval university students never participated in lectures, and most disputations were professional occasions, in which masters and advanced students participated). But medieval Italian civic universities, including civic mendicant *studia*, were not rigidly organized and exclusive institutions; throughout their history lay citizens frequently attended lectures and other forms of teaching as informal and unmatriculated auditors. It was from some such teaching at the Florentine mendicant *studia*, so Dante recounts, 'that in a short time, perhaps in thirty months, I began to sense philosophy's sweetness', to such an extent that its love 'chased away and destroyed every other thought' (*Conv.* II, xii, 7). The later chapters of *Vita nova* suggest the beginnings of Dante's philosophical interests, although he implies that his intensive study of philosophy and his love poetry in that work, although overlapping, did not coincide.

One of the Florentine mendicant *studia* that Dante probably frequented was at the Dominican convent of Santa Maria Novella, where a *studium* in theology was instituted in 1281. By 1288 it was more important than similar *studia* in Naples and Rome, and in 1311 it became a *studium generale*, a prestigious general institution of theological studies. The leading figure at Santa Maria Novella's *studium* in Dante's lifetime was Remigio de' Girolami (*c.*1235–1319). A pupil of Aquinas in Paris, after his return to Florence in the mid 1270s Remigio taught theology and philosophy at Santa Maria Novella for more than forty years. He remained a close follower of Aquinas. It has been argued that, as a layman, Dante would not have been able to follow Remigio's courses; yet, at the same time, it is likely that he heard him preach and it cannot be ruled out that Dante benefited from Remigio's teaching, including lectures and disputations, as well as quodlibetal discussions. Such contact would account for several strikingly specific parallels between Remigio's technical theological treatises and Dante's writings.

Dante may also have attended the *studium* at the Franciscan convent of Santa Croce in Florence. Pietro Olivi (1248–98) and his pupil Ubertino da Casale (1259–*c*.1330), both adherents of the order's radical spiritual wing, taught at Santa Croce from 1287 to 1289. This was before Dante's burgeoning interest in philosophy, but Olivi's legacy at Santa Croce remained powerful after his and Ubertino's departure and throughout the fourteenth century. The influence of spiritualists' ideas in Dante is potent: for example, their doctrine of poverty and their eschatological and apocalyptic notion of a degraded Church about to experience renewal through a saviour. Indeed, Ubertino is celebrated in *Paradiso* XII, 124. Dante does say that he attended religious 'schools' (*scuole*) in the plural, and so it is an attractive hypothesis that he frequented Santa Croce as well as Santa Maria Novella.

It has sometimes been suggested that Dante had contacts with the University of Bologna, but explicit evidence is lacking. His knowledge of Roman law could have derived from his own reading or from contact with his friend and fellow poet, the famous lawyer Cino da Pistoia (1270–1336/37). An interest in the classics was developing in Bologna at the beginning of the fourteenth century, culminating during the early 1320s in the university teaching there by Dante's correspondent, Giovanni del Virgilio. It has been speculated that Dante furthered his literary and classical knowledge at Bologna after his exile from Florence in 1302, but he had already developed extensively in that direction by the time he composed *De vulgari eloquentia* between 1303 and 1305; as has been seen, he had been laying solid foundations in the classics since the early 1290s.

The university experience for students at Italian universities in the later Middle Ages consisted of a total of about 180 teaching days. The academic year normally commenced in mid October, with formal teaching starting at the beginning of November. There were four kinds of professors: ordinary, extraordinary, holiday, and student. There were normally several ordinary professors in major subjects such as civil law. Subjects considered of lesser importance (for example moral philosophy) were taught on holidays. Extraordinary professors taught the same subjects as ordinary professors, but at different times of day. Student lecturers often taught for one year only; they normally had completed a formal disputation but had yet to take their final public examination. Lectures were distributed

## Education 275

throughout the day; professors normally lectured for an hour, occasionally for two. Attendance at lectures could range from ten to more than a hundred students.

Lectures normally consisted of reading and commenting on set texts: in philosophy, normally by Aristotle; in theology, the *Four Books of Sentences* by Peter Lombard (*c.*1096–1164); in civil law, Justinian's *Institutes* and *Corpus iuris civilis* (Body of Civil Law); in canon law, the *Decretum* (Decree) by Gratian (*fl.* 1140s); in rhetoric, Cicero's *De inventione* and the pseudo-Ciceronian *Rhetorica ad Herennium*. Grammarians would lecture on classical authors: Dante's correspondent Giovanni del Virgilio was appointed to lecture on Virgil, Statius, Lucan, and Ovid at Bologna in 1321. The professor read out a passage from the text, and then made comments on it. In the case of classical texts, these comments included paraphrase, grammatical analysis, rhetorical figures, historical, geographical, and mythological references, metrical analyses (in the case of poetry), moral aphorisms (*sententiae*), and allegories. Often the commentary was far longer than the text that had been read out. Important professors such as Giovanni del Virgilio had their commentaries disseminated in manuscript copies, a form of publication anticipating the widespread multiplication of university-level commentaries that occurred with the arrival of the printing press.

The disputation was a formal debate before an audience. It seems to have developed out of 'questions' exploring contested points raised in lectures. By the mid thirteenth century disputations occurred regularly in North European universities; they were well-established features of Italian universities certainly by the late fourteenth century. Eventually university statutes required professors and students to engage in formal disputations: in Padua professors who had not disputed twice a year could be fined. Some universities required 'circular disputations': professors and students had to gather in a circle outside the classroom to dispute conclusions arrived at in lectures.

To sum up, Dante's education was anything but conventional for a man of great learning in the later Middle Ages. He came to the classics as an adult, and his Latinity, both in terms of language and literature, was largely self-taught. He did not study philosophy or theology at university, but was an informal hanger-on at mendicant schools in Florence: he probably heard sermons and disputations, and arguably even lectures by the likes of Remigio de' Girolami at Santa Maria Novella, and he may have been influenced by spiritual Franciscan teaching at Santa Croce, but, again, most of his profound knowledge

# Robert Black

of philosophy and theology must have been self-taught. Signs of his patchy formal education remained with him for life: he never seems to have read Sallust's *Catiline* or *Iugurtha*, although these were the great prose staples of Italian grammar schools in the later Middle Ages; similarly, although he knew Horace's *Ars poetica* intimately, he never seems to have read his *Epistulae*, although these two works continued to be paired together as an anthology in Italian grammar schools throughout the thirteenth century. Dante demonstrated every sign of the self-taught genius: great depth of knowledge for texts he had come to himself, but glaring deficiencies inconceivable for a formally and conventually educated Italian of the later Middle Ages.

## Notes

1 Giovanni Villani, *Nuova cronica*, ed. G. Porta, 3 vols. (Parma: Guanda, 1990), XII, 94.
2 R. Black, *Education and Society in Florentine Tuscany: Teachers, Pupils and Schools, c.1250–1500* (Leiden: Brill, 2007), p. 737.
3 S. Debenedetti, 'Sui più antichi *doctores puerorum* a Firenze', *Studi medievali*, 2 (1906–07), 327–51, at 333, 346.
4 *De vulgari eloquentia*, trans. S. Botterill (Cambridge University Press, 1996), p. 65.
5 *Une grammaire latine inédite du XIIIe siècle*, ed. C. Fierville (Paris: Imprimerie nationale, 1886), pp. 10, 29, 31–3, 37, 38, 56, 59, 65, 74, 132, 161, 162, 164, 165.
6 *Une grammaire latine*, p. 180.
7 Translated from the original texts provided by Giorgio Brugnoli in his article 'Prisciano' in *ED*, IV, pp. 679–80.

CHAPTER 17

# Rhetoric, literary theory, and practical criticism

*Ronald L. Martinez*

Over the last thirty years, Alastair Minnis and his collaborators have revived the study of literary criticism and theory during the Middle Ages, putting to rest prejudice that the period lacked sophisticated reflection about texts.[1] Thanks to these scholars students of late medieval European literature have learned that in regard to literary training, canon formation, the theory of genres, practical criticism, and the dialectic of continuity and innovation, medieval writers reflected on the texts they studied and wrote chiefly through *accessus* (introductions to works) and by means of commentaries on matters from grammar and etymology to textual organization, authorial intention, and ideology.

The late medieval toolbox for literary theory and criticism was, if anything, overfull: manuscript culture changed slowly and retained ancient and early medieval precedents, so that critical categories multiplied. Mixing what for moderns are categories of mode or genre with those of content and intention, Conrad of Hirsau (*c.*1070–1150) identified nine 'kinds' of verse composition: bucolic, comic, tragic, satyric, lyric, apologetic, panegyric, epithalamic, epitaphic, chronical (*cronicum*),[2] and elegiac, while the encyclopaedist Vincent of Beauvais (*c.*1190–*c.*1264) fused two traditional classifications to list seven species of poetry: comedy, tragedy, invective, and satire; and fable, history, and argument – something that might possibly be true (*Speculum doctrinale* III, 109). Indeed, late medieval paratexts deploy more than a dozen categories for characterization of written texts. First was the category of the written text itself (*scriptura*), which could be parsed into broad divisions: as to language (Latin or vernacular); as to whether it was verse or prose; or as to its interpretation (literal or allegorical); or according to its part of philosophy (as in understanding Ovid, the author of the *Metamorphoses*, as a *phisicus* (natural philosopher)); or according to the status of the author or writer (whether an *auctor*, worthy of faith, obedience, and artistic imitation, and hence an 'authority', an *auctoritas*, and thus deserving

277

of commentary, or a mere editor, compiler, or copyist). Distinctions of genre, kind, or level, or style, or of degree of veracity, like those listed by Vincent of Beauvais, because they were inherited from ancient commentary, were often idiosyncratically understood; however, even specific rhetorical techniques, such as amplification and abbreviation, or the use of 'difficult' or 'easy' kinds of figurative speech (a part of *elocutio* (verbal expression) – *ornatus difficilis* was based on tropes, while *ornatus facilis* relied on figures of thought and of words), might be a basis for classifying works.

Minnis and Scott omitted the rhetorical tradition from their anthology, considering the subject well covered by existing studies; and both their anthology and their volume for *The Cambridge History of Literary Criticism* largely bypass vernacular and Latin contexts of thirteenth-century Italian criticism *before* Dante. Yet rhetorical training and the critical discussion of literature in Duecento Italy were for historical reasons *sui generis*. As an example, a preliminary idea of the differences between an established vernacular tradition of narrative in Old French and the literary-critical context of late Duecento Italy can be gained by comparing the *Romance of the Rose* with the *Fiore* (Flower). Written by two authors of different, not to say antithetical views, Guillaume de Lorris (*c.*1200–*c.*1240) and Jean de Meun (*c.*1240–before 1305), the long Old French romance, focused on the subject of love while treating a wide variety of subjects, was in significant measure shaped by ideas found in *accessus* and commentary, and thus to a high degree typified a thirteenth-century aesthetic of both heterogeneity and plenitude. Between about 1285 and 1320, an Italian writer not yet convincingly identified, though many scholars believe him to have been Dante, translated the *Rose* from the octosyllabic couplets of Old French narrative poetry into 232 sonnets, an 'inappropriate' lyric form, eliding most of the natural-scientific content in favour of dialogues involving the Lover and Love, Reason, the Old Woman, and so on. Through parody, irony, and hyperbole the *Fiore* not only contests the French cultural influence represented by the *Rose*, but, closer to home, critiques the tradition of love lyric in Italy in the thirteenth century as practised by Tuscan poets Guittone d'Arezzo (*c.*1235–94), Chiaro Davanzati (*c.*1240–*c.*1304), and Monte Andrea (*fl.* 1265–75). The *Fiore* attests to more than a half century of Italian vernacular literature poor in narratives (Dante excepted) but rich in canzoni and sonnets, including exchanges of *tenzoni*, or poetic debates, and thus echoes the dialogic and critical spirit that marks the Duecento Italian tradition (see the closing subsection below).

## Rhetoric in the Duecento city-state

For the later Italian Middle Ages, as the legacy of the classical past regarding the verbal arts – especially from Cicero (106–43 BCE), Horace (65–8 BCE), Augustine (354–430), and Boethius (*c.*475–*c.*526), as well as the grammarians Donatus (*fl.* 350) and Priscian (*fl.* 500) – was compiled, rhetoric came to identify all speech or writing that persuades, moves, or delights. Although Aristotle's (384–322 BCE) *Rhetorica* was not an influential source in the Italian Duecento, the philosopher's definitions, taken over by Latin writers (Cicero, *On Invention* I, 7; *Rhetoric to Herennius* I, ii; Boethius, *On Different Topics* IV, 1208A–C), are usefully concise: rhetoric has three main kinds – spheres of action, procedures, and ends: when forensic or judicial, its province is the court of law, its method accusation and defence, its end justice; when deliberative, a speaker exhorts or dissuades in council to achieve the useful or expedient; when demonstrative or occasional (epideictic), praise or blame is declaimed in public forums or in written panegyrics (or vituperations) to bring honour or opprobium (Aristotle, *Rhetorica* I, iii, 1–5). In views that persisted into the late Middle Ages, Augustine, himself a trained rhetorician, who legitimized formal rhetoric – despite its utilitarian amorality and tendency to elevate virtuosic style over content – for its usefulness in preaching the Gospel, echoed Cicero's *Orator* (XXI, 69–70) in identifying as functions of the art teaching, pleasing, and persuading ('ut doceat, ut delectat, ut flectat'), associating these with a plain and subdued, a middle or temperate, or an elevated style, respectively (*On Christian Doctrine* IV, xii–xiv, 17–26). Although Emperor Frederick II of Hohenstaufen (1194–1250) had mocked over-elaborate preambles by ambassadors to his court, witnesses such as Konrad von Mure (1210–81), author of a rhetorical treatise, the *Summa de arte prosandi* (Sum of the Art of Writing Prose, *c.*1275), acknowledged Italians as skilled orators (*arengatori*).

As Italian cultural production ramped up after the peace of Constance (1183), much of what might now be called literary criticism and discursive theory, along with the rhetorical disciplines, were represented by three discernible traditions of instruction in rhetoric and poetics, although by the early Duecento these come to overlap in the increasingly compendious manuals that transmitted them. In ascending order of importance for writers, these traditions were, first, the *ars dictaminis*, the art of letter–writing, closely identified since the early twelfth century with the Bolognese schools (only later with the university), whose ambitious and creative *dictatores* taught epistolary composition but also other kinds of writing skills

280                           Ronald L. Martinez

(e.g., the *ars notaria*, for drafting legal documents) for growing numbers of notaries, law students, and clerics, including instruction, drawn from the *Rhetorica ad Herennium*, in rhetorical *ornatus*, or figurative language. Teachers of *dictamen* such as Boncompagno da Signa (*c.*1170–*c.*1240), Guido Faba (*c.*1190–*c.*1243), Thomas of Capua (*c.*1185–1239), and Mino di Colle Valdelsa (*c.*1250–*c.*1290) proclaimed rhetoric the 'art of arts' or 'queen of the sciences', the chief conduit to learning. An important resource for *dictamen* were the anthologies of letters and documents by varied hands, but circulating under the name of Pier delle Vigne (*c.*1190–1249), Frederick II's chancellor and secretary. Deriving from the imperial–papal struggles of the mid thirteenth century and written in the curial 'high' style (*stilus supremus* or *rhetoricus*), they injected controversy into a 'consensus' tradition of epistolography. The *dictatores* arrayed themselves on either side of the language debate (see Chapter 15): Guido Faba produced sample letters in both Italian and Latin, but Buoncompagno and Mino di Colle looked down on oratorical performance in the vernacular. The period after the defeat of the Ghibellines at Benevento (1266) was propitious in that three vernacular versions of Cicero's rhetorical works, Brunetto Latini's (*c.*1220–93) *Rettorica* and *Tresor* (Treasure, 1262–66), which translate and adapt the *De inventione*, and Bono Giamboni's (*c.*1240–*c.*1292) *Fiore di rettorica* (Flower of Rhetoric), an abridged translation of the *Ad Herennium*, were available by around 1270. Thus for both study and governance the vernacular outstripped Latin, although interest in Cicero's texts surged in the 1280s with the appointment of Jacques of Dinant (*fl.* 1275–95) and, a few years later, of Giovanni di Bonandrea (d. 1321) to chairs of rhetoric at Bologna, thereby marking the end of a period in Italy many scholars see as poor in the study of classical texts.

Second is the Ciceronian tradition itself. Although Cicero's *Rhetorica vetus* (Old Rhetoric, the *De inventione*) and *nova* (New, the *Rhetorica ad Herennium*, attributed to him) had been designed to prepare Roman students for courtroom disputation, and enjoyed academic exposition in twelfth-century commentaries, especially in Francia, where co-option of the two works as instructional texts for deliberative rhetoric breathed new life into the tradition. After having gone silent from the time of the Caesars and during medieval monarchical feudalism, political debate enjoyed a resurgence in Italy thanks to the rise of city-republics whose internal governance and foreign affairs were conducted by elected councils. As one of the chief fosterers of a writing practice grounded in civic engagement, Brunetto Latini, a Florentine, translated into the vernacular, and commented on, part of Cicero's *De inventione* and included a

## Rhetoric, literary theory, and practical criticism

section on speaking in the second book in his encyclopaedic *Tresor* (II, 62–7), and on rhetoric in the third (III, 1–72). Taking over the boasts of the *dictatores*, Brunetto (*Rettorica* I, 1) proposed rhetorical study as preparatory to virtually all speechifying (*dire*) and writing (*dittare*), from conciliar debate and ambassadorial speeches to love poetry, for he understood most formal discourse as adversative, as *tencione* (*Rettorica* LXXVI, 2–6).[3] Councilmen in the Guelph republic that dominated Florentine politics after Benevento also relied on the unofficial arts of speechifying (*ars arengandi*) that furnished some of the earliest examples of vernacular prose, as in the Florentine Giovanni da Vignano's (*fl.* 1300) *Flore del parlare* (Flower of Speech), a reworking of the *Arringhe* (Speeches) by Matteo dei Libri.

Finally, instruction in and examples of poetic composition were disseminated in the arts of poetry that reflected the study of classical Latin poetry in the traditional grammar curriculum of medieval schools and universities, especially at Chartres, Orléans, and Paris. The arts depend heavily on Horace's *Ars poetica* (Art of Poetry, also referred to as the *Poetria*, Poetics) and its commentaries, but also on the *Ad Herennium*, especially for its account of levels of style and its catalogue of figurative language in the fourth book. Of these manuals, the *Poetria nova* (New Poetics, *c.*1208–13) of Geoffrey of Vinsauf (*fl.* 1200; rumoured to have taught in Bologna in 1188–90), a didactic poem in 2121 hexameters, and the *Ars poetica* itself, equipped with influential commentaries (for a fuller discussion, see below 'The Horatian legacy'), were important for poets, and may have guided the theoretical reflection of poets writing in literary Italian in Sicily, Tuscany, and Bologna, as well as influencing Duecento compendia of epistolary, rhetorical, and poetic arts such as the *Candelabrum* (Candle-holder, 1227) of Bene da Firenze (d. *c.*1240) and the *Parisiana poetria* (*c.*1231–5) by John of Garland (*c.*1185–1272). John's book gives an idea of the extent to which a preceptive 'art of poetry' might have furnished a full curriculum for composition: treated are the five traditional parts of rhetoric (*inventio*; *dispositio*, the order of topics; *elocutio*, including levels of style, and selection of tropes, that is, figurative language; *pronuntiatio*, delivery, and *memoria*, are less emphasized), and the six parts of the oration (*exordium*, narration, division, confirmation, confutation, conclusion; *Ad Herennium* I, 3). To this theoretical basis are added the rules of letter-writing or *dictamen*, as well as instruction in metrical and rhymed verse (*metrica* and *rithmica*), and in the mechanics of prose, including the *cursus*, the rules for accentual patterns ending clauses. The last book includes sample texts: a verse tragedy, prose letters for various functions, and Latin metrical compositions. When supplemented by the traditions of commenting on the Latin classics – notably the *accessus ad auctores*, as it was modified in the thirteenth century and discussed in the next section – materials for instruction in composition available in the mid-to-late Duecento are all but complete.

## Approaching the authors: the *accessus ad auctores*

Malcolm Parkes remarked: 'it is a truism of paleography that most works copied in and before the twelfth century were better organized in copies produced in the thirteenth century, and even better organized in those produced in the fourteenth.'[4] The trend toward better organization of texts was conspicuous in editorial and critical paratexts, which were transformed by Aristotelian categories and methodology. Secular and religious texts in the twelfth-century 'renaissance' had typically been introduced by the 'type C' prologue, in its short form *materia* (subject-matter), *intentio* (aim), *finis* (goal, purpose) or *utilitas* (usefulness), or in its long form *materia*, *titulus* (title), *intentio*, *modus agendi* (manner of treatment), *utilitas*, and *pars philosophiae* (the part of philosophy to which the text belonged). The 'type C' prologue had in large measure displaced the Servian prologue or *accessus* known from commentary on the *Aeneid* (the so-called 'type B', with emphasis on the poet's life, the title, type of verse, intention, number and order of books) and the 'seven circumstances' or 'type A' prologue, 'who, what, why, how, when, where, by what means'.

Some parts of an *accessus* – the *nomen auctoris* (author's name), *titulus*, and *materia* – serve to label or individuate a work, indexical functions crucial to a manuscript culture, since the title was often the *incipit*, the first words, as in John of Garland's *Parisiana poetria*: 'the title is taken from the first word of the book'.[5] The *intentio auctoris* and *utilitas* reflect value judgements and implicit ideology, since books worthy of critical attention were assumed to have edifying content: thus Statius' epic *Thebaid* and Lucan's poem on Rome's civil war, *Pharsalia*, both blood-drenched by any standard, were thought to dissuade civil conflict. Only a relatively small number of Latin writers were deemed to be 'authoritative', and these were distinguished between 'major' and 'minor' authors. What remained unclear was which *auctores* belonged to which group, although, in essence, there was a group of ten major authors: eight poets – Juvenal, Lucan, Horace, Ovid, Persius, Statius, Terence, and Virgil – and two writers of prose, Cicero and Sallust. Supreme among these was Virgil, who was judged to excel in all the literary styles and was considered the 'fountain' (*Inf.* I, 79) of wisdom. Lists of 'minor' authors were extremely fluid,

# Rhetoric, literary theory, and practical criticism

though these often included introductory school texts, such as versions of Aesop's fables. *Modus agendi* or *tractandi* (manner of treatment) and the *pars philosophiae* classify works within known categories and the traditional curricula of arts and sciences. For non-sacred literature the 'part of philosophy' was usually ethics, given that moral, or in the case of Ovid's *Amores*, immoral, behaviour was often at issue. Potentially the richest descriptor is *modus tractandi*, which might specify the work as dramatic, lyric, or narrative; or as comedy or satire or tragedy: genres or types associated with the three levels of style, mixed, low, and high (*Ad Herennium* IV, xi; Horace, *Ars poetica*, 89–91). The three levels were later codified by John of Garland to express a 'material' concept of styles coordinated with social status. Furthermore, a work might be history, *argumentum*, or fable, according to its veracity or fictionality (*Ad Herennium* I, viii, 13; Isidore, *Etymologiae* I, xliv, 5); or it could be in prose, verse, or *prosimetrum*, a mixed category that reflects the prominence of classics such as Boethius' *Consolation of Philosophy* (*c.*524), and, for the thirteenth century, ways in which Occitan and Italian lyric anthologies were organized.

The translation into Latin of most of the Aristotelian corpus and its incorporation into the curricula of European universities and *studia* precipitated a reorganization of the disciplines, giving new emphasis to natural science, including medicine, and galvanizing philosophy and theology. Propelled in part by the teaching and preaching needs of the rapidly expanding mendicant orders, these innovations brought with them new ways of classifying texts that allowed an increasingly literary and rhetorical approach, especially to sacred writings. Although the 'type C' prologue continued to be used, by mid-century teachers were prefacing both secular and biblical texts in terms of the four causes familiar from Aristotle's *Physics* (II, 3: material cause, formal cause, efficient cause, final cause), which largely replaced *materia*, *modus*, *nomen auctoris* and *intentio*, and *utilitas* or *finis*, respectively. Significantly, the four causes were logically ordered in relation to each other. The final cause, the purpose (*finis*) of the thing made, because it necessitated making the artefact, was also the first, originating cause (Aquinas, *Summa theologica* I, q. 44, a. 4). Next was the efficient cause, which could be subdivided into primary efficient cause and instrumental efficient cause(s), to distinguish divine authorship from that of human authors inspired by the Holy Spirit. The formal cause, the idea or pattern in the mind of the artificer imposed on the thing made, was next – subdivided into *forma tractandi*, which comported the categories enumerated above, and *forma tractatus*, the division of the work into parts, like books and chapters, themselves understood as analytically

284 Ronald L. Martinez

hierarchical. In last place was the material cause, which in literary terms was the subject-matter or theme, what was found or chosen through the rhetorical exercise of *inventio* and *electio*.

Distinguishing the primary from the secondary efficient cause gave exegetes freedom to focus on the existential circumstances of biblical writers, whose private intentions could be isolated from God's, thus drawing attention to the literal sense of the text, since this no longer needed to be wholly accommodated to a divine intention often deduced (or imposed) through allegorical interpretation (allegoresis; and see the next subsection). Aquinas (1225–74), for example, defined as the 'literal' sense of a text the entirety of the human author's *intentio*, including tropes, metaphors, even the allegory (*Summa theologica* Ia, q. 1, art. 10). The motives of authors could be understood as complex, even multiple; thus, although the Psalms were still held to express the divine will, the assessment of David's status as a sinner and a divinely sanctioned author exercised exegetes from Abelard (1079–1142) to Aquinas and Nicholas of Lyra (1280–1349). Attention to the psychology of historically conditioned authors and readers also permitted analysis of sacred texts as persuasive discourse, that is as rhetorical. Abelard had emphasized the persuasive force of Scripture, and Aquinas saw the *modus tractandi* of the Bible as including historical, prophetic, and lyrical 'literary' genres. Job's questioning and Paul's harangues of his addressees could even exemplify a *disputative* mode. The rhetorical intention of the Song of Songs – nuptial songs promoting divine love – was contrasted with the mournful mode of Lamentations, which was also analysed for its use of rhetorical figures drawn directly from Cicero's *De inventione*.

The distinction of 'intellectual' and 'affective' approaches to biblical exegesis and theology (which roughly speaking reflected Dominican and Franciscan approaches, respectively, to devotional practice) emerged as well in the formalization of distinct 'modes of treatment': one, for the rationally based sciences, was analytic (*divisivus*), drawing on proofs (so, *probativus*), and assembling arguments (thus, *collectivus*); while the other relied on examples (thus *exemplificativus*), exhortation (*exhortativus*), and figurative language (making it *transumptivus*), and described how to move the auditor or reader for purposes of indoctrination, or to bring out the imaginative aspects of Scripture and literature. Some texts might combine all the above.

Spotlighting the human author also required that the originating *auctores* (Evangelists, Aristotle) be distinguished from their copyists and interpreters, who though secondary in importance as commentators,

*Rhetoric, literary theory, and practical criticism* 285

editors, and compilers, yet shared in a reflected, subordinate authorship. Subordination also governed the articulation of the 'form of the work', which lay in the artistic province of the human author in the material and structural sense, as divided into books, chapters, verses, or otherwise arranged in parts. Chaptering of the Bible, standardized for Paris Bibles by the mid thirteenth century, made possible new ways of indexing the text, as well as new ways of thinking about how the various parts of a work related to each other. The complex arrangements of the compendious *summae* of the thirteenth century (in theology, natural science, history, law, medicine) led Erwin Panofsky to identify their schemata as homologous with the design principles of Gothic cathedrals, whose articulation and proportions evidenced 'clarification for clarification's sake', a 'system of homologous parts, and parts of parts', and the 'acceptance and reconciliation of contradictory possibilities', reflecting the structure of the scholastic *quaestio*.[6]

By the late Duecento, the methodological implications of the four-cause scholastic *accessus*, as well as the accretion of older types and the *forma tractatus* with parts hierarchically arranged, had become devices for organizing whole works. The vast *Speculum naturale* (Mirror of Nature) of Vincent of Beauvais ordered its subject-matter (mineral, vegetable, and animal) according to the days of their creation in Genesis, while Aquinas' *Summa theologica* (Sum of Theology) was articulated to reflect how God, angels, man, and the history of redemption enact a scheme of procession from and return to God. Albertanus da Brescia's (d. 1253) *Liber de doctrina loquendi et tacendi* (Book of the Teaching of Speaking and Keeping Silent) of about 1230, and repeatedly vernacularized, recaptures six of the 'seven circumstances' of the oldest *accessus* scheme to serve as rubrics for its six chapters. Brunetto Latini's *Rettorica* discusses the relation of rhetoric to politics within an Aristotelian division of the sciences into theoretical, practical, and logical (or verbal) branches (*Rettorica* XVII). More significantly, Brunetto prefaced his work with an extensive *accessus* (*Rettorica* I, 1–11) that combines the four-cause *accessus* with the familiar 'type C' *accessus*. Brunetto boldly affirmed himself as a second author, and not merely a commentator, translator, or compiler (*Rettorica* I, 6). Finally, Guittone d'Arezzo's collection of sonnets against love (*Del carnale amore*, On Carnal Love) deploys an argument against courtly *Amor* constructed as a dialectical syllogism over all thirteen sonnets, and within each individual sonnet. Highly organized, the thirteenth century explored how division and organization might be subjects of the work itself.

## 3 Allegory/allegoresis

Allegory, to which fleeting mention has already been made, was a technique of both composition (*allegoria*) and of interpretation (*allegoresis*). In the Middle Ages allegory was understood as verbal expression in which 'one thing is said, another is signified'. Especially influential was Isidore of Seville's (*c* 560–636) definition of allegory as *alieniloquium*, 'other' speech (*Etymologiae.*, xxxvii, 22). Allegory was thus present in just about all the literature read and composed during the period, and had its theoretical roots in Hellenistic literary criticism and then in early Scriptural exegesis. Origen's (*c.*185–254) threefold division of the Bible into historical, moral, and spiritual senses was developed by Jerome (*c.*347–420) and Augustine into a 'figural' or 'typological' system, whereby the historical events and the descriptions of the created universe evoked in Scripture signified divine truths (Christ is foreshadowed by the Old Testament patriarchs; the Red Sea 'prefigures' the spilling of His blood on the cross). Scriptural allegory was predicated on a providential idea of reality as events ordained and things made by God (*in factis*), and not simply on things said, as in human speech and writing (*in verbis*). John Cassian (*c.*360–435) equated the Bible's historical dimension with its literal sense or *lictera* (letter) – Jerusalem was the city in Judaea – while the allegorical, mystical, and spiritual senses were arranged in a tripartite scheme that expressed historical and spiritual development. Thus Jerusalem signified the community of the faithful (allegorical sense proper, the faith established by Christ); the human soul (tropological sense, expressing moral choice); and finally, Paradise, the celestial city (spiritual or anagogical sense, the reward and home of the blessed). In the later Middle Ages students apprehended this scheme thanks to a mnemonic attributed to the philosopher Augustine of Dacia (d. 1282): 'The letter indicates the deed; allegory what you should believe; the moral how you should behave; anagogy where you soul is heading'. Ever since the fourteenth century (see Chapter 30), readers of the *Commedia* have debated whether or not Dante wished his 'divine' poem to be interpreted according to this scheme. If this were indeed the case, then its application to his masterpiece would constitute yet another aspect of the *Commedia*'s originality, since human writing was normally read according to the twofold *in verbis* system. Thus the *lictera* was equated with the literal fictional or historical dimension of the text, while its allegorical sense was generally associated with its ethical and didactic values.

Given its structural prominence in religious and secular texts ranging from Prudentius' (348–*c.*405) *Psychomachia* (Conflict of the Soul, namely

*Rhetoric, literary theory, and practical criticism* 287

the battle between the vices and the virtues) to the *Roman de la rose*, personification, or prosopopeia, which both antiquity and the Middle Ages deemed not to be allegory but a rhetorical figure, continues to be treated by modern scholars as typical of medieval allegory generally. Although medieval readers and writers were able to distinguish between different types of allegorical composition and interpretation, in practice the nomenclature and uses of allegory were freely transposed. Thus, *allegoria* was employed to refer to Biblical exegesis, to fictions using personifications, and to the moralizations of fables and secular works, as well as to riddles and emblems – essentially, to any text in which 'one thing is said, another signified'. Furthermore, a panoply of other Latin terms was synonymous with *allegoria*: *enigma*, *figura* (figure), *forma* (form), *imago* (image), *mysterium* (mystery), *parabola* (parable), *sententia* (meaning), *sacramentum* (sacrament), *signum* (sign), *symbolum* (symbol), *typus* (type), *umbra* (shadow), and *velamen* (veil). The proliferation of terminology is a mark of the centrality in medieval culture of interpretation – no 'authoritative' text whether religious or secular was left bereft of commentary – and of critical reflection – the commentaries, especially in their *accessus*, as has been noted, were a major source of ideas on the practice and theory of literature. Understood broadly, allegory is a testament to the creative and hermeneutic sophistication of the Middle Ages, which found its culmination in Dante's writing and literary theoretical considerations.

### The Horatian legacy

The rhetorical works of Aristotle, Cicero, and Boethius aside, the chief surviving classical treatise on poetics, literary theory, and practical criticism for the Middle Ages was Horace's brief *Ars poetica* (473 Latin hexameters). The *Ars* is preceptive, not like a schoolmaster but as a friendly adviser to the otherwise unknown Piso brothers, the supposed writers of comedy and satire who are the named recipients of the verse epistle. With its stress on decorous consistencies, the poem seems a far cry from late medieval polygeneric, stylistically hybrid 'comic' works (*Romance of the Rose, Commedia, Canterbury Tales*), but medieval glossators treated the work as an indispensable *auctoritas* and regularized its unsystematic sequence of topics with terminology and categories from Cicero's rhetoric. In the 'type C' *accessus* to the twelfth-century *Materia* commentary on Horace's poem (discussed below), after listing *materia* and a double intention, both common and special (to teach everyone, to teach the Pisos), the 'usefulness' of Horace's poem is determined as 'knowledge of how to

288  Ronald L. Martinez

write poetry' (*scientia poetandi*).[7] Detailing the intention of the work to teach poetic art, however, the *accessus* digresses to list – taking them as implicit in Horace's first thirty-seven lines – six vices (*vitia*) of incongruity to be avoided (*vitanda*) in the organization and style of literary works. Circulating independently, the *accessus* magnified the influence of the enumerated vices.

From its opening description of bad writing and painting as a monster of incongruous parts, Horace's poem advances principles of propriety, or *convenientia*, with reference to styles and genres (tragedy, comedy, satire) and treatment of characters, while also allowing, if tempered by taste and judgement (*discretio*), a certain licence and mixing of genres and styles (89–98), of fiction and fact (151–2), of the 'useful and the agreeable' (*utile dulci*; 343–4). The originary moment of *discretio*, the choice of subject, is crucial, for from it ensue both good arrangement and good words (38–40) – an association that recurs in the poem, and that was seized on by commentators, as it permitted linking *inventio* to *dispositio* and *elocutio*. More ambitious readers, such as Geoffrey de Vinsauf and Dante, saw in the work a programme for fashioning a *poeta* worthy of the name, a true maker (306–7). Thus the *Materia* commentator, after identifying the title of Horace's work as *incipit liber poetrie Horatii* (here begins Horace's book on poetry), parses the term *poeta*: 'for *poio, pois* is "I fashion", "you fashion". Hence poesy or poetry is fiction, or figment; and the poet is a maker, a fashioner'.[8] For Horace, mediocre versifiers are in fact unworthy of the name of poet (372–3). Great poetry requires respect for convention (86–7), imitation of Greek models (268–9), and a mix of natural talent, training, and sweat (408–15); but poets are also bound to renew the language (47–59), leave nothing unattempted (285–8), and be unafraid of risks (9–10, 263–8). Consistent with his emphasis on assiduous craft, the *labor limae*, the work of the file, Horace compares poets with painters, sculptors, potters, weavers, musicians, and even smiths. Poets transcend artisans, however, in drawing from philosophical wisdom (308–10), and, like the mythic civilizers, Orpheus and Amphion, poets prescribe laws and customs (391–401). So they ought to be rhetorically effective, teaching and pleasing in equal measure (344).

It may be that the passage of grammar and literature-based approaches from France to Italy at the beginning of the thirteenth century, tempering traditional emphases on training in *dictamen* and skills useful in law, was in part the result of the *Materia* commentary to Horace's *Ars poetica*. Compiled in France between 1125 and 1175, though based on previous commentaries, the *Materia* commentary was relied upon by Matthew of

# Rhetoric, literary theory, and practical criticism

Vendôme in his *Ars versificandi* (Art of Versifying, 1170–5) and Geoffrey of Vinsauf (*Poetria nova*), and subsequently by the Italian masters who expanded the neo-Horatian tradition to prose and *dictamen* in rhetorical manuals: Bene da Firenze (1220–40), Guido Faba (1230), and Brunetto Latini, (1260s), and in the early fourteenth century to humanist glossators such as Bartholomeo da Pisa (*fl.* 1375–80).

Geoffrey's *Poetria nova* (also called *Liber de artificio loquendi*) seems to announce its relationship both to Cicero's *Rhetorica nova* (the pseudo-Ciceronian *Ad Herennium*) and to one of the medieval titles of Horace's *Ars*, namely *Poetria*. It self-consciously emulates significant twelfth-century poetic achievement displayed in Alan of Lille's (1116–1202) *Anticlaudianus* (Against Claudian), the *Cosmographia* (World-description) of Bernard Silvestris, and Walter of Chatillon's (1135–1204) *Alexandreis* (Alexandreid). Geoffrey's poem was vastly popular, surviving in ten times the number of manuscripts of any comparable treatise (220 manuscripts overall, of which 10 come from thirteenth-century Italy). Geoffrey counsels innovation through surprising verbal combinations (*iuncturae*, as advised by Horace, *Ars* 47–8) and transformation of terms through *transumptio* and *conversio*, but also through the planning of the whole work: his eight forms of beginning at the middle or end, using artificial order and combined with proverbs, was absorbed by Bene, Guido Faba, John of Garland, and Brunetto Latini. Most significantly, like Horace, Geoffrey is both preceptor and poet; he strives to exemplify what he teaches in a work that is both *de arte* and *ex arte*. His emphasis on arrangement (*dispositio*) thus includes that of his own text: since the work is mapped out in advance (*Poetria nova* 30–70), it has an internal, poetic coherence beyond its structural framework, drawn from Cicero and pseudo-Cicero, around the five parts of rhetoric and six parts of the oration. Furthermore, in his own prologue, giving a preview of, especially, *elocutio*, Geoffrey transforms Horace's verses on the monster of incongruities (*Ars* 1–9: part human, part bird, part fish) by conjuring instead a triply defective scarecrow, with frizzy hair, a patchwork garment, and unfinished details.

The passage just discussed in fact anticipates Geoffrey's belief, in Horace's wake, that wise choice of subject (*inventio*) leads to effective order (*dispositio*) and felicitous clothing in words (*elocutio*). But the passage also reflects Geoffrey's emphases, which favour *elocutio* over *dispositio*, and both of these more than *inventio*. Thus, in borrowing Horace's canonical advice on choosing subject-matter – taking on a topic appropriate to what one's shoulders can bear (*Ars* 38–40) – Geoffrey alters it to describe discretion in harmonizing language with meaning. Having alluded freely to Horace, Geoffrey later cites him more directly, at *Poetria nova* 292–303, where he exemplifies apostrophe with an address to a proud man to shoulder a lesser burden if he is weak. The same vocabulary is used when Geoffrey counsels adjusting the diction of a speech (*oratio*) to the audience's shoulders (1090–1), and again when advising memorizing small bits at a time, according to what the shoulders will bear (1995–8). Geoffrey's recurring use of 'take on', 'shoulders', and 'weight' stretches out Horace's metaphor so that it touches all five parts of rhetoric, exemplifying the consistency through beginning, middle, and end recommended in Horace's manual. And Geoffrey also exemplifies his own command about measuring the work in advance – like weighing subject-matter, using Horace's artisanal image of perfecting texts with the 'slow work of the file' (289), which he made his own, as with the 'Take on a subject' image, by creatively developing its connotative associations.

Geoffrey's example was widely, if variously, assimilated. Since Bene da Firenze perhaps taught Pier delle Vigne, and Guido Faba may have taught Brunetto Latini, who copied Pier's exemplary letters, the chief traditions of teaching of rhetoric and poetics find their Florentine convergence in Brunetto. Cicero, Horace, and Geoffrey thus combine in Brunetto's *Rettorica*, where the expositor (*sponitore*), for instance, treats the *causa* as the basis for ordering the discourse, in terms that echo both Horace and the *Poetria nova* (LXXV, 2). Similar debts emerge in the rhetorical book of his *Tresor* (III, 11–3).

Mediated by commentary and the arts of poetry, Horace's advice reached deep into the theory, criticism, and rhetorical teaching of the Duecento. Did his counsels, delivered as poetry, directly affect poetic composition as well? One of the 'comic' sonnets of the Tuscan Rustico Filippi (*c.*1240–1300), 'Quando Dio messer Messerin fece' (When God made Mr Misterling), attributes to God's mischievous creative moments a mixture of bird, beast, and man[9] with features suited to each. Critics have seen in the sonnet a riddle, whose meaning has been viewed as a parody of the court lady assembled from the best parts of others; or as an extended comparison with the male member; or as an inversion of Brunetto Latini's account of Cicero's praise of human eloquence. Since both Cicero's *De inventione* and Brunetto's *Rettorica* are invoked, it is worth noting that the blend of man, bird, and beast also conforms to Horace's incongruous hybrid of a woman's head, a feathered body, and a fish's tail. In this light, Rustico's sonnet, showing the kind of mixture that, on Horace's authority, cannot fail to make us laugh (*Ars* 9), would be a 'divine' etiology of 'comic' writing, and testify to a sophisticated use of Horace's treatise

*Rhetoric, literary theory, and practical criticism*         291

between about 1260 and 1290. An exchange of sonnets (a *tenzone*) from the last decades of the thirteenth century also suggests that the Horatian influence on pre-stilnovist and stilnovist lyric poets is plausible. The five sonnets exchanged by Gonella (late thirteenth century), Bonagiunta Orbicciani (*c.*1220–*c.*1290), and Bonodico of Lucca (late thirteenth century), titled 'Questione di messer Gonella degli Anterminelli da Lucca' (Problem posed by Master Gonella of the Anterminelli of Lucca),[10] take up the scientific problem of how iron can be modified to cut other forms of the metal. However, its real subject, manifest in multiple references, is the relationship between nature and art. The *tenzone* instantiates Horace's presentation of the nature–art relationship as, precisely, a *quaestio* (*Ars* 408–9: 'whether a poem is praiseworthy due to natural talent or art, is the question'), while the idea of iron grinding down iron[11] echoes Horace's *labor limae* (*Ars* 230). The *Materia* commentary in fact compares the correction of verses to the file whittling away iron.[12]

## 5 Canons and the poetry of criticism: lyric anthologies and *tenzoni*

The Italian literary landscape at the end of the Duecento is mapped by three vernacular anthologies, known from the libraries that house them as the P(alatino), L(aurenziano), and V(aticano). Their full designations are Palatino 418, Laurenziano Rediano 9, and Vaticano 3793. All three testify to the cultural prominence of Tuscany in the production of Italian verse (P is Pistoian–Luccan, L largely Pisan, V chiefly Florentine), but also present differences in organizational criteria, in judgements on canonicity, literary value, and artistic priorities, and in the status, class, and training of their compilers and copiers, and of their implied audience.

The smallest, P (180 poems), has illuminated portraits of the poets within the initial letters of the poems, akin to the illuminated Occitan *chansonniers* assembled in Italy in the mid-Duecento; the portraits are keyed to the compositions as if graphic glosses. Copied for aristocratic readers, of the three only P includes *ballate* (strophic poems with refrain; one quire, 22 compositions), inserted between canzoni (8 quires, 104 compositions) and sonnets (52, one quire). The hierarchy of canzoni, ballads, and sonnets, which P represents with progressively smaller initials for each group, roughly echoes the principal Occitan anthologies divided into sections for *cansos* (odes), *tensos* (debates), and *sirventes* (satires), arranged by author, but also reflecting hierarchies of both importance and the social rank of the troubadour. P's compiler acknowledges Guittone d'Arezzo's prominence by beginning with a *canzone* by him and all but concluding the *canzone* selections with his compositions.

L is more than twice as large (432 texts, 18 quires) and is dedicated overwhelmingly to Guittone, including nearly his entire output, with a secondary emphasis on Pisan poets. Guittone's poems begin both the *canzone* and sonnet sections, and the poetic texts are preceded by Guittone's prose and verse letters. The anthology is titled by reference to Guittone; and most significantly, the collection embodies the existential divide in the poet's life, with rubrics distinguishing the earlier love poetry from the moralizing verse he wrote after his entry into the Frati Gaudenti (Jovial Friars) in 1265. The arrangement of the collection in terms of the conversion of the most conspicuous poet of the age suggests that the anthologist-compiler, himself a disciple of Guittone and possibly a Frate Gaudente, honoured his master's intentions for an author's book. The single-author anthology is also attested by the *libre* of the troubadour Giraut Riquier (*c.*1230–92), compiled by the author around the time the Tuscan anthologies were being conceived and assembled. Given that Dante's *Vita nova* was completed by about 1295, the assembly of the Laurenziano anthology, now placed around 1290–1300, is synchronous with other experiments in the single-author book that offer clear evidence of the growing interest in authorship in Romance lyric vernacular circles.

L and P are courtly reading-books copied by professional scribes; V, however, is a large lay anthological book more than twice again as large as P, with a numerical preponderance of sonnets (669 out of 995 compositions). The principal hand is not that of a notary or professional scribe, and though not uninfluenced by library hands, employs *mercantesca* script, marking the writer as embedded in the merchant society of late Duecento Florence. Indeed, the collection has struck scholars as homologous with merchant culture itself, with poems organized on the page like financial transactions in account books, and with blanks at the ends of quires to allow new entries. The principal copyist, almost certainly also the compiler, had a sweeping historiographic and geographic sense for the poetry extant in Italian, demarcated by the assignment of quires: II–V Sicilians (but quires IV–V include Tuscan imitators), VI Emilians, plus Pisans, Sienese, and Lucchesi; VII–VIII Guittone d'Arezzo; IX Florentines; X–XII Chiaro Davanzati; XIII Monte Andrea; XIV–XV miscellaneous and anonymous additions; XVIII–XXI sonnets by Sicilians, Guittone, Florentines; XXII–XXIV *tenzoni*; XXV Rustico Filippi and *tenzoni*, and sonnets by the so-called 'Friend of Dante'. V thus emphasizes the continuity of the Sicilian 'origins' of Italian vernacular lyric with transitional

## Rhetoric, literary theory, and practical criticism 293

figures such as Bonagiunta and with the Tuscans Guittone d'Arezzo, Chiaro Davanzati, and Monte Andrea. These last two, both Florentines, are preponderant numerically and mark the culmination of the anthology, although a prominent role is reserved (as in L) for the Bolognese Guido Guinizzelli (c.1230–76), who opens the first quire after the Sicilians (VI). By receiving a large collection of Sicilian lyrics in a language previously Tuscanized, V represents the whole lyric tradition in Tuscan idiom; furthermore, by giving scant space to religious verse, it signals a powerful lay alternative to ecclesiastic culture.

In their sonnet sections, the three anthologies all concede substantial space to the dialogic form. Somewhat like the Occitan *joc partit*, a staged debate, *tenzoni* are ritualized forms of both amicable and combative dialogue, subject to rules and etiquette. The form reflects the persistent prominence of the *contentio* or *contrasto* (dispute or debate) as a discursive form of the twelfth and thirteenth centuries. The 'minor' scholastic text, the *Ecloga Theoduli* (Eclogue of Theodulus; ninth or early tenth-century), a Latin *altercatio* or quarrel in alternating stanzas between Christian and pagan doctrine (as voiced by Truth, *Alethia*, and Falsehood, *Pseustis*), had long been influential as one of the 'minor' authors used in schools. William of St Thierry wrote on Christian love as a dispute with Ovid; and as we saw, a 'disputational' mode was recognized in biblical books.

A long literary tradition, as well as the contemporary political complexity of Guelf republican Florence, thus lies behind the 'democratic' Vaticano, in which dialogue and debate may be seen as a general principle of the anthologist, the first hand who assembled the collection, as well as of the second hand who completed it. Giacomo da Lentini (*c*.1201–*c*.1260), treated as the originator of vernacular Italian lyric in all three anthologies, and the putative inventor of the sonnet form, inaugurates the sonnet section with a *tenzone* on the nature of love, followed by a second *tenzone*, so that the shift to *tenzoni* in quires XXII–XXV is announced at the beginning of the sonnet section. The Tuscans with which the anthology culminates, Chiaro and Monte Andrea, excel in the frequency of their *tenzoni*. Looking to larger patterns of contrastive dialogue, the consecutive inclusion in V of the 'comic' and 'courtly' collections of Rustico Filippi sets up a stylistic dialectic or *contentio* between Rustico's sonnets. Appended to Rustico's texts, the sixty-one sonnets of the 'Amico di Dante' embed a fictitious *tenzone* with *madonna*, while the central poem is a 'reply' to an *amico*. Even the first of the 'Amico di Dante' canzoni, is entered as a response to the sole poem of Dante's in the collection, originally included without attribution), 'Donne ch'avete intelletto d'amore' (Ladies who have understanding of love). Thus the closing sections of V ratify the prominence of dialogic patterns in the collection.

As if in illustration of Brunetto's principle in the *Rettorica* (LXXVI, 2–6) that not only orations and epistles but even the love *canzone* stages a debate, both political and erotic *tenzoni* have a markedly interrelated presence in V. Although the five political *tenzoni* in V are far exceeded numerically by those on love, two celebrated stridently pro-Guelph political canzoni, by Guittone and Chiaro, begin quires VIII and XII, introducing the polemical, factional positions assumed subsequently in the political *tenzoni*, where the Guelph–Ghibelline rivalry is granted expression. The most elaborate of these apportions seventeen sonnets among six Florentines, including two notaries, two magnates, a banker-poet (Monte Andrea), and a poet (Chiaro, of unknown affiliation). The group represents the aristocrats, lay professionals, and men of business (of the guilds, the *Arti*) who made up the city's governing class. Their poetic exchange models in microcosm Florence's mediation of tensions through discourse, and perhaps V's organization itself. Thus the city was mirrored in its book: as Brunetto had observed, citing Cicero, the rule and life of the city required both acts (*fatti*) and speech (*detti*), so that the speech of rhetoric was balanced by 'the art of smiths, of tailors, of drapers' *Rettorica* XVII, 4).

The *tenzone* principle thus helps to shape the forms of Duecento vernacular texts and define the terms for discussing poetic practice and language. Friar Guittone's first *canzone* in L challenges the amatory and poetic creed of the troubadour Bernart de Ventadorn (*fl.* 1170–80). By the same logic, the division of Guittone's canzoni and sonnet sections articulate a debate on different kinds of love: one sacred, the other secular and 'libertine'. Furthermore, a sonnet by Guido Cavalcanti (1250/59–1300) savaging Guittone's arguments ('Da più a uno face un sillogismo', A syllogism makes one of the many) has been seen as an answer to Guittone's sonnets against love; indeed, his anti-erotic diatribe may very well have inspired Guido Cavalcanti to write his great *canzone* 'Donna mi prega' (A lady asks me) and Guinizzelli to compose his equally famous *canzone* 'Al cor gentil rimpaira sempre Amore' (Love is always drawn to the noble heart). Key texts of Italian literary history thus arise as provocations or answers to literary-critical debates; the tradition is fundamentally dialogic and metapoetic The *Fiore*, as we saw, in a bid to supplant for Italian letters the most prestigious narrative text of French high medieval culture, proceeds with exchanges of sonnets between identified participants, harnessing the *tenzone* pattern to continuous narrative.

# Rhetoric, literary theory, and practical criticism

Two *tenzoni* (L278–79 and V785–86) implicitly debate issues of poetics, and diagram the epochal shift in style and manner from the central Tuscans, represented by Guittone, Monte, Chiaro, and the post-Sicilian Bonagiunta, to the pre-stilnovism of Guinizzelli, who would become the most significant predecessor for Cavalcanti, Dante, and Cino da Pistoia (1270–1336). The more significant of the two *tenzoni* involved Bonagiunta and Guinizzelli and was strategically placed in the Laurenziano anthology. The *tenzone* participates allusively in a cluster of poetic debates, and represents a kind of *summa* of poetic dispute. Bonagiunta's reproach of a shift in style, 'Voi che mutata avete la mainera / de li piacenti ditti de l'amore (You who have changed the style of pleasing poems of love, V785), chastises Guinizzelli for abandoning the example of poets such as Bonagiunta himself. With the reference to 'force of writing' ('forsa di scrittura',) and 'Bolognese wisdom' ('senno ... da Bologna'), Bonagiunta's accusation of excessive obscurity likely refers to university training in law and philosophy. Indeed, in light of Guinizzelli's *canzone*, 'Al cor gentil', with its ostentation of the matter-form, potency-act dyads championed by scholastic reception of Aristotle, Bonagiunta indicts the panoply of new learning that affected everything from the *modus tractandi* to scriptural exegesis. No slouch himself, Bonagiunta parodies Guinizelli's learned terms. Guinizzelli's response, 'Omo ch'è saggio non corre leggero' (The wise man does not run fast, V786), rich in critical vocabulary, enlists parody as well to call into question Bonagiunta's intellectual and poetic standing. Furthermore, the scriptural citations in Guinizzelli's first and final lines (Prov. 28, 26; Eccles. 20, 7) nod to rhetorical prescription for beginning with a proverb (Geoffrey of Vinsauf, *Poetria nova* 126–33). The density of Guinizzelli's scriptural allusion throws back in Bonagiunta's face the reproach regarding the effectiveness of his writing, the 'forsa' of his 'scrittura'. The sonnet's biblical intertexts thus also recall Albertanus' *Liber* on the government of speech and the harm that can be done by an unbridled tongue. Guinizzelli recalls too Geoffrey's restraining advice: 'let the poet's hand not be swift to take up the pen, nor his tongue be impatient to speak' (*Poetria nova* 50–1). Though proverbial, such advice is also exquisitely Horatian and neo-Horatian, as in Geoffrey's *servate modum*, 'keep to the measure' (*Poetria nova* 299). Repeatedly copied in early manuscripts, including eight instances in the *Memoriali bolognesi*, the centralized record of notarial activity in Bologna between 1265 and 1333, Guinizzelli's sonnet furnished a touchstone for late Duecento critical discourse.

# 296                                   Ronald L. Martinez

Guinizzelli's answer to Bonagiunta resurfaces transformed in Dante's *Purgatorio*, where, in a kind of implicit *tenzone*, Guinizzelli reproves hasty and ill-advised praise of Guittone d'Arezzo (*Purg.* XXVI, 115–26). Concerns about the intention, force and danger of speech, oratory, counsel – and of course, poetry – return to inform not only the Ulysses canto in *Inferno*, but also Dante's extended meditation on political, erotic, and verbal discipline in *Purgatorio*, where 'the bridle of art' – the 'art' Dante learned from Cicero, Horace, and his native tradition – prescribes the limits of the poem (*Purg.* XXXIII, 139–41; see Chapter 22 for more information on the poets discussed in this section).

## Notes

1  See A. J. Minnis, *Medieval Theory of Authorship: Scholastic Literary Attitudes in the Later Middle Ages* (London: Scolar Press, 1984); *Medieval Literary Theory and Criticism, c.1100–1375, The Commentary Tradition*, ed. A. J. Minnis and A. B. Scott with D. Wallace, rev. edn (Oxford: Clarendon Press, 2003); A. Minnis and I. Johnson (eds.), *The Cambridge History of Literary Criticism. II. The Middle Ages* (Cambridge University Press, 2007).
2  *Accessus ad Auctores, Bernard d'Utrecht Conrad d'Hirsau Dialogus super auctores*, ed. R. B. C. Huygens (Leiden: Brill, 1970), p. 76.
3  Brunetto Latini, *La rettorica italiana*, ed. F. Maggini (Florence: Galletti e Cocci, 1915).
4  M. Parkes, 'The influence of the concepts of *ordinatio* and *compilatio* on the development of the book' in J. J. G. Alexander and M. T. Gibson (eds.), *Medieval Learning and Literature: Essays Presented to R. W. Hunt* (Oxford: Clarendon Press, 1976), pp. 115–41, at p. 115.
5  *The Parisiana Poetria of John of Garland*, ed. T. Lawler (New Haven and London: Yale University Press, 1974), 3.
6  E. Panofsky, *Gothic Architecture and Scholasticism* (New York: New American Library, 1976; original edn 1951), pp. 35, 45, 64, respectively.
7  K. Friis-Jensen, 'The *Ars poetica* in twelfth-century France: the Horace of Matthew of Vendôme, Geoffrey of Vinsauf, and John of Garland', *Cahiers de l'Institut du Moyen Age Grec et Latin*, 60 (1990), 319–88; the *Materia* commentary may be found at pp. 336–84.
8  Friis-Jensen, 'The *Ars poetica* in twelfth-century France', p. 338.
9  Rustico Filippi, *Sonetti satirici e giocosi*, ed. S. Buzzetti Gallarati (Rome: Carocci, 2005), pp. 162–6, 3.
10  *Poeti del Duecento*, ed. G. Contini, 2 vols. (Milan-Naples: Ricciardi, 1960), vol. I, 278–86; other poems to which reference is made in this chapter may be read in this fundamental collection.
11  *The Parisiana Poetria of John of Garland*, I, 2.
12  Friis-Jensen, 'The *Ars poetica* in twelfth-century France', p. 366.

CHAPTER 18

# Classical antiquity

*Robert Black*

The heritage of classical antiquity and in particular the status of the great Latin authors vacillated throughout the centuries, both during and since ancient times themselves: not only did particular authors rise and fall in favour, but there were even periods when the very study of the great classics went into eclipse. Interest in the Latin classics and particularly the study of the ancient Latin authors dwindled in Italy during the sixth, seventh, and eighth centuries, and it was mainly in the ninth century that a significant revival of the ancient literary curriculum based on a study of classical authors was launched.

The apogee of classical studies in medieval Italy was reached in the twelfth century. According to Otto of Freising (*c.*1114–58), the Lombards in the first half of the twelfth century retained 'the elegance of the Latin language', and Roffredo da Benevento (*c.*1170–*c.*1243) referred to the flourishing state of Latin literary study in Arezzo at the turn of the thirteenth century. A striking literary text written in twelfth-century Italy is Henry of Settimello's (*fl. c.*1190) famous *Elegy*, the most significant piece of classicizing Latin poetry composed in Italy before Lovato Lovati (1241–1309) and the emergence of Paduan humanism. It shows the direct influence of Ovid's poetry of exile and echoes of Virgil and Horace are evident; there are numerous references to the classical world, while biblical allusions are rare, and Henry's Stoic philosophy was possibly stimulated by Seneca. Henry was drawn to the classicizing French Latin poets of the twelfth century, such as Walter of Châtillon (1135–1204), Alan of Lille (1116–1202), and Matthew of Vendôme (second half of twelfth century), whose verse techniques and stylistic eccentricities he appropriated.

The clearest direct evidence of the trend is the survival of classical Latin authors used as schoolbooks. In a survey published in 2001, it was possible to identify forty-one Italian manuscript texts of classical authors used as schoolbooks and produced in Italy during the twelfth century and now housed in Florentine libraries, but of course they do not all originate from

Florence or even Tuscany.[1] The strong presence of Latin classical authors in twelfth-century Italy, as revealed by the Florentine census, was further confirmed by a continuing survey outside Florence. In 2006 a subsequent publication identified 127 Italian-copied manuscripts of classical Latin authors produced or used as schoolbooks in twelfth-century Italy and now housed outside Florence.[2] Work on this survey has continued, extending beyond Italian libraries to collections in Great Britain and North America. So far, the total number of Italian-copied manuscripts of classical Latin authors produced or used as schoolbooks in twelfth-century Italy, as revealed by this census, is 223.

Indirect evidence for indigenous Italian twelfth-century classicism comes from the polemics of the eminent Bolognese professor of rhetoric, Boncompagno da Signa (*c*.1170–*c*.1240). Boncompagno declares that he had never imitated Cicero nor indeed ever lectured on him, and he goes on to reject his predecessors' methods of teaching the *ars dictaminis*, the art of letter writing, accusing them of too much reliance on the ancients: of the traditional five parts of the letter, only three were actually essential; if this was against the doctrine of the ancients, then their teachings had been useless and damaging. He derides the methods of writing letters before his day: masters had spent huge amounts of time adorning their epistles with vivid displays of verbiage and learned quotations from the authors, who were believed to provide the seal of approval for their literary productions. He was reprimanded, so he says, for rejecting the traditional practice of padding his prose with classical quotations and rarified terminology, complaining that he was ridiculed for lacking knowledge of Latin literature, and for drawing examples from the present day. In the late-twelfth century the school of Orléans was particularly associated with the traditional study of the classical authors, and Boncompagno accuses his academic opponents of too much indulgence in Aurelianism (Orléans = Aurelianum).

It is important to appreciate the revolutionary nature of Boncompagno's programme at the turn of the thirteenth century. Traditional Italian educators now felt threatened by the new anti-classical current rapidly developing at the University of Paris in the twelfth century, and so attacked Boncompagno as a prominent member of the avant-garde; in response, he highlighted his educational radicalism, vilifying the school of Orléans as the bastion of reactionary classicism. Boncompagno was in fact criticizing the traditional author-based approach to grammar and rhetoric that had long been practised in Italian schools, and that had underpinned the early development of medieval rhetoric (*dictamen*), which he now

*Classical antiquity* 299

wanted to displace with a more rigidly practical training. The fact that Boncompagno strode forth as a modernizer onto the Italian educational scene suggests that there had been a traditional educational establishment long in existence when he was writing.

What is important here is the geographical context of this battle for and against the ancient authors. The source of this classicism was to some extent French Aurelianism, but crucial is the fact that Boncompagno presents himself as an innovator, revising the methods of his predecessors. Boncompagno was attempting to replace the kind of classical teaching practices traditionally employed in Italy. Boncompagno's self-advertisement as an innovator and a radical implies that classicism was flourishing, not declining, in twelfth-century Italy.

It is true that, ultimately, the emergence of *ars dictaminis* in Italy would result in a less classicized approach to rhetoric, but this anti-classical direction emerged only gradually. Alberic of Montecassino (d. 1105), usually seen as the parent of *dictamen*, still focused on the conventional Ciceronian rhetoric taught in the schools, while drawing also on Virgil, as well as Ovid, Lucan, Sallust, and Terence. Adalberto Samaritano (*fl.* 1115–25), often cited as first among Alberic's successors, opened his *Praecepta dictaminum* (Precepts of Rhetoric) with a pretentious classicizing prologue heavily based on the *De inventione* that included a citation from Ovid's *Metamorphoses*. Bene da Firenze (d. *c.* 1240), Boncompagno's great rival at the University of Bologna, stressed the need to read widely and expected his students to acquire some knowledge of the *Rhetores Latini Minores*, Quintilian's *Institutio oratoria*, Cicero's *De inventione*, the *Ad Herennium*, and the *artes poetriae*.

In contrast, the early thirteenth century represented not a period of slowly rising classicism in Italy, but the collapse of traditional Italian classically based secondary education – a development confirmed by the above-mentioned survey of schoolbooks now housed in Florentine libraries. In comparison with the forty-one manuscripts of classical Latin authors produced as schoolbooks in twelfth-century Italy, the figure for the next century drops to a total of only ten. This pattern, to some extent, mirrors the drop in overall numbers of classical manuscripts being produced in Europe as a whole in the thirteenth century, but the extreme nature of the fall suggests that the shift away from the classics was particularly cataclysmic in Italian schools of that century.

This original census of thirteenth-century Italian manuscripts of the Latin classics is now being extended beyond Florence to collections in the rest of Italy and beyond. So far it has been possible to identify sixty-nine further manuscripts of Latin classical authors produced in Italy during the thirteenth century. So at the present time, the totals for the entire survey are 223 manuscripts of Latin classical authors produced and used in Italy during the twelfth century, in contrast to sixty-nine produced in Italy during the thirteenth century. This survey is still continuing, and doubtless more thirteenth-century Italian manuscripts will be identified both in Italy and beyond; nevertheless, it is impossible for the strong tendency already identified to be negated, given that major collections on the Italian peninsula, including all Florentine libraries, all Milanese libraries (including the Biblioteca Ambrosiana), the Biblioteca Marciana in Venice, and the Vatican Library have been completely investigated, as well as the British Library and Bodleian Library in Great Britain, and the major libraries in the north-eastern United States (Harvard, Yale, Princeton, and Columbia University Libraries, the New York Public Library, and the Pierpont Morgan Library).

The causes of this decline in Italian classical studies during the thirteenth century were twofold. In the first place, there was a powerful anti-classical current flowing from France. One source was the new Parisian logical school of grammar, developed by teachers such as William of Conches (*c.*1100–d. after 1154) and particularly Petrus Helias (*c.*1100–d. after 1166). This systematic and logical approach to language was brought down to the humbler levels of the educational hierarchy in the most decisively imaginable manner at the very beginning of the thirteenth century. In 1199 Alexander of Villedieu (*c.*1175–1240/50) composed what must be one of the most influential and innovatory works in the history of education, *Doctrinale*. One aim of this textbook was to provide a practical substitute for Priscian's (*fl.* 500) *Institutiones grammaticae* (Foundations of Grammar). *Doctrinale* had a further purpose in common with a number of other works composed at the beginning of the thirteenth century: the displacement of the Roman classics from the school curriculum. This was not only an explicit objective of *Doctrinale* but also of Alexander's *Ecclesiale*, where he emerged as a declared opponent of the school of Orléans. Alexander's anti-classicism not only indicated a new direction for the literary side of the curriculum but also a new approach to the teaching of syntax in the classroom: the traditional method of immersion in the authors was to be put to one side and replaced by grammar based on logic and philosophy.

Although *Doctrinale* and the other great French verse grammar, Everard of Béthune's (d. before 1212) *Graecismus* (*c.*1210), were both northern French works, they reached Italian schools during the thirteenth century.

## Classical antiquity

Conclusive evidence here comes from Italian grammars written in the thirteenth century. Pietro da Isolella's *Summa* (1252) contains material taken from *Doctrinale* and *Graecismus*, as does Giovanni Balbi da Genova's (d.? 1298) *Catholicon*, completed in 1286. Most important is the testimony of the Piedmontese grammarian Mayfredo di Belmonte, who in 1225 composed a grammar in Vercelli, giving it the title of *Doctrinale*, in imitation of and homage to Alexander. This new style Parisian grammar imported to Italy corresponds in its anti-classicism to the contemporary anti-classical verse textbook on rhetoric, Geoffrey of Vinsauf's *Poetria nova*, datable between 1208 and 1213, raising the possibility that Geoffrey may have taught in Italy. Moreover, the *Poetria nova* was the most influential treatise on rhetorical style in Italian schools from the time of its publication to the end of the fifteenth century. The kind of style Geoffrey taught had nothing to do with classical prose, but rather represented an abstract elegance: Geoffrey quoted no classical examples in his work.

The second cause was indigenous to Italy. The burgeoning Italian administrative, clerical, notarial, legal, and academic classes could not be satisfied with the painfully slow traditional methods of artificial immersion in the authors; these were aspiring professionals with careers to pursue and quicker progress was needed. Fundamental here was the rise of the professional Italian universities concentrating on the study of law and medicine. These put pressure on the grammar schools to streamline their curricula, focusing on practical and rapid learning of Latin and eliminating the redundant study of Latin literature, previously at the heart of the grammar syllabus. In place of the authors there now burgeoned practical manuals for the study of secondary Latin in thirteenth-century Italy, a genre that before had hardly existed south of the Alps. The thirteenth century saw the first great flowering of Italian grammatical studies; this was also a period in which many copies were made in Italy of Alexander's *Doctrinale* and Everard's *Graecismus*. In some sense, the latter two works came to serve a dual purpose in thirteenth-century Italy: on the one hand, they reinforced previous grammatical knowledge, providing rules and lists in an easily memorized verse format; on the other, they provided a type of substitute for the study of the authors themselves, and were accordingly glossed repeatedly in the traditional school manner.

However, the end of the thirteenth century saw a reaction in Italy to the overwhelming anti-classical tendencies of the previous hundred years. The trendsetter was the Paduan lawyer, Lovato dei Lovati (1241–1309). Here the rise of Occitan and Italian vernacular poetry in early thirteenth-century Italy is crucial. This period is famous for the birth of the Italian literary vernacular, and the trend can in part be connected to the anti-classicism characteristic of Italian grammar and rhetoric teaching in schools and universities at the same time. What Lovato's humanism represented was a reaction against the overwhelming anti-classicism of the preceding generations. Writing around 1290, Lovato ridiculed a singer 'bellowing the battles of Charlemagne and French exploits' in French, 'gaping in barbarous fashion, rolling them out as he pleased, no part of them in their proper order, songs relying on no effort'. In contrast, he intended to write Latin poetry in the classical manner. 'Do you despise him [the courageous poet] because he believes that one must follow in the footsteps of the ancient poets?'[3] Lovato's humanism was a reaction, not just against the vernacular but also in opposition to the anti-classicism of the entire 'century without Rome'.[4]

Lovato's Latin verse epistles possess a new classical quality, demonstrating a sophisticated understanding of classical poetry that drew on and refashioned an impressively wide range of Latin poetry. Direct familiarity with a wide range of rare Latin classics has been claimed for Lovato, although a number of such attributions have been disputed or refuted. What does not seem in doubt is that Lovato exploited the manuscript riches of the library of Pomposa in the Po delta, and that he emerged as the first serious post-antique student of Seneca's tragedies, which had remained little known in the Middle Ages.

Lovato communicated this new enthusiasm for the Latin classics to his contemporaries. Another Paduan lawyer in his circle, Geremia da Montagnone (c.1255–1321), compiled a collection of quotations revealing not only a familiarity with Latin poets rarely encountered in the thirteenth century (Catullus, Martial, Horace's *Odes*, Ovid's *Ibis*, and Lovato's Senecan tragedies), but also an acute distinction between ancient and medieval literature, differentiating the classical *poeta* from the medieval versifier (*versilogus*). Lovato's true intellectual heir was his friend and compatriot from Padua, the notary Albertino Mussato (1261–1329), who extended Lovato's interest in Senecan tragedy, explaining its metres to the great political theorist and fellow Paduan, Marsilius (c.1280–c.1343), as well as composing a set of plot summaries. Mussato wrote histories imitating Livy, Sallust, and, to a lesser extent, Caesar. His greatest achievement was his own Senecan tragedy, *Ecerinis*, which recounted the rise and fall of Padua's despot, Ezzelino da Romano (1194–1259). The play – composed to be read and not acted – was the first tragedy written in classical metres since antiquity, and it led to a further neoclassical revival: no poet had been crowned with laurels since the era of the Roman emperor Domitian

## Classical antiquity

in the first century CE, but now the practice was revived for Mussato by his fellow Paduans in 1315.

The Paduan circle of early humanists extended to nearby Vicenza, where Benvenuto Campesani (1255–1323), showing an unusual enthusiasm for the classics, hailed the rediscovery of Catullus in about 1300 with a celebrated epigram, as well as to Verona. Here the cathedral's custodian, Giovanni de' Matociis (*fl.* 1306–20), using the resources of the city's rich chapter library, composed one of the first examples of historically sensitive literary criticism. Giovanni, familiar with the library's copy of the younger Pliny's letters (a work otherwise unknown in Italy) and using Suetonius' life of the elder Pliny, proved that there were in fact two Plinys, not one as had been assumed in the Middle Ages.

The Veneto was the cradle of early humanism, but the movement extended further south to Bologna, where the canon lawyer Giovanni d'Andrea (*c.*1270/75–1348) was acquainted with the newly recovered letters of Pliny the younger and where Giovanni del Virgilio (late thirteenth century–*c.*1327) showed an enthusiasm for classical Latin verse and corresponded with the Paduan circle. In Florence mythological studies were pursued, laying the basis for Boccaccio's (1313–75) *Genealogy of the Gods.* In particular, Dante's contemporary, the vernacular poet Francesco da Barberino (1264–1348), added Latin glosses to the autograph of his Italian poem, *I documenti d'amore* (The Documents of Love, *c.*1310), demonstrating a wide familiarity with ancient sources. But the true equivalent figure to Lovato and Mussato in Tuscany was the lawyer, Geri d'Arezzo (*c.*1270–1339). Most of his works are lost or survive only in fragments, but what remains shows a remarkable knowledge of classical antiquity. It is clear that he attempted to model his Latin writing style directly on classical authors, rejecting at least in part the medieval traditions of *dictamen.* He knew classical texts almost unread in the Middle Ages, such as Pliny's letters, and he exercised critical judgement on ancient texts, realizing that the *Gallic Wars* was a genuine work by Caesar. He revived classical literary genres such as the dialogue, and, on the model of classical authors such as Cicero, he collected his own correspondence, anticipating Petrarch (1304–74). Moreover, he formed his own circle of humanist friends similar to Mussato's and Lovato's group in Padua. Geri and Mussato were singled out by Coluccio Salutati (1331–1406) as the founders of the humanist movement.

Dante was the contemporary of all these early representatives of humanism: Francesco da Barberino made one of the earliest references to *Inferno*; Dante corresponded with Giovanni del Virgilio and he lived in

304 Robert Black

Verona when Giovanni de' Matociis was engaged in his intensive study of classical texts in the cathedral library. What was Dante's attitude to the classical authors who were being so vigorously studied and revived by his contemporaries? What were Dante's affiliations to the burgeoning humanist movement?

Dante himself drew up several literary canons: in *De vulgari eloquentia* II, vi, 7, the four poets who followed the rules of the loftiest style (Virgil, Ovid in the *Metamorphoses*, Statius, and Lucan) are paralleled by four writers of the loftiest prose (Livy, the elder Pliny, Frontinus, and Orosius). The poets of the 'beautiful school' include Homer, Horace, Ovid, Lucan, Virgil, and Dante himself (*Inf.* IV, 86–102). These lists include authors whom Dante could not (Homer) and certainly did not (Frontinus) read directly. Like many medieval writers, Dante cited and alluded to many authors whom he knew only by reputation. In attempting to assess the range of Dante's knowledge of the classical authors, the fundamental methodological principle of economy should prevail. Dante's access to books was severely restricted both in Florence and during his exile. This biographical fact means that possible sources ought not to be multiplied but rather reduced to his essential and assiduous familiar reading.

## Virgil

Virgil (70–19 BCE) had been at the heart of Italian classicism in the twelfth century, with the above-mentioned survey registering twenty-four manuscripts produced in Italy and used in Italian schools that century; the following century, by contrast, only three manuscripts of this type have emerged in the census. Dante points to Virgil as the leading light for him among classical authors; however, his interest in Virgil was far from typical for Italian readers in the thirteenth century. So with his Virgilian preoccupation Dante was moving onto a new path at the beginning of the fourteenth century; in this respect he was a trendsetter, given that Virgil began to make a recovery after 1300, with five relevant manuscripts from the fourteenth century identified in Florentine libraries.

It is unlikely that Dante read Virgil as a schoolboy, given his own limited early Latin education and Virgil's decline in the Italian classroom during the thirteenth century. Dante first cites Virgil in *Vita nova* XXV, a fact suggesting that his early reading of *Aeneid* was part of the study of the Latin classics undertaken following Beatrice's death in 1290. In the first instance, Virgil's influence on Dante was literary. He acknowledges Virgil as his only teacher of 'the beautiful style' in *Inferno* I, 87. The *bello stile*, valid in both Latin and the vernacular, is the equivalent for Dante of the 'tragic style', the 'illustrious vernacular', the 'highest level' of construction, an artistic language distinct from other literary registers and from crude, everyday, or regional parlance. Dante claims that it was through Virgil alone that he was able to win honour (*Inf.* I, 87): here he may be referring to the didactic and philosophical poetry that he began to write in the 1290s, some of which is included in the *Convivio*.

Virgil was also a formative influence on Dante's ideology of empire. In *Aeneid* I 278–9, speaking through the words of Jupiter to Aeneas, Virgil declares that the Roman empire will be unending and unlimited: 'For [the Romans] I set neither bounds nor periods of empire; dominion without end have I bestowed.'[5] These lines from Virgil became the cornerstone of Dante's political thought, according to which the Roman empire was divinely and providentially ordained to secure peace and well-being for mankind – an idea first articulated in *Convivio* IV, iv, 11: 'this office [of empire] … the Roman people secured … by divine providence'. Virgil concurs in this in the first book of the *Aeneid* when, speaking in the person of God, he says: 'To these (namely the Romans) I set no bounds, either in space or time; to these I have given empire without end.' This imperial ideology would become the basis of *Monarchia*.

In *Convivio* (as in the *Commedia* and *Monarchia*) Dante christianizes Virgil's imperialism. In the Middle Ages there had been a persistent tendency to assimilate classical literature to Christianity. Thus Dante, in line with tradition, reads the opening of Virgil's fourth eclogue (5–10) in Christian terms. For Virgil, a new golden age under Augustus was dawning, connected with the birth of an unidentified child. A Christian, messianic reading of these lines developed early in the fourth century and remained popular throughout the Middle Ages. Dante thus presents Virgil as an unwitting prophet of Christ's coming: 'you did like him that goes by night and carries the light behind and does not help himself but makes wise those that follow, when you said: "The age turns new again; justice comes back and the primal years of men, and a new race descends from heaven"' (*Purg.* XXII, 67–72). Dante follows Virgil's original meaning more closely in *Monarchia* I, xi, 1–2 and in *Epistola* VII, 5–6, interpreting the lines as a reference to an imperial revival and likening Henry VII of Luxembourg (*c.*1275–1313) to Augustus.

Another example of Virgil's Christian transformation in Dante's hands concerns the ancient Trojans. For Virgil, the destruction of Troy had been the whim of the gods: the Trojans' pride had been nothing but positive, and Troy's fall had been undeserved (*Aeneid* III, 1–3). For Dante, in

306 Robert Black

contrast, the fall of Troy was just punishment for the sin of pride (*Inf.* I, 75–6; XXX, 13–4). In his commentary, Francesco da Buti (*c.*1324–1406) suggests that Dante deliberately imposed his own interpretation on Virgil: 'authors make a habit of reading their own meaning into another's authoritative statement when they can appropriately do so, notwithstanding the fact that whoever said it meant it in another sense; and so our author [Dante] does in this instance'.[6]

Although Virgil was above all, for Dante, the greatest Latin epic poet, Dante does refer once to him as 'the singer of bucolic poems' (*Purg.* XXII, 57), and Virgil's *Eclogues* provided the model for his only Latin poems, two *Egloge* directed to Giovanni del Virgilio in 1319 or 1320; Boccaccio stated that bucolic poetry after Virgil was of no account, so suggesting that, in the fourteenth century, there was no classical model for this genre other than Virgil.

## Statius

Statius (*c.*45–*c.*96) had not been favoured in Italian schools even during the twelfth century, with only six Italian manuscripts emerging in the above-mentioned survey for that period, and none at all for the following century. This trend was in contrast to northern Europe. Although *Thebais* and *Achilleis* were widely read as school texts in northern Europe by the twelfth century, this was not the case in Italy: few Italian schoolbooks with either text predating the fourteenth century have so far emerged in the ongoing census; *Achilleis* became a particular favourite in Italy only from the last quarter of the fourteenth century.

Dante's acquaintance with Statius as author of the two epics *Thebais* and the incomplete *Achilleis* could hardly have preceded his classical studies following Beatrice's death. Dante several times alluded to the latter poem at first hand, and he knew that Statius had left *Achilleis* incomplete (*Purg.* XXI, 93); *Thebais* is cited once by name in *Convivio* (III, xi, 16), and is a clear source throughout the *Commedia* and especially in *Inferno*.

Like Virgil, Statius was an exemplar of the loftiest poetic style for Dante. Alongside Virgil, he is named as one of the *regulati poetae*, the poets who respect the rules of the most illustrious poetry (*Dve* II, vi, 7). He is not included among the poets of the *bella scola* in *Inferno* IV because, unlike his pagan colleagues, he is destined to be saved and will not remain for eternity in Limbo; this relegation also reflected medieval lists of *auctores* in which Statius was sometimes presented as belonging to a second and lower order of writers.

# Classical antiquity

Dante provides a substantial life of Statius in *Purgatorio* XXI–XXII, placing him among the trangessors expiating the sins of avarice and prodigality, Statius being guilty, according to Dante, of the latter vice (*Purg.* XXII, 52–4). Commentators generally agree that Dante took this information from the seventh satire of Juvenal (87). Dante erred with regard to Statius' birthplace (Toulouse instead of Naples), following the wrong track indicated by Jerome (*c.*347–420) and Fulgentius (*fl.* late fifth–early sixth century), who had confounded him with the contemporaneous grammarian and rhetorician L. Statius Ursulus of Toulouse (*fl.* 41–54). What is surprising is that Dante added to a biography otherwise based on authoritative sources the claim that Statius was a secret convert to Christianity. No specific source for this astonishing claim has ever emerged. It is generally thought to have been in part influenced by the medieval belief that Statius was Virgil's most fervent follower. Dante further asserts that Virgil's admonition in *Aeneid* III, 56–7 regarding the dangers of materialism freed Statius from the sin of avarice (*Purg.* XXII, 38–41). Virgil's fourth eclogue, with its supposed messianic prophecy of Christ's coming, then revealed to Statius the truth of the Christian message (67–72). For Dante it was historically fitting that Statius had flourished under the Emperor Titus (b. 39; reign 79–81), who avenged Christ's crucifixion with the destruction of the Temple at Jerusalem (*Purg.* XXI, 82–6).

From Dante's perspective, starting from the Virgilian example and tradition, Statius represented a further Christian transformation of the Latin epic. He assumed the role of the redeemed soul ready to ascend to Heaven and to assume the task of Dante's further education, joining Virgil as Dante's teacher. Dante placed Statius at the summit of antique Latin spirituality. He became the mediator between pagan wisdom and Christian truth, a figure of Dante himself: when Statius says that through Virgil he learned not only the way to poetry but to Christianity (*Purg.* XXII, 73), he speaks as Dante's alter ego.

## Ovid

Ovid's (43 BCE– CE 17/18) *Metamorphoses* had been a favourite in the Italian classroom during the twelfth century, with thirteen manuscripts from that period in the ongoing survey, and its presence continued, albeit much diminished, during the thirteenth century, with four manuscripts in the census. In twelfth-century Italy Ovid's other works had a noteworthy appeal, with three manuscripts of the *Fasti*, four of the *Tristia*, and three of the *Heroides* so far appearing in the survey; this trend continued unabated and was even stronger in the thirteenth century, with the census showing five manuscripts of *Ex Ponto*, three of the *Tristia*, and one each of the *Heroides*, *Ibis*, and the amorous verses (*Ars amatoria*, *Remedia amoris*, *Amores*).

Dante's first mention of Ovid was in *Vita nova* XXV, 9 where he quotes *Remedia amoris* 2, but such acquaintance could not have been a remnant of his school experience, Ovid's love poetry having been excluded from the medieval Italian grammar curriculum prior to the fourteenth century. Given his limited Latinity before 1290, it is unlikely that Dante's early vernacular amorous verse was stimulated by Ovid's example. Even after turning to the classics, Dante's interest in Ovid as a poet of love remained minimal: a few allusions to *Ars amatoria*, *Remedia amoris*, and *Heroides*. Influence of the remaining shorter Ovidian works was similarly marginal. For Dante, Ovid was *Ovidius maior*, the author of *Metamorphoses*; his knowledge of the rest of the Ovidian corpus may have been indirect and not based on a first-hand knowledge of the texts.

It is conceivable that Dante had encountered *Metamorphoses* at school. More likely, Dante developed his interest in Ovid as his ambition to write weighty vernacular verse developed: Ovid was, for him, a member of the *bella scola* (*Inf.* IV, 90). Dante singles out 'the Ovid of the *Metamorphoses*' (*Dve* II, vi, 7) as one of the *regulati poetae*: the Ovid who counted as far as he was concerned was the author of the monumental poem that for him was an epic, charting in a continuous narrative the vast course of universal history from the great first metamorphosis of chaos into order to the final metamorphosis, the apotheosis of Caesar.

Christianization is evident in Dante's tendency to transform punishment encountered in *Metamorphoses* from the vengeance of the gods to the fitting outcome of divine justice: Niobe 'threw herself on the cold bodies [of her sons], and without regard for due ceremony, gave all her sons a last kiss' (*Metamorphoses* VI, 277–8),[7] while Ugolino della Gherardesca (*c.*1220–89) 'gave himself, now blind, to groping over each [of his sons], and for two days [he] called on them after they were dead' (*Inf.* XXXIII, 72–4); the death of Niobe's children was provoked by her insults to Latona (*Metamorphoses* VI, 146–312), but, in the case of Ugolino, his desperate pawing was part of a just punishment for his treason inflicted by a providential divine order.

## Lucan

Lucan's (39–65) *Pharsalia*, a favourite in the Italian classroom during the twelfth century, with thirty-six manuscripts in the survey, maintained a much diminished presence there during the next hundred years, with only six manuscripts.

Like Ovid, Dante first cited Lucan (*Pharsalia* I, 44) in *Vita nova* XXV, 9; he is one of the *regulati poetae* (*DVE* II, vi, 7), and a member of the *bella scola* (*Inf.* IV 90). Like *Metamorphoses*, *Pharsalia* could conceivably have been one of Dante's grammar school texts.

Lucan, who loathed Caesarism and its founder, might have represented a negative republican critique of Virgil's providential Roman imperialism, but this contrast was not appreciated by Dante, who tended to integrate Lucan's and Virgil's ideologies, seeing the heritage of antiquity largely as a block. Thus Dante elided the contradiction between the pro-Caesarism at the end of *Inferno* and the anti-Caesarism, based on Lucan, of placing Cato as the guardian of Purgatory, Dante's portrait being based in part on *Pharsalia* II, 326–91. Instead Dante sees Cato and Caesar as joint heroic examples of Rome's perennial heritage: their moral superiority, as revealed by Lucan and Virgil, serves to justify his idea of universal empire through Roman history. Cato and Caesar represent a complementary antithesis, underpinning the fundamental ideology of the poem: the empire as representation of superior ethical values in terrestrial life to prepare for eternal salvation.

With regard to Lucan, Dante maintains his Christian perspective, as was typical in the Middle Ages. In *Inferno* XXV, 94–102 he proclaims, in conceiving a transformation, his own superiority over Lucan (as well as Ovid) not just because of his more complex poetic invention, but also because he believes that, as a Christian poet, he has been privileged to penetrate more deeply into the hidden ways of divine justice and its effects on human destiny.

## Horace

In Italian schools, Horace (65–8 BCE) was widely read during the Middle Ages, reaching a highpoint during the twelfth century, with thirty-two manuscripts in the census. He maintained a significant, if lesser, showing (with fourteen manuscripts in the survey) when interest in the classics diminished over the next hundred years. In the twelfth century the entire Horatian corpus was read in the Italian classroom, but by the thirteenth century school manuscripts of only the *Ars poetica*, the *Epistulae*, and the *Sermones* are found: the *Carmina* (Odes) had virtually dropped from the curriculum.

Horace is first cited by Dante in *Vita nova* XXV, 9, where he quotes *Ars poetica* 141; the poem is also cited directly elsewhere (for instance, *Dve* II, iv, 4; *Conv.* II, xiii, 10; and *Par.* XXVI, 137–8). The *Ars* and its rich commentary tradition were important sources for Dante's grammatical and rhetorical theories, but it seems that his direct acquaintance with Horace stopped there. No convincing evidence has been produced to demonstrate first-hand knowledge on Dante's part of the remaining Horatian *oeuvre*. Horace figures as a member of the 'beautiful school' (*Inf.* IV, 89). For Dante, Horace did not reach the top rank of Latin poets, failing to be mentioned as one of the *regulati poetae*. Dante may refer to 'Orazio satiro' (*Inf.* IV, 89) because of the great regard Horace enjoyed in the Middle Ages as a moralist (satire as a genre was generally associated with praising virtue and attacking vice). Dante wanted perhaps to suggest, by analogy, the moral and satirical qualities of his own *Commedia*. Like Pliny the Elder or Livy, 'Horace the satirist' may have been singled out by Dante not because of direct personal knowledge of his writings, but because of his high and widespread medieval reputation. Several medieval 'arts of poetry' had been based on the *Ars poetica*. Indeed, Horace's rich medieval reputation was in part based on his unique status as both author and literary preceptor.

## Cicero

Cicero's (106–43 BCE) shorter moral treatises were widely read as examples of Latin prose writing in twelfth-century Italian schools, with twenty-three manuscripts in the survey, but his position declined disastrously over the next hundred years with only one manuscript in the census.

For Dante, Cicero was above all a moral philosopher, not an orator: out of sixty or so direct Ciceronian quotations, only one is from a speech and a small number from rhetorical works; the rest are from his philosophical treatises. Here Dante is in the main line of the medieval tradition, like Conrad of Hirsau (*c.*1070–1150), who knew only *De senectute* (On Old Age) and *De amicitia* (On Friendship), or Abelard (1079–1142), who showed particular enthusiasm for *De officiis* (On Duties). It was *De amicitia* (together with Boethius' *Consolation*) that led Dante onto the road to philosophical wisdom (*Conv.* II, xii, 2–4). In *Inferno* IV, 141 Cicero is placed in the 'philosophic family' (*Inf.* IV, 132) crowned by Aristotle. In *Monarchia* I, i, 4 he asserts that no one would dare to defend old age after Cicero's *De senectute*, putting him on a par as an authority with Aristotle and Euclid. His theory of love in *Vita nova* was shaped by the vernacular Romance tradition and Christian ideology; nevertheless also significant was the Ciceronian concept of friendship in *De amicitia* as the union of virtuous individuals. He quotes *De finibus* (On Ends, I, ii, 4) for his defence of the Italian vernacular against the rival usage of Occitan (*Conv.* I, xi, 11–4). He translates *Paradoxa stoicorum* (Paradoxes of the Stoics, I, i, 6) in *Convivio* IV, xii, 6 to condemn riches. He repeatedly cites from and uses a wide range of Cicero's philosophical treatises.

As was typical among medieval writers, Cicero was not a stylistic model for Dante, and was absent from the list of authors 'who have written excellent prose' (*Dve* II, vi, 7). But Ciceronian rhetoric was the ultimate source of Dante's rhetorical theory. *De inventione* (On Invention) is quoted verbatim in *Monarchia* II, v, 2; although he takes no direct citations from the pseudo-Ciceronian *Rhetorica ad Herennium* (believed to be a genuine work of Cicero's throughout the Middle Ages and Renaissance), Dante's word choice in *De vulgari eloquentia* II, iv, 7 echoes *Ad Herennium* IV, viii, 11, so suggesting direct dependence. Dante's doctrine of the three rhetorical styles (*Dve* II, iv, 5) has its conventional roots in the three stylistic genres of *Ad Herennium* IV, viii, 11.

In terms of political theory, Dante transforms Cicero's phrase 'glory of dominion' (*imperii gloria*, *De officiis* I, xii, 38) into 'imperial crown' (*imperii corona*, *Mon.* II, ix, 4). Cicero maintained that wars fought to obtain glory through conquest must be fought less harshly and with due respect for the vanquished, unlike a bitter life-and-death struggle with an implacable and ruthless foe, who must be destroyed at all costs. Dante transforms the passage into an account of a divinely supervised war, seen as a duel for the imperial crown in which God's justice determines the outcome, and in which the victor exercises due restraint over the vanquished. Dante transforms Cicero's words into the Christian context of trial by combat to be determined by God's judgement according to divine justice and in terms of the struggle for the crown of the Christian Holy Roman Empire. Dante's thought here is in line with medieval teachings, whereby Cicero's idea of the just war had been given a Christian slant by Augustine, who had emphasized God's essential role in establishing human justice.

## Seneca the moralist, Juvenal, Persius

Seneca the Younger (*c.*4 BCE–CE 65) numbered among the most widely exploited moral philosophical authorities in the Middle Ages; he was a principal source for the survival of Stoicism in medieval thought. In the twelfth century he came to rival Cicero as an authority for moral philosophy; he was a favourite of William of Malmesbury (*c.*1095–1143),

John of Salisbury (1110–80), and Gerald of Wales (*c*.1146–*c*.1223). His status was enhanced by his widely accepted apocryphal correspondence with St Paul. Nevertheless, Seneca the moralist never occupied a place in the Italian medieval grammar syllabus (as evidenced by the absence of Italian school-level glossed manuscripts): his work belonged to the genre of moral philosophy, which was an advanced subject in the medieval Italian educational curriculum. Given Seneca's importance as a philosophical authority in the Middle Ages, it comes as no surprise that Dante knew and used the philosophical writings of the younger Seneca, including *De beneficiis* (On Benefits), *Epistulae* (Letters), *Naturales quaestiones* (Natural Questions), *De remediis fortuitorum* (On Remedies to Chance Happenings, probably an epitome of a genuine Senecan work), as well as pseudo-Seneca *De quatuor virtutibus* (On the Four Virtues), actually by Martin of Braga (*c*.520–80). Although Seneca was extensively quoted by secular and religious medieval authors, textual evidence suggests that Dante's knowledge of Seneca as a moral philosopher was based on direct reading of his philosophical works, which were ubiquitous in medieval libraries throughout Europe, including Italy.

Juvenal (late first–early second century) had been a widely read poet in twelfth-century Italian schools with twenty-six manuscripts registered in the census, but his position collapsed during the following hundred years, with no manuscripts in the survey. His fellow satirist, Persius (34–62), had had a marginal currency in Italian schools, with four twelfth-century Italian manuscripts in the survey, but, like Juvenal, his presence, according to the census, dwindled to nothing in the thirteenth century. On the other hand, Persius was widely read in northern schools during the twelfth century. In Italy he found a solid place in the grammar school curriculum only in the fifteenth century.

It has usually been assumed that Dante did not have direct knowledge of either Juvenal or Persius: his extensive paraphrase of the opening of Juvenal's eighth satire (1–24, 30–4, 54–5) in *Convivio* IV, xxix, 4–5 is dismissed as second-hand acquaintance, while his mention of Persius by name in *Purgatorio* XXII, 100 is attributed to Persius' high reputation in the Middle Ages and to the prestige enjoyed by satire. In light of the evidence from the above-mentioned survey, it is unlikely that Dante had encountered either satirist while at school.

Nevertheless, there is evidence to suggest that Dante may have had direct knowledge of both satirists. The frequency of his references, the ease with which he makes Juvenalian citations in different locations, the precision with which he identifies the location where he took the citation – such considerations suggest that Dante knew Juvenal directly. In fact, the wording of *Convivio* IV, xxix, 4–5

Classical antiquity 313

recalls the opening of Juvenal's eighth satire literally. Similarly there are direct borrowings from Persius, *Paradiso* XI, 1–3 thus recalling *Satire* I, 1. Equally, as with Seneca, quotations from Juvenal and Persius did circulate independently. But *Florilegia* were disseminated more extensively in Northern Europe in the thirteenth and fourteenth centuries than in Italy, where they were comparatively rare. Unless a specific *Florilegium* can be cited and a case made that Dante could have had access to it, then the presumption should be that Dante quoted from original sources available in Italian manuscripts, rather than from a hypothetical *Florilegium*.

## Homer

In the Middle Ages Virgil had seized the limelight to such an extent that Homer could retreat to the backdrop. *Iliad* and *Odyssey* lacked medieval Latin translations, although Latin and vernacular rewritings of aspects of *Iliad* in particular were far from uncommon, and so, as for medieval authors in general, Dante's knowledge of Homer came at second hand. In *Inferno* IV, 86–8, Homer is placed before all other poets; to him even Virgil defers, declaring to Dante, 'Mark him there with sword in hand who comes before the three as their lord; he is Homer, the sovereign poet'. Such a judgement is reinforced in *Purgatorio* XXII, 101–2: 'that Greek whom the Muses suckled more than any other'. Here Dante was reversing some contemporary opinion: the early thirteenth-century Sicilian jurist and poet Guido delle Colonne had singled out Homer as a sinner and a liar. Although Homer was regarded with reverence in commentaries to Horace's *Ars poetica*, nevertheless it needs to be explained why Dante held Homer in such high regard. He will have recognized and valued Homer as Virgil's predecessor and model; he had a more positive view of Greek culture than was normal in the Middle Ages. Furthermore, Homer commanded the authority of Horace, whose translation of *Odyssey*'s opening in *Ars poetica* 131 Dante cited in *Vita nova* XXV, 9. He would have been impressed as well by the authority of Aristotle, to whose citation of *Iliad* XXIV, 258–9 in *Nicomachean Ethics* VII, i, 1145a he referred three times (*Vn* II, 8; *Conv.* IV, xx, 4; *Mon.* II, iii, 9). He may have been affected by Augustine's philo-Hellenism (a consequence of the latter's hostility to Rome) or by Hugh of Trimberg (*c.*1230/35–after 1313), who, unusually, regarded Homer as superior to Virgil.[8]

## Sallust, Valerius Maximus, Terence

Sallust (86–*c.*35 BCE) had been, together with Cicero, the key prose author of the medieval Italian grammar syllabus, with twenty-four manuscripts in the census; however, unlike Cicero he continued to maintain a significant, if diminished, showing throughout the thirteenth century, with eight manuscripts in the survey. Neither *Catiline* nor *Iugurtha* ever seem to have particularly appealed to Dante. The opening of *Monarchia* ('Omnium hominum quos') seems to recall the beginning of *Catiline* ('Omnis homines qui'), but Dante here was more likely to have relied on an intermediary such as Isidore of Seville (*c.*560–636), who quoted the same passage (*Etymologiae* XI, i, 15). Similarly it can be shown that *Inferno* XXIV, 148 does not depend on *Catiline* LVII, 1–2, nor *Purgatorio* I, 71–2 on *Catiline* XXXIII, 4, but on Servius' (late fourth–early fifth century) commentary to *Aeneid* I, 195, where the latter Sallustian passage is quoted.

Although becoming a staple of the Italian classroom during the fourteenth and fifteenth centuries, Valerius Maximus (*fl.* CE 30) had played no part in the Italian grammar curriculum during the Middle Ages. Dante does not cite Valerius directly. Several possible affinities are either to be eliminated in favour of more probable sources or are inconclusive. If Dante had known Valerius directly, it seems likely that the citations would have been numerous and striking, so close was Valerius to the normal moralizing approach of medieval authors. Thus the first commentators on the *Commedia* did not fail to cite Valerius for parallels to Dante's text or in support of their own arguments.

Terence (*c.*195–*c.*159 BCE) occupied a noticeable but secondary position in the twelfth-century Italian curriculum, with eight manuscripts in the census, but none at all in the following hundred years, moving to the forefront of the classroom in Italy only during the fifteenth century. He was widely read in northern European schools during the Middle Ages, but not so in Italy; Plautus (*c.*254–184 BCE) was hardly known at all. If Roman comedy enjoyed a particular medieval currency, it was north of the Alps. Dante would not have read Terence at grammar school, nor did he appear to gain a direct knowledge of his works later in life. He, together with other writers, is named in *Purgatorio* XXII, 97–8 according to the model of *Ars poetica* 53–5. Dante's naming of Terence does not in itself suggest direct knowledge, given that in the canto he mentions others (Caecilius Statius, Plautus, Varius at line 98, as well as shortly later, at lines 106–7, Euripides, Antiphon, Agathon, and Simonides) of whom he knew little or nothing. But because Terence is mentioned directly in the letter to Cangrande della Scala (1291–1329; *Ep.* XIII, 29; for the dubious authenticity of this text, see below) and because Terence was widely known during the Middle Ages, it has frequently been assumed that Dante was citing *Eunuchus* III, 1 directly in *Inferno* XVIII, 133–5. However, it has been shown that he was quoting here at second hand via Cicero's *De amicitia* XXVI, 98 (where the same passage from *Eunuchus* is cited), with additional information gleaned from the Latin verse version of Aesop (which Dante knew; see Chapter 16). Terence is one more classical author whom Dante knew by reputation alone.

## Seneca the tragedian

Seneca the tragedian was another author known only by reputation. Up to the end of the thirteenth century, his tragedies were unread in Italian grammar schools, although during the following hundred years they rapidly became classroom favourites. Such a development mirrors the history of their transmission, which had been limited in the extreme before the late 1200s but was stimulated by the early Paduan humanists Lovato and Mussato, and then by interest at Avignon, leading to Nicholas Trevet's (*c*.1257–*c*.1334) influential commentary. Dante would not have read the tragedies at school.

Ostensibly Dante might have gained familiarity with Seneca the tragedian while resident at the court of Cangrande from 1312 to 1318. He was in close contact with Giovanni del Virgilio, who in turn was intimate with Mussato. The letter to Cangrande includes this definition of tragedy: 'tragedy at the beginning is admirable and placid, but at the end or issue is foul and horrible. And tragedy is so called from *tragos*, a goat, and *oda*; as it were a "goat-song", that is to say foul like a goat, as appears from the tragedies of Seneca.' Such a statement might suggest more than a generic familiarity and possibly an acquaintance with the tragedies' plots.

However, Dante consistently identifies Seneca as a philosopher. He is called 'Seneca the moralist' (*Inf.* IV, 141) alongside Cicero (*Inf.* IV, 141), included in the 'philosophic family' (*Inf.* IV, 132) presided over by Aristotle; in *Convivio* III, xiv, 8 he is placed among other philosophers including Plato, Aristotle, and Socrates. In the letter to a Pistoian exile (*Ep.* III, 8), he is referred to as the 'most famous of philosophers'. Vincent of Beauvais (*c*.1190–*c*.1264) had pointed to the same Seneca as both philosopher and tragedian (*Speculum historiale* IX, 102), and so it is striking that Dante specifically identified Seneca as a moralist, in distinction to all the other philosophers, who go without epithets in *Inferno* IV. Dante may have been aware that Seneca was also a tragedian, but he appears to have wanted to emphasize that, as far as he was concerned, Seneca was a philosopher.

There is thus a divergence between the author of the letter to Cangrande with its mention of Seneca the tragedian and Dante's focus on Seneca the philosopher. Such a gap becomes all but unbridgeable if the definition of tragedy is further considered. According to the definition in the letter, *Aeneid* would have to be regarded as a comedy, because it begins with sad events (the fall and destruction of Troy) and ends happily (the foundation of Rome), whereas in *Inferno* XX, 113 Dante himself, speaking through Virgil, defined *Aeneid* as a tragedy: 'my high tragedy'. Moreover, the letter is a highly conventional *accessus ad auctorem* (introduction to an author), closely conforming to the norms of an academic genre that Dante, with his style of textual commentary in *Vita nova* and *Convivio*, had already long left behind in creating the highly original metaliterary structures that characterize all his major writings from the *Vita nova* to the *Commedia*. The letter to Cangrande is simply too conventional to have been written by the always individual and unconventional Dante (and see Chapter 28).

Nearly all the allusions alleged to refer to Seneca's tragedies can either be found in other authors familiar to Dante, such as Virgil and Ovid, or are scriptural. The overwhelming number of supposed references to Seneca's tragedies occur in *Inferno*, a fact that would imply Dante's knowledge of the tragedies in a period before his contacts with Mussato's circle, under whose auspices he is meant to have become familiar with Seneca the tragedian. Acquaintance with the tragedies at the time of *Inferno*'s composition is contradicted by the fact that no allusion to them has been suggested for any work composed before the *Commedia*. Dante had no direct knowledge of Seneca's tragedies.

### Dante the Renaissance humanist?

The Latin classics held a profound interest for Dante, who, with his panegyric of Homer and his admiration for Greece's learning and political order, even showed an intuitive attraction to Greek antiquity. Dante cited Horace's *Ars poetica* not Geoffrey of Vinsauf's *Poetria nova*, Virgil's *Aeneid* not Walter of Châtillon's (1135–1204) *Alexandreid*, Boethius' *Consolation* not Henry of Settimello's *Elegy*.

And yet Dante was no Lovato or Mussato or Geri d'Arezzo. He did not participate in the recovery of Seneca's tragedies. There is little to link him to the Paduan humanist circle: his connection to Giovanni del Virgilio led to no known contact with Mussato. The early humanists of the Veneto wanted a Latin revival; Dante focused on an affirmation of the vernacular.

# Classical antiquity

Giovanni del Virgilio wanted Dante to come to Bologna to compose Latin poetry and receive the laurel crown; Dante replied ironically with two Latin eclogues reaffirming his anti-humanist position, reasserting the dignity of vernacular poetry, and refusing the invitation to seek glory in Latin poetry: if Dante were to be crowned poet laureate, it would have to be, as far as he was concerned, in Florence, the hub of the Italian vernacular. Unlike Lovato, who wanted to follow 'the footsteps of the ancients', Dante thought he could better the likes of Ovid and Lucan. Dante made no attempt to debunk medieval myths but on the contrary added his own, making Statius a closet Christian. Boccaccio would contest the veracity of Jove's prediction in *Aeneid* of Roman Imperial eternity,[9] which, in contrast, formed the cornerstone of Dante's political theory. Dante placed Virgil and Livy on the same footing as historical sources: 'Virgil … testifies … Livy … confirms' (*Mon.* II, iii, 6). Cicero the orator held no attraction for Dante, unlike Brunetto Latini (*c.*1220–93), who translated three of his orations into the vernacular.

Dante's Latin was strictly medieval; it is the *lingua franca* of the medieval universities. The technical vocabulary of *De vulgari eloquentia* comes from medieval Italian rhetorical schools, influenced by dictionaries, such as Uguccione da Pisa's (d. 1210) *Magnae derivationes* (Great Derivations), and with roots in late Latin, the Vulgate, and the Church Fathers. Although in the *Commedia* Dante often imitates and emulates stylistic elements that can be linked to a classical source, he was above all interested in the exemplary contents of classical literature. Similar to other medieval readers, Dante did not read classical texts philologically or historically. He read the classics not for themselves, but to transfer the texts to his own age, and to exploit them as a means to express his own needs and those of his own culture. Dante's division of learning into the seven liberal arts in *Convivio* II, xiii–xiv was typically medieval; he showed none of the tendencies to specialization in grammar and rhetoric that would become the hallmark of Renaissance humanism. For Dante, classical learning was a step on the ladder of knowledge that would ultimately lead to theology, the queen of the sciences. Dante represented the summit of medieval learning, not the foothills of humanism: he marks the boundary between the Middle Ages and the Renaissance.

### Notes

1 R. Black, *Humanism and Education in Medieval and Renaissance Italy: Tradition and Innovation in Latin Schools from the Twelfth to the Fifteenth Century* (Cambridge University Press, 2001), pp. 186–92.

318 Robert Black

2 R. Black, 'The origins of humanism' in A. Mazzocco (ed.), *Interpretations of Renaissance Humanism* (Leiden: Brill, 2006), pp. 37–71, at pp. 59–70).

3 Quoted in R. G. Witt, *'In the Footsteps of the Ancients'. The Origins of Humanism from Lovato to Bruni* (Leiden: Brill, 2000), pp. 53–4.

4 G. Toffanin, 'Il secolo senza Roma' in his *Storia dell'umanesimo dal XIII al XVI secolo* (Naples and Città di Castello: Perrella, 1933).

5 Virgil, *Eclogues, Georgics, Aeneid I–VI*, trans. H. R. Fairclough, rev. edn (Cambridge, MA: Harvard University Press, 1974), p. 261.

6 Cited in A. Ronconi, 'Virgilio Marone, Publio' in *ED*, V, p. 1045.

7 Trans. A. S. Kline, http://etext.virginia.edu/latin/ovid/trans/Metamorph6.htm.

8 *Das 'Registrum multorum auctorum' des Hugo von Trimberg: Untersuchungen und kommentierte Textausgabe*, ed. K. Langosch (Berlin: Ebering, 1942), p. 163.

9 *Esposizioni sopra la Comedìa di Dante*, ed. G. Padoan (Milan: Mondadori, 1965), p. 620.

CHAPTER 19

# Religious culture

*Peter S. Hawkins*

Even today, more than seven hundred years after the historical purview of this volume, a visit to any of the cities where Dante lived affords a sense of the pervasive religious character of the poet's culture. Cathedral, free-standing baptistery, the massive churches of the monastic orders along with the monasteries themselves, smaller parish churches, tiny neighbourhood chapels, street-corner shrines: all bear witness to a spiritual matrix that once undergirded every aspect of the medieval city's life. Although some of these structures continue to serve the religious needs of the present community, inevitably many have been repurposed as museums, schools, police headquarters, hospitals, or shops. Even those still functioning, however, have fallen victim to global tourism and the consumer ethos it encourages: churches are sights to be seen and photographed as much as houses of worship. It takes an effort, therefore, for a predominantly secular twenty-first-century person to enter into a world so completely shaped by Catholic religion, or to imagine, more specifically, how a late-thirteenth-century layman like Dante might have been formed as a believer.

## The Christian life

Such an imaginative reconstruction might well begin with the Christian rite of initiation, baptism, which in the Florence of Dante's day was a large public affair held on Holy Saturday, the eve or vigil of Easter, in the communal baptistery dedicated to St John the Baptist, one of the city's patrons. Godparents were trained weeks ahead of time to impart to their wards the essentials of Catholic faith and practice: the Paternoster, the Ave Maria, the Salve Regina, and the Apostles' Creed. The infants were exorcised, signed with the cross on their foreheads, and breathed on by the priest in an invocation of the Holy Spirit. At the baptism itself, in the presence of parents and godparents, priests immersed the children in

319

assembly-line fashion, and in water that had been blessed by the bishop. (The same water would be used for baptisms held later in the year, either at a mass observance at Pentecost or privately, at any time, if the infant was in danger of death.) Immediately afterwards, the newly baptized were given another sacrament, confirmation, and anointed with holy oil (chrism) as the sign of the cross was made on the forehead. Their heads were then wrapped in a cloth 'crown' that remained in place for the eight days following – a symbol of their readiness to be crowned with the saints in Heaven. The entire ceremony took place under the baptistery's magnificent cupola mosaics assembled at great civic expense over the course of the thirteenth century. Within the cosmic story they depict, stretching from Creation to Last Judgement, each set of newborn souls found their place in the story of salvation.

Baptism not only made one a Christian but also a 'member incorporate' in the life of the city. With that membership came the responsibility to live according to God's will, 'on earth as it is in heaven'. To this end, in a 1301 speech delivered in the Florentine baptistery, Dino Compagni (c.1255–1324) reminds his warring neighbours of the fundamental connection they share despite their bitter factional disputes. At the communal site where the most sacred oaths were made, he urges them to remember the 'womb' from which they had all come: 'Dear and worthy citizens, who have alike received sacred baptism at this font, reason compels and binds you to love each other like dear brothers, and especially since you possess the most noble city in the world.'[1]

## Church

The baptistery of the commune marked one's initiation into the local *societas christiana*, but neither it nor the cathedral was the primary place for sacramental life. Instead, the parish church was where a layperson customarily 'grew up' spiritually from cradle to grave: made a confession, took the Eucharist, was married, and received the rites of Christian burial. (As for the other sacrament, holy orders, those who became priests were ordained in the city's cathedral while those who took vows as monks or nuns did so in the chapel of their new community.) Quite distinct from either the cathedral or from the imposing churches of the religious orders built over the course of the thirteenth century – Augustinian, Franciscan, and Dominican, most notably – these neighbourhood chapels or *cappelle* lay in close proximity to one another within the city walls. They could be substantial or only room-size. In early fourteenth-century Bologna, for

*Religious culture* 321

instance, there were roughly 150 urban and suburban chapels for an estimated population of 50,000. Small was the norm: a typical chapel served thirty to forty households or fewer. According to the chronicler Giovanni Villani (*c*.1276–1348), Florence in 1340 boasted as many as 55 neighbourhood chapels, 5 major monasteries, 24 convents of women, 10 mendicant houses, and 30 hospitals for its 90,000 inhabitants.[2] (The commune managed diocesan institutions; the monastic orders those proper to them.)

A larger-than-average church might be served by two or more priests, or even a 'college' of several; most parishes, however, got by with only one priest, who might be assisted in his work by deacon or subdeacon. The sanctuary itself was typically divided by a screen into zones: choir and nave. The more monumental of these, built with a central door and side windows, gave the laity a view into the clergy's precinct but also kept them out except on special occasions. Whereas choir and high altar were controlled by the clergy, the nave (with side chapel altars) belonged primarily to the people. When services were not being held, it was likely to function as a mundane place for folk to gather, to store goods, and to negotiate the noisy details of commercial and civic life. Religious festivals, even carnivals, made easy transition between the church's nave and the commune's public square.

## Liturgy

The primary responsibility of the parish priest and his assisting clergy was to lead daily public worship. This meant saying the monastic hours in the morning, during the day, and after dark. Each service was composed of scriptural readings, set prayers, hymns, and the chanting of psalms – all 150 of them to be heard over the course of a week. The communes were vigilant that this observance should take place. In 1252, for instance, Piacenza levied fines on clergy who did not fulfil their duty to the divine office. Lucca acted more positively: in 1253 it ensured that no matter how small the chapel, there was always to be at least one 'scholar' on hand to assist the parish priest in reading and chanting the hours. Over the course of the thirteenth century lay people increasingly attended these services at Matins or Vespers, especially on Sundays and feast days. But even for the majority who were not in church on such occasions, bells rang throughout the city to signal the liturgical hour and to bid the faithful offer a Paternoster or an Ave Maria wherever they were.

The core of the Catholic liturgy was the Mass, celebrated daily as the occasion when Heaven and earth met together as bread became Christ's body and wine his blood. Although there were variant liturgical forms of the Eucharist, most churches in central and northern Italy followed the Roman rite with some local variation. Typically, men sat on one side of the church and women on the other. The service was largely in Latin (readings, prayers, responses), with the exception of the sermon delivered in the language of the people. This does not mean, however, that the congregation listened in ignorance throughout the Mass, especially in Italy, where the vernacular was close enough to Latin to be at least partially understood even by those who were not in the technical sense of the term 'literate'. Everyone knew (and often recited) the Latin Paternoster, Ave Maria, and Credo, either when bidden by a priest or spontaneously in private acts of devotion. The church was filled with things to look at, the liturgy an occasion for movement and gesture that together formed an ecclesiastical language of its own.

Once the congregation made its offering of money or of 'goods in kind', priests in communal Italy addressed the congregation in the vernacular and bid them pray silently for peace, for the clergy, for those who were sick, and for the dead. What followed thereafter was the canon of the Mass, the consecration of bread and wine, and the literal 'high point' of the ceremony, the elevation of the Host amid the ringing of bells and a cloud of incense. While the clergy consumed the elements, the people by and large made other kinds of communion. They adored what they could see when the celebrant raised the host; they also received in their hands the Pax, an object that took any number of symbolic forms in wood, glass, or metal (e.g. a crucifix, or an image of the Lamb of God). Along with a kiss the Pax was passed down from the high altar to a succession of clergy in their various ranks, and then on to the laity, first to the men on their side of the nave and then to the women on theirs. 'Ite Missa Est' (Go, the Mass is over) would officially end the liturgy, but on Sundays and feast-days the celebration was incomplete until the distribution of the *eulogia* or blessed bread, prepared by the same women of the parish who prepared the hosts for Mass. The laity could feed as well as be nurtured and fed.

Vernacular preaching was part of the parish Mass. Few of these parochial sermons remain, but we can assume that they were straightforward affairs that aimed to instil the basics of the faith as found in the articles of the Creed and to inspire Christian behaviour in everyday life. They might enjoin devotion appropriate to Advent, Lent, or a patronal feast day; or, regardless of the season or feast, issue the perennial call to repentance. The themes of the Church year would play an important part in what people heard in scriptural readings, sermons, and music; or in what they

*Religious culture* 323

viewed in the changing liturgical trappings of vestments and hangings. The Church's calendar tracks the life of Christ, from the expectation of his coming in the season of Advent, to his birth at Christmas, his ministry in Lent, and, thereafter, the feasts of his Passion, Resurrection, and Ascension. These commemorations would be followed by the descent of the Holy Spirit at Pentecost, the Feast of the Holy Trinity the week following, and the long stretch of Sundays through Summer and Autumn. The year then begins once again in Advent.

Added to this unfolding sequence of Masses centred on Christ and the Holy Spirit were the feasts of the Virgin Mary, of the Apostles and major saints of the universal church, as well as of those local *santi* who were of particular importance to a city or region. Communal Italy had an especially large number of lay saints who were revered quite shortly after their deaths and mostly as exemplary neighbours and citizens. The blessed, in other words, were made up not only of those who lived long ago and were known throughout the Church, but also by those who were contemporary, close-at-hand sources of *caritas* (charity). One of these, the pious Sienese comb-maker, Pietro Pettinaio (1180–1289), is recalled in *Purgatorio* XIII, 124–9 by a soul notorious for her pride. Sapia tells the pilgrim that the penitential debts she still owes would have been considerably greater had it not been for Pietro, who simply out of love, 'per caritade', remembered her in his 'holy prayers' and thereby assisted her progress on her purgatorial journey. Sanctity, in other words, could be found as locally as the Sienese Campo and in people as commonplace as an artisan-vendor.

## Priest and people

Although the bishop was the commune's spiritual head and central authority, the parish priest was the shepherd most immediately charged with the care of a flock. Unlike the 'regular' clergy, who lived apart and according to a rule, the 'secular' priest inhabited the same profane world as his people. Later prohibitions give an accurate sense of what had become prevalent over the centuries: 'parish clergy lived very much like their parishioners: they dressed like them, talked like them, worked with them, ate and drank with them, gambled with them, fought with them, slept with them.'[3]

Distressed by the state of the Church at the opening of the thirteenth century, Pope Innocent III (b. 1160/61; papacy 1198–1216) at the Fourth Lateran Council (1215) spelled out in seventy canons what the minimum standards of parish behaviour were meant to be. Of particular importance to the laity was the Pope's stipulation in canon twenty-one that, as a minimum requirement, they should make a full confession to their parish priest at least once a year. They were also to receive communion from him at least once annually, preferably at Easter. Failure to meet these duties would lead to excommunication and the denial of a Christian burial.

Innocent placed a far greater burden on the clergy, who were called to serve the people as preachers and confessors with new diligence. Groups the Church considered heretical were making inroads, which meant that the clergy needed to be doing more to make (as well as keep) faithful Catholics. The Pope first addressed his bishops. If for some reason they could not fulfil their task as the primary teachers of the diocese, they needed to appoint 'suitable men, powerful in work and word, to exercise with fruitful result the office of preaching'.[4] But it was the failure of the lower clergy that especially preoccupied him. They indulged in drunkenness and sexual licence, went hunting and fowling, attended ribald performances of 'clowns and buffoons', dressed extravagantly, slept through the morning office or neglected to say Mass but four times a year, misused the church building as a storehouse for their own belongings, irresponsibly revealed sins confided in confession, charged for burials and marriage blessings that were supposed to be offered gratis, and in addition were often too incompetent and uninformed to proclaim the faith effectively, let alone defend it against its enemies.

There is no reason to assume that all secular clergy were derelict; nonetheless, Pope Innocent deemed the general situation dire enough to warrant such detail. Where, then, was the laity to turn if their parish priest was so lacking in integrity and competence, and the local parish unable to provide the spiritual nourishment they increasingly sought? The need to redress the situation was particularly pressing given the success of Christian movements openly critical of Catholic practice, such as the Waldensians, as well as by those proselytizing on behalf of another religion entirely, such as the Cathars. Both groups were especially successful among artisans and tradespeople, many of whom aspired to live some approximation of the apostolic life, and believed they had the right to spread the gospel on their own. The heretics affirmed these lay longings. They also offered a vernacular world that held out opportunities for leadership and expression (to women as well as men) not readily found in the Church. In contrast to a corrupt Catholic clergy, moreover, they seemed to speak the people's language with moral integrity, and to practise what they preached.

## The mendicant orders

As if in response to Pope Innocent's concerns in Lateran Four, there rose up from the ranks of the early-thirteenth-century Church two men who would change the course of medieval Christianity, Francis of Assisi (*c*.1181–1226) and Dominic de Guzmàn (1170–1221). At virtually the same time they established mendicant orders that aimed specifically to evangelize the Catholics of Europe and to enable the Church to combat more effectively the forces of heresy. Both appealed to the ideal of poverty and used powerful, imaginative preaching as a primary means to spread their message. In time they would absorb many men and even more women into their lay 'third' orders (priests comprising the 'first' and brothers and nuns the 'second'). Some of these third-order laity would eventually end up in the monastic life. Yet what the mendicants had to offer even those who chose to stay 'outside' their official ranks was substantial: monumental places to worship, communities of fellowship, powerful preachers, skilled confessors, and opportunities for study and learning. Much to the chagrin of the secular clergy, who found their pious parishioners increasingly drifting away (and with them, the financial resources owed to the parish), both Franciscans and Dominicans provided a more vital engagement with the faith than could readily be found elsewhere.

The orders also had a profound impact on the development of religious devotion. In word, image, and song they promoted a new emphasis on Christ's human vulnerability as found especially at the moments of his birth and Passion. They cultivated the pathos of the 'Word made flesh' when held in his mother's embrace at the beginning of his life and in his death – nativity and Pietà. Francis fostered both the cult of the crèche and of the battered redeemer; his stigmata bore silent witness to this identification with the redeemer's five wounds. One thinks as well of the Man of Sorrows, in which Christ is depicted naked from the waist up, marked by wounds on side and hands, and crowned by thorns. Dominic, in his turn, is credited with popularizing the rosary as well as devotion to the Virgin Mary – a profusion of prayers, hymns, and images celebrating her person and her powers of intercession. Because the Cathars denied her divine motherhood, the Marian cult was another way for Dominicans to counteract this heresy.

Both mendicant orders were dedicated to evangelization. To assist this enterprise they constructed churches and convents that competed both in size and beauty with the commune's cathedral. (These buildings would be fronted by large piazzas to handle overflow crowds or offer sites designed expressly for outdoor preaching.) At the core of their evangelical task was catechesis: the teaching of the Catholic faith, the conversion of the merely nominal Christian to a deeper and more reliably orthodox life. This was partly accomplished by a wider dissemination of their own Latin training as priests and friars into forms suitable for a more-or-less sophisticated lay audience. Their effort was to turn the erudition of their monastery schools and the devotional practices of their community worship into a dynamic spiritual vernacular that spoke to the concrete realities of secular life. They wanted to win minds as well as hearts.

They did so, moreover, by cultivating different theological emphases, as Dante recognized in *Paradiso* X–XII, when the Dominican Thomas Aquinas (1225–74) celebrates Francis and the Franciscan Bonaventure (1221–74) praises Dominic. Dante revels in the contrasts between the 'seraphic fire' (*Par.* XI, 37) of the one and the 'cherubic splendour' (*Par.* XI, 39) of the other, in Francis as the lover of Lady Poverty and Dominic the militant opponent of heresy. The standard depiction of the two is telling. Typically, we see Francis in ecstasy, receiving the stigmata from a fiery six-winged seraph; Dominic, by contrast, stands resolutely, a book in hand. The one is a poet clad in brown homespun: at home in the world of Brother Sun and Sister Moon, he talks to birds and charms wolves. The other, dressed in the elegant black and white of his order, either gazes up lovingly at the Virgin Mary or is shown to be a champion of the Church against its foes.

There was also a marked difference in the preaching style of the mendicant founders that had a formative influence on the subsequent development of the orders. Contemporary accounts of Francis recall the unsettling way he could grab the attention of a crowd. According to Thomas of Spalato (*c.*1200–68), 'He spoke so well and sensibly that this preaching of an unlettered man stirred the very enthusiasm of even the especially erudite people who were there. He did not, however, hold to the classical manner of preaching but just shouted out practically whatever came to mind.'[5] Dominic was no less fervent, even if, like his Order of Preachers, he pitched the gospel at a higher, more erudite level than the Friars Minor. (From their beginning, the Dominicans were intellectually renowned; the considerable learning of the Franciscans came later.) At Dominic's 1234 canonization proceedings, for instance, he was remembered for dedicating himself to preaching with such passion 'that he exhorted and constrained his friars to announce the Word of God day and night, in churches and homes, in the fields and on the road, everywhere in short,

## Religious culture

and never to speak of anything but God'.[6] One imagines he was more effective in churches than in fields, which were more 'naturally' Francis' proper domain.

Not surprisingly given the distinct qualities of the two founders, the friars developed different styles of communication that appealed to different populations. It would be wrong to draw lines too sharply here, but one can say that the Franciscans took a *sermo humilis* (humble register) approach that turned to narrative, emotion, and the language of the marketplace. They had a strong following among the humbler ranks of artisans, craftspeople, and shopkeepers, who responded, as do most people today, to the well-told story that catches the attention and stays in the mind long after the 'point' has been forgotten. The late thirteenth-century *Meditations on the Life of Christ* attributed to Giovanni de' Cauli gives us a sense of what lay people would hear from Franciscan pulpits: examples and models of poverty, of accepting tribulations, humility, charity, the superiority of the active life over the contemplative and intellectual. The Dominicans by contrast appealed to a higher class of merchants, bankers, and lawyers – the well-to-do *popolo grasso* who had dominated Florentine politics and society since the late thirteenth century. In contrast to the Franciscans, they preached the excellence of the contemplative life and the usefulness of scholastic *ratio*. To their more patrician congregations they emphasized the virtues of political stability, economic responsibility, and the proper use of secular gifts for the well-being of the commune. Leaders of both orders, however, stressed that preachers should strive to address large audiences of people from a variety of backgrounds. They should stick to the core of the faith rather than flatter themselves with deep argument, to speak 'in the vernacular language and without any fantastic web of subtle distinctions'.[7]

## The laity

It would be wrong to assume that Catholics in the communes were entirely dependent on the proclamations of a pope or the evangelization of the mendicant orders. Simultaneously with the founding of the Franciscans and Dominicans, in fact, lay people, both men and women, were gathering in confraternities determined to build up the faith and inspire devotion, to organize acts and institutions of charity, and to claim a measure of independence in their spiritual affairs. The friars often provided inspiration and guidance for these groups, but the confraternities retained a distinct identity of their own.

328                    Peter S. Hawkins

Historians speak of a rehabilitation of the lay status in the early thirteenth century. A convenient starting point is Pope Innocent's 1199 command to the Bishop of Metz to reverse a decision earlier handed down
against a group of Lombard men and women called the Umiliati. These
people felt called to live a penitential life within their own families and
homes, to engage in charitable work among the poor, and to offer Christian
fellowship among their own kind, people working in trade, especially
those in textiles and leather goods – a target population for the Cathars.
They wanted to restrain the excessive tendencies of secular life rather than
renounce them entirely, to attempt a merger of family home, marketplace,
and monastery. They also wanted to preach. With an eye to the greater
freedom that heretical groups offered to their recruits, Innocent specifically approved the Umiliati's desire to witness to one another, to exhort the
gospel and to call each other to repentance. What they were forbidden to
do, however, was preach in public – the prerogative of the clergy alone – or
to openly discuss doctrine and the more controversial aspects of theology.

By the mid-fourteenth century, therefore, an Italian cardinal could note
Also in 1199, Pope Innocent canonized Omobono of Cremona (d.
1197), who had died just two years earlier but was already revered for his
emulation of the apostolic life, his acts of charity such as fostering other
people's children, feeding the poor, and for his intense piety. His sanctity
was thrown into high relief, moreover, when his death occurred during the
Mass at his parish church. (Religious ceremony was often the place where
many of these exceptional laity had their visions and mystical encounters
with the divine – an everyday communal setting for extraordinary private experience.) What is especially noteworthy is that, unlike previously
canonized laypersons, who were kings and queens, Omobono was a mere
artisan, a draper-tailor, and a married man. Suddenly the Church made it
possible to see that it was new birth rather than royal blood, martyrdom,
or clerical vow that made an exemplary Christian. Also, while celibacy
was still held to be the highest calling, it was by no means a requirement
for canonization. Indeed, canon one of Lateran Four made it explicit that
'not only virgins and the continent but also married persons find favour
with God by right faith and good actions and deserve to attain to eternal
blessedness'.

By the mid-fourteenth century, therefore, an Italian cardinal could note
that it had become possible to speak of a *laicus religiosus* (lay religious)
when referring to people who lived in their own homes, engaged in commercial life, and apart from any established rule of life, but whose lifestyle
was distinctive, 'simpler and more rigorous than that of other laypeople, who live in a purely worldly manner'.[8] According to the *Memoriale*

*propositi* (Memorandum of Purpose, 1221), an important document that served as a charter for many lay groups (as well as for the Franciscans in their earliest stages of formation), all that such converts needed do to indicate their penitential status was to wear distinctively 'humble' clothing, eat and fast with moderation, observe the requirements of the Divine Office, confess their sins and receive the Eucharist, and refrain from bearing arms or making oaths. (The latter abstentions caused controversies in the communes.) In addition, they were obliged to perform those acts of 'corporal' mercy enjoined by Christ: feed the hungry, give drink to the thirsty, clothe the naked, shelter the homeless, visit the sick, ransom the captive, and bury the dead. If married, they were expected to practise periodic sexual continence according to the fasts of the Church year. A 'chaste marriage' entirely without sex was also an option if mutually agreed upon. It could serve those who did not want to wait for the death of a spouse to free them from the 'marital debt'.

## Lay confraternities

The sheer variety of these lay groups is impressive. In Florence, for instance, the number of confraternities rose from six in the mid thirteenth century to thirty-three by the middle of the fourteenth, and then jumped to ninety-six over the course of the fifteenth. Although many of these groups were initially formed and led by males, women increasingly swelled the ranks; this led eventually to same-sex confraternities becoming the norm. Some women lived as anchorites or recluses on their own, often in city centres (which were hardly sites of reclusion at all). Those who were single or widowed (called alternately *beguines*, *bizoche*, *mantellate*, *beatae*, or *pinzochere*) could take on a modified habit and live at home, whether or not as vowed celibates. They were often lay sisters to a community of friars, living in 'microconvents', who might subsequently take vows and become nuns. Clare of Montefalco (*c.*1268–1308), for instance, was a devout Umbrian laywoman who began her 'converted' life as a third-order Franciscan before becoming an Augustinian nun. Women like her, who took the veil, entered an enclosed life within convent walls, as in the Order of the Poor Ladies or Clarisses founded by Clare of Assisi (1194–1253) and Francis in 1212. Those who kept their lay status retained a larger measure of freedom but also occupied an ambiguous place uneasily situated between lay and religious. Mysticism flourished in their circles, and with it, extremes of devotion that raised the suspicions of the hierarchy. In the case of Marguerite Porete (*c.*1250–1310), talk of union with

God and the fervour of 'unregulated' piety led to her death at the stake. A happier fate awaited such Italian lay mystics as Umiliana dei Cerchi (1219–46), Gherardesca of Pisa (*c.*1200–*c.*1260), and the redoubtable Margaret of Cortona (1247–97), whose colourful life gives us a sense of a devout laywoman's many options. After bearing a child out of wedlock, Margaret was alternately a recluse and a third-order Franciscan; she publically scolded worldly bishops and lackadaisical priests, founded a hospital and an order of nursing sisters (*le poverelle*), repaired a ruined church, spoke regularly with Christ, and had visions in the course of the Mass. She was a force to contend with.

Both men and women made up the flagellant confraternities that adapted for lay use a practice of mortification first developed in the monasteries. What was once largely a private experience came to be shared within a fellowship. It also 'went public' in dramatic processions that called for mass repentance, made a plea for divine mercy in a time of crisis, and imitated the sufferings of Christ.

Those who formed themselves into *misericordiae* (associations of mercy) made the practice of good works central to their activity, both on behalf of their own membership and for the well-being of the larger community. Having a good time together was also no doubt a motive for confraternity membership, and some groups, like the *frati gaudenti* or 'jovial friars', were as well known for their parties as for their ostensible role as peacemakers in the communes. (See Dante's withering portrait of the failures of Catalano and Loderingo in *Inferno* XXIII).

And then there were the *laudesi*, who dedicated themselves to singing the praises (*laude*) of the Virgin Mary, both her joyful and sorrowful 'mysteries', and most especially her participation in the suffering of her Son. Originating in Tuscany and Umbria, and often taking the name and patron saint of the church in which they met, these groups sang poetry written in both Latin and the vernacular. The *Stabat Mater* (Mother was standing) of Jacopone da Todi (1236–1306) is perhaps the best-known example of the genre, an emotive account of the Virgin's suffering at the foot of the cross that gives a specifically Marian focus to the Passion. Along with the mendicant orders, the *laudesi* were responsible for the popularization of the cult of Mary throughout the communal region. To the repertory of standard Catholic devotion, they added not only new hymns (treasured in each community's *laudario* collection), but also the habitual recitation of the Ave Maria and Salve Regina, the commissioning of altarpieces, and the dissemination of such affective images as the sheltering Madonna of Mercy.

*Religious culture* 331

Although musical services were the defining characteristic of *laudesi* worship, the companies also developed other kinds of performance. Liturgical drama or *sacre rappresentazioni* emerged unevenly. For instance, in early-fourteenth-century Perugia, Assisi, Gubbio, and Orvieto, the morning office of Lauds, named after the theme word of its closing Psalms (148, 149, and 150), was turned into a *lauda drammatica*. Florence, by contrast, was a century behind this turn towards drama, but made up for lost time with plays of the Ascension, Pentecost, the Annunciation, and the Raising of Lazarus staged at major churches throughout the city.

Other para-liturgical developments within the confraternities include *ceri*, wax images of the group's patron saint, whose face, hands, and feet were painted in flesh tones, and their bodies dressed in emblematic clothing. Wax was a highly prized commodity among the faithful, with candle offerings and processions not only central to the lay devotion of the confraternities but also a feature of civic piety and pride. Also popular as devotional objects were the large golden *stelle* or stars that the *laudesi* companies displayed in Florence's major churches. With an image of Christ or the Virgin Mary at the centre of a star-shaped frame, surrounded by painted angels and illuminated by candles, the whole elaborate construction was raised to the church ceiling while appropriate *laude* were sung by the community.

Confraternities typically 'owned' a side chapel that they would decorate with votive images and use to store their candlesticks, books, and other worship materials. Members met on weekday evenings after the night service of Compline for a brief ceremony of readings, prayers, and a few psalms or *laude*. There would be a short 'oration' delivered by a member of the community or by a presiding priest chosen by the confraternity. (The ability to select confessors and preachers, rather than simply accepting by default the offices of the parish priest, was part of the appeal of such groups.) The service concluded with a public 'confession of faults' similar to what would be found in a monastery.

In addition to these evening services held during the week, confraternity statutes specified a monthly gathering. Great emphasis was placed on the proclamation of these statutes to the group as a reminder of who they were and what they stood for. There was also common worship. In 1326, for instance, the Florentine company of St Zenobius met at a church celebrating a Mass in honour of the Virgin Mary at the 'third hour', about nine o'clock in the morning. After the reading of the Gospel and the preaching of a sermon, members left the congregation and, two by two, followed behind a pair of torchbearers, each carrying a lit candle. Singing

332 Peter S. Hawkins

a *lauda* in procession under the direction of a cantor positioned at the head of the line, they ended up in the choir, before the high altar, and there relinquished their candles to the priest in charge. At that point, they would stay in the priest's domain rather than return to their fellow laity in the nave, thus signifying their special status.

## Eucharistic piety

The altar was not the only place where the body of Christ was elevated and adored. The same Lateran council that spelled out the responsibilities of clergy and people also made the Eucharistic doctrine of transubstantiation dogma. Responding to efforts of an early-thirteenth-century Belgian nun, Juliana of Cornillon (*c.*1191–1258), who believed that the Eucharist had not yet received its full due, Pope Urban IV (b. *c.*1195; papacy 1261–4) promulgated the feast of Corpus Christi in 1264. To mark the occasion, he commissioned Aquinas to compose services for the feast's Mass and liturgy of the hours, which include *laude* that reveal the great systematic theologian to be a poet of some ability and that remain popular in the Church's repertory.

Corpus Christi builds upon the notion that the elevation of the Host is the climax of the Mass and indeed for many of the pious the primary 'reason' for going to church. But the feast effectively allowed sacramental devotion not only to be independent of the Eucharistic liturgy but also of the sequence of penance, absolution, and communion. One could receive the sacrament by adoration, whatever the state of spiritual readiness. With the host displayed in an often-spectacular sunburst-shaped monstrance, clergy and people typically processed from the church and moved throughout the city. These processions led to guild-sponsored, laity-performed 'mystery plays' that put the consecrated host in the larger context of salvation history from Creation to Last Judgement. The feast's robust celebration of the sacrament was also a dramatic public repudiation of the Cathars, who held the doctrine of transubstantiation (along with much devotional practice) in contempt. Primarily, however, the purpose of the feast and its civic procession was to take the faith, instantiated in the host, beyond the confines of the church. With a sacrament on the move, Corpus Christi extended the reach of the Catholic faith into the contemporary profane world.

## Pilgrimage

The open road could also be the site of pilgrimage, which pious laypeople undertook to mark a conversion of life or to make an extended act of

# Religious culture

penance. The destination might be Jerusalem, Rome, Compostela, or, as Chaucer reminds us, Canterbury. It could also be a designated holy place in one's own town, such as the 'Holy Jerusalem' complex constructed in Bologna's pre-eleventh-century monastery of Santo Stefano. The faithful set off for many destinations. For instance, a shoemaker in Piacenza, Raimondo Palmiero (d. 1200) – his surname signifying him as a 'palmer' or pilgrim – went to the Holy Land in his youth and then to Compostela and Rome after the death of his wife. Intending to go to Jerusalem once again, he received a vision of Christ who told him instead to tend to the poor and needy of Piacenza. In lieu of a lengthy journey, therefore, one could, like Raimondo, make a local pilgrimage within the city walls and do the work of atonement by performing 'suffrages' of various kinds around town: saying prayers and attending Masses for the dead, performing acts of mercy for the living, giving relief to the poor.

A pilgrimage to Rome, however, was increasingly popular after Pope Boniface VIII's (b. *c*.1235; papacy 1294–1303) proclamation of a Jubilee Year in 1300. This is also the time when Dante set the *Commedia*, during Holy Week, which enabled him both to affirm the holy purpose of the Roman pilgrimage in *Purgatorio* and be highly ironic about it in *Inferno* XVIII, 22–33. In the bull *Antiquorum fida relatio* (A Trustworthy Report of the Ancients), Boniface declared 'not only full and copious, but the most full, pardon of all their sins' to any who, after sincerely confessing their sins, visited the basilicas of Saints Peter and Paul at least once a day for a specified period: thirty days for Romans, fifteen for anyone else. Over 200,000 people made their way to Rome over the course of the holy year. The Jubilee, therefore, was a triumph for the pope (who turned an apparently spontaneous lay movement into a papal invention), for the coffers of the city, and, perhaps especially, for the doctrine of Purgatory. A pilgrimage could lessen the duration not only of one's own afterlife penance but also that of deceased loved ones who were already in the refining fires. The granting of indulgences also heavily motivated the impulse to go on another kind of pilgrimage, a crusade, whether to the distant Holy Land or to the Cathar-held cities of southern France.

If 1300 marked a high point of medieval pilgrimage, it by no means signalled its decline. In 1335 Venturino da Bergamo (1304–46) gathered a group of roughly 3,000 from the city and surrounding countryside, then began a circuitous journey through the cities of north and central Italy to Rome that gradually picked up thousands more along the way. Flagellant groups were especially eager to take their devotional practice on the road, using it as a call for general repentance and, at a time of constant factions and feuds, as a plea for peace and reconciliation. For the intensely devout

334 Peter S. Hawkins

and seriously minded, to follow the path of the crucifix, barefoot and over rough terrain, was the way to begin anew. For others, less driven by penitence but looking for the resources of new life, there were the milder pleasures of pilgrimage: the joy of fellowship with the like-minded, the luxury of a spiritual focus, the delight of simply getting away and seeing new places, holy and otherwise.

## The mendicant schools

Whereas we have no knowledge of Dante's involvement with any of the penitential confraternities sketched above, we know from the *Convivio* that after the death of Beatrice he sought consolation in 'the schools of the religious and the disputations of the philosophers' for a period of 'perhaps some thirty months' (*Conv.* II, xii, 7). The schools referred to here are almost certainly the schools of the Franciscans at Santa Croce and the Dominicans at Santa Maria Novella. In a city that had as yet no university, these two monastic houses were important places of learning. Established to train friars, both drew teachers as well as students from throughout Europe. Moreover, it would seem from scattered evidence, as well as Dante's *Convivio* account, that they were also open to lay people. Such access would have been limited and selective. Contemporary statutes from the Dominicans' Roman Province explicitly ban 'seculars' (both parish priests and laypeople) from attending lectures in philosophy and science (see Chapters 10 and 16).

What could be found in the mendicant schools towards the end of the thirteenth century? We can assume that each community cultivated a devotion to their founder most probably based on their respective *Lives*: St Bonaventure on Francis and Jordan of Saxony (*c.*1190–1237) on Dominic. Each would also have as its leading lecturers and preachers men who were trained at the University of Paris and were therefore 'up to date' in theological matters.

At the heart of the curriculum of the mendicant schools, not to mention of the Church itself, was the Bible. Scripture underwrote the entire culture: from the liturgy of the Mass and of the hours, to church preaching and communal discourse, to iconography of every kind. Lay literacy in communes such as Bologna and Florence – the one with its famous university, the other with its population of judges and notaries, bankers and merchants – was high for the period, 10 per cent or so, although more in the vernacular than in Latin. Scripture (in Latin) informed all three components of clerical education: *lectio*, the reading of the Bible, and

*Religious culture* 335

always with extensive commentary ranging from the Church Fathers to more contemporary authorities; *disputatio*, discussion of questions arising out of problematic texts; and *praedicatio*, preaching.

Such study was based on certain basic assumptions: the Bible's divine authority, the typological relationship between Old Testament 'figure' and New Testament 'fulfilment', and the four 'senses' of Scripture, whereby the literal text was understood not only to be true in itself but also to contain an additional set of spiritual meanings (allegorical, moral, anagogical). Thus the Exodus of the Hebrews out of Egyptian slavery, a literal and historical event, also indicated redemption in Christ, foreshadowed the sacrament of baptism, the moral journey away from sin to virtue, and the afterlife entrance of the believer into Heaven's 'promised land'.

Scripture was not only a multilayered text but also a highly mediated one: the pages of a medieval Bible are typically filled with commentary that surrounds (and often threatens to overwhelm) the scriptural text itself. By the close of the twelfth century, the *Glossa ordinaria* (Ordinary Gloss) was assembled to guide the reader's interpretation with the help of an assembly of witnesses, both ancient and contemporary. Also essential were two other works heavily based upon the Bible, Peter Comestor's (d. *c.*1178) *Historia scholastica* (Scholastic History, *c.*1173) and Peter Lombard's (*c.*1096–1164) Book of Sentences (*c.*1140). At least in the schools and universities, scholars tended to gloss or comment upon these glosses to Scripture rather than on the holy book itself. For most people, the 'sacred page', in the form of St Jerome's (*c.*347–420) Latin Vulgate, was neither owned nor read: it was the physical property of the Church and the privileged few. That said, the Scriptures were everywhere in the culture: ceremonially reverenced in a gospel procession; heard when chanted, preached, or read aloud in church; referred to in earnest or in jest in daily life; and seen when 'translated' into visual imagery not only in church but also throughout the city. In short, biblical literacy did not require reading.

For those like Dante, however, who shared literacy and bookish traits with the learned religious, there was a likely source for direct access to the entirety of Holy Writ, the so-called *Exemplar Parisiensis* or 'Paris Bible'. It was developed in the thirteenth century to meet the needs of both clerical students in the classroom and mendicant preachers on mission. Compact and one-volume, it made crucial innovations in how the Bible was subsequently presented: a book small in size, written on thin parchment, with chapter divisions (verses came somewhat later). These Bibles often included prefaces by St Jerome, as well as an array of tools that made the text eminently 'searchable': lists of biblical names, concordances, and

# Peter S. Hawkins

short passages to be used expressly to combat heresy. They were designed for reference as well as reading, to be both Bible and handbook.

Such material transformations in size and format suggest changes in the way Scripture was read and by whom. Stable Benedictine monastery communities, usually located outside the cities, continued to favour the large multi-volume Bibles in their ancient libraries. By contrast, the new, portable texts became the theological student's affordable book and the *vademecum*, or travelling companion, of the mendicants. The great proliferation of the 'Paris Bible' suggests a growing number of individual rather than community readers, an educated elite that gravitated to the universities or schools of the friars, who filled administrative positions in Church and State alike, and who actively used their Bibles to spread the evangelical word.

## Preaching

Preachers' manuals of the period presented the *ars praedicandi* as a way to improve the quality of the clergy's efforts. They recommended the sermon *ad status*, which aimed at a target audience and an appropriate level of discourse for soldiers, judges, princes, nuns, priests, married people, widows, and virgins. To engage these various congregations, concrete illustrations (*exempla*), taken from literature or from everyday life, were popular: they made the abstract concrete and memorable. So too did a careful sermon structure. Whereas the *modus antiquus* (old manner) attempted to explicate an entire passage apportioned for the liturgy of the day (for example, the gospel reading at Mass), the *sermo modernus* (modern discourse), especially favoured by the Dominicans, suggested an extended elaboration on a particular theme within a lection, one that that might be articulated pithily in a single verse: 'Jesus wept', 'Mary has chosen the better part', or 'He who loses his life shall find it'. Once the theme was stated, the preacher could then ring the changes. It might be divided into several parts, and then analysed with the help of definitions, theological distinctions, *exempla*, other germane biblical passages, or 'supporting evidence' gathered from the Church Fathers and made available in collections of 'quotable quotes'. After this work was done, the sermon ended with a brief conclusion summing up the analysis as a whole. A brief doxology followed.

One master of the art of preaching was the Dominican Giordano of Pisa (c.1255–1311), who came to Florence's Santa Maria Novella in 1303, shortly after Dante's exile from the commune. He was immensely

*Religious culture* 337

popular, so much so that more than 700 of his sermons still remain, preached in the vernacular and taken down by anonymous laypeople who wanted to preserve the homiletic moment for themselves and others. Bishops would often give incentives to the laity to attend sermons by offering indulgences; with Giordano, however, no such effort was needed. According to one of his hearers, he could soften the hearts of even the most obdurate men, who then 'turned their enmities into friendships, and many having renounced all vices, baptized themselves in this same Jordan [i.e. Giordano] with their tears, [and] changed their lives for the better'.[9] Like Dante, Giordano moved freely between the reality of everyday life in city and countryside and the realms of science, philosophy, and theology. Both addressed not only those who had a formal Latin education, such as judges, notaries, and clerks, but also the far larger number of those whom Armando Petrucci has termed vernacular 'monolingual literates': 'merchants, artisans, shopkeepers, artists, accountants, shop or banking employees, as well as some workers and some women'.[10]

Refreshingly down to earth with his audience, full of wit and charm, Giordano's sermons give us a sense of the spiritual lives of the people for whom Dante also wrote the *Commedia*. In one, preached in 1305, on the feast of Mary Magdalene, he argued that true penitence requires deep inwardness rather than the superficial acts of penance that presumably many of his listeners were performing. He tells his congregation that it is better to think of your Creator and sincerely bewail your manifold sins and wickedness than to undertake a pilgrimage to some distant location (which can easily become the occasion for mortal sin), or fast ('not necessary for eternal life'), or wear hair shirts.[11] Because preaching and penance were so intimately connected in the work of the friars, it is easy to imagine that someone as skilled in the pulpit as Giordano was also frequently on call to administer penance. Hearing confession, granting absolution, and determining an appropriate penance was a responsibility that the mendicants often took over from the parish priest, much to the dismay of the latter.

One can understand why they were in demand. The friars had the sophistication and training that the secular clergy lacked. They were also willing to spar with the reluctant penitent, to engage in a war of wit. According to Archbishop Federigo Visconti of Pisa (*c.*1200–77), 'it is fitting that, as one knight fights another powerful, rebellious knight, the friar struggle and do battle with the spears of reason and persuasion against the sinner, that he may conquer him spiritually'.[12] Careful preparation for the sacrament was also expected. There was to be no subterfuge: penitent self-revelation required that one be humble, direct, and hold nothing back. The penitent was to review his or her behaviour honestly in light of the Ten Commandments or, more often, of the seven deadly or capital vices: pride, envy, wrath, sloth, avarice, gluttony, and lust. Brunetto Latini's (*c*.1220–93) mid-thirteenth-century allegorical poem *Tesoretto* (Little Treasure) lines up the vices in the order established by Gregory the Great (*c*.540–604) precisely to prepare the reader to make his or her confession after finishing his book.

Other penitential handbooks offered ways to analyse sin with reference to the five senses, the seven sacraments, and the twelve articles of the Apostles' Creed. Perhaps best known among these was the Dominican William Peraldus' (*c*.1190–1271) *Summa of Vices and Virtues* (*c*.1250), which assembled a full range of contemporary moral thinking to assist a confessor in helping the penitent move from one spiritual state to another. Peraldus devotes the second book of his treatise to the seven capital vices. Their potency is demonstrated by the fact that the seven spawn more than 120 distinct individual sins. He also forges a one-on-one relationship between the vices and their corresponding virtues, which then develops into elaborate comparison-contrasts *in malo* and *in bono*: the symmetry of flesh versus spirit, bad fruit versus good, army of vice against army of virtue. Perhaps most significant for Dantists, Peraldus shows how disordered love is the source of the seven capital vices and the key to their understanding and remediation. So too does Virgil in *Purgatorio* XVII, the *Commedia*'s central canto.

Although canon law mandated confession only once a year, the statutes of lay confraternities urged greater frequency; so too did the natural desire of many devout laypeople. Making a confession need not be restricted to the three times a year when most of the faithful in Dante's day received communion, at Christmas, Easter, and Pentecost. Nor did penance need to be the preamble to the Eucharist; it was a sacrament in its own right – a joy rather than a duty, and perhaps the one occasion when a layperson might receive spiritual direction and even personal advice from someone with skills in discernment.

In addition to penitential manuals and handbooks, another resource invaluable for both preachers and confessors were the lives of the saints. These collections were available in many forms, visual as well as textual. The most influential of them was the *Golden Legend* (*c*.1260) by Jacobus of Voragine (*c*.1230–98), a Dominican friar and Bishop of Genoa. He organized this extraordinarily popular compendium of hagiographical lore according to the liturgical year. An account of individual saints appears on the day of their feast. He also includes a 'History of the Mass' and the 'Twelve Articles of the Faith'. Often beginning with an etymological analysis of a saint's name, Jacobus goes on to recount the life, the 'signs and wonders' associated with it, and the posthumous miracles wrought by intercession, relic, and holy place. Scripture is a constant point of reference throughout the work, in part to create an authoritative context for the saint or feast day in question, in part to ground the narrative of holy lives in Holy Writ. Although written originally in Latin, and no doubt intended primarily for priests, the *Legend* had many vernacular translations and survives in over 1,000 manuscripts. For layperson as well as friar, it offered a digest of the Church's faith conveniently organized according to its cycle of yearly worship and daily observance. In its pages the preacher could find rich fodder for sermons, the confessor exciting examples of virtue, and pious laity inspiration for their own lives.

It is in the pages of the *Commedia*, however, that we find not only the fullest flowering of medieval Catholic belief and practice, but also the freedom of a poet to make received tradition his own. Dante took advantage of the late medieval preoccupation with the afterlife to present this mortal world as God might judge it. He weighed his entire culture, lay and religious, and found it severely wanting, both from the perspective of Scripture and from the point of view of the faith's glorious champions: apostles, patriarchs, the founders of the monastic orders. Together with his lay spokesperson Beatrice, the poet voices a devastating critique of the contemporary scene – its papacy, prelates, monks and priests, not to mention its allegedly Christian rulers. At the same time, the *Commedia* offers an ample sense of the religious fervour that fired this critique and indeed animated the historical period and region in which Dante wrote. The poem is at once a demanding penitential appeal aimed at bringing about the reader's conversion and an extended *lauda* in praise of the Trinity, the Virgin Mary, and all the saints.

## Notes

1 Dino Compagni, *Cronica* II, 8, cited by R. Trexler, *Public Life in Renaissance Florence* (New York: Academic Press, 1980), p. 48.
2 For these statistics, see A. Thompson, *Cities of God: The Religion of the Italian Communes 1125–1325* (University Park: Pennsylvania State University Press, 2005), p. 39 (Bologna), p. 42 (Florence). I am greatly indebted to Thompson's book.

340                          Peter S. Hawkins

3 See D. E. Bornstein, *The Bianchi of 1399: Popular Devotion in Late Medieval Italy* (Ithaca: Cornell University Press, 1993), p. 16, whose characterizations of the clergy are taken from the strictures on their behaviour issued at the Council of Trent.

4 Canon 10, Fourth Lateran Council (www.fordham.edu/halsall/basis/lateran4.asp).

5 Thomas of Spalato, cited by L. K. Little, *Religious Poverty and the Profit Economy in Medieval Europe* (Ithaca: Cornell University Press, 1978), p. 163.

6 Cited by A. Vauchez, *The Laity in the Middle Ages: Religious Belief and Devotional Practices* (University of Notre Dame Press, 1993), p. 100.

7 Hubert of Romans, cited by Little, *Religious Poverty*, p. 187.

8 Henry of Susa, *Summa aurea*, cited by Vauchez, *The Laity in the Middle Ages*, p. 113.

9 Cited by K. L. Jansen, 'A sermon on the virtues of the contemplative life' in M. Rubin (ed.), *Medieval Christianity in Practice* (Princeton University Press, 2009), pp. 117–25, at p. 122).

10 A. Petrucci, *Writers and Readers in Medieval Italy: Studies in the History of Western Culture* (New Haven: Yale University Press, 1995), p. 140.

11 Giordano of Pisa, cited by Jansen, 'A sermon on the virtues of the contemplative life', p. 124.

12 Cited by Little, *Religious Poverty*, p. 199.

CHAPTER 20

# Visions and journeys

## Eileen Gardiner

When Dante began writing his *Commedia* around 1306, European literature was rich with works that provided a fertile ground for constructing his
account of a journey in the otherworld. The two closely related genres –
voyage and vision – were integral aspects of this literary domain. While
the distinction between these two venerable forms should be quite clear
to the modern reader, in the Middle Ages voyage literature could often be
as hypothetical as vision literature. Both shared a common projection of
the hero into the unknown – an experience that often engendered a crisis, resulting in the opportunity for the hero's personal conversion based
on accumulated experience, knowledge, and insight. Epic stories from the
classical period often combined voyage and vision. Heroes like Odysseus
and Aeneas wandered a Mediterranean both real and imaginary, and both
visited the underworld in tales that are mirrored in quite a significant
body of medieval vision literature, including especially the *Commedia*.
Despite their commonalities, it is best to consider these genres of voyage
and vision separately to appreciate fully their vitality and complexity at
the beginning of the fourteenth century.

Let us begin with the voyage. Although the great age of discovery
was still two centuries in the future, fourteenth-century Europe was not
without an interest in the outside world, in travel and adventure, in foreign lands and peoples. Although real travel was circumscribed for most
medieval people, many accounts were careful records of actual journeys.
Travellers embarked on journeys for much the same reasons as they have
always done. The first reason would have been intellectual, motivated
by curiosity and a quest for knowledge about the surrounding world.
The second would have been personal – the journey taken in search of
self-transformation. Under this rubric would be counted both pilgrimage and adventure, including crusade, which had aspects of both military
adventure and spiritual pilgrimage. The third would have been pragmatic,
pursuing trade, diplomacy, or patronage in distant lands. Often travellers'

## 342              Eileen Gardiner

accounts reveal a combination of motivations, and sometimes no clear motivation at all.

Yet many travel accounts relied on imagination and fantasy. Imaginary worlds were created on top of the real world as background and setting for heroic tales. The origins for this practice date back as far as the epic of *Gilgamesh* (eighteenth century BCE). But like the works of Homer (late eighth century BCE?), this and many other ancient works were not directly known in the Middle Ages. Yet Virgil's (70–19 BCE) *Aeneid* (29–19 BCE), which was well known in the Middle Ages in various forms, stands in for all this ancient literature, presenting the outlines of the hero's ordeal as he travels the world, a testing-ground for his outer mettle and inner character. There were other examples as well. The third-century BCE *Romance of Alexander* attributed to Pseudo-Callisthenes was a popular work, recast over centuries in numerous versions, combining the tales of a famous hero with a taste for the wonders of the East. Many later medieval romances would continue this tradition and use the broad outline of geographical knowledge with fantastic supplementary features, such as castles, bridges, rivers, and mountains, as appropriate backgrounds for the adventures of a medieval knight – such as Parsifal or Roland – seeking his place in the world.

In the Western Latin tradition more scientific interest in the surrounding environment can probably be traced to Pliny the Elder (23–79 CE) and his letters describing his encounters with the natural world. But even actual accounts of places visited and described were enhanced by imaginative constructions that combined what actually was, or might be, beyond the horizon with compelling and fantastic speculation. The Anglo-Saxon *Wonders of the East* from about 1000 concentrates on the most astounding things that might be found in that direction. Travelling in the other direction, toward the West, there were fewer, although similar descriptions and fabrications. The ninth-century *Navigatio Sancti Brendani* (Voyage of Saint Brendan) is believed to be based on some exploratory Irish voyages to the Hebrides, Shetlands, Faroes, and Iceland, and perhaps even beyond. This account was supplemented by encounters with imaginary places and unlikely people, such as Judas Iscariot, clearly outside the realm of actual experience. *The Voyage of Saint Brendan* was widely known and very popular throughout the Middle Ages from the time of its composition, and it appears in manuscripts throughout Europe in various translations.

In addition to these well-known works, the earliest pilgrims to Rome and the Holy Land wrote accounts and descriptions of their travels, comprising both natural features and holy places. From the fourth century

*Visions and journeys* 343

come the description by the Bordeaux Pilgrim (333), an account of the pilgrimage of Silvia of Aquitaine or Egeria (*c*.381–84) and the letters of Paula (347–404) and of her daughter Eustochium (*c*.368–419/20), who travelled to the Holy Land perhaps in the company, but at least under the influence, of St Jerome (*c*.347–420). Although brief, their letter to their Roman friend Marcella, written to persuade her to join them in the Holy Land, lists the sacred sites that attracted them to, and then keep them in, Palestine. In the late seventh century the travels of the Frankish Bishop Arculf became the basis for *De locis sanctis* (On Holy Places) by the Bishop of Iona, Adamnan (627/28–704).

This tradition of the pilgrim's account matured into actual guidebooks for pilgrimage. There is rich evidence for the robust production of such guidebooks, a genre that includes the *Einsiedeln Itinerary* of the mid-ninth century, which lists for pilgrims a series of eleven paths through Rome with the sites to be seen on either side, and the *Mirabilia* (Marvels) guidebooks to the same city written both by Benedict, a canon of St Peter's, in around 1143, and the even more secular guide written at approximately the same time by Master Gregory. Guidebooks to the Holy Land were written by numerous pilgrims such as Saewulf (1102/03), the Russian Abbot Daniel (1106/07), John of Würzburg (*c*.1170), Theodoric of Würzburg (*c*.1172), and Johannes Phocas (*c*.1185). Although many now survive in only a manuscript or two, like the twelfth-century *Pilgrim's Guide to Santiago de Compostela* in northwestern Spain, they are nevertheless a testament to a tradition of pilgrims writing about their journeys and describing their observations for those who would follow. However, even when these were intended as reliable accounts of well-documented places, the fascination for the marvellous would creep in, as for instance in the description of the Roman Forum in Canon Benedict's *Mirabilia urbis Romae* (Marvels of Rome): 'Nearby is a place called Hell because in ancient times it burst forth there and brought great mischief upon Rome. Here a certain noble knight, intending that the city should be saved after the gods had given their oracle, put on his harness and cast himself into the pit, and the earth closed. So was the city delivered.'[1]

Early Christianity had also produced a corpus of travel accounts that were less interested in geography and more interested in the work of conversion and in exotic descriptions of the East. The third-century apocryphal *Acts of Thomas*, for instance, recounts the missionary activity of one of Christ's Apostles in India. This work probably spawned in part the legend of Prester John, who moved from India to farther and farther distant locations as travellers reached the hitherto 'farthest reaches' and failed

344                                    Eileen Gardiner

to find traces of this Christian king. The later twelfth-century *Letter of Prester John* provides evidence of a continuing fascination with the wonders of the East, as well as a knowledge of earlier literature like the *Acts of Thomas*.

By the thirteenth century mendicant missionaries began their exploration to the ends of the known world to convert pagans to Christianity or to form alliances against Islam with non-Western Christian communities. While they were engaged in this work, some compiled extremely important descriptions of the places they visited partly based on earlier travel conventions and partly from their first-hand experiences. One of the first Franciscans, Giovanni da Pian del Carpine (*c*.1182–1252), travelled from his native Italy to the Mongol court and, in his *Ystoria Mongalorum* (History of the Mongols), provided the earliest anthropological, geographic, and historical account of the people and regions of central and northern Asia. Not long afterwards another Franciscan, the Flemish William of Rubruck (*c*.1220–*c*.1293), wrote a description of his journey to convert the Tartars, which provided a remarkably accurate account of central Asia. Yet another Italian Franciscan of a later generation, Giovanni da Montecorvino (1246–1328), wrote two letters, important for their geographical report on the regions of China and India. Even though the original reports of missionary travellers, particularly Franciscans and Dominicans, may survive in only a relatively uncirculated letter or a few copies, many of their accounts were known through being incorporated into histories and treatises, like the *Speculum historiale* (Mirror of History) of Vincent of Beauvais (*c*.1190–*c*.1264), which circulated widely.

Rather than seeking to convert or conspire with far-flung peoples, the goal of many other travellers was trade, diplomacy, or simple curiosity. Benjamin of Tudela (1130–73) set off from his native Navarre in Spain and travelled through Spain, then around the Mediterranean, visiting southern France, Italy, Greece, Constantinople, and the Holy Land, which may have been a pilgrimage destination for him as well. According to his account, now known as *The Travels of Benjamin of Tudela*, he may have even set off East toward Baghdad and Persia before continuing his travels through North Africa. While he made particular note of Jewish communities in each of the places he visited, his work is also more broadly important as a geographic and ethnographic study of the Middle Ages. For instance, he describes Amalfi thus:

> Thence [from Salerno] it is half a day's journey to Amalfi, where there are about twenty Jews, amongst them R. Hananel, the physician, R. Elisha,

*Visions and journeys* 345

and Abu-al-gir, the prince. The inhabitants of the place are merchants engaged in trade, who do not sow or reap, because they dwell on high hills and lofty crags, but buy everything for money. Nevertheless, they have an abundance of fruit, for it is a land of vineyards and olives, gardens and plantations, and no one can go to war with them.[2]

Marco Polo (*c*.1254–1324) is perhaps the best known of the later medieval commercial travellers. Working with his father and uncle, he journeyed from Venice throughout central Asia to China. During a brief imprisonment upon his return, he dictated an account of his journey, published originally under the title *Il Milione*, but now well known as the *Travels of Marco Polo*. Marco was a contemporary of Dante, and whether or not his work was known to the poet, the popularity of his writing is strong evidence of a keen interest in voyage literature among literate citizens of the Italian city-states.

Some medieval travellers even sought out the otherworld, which would be described as if it were accessible directly from a particular point on the earth – as if this and the other world inhabited connected planes. 'Mohammed's Night Journey and Ascent into Heaven' (*Life of Mohammed*, 263–71), from the mid-eighth century and translated into several European languages toward the end of the thirteenth century, combined both an earthly journey from Mecca to Jerusalem on a fabulous animal and an otherworld ascent via a fine ladder. The otherworld journey as background for part of a hero's adventure was again based on classical models. While many of those ancient works were not known directly to writers in the Middle Ages, their otherworld landscapes were communicated through known authors and works. For instance, Virgil's description of Aeneas' descent into Hades in *Aeneid* VI, which was well known to Dante and other medieval authors, was modelled both on the descent of Ulysses found in Homer's *Odyssey* (Book XI) and on the tale of Er in Plato's *Republic* (*c*.380 BCE, Book X), two Greek works that medieval authors apparently did not have an opportunity to know directly. Such descents to the underworld can be traced back ultimately to ancient Near-Eastern myths and were even transformed into humorous reinterpretations in the hands of writers such as Aristophanes (*c*.446–*c*.386 BCE), who brought his hero Dionysius on a romp through the underworld in *The Frogs* (405 BCE).

Descents to the underworld also figured in other ancient works well known to medieval readers. Examples include the tale of Orpheus and Eurydice in Book X of Ovid's *Metamorphoses* (8 CE), the descent of Psyche to Tartarus in Book VI of Apuleius' *Golden Ass* (*c*.170 CE), and *Menippus*,

346                    Eileen Gardiner

*or the Descent into Hades* by Lucian of Samosata (*c.*125–after 180 CE). The *Purgatorio Sancti Patricii* (St Patrick's Purgatory, *c.*1153) is one example of this type of descent in medieval literature. To repent for his sins, the knight Owein ventures on pilgrimage to an Irish otherworld entry on an island in Lough Derg (Donegal), much the way Aeneas sought out an entrance to Hades at Lacus Avernus near Naples.

Most of the great flourishing of this otherworld literature in the Middle Ages, however, was written not as journey, but as vision and dream. But there is also the broader genre of vision literature, which may be divided into many types, including apocalyptic, political, mystical, theological or philosophical, and moral. A work like Dante's *Commedia* incorporates elements of all of these.

The most important apocalyptic visions are associated with the Bible as either canonical or apocryphal texts. The *Book of Revelation*, or the *Apocalypse of St John*, became canonical, and its vision of the last days and the end of time is perhaps the most significant piece of this literature, but several other apocryphal visions were also influential. These include the first *Book of Enoch* – which is part of the Jewish but not the Christian canon – and the apocalypses of St Peter, St Paul, and Mary. Each tells the story of the end of time with differing narratives and imagery. The apocalyptic *Sibylline Prophecies* became part of the Christian tradition through their dissemination in both Augustine (354–430) and Lactantius (*c.*240–*c.*320). Augustine's *City of God* concludes with descriptions of both the apocalyptic *visio pacis* (vision of peace) – a contemplation of the heavenly Jerusalem – as well as a beatific vision. The apocalyptic visions were powerful documents emanating from different communities that imagined the last days were near, and that punishment would be imminently meted out to heretics and non-believers as rewards were disseminated to the faithful. Except for the *Apocalypse of St Paul*, which had a continuing importance and influence throughout the Middle Ages in various versions, these vision narratives of the Apocalypse were not imitated so much as transformed into works of prophecy and commentary found in authors such as Ekkehard of Aura (d.1126), Joachim of Fiore (*c.*1135–1202), and Jacopone da Todi (*c.*1230–1306), and in works such as the *Oracle of Balbek* (after 500 CE), the *Vision of the Prophet Daniel* (ninth century), and the 'Sayings of Merlin', from their debut in Geoffrey of Monmouth's *Historia Regum Britanniae* (History of the Kings of Britain, *c.*1136) to their later incarnation as in the *Prophecies of Merlin* (1275). Many of the apocalyptic elements of these works were also used repeatedly in the descriptions found in otherworld visions.

*Visions and journeys* 347

Like John of Patmos' original *Book of Revelation*, medieval visions were on occasion used as political tools. This was accomplished in large part by use of the trope *vaticinium ex eventu*, or foretelling of events, which allowed for a visionary to bear witness to a truth as yet unknown to living contemporaries. Those who had already passed away were revealed to be blessed or cursed depending on where their souls were discovered in the afterlife. The *Visio Karoli Crassi* (Vision of Charles the Fat), which was incorporated into several well-known works during the Middle Ages, is one of the best examples of the political use of vision literature. Although actually written around 900, this vision was supposed to have taken place in 885. In this vision Charles the Fat (839–88) meets his cousin Louis in the otherworld. Louis advises Charles to abdicate his throne in favour of Louis' own grandson, also named Louis – the historical Louis the Blind (*c.*880–928). Charles had done just that and had been severely criticized for it and labelled a traitor and a coward. His supporters, and those of Louis, obviously constructed a *post facto* justification for Charles' abdication, and also took advantage of the opportunity to show the punishment of many of his relatives – including his own father – and their supporters. The *Liber sermonum Domini* (Book of the Sermons of the Lord) and *Liber visionum* (Book of Visions) of Robert of Uzès (d. 1296) similarly use dreams or visions as a tool of political prophecy. Dante makes masterful use of this trope, placing political enemies in Hell and political friends in Heaven.

Although the word 'mystical' has at times been applied quite loosely to various types of visions, mystical visions are generally recognized as describing a personal experience of the divine during an altered state of consciousness. This literature is influenced by, and derives from, earlier Jewish mystical and biblical texts and apocalypses, Greek philosophy, Christian Greek monasticism, and the early Christian Fathers. The New Testament provides an early-Christian example in II Cor. XII, 2–4, where Paul writes:

> I know a man in Christ who fourteen years ago – still in the body? I do not know; or out of the body? I do not know: God knows – was caught up right into the third heaven. And I know that this man, – still in the body? or out of the body? I do not know, God knows – was caught up into Paradise and heard words said, that cannot and may not be spoken by any human being.

Paul's own experience described in I Cor. XIII, 12 – 'Now we see only reflections in a mirror, mere riddles, but then we shall be seeing face to

348                              Eileen Gardiner

face' – is, on the other hand, a classic example of another mystical path, that of 'unknowing' (*agnosia*) in the present life and the promise of beatific vision in the next.

In Western Christianity, except for some early and disparate examples, the mystical vision is a late form. The visions of St Augustine at Milan and Ostia described succinctly in his *Confessions* (VII and IX, respectively) are generally counted as among the first personally described Christian mystical visions. The shared vision at Ostia of Augustine and his mother Monica was of 'that which is' and occurred shortly after his conversion and just before her death. Although his earlier vision at Milan was an important experience for him on his path to conversion, it was not the complete unification and illumination that he achieved at Ostia, which became an influential part of early Christian mystical vision literature. Pseudo-Dionysius the Areopagite (late fifth–early sixth century), who may indeed have been a mystic himself, did not devote his writings to his own personal experiences, but instead drew on the experiences of Moses, St Paul, Carpos, and his own teacher Hierotheus to describe how 'one is supremely united by a completely unknowing activity of all knowledge. And knows beyond the mind by knowing nothing' (*Theologia Mystica* I, 3).

There is a significant chronological gap between these recorded visions and those of Hildegard of Bingen (1098–1179), who appears to be the next Christian visionary mystic and who appears also to be unique in having experienced visions throughout her life. She recorded many, both as texts and illustrations, in her *Scivias* (1151/52), the *Liber vitae meritorum* (Book of the Rewards of Life, 1163), and the *Liber divinorum operum* (Book of Divine Works, 1173). Her near-contemporary Elisabeth of Schonau (1128/29–64/65) also experienced an extraordinary number of visions, which were recorded in three books. Hildegard's visions appear to have been achieved during deep meditation, while Elisabeth's seem to have occurred during trance-like states. If one can make a sharp distinction between mystical visions and spiritual or religious visions, some of those considered mystics, like Elisabeth, left behind writings that indicate the achievement of profound enlightenment yet fail to describe the unitive moment, a silence that looks forward to Dante's own concluding remarks in *Paradiso*.

Since the way to knowledge of, and even the promise of union with, the divine was part of the foundation of much of the monastic enterprise, it is likely that those who wrote about mystic experience in the interim between Augustine and Hildegard and beyond were less concerned with recording personal experiences and exploring their own personal development than with lighting the path for others by recording the rich tradition of the mystical saints or applying the tools of human reason to the outer limits of speculation on the divine.

Of the latter, Joachim of Fiore was one of the most influential and well-known visionary writers, combining mystical with historical speculation. Others include the renowned abbots of St Victor in Paris, Hugh (*c*.1096–1141) and Richard (d. 1173). Their writings do not necessarily describe a personal mystical experience – that is a direct experience of the divine – but rather vivify a sacred concept, individual, or moment. Such visions were, by and large, built upon intellectual foundations and disciplines tied closely to theological principles and philosophical speculation. Thomas Aquinas (1225–74) could thus be known both as the supreme intellectual systematizer of the Middle Ages and as a deeply theological inquirer into the nature of divinity. He gave definition to the greatest spiritual vision, the beatific vision. This vision of the divine, and whether it was attained only at the end of time, would be a controversial topic during the first half of the fourteenth century just as Dante was completing his own vision of the unspeakable divine.

In contrast to the intellectual and philosophical vision, the seraphic vision of Francis of Assisi (*c*.1181–1226) has been categorized more strictly as spiritual, influencing the heart and will rather than the intellect of the visionary. As St Bonaventure (1221–74) describes it in his *Legenda Maior* (*Life of St Francis*):

> On a certain morning about the feast of the Exaltation of the Cross, while Francis was praying on the mountainside, he saw a seraph with six fiery and shining wings descend from the heights of heaven. And when in swift flight the seraph had reached a spot in the air near the man of God, there appeared between the wings the figure of a man crucified, with his hands and feet extended in the form of a cross and fastened to a cross. Two of the wings were lifted above his head, two were extended for flight and two covered his whole body. When Francis saw this, he was overwhelmed and his heart was flooded with a mixture of joy and sorrow. He rejoiced because of the gracious way Christ looked upon him under the appearance of the seraph, but the fact that he was fastened to a cross pierced his soul with a sword of compassion.[3]

The influences of all these types of vision pervaded the intellectual and cultural atmosphere of Dante's time and became integral parts of the political, apocalyptic, theological, and mystical structure of his own great work.

But probably the most obvious influences on the narrative structure and moral underpinning of the *Commedia* were the extremely popular and widely circulated visions of the otherworld – of Heaven, Hell, and eventually Purgatory – which were written down, widely translated and disseminated, and often incorporated into larger histories and chronicles.

As noted above, visits to Hades were found in the epic literature of the ancients including the *Odyssey*, the *Aeneid*, and others. The 'Vision of Thespesius' from the *Moralia* (81 CE) of the Greek historian and philosopher Plutarch (*c.*46–120 CE), tells of a man of greed and iniquity who visited 'with his intellect' a place where he witnessed the three types of punishment meted out to the wicked in special pools. He describes how:

> as the souls of those who die came up from below they made a flame-like bubble as the air was displaced, and then, as the bubble gently burst, came forth, human in form, but slight in bulk, and moving with dissimilar motions. Some leapt forth with amazing lightness and darted about aloft in a straight line, while others, like spindles, revolved upon themselves and at the same time swung now downward, now upward, moving in a complex and disordered spiral that barely grew steady after a very long time.[4]

Thespesius is advised by a relative, whom he meets in the underworld, to mend his ways, and after two days he finally returns to life just as his body is about to be buried. Heeding the moral directive of his vision, he does reform his life.

In the fifth century CE the Roman grammarian and philosopher Macrobius wrote a commentary on the *Somnium Scipionis* (Dream of Scipio) by Cicero (106–43 BCE), from his *De Republica* (Book VI). This work was known in the Middle Ages only through Macrobius' commentary, which quotes much of Cicero's original while creating an encyclopaedic and Neoplatonic digression over fifteen times the length of Cicero's original. In the dream, Scipio Aemilianus meets his grandfather, Scipio Africanus, and while he looks down with his grandson on the world, he explains the nature of the universe, the heavenly spheres, the music of the spheres, the insignificant and transitory nature of fame, the nature of the soul, and finally the moral responsibility of the individual to disdain earthly reward and focus on the good of the commonwealth.

After Macrobius the medieval form of these otherworld visions almost universally served a similar purpose: warnings to the living to follow a moral life and to concentrate on the punishments and rewards of the otherworld instead of the vanities of this world. Gregory the Great (*c.*540–604) is perhaps the first great popularizer of this vision genre. Three short examples ('The Vision of Peter', 'The Vision of a Soldier', and 'The Vision of Stephen') are included in his *Dialogues* IV, 37. There is evidence of Coptic and Ethiopic visions from this early period as well, but it is unlikely that they were generally known, and their influence is hard

# Visions and journeys

to trace. Other visions also appear during the same time. For instance, the very brief 'Vision of Sunniulf' (late sixth century) is integrated into the *Historia Francorum* (History of the Franks) by Gregory of Tours (*c*.538–94), and thus became well known throughout the Middle Ages. It is noteworthy that these early visions included geographical and topographical details generally found in voyage literature. Both the 'Vision of Sunniulf' and Gregory the Great's visions include rivers or lakes and bridges, which are employed to test and punish souls after death. Even the much earlier 'Vision of Thespesius' included three pools of liquid as places for punishment, a motif repeated throughout medieval otherworld visions.

Like Gregory the Great and Gregory of Tours, the Venerable Bede (672/73–735) was a great compiler of stories, and in his *Historia ecclesiastica gentis Anglorum* (Ecclesiastical History of the English People) included two important, often-imitated, and often-cited visions, the 'Vision of Furseus' (III, 19) and the 'Vision of Drythelm' (V, 12). As a result of their otherworld experiences, both Furseus and Drythelm reform their lives and live until the end of their days in ascetic devotion. Significantly, the 'Vision of Furseus' is one of the first surviving Christian visions where the visionary is actually punished in the otherworld and bears the marks of this punishment when he returns to this world. Drythelm, on the other hand, has the unusual experience of seeing the souls of the dead near the mouth of Hell rise and fall in little globes of fire, a motif already seen in the 'Vision of Thespesius'.

The ninth-century *Visio Wettini* (Vision of Wetti), recorded by both Heito (763–836) in prose (824) and Walafrid Strabo (*c*.808–49) in verse (827), is influenced by previous vision literature and is in turn itself referred to in later vision texts. While Wetti lies in bed in the monastery at Reichenau, debilitated and verging on death, he asks his brothers to read to him from the *Dialogues* of Gregory, which, while encompassing a vast array of different topics, had come to be regarded as a progenitor of this particular genre.

From this point the otherworld vision could be found disseminated in chronicles and histories, reported in letters, and written down in verse and prose. The visionaries might be poor beggars, monks, counts, or kings, but almost all have a similar story. Their souls are transported either in sleep or seeming death from this world to the otherworld by a guide – often a saint of particular devotion – and led on a tour of the punishments allotted for different sins, often gruesomely described, and of the rewards of the blessed. The tour almost always concluded with instructions for leading a reformed life upon the inevitable return to this world and often also with advice for helping the souls in torment through prayer and good works.

By the twelfth century reports of these visions were widespread. Many that began as local stories were translated numerous times and frequently copied in manuscript form. No doubt many, because they were good stories as well as good lessons, were also orally disseminated. The *Vision of Alberic* was written down around 1121/23 and survives in only one manuscript, and yet it was thought to have been quite influential. It tells of a young monk from Monte Cassino, near Naples, who lies sick for nine days, before he is visited by St Peter, who with two angels takes him to view Hell, a river of Purgatory, the seven heavens, a land that cannot be spoken of and finally the fifty-one provinces of the earth. This work shows the influence of many earlier visions, so that whatever greater influence has been attributed to it is most likely that of other similar visions that were more widely disseminated.

The *Visio Tnugdali* (Vision of Tundale, 1149), written in Latin in Regensburg by an Irish monk, was translated into at least thirteen languages. Numerous medieval manuscripts survive. This work is perhaps the most elaborate, lengthy, and highly developed surviving Western otherworld vision before Dante's *Commedia*. Tundale, like Furseus, is punished in Hell, a place that is elaborately sectioned according to sins and their appropriate punishments. Tundale's guide is an angel, and the dialogue between the visionary and his guide on the nature of divine mercy and justice is a vibrant precursor to the ongoing dialogue between Dante and Virgil. As Tundale tries to cross a bridge a thousand feet long and only one foot wide, he says to his angel guide:

> 'Alas, misery to me. Who will free me from the journey of this death?' But looking at him with a joyful face the angel answered saying, 'Do not be afraid. You will indeed be freed from this punishment, but after this you will suffer another.' Going first the angel led him across the bridge. After crossing the narrow way, safe now, the happy soul said to the angel, 'I beseech you lord, if it pleases you, tell me what souls are these that I see tormented in this way?' And the angel said to him, 'This place is the most horrible valley of the proud. The putrid and sulfurous mountain is the punishment of flatterers.' And he added, 'Let us go until we come to another that this cannot compare with.'[5]

To understand the context for Dante and his great work, it is important to realize that the vision of Heaven and Hell, which was essentially the form that the *Commedia* adopted to narrate its tale, gathered its force and complexity from all the different varieties of voyage and vision literature that were part of the narrative culture of the fourteenth century. All contributed raw materials. Voyage literature provided the concrete form of an outer adventure story with a strong sense of location and progression. It suggested landscape, which might resemble the known world in many of its geographical and topographical features, but was also a canvas for speculation and fantasy. Vision literature, including eschatological texts and those with mystical and speculative, spiritual, moral, and political underpinnings were the rich and diverse milieu for Dante's description of the soul's inner journey toward transformation, conversion, and salvation.

## Notes

1 F. M. Nichols and E. Gardiner, *The Marvels of Rome = Mirabilia Urbis Romae* (New York: Italica Press, 1986), p. 41.
2 Benjamin, *The Itinerary of Benjamin of Tudela: Travels in the Middle Ages* (Malibu: J. Simon, 1983), p. 66.
3 Quoted in E. H. Cousins, *Bonaventure* (New York: Paulist Press, 1978), p. 305.
4 Plutach, *Moralia*, ed. G. P. Goold, trans. P. H. De Lacy and B. Einarson (Cambridge, MA: Harvard University Press, 1959), vol. VII, pp. 273–5.
5 E. Gardiner, *Visions of Heaven and Hell Before Dante* (New York: Italica Press, 1989), p. 158.

CHAPTER 21

# Historical and political writing

John C. Barnes

Clio has seldom if ever been wholly indifferent to social relations involving authority or power. At some level the writing of history is at least likely to embody some political agenda, while a discussion of politics is unlikely to get very far without some appeal to the historical record. To a large extent, then, this chapter will treat historical and political literature as overlapping categories, though it will also tend to proceed from comparatively pure politics to comparatively pure historiography.[1]

## Scholastic political theory

No account of political writing in Dante's time should ignore the theorists. Political theory in the thirteenth century was handled as a branch of theology, and as such was invariably written in Latin. Without question the brightest star in the theological firmament was the university of Paris, where most of the leading theologians of the period were trained, and where in the mid thirteenth century recent Latin translations of Aristotle's *Ethics* and *Politics* were accessible; and since the world of scholarship was an international one, an exclusive focus on Italy would be misleading, even though a good number of those leading theologians were Italian by birth – those who engaged with politics include Thomas Aquinas (*c.*1225–74), Tolomeo Fiadoni of Lucca (*c.*1236–1327), Giles of Rome (Egidio Colonna, *c.*1245–1316), James of Viterbo (*c.*1255–1308), Remigio de' Girolami of Florence (*c.*1235–1319), John of Naples (*fl. c.*1300–*c.*1350), Marsilio of Padua (1275/80–1342/43), and Augustine of Ancona (*c.*1241–1328). Of these, however, only Tolomeo and Remigio pursued their careers mainly in Italy, though as it happens James, John, and Augustine all penned relevant texts in Naples.

Two key issues may be seen as having underpinned western ideas about politics between 1250 and 1350: the relative merits of different types of constitution by which a political community could be governed, and the

354

*Historical and political writing* 355

relationship between the authority of temporal rulers and the authority of the pope. Regarding the first of these, it was natural that scholars accustomed to living in France should tend to favour monarchy, as Thomas Aquinas clearly did in principle, though his position is nuanced by the view that in practice a king's power should be 'tempered' by an advisory council of the wise to prevent monarchy from turning into tyranny. On different occasions Aquinas also suggests that ultimate authority rests with the whole people, that a mixture of monarchy, aristocracy, and democracy is best, or that the best form of government depends on the particular people, place, and conditions. Ultimately he emerges as a consistent supporter of a theory of mixed constitution, because the rule of law (rooted in the people) must prevail over the rule of the king's wishes. These ideas were developed in *De regimine principum* (On the Rule of Princes), written around 1277–80 by a former student of Aquinas, Giles of Rome, in his capacity as tutor to the sons of Philip III of France (b. 1245; reign 1270–85), and dedicated to Giles' erstwhile charge Philip IV (b. 1268; reign 1285–1314) in the early years of his reign. These circumstances may help to explain why on almost every point where Aquinas wanted limitation of kingship Giles comes down on the side of uncontrolled rule, theoretically placing the king above the law and rejecting any role for the multitude, while recognizing the practical need for the monarch to take counsel with a wise few whom he himself chooses. One of the most influential texts of scholastic political thought, this book was immediately and widely disseminated in Latin and quite faithfully translated into French and Italian – eventually at least five times into the latter. At the same time Peter of Auvergne (1240s–1304), dubbed by one contemporary as Aquinas' most faithful disciple and evidently writing in and after the 1270s, moved in the opposite direction, believing that while a sovereign individual may be the best arrangement in absolute terms, for both theoretical and practical reasons he must share his power with the wise, the nobles, and the whole people; ideally the sovereign should be elected and corrected by the multitude at the suggestion of the wise, though a hereditary monarchy is to be preferred on pragmatic grounds (no doubt inasmuch as it is already well established). Even so, the king can still be corrected, and councils to advise and judge him are presumably to be constituted independently of him.[2]

Thus was the stage set for one of the two most revolutionary political theorists of the Middle Ages (both of whom were Italian). Unlike other medieval writers, Tolomeo Fiadoni dismisses kingship as a form of despotism unworthy of a virtuous people (since a king is by nature above the law) and sings the praises of republican rule; that his own background was in a republican city-state may be no coincidence. In his continuation of Aquinas' unfinished *De regno sive de regimine principum* (On Kingship, or On the Rule of Princes, *c.*1302), he envisages an ideal republic characterized by plurality of participation, mild rule regulated by popularly sanctioned statute, an alternation and election of salaried rulers, and judgement of past rulers. Such a regime – or a regime combining at least some of these qualities – is the best wherever it is possible, which in most places and for most peoples, as well as for large kingdoms, it is not; there Tolomeo favours regal rule. Where he champions republicanism is in city-states such as those of northern Italy and especially Rome, whose citizens are too virile and self-confident to put up with kings and despots: only the exceptional community blessed with a favourable climate, a fortunate configuration of stars, and great virtue can profit from political rule. Tolomeo's principal example of such a government is the ancient Roman Republic, which was ended by the usurping tyrant Julius Caesar (thought in Dante's and Tolomeo's time to have been the first Emperor): Rome's republican heroes were the servants rather than the masters of their state. The consuls depended for their power on the multitude, who could judge them, so that, fearing the citizens' wrath, most consuls ruled moderately, while the institution of the tribunes added a truly democratic element. For Tolomeo the Republic was most praiseworthy when the greatest number of citizens had a share in its government. This admiration for pre-imperial Rome at the expense of the Empire upended a tradition that was over a millennium old, and foreshadowed an attitude more commonly associated with Petrarch (1304–74).[3]

The relationship between the authority of temporal rulers and the authority of the pope had been a theme of political theology since at least the early thirteenth century, when Pope Innocent III (b. 1160/61; papacy 1198–1216) had articulated the doctrine of papal *plenitudo potestatis*, the doctrine, that is, that the exercise of papal authority in spiritual matters could and should extend to cases which required direct intervention in temporal jurisdiction. This became a burning issue from the mid 1290s onwards as a result of heightened tension between King Philip IV of France and Pope Boniface VIII (b. *c.*1235; papacy 1294–1303). Battle-lines – in the shape of councils – were drawn up on both sides. Boniface's council was held in November 1302 and formed the backdrop to the composition of three of the most significant political treatises written by medieval scholastic theologians. Their authors were Giles of Rome, James of Viterbo, and John of Paris (*c.*1255–1306), and they all remained influential throughout

# Historical and political writing

the next two centuries. Already, around 1278, Tolomeo Fiadoni had written for Pope Nicholas III (b. *c.*1225; papacy 1277–80) a *Determinatio compendiosa de iurisdictione imperii* (A Brief Definition of the Jurisdiction of the Empire), which had rigorously and efficiently outlined the whole theoretical basis and extent of papal supremacy over the empire, connecting the papacy to pre-imperial Rome and reinterpreting the Donation of Constantine as a restitution of what the emperors had thitherto held unlawfully. Now, in support of Boniface's position, Giles developed the hierocratic theory more extensively. In *De regimine principum*, directing his discussion towards the relationship between justice and mercy, he had carefully steered his reading of Book III of Aristotle's *Politics* away from any interpretation that might compromise the power of a king of France. With his *De ecclesiatica potestate* (On Church Power, 1301–2), however, the boot was on the other foot.[4]

The core of Giles' argument in his second treatise is that there can be no true lordship and no justice unless there is a corresponding relationship towards God and, by extension, towards the pope as God's representative on earth. As the soul's goal (eternal happiness in Heaven) is superior to the body's (material well-being on earth), the body's goal must be directed towards the attainment of the soul's goal; and since material well-being on earth must be ordered towards the attainment of eternal happiness in Heaven, the power responsible for the soul (the spiritual power) must supervise and direct the power responsible for the body (the temporal power).

*De regimine christiano* (On Christian Government, 1302) by James of Viterbo reaches Giles' conclusions by a different route. James' starting-point is the Aristotelian tenet that the function of life in a political society is not just to live but to live well, not merely to achieve material self-sufficiency, peace, and security but also to lead a life of moral virtue. Virtue is a good of the soul, which is by definition the responsibility of the spiritual power; and political authority, in order to be complete ('perfect'), needs to be guided by grace (the action of the spiritual power). Any definition of political authority that had virtue at its heart necessarily implied subordination to the Church, though unlike Giles, James concedes that temporal power on its own could be legitimate, albeit imperfect. Despite that concession, however, James' case for papal *plenitudo potestatis* is even stronger than that of Giles.[5]

The third important treatise connected with Boniface's council is *De potestate regia et papali* (On Royal and Papal Power) by John of Paris, who positioned himself as an opponent of hieratic papalism and effectively as

358                              John C. Barnes

a supporter of Philip IV. While he steered well clear of dismissing the concept of *plenitudo potestatis* out of hand, he did his best to mitigate its implications. He insisted on the possibility of exercising perfect moral virtue in the absence of grace, which meant that despite its moral purpose the temporal power was not necessarily subordinate to the supervision of the Church. Moreover (in answer to Giles), even if the Church was superior in intrinsic worth and dignity, this did not necessarily make it absolutely superior in command or authority; both the pope and the king received their power directly from God. John did not deny the capacity of the spiritual power to exercise a 'casual' or 'incidental' power of jurisdiction in the temporal sphere; but he did show that the temporal power had a reciprocal right of casual and incidental intervention in the spiritual sphere, in cases of 'urgent necessity' and 'evident benefit', that is, if such action would secure the common good of the whole community. This might be translated into supporting any attempt a council of the Church might make to remove a heretical, corrupt, or incompetent pope. Thus, while accepting a theoretical definition of papal plenitude of power, John made the pope accountable for its abuse.[6]

As it turned out, John's efforts were in effect brushed aside, at least in Rome, with the post-council promulgation of Boniface's bull *Unam sanctam ecclesiam* (One Holy Church), which revived Innocent III's maximalist stance regarding papal supremacy and is indebted to Giles' *De ecclesiastica potestate*. According to this document the temporal power is instituted by the spiritual power, which judges it if it errs. The pope, in unshared headship, rules the Christian community as the Vicar of Christ. He therefore has such power as the general good of souls requires, his judgement of what constitutes that good is absolute, and therefore obedience to what he decides is essential, as the good of the soul is necessary for salvation. This jurisdiction covers every aspect of morality, and thus kingship and the temporal order are not exempt from it.[7]

*Unam sanctam ecclesiam* represents the most obvious provocation to which Dante responded a decade later in *Monarchia* and certain passages of the *Commedia*, where he espouses the view that Church and empire should be constituted as equal and separate authorities. In the decade after *Monarchia* another refutation of the bull, in the context of renewed conflict between Emperor-elect Ludwig of Bavaria (1282–1347) and Pope John XXII (b. 1244; papacy 1316–34), was the purpose of Marsilio of Padua's *Defensor pacis* (The Defender of Peace, 1324). Marsilio – the second of 'the two most revolutionary political theorists of the Middle Ages' – goes further than John of Paris by dispensing with the life of virtue as part of

*Historical and political writing* 359

the goal of political authority and identifying that goal solely as the life of material self-sufficiency. He also emphasizes the spiritual nature of the Church, advocating the New Testament ideal of apostolic poverty, and essentially restricting the clergy's activities to preaching and administering the sacraments. Marsilio elaborately denounces the papacy's claim to *plenitudo potestatis* as the principal cause of civil strife, and insists that each state should control the Church within its borders.[8]

The hierocratic position, however, was not so easily overcome. One demonstration of this is provided by the Dominican philosopher Guido Vernani (d *c.*1348), who taught in the university at Bologna and from around 1320 was based in Rimini. Among other works he wrote two texts redeploying typical papal hierarchical theories, a commentary on *Unam sanctam ecclesiam* and a treatise *De potestate summi pontificis* (On the Power of the Supreme Pontiff, 1327). The following year he completed a caustic 'reprobation' of Dante's *Monarchia*, full of scorn for its author, whom he never names but calls a 'vessel of the Devil' open to Averroistic heresy and a fraudulent seducer of readers' minds. His rebuttals range from the cogent to the absurd.[9]

Meanwhile the controversy foreshadowing *Unam sanctam ecclesiam* had borne other fruits. One of these was the theorizing of Remigio de' Girolami, a Dominican trained in Paris who was lector in theology at Santa Maria Novella in Florence and whose sermons Dante may have heard. Remigio did not neglect to elaborate his own view on papal *plenitudo potestatis*: part of his *Contra falsos ecclesie professores* (Against Heretical Teachers of the Church), probably written in about 1297, argues for the theoretical supremacy of the spiritual power while attempting to restrict the practical exercise of that power over matters of temporal jurisdiction. But he subsequently wrote two explicitly political treatises, *De bono comuni* (On the Common Good, 1302–03) and *De bono pacis* (On the Good of Peace, 1304), which, although prompted by papal interventions in Florence's political affairs, have as much to say about citizenship as about papal prerogatives. He thus provided a detailed commentary both on the factionalism endemic to late thirteenth- and early fourteenth-century Florence and on the series of particular events that that factionalism had precipitated, most notably Boniface's invitation in 1301 to the King of France's brother, Charles de Valois (1270–1325), to restore Tuscany to 'peace and order'. Remigio consistently maintains that the goal of the temporal ruler is to provide peace and harmony, and develops the ideal of citizenship as love, insisting on the integration of the individual citizen into the *civitas*. Not to be a citizen, he affirms (with Aristotle) is not to be

# John C. Barnes

a man. *De bono comuni*, a direct response to the expulsion of the White Guelf faction from Florence, was written with the patriotic purpose of urging Florentines to demonstrate their love for the common good, while *De bono pacis*, written in connection with the peace initiative of Cardinal Niccolò of Prato (*c.*1250–1321), is, with its translation of the common good into the mutual benefit of peace, a precise demonstration of how this principle could be put into practice in a bitterly divided community.[10]

## Vernacular political writing

Although both Remigio's political treatises, written in Latin, represent a practical application of scholastic ideas to the politics of a city-state, their author was more a preacher than a speculative theologian, and as such may be perceived as tending towards a less academic kind of political writing that typically made use of a vernacular – generally an Italian one but in one early case French, though *Li Livres dou tresor* (The Book of the Treasure), written in the 1260s by the Florentine Brunetto Latini (*c.*1220–93), was translated into Tuscan within a few years of its completion. It is an encyclopaedia of primarily classical material for the use of those not trained in Latin. The second of its three books, much of which translates an anonymous Latin compendium of Aristotle's *Ethics*, makes occasional references to politics, including the statement that the lordship of the *comune*, where government is based on love and friendship, is better than the lordship of one man, whether king or *signore* (II, 44). But the last part of Book III (chapters 73–105) is devoted entirely to the *comune*'s governance (other types of regime are ignored), this being – as for Aristotle – 'the highest science and the most noble office there is on earth' (III, 73, 1). Basing these chapters on a lost source, Brunetto offers a veritable manual for the day-to-day running of any government conforming to Italian republican practice, from the selection of a new *podestà* (with a model letter of invitation in III, 77), through such matters as his entry into office, his dealings with councils and wise advisers, his administration of the law, and his conduct of war, to the handling of the end of his term of office.[11]

Brunetto's writing on politics remains an isolated phenomenon in that vernacular political literature generally commented on major contemporary events. This is exemplified by Guittone of Arezzo (*c.*1230–94), an early epistolographer of whose work thirty-four letters survive. As well as rhetorical exercises these are fundamentally essays, or sermons, with moral and religious objectives, although Letter XIV (*PrD*, pp. 60–7), expressing the writer's dismay at the outcome of the Battle of Montaperti (1260), is clearly political. The same battle inspired two of Guittone's finest political canzoni, 'Oh unfortunate, now is the season of great pain' (*PD* I, pp. 206–9), a more partisan and harshly sarcastic first response to the perceived calamity, and 'O sweet Aretine land' (*PD* I, pp. 222–6), directly addressed in similar terms to Guittone's home town (which had been one of Florence's Guelf allies). In the earlier 'Persons unpleasant and boorish' (*PD* I, pp. 200–5) Guittone explains that he has left Arezzo because of its bad (Ghibelline) government, its corruption and its lack of justice, whereas 'Great barons certainly and almost kings' (*PD* I, pp. 235–40), addressed to Count Ugolino (*c*.1220–89) and his grandson Nino Visconti (d. 1298) (of *Inf.* XXXII–XXXIII and *Purg.* VIII, respectively) on their joint appointment as *podestà* of Pisa in 1285, exhorts them to uphold the connections between love, justice, and good government. Dante must have been impressed by these texts and known the agony of their influence.

From Guittone to Petrarch, political verse never accounted for more than a tiny proportion of the overall production, and in no single poet's *canzoniere* is there more than a handful of such compositions. Many poets operated more or less in Guittone's shadow. Most immediately, one might single out Monte Andrea, a thirteenth-century Florentine Guelf who adopts a fiercely partisan stance in his political poetry. All of this takes the form of *tenzoni* (exchanges of poems between two or more participants), the best known of which (*RMA*, pp. 246–66) consists of seventeen sonnets and relates to the coming of Charles of Anjou (1226–85) to Italy in 1265.

A refreshingly different, 'comic' (non-polite) style was cultivated by the Florentine Ghibelline Rustico di Filippo (1230/40–1291/1300), who in one of his political sonnets, 'To you, who went away because of fear' (*Rcr*, pp. 115–6), written after the Battle of Benevento (1266), sarcastically points out to Guelfs of his city that, having timorously left in 1260, they can safely return home and start persecuting Ghibellines again now that the latter are defeated.

Three decades later factional strife flared up again, between the Black and White Guelfs. This, too, is reflected in contemporary poetry. Cino of Pistoia (*c*.1270–1336/37), a Black Guelf who was exiled from his native city in 1303–06, left a small number of poems (*RCP*, pp. 76, 91–2, 211) bewailing the civil strife, for him all the worse because the lady he loves is a member of a White family. Exile was a very common fate in that pugnacious milieu, and several poets express their consequent homesickness.

In 1310 Henry VII of Luxembourg (*c*.1275–1313) crossed the Alps to begin his Italian expedition, to a chorus of approval from poets as diverse

362                                    John C. Barnes

as Dante and the Anonimo Genovese (*fl.* 1270–1311; *PD* I, 713); the latter welcomed the emperor-elect as the champion of the Church. Both Dante's friend Cino and Petrarch's future Florentine friend Sennuccio del Bene (*c.*1275–1349) threw themselves more actively than Dante into Henry's campaign, and on his premature death in August 1313 they both composed canzoni lamenting his passing and that of the opportunity he represented (*PD* II, 678–9; *PmT*, pp. 49–52). Both poems combine threnody with eulogy though each also has a prominent personal element.

Before long another focus of poetic activity was emerging in the north-east, at the Veronese court of Cangrande della Scala (1291–1329), the exiled Dante's host between 1312 and 1318. The Jewish philosopher and 'comic' poet Immanuel Romano (*c.*1265–before 1331), who had also written two sonnets pledging support to whatever political faction or religion happened to hold sway (*Rcr*, p. 546–9), composed a 212-line poem (which he called *Bisbidis*) extolling Cangrande's splendid court and describing its lively life (*Rcr*, pp. 551–60). Of a contrasting persuasion was the lawyer Niccolò de' Rossi (*c.*1280/90–*c.*1350), fearful lest his native Treviso succumb to Cangrande's expansionist policies (as was indeed to happen in 1329) and – since neither Padua nor the avaricious King Robert (1278–1343) will help – exhorting the Trevigiani to seek the protection of the pope (*RT*, pp. 693–4).

Not all the political writing arose from specific circumstances. It could take the form of praise of one's own city-state inspired by patriotic pride, as with *De magnalibus Mediolani* (The Wonders of Milan), a detailed account of the topography, demography, and architecture of the city and its *contado* written in Latin prose around 1288 by Milan's most accomplished thirteenth-century writer Bonvesin da la Riva (*c.*1240/50–*c.*1314);[12] or as with certain vernacular poems by the prolific Anonimo Genovese, which (e.g. *PD* I, 751–61) celebrate Genoa in a lively manner, rich in detail of civic and maritime life. Bonvesin, as the first poet to write in Milanese, composed a 736-line *Disputatio mensium* (The Argument of the Months), in which the months from February to December rebel against the despotic rule of January (*OvBR*, pp. 3–27), the poet in the end evidently endorsing January's legitimacy.

All this prose and poetry, whether in Latin or a vernacular, was written for a relatively educated readership. There was also, however, a more demotic production line, of which occasional anonymous traces remain. A unique example is *La sconfitta di Monte Aperto* (The Defeat at Montaperti; extracts: *PrD*, pp. 937–46), a passionate, partisan account of the 1260 battle in Sienese prose by a Sienese participant in it, which

*Historical and political writing* 363

is preserved in various redactions. In verse there survive two incomplete Romagnole compositions of the 1280s (and possibly 1270s), which may have been intended for oral recitation; they reflect a period of extreme turbulence in Romagna and perhaps provided grist to that subject for Dante's mill (*PD* I, pp. 843–81).

### Latin and vernacular historical writing

By and large, the texts considered so far in this chapter have been overtly political. But a political objective can also be at least thinly camouflaged, as Nicolai Rubinstein was thinking when he entitled one of his articles 'The beginnings of political thought in Florence': the main works he there discusses are two chronicles, the anonymous *Chronica de origine civitatis* (Chronicle on the City's Origins) and Sanzanome's *Gesta Florentinorum* (The Deeds of the Florentines), both written in the first half of the thirteenth century, not long after Florence had shaken off the yoke of imperial control, and embodying a militant patriotic outlook, emphasizing the city's status as Rome's daughter and characterizing the recent past as a period of territorial expansion.[13] Florence was by no means the first to express such self-confidence in chronicle form, chronicles being a standard vehicle for implicit 'nationalist' propaganda. Cities which had a flourishing tradition of chronicle-writing well before 1250 include Genoa, Milan, Cremona, Faenza, Venice, Vicenza, Pisa, and Viterbo.

Despite their essentially local focus many chronicles also had a universalizing dimension. This came partly from the religious climate, historical events being viewed as favours or punishments meted out by God in recognition of a community's virtue or vice; and this sense of context often resulted in the historical record being made to begin with Adam and Eve. The universalizing dimension also came partly from an encyclopaedic impulse, exemplified in the work of Vincent of Beauvais (*c.*1190–1264), whose *Speculum maius* (The Great Mirror) was the largest, most comprehensive medieval work of reference, incorporating sources from classical to contemporary, and was greatly influential during the late Middle Ages and beyond. One of its three parts is a *Speculum historiale* (The Mirror of History), a compilation of narrative *exempla* furnished with suitable moralizing tailpieces, which at some time after Vincent's death an unknown writer partially translated into Tuscan as the *Fiori e vita di filosafi e d'altri savi e d'imperadori* (Exemplary Deeds and Lives of Philosophers and Other Wise Men and Emperors; extracts: *PrD*, pp. 521–32).

*Li Livres dou tresor* has a section devoted to history (I, 6–98), beginning with Adam, incorporating much matter from the Bible but finishing with the end of the Hohenstaufen line at the Battle of Tagliacozzo (1268), having devoted several pages to Emperor Frederick II (1194–1250). As we have seen, Brunetto's encyclopaedic work was translated into Tuscan at an early stage and quickly acquired a readership in Italy. Nor were it and Vincent's *Speculum* by any means the only historical works read in Italian translation. A text written in Romanesque in the 1260s is the *Storie de Troia e de Roma* (Stories of Troy and Rome; *PrD*, pp. 375–426), which was the first of three Italian translations of the Latin *Liber ystoriarum Romanorum* (The Book of Stories of the Romans). Also in Romanesque and evidently dating from the same decade is *Le miracole de Roma* (The Wonders of Rome; *PrD*, pp. 427–39), which reworks one of the earliest redactions of the evergreen *Mirabilia urbis Romae* (Wonders of the City of Rome), a historical and archaeological guide to the Eternal City's monuments. The late thirteenth-century *I fatti di Cesare* (The Deeds of Caesar; extracts: *PrD*, pp. 453–88) is a free translation of *Li Fet des Romains* (The Deeds of the Romans), an early Duecento French compilation of matter mainly from Lucan, Sallust, and Suetonius, outlining events and persons connected with the career of Julius Caesar – and of which at least seven versions of varying proportions survive.

Except perhaps in Rome, the political significance of these translations seems negligible, partly because they do not engage with contemporary events. The opposite extreme is exemplified by the *Cronaca* written in the early 1260s by Rolandino dei Baialardi (1200–76), one of the masterpieces of medieval historiography.[14] Rolandino was a notary, prominently employed in the public service of his native Padua, and a teacher of grammar and rhetoric in the city's *studium*. His *Cronaca*, in twelve substantial books, covers the period 1200–60 and focuses on Padua in the exclusive context of the March of Treviso (that is, Venetia without Venice or Rovigo), mainly in the years between 1237, when the city-state fell under the tyrannical rule of Ezzelino III da Romano (1194–1259; of *Inferno* XII and *Paradiso* IX), and 1256, when Ezzelino was driven out. Ezzelino's was the first instance of a new species of tyranny, and from his experience of it Rolandino learned the value of a unified ruling class; this he therefore insists on, developing the idea of a conflict between the *comune* (representing the whole citizenry) and factions, which seek domination in pursuit of their own ends. He was the first writer in medieval Italy to enunciate the principle that justice is bound up with the community's consent. The *Cronaca* has a compact, organic structure as a celebration of

# Historical and political writing

liberty regained in parallel with the tragedy of the tyrant. The viewpoint is restricted to Padua's indigenous ruling class, with the dynamics of the bigger picture accommodated only insofar as they impinge on the local situation.

In almost complete contrast to Rolandino's *Cronaca* is another *Cronica* in a Latin heavily inflected with the lexis and syntax of Italian, by the Franciscan Salimbene de Adam (1221–88/89).[15] The two works may be taken to illustrate the difference between chronicle, which is structured according to the haphazard occurrence of events, and history, which derives its form from an ideological purpose and narrates events selectively in the service of that purpose. Although Rolandino's text lies well inside the grey area between chronicle and history, all thirteenth- and possibly all fourteenth-century Italian historiography falls into the former category: full-blown 'history' in post-classical times is customarily reckoned to begin in the Quattrocento.

The proud northern maritime republics continued to produce vigorous chronicle traditions.[16] Among the inland cities of the north, Asti stood out with a fine local chronicle, full of civic pride, by the city archivist Ogerio Alfieri (*c*.1230–*c*.1294), continued – but overlapped with – by the *Memoriale* of Guglielmo Ventura (*c*.1250–*c*.1325), a prosperous spice merchant, whose narrative begins in 1260 and includes events unfolding elsewhere in Italy and Europe. Further south, Pietro Cantinelli (*c*.1235–after 1305), a Bolognese notary in exile at Faenza, wrote a *Chronicon* about events in Romagna between 1228 and 1306, especially Bologna until 1274 and Faenza thereafter. Meanwhile another notary, Riccobaldo of Ferrara (*c*.1245–1318), had begun a sequence of several chronicles in different styles, using different methods and sources, for different readerships, of which the first and best known is his *Pomarium Ravennatis ecclesiae* (The Orchard of the Church of Ravenna); his other chronicles include an influential *Historie* and a *Chronica parva ferrariensis* (A Short Chronicle of Ferrara). Dante may have known him in Verona and seems to be indebted to him at least for the story about Boniface VIII and Guido da Montefeltro (*Inf.* XXVII). One of those who drew on the *Historie* was the Dominican Francesco Pipino of Bologna (*c*.1255–*c*.1330), whose *Chronicon* covers the years 745–1322. Another was Benzo of Alessandria (*fl.* 1311–29), whose *Chronicon a mundi principio usque ad tempora Henrici* (Chronicle from the Beginning of the World to Henry's Times) reveals less interest in historical events than in legends, geography, philosophy, and the deeds and sayings of famous men.[17]

None of these texts is in any variety of Italian: in northern and central Italy Latin remained entrenched as the language of chronicling – except in Tuscany, where surviving texts include a 61-line Pisan verse chronicle written in 1279 and a late-Duecento or early-Trecento *cronichetta* of Lucca (there are two redactions, one ending at 1260, the other at 1304), both in Tuscan and both anonymous (extracts: *PrD*, pp. 901–6). The thirteenth-century vernacular scene is also haunted by a ghost chronicle of somewhat larger proportions, the lost *Gesta Florentinorum* (no relation to Sanzanome's work with the same title), which recounted Florence's story from 1080 to the 1270s and has been confidently reconstructed on the basis of its numerous extant epigones (extract: *PrD*, pp. 927–35). The most substantial early vernacular chronicle is also Florentine and is known as the chronicle of pseudo Brunetto Latini, because it was once erroneously attributed to Brunetto. It spans the years between 1002, when Henry II was elected emperor, and 1303, and is notable for an extraordinarily full account of the Buondelmonte murder in 1216 and its consequences.[18] It seems clear that Dante knew at least some of the Florentine chronicles mentioned here and earlier.

After 1300 Florence produced the two masterpieces of Italian medieval vernacular historiography. The first of these is the *Cronica* written in 1310–12 by Dino Compagni (*c.*1246–1324). A modestly prosperous silk merchant and politician, Compagni was the most senior of the six priors unseated when Florence was overrun by the troops of Charles de Valois in November 1301, a reversal that ushered in the permanent subjection of the White Guelfs (including both Compagni and Dante) to the Blacks.[19] Unlike Dante, Compagni had the good luck not to be exiled, but he did fall into obscurity. A decade after that turning-point in his and Florence's fortunes he was stimulated to write the *Cronica* by the onset of Henry VII's Italian campaign, which held out the prospect of Florence's being rid of the Black Guelfs and restored to the more democratic and law-based regime he had always favoured. On this optimistic note his book closes. Compagni is mindful of the example of the ideologically driven historians Sallust and Orosius, and it seems likely that he learned his craft partly from Rolandino's Paduan *Cronaca*. Despite its title his monographic text has the shape and structure of history rather than chronicle: spanning the years 1280–1312 and divided into three books following a short proem, it is effectively articulated as a tripartite drama. The prose, too, is of an outstandingly high quality. As a seasoned orator Compagni seems to draw more on patterns of speech than most contemporary writers, though he is also conversant with the prevailing norms of written discourse, of which he makes extensive and well-judged use. Thus his *Cronica* has real literary stature as the embodiment of a well-informed citizen's passionate but

# Historical and political writing

coherent outlook on strictly local affairs. Cruelly, though – presumably because Henry's mission collapsed – it evidently remained unread until the late Trecento.

The second masterpiece, the *Nuova cronica* (New Chronicle) by Giovanni Villani (*c.*1276–1348), is quite different.[20] Consisting of thirteen books that become progressively longer, rather than a history, it is unmistakably a chronicle, the most ambitious and comprehensive of those produced in Tuscany. While the spotlight falls principally on Florence, this is the story of the known world from the Tower of Babel onwards (1280 is not reached until chapter 56 of Book VIII); material is included concerning such remote corners of the known world as Scotland, Armenia, and Tunisia, because the writer is aware that, potentially, at least, it could be relevant to Florence. Villani, a moderate Black Guelf, belonged to a successful merchant family, and with Compagni is one of a number of Tuscan merchant historiographers: merchants, like notaries, were constantly writing and lived their lives surrounded by written texts. Villani had access to statistical information and official documents that provided valuable content for his chronicle. The *Nuova cronica*, however, has many other kinds of sources, including the wide experience of its author, who also displays a respectable classical education (unusual for a merchant) and a considerable knowledge of the Bible. Although he is archaic in his superstition and his providential view of history (calamities are God's punishments for wrongdoing), he is progressive in a notable concern with causes and effects and in his attention to practical detail – financial, for example. Villani probably began his chronicle around 1322; he revised it, apparently after 1332, and continued to extend it until his death.

Meanwhile the north-east was experiencing the wind – or at least a breeze – of change commonly labelled pre-humanism. Prominent here was the Paduan Albertino Mussato (1261–1329), another notary, as well as a politician and diplomat, and an acquaintance both of Marsilio (the author of *Defensor pacis*) and of Dante's correspondent Giovanni del Virgilio (late thirteenth century–*c.*1327; he appears to be alluded to in Giovanni's and Dante's *Egloge*, II, 45–7 and III, 88–9). Mussato's *Historia augusta* (A Venerable History) was published in 1315. It is an account of Henry VII's Italian expedition, with which the writer had been associated. Mussato successfully combines an acute grasp of detail with a highly original recreation of classical style and syntax, where the conventions of the *artes dictaminis* are boldly jettisoned. Mussato followed the same strategies in a sequel, *De gestis Italicorum post mortem Henrici VII* (On the Deeds of the Italians after the Death of Henry VII), which, written at the end of

# 368 John C. Barnes

his life and interrupted at 1321, presumably by his death, is designed to forge a parallel between the decline of the Roman republic and the extinction of the Paduan *comune* in 1328. In both works Mussato, truthful, well informed and generally impartial, brings the events to life with a civic passion that seeks to harmonize city-state freedom with the universalist ideals of Church and empire. His historical works were a major source of inspiration and material for the Vicentine notary and scholar Ferreto de' Ferreti (1294/97–1337), who around 1330 completed a huge account of Italian affairs (particularly those of Venetia) between 1250 and 1318.[21]

This, however, was where the pre-humanist flame of Padua and Vicenza flickered out. Padua had been pre-humanism's nerve centre and Mussato its more recent paragon: after Mussato's exile in 1325, his death in 1329, and the end of Paduan liberty in 1328, the torch would be relit elsewhere.

## Notes

1 I thank Andrew Johnstone and Matthew Kempshall for helpful comments on a preliminary draft of this chapter and Antonio Corsaro for checking a detail in Florence's National Library. Hereafter I use the following abbreviations: ISI: Istituto Storico Italiano; *OvBR: Le opere volgari di Bonvesin da la Riva, volume primo: testi*, ed. G. Contini (Rome: Società Filologica Romana, 1941); *PD* I, *PD* II: *Poeti del Duecento*, ed. G. Contini, 2 vols. (Milan and Naples: Ricciardi, 1960); *PmT: Poeti minori del Trecento*, ed. N. Sapegno (Milan and Naples: Ricciardi, 1952); *PrD: La prosa del Duecento*, ed. C. Segre and M. Marti (Milan and Naples: Ricciardi, 1959); *RIS: Rerum Italicarum Scriptores ab Anno Aerae Christianae Quingentesimo ad Millesimum Quingentesimum*, ed. L. A. Muratori *et al.*, 25 vols. in 28 (Milan: Società Palatina, 1723–51); revised, corrected and extended as *RIS2: Rerum Italicarum Scriptores: Raccolta degli storici italiani dal cinquecento al millecinquecento*, ed. G. Carducci *et al.* (Città di Castello: Lapi; Bologna: Zanichelli; Rome: Istituto Storico per il Medioevo, 1900–); *RMA*: Monte Andrea, *Le rime*, ed. F. F. Minetti (Florence: Accademia della Crusca, 1979); *Rcr: Rimatori comico-realistici del Due e Trecento*, ed. M. Vitale (Turin: UTET, 1956); *RCP: Le rime di Cino da Pistoia*, ed. G. Zaccagnini (Geneva: Olschki, 1925); *RT: Rimatori del Trecento*, ed. G. Corsi (Turin: UTET, 1969).

2 Giles of Rome, *De regimine principum libri III* (Rome: Blado, 1556; reprinted Frankfurt: Minerva, 1968); *Del reggimento de' principi di Egidio Romano: volgaizzamento trascritto nel MCCLXXXVIII*, ed. F. Corazzini (Florence: Le Monnier, 1858); Petrus de Alvernia, *In politicorum continuatio* in *S. Thomae Aquinatis opera omnia*, ed. R. Busa, 7 vols. (Stuttgart and Bad Cannstatt: Frommann and Holzboog, 1980), vol. VII, pp. 412–80.

3 Tolomeo Fiadoni, *De regimine principum ad regem Cypri* in Thomas Aquinas, *Opuscula omnia necnon opera minora, tomus primus: Opuscula philosophica*, ed. R. P. J. Perrier (Paris: Lethielleux, 1949), pp. 221–445.

# Historical and political writing 369

4 *Determinatio compendiosa de iurisdictione imperii auctore anonymo ut videtur Tholomeo Lucensi,* ed. M. Krammer (Hannover and Leipzig: Hahn, 1909), pp. 1–65; Giles of Rome, *De ecclesiastica potestate,* ed. R. Scholz (Stuttgart: Scientia Aalen, 1961).

5 James of Viterbo, *De regimine christiano,* ed. H.-X. Arquillière as his *Le Plus Ancien Traité de l'église: Jacques de Viterbe, 'De regimine christiano'* (Paris: Beauchesne, 1926).

6 John of Paris, *De potestate regia et papali,* ed. J. Leclercq, in his *Jean de Paris et l'ecclésiologie du XIIIe siècle* (Paris: Vrin, 1942), pp. 173–260.

7 For *Unam sanctam ecclesiam* see *Corpus iuris canonici,* ed. E. A. Friedberg, 2 vols. (Leipzig: Tauchnitz, 1879–81), vol. II, cols. 1245–6.

8 *The 'Defensor Pacis' of Marsilius of Padua,* ed. C. W. Prévité-Orton (Cambridge University Press, 1928).

9 Guido Vernani, *Expositio super decretali 'Unam Sanctam',* ed. M. Grabmann in his *Studien über den Einfluss der aristotelischen Philosophie auf die mittelalterlichen Theorien über das Verhältnis von Kirche und Staat* (Munich: Bayerische Akademie der Wissenschaften, 1934), pp. 144–57; *Tractatus de potestate summi pontificis,* ed. F. Cheneval in his *Die Rezeption der 'Monarchia' Dantes bis zur Editio princeps im Jahre 1559: Metamorphosen eines philosophischen Werks* (Munich: Fink, 1995), pp. 423–45; *De reprobatione Monarchie,* ed. N. Matteini in his *Il più antico oppositore politico di Dante: Guido Vernani da Rimini: testo critico del 'De reprobatione Monarchie'* (Padua: CEDAM, 1958), pp. 91–118.

10 Remigio de' Girolami, *Contra falsos ecclesie professores,* ed. F. Tamburini (Rome: Pontificia Università Lateranense, 1981); *De bono comuni* and *De bono pacis,* ed. E. Panella in his *Dal bene comune al bene del comune: i trattati politici di Remigio dei Girolami († 1319) nella Firenze dei bianchi-neri* (Florence: Nerbini, 2014), pp. 146–221 and 222–47.

11 Brunetto Latini, *Li Livres dou tresor,* ed. F. J. Carmody (Berkeley and Los Angeles: University of California Press, 1948); *Il 'Tresor' di Brunetto Latini* [extract] in *Volgarizzamenti del Due e Trecento,* ed. C. Segre (Turin: UTET, 1953), pp. 59–84.

12 Bonvesin da la Riva, *Le meraviglie di Milano (De magnalibus Mediolani),* ed. and trans. P. Chiesa (Milan: Fondazione Valla/Mondadori, 2009).

13 N. Rubinstein, 'The beginnings of political thought in Florence: a study in medieval historiography', *Journal of the Warburg and Courtauld Institutes,* 5 (1942), 198–227.

14 Rolandino, *Vita e morte di Ezzelino da Romano (Cronaca),* ed. and trans. F. Fiorese (Milan: Fondazione Valla/Mondadori, 2004).

15 Salimbene de Adam, *Cronica,* ed. G. Scalia, 2 vols. (Turnhout: Brepols, 1998–89).

16 Oberti Stanconi, *Iacobi Aurie Annales, ann. MCCLXX–MCCLXXIX* in *Annali genovesi di Caffaro e de' suoi continuatori,* ed. L. T. Belgrano and C. Imperiale di Sant' Angelo, 5 vols. (Rome: ISI, 1890–1929), vol. IV, pp. 127–86; *Iacopo da Varagine e la sua Cronaca di Genova dalle origini al MCCXCVII,* ed. G. Monleone, 3 vols. (Rome: Istituto Italiano per il Medio Evo, 1941); *Origo*

370 John C. Barnes

*civitatum Italie seu Venetiarum (Chronicon Altinate et Chronicon Gradense)*, ed. R. Cessi (Rome: ISI, 1933); Paolino Minorita (Venetian), several unpublished chronicles; Martin da Canal, *Les Estoires de Venise*, ed. A. Limentani (Florence: Olschki, 1972).

17 *Chronica Astensia ab anno MLXX usque ad annum circiter MCCCXXV auctoribus Ogerio Alferio et Guilielmo Ventura* in *RIS*, vol. XI, cols. 133–268; *Petri Cantinelli Chronicon*, ed. F. Torraca in *RIS2*, vol. XXVIII, 2; *Ricobaldi Ferrariensis Pomarium Ravennatis ecclesiae* in *RIS*, vol. IX, cols. 97–192; *Historie*, unpublished; *Chronica parva Ferrariensis*, ed. G. Zanella (Ferrara: Deputazione Provinciale Ferrarese di Storia Patria, 1983); *Chronicon Fratris Francisci Pipini Bononiensis* in *RIS*, vol. IX, cols. 580–752; Benzo of Alessandria, *Chronicon* (1313–20), unpublished except for Book XXIV, ed. M. Petoletti in his *Il 'Chronicon' di Benzo d'Alessandria e i classici latini all'inizio del XIV secolo: edizione critica del libro XXIV, 'De moribus et vita philosophorum'* (Milan: Vita e Pensiero, 2000).

18 *Cronichetta pisana scritta in volgare nel MCCLXXIX*, ed. E. Piccolomini (Pisa: Nistri, 1877); *Die Annalen des Tholomeus von Lucca in doppelter Fassung*, ed. B. Schmeidler (Berlin: Weidmann, 1930); *Cronica fiorentina compilata nel secolo XIII* [erroneously attributed to Brunetto Latini] in *Testi fiorentini del Dugento e dei primi del Trecento*, ed. A. Schiaffini (Florence: Sansoni, 1926), pp. 82–150.

19 Dino Compagni, *Cronica*, ed. D. Cappi (Rome: Istituto Storico per il Medioevo, 2000).

20 Giovanni Villani, *Nuova cronica*, ed. G. Porta, 3 vols. (Parma: Fondazione Bembo/Guanda, 1990–91).

21 *Albertini Mussati de gestis Heinrici VII Caesaris Historia augusta* and *Albertini Mussati de gestis Italicorum post mortem Henrici VII Caesaris Historia* in *RIS*, vol. X, cols. 1–568 and 570–768; Ferreto de' Ferreti, *Historia rerum in Italia gestarum ab anno MCCL ad annum usque MCCCXVIII*, vols. I–II of *Le opere di Ferreto de' Ferreti*, ed. C. Cipolla, 3 vols. (Rome: ISI, 1908–20).

CHAPTER 22

# Vernacular literatures

## Paolo Cherchi

Dante wrote the *Vita nova* around 1292–95, and included in it poems written previously at dates difficult to establish. Around the same time Guiraut Riquier (b. *c.*1230), the last of the troubadours, died (1292); Guittone d'Arezzo (b. *c.*1235) died soon after (1294), as did Brunetto Latini (1293; b. *c.*1220). The composition of the *Vita nova* fell between the death of Guido Guinizzelli (1276; b. *c.*1230) and that of Guido Cavalcanti (1300; b. 1250/59). Also during those two decades the *Libro di cento novelle* (Book of One Hundred Tales), better known as *Il novellino*, the first major work in prose written in an Italian vernacular, was composed. Dante's entry into the literary scene took place at a time of generational and cultural change of which the poet was a pivotal cause and protagonist.

By the time the *Vita nova* began to circulate towards the end of the Duecento, the literary panorama of the Italian peninsula had altered into being indisputably 'Italian' in the linguistic sense, abandoning Occitan and Old French as literary languages. The change came about slowly but decisively; nor did it imply the rejection of what had been written before, but rather an adaptation and reassessment of this, otherwise it would be difficult to understand the sudden blossoming of Italian literature, its reaching a peak of excellence in a very short period.

Besides Occitan and Old French, the other language that was primarily written on the Italian peninsula was Latin. The spoken languages were regional forms of the Italian family, but the written documentation in local vernaculars is quite limited, and in any case it is not deemed worthy of being considered 'literature' (see Chapter 15).

The birth of Italian literature is strikingly late when compared to its Occitan and Old French counterparts: the earliest troubadours were active around 1100 and the *Song of Roland* was composed about the same time. This chronological discrepancy has inevitably caused literary historians to wonder why Italian literature began so much later than that of other Romance cultures. One of the problems facing Italians was that whatever

371

language of their own native land they used, this had not reached the formal standardization attained by the languages of the south and north of France. Italians were therefore the first in Europe to face a 'question of the language', as is made evident by Dante's *De vulgari eloquentia*: they had to overcome regional linguistic fragmentation and decide to adopt a language that, for its aesthetic qualities and for its historical and cultural prestige, could serve as 'standard Italian', namely as the linguistic standard for all inhabitants of the peninsula regardless of the area from whence they came.

The contacts between Italy and the Occitan troubadours were numerous and occurred relatively early. The presence of troubadours was most visible in the courts of northern Italy, which were closer to southern France. The most frequented were the court of Monferrato in Piedmont (which geographically was very close to Savoy, where many troubadours resided), the court of the Malaspina in Lunigiana, that of the Este in Ferrara, and above all that of Treviso, which attracted many troubadours. However, troubadours crossed the Apennines as well, reaching Florence and southern Italy. Their presence is documented as early as the first decade of the thirteenth century. They praised Italian ladies and Italian rulers, and sang of Italian events, mostly of a political nature. They also brought into the peninsula the courtly culture of *fin'amors* (refined love), in a version that was fairly conventionalized, typical of troubadours who flourished after the greatest and the most creative troubadours of the so-called generation of 1180. The style and the language these troubadours imported were those of the *trobar leu* or plain style, which was better suited for non-native speakers. Equally numerous were the poets of Italian origin who wrote lyrics in Occitan. The first of the Italian troubadours was Peire de la Cavarana (middle to late twelfth century) about whom practically nothing is known. Only one *sirventes* of his remains, in which he exhorts the Lombards to oppose the domination of the Emperor. Since this emperor is supposedly Henry VI (b. 1165; reign 1191–97), the poem has been dated to 1194 and inaugurates the tradition of political *sirventes* that became so successful in Italy, no doubt on account of its political fractiousness.

Another early troubadour is Rambertino Buvalelli (*c.*1170–1221) from Bologna who held important political posts and duties, from *podestà* to ambassador. He flourished in the period 1201–20. Seven of his *cansos* (songs), all 'love poems', are extant. The Italian troubadour with the largest corpus of poems that have survived is Lanfranc Cigala (d. before 1274) from Genoa, whose activity as poet spans the years 1235–57. He must have been an influential person, since he is remembered as a judge in his

# Vernacular literatures 373

native city. He embodies a typical phenomenon of Italian culture, where men of letters came most often from the judicial ranks, or even more frequently from the notarial class. Thirty-two poems of his are extant, and they are a mixed body of love and religious poems, *sirventes*, some poetic debates (four with another Genoese troubadour, Simon Doria (*fl.* 1250–93), and one with Giacomo Grillo (*fl.* 144–62), yet another Genoese poet (it is interesting to find three poets, all from Genoa, debating in Occitan!) and an interesting *planh* (lament) for a lady. Cigala is second only to Sordello (1200/10–69?) among the Italian troubadours for the quality of his poetry. Born to a noble family in Goito, Lombardy, around 1200, Sordello lived in several Italian courts, as well as in Provence and in Spain. He spent the last part of his life at the Anjou court in Naples, and died in Abruzzo in a castle he owned. Today his name is familiar to all Dante's readers for his role in *Purgatorio* VI–VIII.

Among other Italian troubadours, one ought to mention the Genoese Bonifacio Calvo, active between 1253–66; the Venetian Bartolomeo Zorzi, active between 1266–73; and others of lesser importance, such as Luchetto Gattilusio (*fl.* 1248–1307) and the Genoese Percivalle Doria (d. 1264). What matters rather more than this minor production is the fact that the *vidas* or biographical sketches of troubadours were compiled in Italy, as well as some of the most important collections of their poems. In addition, several of the earliest grammars of Occitan were also composed in Italy, such as that by Terramagnino of Pisa, the *Doctrina d'acort* (Doctrine of Concordance; *c.*1280); and even the earliest, the *Donatz proensal* (Provençal Donatus; *c.*1250), was written by Uc Faidit while residing in Italy. Evidently Italians were passionate and professional students of the poetry and language of the troubadours, an interest that opened the way for vernacular poetry in Italian. Thus the earliest production of Italian poetry developed side by side with Occitan for almost a century.

Occitan was not the only language competing for an Italian audience. The *langue d'oil*, used in Northern France, was the language of prose romances or narratives, of epic poetry, and of every kind of prose writing, all of which had achieved a high degree of popularity. Several Italian authors wrote in French. The best known was Brunetto Latini, who justified his linguistic choice for his *Livres dou Tresor* (Books of Treasure) on two grounds: one because he composed his encyclopaedic compendium during his exile in France (1260–66); the other because French was the most delightful and most widely understood language in the world. Other works by Brunetto, the *Tesoretto* (Little Treasure), the *Favolello*, and the translation of Cicero's *De inventione*, the *Rettorica*, are in Italian. Other

374 Paolo Cherchi

authors who wrote in French are Aldobrandino da Siena (d. 1296?), author of *Le régime du corps* (The Bodily Regimen, 1257, a treatise on diet and hygiene); Filippo da Novara (*c.*1200–*c.*1270) in *Des quatre tenz d'aage d'ome* (The Four Ages of Man, 1265) and other works; the Venetian Martin da Canal (d. after 1275) in his *Estoires de Vénise* (Histories of Venice, 1267–75); Rustichello da Pisa (d. after 1298), author of the *Meliadus* (1272–98), which is based on the romances *Guiron le Courtois* (Guiron the Courtly) and *Tristan en prose* (Tristan in Prose), and who used French to acknowledge its role in creating the Arthurian tradition. Rustichello da Pisa was prisoner of the Genoese together with Marco Polo (1254–1324), who dictated to him the *Divisament dou monde* (The Description of the World, 1298), better known as *Milione* in its Italian versions. Marco Polo's text is in French mixed with some elements of Venetian language. However, this occurs in only some manuscripts; if this mixture were in the original, the *Milione* would belong to Franco-Venetian literature, another manifestation of the plurilingual situation found in Italy in the Duecento. It is worth noting that, when the *Milione* and the *Meliadus* appeared, Dante had already published the *Vita nova*.

Far more influential and long-lasting was the impact of epic writing on Italian culture. This tradition reached an audience larger than that reached by any other type of literature. Moreover its influence remained constant until the end of the sixteenth century. Initially it was diffused by minstrels, spreading out from the Veneto (especially the Marca Trevigiana) and reaching as far as the entire Po valley, to Ferrara in the south-east and Monferrato in the north-west. They disseminated the stories of Charlemagne and his knights, of the traitor Ganelon and his family, of Roland's infancy and youth, and of numerous other chivalric deeds. This imported tradition very soon stimulated a local production, and by the beginning of the Trecento and possibly earlier, Italian authors began to compose texts that mixed traditions and narrative 'cycles', and used a language that was basically French though highly contaminated by regional elements of the Veneto area, hence giving origin to the literature now termed Franco-Venetian. Of the many works belonging to this tradition, the most significant are the *Chanson d'Aspremont*, which is a Trecento adaptation of a French original of the thirteenth century; the *Berta da li pè grandi* (Big-footed Berta) from an original *Bert au gran pied*; the *Beuve d'Antone*, of the first half of the Duecento, had two Franco-Venetian versions in octaves and several in prose, one of which was included in book IV of the *Reali di Francia* (Royal Houses of France) by Andrea da Barberino (*c.*1370–1431/33); and the *Huon d'Auvergne*, which was perhaps originally in Italian – it belongs to the middle years of the Trecento and contains an episode that seems to imitate Dante's *Inferno*.

Franco-Venetian was a *koiné* used not only for epic literature, but also for didactic works, such as the *Enanchet* (1287), which contains moral teachings and precepts on love based on the twelfth-century *De amore* by Andreas Capellanus.

If the 'Carolingian' literature found its best medium of diffusion through Franco-Venetian, the 'Arthurian' or Breton literature found its most successful form in Tuscan prose. Many texts have survived confirming the popularity of this tradition in the early Duecento, including manuscripts in French copied in Italy, paintings of the heroes, and their names widely used to designate persons and places. Arthurian literature was adapted and translated into various Italian vernaculars. The best example of this rich tradition is the *Tristano Riccardiano* (its major manuscript is found in the Riccardiana Library in Florence, hence its name), which translates, at the beginning of the Trecento, the French *Tristan en prose* written at the beginning of the previous century. The Italian syntax imitates the linear word order of the French, a fact that is typical of Italian prose until Boccaccio, who imitated Latin syntax. There are some noteworthy exceptions to this trend: one is Dante's *Vita nova*, with its musical or poetic effects in prose, and the other is the *Convivio*, with its doctrinal prose that in part follows the logical patterns of the demonstrations employed by scholastic authors.

Works of history and doctrine were also translated from French sources (see Chapter 21). Among the earliest is *I fatti di Cesare* (The Deeds of Caesar), which is a partial translation and adaptation of the *Li fet des Romains* (The Deeds of the Romans), a work that draws on many Latin historians and poets and was widely used by Romance authors. The Italian translation survives in numerous versions, some more complete than others, and the oldest and most complete of these can be dated to the middle of the thirteenth century. The *Istorietta troiana*, which translates a prose version of the *Roman de Troie* by Benoît de Sainte Maure, belongs to the end of the same century. Many doctrinal works were also translated from French, most notably, Brunetto Latini's *Tresor*, probably translated by Bono Giamboni (*c*.1240–92?), and Marco Polo's *Milione*, translated by an unknown writer before 1309. Other works were of a moral and didactic character – such as the *Livre dou gouvernement des rois*, which was a translation of Giles of Rome's (Egidio Colonna, *c*.1245–1316) *De regimine principum* (On the Rule of Princes), and was then rendered into Tuscan (more precisely into Sienese) from the French version in 1288. Yet other

376                              Paolo Cherchi

works were of an exemplary and narrative nature, as is the case with the *Libro dei sette sav* (Book of Seven Sages), which reached the West via Arab Spain, and was translated into Latin (*Dolopatos*) and into French, and subsequently from French into Tuscan, whereas the Latin version was translated into Venetian. These translations and adaptations are known as *volgarizzamenti*, namely 'vernacularizations'.

Italian prose writing gained further confidence and dignity as a result of many translations from Latin. Indeed, over time, Latin *volgarizzamenti* became predominant and had a major impact on literary prose style, especially as regards syntax. History was given pride of place, but the historians translated were not necessarily those of ancient Roman. One of the earliest translations into a Roman vernacular was the *Storie de Troia e de Roma* (*c.*1258) based on *Multe ystorie et troiane et romane* composed in the mid-twelfth century. A similar text was *Le miracole de Roma* (The Wonders of Rome), a thirteenth-century translation into Roman vernacular of a medieval *Mirabilia urbis Romae*. Ethics was another subject that attracted translators: for example, the *De arte loquendi et tacendi* (On the Art of Speaking and Being Silent, 1245) by Albertano da Brescia (*c.*1195– *c.*1251) was translated by an anonymous Florentine writer in the fourteenth century. Albertano's *De amore et dilectione Dei* (On God's Love) was translated in 1268 by Andrea da Grosseto, while his *Liber de consolatione et consilii* (Book on Consolation and Advice, 1246) was translated in 1275 by Soffredi del Grazia di Pistoia (*c.*1240–97). Bono Giamboni translated, or rather adapted, the *De contemptu mundi* (On the Contempt of the World) by Lotharius, later Pope Innocent III (b. 1160/61; papacy 1198–1216), as *Della miseria dell'uomo* (Man's Misery). There is little point in listing other *volgarizzamenti* as they are too numerous, and the examples given ought to suffice to make clear that the Italian reading public was educated by these, while Italian authors were stimulated and guided by them to create their own original works.

Religion was an area where Italian culture made a substantial, original, and influential contribution to the medieval context. It is enough to think of Popes of the stature of Innocent III and Boniface VIII (b. *c.*1235; papacy 1294–1303), who straddle the thirteenth century, which also saw figures of the stature of St Francis (1181/82–1226), Thomas Aquinas (1225–74), Bonaventure (1221–74), a spiritual leader of the importance of Joachim of Fiore (1130/35–1202), and the hagiographer Jacobus of Voragine (*c.*1230–98), author of the *Golden Legend* (*c.*1260). However, the language predominantly employed by these authors was Latin and not Italian. Nonetheless, works in Italian have especially strong

*Vernacular literatures*  377

ties with spiritual and political culture, which is why Francis' *Canticle of the Creatures* is considered as the first manifestation of Italian literature. Italy, like France and other parts of Europe, was characterized by that peculiar mix of rationalism and spirituality, respectively associated with scholasticism and apocalyptic and pauperistic movements nourished by an intense longing for a renewal of all areas of life, from the organization of academic disciplines and the monastic orders to the political system (see Chapter 7). The thirteenth century was fundamentally marked by the revival of interest in Aristotle, while also demonstrating a continued commitment to crusading; it was a century that was aware of standing at the threshold of historical change. Although Italy was part of the Holy Roman Empire, it had progressively gained a considerable degree of independence from the imperial power, resulting in a new form of political organization represented by the *comune* or 'city state'. The ensuing fragmentation added a political and local dimension to religious life, as demonstrated by the phenomenon of the *laudi*, songs of praise, which were present in some regions (mostly in Tuscany and in Umbria) but not in others, where the prevailing civic sentiment inspired different types of literary texts (for example, in Milan, Bonvesin de la Riva's (*c.*1240–*c.*1315) writings discussed below). There is no denying, however, that Christianity inspired the birth of a literature that can be considered Italian in all respects (see Chapter 19).

Francis' *Canticle* is a brief hymn in which the primary elements of life (light, water, air, etc.) are exhorted to praise God's majesty. The poem – meant to be sung like a psalm – is remarkably simple; nonetheless, it expresses the saint's notion of God's circularity: God praises Himself through His creatures who, by praising Him, find their sense of being as part of the universe. This circularity is all the more significant, since it challenges the dualistic viewpoint of several powerful heresies of the time, especially Catharism (see Chapter 7).

Popular devotion found its most successful expression in the *lauda*. It was normally structured in the form of the *ballata*, having a refrain typical of choral and dance poems, and was sung in processions and at other religious ceremonies. These poems are mostly anonymous, as they were written by poets appointed as official composers of a congregation or a religious order. We know the names of only a few such composers, one of them being a ser Garzo, who for a time was thought to be Petrarch's (1304–74) grandfather. Several collections of *laudi* survive; and some lyric poets adopted the genre, among these, Guittone d'Arezzo who composed four *laudi*. The most original composer of *laudi* was Jacopone (1236–1306),

378                                    Paolo Cherchi

who only used the *lauda* form, although his poems were not meant to be sung.

Jacopone was from Todi in Umbria, the region of St Francis, and ranks as one of the most powerful and disconcerting poetic voices of the century. He was a notary who became a minorite, a Franciscan monk, in 1270, and belonged to the spiritual current of the Franciscans. In 1297 he signed a petition to remove Boniface VIII from the papacy, and as a result he was imprisoned until 1303, dying three years later. It is difficult to classify Jacopone's poetry. On the one hand, he ostensibly ignores rhetorical embellishment and employs a harsh language with realistic effects that is unrivalled in his presentation of vices, the lewdness of the flesh, and the horrors of imprisonment and wealth. On the other hand, however, he was a master rhetorician who used the 'low' style to achieve powerful effects of disgust and repulsion. Not inappropriately one might think of him as a radical ascetic, who detested any sort of sensual pleasure and dreamt of the dissolution of anything human. Yet, if many of his *laudi* preach total annihilation, many others exalt a different kind of dissolution – one that is a type of contemplative annihilation in the love of God. Christ's death on the cross is the model of the perfection of this death, a total abnegation of the human body. It is a form of violent death, but at the same time it is a form of violent love, almost ineffable in its intensity. The love sung in Francis' *Canticle* is of equal intensity to that expressed by Jacopone, but with one fundamental difference: Francis' love is joyous, while Jacopone's is tragic and pessimistic. Such tensions grant great intensity and a powerful expressionistic force to Jacopone's poetry – one indeed that comes close to rivalling Dante's.

Religious literature found its expression in various other genres, including sermons, lives of saints, visions, and allegorical conflicts between vices and virtues, all of which contributed to creating confidence in the artistic potential of the vernacular. One writer in particular, Bonvesin de la Riva is worthy of mention. He is often remembered as a precursor of Dante, since his *Libro delle tre scritture* (Book of the Three Scriptures) depicts the otherworld, as does the *Commedia*. The similarities between the two works, however, are limited to only this one structural element. Nonetheless, Bonvesin's poem shows clear signs of rhetorical control and a clear mastery over apocalyptic and eschatological themes.

A genre in which Italian achieved a noteworthy degree of originality was that of *parlamenti* and *epistole*, namely diplomatic speeches and letters. Italy in fact pioneered the rhetorical teaching of these subjects (see Chapter 17). The *Gemma purpurea* (Purple Bud, 1239–42) by Guido Faba (*c*.1190–*c*.1243) from Bologna inserts into a Latin frame examples of letter-writing in the vernacular; while in the *Parlamenta et epistole* (1243) Guido presents different themes followed by three letters in Latin, each one treating the same subject but with different degrees of formal elaboration. Guido Faba demonstrated how rhetorical precepts could be applied to vernacular prose. Indeed, if we examine the epistles written by Guittone d'Arezzo and his followers, we note the birth of a new kind of stylistically refined prose that employed every type of rhetorical device, from elaborate syntactic construction to the *cursus* or rhythmic prose. It is important to remember that Italy developed the *ars dictandi* (art of letter- and prose-writing) in opposition to the *ars poetriae* (art of poetry) that flourished in France. The main reason for this is that political and economic life in the *comuni* encouraged a class of notaries and lawyers to flourish, while also stressing the importance of oratorical, diplomatic, and forensic skills. This is the principal reason why Brunetto Latini composed the *volgarizzamenti* of Cicero's *De inventione* and of the *Rhetorica ad Herennium*, which at the time was attributed to the great Roman orator.

Prose writing acquired such dignity that it intruded into areas hitherto reserved to Latin and French, namely ethics and science. In the field of ethics, special mention ought to be made of Bono Giamboni, who, as well as *volgarizzamenti*, composed *Il libro de' vizî e delle virtudi* (The Book of Vices and Virtues, after 1272), an original synthesis of moral teaching and allegorical voyage narrative, which furthermore used a highly homogeneous and polished language that was quite novel. In the scientific field, Ristoro d'Arezzo made an important contribution with his *La composizione del mondo* (The Composition of the World, c.1282). Its prose is somewhat monotonous and inelegant, but it is nonetheless a remarkable attempt to use the vernacular to compile an encyclopedia of cosmological and anthropological matter.

The *Novellino* appeared at about the same time. Written during the last twenty years of the Duecento, it demonstrates that Italian prose had reached a high artistic level. The *Novellino* belongs to the tradition of *exempla* – short anecdotes with a moral purpose; however, it develops these into a collection of short stories, which highlights its artistry by selecting stories, developing characters, amplifying witty dialogues, and drawing on rhetorical expedients to free traditional *exempla* from their abstract and simple narrative constraints. The *Novellino* is a worthy precursor of the *Decameron*. By the time it appeared, Dante was writing the *Vita nova*, and vernacular prose had achieved such versatility as to allow the poet, a decade later, to fashion a work of the novelty, sophistication, and ambition of the *Convivio*.

Italian made its most original contribution to the field of lyric verse. Its earliest expression was that of the so-called 'Sicilian school', which flourished in the brief period between 1230–60, when other Italian poets were still composing in Occitan. Dante – who was the first historian of Italian literature – coined the designation, as it was a poetic movement that had its centre in the Sicilian court of Frederick II (1194–1250). The court hosted intellectuals from all parts of Italy and Europe, and was located in a region that served as the crossroads of Latin, Greek, Arabic, Italian, French, and Norman cultures. The language of this poetry was a local Sicilian vernacular purified of all strongly regional elements and embellished with borrowings from Occitan and Latin. The result was a 'curial language', as Dante called it, namely, an 'aristocratic' language used at court by non-native speakers.

There is no evidence of any pre-existing poetic tradition, other than those in Occitan and French, that may have provided the models for the lyrics of Giacomo da Lentini, the first poet of the Sicilian school, whose striking formal perfection is unthinkable without the example of the troubadours. Giacomo was a notary, and therefore familiar with rhetorical teaching. This kind of education was common among the poets of the Sicilian school. They were high-level administrators rather than gentlemen poets; they were experts in law, and, for them, poetry was a refined exercise. In their poetry of love, one finds the typical courtly themes and motifs, but not the basic troubadouric notion that love leads to moral perfection. The Sicilian poets focus on the physiological nature of the emotions, preferring to debate about the nature of love and to define it in philosophical and medical terms, thereby leading them to introduce the language of science into their verses. At the same time, they almost never refer to historical persons or events; they do not write political or moral poetry such as the Occitan *sirventes*; and they do not send their song to a lady or to any other person. Their poetry does not establish a culture of gentility nor develop the figure of the nobleman. Instead they did create an autonomous Italian tradition of love poetry that investigated the nature of love, and therefore looked at the courtly tradition with a critical eye, thereby modifying its conventions and purview.

Giacomo da Lentini, also known as the Notary, was a sophisticated poet (about fifty or so of his poems have survived), who wrote in an elegant language and employed different metrical variety (*canzoni, canzonette, discordi, tenzoni*). He is primarily remembered as the inventor of the sonnet. Noteworthy among the other poets are Pier delle Vigne (*c.*1190–1249), Stefano Protonotaro (*fl.* 1261), Giacomino Pugliese (*fl.* 1239–46), the

*Vernacular literatures* 381

Emperor Frederick II, and Guido delle Colonne (*c.*1210–*c.*1287). It is important to remember that only two of their compositions have come down to us in the original Sicilian. The remainder of the poems have reached us in their Tuscanized versions, the language into which Tuscan scribes transcribed them (see Chapter 15). Dante read the poems in this guise, and for this reason thought that their language was to be held up as the model of 'curial language', which, as the most refined, he considered the best for transregional Italian lyric poetry. The Sicilian school largely disappeared after Frederick's death in 1250 and that of his son Enzo (b. *c.*1218) in 1272. However, the poets' experience, example, and diffusion were fundamental for the development of Italian poetry. The Sicilians not only dealt with the problem of love in a way that developed a specifically Italian approach, but also introduced some important technical innovations, most notably the invention of the sonnet.

A second generation of lyric poets flourished in Tuscany, at the time the most prosperous Italian region. Arezzo, a major cultural centre for a good part of the century, became the new focal point for poets from right across the region. Panuccio del Bagno and Bonagiunta degli Orbicciani (d. before 1300) were from Lucca: Paolo Lanfranchi (*fl.* 1282–95) was from Pistoia: Chiaro Davanzati (d. 1304), Monte Andrea, and Dante da Maiano were from Florence; and the greatest and most influential of these poets, Guittone, was from Arezzo. These poets are normally designated as 'Sicilian–Tuscan', since it is claimed that they follow on from the Sicilians. In fact, the Sicilians' chronological priority is problematic, given that some Tuscan poets begun composing before 1266, when, at the battle of Benevento, the pro-imperial forces were definitively defeated. The major poet of this group is Guittone d'Arezzo, who was regarded as the poetic leader of his generation. He left a large body of poetry, which he organized in a fashion that foreshadows Petrarch's *Canzoniere*, since it is structured to convey his personal history. Guittone's poems are divided into two groups: the first celebrates love and its power, while the second views love as a negative and irrational passion. Initially Guittone accepted the traditional courtly notion that love generates virtue; however, subsequently he believed that love impedes reason, and hence the acquisition of virtue. He also believed that poetry must be guided by justice to fulfil its moral functions. This is an important innovation, which explains why Guittone is the first Italian poet to write about political themes, a lesson that will not be lost on Dante. Guittone preferred the style of the *trobar clus*, the difficult and obscure style, in contrast to the *trobar leu*, the light and plain style preferred by the Sicilians. His poetry is often extremely difficult on account of its convoluted syntactic construction, its lexical choices – which draw on local and regional forms for realistic effect – and its recourse to rhetorical inversion and ambiguity that became the mark of *guittonismo*, the imitation of Guittone. This type of realism prompted Dante to define Guittone's style as 'plebeian'. Guittone was one of the most powerful poetic voices of his generation, highly respected for his moral rigour and for the new function he assigned to poetry in the 'political' culture of the *comune*. He also lived long enough to see his role as poetic leader challenged.

A third generation of poets was emerging, who came to be called the poets of the *dolce stil novo*, the sweet new style, from a designation formulated by Dante in *Purgatorio* XXIV, when the pilgrim meets the Guittonian Bonagiunta da Lucca. This movement's founder was the Bolognese Guido Guinizzelli. He began by imitating Guittone, but in a sort of poetic manifesto, the *canzone* 'Love always repairs to the noble heart', he departed from his teachings and insisted that love can only be present in a gentle or noble or virtuous heart. In other words, he did not maintain that love causes nobility of the soul, but rather that only a noble mind was fit to being in love. Guinizzelli presented his views by appealing in part to philosophical argument, so that Guittone reproached him for 'having changed the ways' of writing love poetry. This was not the poem's only innovation: the noble lover would no longer ask his lady for her love, but instead would praise her beauty as if she were an angelic figure, a manifestation of God's power.

Guinizzelli opened the way to a different kind of poetic imagery and style, which was followed by Guido Cavalcanti, Dante, Cino da Pistoia (1270–1336/37), Gianni Alfani, and Dino Frescobaldi (1271–*c.*1316), the poets who constitute the *dolce stil novo*. Was it really a school? If we consider their poetic language, there is little doubt that it can be defined as such: it was *dolce* and Tuscan, without any of the harshness and rhetorical complexity of the Guittonian poets. If we consider its way of understanding love, their commonality disappears, since we find them engaged in presenting different and even opposite points of view. This is certainly true in the case of the major two poets, Cavalcanti and Dante.

Cavalcanti was attracted to examining the nature of love in philosophical terms. Most notably, he wrote a *canzone*, 'A lady asks me', which interprets love in a negative key. The poem has been discussed for centuries, and to this day challenges its readers. It is a Guittonian composition in the tradition of the *trobar clus*, and essentially asserts that love is the enemy of reason and impedes rational knowledge. Thus, far from being a

*Vernacular literatures* 383

source of virtue, love is a fatal accident that takes over the mind of a person who can only see the damage it causes, since the self has no means to defend itself against love. Elsewhere in Cavalcanti's poetry – altogether about fifty compositions – such a philosophical approach is not present. Instead, he concentrates on the analysis of, and on the sense of shock in the face of the devastation that love causes in him, as well as his powerlessness before the splendour of the lady's beauty – a beauty that reaches the innermost recesses of his soul leaving only pain and an awareness of the impossibility of capturing and knowing the beloved's image. The prevailing tone of Cavalcanti's poetry is one of elegiac sorrow for this intellectual defeat. It is most beautiful and sophisticated poetry of the Duecento, with dramatic sonnets that perfectly describe the vision of his beloved or the anatomy of his tortured soul, and with exquisitely melancholy ballads.

Cavalcanti died in exile in 1300. He had been banished from Florence by the city's priors, one of whom was Dante. Yet Dante presented Cavalcanti as his 'first friend' and dedicated the *Vita nova* to him, which, however, can be read as a rebuttal of the idea that love is incompatible with virtue. Dante made love the central idea of the universe, and Beatrice, who embodies this notion, is a vital presence in his work. Dante began by presenting love as a strongly passionate emotion, but subsequently understands that real and lasting love is one that consists in the selfless praise of the lady without asking for anything in return. Such praise is appropriate because Beatrice appears as a miraculous creature bearing a divine message that leads to salvation (see Chapter 9, Contemplation, love, and grace). It is a complex ideological narrative that is developed throughout Dante's work, from the *Vita nova* to the last canto of *Paradiso*, and which is discussed elsewhere in this volume (see Chapter 28). Here it is important to highlight its origins in the debates of the *dolce stil novo*. In this context, however, it is also worth noting that, in the *De vulgari eloquentia*, Dante had in mind the melodiousness and 'light' style of the *stilnovo* poets when he presented a linguistic model for Italian lyric poetry.

Dante was exiled from Florence soon after Cavalcanti, and felt the need to acquire great intellectual range and sophistication in order to be able to serve as a political adviser and ambassador. At the same time, he also felt that the personal injustices that he had suffered authorized him to speak out against social and political problems that were essentially moral in nature. To this great cause he devoted his mature works, the *Convivio*, the *Commedia*, and the *Monarchia*. The preceding fifty years of Italian literature had given him the principal literary tools with which to carry out this grandiose project. The Sicilian poets gave him the idea that Italy could

384 Paolo Cherchi

have an independent voice thanks to its own language; religious literature had demonstrated that, even when it used allegory, it could attract a
large audience; Guittone's political and moral poetry revealed that politics
could be a powerful theme; the stilnovist notion of love had opened for
him a personal way of thinking about salvation; the prose writings of the
*volgarizzatori*, the story-tellers, and the philosophers had provided new
openings to all types of discourse; the masters of the *artes dictandi* granted
formal dignity to the writing of literature – everything was there for a
creative and intellectual genius like Dante to bring the youthful Italian
literature to levels that had never before been reached by any vernacular
language.

Yet our survey has so far failed to address other manifestations of
thirteenth-century literary culture that also played a key role in the making of the *Commedia*. One such tradition is poetry in the 'low' style.
Alongside the highly formalized poetry there thrived a 'comic' poetry that
in part parodied the 'higher' one, and in part developed its own tradition using themes and language that were deemed inappropriate for the
'high' style. This tradition has been designated 'comic-realist', because its
aim was to provoke laughter and because it rejected abstract and refined
vocabulary. Important representatives of this current are: Rustico Filippi
(*c.*1235–before 1300), who even descended to obscenity for comic effect;
Cecco Angiolieri (*c.*1260–1331/33), who also wrote love poems in the 'high'
style; and Folgore da San Gimignano (before 1280–before 1332), who is
remembered mostly for his poetry dedicated to the pastimes of an aristocratic company during each month of the year. These poets were all
Tuscans and wrote sonnets – a metrical form that, over time, revealed its
ability to introduce into poetry daily life and minor philosophical debates.
The sonnet would become one of the greatest contributions to Western
literature. It is important to remember that Dante used 'comic-realist'
poetry in his poetic exchange with Forese Donati (d. 1296), an experience
that he seems to recant in *Purgatorio* XXIV. Moreover, some parts of the
*Commedia*, especially the cantos of Malebolge, recall this 'comic' register.
In fact, one of the ways in which Dante defined his new and experimental
'epic' 'comedy' was in light of the 'comic-realist' tradition.

Another literary tradition clearly present in the *Commedia* is that of the
historical chronicle (see Chapter 21). The politics of the *comune* had stimulated interest in and the need to record the events that brought turmoil
and greatness to the city-states. The *Commedia* can be seen as a chronicle
of its world, touching upon both major occurrences and local minor figures, treated at times with gossipy pleasure or antipathy. In light of this

*Vernacular literatures* 385

approach, the historians who come closest to Dante are the Florentines Ricordano Malaspini (d. before 1323) with his *Istoria fiorentina* (Florentine History), covering the years up to 1281, and Dino Compagni (*c.*1246–1324), whose *Cronica* is indispensable reading for helping to clarify several episodes in the *Commedia*. Another chronicle was by Giovanni Villani (*c.*1276–1348), who began it around 1300 but left it incomplete. Villani's work presents history in 'providential' terms, as divinely ordained, beginning with the Tower of Babel. The same universalizing sacred perspective also structures the *Commedia*, although we should not think that Dante borrowed it from the chronicle tradition, since it was fundamental to the medieval understanding of history. Providential history is at the core of the *Monarchia*; and referring to the *Monarchia* reminds us that Dante was also the author of Latin works.

As vernacular literature developed, Latin had not ceased to be a literary language. In fact it was *the* universal language, because it was 'universally' used, and, in the *Convivio*, Dante ranked it as more sophisticated than vernacular, though, in the *De vulgari eloquentia*, he reversed his view, while the *Commedia* leaves no doubt that he considered the vernacular as superior to Latin. Dante used Latin in the *De vulgari eloquentia*, the *Monarchia*, in his letters, and in two eclogues. His Latin bears the imprint of his expressive genius: lucidity of argument, brilliant rhetorical energy, and vigorous moral conviction. In fact, it was an excellent medium through which to showcase the eclecticism of his learning. But it also bears the imprint of the Latin of his day: 'scholastic' doctrinal and abstract vocabulary, a language learned from the manuals of grammar rather than from the regular reading of the classics. When Giovanni del Virgilio (late thirteenth century–*c.*1327) reproached Dante for having written in the vernacular a poem that dealt with divine matters and justice, Dante replied with an eclogue in elegant Latin saying that he wrote the *Commedia* in the 'ever-changing' vernacular in order to reach as broad an audience as possible.

The thirteenth century in fact saw various attempts at reviving the language and literary models of ancient Rome. The Paduan Albertino Mussato (1261–1329) – a close contemporary of Dante's, whom the poet possibly met, and with whom he shared an admiration for the emperor Henry VII (*c.*1275–1313) and a staunch opposition to any form of tyranny – was the leading promoter of this revival. He expressed great admiration for classical culture, and, contrary to the contemporary deprecation of the moral lassitude of pagans, he saw the ancient world as a model of moral and political, as well as literary, values. He strongly advocated a return to classical

386                          Paolo Cherchi

models, the principal reason why he is considered a proto-humanist. In 1315 the University of Padua conferred on him the title of poet laureate. He was the first modern to receive the honour, which had fallen into disuse since antiquity. Mussato also wrote the first modern tragedy, *Ecerinis*, composed in Latin and following the model of Seneca's tragedies. Mussato was a student of Lovato Lovati (1241–1309) who established a school of rhetoric in Padua and discovered and transcribed important manuscripts of ancient works, initiating the philological trend later followed by Petrarch and by the humanists. He wrote a metrical epistle addressed to a Milanese friend in which he presented aesthetic principles that followed those of Horace's *Art of Poetry*, and firmly maintained that ancient poets were to be strictly imitated as far as metrical matters were concerned. In Verona, where Dante spent a significant part of his exile, interest in the ancient world was also steadily increasing. It can be seen in Geremia de Montagnone's (1255–1321) collection of *Flores* (Flowers), which contains passages from many classical texts that had been largely forgotten. The historian Benzo d'Alessandria (d. 1333), who in his *Chronica* shows a particular taste for antiquarian matters, illustrating ancient and recent inscriptions and seals of many cities, also lived in Verona. Vicenza, which is close to Padua, was another centre where classical culture attracted new attention. Here we find commentators of Mussato's *Ecerinis*, a fact that indicates the success of the revival of ancient tragedy. Among these were Pace da Ferrara (d. *c*.1310) and Castellano da Bassano (1270–*c*.1333) who, together with Guizzardo da Bologna (*fl.* 1290–1323), prepared an extensive commentary on the play that examined many metrical questions. Interest in the genre of tragedy was alive in Tuscany as well. Cardinal Nicolò da Prato (*c*.1250–1321) introduced tragedy into the papal court at Avignon, where the Englishman Nicholas Trevet (*c*.1257–*c*.1334) composed a very important commentary on Seneca's plays. Signs of this change in attitude were also felt in Naples at the court of the Anjou. It is enough to remember Pietro Piccolo da Monteforte (1306/08–84) whose work inspired the defence of poetry undertaken by Boccaccio in the last two books of his *De genealogia deorum* (On the Genealogy of the Pagan Gods).

Naples and Southern Italy also fostered a revival of first-hand interest in Greek traditions. This may have been a minor contribution, but an extremely interesting one nevertheless, if we recall that direct knowledge of Greek culture had been practically extinct for centuries in the West. Cases such as those of John of Salisbury (*c*.1115–76) and of Burgundio of Pisa (d. 1193) were exceptions. In Naples at the Anjou court, this revival was encouraged by Barlaam Calabro (*c*.1290–1348) and by Leonzio Pilato

# Vernacular literatures 387

(d. 1364) who translated Homer and who was consulted by Boccaccio on mythographical questions. Another intellectual involved directly with Greek culture was the Paduan Pietro d'Abano (*c.*1257–1315). Pietro travelled to Turkey and acquired a functional knowledge of Greek, so that he was able to read Aristotle in the original. Pietro was a scientist and played a noteworthy role in the intellectual world of his day, especially with his work *Conciliator differentiarum quae inter philosophos et medicos versantur*, which is a vast collection of *problemata* in the manner of Aristotle and of Alexander of Aphrodisia, and a work that tries to find agreement in the conclusions reached by philosophers and physicians on particular questions or *problemata*. When in Dante and his contemporaries we find words of Greek origin, these were possibly the result of this recent interest in Greek culture, though some can be explained as Latin borrowings.

Cultural change was in the air at the start of the Trecento, although it was still only a trend limited to a small group of notaries and teachers of rhetoric active in a few cities. However, fairly soon this trend would gain a considerable following and lead to the establishment of humanism. A final glance at the field of *volgarizzamenti* may offer a sense of the changes that were taking place. The *Arrighetto*, an anonymous early Trecento *volgarizzamento* of the *Elegia sive de miseria* (Elegy or on Misery) written by Enrico da Settimello (*fl.* 1190) in imitation of Boethius, is a lively but 'low style' translation. Around the same time, Alberto della Piagentina (d. 1332) translated Boethius' *Consolation of Philosophy*. The difference between the two texts is obvious: Alberto's decision to base himself on the original text, as well as the quality of his translation into a language that aims to equal the severe beauty of the Boethian text, is the clear mark of a very different cultural attitude.

The changes introduced by these pre-humanist trends affected many aspects of late medieval culture, from the literary canon and the language appropriate for literature to attitudes towards ancient authors. The discoveries of texts that for centuries had been buried in unvisited libraries revealed the existence of many old yet 'new' authors, and the change in taste made them the object of imitation, which affected not only composition and subject-matter, but also the choice and quality of language. However, the most fundamental change occurred in the way history was viewed. The new appreciation of antiquity made it clear that the ancient world was not a link in the chain of history that, in the Christian view, was extending towards an ending, a *plenitudo temporum*. Instead, it was a phase in the history of humanity – a phase in which people acted and spoke differently to moderns, while, in many other respects, they were no different to the generations that had come after them. Studying the human dimension in the past is precisely the goal of literary studies; hence they are appropriately termed 'humanistic studies'. Antiquity is an autonomous moment in human history, and we can learn a great deal about our own *humanitas* by observing how our ancestors thought and acted. Dante had a different notion of history: he shared the medieval idea that history was the realization of a divine design. This notion was the basis for his unique *oeuvre* and for his ethical and religious views. However, while he was carrying out his monumental work, that vision was undergoing significant change. Dante shows no awareness of this. Nevertheless, this lack of perception does not in any way diminish Dante. On the contrary, it makes his vision of the world that much more poignant, with its mixture of pessimism and utopianism. Dante was in tune with the world in which he lived. Indeed, he was so committed to it that, when change overwhelmed that world, his human and literary lesson continued to resonate across the centuries.

CHAPTER 23

# *Popular culture*

### *Jan M. Ziolkowski*

The lofty status of Dante's *Commedia* may blind us to the potential of the poem to embrace folklore and other popular material. Dante's masterpiece may be regarded as embodying consummately high culture, and high culture is often presented as antithetical to popular culture. The divine or heavenly is set off against the earthly, and this opposition falls into place alongside other dichotomies, such as ecclesiastic and secular, clerical and lay, literate and illiterate, learned and unlearned, written and oral, and Latin and vernacular. As a consequence, a composition that has been stamped by its very author as sacral (Dante refers to it as 'sacred poem' in *Paradiso* XXIII, 62 and XXV, 1), and that has been hallowed for centuries by readers as 'divine' – hence the *divine* element in its conventional title – might seem to hold scant promise of incorporating popular religion, folklore, and other manifestations of earthliness.

Yet among Dante's works the *Commedia*, followed by first *De vulgari eloquentia* and then *Monarchia*, affords the richest resources in his *oeuvre* for an investigation and appreciation of the popular culture that surrounded him. The explanation for this is not far to be found. Whereas the other texts by Dante are more learned and literary, the *Commedia* has earned unique stature by virtue of its very comprehensiveness, as an encyclopaedia not only of lore but even of life as a whole. Its imaginative sweep takes in everything from Heaven to Hell, with a robust sampling of all (and not just Purgatory) that intervenes between the two.

In the poem Dante showed himself to be anything but walled off from the great wash of cultures and subcultures to which he won exposure during his journeys and sojourns in northern and central Italy. To all appearances, he clambered with the same freedom up and down the social ladder as he traversed the geographical space of the regions in which he wandered. In fact, he managed to achieve a startlingly inclusive panorama of the multifarious social world he inhabited, in the process absorbing alongside the obvious glitter of Latinate cultural literacy the varied vivacity of vernacular orality. Despite being present and plentiful, the non-literate elements in Dante's text that can be and have been attributed to medieval popular culture have received relatively little heed, and the task of coming to grips with that culture grows only ever harder for us as we become further removed from agrarian life and the peasantry, illiteracy and orality, absence of electronic media, and assorted other characteristics that make the Middle Ages differ strongly from the twenty-first century.

Popular culture in central and northern Italy between 1250 and 1350 had next to nothing that overlaps with mass entertainment today, which is disseminated commercially through the constantly evolving and enlarging media that typify culture in the developed and developing world of our times. As the adjective 'popular' presumes, popular culture would have belonged to the people. But who were they? In modern usage, popularity is often presumed to stand in contradistinction to such categories as elitism and education. As such, it dovetails poorly with the attestations of the noun *popolo* in the vernacular of Dante's day, which designated not the opposite of the nobility but rather a class between it and the plebs. The more widespread denotation of 'popular' nowadays does accord with presumptions underlying the Latin derivatives 'vernacular', which has embedded within it the noun for a slave, and 'vulgar', stemming from a word that equates roughly to 'common herd'.

The English language has the alternative expressions 'popular culture' and 'folklore'. The compound noun, first documented in 1846, arose out of an effort to pair the Latinate popular and culture. By attraction among such closely related expressions, the notion of the popular relates loosely to such terms as folklore, folk tale, and folk song that are flagged explicitly as pertaining to the folk, and that are perceived, sometimes arbitrarily, as belonging to oral rather than written culture. Such terminology is all relatively recent, having originated under the lingering spell of Romanticism in the nineteenth century.

Beyond the issue of determining who the people were looms the question of what passes muster as popular, and what does not. Does popularity encompass whatever lies outside the official culture of monks and clerics, and any other culture restricted solely to the upper reaches of the nobility? Is there popular religion, or is the very formulation a contradiction in terms? Should we be particularly alert to verbal lore, or instead to art, dance, and music? In the quest for popularity, should we attend especially to beliefs and practices found among peasants, such as the shape of haystacks or the nature of festivals connected with the agricultural calendar?

*Popular culture* 391

Should we enlarge the picture from the purely medieval by considering popular beliefs and practices from antiquity that Dante relates?

The quality of popularity is often associated with medieval entertainers who purveyed song and stories, while also performing mime, sleight of hand, and more physical stunts. In English we might call such professionals minstrels. In Italian the term *giullare* is often deployed, deriving proximately from the Occitan *joglar* but ultimately from the Latin *ioculator* (from which descend both *juggler* and *joker*).

Humbler performers of these sorts plied their trade in Florence as elsewhere. A Florentine poet of the thirteenth century who has been seen as perhaps being influenced by this class of humble artist is Ciacco dell'Anguillaia, a near contemporary of Dante's, and possibly the homonymous character to whom *Inferno* VI, 52 refers, but neither the identity of the poet and the character, nor the connection with *giullari* rests on solid foundations. Dante alludes in *De vulgari eloquentia* I, xi, 13 to the so-called 'Castra's song' (1260–80). Devised by a Florentine to mock the dialect current in the region of the Marche, this is a product of Dante's hometown that may have a nexus with popular literature. The 'Dialogue of the woman from Djerba', a ballad of sorts that relates an exchange between a sailor and the mother of a woman (from the Tunisian island of Djerba) he has seduced, is another text that has been subsumed in this category. Dante does not quote from such poems, but he does conjure them up to enrich the texture of his own. Likewise, he refers to the practice of singing love songs at daybreak (*Par.* X, 141) that is familiar from the genre of secular love poetry known as *alba* in Italian or *aubade* in French.

The archetypal genre of literature at the junction between oral and written as well as between popular and learned was hagiography: it is no accident that the word *legend*, which denotes literally 'what is to be read', has devolved from relating specifically to the deeds of saints into a term for stories of historical personages who have progressed definitively beyond reliable truth. Such a transition may be detected between the presentations of St Paul early and late in the *Commedia*. In *Inferno* II, 32 he is Paolo, on a par with Aeneas; in *Paradiso* XVIII, 131 and 136 he is first named in customary fashion but then treated irreverently, from the mouth of a pope, by the more colloquial – the more popular? – Polo.

To take another example, Dante retells the legend of St Nicholas and the three girls (*Purg.* XX, 31–3), according to which the good Bishop of Myra dropped purses of gold through a window into a house so as to provide three poor sisters with dowries to marry, and thus to escape prostitution. In what sense does this tale merit being regarded as popular? Like many

## 392          Jan M. Ziolkowski

motifs and miracles attributed to saints, the episode would have been so commonly known that an author who wrote about it could have been conversant with it even without having ever read it, and many in the audience who chanced upon it in his writing would have known it beforehand from preaching, art, or other such channels. The question arises once again of whether or not such commonality should be equated with popularity.

To shift from legend to myth, the *Commedia* contains modifications of ancient myth, such as the tail that Minos acquires or the hoariness that distinguishes Charon, which may have evolved from popular tradition. Similar questions bulk even larger where the character of Virgil enters the picture: readers both before and after Domenico Comparetti[1] have wondered over the relative debt to learned and popular tradition in the traits assigned to the Roman poet as he is depicted in *Inferno* and *Purgatorio*.

For all the many literary intersections, the concept of popularity would be unduly restricted by overemphasizing its manifestations in literature. Popular culture stretched beyond poetry to other forms of verbal expression such as words and proverbs, to say nothing of types of expression beyond words, such as ritual, agricultural practices, non-verbal manifestations of superstition, and much more.

Dante does not record the wording of a lullaby, but his mention of *nanna* (*Purg.* XXIII, 111) confirms the obvious inference that he is acquainted with the genre. Within the *Commedia*, *Inferno* in particular contains linguistic registers that display symptoms of popular comedy and popular humour. The exuberant names of the devils in Cantos XXI–XXIII may be relevant: designated collectively as the Malebranche (evil claws); these guardians of Malebolge (evil ditches) are led by Malacoda (evil tail), and are named Scarmiglione (troublemaker), Alichino (harlequin), Calcabrina (grace-stomper), Cagnazzo (nasty dog), Barbariccia (curly beard), Libicocco (Libyan cook), Draghignazzo (nasty dragon), Ciriatto (wild pig), Graffiacane (dog scratcher), Rubicante (red-faced), and Farfarello (goblin).

Other examples may be forthcoming in incomprehensible words. Plutus' famous 'Pape Satàn, pape Satàn aleppe!' (*Inf.* VII, 1) may be called popular: it is certainly not Latinate. Nimrod's outburst of nonsensicality could fall into the same category: 'Raphèl maì amècche zabì almì' (*Inf.* XXXI, 67). At the same time, it is not immediately apparent how much the label 'popular' helps to explain either of these outcries or the nature of popularity itself.

Proverbial sayings come to the fore across Dante's *oeuvre*. Yet it can be challenging to pinpoint which of them qualify as popular, since

*Popular culture* 393

proverbiality and popularity are far from identical. Some of these dicta may have ben disseminated in a constant stream of *sententiae* and aphorisms from the schoolroom, library, and pulpit into less formal and learned settings. In fact, most proverbs and proverbial turns of phrase in the *Commedia* have demonstrable roots in learned sources.

Holy Scripture is one deep wellspring. For instance, Catalano's report that in Bologna he heard the Devil called 'a liar and the father of lies' (*Inf.* XXIII, 144) is a citation drawn from Scripture (John VIII, 44). Similarly, Marco Lombardo adapts words from the Sermon on the Mount (compare *Purgatorio* XVI, 113–4 with Matthew VII, 16–7 and Luke VI, 44). Such turns of phrase are undeniably sententious, but they did not emanate from the common folk – or at least not from the common folk of medieval Italy, since theoretically they could have emerged from the back alleys and byways of the Holy Land in the days of Jesus.

Another resource upon which Dante may have drawn is his grasp of classical Latin language and lore. Cacciaguida utilizes the construction 'a Cesare noverca' (a stepmother to Caesar, *Par.* XVI, 59), which concludes with a perfectly normal Latin noun that surfaces in a few ancient Roman proverbs but only once elsewhere in Dante's Italian (*Par.* XVII, 47). It would be difficult to frame a convincing argument that he was led to this phraseology by either peasant or broader, non-elite oral culture.

In contrast, little debate rages over the proverbiality and therefore the popularity of such instances as 'in church with saints, and with guzzlers in the tavern' (*Inf.* XXII, 14–5), and even less over medieval proverbs obsolete today that are presented outright as having been 'said', as with the saying 'what is done is done' (*Inf.* XXVIII, 107, author's translation), which is ascribed to the Florentine Mosca, or that match proverbs still in vogue nowadays, as with 'one swallow doesn't make spring' (*Conv.* I, ix, 9). In other cases the specialists, paremiologists, have classified as proverbs sayings in Dante for which no other attestations have been found in either the Middle Ages or modern times, but which have a proverbial ring. Thus Cacciaguida couples two images: 'and a blind bull falls more headlong than a blind lamb, and often one sword cuts more and better than five' (*Par.* XVI, 70–1).

In appraising not only possible proverbs but also any other features that may hold promise of being popular, we can secure considerable help from commentators on Dante, especially from those closest to him chronologically and culturally (see Chapter 30). Let us look at one example of bird lore as justification for the utility of consulting the commentary tradition. In *Purgatorio* the Sienese Sapia (*c.*1210–*c.*1278) tells of shouting to

394          Jan M. Ziolkowski

God, 'Now I fear you no more!', and explains her behaviour with a simile 'as did the blackbird for a little sunshine' (*Purg.* XIII, 122–3). To clarify this avian allusion, the commentator Francesco da Buti (*c.*1324–1406) recounts a fable in which the blackbird comes out after bad weather has ended, mocks other birds, and proclaims that it has no fear of God, now that winter has passed.

For self-evident reasons, we will never gain access to peasant informants whom we can survey about their relative knowledge or ignorance of items such as the fable of the blackbird. As a result, the effort to gauge the relative folkishness or folklorishness of a given expression or custom may require assessment of non-verbal sources in which it may be attested. The consideration of artistic evidence, even if speculative, can be enlightening.

Furthermore, we must always reckon with the likelihood that constant interchange took place among social classes, and that images and practices filtered from below to above, and from above to below, besides being created by individuals who cannot be classified rigidly as either high or low. Here a representative instance would be 'and if fire is inferred from smoke' (*Purg.* XXXIII, 97). Dante was indubitably aware of the sign theory expounded by Augustine in *On Christian Doctrine* II, i, 1: 'when we see smoke, we know there fire is underneath'.[2] Just as certainly he would have happened upon formulations – biblical, classical, and medieval alike – along the lines of our 'where there's smoke, there's fire'. In such circumstances it would be absurd to put ourselves under the obligation to choose between the one or the other designation, learned or popular. Medieval culture, like our own, benefitted from a constant up and down exchange. Better still would be to view the movement less hierarchically as shuttling back and forth.

Popular culture extended to folklore and folk practices that stretch across a great spectrum. Little of this lore, and few of these activities, are designated outright as emanating from the common people. For example, popular culture comprehends civic sports, tournaments, and games (see Chapter 8). Dante makes little mention of such pastimes, but he does tuck into the *Commedia* coverage of some.

In *Inferno* he touches upon the footrace known as the *palio* (*Inf.* XV, 121–4) that was staged in Verona each year on the first Sunday of Lent. In *Paradiso* he refers to the horse race run along the Corso in the Florentine festival to honour St John the Baptist on 24 June (*Par.* XVI, 40–2). St John's Day is unusual as a feast day for at least two reasons. First, it commemorates the saint's birth rather than death. Second, the eve of the feast coincides with Midsummer Eve, the summer solstice. In the celebration of St John's Eve fire rituals are widespread, such as the lighting of true bonfires (actually 'bone-fires') and kindling of torches. Also common are elements relating to fertility, such as the use of greenery, herbs, and flowers. Such features of St John's Eve would have sprung to the mind of anyone from Florence who perused the lines in *Paradiso* – but Dante refers to none of these practices explicitly, beyond the race itself. Dante does allude once to the flowering branches borne in processions for May festivals (*Purg.* XXVIII, 36).

To shift to games, we cannot pinpoint for sure which games of chance would have been popular in any sense of the word. Dante builds a simile about winning and losing that relies upon *zara*, a game played with three dice (*Purg.* VI, 1–9). The name for this game of chance derives, by way of French and Occitan words related to the English *hazard*, from the Arabic *zahr* for a die. A craps-like form of entertainment, *zara* belongs squarely within popular culture as it is conventionally defined. The same can be said of the game in which children amuse themselves by 'whipping' a top (*paleo*) to make it spin (*Par.* XVIII, 41–2; compare *Aeneid* VII, 378).

Among other entertainment, the poet evidences familiarity with group encounters in tournaments with swords, and individual jousts with lances (*Inf.* XXII, 6). He can speak knowledgeably about falcons and falconry (*Purg.* XIX, 64–6), as well as about boar hunting (*Inf.* XIII, 112–4). Both forms of sporting would have involved not only the most privileged noblemen but also their retinues of servants. More important, the last example relates loosely to a folkloric motif known as the Wild Hunt, in which a viewer stumbles upon a supernatural phantasm of hunters, horses, and hounds.

Dance was a recreation that cut even more broadly across social classes, despite the injunctions against it by the ecclesiastical authorities. The earliest mention of this diversion in the *Commedia* refers to the dancers as *la gente*: 'so it is necessary that the people here dance the round dance' (*Inf.* VII, 24, author's translation). Later Dante resorts to two different expressions to refer to dancing in a round. The first involves the noun *rota*: 'those who dance in a round' (*Par.* XIV, 20). The second is based upon idea of dancing a *carola* (*Par.* XXIV, 16–8; compare XXV, 99). Dante also draws upon a rollicking peasant dance, the *tresca*, for a metaphor to describe the motion of hands: 'the dance of the wretched hands' (*Inf.* XIV, 40; compare *Purg.* X, 65). The word *ballo* he employs in reference to women (*Par.* X, 79), once specifically to a virgin joining a dance to honour a newly wed bride (*Par.* XXV, 103).

Among other non-verbal means of expression, Dante shows an awareness of traditional gestures. Thus a usurer sticks out his tongue in mockery, like an ox that licks its nose (*Inf.* XVII, 74–5). Vanni Fucci (d. after 1295) makes with both of his hands the obscene sign of the 'fig' that signifies the female labia, by inserting his thumb between his middle and index fingers, and at the same time he shouts to God 'Togli!' (take them!, *Inf.* XXV, 1–3; author's translation). A thief spits to ward off the devil (*Inf.* XXV, 138).

Among customs connected with rites of passage, the first in the course of a lifetime would be when a woman calls out the name of the Virgin Mary immediately upon giving birth (*Purg.* XX, 19–21). The second would be betrothal and wedding. Here we have, alongside extensive comments in *Vita nova* (XIV, 1–15), inconclusive mentions of: a ring in the speech of Pia (*Purg.* V, 130–6), which need have nothing to do with popular culture; the singing of a dawn song by the bride of God (*Par.* X, 140–1); the size of dowries (*Par.* XV, 103–5); and the honouring of a new bride in a dance (*Par.* XXV, 105). A third, and definitive, stage in the course of life would be death and burial. These last rites are represented somewhat enigmatically in the cairn raised over the corpse of Manfred (1232–66), the bastard of Frederick II of Hohenstaufen (1194–1250), and in the later transfer of his remains, with candles inverted and extinguished, to a new gravesite (*Purg.* III, 112–32). How much, and how, the treatment of Manfred's body owes to his having been excommunicated is not at all clear.

Many beliefs and superstitions related in the *Commedia* would have run counter to official Church doctrine. *Inferno* and to a degree *Purgatorio* are by definition taken up with depicting the fate of individuals who through their sins violated basic tenets of Christianity. Although as a category sinfulness is not coterminous with popularity, at the same time Dante portrays many sinners whose sins prompt him to describe activities that could qualify as popular. For example, he devotes lavish attention, especially though not exclusively in *Inferno* XX, to magicians, astrologers, soothsayers, pseudo-prophets, necromancers, and diviners, from antiquity down to his own time, who presumed that the future could be foretold through astrology, geomancy, or other related means. Thus we learn of Guido Bonatti (d. 1296/1300; *Inf.* XX, 118), Maestro Benvenuto (known as Asdente; *Inf.* XX, 118; *Conv.* IV, xvi, 6), and Michael Scot (1175–*c.*1232; *Inf.* XX, 115–7). In another subcategory fall women who became soothsayers, casting spells with herbs and images – those whom we might regard as witches (*Inf.* XX, 121–3). Not all attempts to acquire superhuman insight into the present or future were necessarily sinful: Dante seems more to ridicule than to condemn the custom of taking augury from sparks that fly up when smouldering logs are struck (*Par.* XVIII, 100–2).

*Popular culture* 397

Astrology could be a valid science, with a niche alongside astronomy in the science of the stars (see Chapter 14). The very first canto of *Inferno* alludes to the astrological belief in the influence of constellations, and other references crop up elsewhere in that canticle as well as in *Purgatorio* and *Paradiso* (*Inf.* I, 41, XV, 55, XXVI, 21; *Purg.* XVI, 73; *Par.* I, 37, XXII, 109). Dante displays a ready command of star science, and when discussing celestial objects such as the moon refers freely to classical mythology: his familiarity with the deity Diana, in her guises as Delia (*Purg.* XXIX, 78), Trivia (*Par.* XXIII, 26), Phoebe (*Mon.* I, xi, 5), and daughter of Latona (*Par.* X, 67), offers confirmation.

Popularity has a better chance of entering the picture when the poet touches upon 'Cain with his thorns' (*Inf.* XX, 126:). Dante lends Cain prominence in the very topography of Hell, by assigning the name of Caina to the first of four zones (or ghettoes) in the lowest circle, where those who betrayed their families endure punishment. The four words linking Cain and thorns allude squarely to a popular tradition. According to it, God afflicted the murderous son of Adam and Eve for his crime against his brother, Abel, by loading him with a bale of thorns and banishing him to the moon. Dante returns to this tradition in *Paradiso*, when his persona asks Beatrice to account for the origins of the dark marks on the moon (*Par.* II, 49–51).

If the superlunary universe could be interpreted so as to explicate the sublunary world, then other ways existed for the future to break into present consciousness. A privileged group was dreams, which could be prophetic (*Inf.* XXXIII, 45), especially at liminal moments such as the early morning; *Purgatorio*, the canticle of the *Commedia* devoted to time and transition, contains repeated examples (*Purg.* IX, 13–8, XIX, 1–7, XXVII, 94–7).

Lore that at first blush might seem popular turns out upon closer examination to be rooted in beliefs that by Dante's time had already been circulating for a millennium or so in widely studied texts. For instance, in describing the punishment of thieves Dante alludes to their inability to make themselves invisible through the use of the heliotrope-stone (*Inf.* XXIV, 93), which is stock from lapidaries. Along similar lines, he draws repeatedly upon lore about both real and legendary animals that was commonplace thanks to the *Physiologus*, an early Christian work that achieved extraordinary popularity in the Middle Ages, and bestiaries, among other sources. The eagle can stare unblinkingly into the sun (*Par.* I, 48, XX, 31–3). Dolphins, by arching their backs, warn sailors of impending danger (*Inf.* XXII, 19–21). Not all such references are popular, in the sense of being old wives' tales. When Dante tells of the death and rebirth of the phoenix every half millennium, he credits the information to 'the great sages' (*Inf.* XXIV, 106–8).

Popular culture is elusive as both a concept and a phenomenon. As a concept, it did not belong explicitly to the toolbox of many medieval authors, leastwise those as erudite as Dante. As a phenomenon, it slips away from our firm grasp because of the paradox that it is preserved most fully in texts that were produced by and for different coteries within an official culture that constituted its natural inverse. Then again, elusiveness does not mean non-existence, and opposition may be an unfruitful way of viewing the relationship between peasants and other common people on the one hand and nobles and churchmen on the other. The fact that popularity, like beauty, is in the eye of the beholder (or hearer) does not call into question its very existence.

### Notes

1 D. Comparetti, *Vergil in the Middle Ages*, trans. E. F. M. Benecke (Princeton University Press, 1997).
2 Saint Augustine, *Teaching Christianity (De Doctrina Christiana)*, trans. E. Hill (Hyde Park, NY: New City Press, 1996), p. 129.

# PART IV

*Visual and performative culture*

CHAPTER 24

# *Illumination, painting, and sculpture*

## Louise Bourdua

Dante is often described as a very visually informed observer. This sensitivity is owed in part to his exposure to the rich visual culture that surrounded him from an early age, in Florence and Tuscany where he spent the first thirty-seven years of his life, in northern Italy (Verona) and Ravenna where he ended his life, and in centres such as Rome, Milan, and Venice on diplomatic missions. Little is known of the relationships he may have had with artists who, like him, were protégés of foreign courts. His writings record very few artists by name. Some of those he does name are well known to us, such as Cimabue (d. 1302) and Giotto (1266/67–1337); others have left few traces, including illuminators, on whom more below. Dante's interest in these men is moralizing: he uses them as agents of sin and of the vanity of artistic pride in particular, and perhaps to explore the connections between poetry and the visual arts. His encounter with painters and illuminators nonetheless serves as an important testimony to reception before the emergence of the history of art. Above all, the world Dante observed included the carved, painted, and built environment, and provided rich and complex metaphors whose effect on his work continues to be debated.

As a boy, Dante would have grown up surrounded by paintings, mosaics, carvings, and reliefs from wood and stone to metalwork and ivory, and would have become intimately acquainted with certain buildings and their decorative programmes, particularly in his native Florence. His Christian journey began at the large stone font of the Baptistery of San Giovanni where he was baptized in 1266 and where he dreamt of being crowned poet laureate (*Par.* XXV, 7–9). The font was demolished in 1576 and thus survives only in fragments, but was probably square or octagonal, decorated with slabs with a delicately carved border and centre, inlaid with green marble and, as was customary, round compartments (*battezzatori*) for the priests to stand in (see *Inf.* XIX, 16–20). Pisa's baptistery font, from the mid thirteenth century, has similar decoration, four *battezzatori*

401

and its central space is lined with multicoloured marble. In the Florentine baptistery, a large section of the tessellated floor is well preserved and displays complex motifs (birds, animals, foliage) in inlaid marble created in two phases and using two techniques. The earlier phase exhibits geometric designs covering three-quarters of the floor space, in *opus tessellatum*, and dates to *c*.1202, while the zoomorphic and anthropomorphic sections in the east and south are *opus sectile* and are dated slightly later but still during the first decade of the thirteenth century. The mosaic programme was partially completed between the 1240s and 1310. The chancel vault presents a messianic programme with a large wheel centred on a Lamb of God and eight Old Testament prophets between the spokes, while more prophets occupy the front and intrados of the entrance arch. Such decorated wheels were known in early Christian and Romanesque art and the meaning here was pretty clear, given that the Baptist saw Jesus as the Lamb of God. At a later date, perhaps after Dante had been exiled, two seated figures of the Virgin Mary and John the Baptist were squeezed between the telamones supporting the wheel. The mosaic programme of the main dome vault was begun earlier than the chancel but work was ongoing during Dante's lifetime. The complete cycle includes a classicizing decorative tier around the lantern, below which stand Christ and the angelic hierarchies. The lower segments portray the Creation, Genesis, and Joseph cycles, Christ's infancy and passion, the life of the Baptist, and, on a larger scale, the Last Judgement.

We do not know where Dante's parents' house stood, let alone whether it held any images, but within the homes of the well-to-do, one might expect to find a small painting of the Virgin and Child or a crucifix in a bedchamber or prayer corner, as shown in the predella of the Master of the San Martino a Mensola altarpiece, dated 1391. Some households did possess psalters or small Books of Hours, and Dante certainly knew his Psalms inside out. More expensive illustrated Books of Hours are rare in Italy until the fifteenth century, but both Franciscans and Dominicans in Florence had fine copies from the 1280s. Outside home and church, Dante would have come across a host of objects of devotion: gilded copper crucifixes with bronze figurines of Christ and incised symbols of the Evangelists and the Lamb of God carried in procession, or reliquaries encrusted with gems; devotional paintings on street corners or in public places, such as the Madonna of Orsanmichele, unveiled weekly during the thirteenth century. Although no Florentine equivalent is identified per se in Dante's writings, the much visited and venerated Holy Face of Lucca, the *Volto Santo*, a twelfth-century polychrome wooden statue of Jesus crucified with a face miraculously made by God, is specifically named by devils in *Inferno*. Corrupt Lucchese politicians are thrown into black pitch and float bottom up, leading the devils to shout in parody: 'The Holy Visage is not here for you. Here the swimming is not like that in the Serchio' (*Inf.* XXI, 48–51).

Unlike devotional works that have survived the test of time thanks to regular maintenance, inscriptions, heraldic shields, or coats-of-arms often perished by being defaced or removed as soon as a family or ruler fell out of grace or was banished. Such heraldic depictions of animals and simple objects were instantly recognizable to those in the know, and Dante sometimes used them to identify sinners. In the seventh circle of Hell, for instance, the fat blue sow on a white sack worn around the neck of the leading usurer was the emblem of the notorious Reginaldo Scrovegni (*Inf.* XVII, 64–75) who identified himself to Dante as a Paduan in the midst of Florentines.

Tales and anecdotes were not only spoken or written acts but were also visual, and Dante was much inspired by visual stories. As well as monumental Last Judgements, he would have known ephemeral secular images such as *pitture infamanti*, defamatory images of political enemies or notorious criminals often known to us now only through written records. Indeed there must have been innumerable other ephemeral secular images, perhaps like the fresco mural of the Tree of Fecundity or 'penis tree', a rare survival set in the wall of the Fonti dell'Abbondanza in Massa Marittima from the late thirteenth/early fourteenth century. He must also have known secular cycles decorating the homes of the powerful, such as that in the great hall of the Visconti castle of Angera around 1280, as well as the still familiar saints' lives, such as that of St Francis painted on panel in the Bardi chapel (Santa Croce, *c.*1250s), the labours of the months (as in the stone friezes on the facade of Lucca Cathedral), signs of the zodiac as in the Baptistery and San Miniato al Monte, Florence, or beasts and monsters grimacing from the capitals of church naves (as in the Romanesque *pieve* (baptismal church) of San Pietro in Romena on the road to the Casentino). The repetition of subjects and styles instilled familiarity and comfort (or horror) in the viewer/devotee.

If Dante did not come across miniatures while sitting on his mother's lap, he would have seen them during his education, and later when he was elected to office. As prior, the books he used would not usually have been decorated (beyond notarial marks and symbols or letters for archiving purposes), but as a member of the Council of 100, he would have glimpsed more elegant copies of statutes, with illuminated initials,

404         Louise Bourdua

and presumably law books including perhaps ornate Bolognese examples. Dante had sufficient knowledge of illuminators to recognize at least one by sight, Oderisi da Gubbio (d. before 1299) – the 'honour' of that city and of 'illuminating' (*Purg.* XI, 79–81) – and another by deed, Franco da Bologna, apparently Oderisi's pupil, but about whom we know little, save that his art surpassed that of his teacher (*Purg.* XI, 83).

Bologna's illuminated book production reached its apogee in the last quarter of the thirteenth century, corresponding with the time of Dante's sojourn in the city. So prized was the industry that books of common manufacture could cost more than the annual wage of a university master. Such expense did not seem to deter purchase or commissions either from academics, students, or other elite groups, including the papal curia, cathedral chapters, and the recently established mendicant orders. It is more difficult to identify the illuminators securely, however, since only one from Bologna, Niccolò, ever signed his work and that was in the second half of the fourteenth century. On the other hand, documents in Bologna from 1268, 1269, and 1271 do record a painter named Oderisi, son of Guido of Gubbio. In 1271 he was employed alongside Paolo di Jacopino dell'Avvocato (*fl.* 1269–94) and Azzone dei Lambertazzi, 'illuminating with a brush in good blue (*azzurro*) eighty-two folios of an antiphonary for nocturnal use for 30 bolognese soldi'.[1] As he never signed his books, there is no way of securely identifying his work, but Dante credits Oderisi as one of the major exponents of Bolognese illumination: '"Oh" I said to him, "are you not Oderisi, the honour of Gubbio and of that art which they call in Paris illuminating?"' (*Purg.* XI, 79–81). Giorgio Vasari (1511–74) followed suit in his Life of Giotto of 1568, and added that Oderigi d'Agobbio, the artist's friend, had been summoned to Rome by the pope to illuminate books for his palace library. As for Oderisi's pupil, Franco da Bologna, Vasari claimed that he was a 'much better master than Oderigi', had worked for the same pope, and drew very fine and beautiful designs 'in painting and in illumination', including an eagle and a lion tearing a tree, now in Vasari's possession.[2] Dante had acknowledged Franco's superiority over Oderisi using the voice of Oderisi himself: '"Brother," he said, "the pages smile brighter from the brush of Franco of Bologna; he has now all the honour, of which part is mine"' (*Purg.* XI, 82–4).

No documents have emerged to substantiate either Franco's existence or his fame. Nonetheless, Vasari's words and their repetition by Carlo Cesare Malvasia (1616–93) in his *Felsina pittrice*, a history of painting in Bologna (1678), have resulted in attributions of at least one Avignon bible

## Illumination, painting, and sculpture

to Franco's hand (Paris, BN ms. Lat. 18). Given our lack of secure knowledge of either illuminator's work, it is not easy to know what Dante had in mind. Did Oderisi's style follow French painting? How did Franco raise the game? Did he follow Giotto, as has been proposed? Can the noticeable shift between two modes of illumination in Bologna during the second half of the thirteenth century, still usually referred to as 'first' and 'second' styles, be linked to Dante's two illuminators?

Although these questions cannot be answered, a comparison of two opening leaves of the Gospel of Matthew showing the genealogy of Christ illustrates the sort of iconographic and stylistic differences at the heart of the problem (Figures 24.1–24.2). One of these, known as the Gerona Bible, has over the years been alternately attributed to Oderisi da Gubbio or Franco da Bologna. The first folio of Matthew in both manuscripts is divided into two columns of text and features a mixture of figurated initials and marginalia. In the centre, both pages share a long and fairly wide historiated initial 'L' (*Liber generationis*) housing the Tree of Jesse. Both illuminators place the recumbent Jesse in the horizontal stroke of the letter, though the later of the two, the Gerona Bible, reverses the direction of the earlier composition. In this earlier version, from around 1267 (Paris, BN, ms. Lat. 22, fol. 346r.), two entwined branches stem from between Jesse's legs and rise up, framing seven medallions of descendants, while the later Gerona Bible places the progeny on the trunk and seated prophets on curved branches. The modernity of the Gerona Bible and its closeness to Byzantine painting of the Palaeologan period sets it apart from the earlier example, as does the extensive use of a blue field and gold leaf. The differences in marginalia also constitute distinctive elements: French *drôleries* in the earlier example, such as the half-dressed man in the centre about to blow into a long trumpet, whose legs disappear into a tail motif, a brown and blue wader with a large fish in his beak on the right, and a lion devouring a hare at bottom left. The Gerona Bible retains some of the animals, but the *bas de page* has been replaced by historiated and figurated roundels.

Dante was in Florence long enough to witness the beginnings of what is still called an artistic revolution in monumental painting and sculpture. Indeed, when he encounters Oderisi in Purgatory, the illuminator informs him that: 'In painting Cimabue thought to hold the field, but now Giotto has the cry, so that the other's fame is dim' (*Purg.* XI, 94–6). Dante surely knew Cimabue's great crucifix, the largest example of its time (433 x 390 cm), completed probably before 1288 for the Franciscan church of Santa Croce, of a type much disseminated by the mendicant

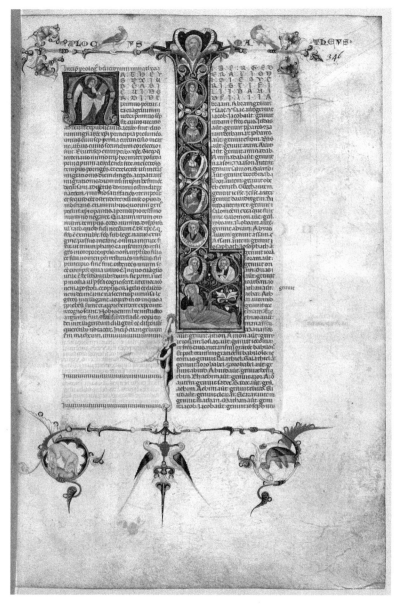

Figure 24.1 Gospel of Matthew, 'L' (*Liber generationis*) depicting the Tree of Jesse, *Bibbia sacra* c.1267 (Paris, BN, ms. Lat. 22, fol. 346r.).

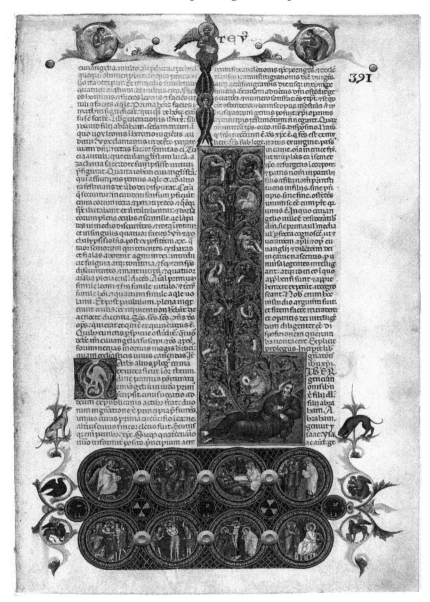

Figure 24.2 Gospel of Matthew, 'L' (*Liber generationis*) depicting the Tree of Jesse, *Bibbia vulgata* also known as 'Bible of Charles V', 1285–90 (Gerona, Cathedral chapter library, MS. 10, fol. 391r.).

Figure 24.3 Cimabue, crucifix, Santa Croce, Florence, before 1288.

orders during the second half of the thirteenth century (Figure 24.3). Its monumentality alone made it stand out, but so did Cimabue's transformation of Christ's body, imbuing his flesh with more naturalistic tones and creating effects of light as yet unseen, enabling his loincloth to become a transparent veil. Dante may just also have caught a glimpse of

Figure 24.4 Giotto, crucifix, Santa Maria Novella, Florence, c.1290.

Cimabue's large gabled panel depicting the Virgin and Child enthroned with angels and prophets peering from beneath her seat, executed for the Vallombrosans of Santa Trinità, most probably before August 1301, when the master can be found working on the mosaics in the cathedral apse in Pisa. Although the solidity of the throne on which the Madonna and

Child sit had already been experimented in the version painted by the same master in the transept of the upper church of San Francesco at Assisi, the novel frontal aspect allowed its inner faces to be displayed. The four Old Testament figures peering out of the openings beneath the base of the throne at Santa Trinità are also without precedent. Dante would never see its rival executed by Giotto for the Umiliati of Ognissanti around 1310. This slightly smaller panel (328 X 205 cm) repeats the familiar formula of the Virgin and Child seated majestically on a throne, but Giotto replaces Cimabue's wooden throne enriched by gold chasing, inlays, mounted gems, and coffering with one combining elements of French gothic micro-architecture. It includes the sought-after work of the Cosmati family of Rome – white marble trimmed with polychrome glass and stone tiles – while a three-sided structure forms a canopy surrounding a bench raised on a stepped platform. The side walls are complex constructions with the lower area divided into two trefoil arcades by a polychrome *colonnette*, and the upper area opening into a trefoil arch topped by a pediment with finials and edicules. Conversely, Giotto's crucifix for the Dominican church of Santa Maria Novella was most probably positioned on its rood screen by the 1290s (Figure 24.4). A great shift occurred in the rendering of Christ's body, no longer curved to the left but now hanging naturally. This in turn has an effect on the position of the arms, hands, head, and chest, all tilted forward, giving the impression that Jesus is suspended by the two nails piercing his palms and restrained by the single nail that now fixes his feet together below. The realism of death by crucifixion is increased through the strain on his arm muscles and expanded chest, yet so too is the impression of calm achieved by depicting Jesus' closed eyes as if he were asleep. Nor do the mourners Mary and John (on the terminals of the arms of the cross) express grief through gesture and eye contact as they had until then, but instead focus on Christ.

Who knows what Dante made of the Rucellai Madonna, executed in 1285 for Santa Maria Novella by the Sienese painter Duccio di Buoninsegna (*c*.1255–1318), Cimabue's and Giotto's predecessor. The conspicuous dimensions of this gable-ended panel could hardly have escaped him. His silence on this painter is not surprising, however, given that even Ricuccio di Puccio, the benefactor of the oil that kept a lamp lit in front of it from 1312, could not recall the painter's name, whereas he could remember Giotto's, whose crucifix in the same church he also endowed with oil for its lamp.

Did Dante ever meet Giotto, and if so, was it in Florence, Rome, or the Veneto? Much depends on the whereabouts of the Florentine painter, whose movements are as contentious as Dante's, and the chronology of

# Illumination, painting, and sculpture

his works, which is still disputed. But if the seventeenth-century historian Ferdinando Leopoldo Del Migliore (1628–96) is correct, Giotto was working in Rome during the pontificate of Pope Boniface VIII (b. *c.*1235; papacy 1294–1303). The acknowledged Roman works usually include a fresco cycle in the Loggia delle Benedizioni of the Lateran Palace commissioned by this pope between 1294 and 1300, destroyed except for one fragment of the pope blessing from a balcony now in San Giovanni in Laterano, although not everyone concurs with this attribution. There is more agreement regarding Giotto's *Navicella*, the large mosaic depicting the rescue of St Peter by Jesus walking on water in the atrium of Old St Peter's, although there is no consensus on its date (*c.*1296, or 1307–08, or 1312–13). Sometime before 1342, Giotto was paid the handsome sum of 2,200 florins by Cardinal Jacopo Stefaneschi (*c.*1260/61–1341 or 1343), remuneration unrivalled in Vasari's experience, which must mean that the master was directing the entire mosaic works, as well as working out the design and painting the walls to set the composition and colours for the mosaicists. Despite early attempts to preserve the mosaic during the demolition of Old St Peter's, just two fragments from its margins survive, and of these only one angel (in the Vatican Grottoes) preserves much of its original mosaic tesserae.

The evidence for Dante's own presence in the papal city in the second half of the Jubilee year is suggestive if not conclusive. Regardless of when he arrived, however, there was plenty to see, for Rome was a vibrant city for artistic production in the last quarter of the thirteenth century. From the papacy of Nicholas III (Giovanni Gaetano Orsini, b. 1212/16; papacy 1277–80) onward, popes, cardinals, and wealthy members of the curia rivalled one another in renewing early Christian basilicas and commissioning mosaics, fresco cycles, and liturgical furnishings. Nicholas sponsored the rebuilding and redecoration of the early Christian chapel dedicated to San Lorenzo in the Lateran Palace, which became known as the *Sancta Sanctorum* (Holy of Holies). As the private chapel of the popes, it housed precious relics including an *acheropita*, a miraculous image of the Saviour made without the intervention of man, covered with silver by Pope Innocent III (b. 1160/61; papacy 1198–1216) to emphasize Christ's face. A unified theocratic and decorative propaganda programme combines mosaics over the relic altar with frescoes on the upper walls of the chapel: episodes from the life of the two papal apostles, Peter and Paul, the deacons Stephen and Laurence, and Saints Agata and Nicholas, the latter reflecting Nicholas' onomastic choice. The frescoes in particular can be singled out not only for their unique imitation of ancient Roman decorative motifs but also because of their relation to the most famous frescoes in Italy for this period, in the Upper Church of San Francesco at Assisi.

Although Dante does not appear to have travelled to Assisi, he made specific reference to St Francis in *Paradiso*, and his knowledge of Giotto would have made him aware of what had occurred there. It is thought that Nicholas III sponsored some of the Assisi paintings, namely the much faded, painted mural cycle by Cimabue in the upper church transepts, depicting Peter and Paul. Although there are again no firm documents to prove it, a later pope, Nicholas IV, a Franciscan from Ascoli Piceno in the Marches (b. 1225/30; papacy 1288–92), is instead often held responsible for much of the nave decoration, which not only presents the most complete cycle of the life of St Francis of Assisi, but embeds it within a cycle of the Old and New Testaments. The extent of Giotto's contribution to these frescoes remains contentious, as does the identity of the numerous other painters involved, usually thought to be Roman and possibly including Jacopo Torriti (*fl. c.*1270–1300) and Filippo Rusuti (*fl. c.*1297–1317).

Nicholas IV certainly pursued the artistic renewal in Rome begun by his predecessor, and together with the archpriest Giacomo Colonna (*c.*1250–1318), commissioned a mosaic and mural painting programme in the newly extended basilica of Santa Maria Maggiore. The apse mosaics of the Coronation of the Virgin and episodes from her life, with twenty-four elders in the apsidal arch were signed by Jacopo Torriti in 1296, while the facade mosaics with a Christological cycle and scenes of the legendary foundation of the basilica were signed by Filippo Rusuti before 1297. Frescoes were left unfinished in the transept, probably as a result of the expulsion of the Colonna, while a possible Last Judgement was executed on the counter-facade. The extant fragments from the transept – heads of prophets and sophisticated architectonic motifs – have been linked over the years to the great painters Gaddo Gaddi (doct. 1320), Pietro Cavallini (doct. 1273–1308), Filippo Rusuti, Giotto, or the sculptor Arnolfo di Cambio (*c.*1240/50–1302/10). Most recently, their links with the frescoes of the Upper Church of San Francesco at Assisi and two episodes of the life of Isaac by the so-called Isaac Master, have refuelled the debate on the origins of the painters active in Assisi.

At San Giovanni in Laterano, Nicholas IV also oversaw the rebuilding of the Constantinian apse and relied on Jacopo Torriti once again for the mosaic decoration, which focused this time on the triumph of Christ, represented by a jewelled cross and a bust of the Saviour that may have incorporated fragments of the fifth-century decoration. The facade was

## Illumination, painting, and sculpture

also adorned with mosaics, but only a small bust of Christ survives on the tympanum of its baroque makeover. Nicholas ensured that in the apse programmes of both basilicas, Francis, the beloved founder of his Order, was prominently included, while he had himself commemorated as a diminutive, kneeling devotee, just to the side of the central focal point.

Rome was the city par excellence of early Christian martyrs and numerous churches dedicated to them also benefitted from the thirteenth-century renewal. Santa Cecilia in Trastevere received a precious silver reliquary statue of the saint from Pope Martin IV (papacy 1281–5) when he was cardinal-titular of the church, and a few decades later this was joined by a monumental Last Judgement in fresco on its counter-facade by Pietro Cavallini and an Old Testament cycle in its nave, probably ordered by another incumbent cardinal, Jean de Cholet (d. 1293). This fashion for commemoration was not reserved to high-ranking ecclesiastics. A case in point is the set of seven mosaic panels added as a sort of *predella* (platform on which an altar is placed) to the earlier apse mosaic of Santa Maria in Trastevere by Cavallini, 1293–1300. In the central panel a layman about whom we know little, Bertoldo Stefaneschi, the brother of a powerful cardinal, kneels below the Virgin and Child, accompanied by Saints Peter and Paul. His family arms are as large as he is, while two metrical inscriptions contextualize his gift more fully. His brother, Cardinal Jacopo, who paid for Giotto's *Navicella* mosaics, would later order a double-sided triptych from Giotto for Old St Peter's.

Tomb monuments abounded in Rome as elsewhere, and were another way of ensuring commemoration, perhaps by having shields inlaid in the bier in the fashion of Cosmati decoration bearing the arms of the deceased, and adding carved effigies that captured their features, such as the tomb of Pope Honorius IV (b. *c.*1210; papacy 1285–7), originally in Old St Peter's. Indeed the sculpted wall tomb became highly developed in Rome and soon included elaborate gothic canopies adorned with trefoil arches, crockets, and figural sculptures. A popular fashion had two angels drawing back curtains to reveal the gisant behind and was pioneered in the tomb of Cardinal Guillaume de Bray who died in Orvieto in 1282 and was buried there in San Domenico. The French custom of adding a frieze of figures in procession can be observed in the fragmentary tomb of the curial notary Riccardo Annibaldi (1200/10–76), now in the cloister of the Lateran. Attending clerics participate in a funeral mass carrying long candles, censers, and an *aspergillum* (device for sprinkling holy water), while a bishop carries his mitre and crozier and a deacon reads the office from a book resting on the head of an acolyte. These commissions all share the same maker, Arnolfo di Cambio, who dominated the trade in Rome from 1275 to 1295. He was identified as *discipulus* in Nicola Pisano's (*c.*1220–78/84) workshop when the latter was carving the pulpit for Siena Cathedral (1266), was recorded later as 'from Florence', and worked for King Charles I of Anjou (1226–85) for some years. The Perugian authorities 'borrowed' him to assist with their second Perugia fountain in 1277. With Rome and its ruins at a stonemason's feet there was no need to quarry the Apuan Alps for marble, and Charles allowed him to export Roman spolia to the city. For King Charles' own seated portrait now in the Capitoline Museum, never finished, Arnolfo re-carved a Roman architrave. Aside from exploiting the ancient city's stone, Arnolfo was much inspired by its classical past and, for example, adapted the commonly found figures of river gods into allegorical reclining females for one of the Perugia fountains.

The carved liturgical furniture of the late Middle Ages that underwent the greatest innovation was the monumental canopy placed over high altars, which in Rome accommodated specific local liturgical practices and enabled the celebrant to face the congregation. Arnolfo di Cambio signed his name on examples in both San Paolo fuori le Mura in 1285 (along with Pietro, his associate, *socius*, who remains difficult to identify), and Santa Cecilia in Trastevere in 1293. Unlike previous canopies, that in San Paolo displays high relief carvings including figures in profile on its spandrels, angels in flight supporting a round window on each gable, more angels on the inside, and saints in the round in corner niches. Of note is the profile figure of the patron, Abbot Bartholomeus, kneeling and offering a model of the ciborium to St Peter on the opposite side. Such compositions were to influence painting in the early Trecento. Arnolfo also made further and bolder use of classical models on the spandrel figures of the back of the San Paolo canopy: Adam owes his ashamed posture (as God interrogates him) to the Venus *pudica* (chaste) type, one hand across his chest and the other covering his fig leaf. The innovative aspects of Arnolfo's carving can be contrasted with the monumental paschal candelabra that had been executed at the turn of the century by Nicola d'Angelo and Pietro Vassalleto (*fl.* 1154–86) for the same church. Three of its eight registers focus on the passion and resurrection of Christ, and the figures, Romanesque in style, are tightly packed with enlarged heads and wide-open eyes, displaying no emotion. Arnolfo meanwhile breathes realism into his figures through hand gestures, open mouths, and individualized facial features approaching portraiture.

Arnolfo di Cambio is also credited with the bronze, life-size seated figure of St Peter, blessing with his right hand and holding the two large

# Illumination, painting, and sculpture

keys of the gate of Heaven against his chest, now in St Peter's Basilica. The tight grip on the keys is repeated in the marble seated portrait of Pope Boniface VIII universally attributed to Arnolfo, now in the Vatican. This was one of many portrait statues of Pope Boniface commissioned by towns displaying their allegiance, such as Anagni, Bologna, Florence, and Orvieto. His funerary chapel, demolished in the seventeenth century but ordered before his death, was placed against the counter-facade of Old St Peter's. It would have been hard for Dante to miss, and one imagines that its opulence seemed appropriate for a simoniac (*Inf.* XIX, 52–4; *Par.* XXX, 146–8). Known to us through watercolours and transcriptions of the inscriptions, it too was designed by Arnolfo, who now signed himself *architectus*, and consisted of a tomb chest with a fine effigy (now in the Grotte Vaticane), a wall mosaic signed by Jacopo Torriti where the kneeling pope is presented with the keys by God, supported by St Peter behind him, and a large canopy vying in size and complexity with contemporary altar ciboria.

Dante is silent about what must have been the talk of town back in Florence, the new Marian sculptural and mosaic programme for the facade of the cathedral, Santa Reparata, thought to have been executed between 1296 and 1302. Whether this is because Arnolfo di Cambio's statues on the facade and Gaddo Gaddi's interior facade mosaic were installed after his departure from the city, or because they were obscured by scaffolding (the works continued until the middle of the fourteenth century), we cannot say (Figure 24.5). The unfinished sculptural facade project, with its emphasis on the Virgin Mary, was the first step of a process that would see Santa Reparata rededicated to Santa Maria del Fiore. We can only reconstruct Arnolfo di Cambio's marble statue groups for the first register and three lunettes: above the central door Mary sat on a throne and held the Christ child accompanied by Saints Zanobius and Reparata and four angels; a Nativity stood over the left door, the Dormition of Mary above the right. We can imagine that, given his appreciation of Roman reliefs, Dante would have approved of Arnolfo's predominant use of marble and indebtedness to classical antiquity. The sculptor's seated Virgin and child group is carved from a single block of marble and is deeply cut, enabling limbs and heads to be observed in the round. The drapery clings to the body nonetheless, and the child's cloak is draped over his shoulder in the manner of Roman imperial philosopher statues; his left hand rests on one end of a scroll propped on his lap. Details such as the rolled-up edges of the scroll, carefully secured with string, had not been seen since antiquity, while the glass eyes add an unprecedented touch of realism.

Figure 24.5 Facade of S. Maria del Fiore, Florence, by Alessandro Nani, after a drawing by Bernardino Poccetti (Archivio dell'Opera di S. Maria del Fiore).

Sculpture certainly played an important part in *Purgatorio*, appearing on the steep bank of the first terrace of Mount Purgatory: 'white marble and adorned with carvings such that not only Polycletus but nature would be put to shame there' (*Purg.* X, 31–3). These reliefs become study aids in humility for the pilgrim through their 'visible speech' (*Purg.* X, 95), and include the Annunciation, David and Michael before the Ark of the Covenant, and Emperor Trajan granting justice to a widow. While precise

## Illumination, painting, and sculpture

visual models for Dante's descriptions remain elusive, various possibilities have been put forward ranging from Giotto's Arena chapel in Padua, Pietro Cavallini's mosaic from the facade of Santa Maria in Trastevere, Rome (1290s), and the carved pulpit of Giovanni (*c.*1248–1318) in Sant'Andrea, Pistoia (1301?). Yet the spatial relationship suggested by Dante's juxtaposition of the Angel Gabriel, the Virgin Annunciate and a 'cart and oxen, drawing the sacred ark', as well as copious details such as 'the smoke of incense' (*Purg.* X, 55–61), recall Roman imperial reliefs such as those on Trajan's column, the Arch of Constantine, and the Aurelian column. This is not the only instance where antique statues held meaning for Dante. He refers to a statue of Mars in his hometown of Florence, reduced to fragments and to be destroyed by flood in 1333, but perhaps originally an armed knight on horseback, which guarded the bridge on the north side of the Arno and was believed to have been erected to appease the god of war (*Inf.* XIII, 143–50; *Par.* XVI, 145–7).

The carved world Dante would encounter in Verona looked rather different. Devoid of much movement or many references to antiquity, Veronese late medieval sculpture was characterized by bulk, expressive facial features and colour, not only in the application of pigments but in the variety of stone available in this region, including the much sought-after red marble, *rosso di Verona*. Sculptors in this city are poorly documented until the 1340s, so attributions have been made to anonymous masters grouped around sculptures sharing stylistic features. These sculptors were particularly active in the Dominican church of Sant'Anastasia and the Benedictine abbey of San Zeno, probably around the 1290s. A life-size painted *tufo* (tuff) figure of St Gemignanus blessing, still in situ in the Dominican church, epitomizes a move away from the Romanesque flatness and stylization of the reliefs of the facade of San Zeno (Figure 24.6). The intensity of the bishop's gaze is achieved through a combination of deep-cutting, judicious use of pigments, and attention to details such as wrinkles around his eyes and the grooming of his beard and moustache. Equal effort was spent on carving the fictive embroidery of mitre, vestments, and gloves, including a Lamb of God within a medallion, and the rich binding and clasps of his gospel.

Verona tombs received comparable attention, and the best example is that of Guglielmo Castelbarco (d. 1320), located over the entrance to the cloister of Sant'Anastasia. Castelbarco, a key ally of Cangrande della Scala (1291–1329), had served Alberto della Scala (d. 1301) as *podestà* in 1285 and divided his time thereafter between his lands in the Val Lagarina and Cangrande's court, carrying out ambassadorial missions. It is difficult

Figure 24.6 Statue of S. Gemignano, tufo, Sant'Anastasia, Verona, 1290s.

to imagine that Dante did not meet him during one of the lavish feasts for which Cangrande was famous. Castelbarco certainly planned his tomb when Dante was still in town, even if the poet did not see it finished and installed. No less than 500 lire were spent on the project before 13 August 1319, the day on which Castelbarco dictated his will and stipulated that a further 1,000 lire should be made available for its completion.

## Illumination, painting, and sculpture

Figure 24.7 Tomb of Guglielmo Castelbarco, above entrance to the cloister of Sant'Anastasia, Verona, c.1320.

It is likely that the first phase focused on the two representations of the deceased – a kneeling figure with enlarged head, and a recumbent, near life-size effigy on the Roman-style sarcophagus: both display distinctive bushy eyebrows, hooked nose, and protruding chin, presumably intended as a likeness (Figure 24.7). Veracity approaching the point of caricature would feature again in Cangrande della Scala's own effigies over the portal of Santa Maria Antica (after 1329); both the mounted figure and the gisant sport a large grin and puffy cheeks.

Guglielmo Castelbarco's trademark profile was even more prominently captured for posterity around 1318 in a monumental depiction on the right of the triumphal arch of the Franciscan church of San Fermo Maggiore by a painter known only as the *Maestro del Redentore* (Master of the Redeemer; Figure 24.8). Dressed in his finest cloak of ermine with matching hat, Castelbarco kneels holding a model of the church he had helped reconstruct. On the opposing side, the tonsured friar responsible for channelling his gift into concrete works, Daniele Gusmerio, also kneels and joins his hands in prayer, wearing his more modest Franciscan habit.

Figure 24.8 *Maestro del Redentore*, Votive portrait of Guglielmo Castelbarco, San Fermo Maggiore, Verona, c.1318.

Guglielmo Castelbarco's prominent coat of arms further ensures visibility and posterity. These two frescoed profile portraits were also clearly modelled on the depiction of Enrico Scrovegni (d. 1336) in Giotto's *Last Judgement* in the Arena chapel, Padua and constitute the earliest extant response to the Florentine painter's work in Verona. Bearing in mind Vasari's claim that Giotto painted an altarpiece in the Franciscan church of Verona as well as a portrait of Cangrande (both lost), the Castelbarco fresco was long mistakenly attributed to the master.

The new painting fashion in Verona epitomized by this double-kneeling portrait was radically different from the previous, linear, elongated style encountered in much of northern Italy and elsewhere. The best-preserved example can still be found in the tower of the abbot's palace at San Zeno, and as a Ghibelline decoration, it could not have escaped Dante. The monastery of San Zeno had been an imperial stopover for German emperors since the final descent into Italy of Otto I (912–73) in 966, and around the middle of the thirteenth century a monumental painted scheme was created to pay homage to the emperor (Figure 24.9). The 'frescoed room',

Figure 24.9 Anonymous master, *Procession*, tower of abbey of San Zeno, Verona, *c*.1260.

as it is known today, was part of a suite of rooms possibly designed with Frederick II (1194–1250) in mind, although we do not know whether he ever set foot there. One wall is divided into four registers with, at the top, an inhabited frieze of red and grey/blue alternating spirals inhabited by monstrous masks and animals or figures. Below, in the central register, a large crowd of well-ordered men divided by station and race emerge from a stone fortress complete with tower and crenellations, and process towards an enthroned, crowned emperor who gestures benevolently (his right hand is lost). Three diminutive figures, now reduced to shadows, kneel at his feet, and a wooden stand holding objects, perhaps a lectern, separates the emperor from his cortège. A hunting scene with hounds and men chasing and killing wild boar occupies the register below, while a griffin assails a deer at the far right. Traces of an early wheel of fortune and the black imperial eagle on a yellow shield can be seen scattered on the other walls underneath a later layer imitating marble. This later decorative scheme, apparently commissioned between 1292 and 1304 by Abbot Giuseppe della Scala (1263–1313), known to Dante as one 'defective in body, worse in mind, and basely born' (*Purg.* XVIII, 124–5), carefully preserved the imperial cortège by covering only the dado level with alternating fictive red and green marble panels. Again, this was reminiscent of Giotto's illusionism and most probably, given the early date, of his early experiments in the church of St Anthony in Padua.

Located some fifty miles east of Verona, Padua called on imperial or papal armies to retain its independence as a commune during the later Middle Ages. During Dante's initial stay in Verona (1303–04), Padua was at war with Venice, while Verona remained neutral. Dante's longer, second stay in Cangrande's court coincided with open hostilities between the two cities, interrupted by an initial peace in 1314 and renewed conflict until a second peace treaty of 1318. Thus, Padua was an unlikely destination for the Ghibelline Dante after 1311. Yet the successful narrative of Giotto's Arena chapel frescoes, including the individualized punishments of sinners in Hell, together with the nineteenth-century claim of local historians that Dante lived in Padua in 1306, gave rise to a tradition that the frescoes had been painted under the influence of the poet himself. The contention that the two men were friends was further sparked by a nineteenth-century discovery of a purported posthumous portrait of Dante frescoed in another Last Judgement, painted by Giotto in the Cappella del podestà (now the Bargello) in Florence. The Bargello cycle is today dated to either shortly after 1322 or around 1332–37.

Giotto was very probably at work in Padua from 1302 to 1305, painting the chapel built within the Arena by Enrico, son of Reginaldo Scrovegni. The Scrovegni chapel is particularly famous for Giotto's Last Judgement fresco, replete with usurers and simoniacs, and its dado of monochrome allegories of virtues and vices. The Last Judgement is, as was usual, placed on the inner facade wall, and therefore the last scene visible on exiting. Jesus dominates the composition in the centre, surrounded by the twelve Apostles, presiding over a heavenly court of angels. Below on the left, a large gathering of the elect await, guided by saints and angels. Naked souls emerge from their tombs to join them. Beneath Christ and immediately to the left of a large cross held up by two angels is the donor, Enrico Scrovegni, who kneels and presents a model of his chapel to three holy women; a cleric intercedes by holding the model church aloft. Jesus looks benevolently at Enrico, while four rivers of fire emerge from his feet and flow down towards the pit of Hell on the bottom right. Here the damned are swept to their eternal punishments, dragged by demons tormenting them in anticipation of their select punishment. These eternal sufferings and the sins themselves are depicted with great attention to detail: tonsured clerics, lay men and women, mostly naked, hang by their neck,

## Illumination, painting, and sculpture

hair or genitalia; bishops bless women or clerics whilst accepting a bag of money; others roast on a spit or are devoured or defecated upon by a gigantic, monstrous Lucifer.

Giotto's hideous realism is also deployed elsewhere in the chapel, as in the personification of Envy painted in monochrome to resemble a stone statue. The painter translates Ovid's description of the venom infusing Envy's tongue and her gnawing at herself into a serpent projecting out of her mouth but curling back to bite her face (*Metamorphoses* II, 752–86). The Vice is further deformed by the addition of goat's horns and enlarged and elongated ears resembling a bat's. The grotesque provoked both scorn and laughter in the viewer, as did other witty features embedded in the continuous Marian and Christological narrative framed by Old Testament vignettes unfolding on the walls. One of the most cited is the pot-bellied wine servant in the Wedding at Cana, wearing an undersized cap, tasting the wine from a fine chalice and resting his free hand in his tight belt. For the most part, however, the narrative is decorous and dramatic, and Giotto's fame stems from his ability to convey emotion and tension through gesture, eye contact, and simple, centrally staged compositions. The Arrest of Christ is a case in point, focusing on the most dramatic moment, the kiss of Judas, the signal by which Jesus would be recognizable to the soldiers (Figure 24.10). Judas embraces Christ and reaches up to kiss him in an exaggerated, almost caricatured manner: puffed up cheeks, puckered mouth, wearing a yellow cloak that envelops the two men. Their gazes meet, with Jesus looking calmly down at the apostle in the act of betraying him. Chaos reigns all around, the action moving from the centre outwards. On the left, Peter lashes out and slices off the ear of Malchus, the servant of the high priest, while just in front of him a hooded man seen from the back reaches out to pull the clothes of another man, trying to flee. The arm gesture resembles the drawing of a curtain as if to shield the horror, a theatricality that has been much noticed. Tightly pressed against Jesus and Judas is a multitude of soldiers: we can make out just a few faces, but the idea of the crushing crowd is achieved by depicting numerous helmets and filling the sky with raised clubs, lances, half-moon halberds, and torches. On the right, other soldiers and civilians march towards the central pair, bearing arms and torches, one sounding a horn. The right foreground is reserved for the finely dressed Pharisee, arm raised in accusation towards Christ, while the cropping of figures on either side of the action leads the viewer beyond the scene to the rest of the narrative.

Venice was the other centre well known to Dante, as evinced by his references to the Arsenal (*Inf.* XXI, 7), the Rialto, and the dialect of the

Figure 24.10 Giotto, *Arrest of Christ*, c.1305, Arena chapel, Padua.

Venetians, 'not worthy to rank as the Italian vulgar tongue' (*Dve* I, xiv, 6). His knowledge of Venice's surroundings, such as Mira and Oriago in the Brenta marshlands (*Purg*. V, 79–81), suggests the poet had travelled there frequently and by a variety of sea and land routes. We know that he acted as ambassador in the lagoon city for Cangrande della Scala and Guido da Polenta (d. 1330). In the political hub of Venice, Dante would have observed the two ancient Egyptian granite columns that formed an impressive entrance for those disembarking near San Marco. The column nearest the ducal palace already supported a medieval capital on which stood the trademark statue of the winged lion, symbol of St Mark. This ancient bronze, looted by the Venetian fleet perhaps during the first crusade, was substantially refurbished using modern materials following a decree of the Great Council in 1293. Its companion statue, the warrior-saint Theodore, was not erected until 1329 according to the

*Illumination, painting, and sculpture* 425

chronicler Francesco Sansovino (1521–86), writing in 1581. Nor had the Palazzo Ducale yet acquired the characteristic gothic envelope of white Istrian stone and pink marble begun in the 1340s, so Dante would have seen something more akin to a medieval fortress.

San Marco was undoubtedly the most impressive building in Venice. It was admired for its five domes, marble cladding and mosaics, carved portals (with allegories, labours of the months, and depiction of trades), numerous reliefs of saints, beasts, and foliate motifs originating from Byzantium and local manufacture, and six bronze doors, including one adapted from Byzantine booty by Master Bertuccio in 1300. The mosaic lunette over the northern portal of the west facade (second half of the thirteenth century) preserves an image of the church's west facade as the background for the solemn translation of the relics of St Mark following their holy theft from Alexandria by two Venetian merchants. Amongst the rich mosaics and marbles, the mosaicist singles out the four ancient bronze horses resplendent and golden above the main portal, depicting them frontally with each pair of horses facing one another, mane caught in the wind and one hoof raised. These spoils of wars had come a long way, dislodged from their original Roman and Greek province and taken to Constantinople in the fifth century, only to be stolen again by the Venetians, most likely during the fourth crusade.

San Marco and the Rialto area were relative newcomers to the Venetian lagoon, replacing the spiritual capital on the island of Torcello and the political centre on Malamocco. On Torcello, a basilica dedicated to Mary had been consecrated in 639 and rebuilt in 1008. It faced the island's council palace and had its own bell tower, a round baptistery and a Greek cross martyrium dedicated to Santa Fosca built in phases between the ninth and twelfth centuries. In the eleventh century the basilica had received the most complete mosaic programme in the region. Its inner facade wall, although much restored, still preserves a Last Judgement that differs somewhat from that in the Florentine Baptistery and the Arena Chapel. The punishments of sinners in Hell are reduced to essential elements, such as worms that devour the eyes of skulls symbolizing the envious. The inspiration for such shorthand stems from earlier apocalyptic literature.

Ravenna, where Dante ended his days, preserved perhaps the most substantial traces of its Roman, early Christian, and Byzantine foundations. In contrast to the great changes the poet witnessed in his peregrinations, Ravenna displayed but a hint of late medieval refurbishment, 'standing as it has done for many a year' (*Inf.* XXVII, 40). The principal gate, the Porta Aurea, constructed in the first century and demolished in the sixteenth,

420      Louise Bourdua

was appreciated for its rich marbles, while the Byzantine churches and baptisteries of the fifth and sixth centuries were famed for their mosaics covering floors, walls, and ceilings. Some of their iconographic motifs may have inspired Dante's descriptions of the blessed and the souls of the elect, such as the processions of male and female martyr saints on a bed of flowers and plants in the Earthly Paradise still visible on the nave walls of Sant'Apollinare Nuovo (*Purg.* XXIX, 83–4, 88). When he described the millions of souls of warriors that form a Greek cross on Mars in the fifth sphere of Paradise (Par. XIV, 97–102), the poet may also have had in mind the large bejewelled cross of the apsidal mosaic in Sant'Apollinare in Classe.

As he travelled, Dante encountered diverse artistic styles. His comments on the styles of Oderisi and Franco, or Cimabue and Giotto show him to be alert to the changes in fashion. As well as fragments of ancient Mars or the new St Reparata in his native Florence, his visual world included the peaks of innovation in Rome and northern Italy, alongside ancient monuments in modern use, such as Rome's Trajan's column or Ravenna's Porta Aurea (Golden Gate). We cannot tie down his relationships with particular artists or know what he made of such works as the Torcello Last Judgement or the Arena Chapel, if he saw them. This chapter has underlined what was new, but early medieval and ancient works were still there to be learned from, and Dante's interest in classicizing models was a feature of the artistic production of the age.

### Notes

1  F. Filippini and G. Zucchini, *Miniatori e pittori a Bologna. Documenti dei secoli XIII e XIV* (Florence: Sansoni, 1947), p. 184.
2  G. Vasari, *Le vite de' più eccellenti pittori scultori e architettori nelle redazioni del 1550 e 1568*, ed. R. Bettarini and P. Barocchi, 9 vols. (Florence: Sansoni, 1966–87), vol. I, p. 105.

CHAPTER 25

# Architecture and urban space

*Areli Marina*

At the end of the thirteenth century Dante, like most Florentines, lived within a few hundred metres of at least one major building site. Half a block from his house on via di San Martino (now via Dante Alighieri) reconstruction of the city's principal Benedictine abbey, the Badia, had been underway since 1288. Across the street from the Badia, the city government broke ground for its first permanent headquarters in 1255, and spent the next half century continually enlarging the complex, now known as the Bargello. Two hundred metres south-west, a new residence for the city's priors (now the Palazzo Vecchio or della Signoria) rose around the nucleus of the former Foraboschi family tower starting in 1299. Further afield, work continued on an ambitious new circuit of walls, as well as on dozens of major and minor projects, including the construction of a larger cathedral to replace the dilapidated basilica of Santa Reparata.

Dante did not only witness this architectural ferment; as an official in the Florentine government, he also promoted the city's metamorphosis. He served on Florence's Council of One Hundred (in charge of fiscal matters) when, on 5 June 1296, it considered a petition to launch one of the most significant urbanistic enterprises in the city's history: the redesign of Piazza San Giovanni, the square between the free-standing baptistery of San Giovanni and the cathedral (Figure 25.1). The cathedral workshop's administrators and the consul of the Arte di Calimala (the powerful cloth merchants' guild) asked the commune for permission to expand the 'confined and small' piazza by removing the tombs surrounding the baptistery and demolishing one of Florence's largest hospitals, San Giovanni Evangelista.[1] (In addition to obstructing the piazza's expansion, the hospital had been superintended by opponents of the city administration; many of the graves belonged to aristocratic families out of political favour.)

As the record of the meeting notes, the proposed larger, unencumbered piazza would provide essential additional space for public religious ceremonies. The bigger square would also create unobstructed views of

427

Figure 25.1 Giovanni Toscani (Maestro della Crocifissione Griggs), *Procession of the Palio dei Barberi standards in Piazza San Giovanni*, from a now-dismembered *cassone*, Florence, c.1425. This painting depicts one of the many ceremonies that took place in Piazza San Giovanni. The standard-bearers for the annual Palio dei Barberi horse race parade between the new facade of Florence cathedral (partially visible to the right) and the baptistery (depicted to the left). The race took place annually on the feast of Florentine patron St John the Baptist (*Par.* XVI, 40–42).

the cherished baptistery and, eventually, the facade of the new cathedral, whose foundation ceremony would take place three months later. Before the vote, Dante addressed the council gathered in the church of San Pier Scheraggio in favour of the proposal. Though his words were not recorded, the petition won the day. Dante and his fellow councilmen acted 'to provide for and procure the beauty and honour of the city of Florence', as the petition exhorted.[2]

More specifically, the council's actions responded to the civic turmoil that had been rending the social and physical fabric of the city for fifty years. City authorities partly redressed those wounds by creating significant public spaces for the rituals that gave material form to the city's faith, political order, and prestige. Simultaneously, the construction of magnificent new buildings imprinted Florence with material embodiments of the ruling faction's sovereignty. The demolition of monuments associated with political rivals, like the hospital and the tombs around the baptistery, removed reminders of their patrons – and their former might – from the heart of the city.

By the 1290s these architectural practices were neither new nor unique to Florence. Italy in Dante's day was a land in transformation. From the expansive Lombard plain on the European mainland to the mountainous peninsula to its south, evolving social practices, demographic shifts, and mutating economic, political, and religious institutions generated – and responded to – substantial changes in the built environment, though their pace and precise timing depended on local circumstances.

Two principal factors conditioned this architectural and urbanistic renaissance. The first was the heritage of ancient Rome, whose physical remains pervaded Italy. Ancient buildings, road networks, and bridges in various degrees of preservation were adapted and reused throughout the medieval centuries. They provided building materials and architectural inspiration, including an enduring preference for masonry construction with assertively solid walls and architectural detailing that expressed the building's structural logic. Certain elements of the Roman architectural vocabulary – especially the extensive use of marble and limestone, vaulting, arcades, colonnades, and the architectural orders – remained closely associated with ancient Roman civilization. When transplanted to new contexts, they imbued them with Rome's enduring cultural prestige. Rome's legacy also established medieval Italy's distinctively urban orientation. The Italian peninsula and the Lombard plain had the ancient empire's highest concentration of towns; many survived the pan-European demographic contraction of the early Middle Ages. As a result, in the century before the Black Death, upper Italy had most of Europe's large cities and the greatest proportion of urban dwellers.

The second factor was political fragmentation. The unresolved conflict between papal and imperial authority in the High Middle Ages created opportunities for other aspirants to sovereignty. In north and central Italy, many cities experimented with representative government and garnered an unusual degree of political autonomy (see Chapter 1). Some managed to extend their authority into the countryside, take over smaller or weaker towns, and flourish as the capitals of independent city-states (see Chapter 2). Not all republican governments succeeded, however. Dissension among the ruling elites and discord between them and other segments of the populace made self-government difficult, and in many cities republican regimes gave way to rule by despots (*signori*).

Republican communes and *signori* alike exploited the expressive qualities of architecture to assert their piety, political legitimacy, administrative ability, and military strength. The churches, bell towers, town halls, market buildings, public squares, family palaces, and city walls that they erected did double duty – they promoted the ideology and interests of their sponsors while enhancing the functionality, appearance, and reputation of the city as a whole. Nor were these changes confined to urban centres. The traditional boundaries between town and country blurred as many cities expanded. Their widening circuits of walls engulfed swathes of the former countryside. Across the landscape the foundation of new subject towns and fortifications enabled, and attested to, the expansionist

430 Areli Marina

territorial policies of urban authorities, whether they were communal governments or individual lords.

In Dante's Italy, two types of cities prevailed: mercantile metropolises such as Florence and Venice, which managed to retain their corporate, republican government into the fifteenth century and beyond, and cities that became the seats of local or regional lordships or *signorie*, such as Ferrara and Verona. This chapter introduces the architecture and urban space of upper Italy by focusing on the two cities Dante knew best: peninsular Florence, where he lived from birth until his exile from the faction-riven republic in 1302, and continental Verona, where he twice found refuge in the della Scala signorial court (in 1303–04 and 1312–18).

Though Verona and Florence had different settings and histories, they shared common roots. Both had been Roman colonies sited near rivers and given the standard Roman camp's quadrilateral layout organized by an orthogonal grid of streets oriented to the cardinal points. (In Verona, the plan was rotated about 35 degrees to make the most of its position inside a tight bend of the Adige river.) At their central intersection, both had a rectangular open space – the forum – that constituted the colony's economic, political, and religious centre, and was framed by its most imposing public buildings. Roman Florence was guarded by the customary quadrangular perimeter wall; each side was pierced by a gate. Roman Verona had walls and gates only along two sides, because the river protected its northern confines. The urban form of thirteenth-century Florence and Verona, like that of many Italian cities of Roman foundation, was grounded in this ancient infrastructure. Both kept much of the ancient street grid, and their principal marketplaces remained on the site of the forum – now called Piazza delle Erbe in Verona and Piazza della Repubblica (once the Mercato Vecchio) in Florence. Verona also retained several well-preserved Roman monuments, including its amphitheatre, a triumphal arch, and two city gates.

However, from late antiquity to the later Middle Ages, dissimilar topography caused each city to develop differently. Florence expanded radially in all directions. The extramural roads or *borghi* that converged at its southern bridgehead and northern, western, and eastern gates blossomed into neighbourhoods serving the growing population. As the city prospered, it built increasingly ample circuits of walls to enclose the new suburbs (see Map 3). The walls of Dante's childhood, which had a postern (the Porta Abbatissae), a five-minute stroll from his doorstep, were superseded between 1284 and 1333 by a new circuit that quintupled the city's area. It encompassed not only newly settled *borghi* but also considerable

*Architecture and urban space* 431

agricultural land. Crenellated battlements with rectangular merlons surmounted the thick sandstone curtain walls of the new enceinte; sixty-three rectangular towers, twelve major gates, and several posterns punctuated its 8-kilometre perimeter.

In contrast to Florence, Verona's situation within a curve of the Adige and close to the steep Alpine foothills inhibited its expansion to the north. The medieval city spread principally to the south and south-west of its ancient core. During Dante's first Veronese sojourn in 1303–04 at the court of Bartolomeo I della Scala (reign 1301–04), the protection afforded by the Adige was supplemented by the latest in a succession of southern fortifications that enclosed progressively greater areas beyond the city's Roman boundary. Dante would have found part of the ancient Roman walls and two of their gates, Porta dei Leoni (Iovia) and Porta Borsari, still standing within the newer defences. Around 1325, Cangrande della Scala (1291–1329) ordered the construction of an even wider circuit whose walls were articulated by alternating bands of red brick and whitish tuff, rectangular towers, and swallow-tailed merlons.

As Cangrande knew, mural fortifications not only protected cities from attack, they also facilitated the authorities' social and economic control. Walls curbed unsupervised circulation, and the gates functioned as tollbooths or customs houses where goods entering or leaving the city could be monitored and taxed. Moreover, as numerous medieval representations attest, these enclosures – complete with their tall towers and imposing fortified gates – were one of the key constituents of the visual image of a city (Figure 25.2).

Following the decline of Roman imperial institutions and the advent of Christianity, these different development patterns altered the distribution of people within each city over time, and challenged the primacy of the former forum as each city's most important public space. In some cases, the political and religious activities that had coincided at the forum migrated elsewhere, changing the monocentric ancient *urbs* into a polycentric city with competing nodes of authority. Although persons of all social orders could be found anywhere within the walls, the oldest and most distinguished families clustered near the older centres of economic, religious, and political administration.

By the early thirteenth century many Italian republics had built government headquarters that accommodated their legislators, judges, administrators, and growing number of records, and that also visibly represented their authority. Florence lagged. Its republican government had no permanent seat for more than 140 years after its inception around 1115; its

Figure 25.2 View of Florence, detail from the *Madonna della Misericordia*, fresco, Loggia del Bigallo, Florence, c.1342. In fourteenth-century Italian art, cities were conventionally represented as surrounded by crenellated masonry walls. In this fresco for the headquarters of a charitable confraternity, the anonymous artist identifies the city as Florence by inscribing its name on the walls, as well as depicting its distinctive baptistery and the Palazzo dei Priori (now Palazzo Vecchio).

councils and officials met at various locations around town. Then in 1255 Florence – controlled at the time by an anti-aristocratic regime now known as the *primo popolo* – finally established a residence for the head of its government, the *capitano del popolo*. The site chosen was neither near the city's principal marketplace on the former forum nor near the cathedral. Those locations within the eleventh-century 'ancient circle' of walls invoked by Dante's great-great-grandfather Cacciaguida (*Par.* XV, 97) were too close to the turreted strongholds of the regime's aristocratic political rivals. Instead, the building rose at a more secure location, a plot to the east of the old ring and nearer a part of the city where supporters of the *popolo* abounded.

As the organization of Florence's government mutated in response to complex local politics, its need for real estate to accommodate councils, committees, and officers continually increased. The government soon outgrew the Palazzo del Capitano and repeatedly expanded its facilities

## Architecture and urban space

on the site in successive decades. (The building's nomenclature evolved too. It was renamed the Palazzo del Podestà after the demise of the *primo popolo*, and finally the Bargello after its role as residence of the chief of police in the sixteenth century.) Morphologically, the complex – which eventually comprised several buildings with few ground-storey openings, two towers, and an enclosed courtyard – resembled the agglomerations of inward-oriented, interconnected houses, courts, loggias, and towers that characterized the urban compounds of the most powerful Florentine families. Despite continual construction, when Dante entered political life in the 1290s, the existing structures still could not satisfy the government's evolving needs. When he served on the Council of One Hundred, it met in the church of San Pier Scheraggio for lack of a suitable council hall. And for some time after the establishment of the priorate in 1282 as one of the commune's most important offices, the six priors of the city's six administrative divisions or *sestieri* spent their short tenures sequestered in the Torre della Castagna, near the Alighieri family's houses.

After more than fifteen years of fruitless proposals for a permanent headquarters for the priors, the old communal complex was superseded in prominence and prestige by a new palace begun in 1299 (Figure 25.3). The site chosen was between San Pier Scheraggio and the empty lot where the banished Uberti clan's properties had once stood. Like its counterparts on the Lombard plain, the new palace had a vast meeting hall on the first floor for the city's largest council. In addition, its upper storeys also included several small chambers to house the priors, staff, and records. An interior courtyard provided light and ventilation to rooms facing inward. Instead of the permeable, arcaded lower storey adopted by most Lombard palaces, the ground storey of the Florentine Palazzo dei Priori (later the Palazzo della Signoria or Palazzo Vecchio) had a closed perimeter. Its rusticated, rough-hewn sandstone exterior and battlements gave it a forbidding appearance tempered by the elegant two-light windows of its upper floors.

The first incarnation of the palace was finished in 1302, too late for Dante to have lived in it during his term as prior in 1300. Subsequent changes shifted the palace's principal facade from the north to the west, doubled the height of its projecting battlements, and added a massive belfry by 1315. After these modifications, the tall palace and its gravity-defying tower loomed monitorially over spectators outside. Though larger and more aggressive in form, in type it resembled other Tuscan town halls, such as the inward-oriented, turreted Palazzo dei Priori of Volterra (1208–54), and its own Florentine predecessors on the via del Proconsolo.

Figure 25.3 Palazzo dei Priori (or Palazzo Vecchio or della Signoria) and Piazza della Signoria, Florence, begun 1299. The Florentine prior's palace's closed ground storey, heavily rusticated masonry, and gravity-defying tower presented a forbidding face to spectators in the piazza below.

To maximize the palace's visual impact, an L-shaped piazza that wrapped around its north-western corner was painstakingly carved from the dense urban fabric around it over the course of sixty years (1299–1362). The completed piazza (now Piazza della Signoria) showcased the height and mass of the building from its principal ceremonial entrance, the street leading to the cathedral and baptistery's portals (now via dei Calzaiuoli). In addition to creating perspectival views of the commune's signature building, the paved piazza performed a host of civic duties. When the palace bells summoned the populace to arms, it was Florence's mustering ground. It was the stage for various official religious and political processions and ceremonies, such as the swearing in of the priors and the official welcome of ambassadors. It was an important link along the chain of streets that connected the city's most important monuments. Though Dante never saw it finished, Florence's Piazza della Signoria shared these functions with many monumental and geometrically idealizing piazzas developed around civic buildings and episcopal complexes throughout upper Italy beginning in the thirteenth century.

*Architecture and urban space* 435

However, the Piazza della Signoria's accessibility and the Palazzo dei Priori's symbolic import also made the site a flashpoint for protest. When in February 1304 Corso Donati (d. 1308) turned against the leaders of his own Black Guelf faction, then in charge of the city, Dino Compagni (*c*.1246–1324) reports that he gathered his supporters and 'came to the piazza armed on horseback and fiercely attacked the palace of the Priors with fire and crossbows'.[3] Corso's assault failed to bring down his rivals' government, but such attacks could be effective. In 1308, for example, the armed mob that massed in Parma's communal piazza succeeded in seizing the civic palaces around it and overthrowing aspiring *signore* Ghiberto da Correggio (*c*.1250–1321). Indeed, in the early fourteenth century Lords Matteo (1250–1322) and Luchino Visconti (1287 or 1292–1349) of Milan routinely sealed off the communal piazzas of newly conquered cities with fortifications to prevent insurrectionists from having access to the spaces and buildings that incarnated the city's previous political authority.

When the exiled Dante arrived in Verona in the spring of 1303 in the hopes of mustering Bartolomeo della Scala's support for the White Guelf cause, he found a city whose magnificence overshadowed Florence's. The grand effect produced by Verona's ancient marble monuments, majestic twelfth-century churches, and newly paved streets had been enhanced by no fewer than five government-sponsored palaces. All of them clustered on or near the ancient Roman forum, the market square now called Piazza delle Erbe. Unlike in Florence, Verona's first communal palace (the Palazzo del Comune or, later, the Palazzo della Ragione) went up soon after the establishment of republican government in the early twelfth century; it was repeatedly remodelled. By the time Bartolomeo became *signore*, the rectangular structure with five towers and multiple porticos dominated the south-eastern edge of the spindle-shaped market square. Red brick and white tuff banding ornamented its exterior perimeter and interior courtyard. Two civic bells had been hung from one of its towers in 1295.

The patron responsible for the transformation of Verona's cityscape was not Dante's patron Bartolomeo, however, but his father Alberto (reign 1277–1301). Like his brother and predecessor Mastino I (d. 1277), who had taken control of Verona after tyrant Ezzelino III da Romano's (b. 1194) assassination in 1259, Alberto coopted the city's surviving republican institutions to consolidate his authority, reinforcing the practice by architectural means. Over his twenty-four-year reign, he improved the city's defences and infrastructure and, most significantly, monumentalized the previously workaday Piazza delle Erbe and inaugurated a Scaliger signorial complex to the piazza's east. Alberto's principal three interventions in the Piazza delle Erbe were the construction of the Domus Nova (New House) and the Domus Bladorum (Grain House), and the reconstruction of the Domus Mercatorum (Merchants' House). The Domus Nova provided lodgings for Verona's *podestà*, as well as additional meeting rooms for its communal councils. It is impossible to recapture the building's original form, since it was rebuilt in 1369 and subsequently altered. There is no question, however, that it was sited for maximum impact – on the square's central intersection, to the north of the Palazzo Comunale, and on the road leading directly from the Ponte Nuovo, the new bridge Alberto built in 1291. The Veronese *signore* continued his appropriation of the piazza's eastern border with the construction of the Domus Bladorum. This shallow but long building extended along the entire northern half of the piazza's eastern boundary, from the Domus Nova to the square's northern terminus. Upstairs, the Domus Bladorum sheltered the public granary (as its name indicates); tradesmen rented the shops along its arcaded ground storey.

Towards the end of his reign, Alberto completed his redevelopment of the Piazza delle Erbe into the city's commercial and political epicentre by rebuilding the Domus Mercatorum, the headquarters of the powerful merchants' council, which was prominently located on the west side of the square, opposite the Palazzo del Comune (Figure 25.4). The transformation of this building from its original wooden forms into a brick and limestone palace must have had particular meaning for Alberto, who held the office of *podestà* of the merchants for 31 years, even after he had been proclaimed the city's Captain-General for life. The Domus Mercatorum had ground-storey arcades around three sides, which were used for commercial and judicial activity. Upstairs, large halls illuminated by two- and three-light windows, and probably decorated by frescoes, served as meeting rooms for the merchants' council and the city's guilds. The magnificence of the well-preserved (and well-restored) palace attests to the grandeur of Alberto's undertakings. *Rosso di Verona* columns and brick piers support the vaults of the ground-storey porticos that wrap around three sides of the building; marble colonnettes divide its upper-storey windows; red-and-white voussoirs ornament its arcades and window frames; swallow-tailed merlons enliven its roof line with reminders of their patron's military might. Buildings of this type abounded across the Lombard plain, and functioned as episcopal, communal, and royal palaces. Extant examples include the communal palaces of Cremona (1206–46), Milan (1228–33), and Piacenza (begun 1281), and the episcopal palace of Parma (given this form *c*.1233). Central Italian variations include the Palazzo del Capitano of Orvieto (after 1250) and Todi (*c*.1290).

*Architecture and urban space*

Figure 25.4 Domus Mercatorum, Verona, begun 1301. The combination of downstairs porticos and upstairs council halls found in Lord Alberto I's House of the Merchants is typical of many civic palaces in upper Italy.

As a result of Alberto's architectural interventions, della Scala-sponsored buildings dominated the Piazza delle Erbe's perimeter and constantly reminded viewers of Scaliger support of the city's economic life and concern for its prudent administration. By contrast, in Dante's time Florence's ancient forum, the site of the Mercato Vecchio, did not contain much in the way of government-sponsored monumental architecture, although private tower complexes and a growing number of guild halls were scattered around its environs. And despite Florence's mercantile orientation, the Bargello, Palazzo dei Priori, and its emerging Piazza della Signoria did not visibly cater to commercial activity.

Alberto's campaign to reify della Scala authority did not stop within the Piazza delle Erbe's perimeter. He also built a new palace for himself beyond its eastern boundary, between the Palazzo del Comune and the church of Santa Maria Antica, which had been rebuilt around 1185. The palace formed the nucleus of what would become an extensive signorial complex arranged around a new, rectangular piazza (Piazza dei Signori) positioned at a right angle from Piazza delle Erbe. Though the precise location and appearance of Alberto's palace cannot be determined, it incorporated towers and battlements, potent signifiers of dominion that his government forbade others to use in the piazza's vicinity.

When Dante returned to Verona in 1312 to join the court of Cangrande, he encountered an even vaster, grander signorial compound consonant with his patron's reputation for magnificence (*Ep.* XIII). In addition to enlarging and improving Alberto's palace near Santa Maria Antica, Cangrande was also the probable patron of the tall palace that defined the eastern boundary of the evolving Piazza dei Signori, begun around 1308 and later continued by Mastino II (b. 1308; reign 1329–51). The building, now known as the Palazzo della Prefettura, consisted of three wings arranged in a U-shaped plan open towards Corso Sant'Anastasia to the north. The partly restored piazza facade of the western wing has a portico with semi-circular arches at the lower level, multiple upper storeys with varied windows, and the typical Veronese array of swallow-tailed battlements across the top. Elaborate trefoil lancet windows articulate the upper storeys of its southern facade. The ensemble was completed by the refashioning of the church of Santa Maria Antica as the clan's palatine chapel. Its exterior cemetery became the della Scala dynastic burial ground – the remains of Alberto, Bartolomeo, Alboino (*c.*1284–1311), and Mastino I rested there by 1311 – though the showy elevated funerary monuments of Cangrande and his successors postdate Dante's time in Verona. While no interior descriptions of the Scaliger palaces during Dante's sojourn survive, later accounts suggest their grandeur. The use of the prized, pink-to-white *rosso di Verona* limestone (considered marble in the Middle Ages), architectural sculpture, and polychrome decoration on the palace's exteriors signalled the sophisticated taste and affluence of its patrons. They must have been fitting backdrops for the peerless splendour of the courtly spectacles for which the della Scala were renowned. Early modern views of the Piazza dei Signori complex still capture the monumental effect that earned the city the epithet 'Verona marmorina' (marble Verona) a generation later (Figure 25.5).

Though Verona's signorial palace complex was one of several built in upper Italy, few survive. They included the Visconti palatine complex near Milan cathedral (by 1335, mostly destroyed), the Bonacolsi complex in Mantua (1273–1328, partly engulfed by the later Gonzaga ducal palaces), and the d'Este complex on Ferrara's cathedral square (from 1242, destroyed and partly rebuilt in neo-medieval style in the 1920s). Their effectiveness as expressions of the authority and identity of a particular lord or lineage rendered them vulnerable to appropriation and transformation by subsequent rulers, and to destruction by enemies. Although the buildings

Figure 25.5 Detail of the Piazza dei Signori, Verona, c.1525, from Niccolò Giolfino, *Gaius Mucius Scaevola Thrusting his Right Hand into the Flame*, tempera on panel, c.1525–1550 (present location unknown). This painting sets the ancient Roman story of the heroism of soldier Gaius Mucius Scaevola (*Par.* IV, 82–87) against the backdrop of the Piazza dei Signori as it appeared in the early sixteenth century, including the palaces of Lords Alberto (to the right) and Cangrande (centre background), and beyond the elevated bridge that connects them, the tomb monument of Mastino II in the Scaliger cemetery of Santa Maria Antica.

sponsored by the della Scala included towers and battlements, they were not intended for long-term protection. This expectation changed in the latter half of the Trecento, when *signori* worried about security commissioned true urban citadels that complemented and sometimes displaced the aulic architecture of the older courts.

Before the construction of those citadels, the only buildings that rivalled the scale of Florence and Verona's civic and courtly palaces were, of course, their great churches. Both cities were ancient episcopal sees. Their cathedrals were part of larger ensembles comprising a bishop's palace, baptistery, bell tower, and residence for the cathedral clergy, and usually placed beyond the Roman city's boundary. Like all important buildings, they were often modified over the centuries. In Verona, the cathedral remained at the city's edge. By contrast, Florence grew in such a fashion that the cathedral's position was no longer marginal by the fourteenth century. Verona's episcopal buildings – the cathedral of Santa Maria Matricolare completed in 1187, the basilican baptistery rebuilt after 1123, the Romanesque campanile, and the episcopal palace – satisfied the city's requirements through the fourteenth century. Santa Maria Matricolare was not new, but it was impressively large and lavishly decorated. Although the church was finally remodelled in the fifteenth century, surviving twelfth-century passages, such as the richly sculpted west portal by Niccolò installed in 1139, attest to the medieval building's distinction.

During Dante's childhood, Florence's most imposing church was not the modest timber-roofed cathedral basilica of Santa Reparata (last rebuilt in the eleventh century) but rather the marble-clad, octagonal, vaulted baptistery of San Giovanni to its west. Though medieval chroniclers recast the Florentine baptistery as an ancient temple to Mars to promote the concept of Florence as the new Rome, in its current form the building most likely dates from the eleventh century; it was consecrated in 1059 and received its golden-globe-surmounted lantern around 1150.[4] Like so much of Florence, San Giovanni attracted further embellishment in the decades around 1300. Its interior was sheathed in multicoloured marble inlay and glass mosaic, culminating with the complex hagiographic and eschatological mosaic cycles of the octagonal vault. In 1329 the Arte di Calimala, the guild in charge of its care, launched a campaign to replace the three sets of existing wooden doors with bronze doors bearing biblical narratives.

Partly because of its height (well over 30 metres), distinctive green-and-white-striped exterior, and pyramidal roof, the baptistery became one of the city's iconic monuments (Figures 25.1 and 25.2). The 'bel San Giovanni' is the only Florentine church Dante identifies by name in the *Commedia* (*Inf.* XIX, 16–18). Not only the poet and his ancestor Cacciaguida (*Par.* XXV, 7–9; XV, 134–35), but nearly every Florentine was baptized at San Giovanni's font until 1935, as surviving baptismal records document. Like its counterparts in other Italian cities, the Florentine baptistery performed other functions as well. These included housing military standards, war trophies, and state gifts, such as the sword of Bishop Guglielmo of Arezzo, who fought for the Ghibellines at Campaldino in 1289, and the pair of porphyry columns given to the city by Pisa in 1114. State councils were sometimes held in baptisteries; prior Dino Compagni chose San Giovanni to host the ill-fated 1299 meeting intended to reconcile the city's rival Black and White Guelf factions, perhaps because he hoped to remind participants of their common citizenship.

Just five years before, Florence's commune, bishop, and cathedral chapter had agreed to improve the environs of the episcopal complex and rebuild the cathedral on a scale and style more consonant with the city's then current status and size. Demolition to clear space for the new church had begun by June 1296, when Dante's council consented to the expansion of Piazza San Giovanni. Construction of a much larger Latin-cross basilica officially began in September 1296, under the direction of master builder Arnolfo di Cambio (c.1240/50–1302/10) and the rotating administrative leadership of the major guilds. Unremarkably for a project of this magnitude, work on the rechristened cathedral of Santa Maria del Fiore proceeded in fits and starts for the rest of the new century and accommodated major and minor alterations in design, notably changes in the number and proportions of the bays of the nave, the incorporation of nave rib vaults, and the substantial enlargement of the church's eastern end, including plans for a massive cupola with a diameter of 42 metres to surmount the crossing of the nave and transept. By the 1350s only the nave and the lower west facade facing the baptistery were well advanced; work on the east end had not yet begun.

Like most of his contemporaries, Dante attended services in the cathedral only a few times a year, on designated Christian and civic feast days. The everyday care of souls in Italy's late medieval cities was not performed by the cathedral clergy (see Chapter 6). Instead, the diocese was subdivided into a network of parishes, each with a principal church officiated by its own priests who served the population's ordinary pastoral needs. In Florence, Santa Margherita de' Cerchi (after 1032), a small, rectangular, one-room stone church tucked into a side street branching from the busy via del Corso, did double duty as the parish church of nearby families and the funerary church of the Portinari clan. Santa Margherita may have been the site of Dante's marriage to Gemma Donati, or the place where as a boy he glimpses, and falls in love with, Beatrice Portinari, as the modern plaques on the building assert, but no evidence survives to either refute or support these claims. The Alighieri family's parish church was San Martino del Vescovo, around the corner from Santa Margherita and adjacent to their homes and the Torre della Castagna.

Urban Christian institutions were not limited to those of the diocesan church. Residents encountered private oratories, collegiate churches, and hospitals all over the city, and monasteries and convents of all sizes could be found inside and outside the walls. Among these, the houses of the new mendicant orders dedicated to serving the spiritual needs of urban populations had the most dramatic impact on the shape of Italian cities at the turn of the fourteenth century. The Franciscans, Dominicans, and Servites, among other mendicant orders, challenged the regular church's monopoly over care of the city's souls. They established friaries – typically comprising a church, a cloister, and other monastic buildings – in the city's sparsely inhabited outer fringes, or even outside its walls, rather than in the crowded, expensive city centres. In the course of the thirteenth and fourteenth centuries, the friars' humble original churches were gradually replaced by vast basilicas designed to accommodate large congregations. These rivalled and sometimes exceeded the size of the cathedral, and attracted believers from parishes all over town.

Florence's Franciscan Church of Santa Croce, founded around 1294 – within a few years of the new cathedral and the new Palazzo dei Priori – is a fine example of the genre. It was built on the site of Florence's original Franciscan foundation, well to the east of the city centre in a neighbourhood populated by artisans and, especially, woolworkers – the city's largest industry. Santa Croce has a Latin cross plan; its 115-metre-long central nave is separated from the lower, groin-vaulted aisles on each side by high, pointed arcades supported by octagonal stone piers. A continuous walkway above the arcade leads the visitor's eye uninterruptedly past the site of the church's erstwhile choir screen to the high altar, which is enclosed in a polygonal apse lit by multiple stained-glass lancet windows. Many lavish, custom-decorated private funerary chapels funded by wealthy families including the Bardi and Peruzzi flank the choir and surround the projecting transept, which was completed around 1300. Though its pointed arches, stone tracery, and lofty height evoke the Gothic features also adopted by the nearly contemporary new cathedral and the Dominican church of Santa Maria Novella at the opposite edge of town, Santa Croce's nave was not vaulted. The date inscribed on its timber ceiling – 1384 – attests to the slow pace of construction, too. The large rectangular piazza that spreads in front of Santa Croce's western facade accommodated the friars' custom of preaching outdoors to crowds eager to hear the word of God in the vernacular.

Though Florence's pattern of establishing mendicant friaries on the city's outskirts is common throughout Italy (as in Parma, Bologna, and Prato, for example), variations were possible. In Verona, some of the most important mendicant establishments are at the edges, but still within, the city's fortified perimeter. The della Scala lords supported new Franciscan, Dominican, and Servite churches. Of these, the nearest to the della Scala

*Architecture and urban space* 443

signorial compound is the basilica dedicated to the Veronese Dominican martyr St Peter (d. 1252) begun in 1292 on the site of the pre-existing church of Sant'Anastasia, by whose name it is now best known. The church's construction was promoted by Cangrande, as attested by the della Scala arms frescoed on the lunette above the apse, but the courtier-condottiere Guglielmo di Castelbarco (*c*.1245–1320), who was lord in his own right of the Lagarina valley, provided most of the funding.

Sant'Anastasia, which is built from brick, has a Latin-cross basilican plan with rounded apses. Inside, along both long sides of the nave, slender cylindrical *rosso di Verona* piers surmounted by low crocket or foliate capitals support a steep pointed arcade, which separates the nave from the side aisles. Above the arcade, stone pilasters, colonnettes, diagonal ribs, and transverse arches demarcate and ornament the nave's square bays. Metal tie rods reinforce the thin walls and high vaults. Construction progressed slowly – by 1323 only the east end of the church, transept, and the first two bays of the nave had been finished. On the still incomplete facade, only the elegant splayed embrasures of its principal portal and the oculus facade above it were finished in the Middle Ages. To the facade's left, above the portal that once led into the conventual complex, a ciborium protects the sculpted *rosso di Verona* sepulchre of Guglielmo di Castelbarco (see Chapter 24, Fig. 7).

Indeed, during the thirteenth and fourteenth centuries, the friars' popularity among the urban population led to a substantial decrease in funerary bequests to the regular church. Castelbarco could have chosen to be interred in the cathedral of Trent, whose construction he had also sponsored, but he preferred to rest with Sant'Anastasia's Dominicans. When Dante died in Ravenna at the court of *signore* Guido Novello da Polenta (reign 1316–30) in 1321, Guido Novello ordered that the poet's remains be carried in a solemn funerary cortège to the convent of San Francesco, where he was buried in a stone sarcophagus placed in a small exterior chapel under the left portico of the Franciscan church.

But the new friaries, cathedrals, signorial palaces, and town halls of upper Italy did not rise in isolation. In Florence and Verona, as in many other cities, they were connected by newly paved thoroughfares, well-maintained canals, and stone bridges that improved sanitation and eased circulation through the city. Lanes were widened and straightened to accommodate increased traffic and admit more light into adjacent buildings. Privileged locations such as churchyards, piazzas, and principal streets acquired expanses of colonnaded porticos to shelter the public. New streets were built, not only through open land recently enclosed within city walls, but also – after much political manoeuvring – through dense inner city neighbourhoods, in order to facilitate access between important central locations and newly developed parts of the city. In fact, in April and May of 1301, during another term on the Council of One Hundred, Dante oversaw a project to straighten and improve via San Procolo (now via dei Pandolfini and via dell'Agnolo), the street that led eastward from the former Porta Abbatissae not far from his house towards the new walls.

Governments and religious institutions energetically undertook the development of the newly intramural areas, transforming agricultural land into residential quarters to accommodate the influx of manufacturing workers into the city. Even the ordinary housing stock improved, as masonry row houses gradually replaced fire-prone wooden ones. In Verona, Cangrande's legislation provided incentives for residents to build at a certain minimum quality. Signorial and republican governments both developed bigger administrative infrastructures to support these enhancements to the cityscape, as attested by the explosion of statutory regulation and minor offices dedicated to the establishment, maintenance, and protection of streets, porticos, piazzas, canals, mills, fountains, wells, and walls. By the middle of the fourteenth century, upper Italy's citizens so closely identified good government and a peaceful and orderly city with a well-maintained urban fabric that the concept inspired Ambrogio Lorenzetti's (*c.*1285–1348) celebrated fresco decoration of the Sala della Pace in the Palazzo Pubblico in Siena, the hall in which the city's leading Council of Nine convened (Figure 25.6). As part of an allegorical representation of good government, the room's eastern wall portrays a harmonious, densely built walled city in which a prosperous citizenry thrives – and continues to add to and improve its buildings.

However, the zeal to protect the city fabric documented by the statute books cannot conceal another notable, but harsher, aspect of Italy's architectural and urban culture – one that Dante experienced first hand. In a milieu in which individual and collective identities were intimately bound to place, banishment was one of the most feared modes of punishment. It typically took the form of the death penalty should the banished party return to the proscribed jurisdiction. Exile was often accompanied by another sanction: the confiscation, destruction (*guasto*), and dispersal of the condemned's movable and fixed property. This penalty had certain benefits for the authorities: it often resulted in the exile's financial ruin, the demolition of his house made the exile's repatriation difficult, and dispersal of his assets generated funds and materials for his accusers. For

*Architecture and urban space*

Figure 25.6 Detail, east wall fresco, Ambrogio Lorenzetti, *Effects of Good Government on the Town*. Siena, Palazzo Pubblico, Sala della Pace, 1338–39. The peaceful, well-governed city has well-maintained buildings and fortifications, as well as ongoing new construction.

example, the Florentine government allocated the materials salvaged from the demolition of the Ghibelline Uberti clan's properties in 1258 to the city's fortifications. More significantly, the practice of *guasto* constituted a kind of *damnatio memoriae*. The devastation of the buildings identified with an exile and his lineage eradicated the most visible record of their existence from the cityscape, and obliterated their memory from civic consciousness.

While some expropriations and demolitions resulted from legitimate judicial procedure, they were also used to settle personal and political vendettas. Dante's long exile from Florence began, not as the product of a formal trial but because the Black Guelfs overthrew the White Guelf regime that Dante supported while he was outside the city. During the first week of November 1301, Corso Donati and the Blacks waged a bloody campaign of terror against their political adversaries, killing many and destroying much of their property. Rather than risk his life, Dante postponed his homecoming. When Dante refused to obey the Black Guelf tribunal's summons to return to Florence for trial, he was convicted of contumacy and ultimately sentenced to death, should he ever return to the city. Although the penalties against him included expropriation and *guasto*, in fact the Black Guelfs had already laid waste to his family's property during the November rampage. One consequence of the wholesale demolitions of 1301 is that modern scholars have never been able to identify the precise location of Dante's home, which adjoined those of other

Figure 25.7 Detail, west wall fresco, Ambrogio Lorenzetti, *Effects of Bad Government on the Town*. Siena, Palazzo Pubblico, Sala della Pace, 1338–39. Ruined masonry structures and men demolishing a building characterize the badly governed city.

Alighieri family members in the vicinity of San Martino del Vescovo. (The Florentine museum known as the Casa di Dante, a neo-medieval structure built *ex novo* in 1911, is near, but almost certainly not on, the site of Dante's own house.)

A now-lost letter by Dante cited by Leonardo Bruni intimates that, later in life, the poet regretted the decision he made while prior in 1300 to banish the leaders of the White and Black Guelf factions.[5] Nonetheless, the suffering *guasti* caused him and his family did not lessen Dante's enthusiasm for that violent practice. In the Epistle to the Florentines dated 1311, Dante self-righteously augurs that the Florentines will see their buildings 'crumble beneath the battering-ram, and devoured by the flames' (*Ep.* VI, 4). The wanton dispersal of assets and degradation of the city produced by *guasti* did not find universal approbation, however. Time and again, contemporaries criticized lords and communal authorities for these destructive practices and praised them for undertaking new building projects. The badly governed city depicted on the west wall of Siena's Sala della

# Architecture and urban space

Pace is characterized not only by the violent acts of murder, robbery, and vandalism performed within its confines, but by the fact that they unfold amidst the ruins of once impressive structures (Figure 25.7).

## Notes

1 G. Biagi and G. L. Passerini, *Codice diplomatico dantesco: i documenti della vita e della famiglia di Dante Alighieri, riprodotti in fac-simile, trascritti e illustrati con note critiche, monumenti d'arte e figure,,* 3rd fascicle. (Rome: Società dantesca italiana, 1898), s.v. "1296 - v di giugno," p. 3.
2 *Ibid.*
3 D. Compagni, *Dino Compagni's Chronicle of Florence,* trans. D. E. Bornstein (Philadelphia: University of Pennsylvania Press, 1993), p. 65.
4 G. Villani, *Cronica di Giovanni Villani a miglior lezione ridotta coll'aiuto de' testi a penna,* 8 vols. (Florence: Magheri, 1823; repr. Rome: Multigrafica, 1980), I, 42, vol. I, p. 60.
5 L. Bruni, *Le vite di Dante e del Petrarca,* ed. A. Lanza (Rome: Archivio Guido Izzi, 1987), p. 36.

CHAPTER 26

# Music

*Michael Scott Cuthbert*

By the late Duecento and early Trecento, music had acquired nearly all the characteristics that we associate with the art form today. Professional musicians coexisted with amateur performers and composers. A well-established and efficient system of notation and means of transmission had been developed. Scholars had written textbooks documenting both the scientific and, to a lesser extent, the artistic fundamentals of music. Music existed to accompany, document, and amplify nearly every aspect of life, from gleeful dancing to solemn ceremony, and from sacred worship to bawdy celebration. Many uses for music and a variety of musical expressions would have been known to Dante – and indeed his writings give ample evidence of his rich learning in this art – but the specific forms of musical expression and the vocabulary used to discuss music, its composition, its study, and its performance are quite foreign today. In addition, apprehending connections between Dante and music is complex since the musical world of Italy at the time he was writing is still little understood. Most studies of Italian music or medieval music begin their focus on the peninsula only after the arrival of the Black Death towards the middle of the Trecento, up to this point centring their discussions of European music history on French traditions.

This chapter provides a background to the music and ways of conceptualizing music that would have been known towards the end of the thirteenth century and into the mid-fourteenth century. It does not focus exclusively on new compositions that were written during the lifetime of Dante and his early readers in and around Florence, but also covers the older music and older musical ideals that were still in currency in the early fourteenth century.

The most important and pervasive musical tradition was also the oldest. Plainsong, or Gregorian chant as it is called today, was a set of codified relationships between music and words sung at the daily Mass and, especially in monasteries and at large churches, at the eight other ceremonies called the hours of the Office. The musical style of plainsong varies greatly, from syllabic settings – that is, with one note per syllable – for long texts, to elaborate, melismatic settings where dozens of notes would be set to a single syllable, such as for those in the word 'Alleluia'. Many syllabic chants were sung largely on a single pitch called the reciting tone or simply *tonus*. The beginnings of chants and the most melismatic parts of chants would be sung by a single soloist or small group of soloists. Other chants, especially simpler ones, were sung by the full choir and congregation, sometimes with the singers divided into two groups that sang each line in alternation (*antiphonal* chant). Because the sheer amount of music needed for the liturgical year was so vast, tunes were often reused. Aiding in the memorization of pieces were the 'modes' into which nearly every piece was classified. This system of eight modes aided singers by giving some sense of the stock phrases that they could expect to appear in the piece, as well as the range of the piece and which notes were the most important, that is the reciting tone and the *finalis*, the note on which the piece would come to rest at or near its end. The range of the piece was described as being either in an *authentic* mode, where the *finalis* would be near the bottom of the range (think *Row, row, row your boat*), or *plagal*, where the *finalis* would be closer to the centre of the range (as in *Happy birthday*). Mode also heavily influenced one of the most important forms of plainsong: the chanting of the 150 Psalms throughout the week. Each Psalm verse ended with one of a set of stock figures determined by the mode, usually to move from the reciting tone to the *finalis*.

In addition to the largely fixed traditions of plainsong, newer sacred musical forms would have been familiar to Dante and his early readers. Although the texts of the Mass and Office were codified long before the end of the thirteenth century (though new Masses for new saints allowed for an expansion of the liturgy), there was still ample space within the Church for new musical creativity. As long as the entire text, and most of the music, was sung, there were no restrictions on additional music that could be added to a service. New verses called tropes, with original words and music, were frequently added to solemn services. Historically, the most significant type of troping was the addition of a second, then third, and sometimes fourth melody on top of the existing chant. These multipart (polyphonic) elaborations originated by the ninth century and were known in Italy by at least the early eleventh century through the writings, particularly the *Micrologus* (1025/26), of the theorist and pedagogue Guido of Arezzo (*c.*991–after 1033), who is also credited with the invention of the musical staff and the names of the notes *do* (which he called *ut*), *re, mi, fa,* and so on, which formed the first syllable of each line of the melody he wrote to the hymn *UT queant laxis, REsonare fibris, MIra gestorum …* (So that [your servants] may, with loosened voices, resound the wonders of your deeds), like a medieval 'Doe, a deer …'.

The added voice or voices in a polyphonic composition could set a single note against each note of the original chant, called the *vox principalis* or, later, *cantus firmus* or tenor (contrary to later usage, the tenor usually designated the lowest voice). This style was common in the earliest repertories throughout Europe and continued to be common in Italy in Dante's lifetime and beyond. By the end of the Duecento, however, another style came to dominate in France and was also present on the peninsula. In 'florid polyphony', the added voices set two, three, or, in the case of the earlier but still circulating compositions of Leonin (*fl. c.*1175) and Perotin (*fl. c.*1200) of Notre Dame in Paris, even up to dozens or hundreds of notes against a single note of chant. Naturally, such settings necessitated singing the original melodies much more slowly than when they were performed as monophonic plainchant.

Theoretical writings about polyphony are primarily devoted to defining the intervals – that is, the distances between pitches sounded together – to be used. The octave, or the distance of eight notes, was always allowed in polyphony, and in fact notes an octave apart are referred to by the same letter name, as in (low) C to (high) C. Musicians have traditionally counted both the first and last note when measuring intervallic distances. For instance, the distance between A and D is a fourth and not a third, since this interval involves four notes, namely, A, B, C, and D. The terminology stems from Greek definitions of intervals as counting the number of strings on a harp that need to be sounded in order to play them. This form of counting leads to counterintuitive results. For example, the interval of a third followed by another interval of a third leads to the aggregate interval of a fifth, not a sixth. The fifth was the other generally agreed-upon proper interval for polyphonic music, though its usage is less straightforward than that of the octave. Of the seven fifths that can be created with the letters A to G, six are 'perfect', that is, consonant, while the seventh fifth, from B to F, is a discordant interval ('diminished') and not to be used as a stable entity.

The person who would have understood these intervals and in particular the mathematical underpinnings of the ratios of string lengths that create them was called a 'musician' (*musicus* in Latin). The term did not mean the same thing it does today. A musician was not just a skilled singer or performer of instruments (for which the terms *cantor* or a specific name such as *tubicen* for trumpeter would have been used), nor a composer (for which no word fitting our definition was commonly used), but was applied only to one who had studied music theory in Latin and whose knowledge by the fourteenth century was increasingly backed up by a university degree. A musician knew that two strings whose lengths were in the ratio of 2 to 1 would sound tones an octave apart and those that were in the ratio of 3 to 2 would sound a perfect fifth. He also knew that the only strings whose tones would produce a consonant sonority were those in the ratios of 1:1, 2:1, 3:1, 4:1 (called multiples) or 3:2 or 4:3 (called superparticulars, that is, in the form n+1:n).

In Dante's time, interval theory was increasingly becoming divorced from compositional practice. While the octave and the fifth remained important consonances, the early Trecento marked the end of a centuries-long phasing out of the fourth as a stable consonance above or below the tenor. While it continued to be acknowledged in theoretical sources as a consonance for over a century, its function was generally being replaced by the third, though the third never appeared at the beginnings or ends of pieces or their larger subdivisions.

The rhythm of polyphonic and to some extent monophonic compositions became more codified and precise during Dante's lifetime and in the decades to follow. The earliest pieces still in circulation were written with repeating rhythmic cells such as Long (L) – Short (B = *breve*); L–B; L, or L–B–B; L–B–B; L. Theorists called these distinct patterns the rhythmic modes and most writers distinguished six of them. The lengths of individual notes were not determined by their individual shapes but rather by patterns in the number of notes grouped together in *ligatures*. For instance, the first pattern (L–B, or mode 1) was created by a group of three notes followed by consecutive groups of two. The second pattern (L–B–B, or mode 3) was created by a single note in isolation followed by groups of three. By the mid-to-late thirteenth century, a second system of rhythm came to be in use where the *shapes* of groups of notes rather than the *number* of notes in a group determined note lengths. Towards the dawning of the fourteenth century, a third system of rhythm began to emerge. In this system, as in modern music notation, the lengths of notes are generally determined by the shape of individual notes and not by their relationships to adjacent notes. The three rhythmic systems are summarized graphically in Figure 26.1. The propriety or superiority of one system over another formed a large part of the philosophical discourse on music of the time. In Italy, the strongest proponent of a new system for notation that distinguished itself throughout the fourteenth century as a national

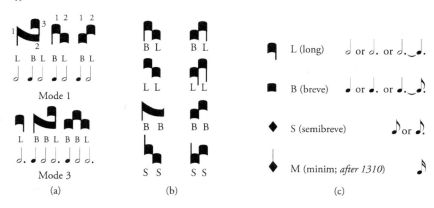

Figure 26.1 Examples of innovations in rhythmic notation arriving (a) *c.* 1200, (b) *c.* 1260, (c) *c.* 1300.

tradition separate from that emerging in France, was the composer and music theorist Marchetto of Padova (b. *c.*1275), who set forth his system in the *Pomerium* written in Naples around 1319.

These new conceptions of intervals and rhythm are found in many of the polyphonic compositions either composed on the Italian peninsula or known to have been imported. The *Ordo* (Order) of Siena (1215) prescribes polyphony for these settings, and even though the music that was sung there does not survive, it gives important information about the feasts that were considered sufficiently solemn to receive special musical treatment. Of the music that does survive from before and during Dante's life, most pieces are settings of the phrase that dismisses the Office, 'Benedicamus Domino' (Let us bless the Lord) with its response 'Deo gratias' (Thanks be to God). This liturgical expression continued to be musically important up to the end of the fourteenth century, and three-part, rhythmic settings of the piece can be found for instance in a manuscript from Perugia (Biblioteca Capitolare, MS 15).[1] A work that may be interpreted in light of the therapeutic power of music expressed in *Purgatorio* is the two-voice sequence *Hec medela corporalis* (This bodily cure) written by one Bonaiutus de Casentino (d. 1312) on the occasion of an illness of his patron, Pope Boniface VIII (b. *c.*1235; papacy 1294–1303).[2] Boniface was a collector of complex music of both Italian and French origin. French 'motets', or polyphonic pieces usually with multiple texts sung simultaneously over slow, often chant-based tenors, would have been known among the educated in Italy.

*Music* 453

The motets of the period often quoted from or were inspired by monophonic secular music with which Dante was certainly well acquainted. The main centres for secular monophony were mostly located in present-day France, separated by language – Northern French and Occitan – by region (south and north), and by chronology (the latter flourishing over half a century after the former). Although many *trouvère* (northern poet-composers) manuscripts, primarily of Artois and Picardy origins, contain musical notation, only two surviving manuscripts dedicated to Occitan troubadour lyrics contain music for the songs. One of these manuscripts was written in Lombardy. Another Italian manuscript contains troubadour songs that have been contrafacted, that is to say, they were given new lyrics in a different language. Together they suggest that there was a wide diffusion of such music in Italy in Dante's time.

Some troubadour songs also yield clues about the largely unwritten instrumental traditions of the time. Raimbaut de Vaqueiras's (*fl.* 1180–1207) *Kalenda Maya* (Calends of May), for instance, is preceded by a *razo* that explains that the song is built upon a melody, an *estampie* (stamping dance), played by two fiddlers. On the staff of Figure 26.2 is a transcription of the melody of *Kalenda Maya* along with the first verse's lyrics. The biggest difficulty in reading and performing troubadour, and most *trouvère*, song is the interpretation of rhythm. Older editions of this music, as well as many recent editions of the related Italian sacred vernacular repertory of the lauda, tend to transcribe the music as if it were written in the 'modal rhythm' of Figure 26.1(a). A transcription following this interpretation, which emphasizes the possible dance origin of the melody, is shown in the upper of the two rhythmic transcriptions in Figure 26.2. More recent scholarship, however, argues that the rhythmic notation of the manuscript does not give any hints at such a rigid framework, and that a freer interpretation, while still taking into account syllabic accent and stress, is more likely to be accurate. The lower rhythmic transcription of Figure 26.2 follows this model, taking its rhythm directly from the noteshapes of one version of the piece.

Dante's first readers would have known several secular musical styles that were only just emerging in Italy at the end of the poet's life and in the decades to come. The three main Italian poetic forms that were set musically during the Trecento were the madrigal, *caccia*, and *ballata*. Early in the Trecento, the madrigal was the most common musical form, though its influence waned as the century progressed. Most madrigals are on Arcadian themes and, with the exception of a single setting by Jacopo da Bologna (*fl.* 1340–*c.*1386) of Petrarch's (1304–74) 'Not so much

Figure 26.2 *Kalenda Maya* with two possible rhythmic interpretations.

did Diana please her lover', Italy's most esteemed poets are absent from surviving musical settings (the unrelated madrigal of the sixteenth century, by contrast, abounds in settings of Petrarch and to a lesser extent Boccaccio and Dante). The madrigal had already been described as a genre by the early fourteenth century, but is never mentioned in Dante's works. Musically, the madrigal was distinguished by two contrasting sections: a repeated section of two strophes termed the *terzetti* followed by a concluding through-composed *ritornello*. The *ritornello* was typically in a different metre from the first section; for instance, in triple time instead of duple. Most poetic lines of the madrigal had long melismas on the first and penultimate syllables, while the intervening syllables were set to a single note or few notes, sometimes in a style close to patter song. Such opening and closing melismas, though unusual to modern ears, appear in most other newly composed Italian musical forms (both sacred and secular) of the fourteenth and early fifteenth centuries, but the lengths of their melismas are rarely so pronounced as in the madrigal. Though musically madrigals can be highly ornamented, many early works actually conceal simple underlying structures, such as a series of perfect fifths in a row and the written sources may be frozen forms of styles of improvisation that are otherwise lost.

The *caccia* is a musical and poetic form for three singers similar in some ways to the madrigal but involving a hunting (or fishing, etc.) scene in dialogue with a canon (round) in the upper two voices. The second voice enters after the first voice has begun and chases it using the same musical material as the first. The *cacce* that survive with music differ from the only known description from near the time of Dante. That description states that the form has up to five singers and involves the passing of high and low material back and forth between two singers (voice exchange). This description seems closer to the type of piece found in England, exemplified by the *rota* (vocal round), 'Sumer is icumen in' (*c.*1250), which has up to four upper voices and a two-voice *pes* with voice exchange. It is probable that lost Italian pieces of the late thirteenth century were similar in construction.

Unlike the madrigal and *caccia* which began their existences as polyphonic genres, the earliest *ballate* (ballads) were monophonic pieces that relied for their musical interest on large-scale terraced descents and rhythmical flourishes. The descriptions of *ballate* singing at the end of each day of Boccaccio's (1313–75) *Decameron* probably refer to this type of *ballata*. Notably on at least three days the entire group sings with the soloist, probably on the *ripresa* (the refrain repeated between stanzas), and one day the performer is accompanied on the lute. The performance of song in the *Decameron* by women and mixed groups is also supported by evidence from other documents, as is the singing of sacred polyphony by women. (Performance of liturgical polyphony by mixed groups is less strongly attested, however.) The name of the genre and its descriptions in the *Decameron* and *De vulgari eloquentia* (II, iii, 5) all imply that the *ballata* was accompanied by dancing, but by the emergence of the polyphonic *ballata* around 1360, the connection between the two art forms was greatly weakened. (Note that the French equivalent, poetically and musically, of the Italian *ballata* is not the *ballade*, whose form is closer to that of the madrigal, but the *virelai*.)

456                    Michael Scott Cuthbert

Although purely instrumental music formed a large part of the medieval sound world, very few instrumental pieces were ever written down or survive. Thus modern performers seeking to recreate the instrumental sounds of Dante's time must extrapolate from scarce surviving examples such as the eight royal *estampies* from a single French – though possibly Neapolitan – manuscript from around 1300, the one surviving keyboard manuscript (the 'Robertsbridge codex' which was formerly thought to be an Italian source from around 1320; the manuscript's new provenance of England around 1360 gives it less authority for understanding Dante's sound world), and, as noted in the discussion of *Kalenda Maya* above, from allusions to instruments and instrumental forms in the texts of vocal pieces or in accompanying illuminations. The organ and *organetto*, an instrument played with one hand while the other worked the bellows, were common instruments in church performance. The harp, psaltery, and lute were the principal plucked strings, while the vielle (*viuola*) was the main bowed instrument. These instruments, along with recorders, were considered suitable for mixing with voices. Among the louder instruments were trumpets and horns of various types, bagpipes (*cornamuse*), loud double reeds such as shawms (*ciaramelle*), and drums such as the two-toned nakers.

As the instrumentation, tempo (speed), pitch level (key), *musica ficta* (sharps and flats), dynamics (volume), ornamentation, and vocal quality of Duecento and Trecento music was not indicated in their scores, modern recordings of the same piece can vary dramatically from ensemble to ensemble and disc to disc. Yet a neutral performance, using only the indications directly given in the manuscript, is inaccurate and impossible. Listeners are thus strongly cautioned not to take any single interpretation of a work as representing the composer's or medieval performers' actual intentions or performance practices. Although much is known and continues to be discovered about music and its performance in the time of Dante and his early readers, much more is unknown and still awaits discovery.[3]

### Notes

1 The earliest polyphonic sacred pieces from Italy, along with some later works in similar styles, are collected in facsimile in F. A. Gallo and G. Vecchi, *I più antichi monumenti sacri italiani* (Università degli studi di Bologna, 1968), and many of the pieces from Dante's lifetime are edited in modern notation in K. von Fischer and F. A. Gallo (eds.), *Italian Sacred Music*, Polyphonic Music of the Fourteenth Century (hereafter PMFC) 12 (Monaco: Editions de l'Oiseau-lyre, 1976).

*Music* 457

2 K. von Fischer and F. A. Gallo (eds.), *Italian Sacred and Ceremonial Music,* PMFC 13 (Monaco: Editions de l'Oiseau-lyre, 1987), no. 42.
3 I want to thank Lauren Jennings and Agostino Ziino for helpful comments during the writing of this chapter.

# PART V

# *Dante: life, works, and reception*

CHAPTER 27

# *Life*

## Lino Pertile

Very little is known with certainty about the life of Dante Alighieri. We do not have a single line, word, or signature written by him; nor do we have a single book or manuscript or object that belonged to him. The Casa di Dante that is shown to tourists in Florence was largely built in the early twentieth century in the area of the city where we know that the Alighieri had their houses in the thirteenth century. Archival documents concerning Dante are very rare too, except for the short period when he served in the Florentine government. Of the little we know about him, most is gleaned from indirect references scattered throughout his works, and hardly any of it is corroborated by independent sources. We must be even more cautious with Giovanni Boccaccio's (1313–75) *Life of Dante*, which is largely a fictional work, written around the middle of the fourteenth century.

### Early life

Dante Alighieri was born into a modest Guelph family under the sign of Gemini, towards the end of May 1265, in the parish of San Martino del Vescovo in Florence, between the Duomo and Piazza della Signoria. He was probably baptized with the name of Durante, which later was shortened to Dante. We know that he was the only child of Alighiero di Bellincione degli Alighieri (d. before 1283) and Bella, probably the daughter of Durante degli Abati. Dante's mother died between 1270 and 1273, and his father married Lapa di Chiarissimo Cialuffi, of a very modest background, who bore him two children, Francesco and Tana (shortened from Gaetana). Documents mention another sister, though we do not know whether she was Bella's or Lapa's daughter.

The Alighieri were minor Florentine nobility who had seen their social status and economic position considerably reduced in the course of the previous two centuries. Dante's great-great-grandfather Cacciaguida

461

(*c.*1091–*c.*1148) was knighted by Emperor Conrad III (1093–1152) and followed him to the Holy Land where he died fighting (*Par.* XV, 139–48). His immediate descendants were aristocrats who married into other families of similar social standing. However, Dante's grandfather and father clearly belong to a different, more modest social class of small businessmen and landowners. Bellincione, Dante's grandfather, was an active Guelph who was banished twice from Florence between 1248 and 1251 and again from 1260 to 1267. He was a modest businessman and money-lender, particularly active in and around Prato. His son Alighiero followed in his father's footsteps; he was an equally wise steward of the family's estate, but in politics he kept a much lower profile. This explains why, after the battle of Montaperti and the Ghibelline takeover of the city in 1260, Alighiero was not banished as most prominent Guelphs were, a circumstance that, incidentally, made it possible for his son Dante to be born in Florence. Alighiero owned the ancestral home in Florence, two good-sized farms in the Florentine territory (one in Camerata, near Fiesole, and the other in Pagnolle, near Pontassieve) and two smaller pieces of land in the parish of Sant'Ambrogio, on the outskirts of Florence. Not a large estate, but enough to feed the family all the year round and keep them warm in winter; enough also to permit the young Dante to pursue his studies, though eventually inadequate to cover the considerable expenses of his public life. There is no doubt that, while in 1100 the Alighieri were a prominent family in Florence, by 1300 they had all but lost that position and, despite their dignified past, they had been socially surpassed by the many newcomers, both noble and not, who, in the changed economic climate, had made large fortunes.

The modern reader will be struck by Dante's absolute silence about the major facts of his life. In 1277 he was betrothed to Gemma Donati (*c.*1265–*c.*1343).[1] Probably in 1285, aged twenty, he married her. During the following fifteen years the couple had three, possibly four, children whose dates of birth have always been a matter of intense speculation: Giovanni born perhaps as early as 1287 (if he ever existed), Jacopo around 1289 (d. 1348), Pietro (d. 1364) and Antonia in the late 1290s. Neither his parents, nor his wife, nor any of his children are mentioned in any of Dante's works; it is as if they never existed. The opposite is true of Beatrice, the love of Dante's life, with whom he hardly had any contact at all. If she actually existed, she is likely to have been Folco Portinari's daughter, who was born in 1266, married Simone de' Bardi in 1287, and died in 1290.

After receiving a modest secular education (see Chapter 16), Dante began to write poetry. He was hardly an adult when his father died between 1281 and 1283, and he found himself at the head of the family.

# Life 463

In 1283 he sent out the sonnet 'A ciascun'alma presa e gentil core' (To every captive soul and gentle heart) and came into contact with some of the most influential Florentine intellectuals and poets of the period, such as Brunetto Latini (*c.*1220–93) and Guido Cavalcanti (1250/59–1300). It was probably the latter, five or so years his elder and a member of one of Florence's noblest Guelph families, who offered Dante the example of a poetry worth emulating. Indeed, lyric poetry, especially love poetry, continued to occupy Dante for the next ten years, though he never stopped writing and reflecting on poetry for at least the next twenty-five or so years, until he started the great poem that would absorb him for the rest of his life, the *Commedia*. The result was an outstandingly innovative body of verse, which has come to be known as *Rime*, and which transformed the history of Italian literature.

Dante's domestic life in the 1280s must have been a considerable challenge. Having lost both his parents, he found himself in charge of a household that included his stepmother and young stepbrother and sister, and, probably from 1285, his newly-wed wife, Gemma Donati, who had not brought much of a dowry with her. As far as we know, Dante went on living in the style of a gentleman of independent means. It is assumed that neither his domestic life nor his extramarital interests kept him from pursuing his poetic training and experimentation. Some scholars believe that around 1286 he wrote the 232 sonnets of *Il fiore*, a bawdy and brilliant Tuscan adaptation of the French *Romance of the Rose*, and the 480 *settenari* of the *Detto d'Amore*. In 1287 he spent a period of up to six months in Bologna, where he came into contact with the poetry of Guido Guinizzelli (c.1230–76), whom he was later to acknowledge as the father of the *stilnovo* (new style, *Purg.* XXVI, 97–9). Two years later he served as a cavalry officer, at his own expense as was expected of Florentine noblemen, at the battle of Campaldino, in which Guelph Florence defeated Ghibelline Arezzo, and at the siege of the Pisan castle of Caprona, both episodes later remembered in the *Commedia* (respectively *Purg.* V, 91–129 and *Inf.* XXI, 94–6). Information about his life in the 1280s is very scant – enough, however, to make us suspect that he could hardly afford the lifestyle in which he lived.

In 1290 Beatrice died, a crucial event in Dante's life, which at first, as he tells us in the *Convivio*, drew him closer to his favourite studies. He read Boethius and Cicero, and their reading changed his life; he discovered Philosophy:

> Pondering these [authors], I quickly determined that Philosophy, who was the lady of these authors, sciences, and books, was a great thing. I imagined her fashioned as a gentle lady, and I could not imagine her in any attitude

464                    Lino Pertile

except one of compassion, so that the part of my mind that perceives truth
gazed on her so willingly that I could barely turn it away from her. I began
to go where she was truly revealed, namely to the schools of the religious
orders and to the disputations held by the philosophers, so that in a short
period of time, perhaps some thirty months, I began to feel her sweetness
so much that the love of her dispelled and destroyed every other thought
(*Conv.* II, xii, 4–7).

By 'the schools of the religious orders' Dante is very likely to mean the
*studia* (schools) of the Dominicans at Santa Maria Novella and of the
Franciscans at Santa Croce, where theological and moral instruction was
given (see Chapter 16); Dante may also have had access to the monastery
of the Augustinians at Santo Spirito, though very little is known about
this school. As for 'the disputations held by the philosophers', or to be
more precise, the lay intellectuals and professors who lectured in the universities, there was no institution in Florence in the 1290s where this kind
of philosophical debate took place. However, Dante may have attended
some debates in Bologna where we know that such discussions did take
place.[2]

In 1294 the young Charles Martel of Anjou (1271–95), King of Hungary,
destined to die one year later, came through Florence, and Dante met
him, perhaps in a private capacity; however, the meeting was important
enough for the poet to assign Charles a major role in the heaven of Venus
in *Paradiso* VIII.

Nothing more is known about the years 1290–95; but all circumstantial evidence indicates that in this period Dante wrote his first book, the
*Vita nova.* In ten years Dante had become a leading practitioner of Italian
poetry. The *Vita nova*, the story of his love for Beatrice, was to prove his
technical and intellectual mastery, and at the same time demonstrate that
he was far from satisfied with his achievement.


## Florentine politics

In the highly confrontational Florentine environment, Dante's position was hardly straightforward. Although he belonged to the nobility
by birth, he was too poor to be a member of the elite. To be precise, he
was not a *magnate*, that is to say a member of a wealthy aristocratic family or of a powerful family of bankers and merchants that had recently
acquired the status of *magnati* or *grandi*. So when in 1293 Giano della
Bella (*c.*1240–*c.*1305), with his anti-aristocratic *Ordinamenti di Giustizia*

_Life_ 465

(Ordinances of Justice), established a long list of families of *magnati*, both Guelph and Ghibelline, and excluded them from public office, Dante was not affected by it. However, Dante was not a *popolano* either, since, as a man of independent means, he did not work and therefore could not belong to one of the professional guilds that held sway in Florence, a condition that was essential for anyone to participate in government. In 1295, however, giving in to aristocratic pressure, the General Council of the commune of Florence made a crucial change to the *Ordinamenti di Giustizia*: noblemen were allowed access to the Priorate, the city's highest office, subject to their being registered with one of the guilds, regardless as to whether they were practising their profession or not. Dante immediately joined the Guild of Physicians and Apothecaries, probably on account of his being a scholar, and while his stepbrother Francesco took care of the ever-shrinking family estate, he became deeply involved in Florentine politics.

His progress was fast. In the following few years he held several positions of importance and was a member of councils that advised the government in significant matters. In May 1300 he attended, as Florentine ambassador, a meeting of the Whites in San Gimignano to devise a common strategy against papal expansionism in Tuscany. Indeed, even within the White faction, Dante's opposition to Pope Boniface VIII (b. *c.*1235; papacy 1294–1303) was particularly fierce. Archival records show that he was the only member of the Council of One Hundred who spoke against extending Florence's military assistance to the Pope. However, he must have had considerable support in the administration, given that he was elected to the Priorate for the period 15 June to 15 August 1300. It was a particularly troublesome moment in the conflict between the Guelph factions of the Blacks and the Whites, the former headed by Corso Donati (d. 1308), who was intransigently opposed to any popular participation in public life, the latter, with whom Dante sided, led by Vieri de' Cerchi (d. 1313), more open to cooperation with the *popolo*, which included a large part of the active population of Florence, from bankers and merchants to doctors and notaries, and shopkeepers and craftsmen. In an attempt to quell factional violence, Dante and his colleagues banished the leaders of both warring factions, including arch-enemies Corso Donati and Guido Cavalcanti – the latter was to die in exile that summer. However, this move failed to pacify the city.

In 1300 Dante is likely to have visited Rome on the occasion of the first Jubilee; the experience would explain his vivid description of the two-way traffic of pilgrims crossing Ponte Sant'Angelo, which he gives at *Inferno* XVIII, 25–33. What is certain is that Dante led a Florentine mission to Rome in October 1301 charged by the White administration with persuading Pope Boniface not to interfere in the internal affairs of the commune. The Pope, overtly delaying any decision, sent the two other ambassadors back to Florence, but kept Dante at his court. Meanwhile, in November 1301, following the Pope's request, Charles of Valois (1270–1325), brother of Philip IV (1268–1314), King of France, intervened in Florence and put the Blacks and Corso Donati back in control. It was a veritable *coup d'état*, immediately followed by the trial of the most active among the White politicians. Among them, Dante was charged with corruption and financial extortion, opposition to the Pope, and complicity in the banishment of the Blacks from Pistoia. Political trials, used by winners to settle old scores and eliminate opposition, were hardly unusual in Florence at the time. In such trials, charges of corruption and extortion were standard, and there is every reason to believe that it was so in Dante's case too. But although charges may have been trumped up, their consequences were real. On 27 January 1302 Dante was sentenced, along with four others, to a huge fine, two years of exile, and a permanent ban from public office. The sentence reached him probably in Siena, as he was on his way back from Rome. Since he refused to pay the fine within the prescribed three days, his property was confiscated and on 10 March 1302, with a group of 14 other White Guelphs, which grew to 600 by the end of the year, he was sentenced to burn at the stake, should he be apprehended by the authorities.

## Exile

Dante never returned home. It was the end of his political career and the opening of a wound that never healed. For two more years he cooperated with the White Guelfs who, formally organized in a political–military association (the *Universitas partis Alborum de Florentia*), were seeking to regain control of Florence. He was at San Godenzo, in the Mugello region north of Florence, in June 1302, at a meeting of the Whites making plans to fight the Blacks. In the autumn he followed the Whites across the Apennines to Forlì, the centre of the Romagnole Ghibellines, who were major allies of the Whites. He was probably in close contact with the Guidi family of Romena, in the Casentino region between Florence and Arezzo. In 1303 we know that he stayed for about ten months with Bartolomeo della Scala (d. 1304)

*Life*                                                                    467

in Verona, unsuccessfully seeking support for the war against the Black usurpers, but taking advantage of one of Europe's richest libraries, the Chapter Library of Verona. It was here that the idea of the *Convivio* was probably born. In this period Dante is also likely to have visited, on behalf of the Scala family, Treviso, Venice, and Padua, where he might well have met Giotto (1266–1337) then at work in the Scrovegni Chapel.

Meanwhile, the hated Pope Boniface VIII had died (11 October 1303) and his successor, Benedict XI (b. 1240; papacy 1303–04), initially raised the hopes of the Whites for peace by entrusting cardinal Niccolò da Prato (*c.*1250–1321) with mediating peace in Florence. The cardinal entered the city in March 1304. Peace seemed imminent and Dante left Verona and rejoined his fellow Whites in Arezzo. From there, although the White camp was divided, he composed, on their behalf, a conciliatory letter to cardinal Niccolò. Alas, contrary to all hopes, the operation failed. In June, inflamed by Corso Donati, the Blacks ran riot in the city. Many homes known to belong to traditionally White families were burnt and ransacked. In fear for his safety, Cardinal Niccolò himself fled Florence, and instead of peace, open war broke out between Blacks and Whites. When they finally engaged in battle, the Whites proved no more skilled at fighting than they were at negotiating peace. They were defeated at La Lastra, near Florence, on 20 July 1304. By that day Dante had already left: utterly disillusioned, he had decided to 'make a party unto himself' (*Par.* XVII, 68–9).

After 1304 few details of Dante's movements are known for certain, and these are clouded by the legends that grew across the centuries around the figure of the lonely exile. We know that Dante's finances were in a disastrous state in 1304. There is evidence that, on 13 May 1304, the poet borrowed twelve gold florins, with the assistance of his brother Francesco, from an Aretine apothecary. Towards the end of the year, in a letter of condolences to the Counts Oberto and Guido da Romena on the death of their uncle Alessandro (November 1304), he excuses himself for his absence from the funeral by referring to his poverty:

> It was neither neglect nor ingratitude which kept me away, but the unlooked-for poverty brought about by exile. Poverty, like a vindictive fury, has thrust me, deprived of horses and arms, into her prison den, where she has set herself relentlessly to keep me in durance; and though I struggle with all my strength to get free, she has hitherto prevailed against me (*Ep.* II, 3).

468 Lino Pertile

Around the same time, a few pages into the *Convivio*, he describes more fully the distressing indigence to which exile had reduced him:

> Since it was the pleasure of the citizens of the most beautiful and famous daughter of Rome, Florence, to cast me out of her sweet bosom – where I was born and bred up to the pinnacle of my life, and where, with her good will, I desire with all my heart to rest my weary mind and to complete the span of time that is given to me – I have traveled like a stranger, almost like a beggar, through virtually all the regions to which this tongue of ours extends, displaying against my will the wound of fortune for which the wounded one is often unjustly accustomed to be held accountable. Truly I have been a ship without sail or rudder, brought to different ports, inlets, and shores by the dry wind that painful poverty blows (*Conv.* I, iii, 4–5).

Dante undoubtedly travelled, seeking protection but all the while feeling the blows of solitude and poverty. Between July 1304 and early 1306 he seems to have been in Bologna, where it is reasonable to assume that he spent most of his time reading for, and writing, the *Convivio* and *De vulgari eloquentia*. Writing provided a measure of consolation, though at this stage its purpose might also have been to obtain an honourable recall back to Florence.

The quiet of Bologna did not last long. In the first months of 1306 the city turned against the White Guelfs and the Ghibellines, and Dante was obliged to leave. According to Leonardo Bruni (*c.*1370–1444), who saw a letter by Dante now lost ('Popule mee, quid feci tibi?', My people, what did I do to you?), the poet, having nowhere left to go, humbly tried to persuade Florence to revoke his banishment, but in vain. He found shelter in the mountainous region of Lunigiana, in north-west Tuscany, as a guest of Marquis Francesco (d. 1339) and Moroello Malaspina (*c.*1268–1315), a family highly praised in *Purgatorio* VIII, 121–32. Here he wrote the great allegorical lyric 'Tre donne intorno al cor mi son venute' (Three women have come round my heart, *Rime* CIV) on the theme of exile. The autobiographical segment of this *canzone* (ll. 73–107) poses significant problems of interpretation. While in lines 73–6 Dante proudly states that he counts as an honour the exile imposed on him ('l'essilio che m'è dato, onor mi tegno'), a few lines later he admits to wanting desperately to go back home, for the desire he feels to behold the fair sign ('l bel segno') – the lily of Florence perhaps or maybe a woman, his wife Gemma – is consuming him. He adds that, if he is guilty of some fault ('s'io ebbi colpa'), many months have passed since he has repented (ll. 88–90). Can this be a reference to Dante's collaboration with the Ghibellines, Florence's historic enemy? The suggestion finds support in a second *congedo*, which Dante,

*Life*                                                                    469

having previously published the *canzone*, added at a later stage – another unusual feature. Here, without renouncing his loyalty to the Whites (the 'white birds'), he asks the Blacks (the 'black hounds') to make him 'a gift of peace' (l. 104). Is this yet another attempt to persuade the Blacks that he is reformed and should be allowed to return?

In 1307 Dante moved again from Lunigiana to Casentino – we do not know exactly where. He found comfort where he could, sometimes unwittingly increasing his troubles in the process. Such is the case of a violent passion for a lady from mountainous Casentino, which is the subject of a *canzone* (known as the 'montanina', *Rime* CXVI) he sent to Moroello Malaspina in 1307. Accompanying the *canzone* is a letter (*Ep.* IV) in which Dante asks his patron and protector to forgive his negligence, for, upon arriving in the wild Arno valley, he was stricken by a merciless passion that now overwhelms him, an obsession even greater than his desire to return to Florence. Here is how the *canzone* ends:

> My mountain song, go your way. Perhaps you will see Florence, my city, that shuts me out from her, void of love and stripped of compassion. If you should enter, say: 'Now my maker can make war on you no longer: he's bound by such a chain in the place I come from that even were your harshness to relax, he is not free to return here' (76–84).

In 1308 we find Dante in Lucca, under the protection of the Malaspina. Here it is possible that his family joined him. A notarial act dated 21 October 1308 mentions a Giovanni, son of Dante Alighieri from Florence. Unfortunately it is the only mention we have of a son of Dante named Giovanni. In 1310 Dante was back in the Casentino, staying in the Castle of Poppi, a guest of Count Guido da Battifolle (1255/60–1322/23). We know very little of what he actually did as a guest of so many local lords. He probably read and discussed his poetry with them; with his presence he gave prestige to their modest courts; occasionally he acted as their envoy or letter-writer. In spring 1311 he wrote three versions of a letter (*Ep.* VIII, IX, and X – only the last was sent) to Marguerite of Brabant (d. 1311), wife of Emperor Henry VII (*c.*1275–1313), on behalf of the Countess Gherardesca, wife of Guido di Battifolle. In 1312 he was already in Verona. The suggestion that in these years he visited Paris has never been substantiated. What is remarkable is that, despite the instability of his circumstances, he found the determination necessary to begin and considerably advance the *De vulgari eloquentia*, the *Convivio*, and, probably in 1307, having interrupted and left unpublished those works, the *Commedia*.

## Henry VII's Italian campaign

In 1310, while he was in the Casentino, Dante's hopes of returning to Florence were suddenly rekindled. Henry VII of Luxembourg was on his way to Rome, invited by the Gascon Pope Clement V (*c.*1264–1314) to be crowned Holy Roman Emperor, take possession of his Italian lands, and put a stop to the peninsula's endemic factionalism. Dante's loyalty to the White cause in the 1290s and early 1300s is beyond doubt, but it seems likely that his seven-year direct experience of Italian politics persuaded him that peace could not be brought to Florence and Italy except by an external force capable of imposing it by military means, if necessary, in the name of its God-given authority. He identified this power with the Holy Roman Empire. Thus in 1310 Henry of Luxembourg came to represent for Dante the only possible solution to both the Italian crisis and his personal predicament. However, Henry was indecisive, and although such Ghibelline cities as Milan and Verona welcomed him, others, especially Florence, fiercely resisted the prospect of losing their autonomy.

Describing himself as *Florentinus exul inmeritus* (a Florentine undeservedly in exile, *Ep.* V, 1; VI, 1) and later as *Florentinus natione sed non moribus* (a Florentine by birth, but not by conduct, *Ep.* XIII, 1), Dante entered the fray by writing public letters to the princes of Italy and to the Florentines, urging them to welcome Henry as God's envoy, and to the Emperor exhorting him to strike at Florence, the heart of the enemy camp. These letters are documents of extraordinary interest, and not only as a powerful witness to the bitterness of Dante's exile. Written at a time when he was almost certainly composing the *Commedia*, they enable us to observe Dante as he engages directly with a historical situation involving Florence, the Church, and the empire. They exemplify how he responds in real life to the moral and intellectual dilemmas that he so compellingly and obsessively feeds into his poetry.

The ideas that Dante foregrounds in his letters are not substantially different from those of the *Monarchia*, the political treatise which he wrote, or began writing, in this period. Yet here Dante abandons any attempt to argue logically for the dualism of Church and empire, using instead Virgil's writings and the Bible as sacred texts for political persuasion. From the time of the struggles between Pope Gregory VII (b. 1020/25; papacy 1073–85) and Emperor Henry IV (1050–1106), the Church had been invoking the authority of the Bible against all those who, like the emperor, attempted to check its power. Now, apparently making common cause with the Spiritual Franciscans, the 'apocalyptic' agitators and other

*Life* 471

'heretical' sects (see Chapter 7), Dante turned the Bible against the official Church and its acolytes. More significantly, in doing so, he affirmed that the State was not a lay but a sacred institution, and that all history, not only biblical and Roman, was sacred history. Henry VII was a new Messiah, another Moses 'who shall deliver his people from the oppression of the Egyptians' (*Ep*. V, 4), Italy's bridegroom, 'hastening to the wedding' (*Ep*. V, 5), the rightful owner of everything on earth, 'the shepherd descended from Hector' (*Ep*. V, 17). As for Florence's resistance to the emperor, Dante identified the city that had exiled him as the root of all evil and rebellion, a new Babylon, the arrogant slave of cupidity:

> She is the viper that turns against the vitals of her own mother; she is the sick sheep that infects the flock of her lord with her contagion; she is the abandoned and unnatural Myrrha, inflamed with passion for the embraces of her father Cinyras; she is the passionate Amata, who, rejecting the fated marriage, did not shrink from claiming for herself a son-in-law whom the fates denied her, but in her madness urged him to battle, and at the last, in expiation for her evil designs, hanged herself in the noose (*Ep*. VII, 24).

Florence responded by excluding Dante from the political amnesty it promulgated in September 1311 in order to strengthen internally the anti-imperial resistance and divide externally the Ghibelline and Guelph pro-imperial alliance. While Henry hesitated, the Pope, who since 1308 had resided in Avignon (France), switched sides, allying himself with Robert of Anjou (1278–1343), King of Naples, and, predictably, with the Black Guelphs. When it finally was mounted, the siege of Florence (September 1312) was a fiasco for Henry and the imperial cause. Dante left Tuscany before it ended, and once again found refuge at the court of the della Scala in Verona, now ruled by the young Cangrande (1291–1329). The following year, the emperor died of malaria at Buonconvento, near Siena (24 August 1313). Dante was left bitterly disappointed and without a glimmer of hope for his own future return to Florence. However, his faith in the empire remained unscathed. In *Paradiso* he assigned Henry a great seat in the rose of the blessed, justifying his failure to pacify Italy with her unreadiness (*Par*. XXX, 133–8), and predicting eternal damnation for the pope who had 'betrayed' Henry (*Inf*. XIX, 82–4).

When Clement V died, in April 1314, Dante wrote yet another letter pleading for the speedy election of an Italian pope. This letter, too, was steeped in biblical allusions. It started with the opening verse of the Lamentations, which, significantly, the poet had used twenty years earlier in the *Vita nova* to describe Florence after the death of Beatrice. Now it was Rome that, like Jerusalem after her fall, sat alone, 'a widow that

472 Lino Pertile

was great among the nations' (Lam. 1, 1). Deprived of her two luminaries (both the emperor and the pope were dead, and the holy see had been transferred to Avignon), she moved to pity even the 'infidels' who believed that her fate was decreed by the heavens. On the contrary, it was the result of choices that the cardinals themselves had made out of sheer greed. 'You', Dante writes directly addressing the cardinals:

> who are as it were the centurions of the front rank of the Church militant, neglecting to guide the chariot of the Spouse of the Crucified along the track which lay before you, have gone astray from the track, no otherwise than as the false charioteer Phaëthon. And you, whose duty it was to enlighten the flock that follows you through the forest on its pilgrimage here below, have brought it along with yourselves to the verge of the precipice (*Ep.* XI, 5).

Dante concluded urging the cardinals to return to the path of righteousness and fight for the spouse of Christ, for Rome, for Italy, and for the whole world in pilgrimage on earth. But again his pleas were not heeded. The Carpentras conclave lasted two more years, and produced a new French pope, John XXII from Cahors (b. 1244; papacy 1316–34), while the papal see remained at Avignon until 1377.

## The amnesty

The period which Dante spent at the court of Cangrande della Scala between late 1312 and, probably, 1318 was the longest and quietest that he enjoyed anywhere during his twenty years of exile. Verona was the most congenial environment Dante could find in Italy, and Cangrande a staunch Ghibelline, indeed the Imperial Vicar, a title that he refused to relinquish even after Henry's death, which brought about his excommunication by Pope John XXII. This situation perhaps strengthened Dante's resolve when, in 1315, he refused to take advantage of the amnesty that Florence offered the White Guelphs in exile on condition that they paid a small fine and publicly acknowledged their guilt. Writing to a friend in Florence, who had probably worked hard to obtain his recall, the poet explained his decision in fiery words:

> This, then, is the gracious recall of Dante Alighieri to his native city, after the miseries of well nigh fifteen years of exile! This is the reward of innocence manifest to all the world, and of the sweat and toil of unremitting study! Far be it from a familiar of philosophy such a senseless act of abasement ... Far be it from the preacher of justice, after suffering wrong, to pay of his money to those that wronged him ...

*Life* 473

No! ... not by this path will I return to my native city. If some other can be found, in the first place by yourself and thereafter by others, which does not derogate from the fame and honour of Dante, that will I tread with no lagging steps. But if by no such path Florence may be entered, then will I enter Florence never. What! Can I not anywhere gaze upon the face of the sun and the stars? Can I not under any sky contemplate the most precious truths, without I first return to Florence, disgraced, nay dishonoured, in the eyes of my fellow-citizens? Assuredly bread will not fail me! (*Ep.* XII, 5–9; Toynbee, IX, 3–4).

Behind these angry words we hear the poet of justice and rectitude, the poet who, in those very same years, probably was writing his *Monarchia*, completing *Purgatorio*, and setting out on the waters 'never sailed before' (*Par.* II, 7) of *Paradiso*. How could he submit to the indignity of the Florentine 'pardon' without making a mockery of his 'sacred poem', that is, of everything he believed in and stood for? Ironically, his writing, though motivated by a desire to be recalled to Florence, ended up by becoming a new obstacle to that recall. The more Dante wrote, the more he compromised his chances of return. The poem is a declaration of militant politics, which was fatally destined *not* to resolve the conflict between Dante and his birthplace but rather to exacerbate it. Unsurprisingly, the 1315 amnesty did not change anything for Dante. The death sentence, to be carried out by decapitation, was now reconfirmed and extended to his children.

## The last years

In 1318 – though again the date and the motivation behind this move are uncertain – Dante left Verona and settled in Ravenna as a guest of Guido Novello da Polenta (d. 1330). As the law required, sons followed their fathers into exile when they reached fourteen, and so did both Jacopo and Pietro Alighieri. Traces of both of them abound in Verona, where the Alighieri enjoyed the protection of Cangrande, while we know that Dante's daughter, Antonia, became a nun in Ravenna and took the name of Sister Beatrice (she died fifty years after her father, on 21 November 1371). The only document attesting to Giovanni's existence places him in Lucca in 1308, where Dante could have been at the time. Giovanni then, if he is indeed Dante's son, would have been the first to be banished as a consequence of his father's exile. The children were allowed to return to Florence after their father's death. Jacopo returned in 1322 and lived there until his death around 1348; Pietro, after returning in 1323, refused

474 Lino Pertile

to abide by the conditions set for his stay in Florence, and, after a period spent in Bologna studying civil law, he settled in Verona where he died on 21 April 1364. We do not know whether Gemma followed Dante into exile, but it is possible that she stayed behind in Florence. She might well have spent time with her husband especially during the first ten or so years of his exile, which he largely spent in Tuscany. Also, as Antonia appears to be in Ravenna in the late 1310s, it is reasonable to suppose that Gemma was there too.

In Ravenna Dante completed *Paradiso*. Between 1319 and 1320 he wrote two other new works: two Latin *Egloge* in which he politely refuses the invitation, extended to him by the Bolognese professor of rhetoric Giovanni del Virgilio (late thirteenth century–*c*.1327), to seek glory in Latin poetry and leave Ravenna for Bologna; and a short scientific treatise in Latin, the *Questio de situ et forma aque et terre*, which he gave as a lecture on 20 January 1320 during a brief visit to Verona. It is probably at this time that Dante wrote a letter, if it is indeed by him, in which he dedicates *Paradiso* to Cangrande, and offers an introduction to the poem as a whole, whose authenticity and critical merits still continue to divide the opinions of Dante scholars all over the world.

In 1321 Dante went on a mission to Venice on behalf of Guido Novello, charged with the task of negotiating a reduction of hostilities between the Serenissima and Ravenna. On his way back, he caught malaria, just like his friend Cavalcanti and his Emperor Henry, and he died on the night between 13 and 14 September 1321 in Ravenna, where he was honourably buried in the Church of San Pier Maggiore, later known as San Francesco.

## Notes

1 In an essay published online as we brought this volume to completion, Isabelle Chabot argues very persuasively that 9 February 1277 was, in fact, the date of Dante's and Gemma's actual marriage, not just of their contract to marry. However, as Dr Chabot explains, a marriage at twelve was extremely unusual for a boy at the time, and in the case of the Alighieri and Donati families there seem to be no circumstances that can help explain it. See Isabelle Chabot, 'Il matrimonio di Dante', *Reti Medievali Rivista*, 15/ii (2014), issue ed. G. Milani and A. Montefusco: http//rivista.retimedievali.it. The issue contains several excellent and original articles on the background to various matters relating to Dante's life.

2 See the footnote to *Convivio* II, xii, 7 by its editor Gianfranco Fioravanti, in Dante, *Opere*, ed. M. Santagata (Milan: Mondadori, 2014), vol. II, pp. 302–4.

CHAPTER 28

# *Works*

## *Lino Pertile*

Dante did not have an easy life. The loss of his mother when he was still a child, and of his father ten years later, which compelled him to take charge of his family when he was barely eighteen; his early, prearranged marriage, admittedly not unusual at the time; the addition of his three or four children to a household that could only count on a modest income; the death of Beatrice in 1290, and that of Guido Cavalcanti (b. 1250/59) ten years later in circumstances for which Dante could feel partly responsible; the bitter disappointment of his political career in Florence; the unspeakable offence of the trial in absentia, and the wound of the capital sentence, extended eventually to his children; the twenty years of exile, spent wandering from court to court without a permanent home for himself and his wife and children; finally, his own death of malaria when he was fifty-six (not young for the fourteenth century, but not old either): this definitely looks like a difficult life. What is astonishing is that, despite the many obstacles, Dante was able to write a body of work that placed him permanently at the forefront not only of Italian literature, but also of Italian language and philosophical studies. There is no doubt that the difficulties he encountered in life stimulated his work as a writer; indeed it can be argued that we owe his masterpiece, the *Commedia*, to his experiences as a politician and his exile. Dante's writing is quintessentially autobiographical, which is not all that unusual in the Trecento. What distinguishes Dante's work is the way in which historical events, poetic autobiography, and reflection on poetry are inextricably interwoven in it. From its very inception, Dante's poetry appears to be a self-conscious elaboration of personal experiences, where the lines between dreams, imaginings, and real events are blurred and crossed. This procedure was conventional among Dante's circle of friends and correspondents; however, the coherence and originality with which he developed it made him unique. Its first, but already mature and refined, result is the *Vita nova*, probably begun in 1292 but certainly written after Beatrice's death in 1290, and before 1295.

476 Lino Pertile

## *Rime*

Dante's lyric production spans twenty-five years, from the early 1280s to 1306–07, when he began to compose his major poem. This production, excluding the poems that he used for the *Vita nova*, makes up what is traditionally known as his *Rime* (Rhymes), his collected verse as arranged posthumously and variously by successive generations of editors. As a consequence, one of the major problems concerning the *Rime* is their chronological ordering; what is beyond dispute is the extraordinary richness of their form and subject-matter.

The first lyrics are in the styles also exemplified in the *Vita nova*, but they include poems dedicated to women other than Beatrice, such as a Fioretta and a Lisetta; and poems, such as 'Guido, I wish that you and Lapo and I', that capture, as a pendant of courtly love and ideals, the exclusive atmosphere of intellectual refinement and male friendship typical of Florentine *stilnovo*, 'new style'.

Yet the influence of Cavalcanti at his most dark and sorrowful is plainly visible in a *canzone* such as 'I pity myself so intensely', which records the destructive power of a fierce lady, perhaps Beatrice herself; or in another early *canzone*, 'The sorrowful love that leads me', where Beatrice – now mentioned explicitly – is the merciless harbinger of death, as in the best Occitan and courtly tradition. It is only when we compare these poems with those in praise of Beatrice included in the *Vita nova* that we begin to appreciate the ideological significance of the poet's selection for the little book and the chasm that this opened between him and Guido Cavalcanti.

What distinguishes Dante's lyric production after the *Vita nova* is, together with its variety and experimentation, a move towards more complex forms and increasingly demanding subject-matter. This is particularly noticeable in the poems he composed after his exile from Florence, which we shall consider below.

Meanwhile, as a direct result of the philosophical studies he undertook after the death of Beatrice, Dante composed throughout the 1290s a series of poems in which philosophical and theological subjects were articulated in the language of love poetry. Among these poems are the first two canzoni on which Dante comments in detail in the *Convivio*: 'O you who move the third heaven by intellection', and 'Love, speaking fervently in my mind'. The lady who inspired them was possibly a real woman, perhaps the 'gentle and compassionate lady' of the *Vita nova*, but in the *Convivio* Dante identifies her allegorically as Lady Philosophy. The critical problem is whether the allegorical meanings that Dante attributes to these poems were originally present (as he would have us believe), or whether they were written into them retrospectively when he wrote the *Convivio*. The difference between the two hypotheses is substantial: in the first case the feminine object of his lyrics is a symbol of Dante's emotional life; in the second, that same feminine object is a symbol of his philosophical fervour and of the moral virtues he aims to pursue by means of his rational faculties. The question is a thorny one and remains largely unresolved.

During the same period the poet was also experimenting in other directions. 'The sweet love-poetry I was accustomed', the third great *canzone* on which Dante would comment in the *Convivio*, marks a turning point in his poetics. No longer focusing on love in the 'sweet new style', the *canzone* discusses the nature of nobility in the manner of a philosophical treatise. Nobility had been oft-debated in antiquity and the Middle Ages; Guittone d'Arezzo (*c.*1235–94) had devoted to it his *planh* (lament) for Giacomo da Leona, 'A shared loss is a shared sorrow'. More recently in Florence, it had become a very controversial topic, and a reason for political strife, as the anti-aristocratic *Ordinances of Justice* were introduced and modified (see Chapter 27). Now Dante takes on the role of poet of righteousness to argue in hard and difficult rhymes that true nobility is neither inherited nor bought: it is a function of the moral virtues that an individual possesses and practices.

Possibly at the other end of the spectrum, the *tenzone* (poetic exchange) with Forese Donati – a friend of Dante's who died in 1296 – is an exchange of sonnets so scurrilous, base, and harsh that they can hardly be accommodated even within the conventions of the burlesque genre; indeed their paternity is keenly contested. Significantly, Dante would later remember this episode with regret (*Purg.* XXIII, 115–7).

Another group of lyrics articulates the theme of love not as a beneficent, saving force, but as a disturbing, invincible reality. For instance, even though she comes from Heaven, love does not touch the young girl of the ballad 'I am a young girl, lovely and marvellous'. Much more hard-hearted and insensitive, the *donna petra* (stony lady) of the *rime petrose* (stony poems) pushes the poet to experiment in the difficult style, hitherto untried in Italian, of Occitan poet Arnaut Daniel (*fl.* 1180–1200). The *canzone* 'I want to be as harsh in my speech' is shocking for the harshness of its sounds and the violence of its imagery; it is a style to which the poet would return, especially in *Inferno*.

During the first years of his exile, Dante also composed some important lyrics characterized by a strong moral content. The language remains that of love poetry, but is now used to convey the poet's ideals of public justice and morality. Dante presents himself as the poet of rectitude, contrasting his own scornful solitude with the disorder, violence, and corruption that prevail in society. In 'Three women have come round my heart' – a *canzone* that was to be commented on in the last, never written, treatise of the *Convivio* – the three women personifying divine justice, human justice, and the law are exiled from a world that has banned all virtue, and the poet, listening to their 'divine speech', 'counts as an honour the exile imposed on him' (76). Clearly, Dante begins here to view his personal predicament as both emblematic and symptomatic of a universal crisis affecting the whole world.

Most editions of the *Rime* include an appendix of poems (sixteen in the De Robertis edition) whose attribution to Dante is considered doubtful. This is an unstable category, as ongoing research can occasionally prove that a poem is undoubtedly authentic. See the case of *Aï faus ris* (Ah, false smile), a famous trilingual (French, Latin, and Italian) *canzone* traditionally considered doubtful, which has recently joined the corpus of Dante's lyric poetry.

### *Fiore*

Published for the first time in 1881 by the French scholar Ferdinand Castets, who discovered it in the library of the École de Médecine, Montpellier, in a manuscript (H 438) containing the *Romance of the Rose*, the *Fiore* is a summary of the *Romance* in 232 sonnets, written perhaps between 1285 and 1290 in a Tuscan vernacular with conspicuous and widespread French borrowings, which partly translate and partly rewrite the French text. Originally anonymous and untitled, the work was called *Il Fiore* (The Flower) by its first editor. The author focuses on the plot, leaving out the long, learned digressions of the French original but attacking the mendicant orders with gusto. The narrative tells the story of the Lover's quest for the 'flower' – a transparent allegory for the female sex, a quest that, aided by the Lover's allies (Venus, Boldness, etc.) and advisor (Friend), resisted by Reason, and impeded by the defenders of the flower (Shame, Fear, Chastity, etc.), ends with the violent storming of the fortress where the flower is kept. Among the longest and most memorable speeches, are those by the cynical Old Woman, who teaches the heroine Fair Welcome how to take advantage of the Lover's folly, by Friend who advises the Lover on the best strategy to conquer the object of his desire, and by False Seeming, the hypocrite who puts forward the viewpoint of the mendicant friars, revealing all their greed.

The paternity of the work was hotly debated from the time of its first appearance, and many names have been suggested as possible authors from Dante da Maiano (late thirteenth century) to Folgore da San Gimignano (before 1280–before 1332), Brunetto Latini (*c.*1220–93), Guillaume Durand (*c.*1230–96), and Cecco Angiolieri (*c.*1260–1311/13). The thesis of Dante's authorship found significant following when it was championed by the eminent Italian philologist Gianfranco Contini. On the basis of considerable linguistic, stylistic, and conceptual resonances with Dante's other works, Contini deemed the work 'attributable' to Dante, and edited and published it as such in 1984 together with the *Detto d'Amore*. Such caution appears to be abandoned in some of the successive editions, which drop altogether Contini's 'attribuibile'. The debate shows no sign of ending, and while the Società Dantesca Italiana, boldly and without qualification, places the *Fiore* under Dante's name, another major edition of Dante's complete works includes it in a volume devoted to 'works of doubtful attribution',[1] and a recent re-examination of the controversy comes down squarely against Dante's authorship.[2]

### Detto d'Amore

Published for the first time in 1888 by Salomone Morpurgo, who found it on four sheets of the manuscript Laurenziano-Ashburniano 1234 of the Biblioteca Laurenziana of Florence, the *Detto d'Amore* (Love's Tale) is a vernacular poem in 480 verses of seven syllables (*settenari*). As the handwriting, the paper, and the style of production is the same as for the *Fiore*, it is safe to assume that it originally belonged to the Montpellier manuscript H 438, and that at a certain point it became separated from it. The poem, which appears to be incomplete and was entitled *Detto d'Amore* by its first editor, is a debate between the Poet, who sings the praises of Love, and Reason, who invites him to be cautious and place his trust on more lasting and reliable goods. Circumstantial evidence locates its composition in Tuscany around 1286–87. The author, who is most likely to be the same as for the *Fiore*, shows familiarity with the Italian lyric tradition from the Sicilian poets to Guittone d'Arezzo and, interestingly, Brunetto Latini.

### Vita Nova

The *Vita nova* (New Life) is a *libello* (little book) in which Dante transcribes from 'the book of *his* memory' the story of his love for Beatrice.

The nature of the project is eminently literary. The poet-protagonist selects thirty-one poems (twenty-five sonnets, five canzoni, and one ballad) out of all those he has written in the previous ten or so years, and sets them within the frame of a prose commentary. This alternation of poetry and prose (*prosimetron*) had influential models, notably Boethius' *Consolation of Philosophy*, the Occitan *razos*, Brunetto Latini's commentary on Cicero's *De inventione* (On Invention), and the glossed manuscripts of the Song of Songs, as well as of classical poets, especially Ovid. Dante's anthology aims to be both a sophisticated autobiography and a treatise on poetry: the exemplary story of a spiritual education coinciding with the development of a poetic career. As such it was not, and could not be, intended for the ordinary reader, but for a select circle of fellow-poets who would be able to understand its complex nature. Among these was Guido Cavalcanti, Dante's 'first friend', who had advised him to write his commentary in Italian rather than Latin. Having been in existence for about one-and-a-half centuries, Italian poetry had developed rules and conventions; but an Italian literary prose scarcely existed.

Taken by themselves, the lyrics of the *Vita nova*, at least up to the crucial chapter XIX, can be viewed as exercises and experiments in the disparate literary traditions of love poetry prevalent at the time of their composition; they are mainly in the courtly style of the Sicilian school and of Guittone d'Arezzo, or they are inspired by the more recent *stilnovo* examples of Guido Guinizzelli (*c.*1230–1276) and Cavalcanti. However, from the outset of the *libello*, Dante's prose-narrative anchors them firmly to the figure of Beatrice, investing them with much more significance than they originally had. The self-commentary brings to the surface the secret order, the meanings, and the inner connections intuited by the poet when he started writing; revealing the universal, exemplary value of an otherwise fragmented itinerary, it gives the *libello* a coherent, unified and progressive structure that the actual experiences, if and when they occurred, did not have. The *Vita nova* thus bears witness to that 'editing' of the self that was to become one of Dante's obsessions.

The agent inspiring Dante's revisitation and revision of his own past is, simply, Beatrice. It is impossible to establish the extent to which this figure corresponds to the real Bice de' Bardi. For, paradoxically, although the *Vita nova* suggests that she is a real woman, Beatrice hardly has any life outside Dante's mind. Her effects on him are physical enough: she makes him sigh, tremble, weep; she overwhelms him. Yet she has neither body nor character of her own; she is a vision, an angel, a divine messenger. Dante does not even try to approach or speak to her; indeed, as the story develops, he becomes incapable of withstanding her presence or her gaze. Once ignited, his passion is totally internalized; it is a desire that feeds on itself, a desire of desire.

These are not unusual ingredients in the theory and practice of courtly love poetry. However, the myth of Beatrice rests on original elements that Dante drew from another, indigenous and exceptionally rich source: the 'popular', hagiographic tradition that, itself feeding on a vast body of writings surrounding the Song of Songs, created the lives of the saints. The contemplative atmosphere of miracles and revelations, of dreams and ecstasies, of visions and prophecies that pervades the *Vita nova*; the structure, fabric, and rhythm of its prose narrative; its allusions to biblical language and the liturgy of the Church: all this is a personal, exquisitely literary elaboration – it is impossible to determine whether religious or aesthetic – of oral and written, 'low-brow' material that was circulating in central Italy towards the end of the thirteenth century. The transformation of Beatrice from courtly lady to saint represents the most mature literary fruit of this relatively humble tradition, just as the Madonnas of the Italian churches of the time are its first artistic expression.

The *Vita nova* is not a story of events and characters, but of gazes from afar, desires, imaginings, and dreams. Dante is nine years old when he first sets eyes on Beatrice; the second time he sees her he is eighteen. These numerical correspondences emphasize Beatrice's providential role in the renewal of Dante's life. She enters into it as a divine agent whose greeting causes the poet to feel at once profound joy and unbearable anguish. When she later refuses him her greeting, he decides he will place all his hopes of future happiness in words of praise for her, something that cannot fail him. At first, however, this theme proves too lofty for his writing, until one day his tongue speaks 'almost as if it moved of its own accord', and he begins:

> Women who understand the truth of love,
> I want to talk with you a while about
> my lady – not because I could run out
> of words and ways to praise her, but to set
> my mind at ease.

This (chapter XIX) is the heart of the *Vita nova* and the start of its most original section. From now on, the poet is driven by a superior force to sing the praises of his lady while expecting nothing in return from her: *Donne ch'avete intelletto d'amore* is the *canzone*-manifesto of this new style. Gone is Cavalcanti's idea of love as a disruptive, negative power that Dante had espoused at the beginning of his *libello*. Even Guinizzelli's vision of the lady as beatifier is surpassed. Now Beatrice is a manifest 'miracle'; she is 'gentleness' and 'grace' personified, the source of every 'salvation'; her beauty delivers the world from everything negative and unworthy; in short, she is a saint, a mirror of Christ.

But the signs of her imminent death are by now unmistakable. Her father dies, then the poet is struck for nine days by a painful sickness. On the ninth day he has a vision in which his own death is announced, and that of his lady too, at which, as at Christ's death, the sun grows dark, airborne birds fall down dead, and the earth trembles violently. Soon afterwards Beatrice actually dies, summoned to Heaven by God himself. The *libello* has become, paradoxically, the story not of the conjoining of two lovers, but of their progressive parting. Beatrice's death, after the withdrawal of her greeting and presence, is the indispensable step in Dante's sublimation of his love for her; by making even her body redundant, the poet establishes the ultimate autonomy of his love.

Dante mourns Beatrice's departure for a year. Then, as one day his thoughts are full of sorrow, he sees 'a gentle lady', young and very beautiful, who is looking at him from a window so compassionately that pity seems to be epitomized in her appearance. A conflict develops within the poet's mind between the memory of Beatrice and the feelings the gentle lady inspires in him, until one day Beatrice reappears to him as young as when he first saw her and clothed in the same crimson garments. Overcome by bitter remorse, the poet recognizes the vanity of every consolation that does not stem from the memory of his beloved. His thought becomes a 'sigh', a 'pilgrim-spirit' that longs to be reunited with her 'Beyond the sphere that turns the widest gyre'. This is the last poem of the *Vita nova*. There follows a mysterious, 'marvellous vision' in which the poet sees 'things' that make him decide to write no more of the blessed Beatrice until he can do so more worthily:

> To achieve this I am doing all that I can, as surely she knows. So that, if it be pleasing to Him who is that for which all things live, and if my life is long enough, I hope to say things about her that have never been said about any woman.
> Then, if it be pleasing to Him who is the Lord of benevolence and grace, may my soul go to contemplate the glory of its lady – that blessed Beatrice, who gazes in glory into the face of Him *qui est per omnia secula benedictus* [who is blessed forever and ever] (XLII, 2–3).

What is the meaning of this ending, which promises, or rather searches for, a new beginning? Had Dante not written the *Commedia*, it could be read as a sublime *praeteritio* – after all, the *Vita nova* had gone so far as to speak of Beatrice in terms that had never been applied to any woman. But the fact that Dante did write the *Commedia* makes the temptation to link the end of the *libello* with the beginning of the 'sacred poem' almost irresistible, even if nothing else in either text justifies such speculation, except the finale of the *Vita nova*. The question must be: was that 'marvellous vision' already present in the original *libello,* or was it added later by the poet, when the idea of the *Commedia* took shape in his mind, in order to connect, through the name of Beatrice, his first and his last book, even if at the expense of all he wrote in between?

Be this as it may, the conclusion of the *Vita nova* forces us to assume that at a certain point Dante began to see 'things' for which his old poetics were inadequate. Thus the *Vita nova* marks the triumph and, simultaneously, uncovers the limitations of the *stilnovo*. When some fifteen years later he publicly resumes his writing for Beatrice, Dante does so on the basis of a much wider and more ambitious perspective.

### *Convivio*

Seen retrospectively from the vantage point of the *Commedia*, the *Convivio* (Banquet) and the *De vulgari eloquentia* inevitably appear as 'minor' works that record Dante's efforts to 'find himself' during the transitional years following his exile from Florence in 1302. But such a view ignores the fact that with these works Dante intended to assert his authority far beyond the field of love poetry, and that, even in their unfinished form, nothing quite like them exists in any European language at the beginning of the fourteenth century. What, therefore, may seem like a slow and hesitant transition was in fact a period of intense activity and of rapid, almost irresistible, intellectual evolution.

After his recent traumatic experience, Dante was radically reviewing his past, seeking to restore his battered self-confidence and reputation, and to find new and more solid ground upon which to base his future. In this enterprise he was aided by his extraordinary ability to absorb and synthesize all forms of knowledge, transforming these into new, personal, and coherent ideas. Besides Cicero and Boethius, he read St Augustine's *Confessions* and probably reread Virgil's *Aeneid,* as well as other major classical authors, but now with a new sense of purpose. He studied the scholastic philosophy and theology of Thomas Aquinas (1225–74), Albert the Great (before 1200–80), and St Bonaventure (1221–74), but also the scriptural commentators, the contemplatives, and, perhaps, such

## Lino Pertile

heterodox thinkers as Siger of Brabant (*c.*1240–*c.*1284) and the speculative grammarians.

When he undertook his two projects, in all likelihood in 1303–06 between Verona and Bologna, Dante consciously aimed as high as he could: the *Convivio* was to bring his philosophical canzoni within reach of a wide Italian audience and at the same time establish their canonical standing; the *De vulgari* was to demonstrate in Latin the formal dignity of his vernacular poetry in the context of a universal theory and history of language and literature. Dante hoped that works of such significance would compel Florence to recognize his merits and revoke his exile.

Like the *Vita nova*, the *Convivio* is a retrospective self-commentary, but its stake is now the status and value of Dante's poetry as purveyor of philosophical truths. There are other, equally substantive differences. The 'gentle lady' of the *Vita nova* now becomes Lady Philosophy, and in this guise she replaces Beatrice as the force that motivates the poet's new quest. Dante no longer addresses himself to a small circle of 'Love's faithful servants', but to all who seek knowledge. This is why he writes in the vernacular. His *Convivio* will literally be a 'banquet' in which the food of knowledge will be offered to all.

The project was extremely ambitious. As an Italian encyclopedia, the fifteen treatises of the *Convivio* were intended to bridge the enormous gulf between academic and 'popular' culture. The first treatise was to serve as a general introduction; the following fourteen were to be critical commentaries on the same number of philosophical canzoni. In the event, only four books were completed, the introductory one plus three commentaries on three canzoni written in the 1290s.

The four treatises contain a vast array of topics whose relevance to the text of the poems is often only superficial. In the first book, Dante's defence of his poetry and of himself as 'undeserved exile', and his praise of the goodness and power of the Italian vernacular, produce pages of remarkable intensity and resonance. In the second book, devoted to the *canzone* 'You whose intellect the third sphere moves', angels and heavens are the protagonists. Caught between his love for Beatrice and that for another lady, Dante turns for consolation to the angels of the third heaven. Each heaven is moved by a different order of angels who draw their power from God; at the same time each heaven is associated with a different branch of learning: the Moon is moved by the Angels and is like grammar; Mercury is moved by Archangels and is like dialectic; Venus is moved by Thrones and is like rhetoric. The book ends with a revelation: the lady at the centre of the *canzone* Dante has been commenting on is 'the daughter of God, queen of all things, most noble and beautiful Philosophy' (II, xii, 9). The following book – a commentary on 'Love, speaking fervently in my mind' – is all about Lady Philosophy as a model of beauty and destroyer of vice. Philosophy for Dante is both quest for knowledge and love of wisdom: it is the 'loving use of the wisdom' (III, xii, 12) that exists in supreme measure in God. The book ends with a hymn to the wisdom that was with God when He created the universe: 'O worse than dead are you who flee her friendship! Open your eyes and gaze forth! For she loved you before you existed, preparing and ordering your coming' (III, xv, 17). The fourth book – on 'The sweet love poetry I was accustomed' – is the longest and in many respects the most accessible, for its ethical and political content makes it feel very relevant to our own concerns. The general topic is nobility, but in connection to this Dante discusses the necessity of the empire in order to achieve happiness on earth; he inveighs against riches, be they inherited or acquired by legal or illegal means; he distinguishes two kinds of happiness on earth, corresponding to active and contemplative life; he refines his definition of nobility as a divine gift made to the individual not on families; finally, he maps out the four stages of human life and explains how each one is enriched and illumined by nobility. What constantly fires Dante's enthusiasm throughout the four books, often producing significant digressions, is his desire to communicate knowledge, to convey to all his faith in reason and human intelligence.

The *Convivio* proves the depth and range of Dante's familiarity with the main currents of thought in thirteenth-century Europe. Central to philosophical debate in the universities was the question – which had endless ramifications in all human sciences – of how to reconcile Aristotelian authority with biblical doctrine: in other terms, how to reconcile philosophy with theology, and reason with Revelation. Different thinkers offered different solutions. Recognizing and simultaneously undermining canonical authority, Dante eclectically echoes now Thomas Aquinas, now Albert the Great, and now even the current to which his friend Cavalcanti had subscribed, and which was later to be called 'Averroism'. His observations range from literary criticism to ethics, metaphysics, cosmology, and politics. The *Convivio* is a work that bursts with ideas, but ideas still in a state of flux, confusion, and even contradiction: this is both its strength and its weakness. What Dante fails to resolve is the tension he set out to overcome for himself and his potential readers, between a rational, humanist, Aristotelian world-view and an idealist, Christian, Neoplatonist one.

The *Convivio* fully reflects the richness and complexity of Dante's intellectual quest in the early years of his exile. In terms of language and style,

486 Lino Pertile

it is a veritable tour de force, proving that one could treat in Italian, effectively and elegantly, even the most arduous philosophical subjects traditionally believed to be the preserve of Latin.

## *De vulgari eloquentia*

The digression on the vernacular in the first treatise of the *Convivio* was developed, probably in 1304–06 in Bologna, into the *De vulgari eloquentia* (On Vernacular Eloquence), a thoroughly original work, planned to include at least four books and to deal with the origins and history of language, and the complete range of styles and forms used in vernacular literature. To convince even the most conservative among the literati of the worth of the vernacular and, at the same time, to pay this the ultimate accolade, the analysis is conducted in Latin. The treatise remained unfinished and unpublished, probably overshadowed, like the *Convivio*, by the dawning of the *Commedia*. Nevertheless, it is of fundamental importance both for the history of the 'questione della lingua' (the debate on which form of vernacular was to be adopted as the national written language, which resurfaced particularly in the sixteenth and nineteenth centuries in Italy), and for what it reveals of Dante's perspectives on language and style.

The first book begins, astonishingly and provocatively, by asserting the superiority of the vernacular over Latin (known also as *gramatica*). To justify his radically unconventional view – the opposite of what he had stated in the *Convivio* – Dante traces a brief history of language from the first word ever spoken by Adam (rather than by Eve, as the Bible states) to the building of the Tower of Babel and the ensuing gradual division, subdivision, and, finally, atomization of idioms that characterize present usage. Dante shows an unprecedented grasp of the historical character of language as a living organism in continuous evolution through time and space. Of the three closely related languages derived from Latin in southern Europe (the languages of *oc* [Occitan], *oïl* [Old French], and *sì* [Italian], the language of *sì* presents the greatest variety. However, none of its many (at least fourteen) dialects is in itself dignified enough to become the literary language of Italy. Such a language already exists, not as an immanent presence but as a transcendent paradigm to which the best Italian poets strive to conform. It is the 'illustrious vernacular', a literary language free from, and superior to, all provincialisms, and already as fixed as Latin within the ever-changing flux of local idioms: effectively, a new *gramatica*.

The second book is Dante's 'art of poetry'. The illustrious vernacular, he writes, is not simply form, but the only language capable of reflecting the writer's moral and intellectual personality. Therefore, it is suitable only for the most excellent poets seeking to express the noblest subjects: arms, love, and rectitude. As to metrical forms, the highest and most convenient for such lofty subjects, and especially for rectitude, is the *canzone*. The illustrious vernacular and the *canzone* are essential components of the superior 'tragic' style.

The major logical contradiction of the *De vulgari* lies in its presentation of the illustrious vernacular as both a historical reality and a transcendent ideal. In his search for a morally and expressively mature model of vernacular eloquence, Dante is obliged to repudiate the spoken language in favour of the literary variety employed by the few writers – namely, the Sicilians and the *stilnovisti*, himself included – who had excelled in the 'high' style. He is seeking one integrated solution to two discrete orders of problems – historical and eschatological – concerning the phenomenon of language. More specifically, Dante interprets the episode of Babel as the crucial second Fall through which humanity irreparably lost its linguistic paradise. After Babel, all the vernaculars became themselves fallen, corrupt, and incapable of fulfilling the primary function of language – universal communication. *Gramatica*, first as Latin and now as illustrious vernacular, represents the only morally valid response to post-Babelic confusion: an attempt to move back from fragmentation to unity, from the hell of individuality and incommunicability to the paradise of universality and communion. Although intellectually exciting and morally uplifting, this idea was a linguistic dead-end.

The *De vulgari* was interrupted in mid-sentence. More significantly, the illustrious vernacular and the tragic style turned out to be totally inadequate when Dante set out to write his poem of salvation. It is an instance, one of many, of how Dante's mind was always ahead of his own experimentation – at least until he successfully attempted that all-inclusive enterprise towards which all his experiments tended, and beyond which no further experiment was possible or necessary.

The *Convivio* and the *De vulgari eloquentia* contain a store of information of the utmost importance for our understanding of Dante's intellectual evolution. Yet they are works that Dante never completed, revised, or published. In Dante's mind, they may well have been entirely superseded by the *Commedia* in which we find them substantially and repeatedly contradicted. The great poem was like an earthquake in Dante's life. It caused his own final revision of his past: principally, the rejection of the double

488        Lino Pertile

project *Convivio/De vulgari*, and possibly the writing of a new ending for the *Vita nova*. The cluster of critical problems surrounding the sequence *Vita nova–Convivio/De vulgari–Commedia* is likely to be the result of Dante's attempt to rewrite his past in order to endow his public image with a unified sense of purpose, a teleology that would demonstrate the extraordinary nature of his artistic calling.

## *Monarchia*

The relationship between Church and empire was a major problem in Italian and European history, and one very acutely felt from the eleventh century onwards (see Chapters 1 and 3). Although it gave rise to many polemical tracts, the question was far from academic, having often involved the two institutions, more or less directly, in open warfare. In the overlapping of temporal and spiritual powers Dante saw one of the principal roots of the social and moral degeneration that afflicted contemporary life. He keenly opposed the Church's holding or exercising any temporal power – something that had become prevalent, especially after the death of Emperor Frederick II (b. 1194) in 1250. It is for this reason that he took the side of the White Guelphs against the interference of Pope Boniface VIII (b. *c.*1235; papacy 1294–1303).

Dante elaborated his views on politics in a Latin treatise entitled *Monarchia*, though when exactly is a crucial and much debated question that affects the interpretation of the work itself. There are at least three proposed dates: 1308, 1312–13, and 1317–18. The treatise is in three books. Book I argues on philosophical grounds for the necessity of a universal monarchy for the fulfilment of all human potentialities in the fields of both action and contemplation. This fulfilment is the supreme purpose of civilization, and can be achieved on the sole condition that the entire world lives in peace: a peace that only a supreme all-powerful monarch can guarantee by impartially administering justice, favouring harmony, and allowing the exercise of individual freedom.

Book II seeks to prove historically that the Roman people are the legitimate holders of universal power, and the city of Rome this power's proper, divinely ordained seat (accordingly, this is also the book where the classics are most often quoted, especially Virgil as the poet of justice). The events of Roman history are treated by Dante in the same way as the events of the Old Testament, that is, as the expression of God's will. The unification of the ancient world under Rome, he argues, was providentially willed so that the sacrifice of Christ could be undertaken under a universal authority, and its fruits benefit the whole of humanity.

Book III deals with the question of the relationship between Church and empire, a theological minefield that one crossed only at great personal risk. Dante did not flinch or compromise, systematically demolishing all arguments in favour of ecclesiastical property and jurisdiction. He particularly refuted the idea that God wanted imperial authority to be subordinated to papal authority, and challenged the validity of the Donation of Constantine, a document forged between the eighth and ninth century – as Lorenzo Valla (*c*.1407–57) later showed – claiming to be the official act by which Emperor Constantine (b. *c*.272; reign 306–37) granted imperial power to the pope. Dante did not doubt its authenticity, but he denied its juridical validity: on the one hand, he argued, the emperor could not give away or divide the empire, for he had been ordained by God in order to preserve its integrity; on the other, the Pope could not receive it, for Christ had ordered him to live in total poverty. For Dante, both imperial and papal authority derived directly from God; the former's proper function was to lead humanity to earthly beatitude through philosophical and moral teaching; the latter's was to lead it to heavenly glory through the teaching of Revelation. The two authorities, and their respective jurisdictions, were complementary but entirely discrete.

These ideas were considered so poisonous by the ecclesiastical authority that in 1328 the Dominican Guido Vernani (d. *c*.1348) wrote a virulent attack on the *Monarchia*, and a year later, at least according to Boccaccio, the treatise was burnt in the public square in Bologna; finally, in 1554 the Church placed it on the list of the prohibited books, where it remained until 1900.

The *Monarchia* is sustained throughout by Dante's firm belief in the unity of society and creation; although based on an academic approach and mode of argumentation, it is fired by a genuine political and religious passion. The critical problem is whether or not it is to be interpreted as an early example of a modern, lay conception of the State. What exactly did Dante have in mind when he thought about the 'State'? Neither the *Monarchia*, nor the *Commedia* with its impassioned treatment of politics, can ultimately reveal his intentions; however, there are some documents that unambiguously illustrate Dante's ideological stance between 1310 and 1314. These are the letters that he wrote on the occasion of Henry VII's (*c*.1275–1313) descent into Italy (*Epistles* V, VI, and VII), and for the conclave of 1314 (*Epistle* XI) (see Chapter 27).

## *Commedia*

The *Commedia* is a *summa* of medieval culture, a synthesis of all facets of reality as an integral whole – earthly and heavenly, physical and spiritual, natural and historical, cultural and ethical. This synthesis was conceived and achieved just as, and because, the ideological and historical premises that underpinned it were manifestly failing, and the unity of the medieval world was irreversibly breaking up under the pressure of historical forces more powerful than any individual will. Dante perhaps dreamed that his poem would somehow reverse this process of disintegration. Such untimely vision is not uncommon among great thinkers. What is unique to Dante is that he achieved it by means of a poetry that is probably unrivalled in the history of Western literature.

### *Birth of a 'comedy'*

The *Commedia* claims to be the account of a real journey through Hell, Purgatory, and Paradise, which the poet Dante undertook, by the explicit will of God and through the intercession of his beloved Beatrice, when he was thirty-five years of age in the year 1300 – a year of crucial significance not only in marking the beginning of a new century and the first holy year declared by Pope Boniface VIII, but also a year when, for Dante, humanity was deprived of its two leaders, the pope and the emperor. The journey, which includes many meetings and conversations between Dante and a significant number of his friends and foes, starts on the night of Good Friday and ends a week later, thus coinciding with the liturgical recurrence of Christ's passion, death, and resurrection. It leads to the salvation of its protagonist and to the composition of a 'sacred poem' whose purpose is the salvation of the whole world.

Even apart from the question of credibility, the work broke all the rules: literary, political, religious. Its subject was deeply serious, but its language vernacular; its stylistic range was unprecedented, mixing the low and base with the lofty and abstract, the 'comic' with the 'tragic', the lyric with the epic, the Christian with the pagan. Politically, it condemned to eternal damnation Guelfs (both Black and White) as well as Ghibellines, ecclesiastic as well as secular leaders. Though it favoured Florence as a target of its indignation and sarcasm, it spared no city in Tuscany or beyond. Above all, it displayed a profound aversion for the new class of entrepreneurs and self-made men who had transformed Florence into a major international centre of trade and industry, and who now exercised

*Works* 491

power over its civil, social, and cultural institutions, its customs and laws, its internal and foreign affairs. Finally, although its theology appeared to be broadly orthodox, the poem was in many ways a veritable scandal: it denounced popes and the customs of the Holy Roman Church, calling for the surrender of all the wealth and power it had accumulated over a thousand years. What was worse, indeed intolerable, its author claimed to be a new Christian prophet, sent to reform the world before its impending end. How could a decent, intelligent, cultivated Florentine have written anything as subversive as this?

The poem begins abruptly, with a directness that is the hallmark of its author. Having reached 'the middle of the journey of our life' (traditionally said to last seventy years), Dante finds himself in a dark forest. We are not told how he got there, nor does he seem to know. Yet the situation is real enough; the forest so 'savage and harsh and dense' (*Inf.* I, 5) that the mere thought of it still terrifies him. From its very beginning, the poem forces us to visualize simultaneously, and as equally true, two separate stages in Dante's life, two kinds of 'present': the stage of the journey, or the present of the narrative; and the stage of its recounting, or the present of the narrator who has accomplished the journey.

As he recounts his extraordinary experience, the narrator often interjects, reflecting and commenting on it and on his present efforts to find adequate words for its retelling. One of the most striking features of the *Commedia* is that it not only narrates a story, but also contains within itself the story of its making. The point where it comes closest to releasing the secret of its origin is perhaps in the Earthly Paradise, when Dante meets Beatrice at the centre of a symbolic pageant representing the history of the world, past, present, and future (*Purg.* XXIX–XXXIII). Beatrice says that, after she died, Dante forgot her, sinking into such moral and intellectual dissipation that it brought him to the brink of spiritual death. The only way to save him was to send him on the journey that he has now more than half completed. The story of Dante's salvation, as told by Beatrice, is a duplicate version of both Dante's journey in the *Commedia* and the story of universal salvation as synthesized in the pageant. Dante's reunion with Beatrice at Easter-time 1300 re-enacts the union of Christ with his Church, as represented in the pageant by the griffin who draws the chariot to the great tree. This timeless pattern, provided by the biblical narrative of the Song of Songs, gives meaning both to the individual life of Dante and to the history of humanity as a whole. As a result of his meeting with Beatrice, Dante's life is renewed, just as the dead tree is revived by the touch of the griffin. Paradise is now opened to Dante, as it was reopened to humanity by the sacrifice of Jesus Christ, and was ritually opened again at Easter time 1300. Suddenly, the pattern of Dante's life, like that of historical man on earth, is transformed.

The title *Commedia* – the adjective *divina*, employed by Boccaccio to describe poet and poem, was added to the title only in 1555 – puzzled and shocked many of Dante's Trecento readers. Indeed it is so original that its motivation and meaning are still a matter of controversy. The most widely held opinion is that *Commedia* was meant to refer to the composite nature of the poem, which mixes different and traditionally incompatible themes and registers, the basest and loftiest subjects, imagery and language. No doubt this is at least partly correct. However, its original motivation may not only be of a rhetorical nature. The title given in the manuscript tradition and in the Epistle to Cangrande is *Comedia Dantis Alagherii, florentini natione sed non moribus* (Comedy of Dante Alighieri, a Florentine by birth but not by conduct), a title that blends the reality of objective experience with that of its narration, Dante the character with Dante the narrator and the man. Quite simply, the poem is called a 'comedy' because it narrates Dante's salvation – an experience that is 'comic' in the medieval sense that it leads to a happy conclusion.

We must assume that something extraordinary happened to Dante around 1306–07, an illumination, an inspiration, a conversion, call it what you will. Suddenly, Dante abandons the *Convivio* at the end of only the fourth book, and the *De vulgari eloquentia* in mid-sentence: what is at stake now is more than his return to Florence and the restoration of his reputation, more even than his own spiritual salvation, for the new project involves the salvation of the world. However, if Dante abandons his other projects, it is also because the new one thoroughly subsumes them. The double vein, creative and self-exegetical, that runs through his previous work finds an organic and fully integrated development in the *Commedia*. What was divided is now perfectly fused. The Florentine, the exile, the literato, the philosopher, the poet, the Christian, the politician become one, and the writing of the poem becomes a mission.

### Composition and early diffusion

When did Dante begin his masterpiece? The consensus among modern scholars is that composition began around 1307 and continued almost to the end of his life. There is some evidence, though open to interpretation and debate, that *Inferno*, or parts of it, became known in 1314, *Purgatorio* in 1315, and *Paradiso* in the last years of the poet's life. It is reasonable to assume that between the 'publication' of *Inferno* and that of *Paradiso* there was a gap of six to eight years (see Chapter 29). There are no signs that the poet ever modified or rewrote any parts of his poem after their initial release, though he might well have revised them previously. This is a most remarkable fact, given the range, complexity, internal cross-referencing, and near-total consistency of the narrative as a whole. The entire poem, from beginning to end, must have been in Dante's mind as he composed each canto. This means that every line was written once and forever, and so was every destiny. As a judge, Dante conceded no appeal.

The poem was widely read as soon as it, or parts of it, became available to the public. After the poet died, it became the object of learned glosses and commentaries, in Latin as well as Italian (see Chapter 30), receiving the sort of attention normally reserved for Scripture and a few classics. Dante himself probably inaugurated this tradition by writing the Epistle to Cangrande (see below).

### Formal organization and language

The metrical and narrative structure of the *Commedia* is based on numerical symmetries that are meant to mirror the unity and symmetry of the universe itself. The poem is divided into three *cantiche* (the term is probably inspired by the *Cantica Canticorum*, the biblical Song of Songs), which are in turn subdivided into *canti*. As there are thirty-four *canti* in *Inferno* (the first serves as a general prologue) and thirty-three each in *Purgatorio* and *Paradiso*, their total is one hundred, a perfect number. The *canti* are made up on average of just under fifty stanzas of three hendecasyllables each, called *terzine*. In this metrical form, the first and third hendecasyllable rhyme with each other, and the second introduces a new rhyme that, in turn, frames the following *terzina* with a forward movement that halts only at the end of each canto with a double rhyme, so that the initial and final rhymes clearly mark the boundaries of each canto. The metrical structures, with the exception of the hendecasyllabic line, and the *Commedia*'s organization are Dante's own inventions and serve as external formal markers of its originality.

The nature of Dante's new work dictated the language in which it was to be written. As a Christian epic and a serious eschatological poem, it would have been normal, if not mandatory at the time, for it to have been written in Latin. However, for Dante the *Commedia* was itself inherently 'vernacular', just as the *sermo* (register) of Scripture was inherently *humilis* (humble). The choice was ideologically, rather than rhetorically,

494 Lino Pertile

determined. As a poem of salvation, his *comedía* would surpass Virgil's *'alta tragedía'* (lofty tragedy), which, lacking the message and model of Scripture, could never be a 'sacred poem'. It would also achieve by itself what the *Vita nova* and the *Convivio*, with their mixture of verse and prose, and the *De vulgari eloquentia*, with its highly wrought Latin, had together failed to deliver: the discovery and revelation of a universal and timeless system of truths.

The language of the *Commedia* still impresses the reader as prodigious in range, energy, and sophistication. Breaking all conventions, Dante extends enormously the 'comic' register, borrowing freely, even inventing, according to his expressive needs. His experimental vein reaches full maturity without losing any freshness and originality. The vocabulary is gathered from a wide variety of sources, both written and spoken: Latin, Tuscan, Occitan, Old French, as well as northern-Italian dialects. The language of science (astronomy, physics, geometry, optics, medicine, philosophy, theology, etc.) coexists with that of the street, the kitchen, and the stable; the sophisticated dispute of the university classroom with the quick repartee of the *piazza*; the sweet sounds of the *stilnovo* with the harsh and grating syllables of the *rime petrose*. This extraordinary linguistic eclecticism is constantly kept under control by Dante's rhetorical sensitivity.

### Allegory and realism

The *Commedia*'s claim to truth radically distinguishes it from the medieval genre of visions and allegorical journeys to which it superficially belongs (see Chapter 20). But above all it guarantees its absolute exemplarity, for the truer the individual experience, the more effective it must be as a moral example. This applies not only to Dante, the poet-protagonist, but also, with a few clearly signposted exceptions, to all the events he witnesses and the characters he meets in the course of his journey, starting with his three guides: Virgil, the Roman poet of the *Aeneid*, who leads him through Hell and Purgatory; Beatrice, who accompanies him through the nine heavens of Paradise; and St Bernard of Clairvaux (1091–1153), the writer and contemplative, who leads him to the final vision of God in the Empyrean.

For Dante, as indeed for any Christian believer, death is not the end of life, but the beginning of a new immortal life in which every soul (immediately in Hell and Paradise, and at the end of purgation in Purgatory) achieves its ultimate reality, its definitive state of being. It is this ultimate and unchanging reality, in which all the souls are fixed forever in the contemporaneity of timelessness, that Dante claims to have visited and to be describing. There is, therefore, little in the *Commedia* that can be read as conventional allegory, where the literal meaning is no more than a beautiful lie, and the 'real' meaning is other, to be discovered by decrypting the text according to a built-in code. Dante does occasionally employ this type of allegory. For instance, the three beasts that, at the beginning of the poem, prevent him from climbing the hill are not meant to have a reality of their own, but to be symbols of lust, pride, and greed. This is no more than a rhetorical device and a literary technique, while the allegory of the *Commedia* is a way of understanding reality in all its interconnected multiple meanings. Such allegory is based on the Christian notion – a commonplace in medieval thought – that all objects, people, and events in space and time, besides signifying themselves in their objective reality, are also signs of the providential design that has created them. 'The world is a book written by the finger of God', writes Hugh of St Victor in the twelfth century.[3] But God is also the author of the book par excellence, namely the Bible, the book that reveals His intervention in the history of humanity. According to the Fathers of the Church, the events of the Old Testament were real – they had actually occurred – while at the same time they prefigured (they were 'figures' or 'types of') events that were to occur later in the New Testament. The subsequent events gave meaning and substance to the former: they were their fulfilment. Figural allegory teaches the hidden network of relations that exists between distant and apparently unrelated events.

In Dante's hands, this approach to reality preserves the irreducible individuality of persons, while revealing their position in the divine scheme. The state of souls after death is the fulfilment of their lives on earth. Virgil is not Reason, and Beatrice is not Theology: they are both the final fulfilment of their historical selves; not personifications of abstract qualities, but what they have become at the end of their journeys, one in Limbo and the other in Heaven. The same is generally true of the many characters whom Dante meets in the three realms of the afterlife. Like Dante-the-character, they furnish examples of individual journeys, now completed, which can guide the readers of the poem who are still *in via*, and can thereby determine their eternal destinies in a kind of moral allegory that coexists in the *Commedia* along with figural allegory.

### Dante's journey

Dante's universe is a moral, as much as a physical, reality. At its centre, motionless, sits the earth. All the land is in the northern hemisphere between the delta of the Ganges and the Pillars of Hercules (Straits of Gibraltar); the mid-point between these two boundaries is Jerusalem. The southern hemisphere is completely covered by water, except for the mountain of Purgatory.

Dante's Hell is in the shape of a huge funnel, located below the surface of the northern hemisphere and extending to the centre of the earth. It is divided into Ante-Inferno and nine concentric circles, sloping down towards the bottom. Here, most remote from God, is Lucifer-Satan. His fall from the Empyrean caused the earth to recoil in horror, creating the chasm of Hell and, on the southern hemisphere, the mountain of Purgatory, which stands in the shape of a cone at the antipodes of Jerusalem. The latter, topographically Dante's original creation, is divided into seven terraces, preceded by the Ante-Purgatory, and followed, at the top, by the Earthly Paradise. Nine concentric, diaphanous spheres rotate around the earth, one for each of the seven planets (Moon, Mercury, Venus, Sun, Mars, Jupiter, Saturn) plus one for the Fixed Stars and one for the Primum Mobile, the invisible heaven which, taking its motion directly from the Love of God, communicates it to the planets below. Beyond the Primum Mobile is the Empyrean, the domain of absolute rest, which contains everything and is contained by nothing. Dante's journey, therefore, takes him across the entire universe, from the centre of the earth to the Empyrean, where both time and space began.

The structural correspondence between the three realms of the afterlife allows the poet to organize his three *cantiche* with a high degree of symmetry. This symmetry, however, is not presented as an arbitrary choice on his part, but as an objective necessity of the subject-matter itself, a mirror of the reality of the afterlife. The topography of the three realms appears to Dante-the-character as the objective manifestation of the ethical system according to which they are inhabited.

The moral system of Dante's *Inferno* is based on a broadly Aristotelian–Ciceronian scheme, but with variations that depend on other, essentially Christian traditions. After the neutrals, who are rejected by both Satan and God, and the virtuous pagans who inhabit the first circle (Limbo), the damned are distributed from the top to the bottom of the funnel in precise relation to the increasing gravity of their sins, beginning with the incontinent who were unable to control their instincts, and proceeding through the heretics, the violent, and the fraudulent to the worst sinners of all, the traitors. At the bottom of the pit, Lucifer chews in his three mouths Judas who betrayed Christ, and Brutus and Cassius who betrayed the empire in the person of Julius Caesar.

In *Purgatorio* the excommunicates, the lethargic, the late penitents, and the negligent rulers await at the foot of the mountain until they may begin their purification. Purgatory proper is structured on the traditional ordering of the seven capital vices. When the penitents enter it, they are made to progress through its seven terraces spending more or less time on each according to the degree of their guilt in respect of each sinful inclination. The seven faults are therefore rectified from the bottom to the top of the mountain according to their decreasing gravity. The first three (pride, envy, and wrath) are a perversion of love; the fourth (sloth) is a sign of defective love; the last three (avarice, gluttony, and lust) represent excessive love. On the top of the mountain is Earthly Paradise, where human history began with the Fall of Adam and Eve.

Though they all 'reside' in the Empyrean, the blessed appear to Dante in the seven spheres that surround the earth, gradually closer to God according to their individual capacity to see Him and partake of His bliss. In the Moon are those who were forced to break their vows, in Mercury the seekers of glory, in Venus the lovers, in the Sun the lovers of wisdom, in Mars the martyrs and crusaders, in Jupiter the righteous rulers, and in Saturn the contemplatives. In the Fixed Stars, Dante sees the Church Triumphant, and in the Primum Mobile the angelic orders. This distribution is replicated in the Empyrean itself beyond space and time. This is also where Dante's journey ends.

### Myth and history

The landscape of Dante's Hell is exceedingly varied. Natural obstacles separate its major divisions, often doubling up as penal places. All circles have guardians and torturers – mythological monsters that embody in essence the moral features of the sinners they rule over and torment. Typical devils are rare in Hell. Only in the fifth ditch, where they are collectively called 'Malebranche' (Evil Claws), do they play a major role, looking and behaving like the devils of the Christian tradition. Most of the other demons, like the topography of Hell generally, are derived from classical sources, especially Virgil's *Aeneid*. However, Dante transforms the fables of the classical past into organic components of the Christian afterlife, revealing the full meanings of old forms by realizing and fulfilling them in the new.

The same holds for the classical figures who appear in *Inferno*. By and large, Dante's characters belong to his own times; most of them are Florentine or Tuscan. However, next to Francesca da Rimini (murdered by her husband *c.*1285) we find Dido and Helen of Troy; next to Guido da Montefeltro (*c*.1220–98), Ulysses and Diomedes. All events and characters – mythological, legendary, historical – become equally real and contemporary in Dante's afterlife. And the reason for this is not his lack of historical perspective, but his belief in an eschatology to which history itself is subservient.

The souls Dante meets in Purgatory are almost exclusively drawn from recent history. There are two major exceptions to this rule. One is Cato, the ancient Roman who, rather than submit to Caesar and lose republican freedom, chose suicide in Utica; his love of freedom, greater even than his love of life, made him guardian of that Christian freedom that now Dante, like all the purging souls, seeks in Purgatory. The other is Statius, the Latin epic poet of the first century CE, who joins Dante and Virgil on the terrace of the avaricious and prodigal (canto XXI), and stays with them through the rest of Purgatory; Virgil's *Aeneid* and fourth eclogue opened his eyes and made a secret Christian of him (XXII, 90).

In Paradise, lest we presume to know the inscrutable ways of God's justice, we find not only the apostles, saints, theologians, holy emperors, and crusaders we might have foreseen, but also unexpected names from both pagan and Christian times. In the heaven of Venus, for example, we meet the notorious Cunizza da Romano, whose many marriages and love affairs were legendary in thirteenth-century Italy. In the eye of the eagle in the heaven of Jupiter, together with Emperors Trajan and Constantine, we meet a humble Trojan warrior by the name of Ripheus (*Par.* XX, 67–9) whom Virgil briefly mentions in *Aeneid* II. Pagans and converted sinners are admittedly few, but enough to prove that God's goodness transcends all appearances.

Dante greatly admires the ancient world; in the Roman empire he sees a model of reason and justice, the indispensable vehicle of God's redemptive plan. Yet its world cannot be saved, for it lacked divine grace. The character of Virgil is the best illustration of this tragic destiny. For Dante, as for his contemporaries, Virgil's *Aeneid* foreshadowed the Christian message, and his fourth eclogue prophesied the coming of Christ. In the *Commedia*, the Latin poet guides Dante through Hell and Purgatory, leading him, like a father, over all the hurdles of the journey and, like a teacher, through all the problems that human reason can solve. However, once they reach Earthly Paradise, Virgil must go back to Limbo: he is not, and never will be, allowed to reach beyond. His figure is a moving symbol of a humanity in every respect perfect but deprived of grace. Virgil lived and died well before Christ, of course; nevertheless, Dante's Christianization of history and mythology entails their subjection to the rigours, and the unfathomable ways, of Christian justice.

### The 'contrapasso'

Christian justice operates throughout Dante's afterlife, ensuring that nothing in it is gratuitous or arbitrary. Assigning every soul to its appropriate place is the law of *contrapasso* (*Inf.* XXVIII, 142), a retributive principle whereby everyone must suffer in the afterlife according to the sin he or she has committed on earth. This suffering is retributive and eternal in Hell, whilst in Purgatory it is remedial and temporary. In Paradise, too, the situation of the blessed is closely related to their earthly behaviour; by appearing in different spheres, they are shown to receive the quality and measure of reward appropriate to each of them. Thus God's justice is done, and is seen to be done, in all three realms of the afterlife.

The *contrapasso* is not Dante's invention. What distinguishes its appearance in the *Commedia* is that it functions not merely as a form of divine retribution, but rather as the fulfilment of a destiny freely chosen by each soul during his or her life. Thus in Dante's afterlife, far from being cancelled, diminished or even altered, the historical identity of each soul is revealed in its very essence and so intensified. In Dante's hands, the *contrapasso* works simultaneously as an instrument of justice and as a powerful narrative device.

### Dante-the-character among the dead

But the *Commedia* is no mere catalogue of crimes and punishments, virtues and rewards. It is a poem of ever-changing human emotions, a poem in which human actions are explored in all the complexity of their public and private, social and psychological motivations. In the darkness of Hell, the damned are whipped, bitten, crucified, burned, butchered, deformed by repulsive diseases; they are transformed into shrubs and snakes; buried alive in flaming graves and fixed head-first into rocky ground; immersed in mud, in excrement, in boiling blood and pitch; frozen in ice and chewed in the mouth of Satan. The sounds and signs of physical pain are present everywhere. What is deeply disturbing is the relentlessness of the conditions in which victims and tormentors are caught by the eye of the passing visitor: the notion that, for instance, Count Ugolino will always gnaw at the skull of Archbishop Ruggieri. It is this implacability of God's justice that makes the dead plead in vain for a second, definitive death (*Inf.* XIII, 118). Nevertheless, despite their atrocious suffering, brutish nastiness, and disgusting cruelty, the damned remain quintessentially human; and it is with that humanity, albeit distorted and perverted, that Dante-the-character time after time engages. As he descends deeper into Hell, his reactions range from horror to compassion, from terror to indignation, from pity to pitilessness. *Inferno* is a Christian exploration of the effects of sin, but also a descent into the darkest recesses of the human soul.

In *Purgatorio*, as the physical and human landscapes change, the poetic register changes too. Like earth, Purgatory exists in time, it has dawns and sunsets, days and nights, visions and dreams. The penitents are not frozen in their earthly individuality; they move on together, at peace with themselves, with each other, and with God. They are all listening to, or looking at, examples of virtues and vices; occasionally, they recount such examples themselves. They suffer physical pain, of course. Yet their pain is internalized; its very existence ensures that it will end, giving way to the joy of Paradise. This is why they are so keen to undergo it. What they feel with much greater intensity is their distance from God. Like a reverse nostalgia, this sense of separation and exile characterizes their ascent, transforming it into a pilgrimage towards the heavenly home. Dante climbs the mountain with them; a pilgrim among pilgrims, he understands and shares their memories of the past and their longing for the future. His encounters in Purgatory often become dialogues about art and poetry, but the thought of earth with its horrors and injustices is never allowed to slip too far away.

With *Paradiso* Dante is proudly aware of sailing 'waters never sailed before' (*Par.* II, 7). Having placed Paradise beyond the confines of human memory and language, what the poet claims to describe is not the reality of perfect bliss, but his experience of approaching it, the desire that propels him from the heaven of the Moon to the Empyrean – for the fulfilment that lies beyond that desire is also beyond the limits of poetry. The narrative devices employed in this *cantica* have the function of anticipating and simultaneously delaying the final vision. In this sense Dante's ascent is not – not at least until its very end – an appeasement, but a constant intellectual and emotional challenge, a struggle to reach beyond, for God's desirability lies in His transcendence, His power of attraction in His distance and His absence. Conversely, it is only by deferring for thirty-three cantos the full satisfaction of desire that the poet creates a space within which the poem may be completed in line with the formal requirements of its overall structure. The blessed, too, are depicted in a state of desire, but their desire is constantly satisfied and constantly rekindled; they always have what they desire, and always desire what they have. They desire God each according to his or her own capacity to enjoy Him, thus preserving and fulfilling in Paradise their individual earthly identity.

No landscapes are depicted in Dante's Heaven, only a spectacular series of ever-changing lights, colours, sounds, emblems, and geometric figures. Nor are there complex characters to be explored, only blessed spirits, all absolutely happy and fulfilled. There are disquisitions on science, ethics, and theology – a demanding banquet for the inexperienced guest. *Paradiso* brings to fruition Dante's enthusiasm for knowledge, and, simultaneously, sets the limits beyond which reason and intelligence cannot venture. The pilgrim's – and the reader's – ascent is meant to be not only emotional and spiritual, but intellectual too; Paradise is not just a contemplative experience, but also a process of enlightenment, light being the external manifestation of an 'internal' process. This does not mean that earth is forgotten. Beatrice, Justinian, St Thomas Aquinas, St Bonaventure, Cacciaguida, and St Peter deplore in the strongest terms the corruption of Church and empire, of religious orders and civil society, of individuals and communities. Indeed, it is in *Paradiso* that Dante's journey receives its final legitimation; in *Paradiso* the prophetic nature of the poem is fully claimed and sanctioned from within the poem itself.

### Florence, the individual and society

The profound ideological crisis that shook the thirteenth century gave rise to a diffused feeling that the end of the world was near. Many people believed that the degeneration of humanity had reached its nadir, and were therefore eagerly awaiting a spectacular and definitive reaffirmation of God's justice over the evil forces of the Antichrist (see Chapter 7). Even apart from apocalyptic expectations, a longing for peace and justice was widespread in Italy, a country torn by internal conflicts and in the throes of social upheaval. As he begins his journey, Dante is lost, a victim of these troubled times; but by the end he is enlightened and saved. What is more, he is authorized, indeed instructed, to don the garb of a prophet and offer in the *Commedia* a fully integrated answer to all the anxieties and fears of his contemporaries.

As we have seen, for Dante the conflict of interests between Church and empire had deprived humankind of its two main guides, essential to its well-being on earth and its fulfilment in Heaven (*Mon.* III, xv, 7–11; *Purg.* XVI, 106–14). As a consequence, *cupiditas*, or greed, the root of all evil, had triumphed everywhere. Possessed by an insatiable craving for material goods and power, contemporary society had become utterly corrupt. Everyone was fighting for individual advantage and material gratification, and nowhere was this more the case than in Florence, a city which had become for Dante the true kingdom of *cupiditas* (*Inf.* XXVI, 1–3). In effect, of the seventy-nine damned that Dante meets in Hell, thirty-two are Florentine and eleven Tuscan, while in Purgatory there are four Florentines and in Paradise, apart from Beatrice, only three.[4]

However, Dante wrote the *Commedia* not merely to castigate Florence, but also to reform and reconquer her; his journey towards the 'sacred poem' (*Par.* XXV, 1) is also meant to be a journey towards his Florentine home. Dante treats Florence just as he treats the Church: with both love and disdain – love for the city as a community capable of fulfilling all human potential; disdain for its people and administrators, all equally corrupted by their lust for power and wealth. But just as he attacks the popes and high clerics and not the Church, so he attacks the Florentines and their government but not the city as institution. And just as he asks that the Church turn back the clock and divest itself of all its possessions and earthly power, so he would have Florence return to former simplicity and sobriety of life and customs. The Dantean utopia of the early Church corresponds to the Dantean utopia of the Florence of the good old days.

The political theme surfaces everywhere in the *Commedia*, but there are certain strategically positioned cantos in which the poet focuses on it with particular vehemence. In canto XVI (73–5) of *Inferno*, he denounces 'the new people and the sudden profits', which he sees as responsible for Florence's moral and political collapse. Of the many profound and irreversible changes that took place in Italy in general and in Florence in particular during the second half the thirteenth century (see Chapter 2) he sees only the negative aspects and internal contradictions. Dante seems to understand that contemporary society finds itself at a historic crossroads: on the one hand, the capitalist way – a dynamic lifestyle that aims to achieve happiness in this life through material progress while letting the afterlife take care of itself; on the other, a subsistence economy, namely, a peaceful life focused on the development of the intellectual and spiritual capabilities of the human persona in view of its eternal happiness, while the economy produces enough to live on but production is never used for gain. Clearly, Florence had already chosen, enthusiastically, the capitalist way, but Dante still believed that the city could change its course: this after all was why he was writing the *Commedia* (*Purg.* XXXII, 103).

Dante was not against the human search for happiness on earth, but he objected to the notion that wealth and power, regardless of how acquired, could make people happier and more fulfilled. He never entertained the idea that the social conflicts of his time could pave the way for a new, more just society; or that any movement, whether individual or collective, which aimed at earthly well-being independently of humanity's eternal destiny, could ultimately be positive. The supreme good for civil society does not lie, according to Dante, in equality and social progress – notions that are foreign to the beliefs of his time and to his world-view – but rather in universal peace, inasmuch as 'universal peace is the best of those things which are ordained for human happiness' (*Mon.* I, iv, 2). Florence, on the contrary, was for him the embodiment of a society that had lost its way, a society that, by obsessively seeking Heaven on earth, had made Hell of life on earth.

The political-ethical theme is taken up again in canto XVI of *Purgatorio*, fiftieth in the poem, by Marco Lombardo, who squarely affirms men's responsibility in the current degeneration of the world. God created the soul innocent and unaware (*Purg.* XVI, 88), but with the instinct to return to the perfect joy of its Maker. Moved by this instinct, the soul searches for happiness in worldly goods, confusing every desirable object, however insignificant, with the supreme good. This is why it needs laws both human and divine to support and guide it towards the highest good. The laws exist, but there is no one to enforce them, since of the two highest authorities meant to do so, the empire is without emperor and the papacy has lost the ability to distinguish between good and evil (*Purg.* XVI, 106–12). Thus it is not human nature that is corrupt, but the institutions delegated by God to guide it, and, in their absence, chaos triumphs in public life while the individual soul is lost in the forest of sin, confusion, and utter despair. In this way the two fundamental themes of the whole poem are woven together: the personal drama of the pilgrim in search of freedom and salvation, and the civil and historical drama of a society lost in disorder, corruption, illegality. Society in its entirety enters into a vicious circle from which it cannot escape without the intervention of an external force capable of rescuing it.

This is exactly Dante's predicament at the beginning of his journey and of the story told in the poem: alone, lost in the dark wood, surrounded by wild beasts, lacking all hope of salvation. Only the intervention of an external force can save him. This is what occurs when Virgil, instrument of Beatrice and voice of reason and poetry, appears before him to guide him on a journey of redemption. The poem narrates the journey that saves the poet, but also foresees that soon a *veltro*, a mysterious greyhound, will come to save Italy and the world. Just as Virgil is the instrument of Dante's salvation, so will the *veltro* be the instrument that saves the world, and Dante, with his poem, will be its prophet.

At the centre of *Paradiso*, Cacciaguida, the poet's great-great-grandfather, endorses the position that Dante voiced at the centre of *Inferno* and Marco Lombardo reaffirmed at the centre of *Purgatorio*. Cacciaguida uses the example of the Florentine women of his own time to illustrate the integrity of the old city and, by contrast, the shocking depravity of the contemporary city. For Cacciaguida, and for Dante, women's customs are an indication of public well-being; their modesty a sure sign of the moral health of society as a whole. Now however – Cacciaguida says – women go about showing their breasts, their bodies covered in chains, coronets, and richly adorned skirts and belts, a far cry from when they devoted themselves to home and family, and integrity reigned in public life (*Par.* XV, 100–26). Into that peaceful, sober, modest city, Cacciaguida was born – writes Dante – and his civic and moral virtues were nurtured. Knighted by Emperor Conrad III (1093–1152), Cacciaguida followed him to the Holy Land, where he died fighting the 'infidels.'

The life and death of Cacciaguida, exemplary citizen and exemplary Christian, are the product and mirror of the city in which he was born and lived. The virtues of the community affect every individual, and in turn every individual contributes with his good work to the well-being of the community. It was one of the poet's most profound convictions that, as he stated in the *Monarchia* (citing Aristotle): 'in bad government the good man is a bad citizen, whereas in good government the good man and the good citizen are one and the same thing' (I, xii, 10). In Cacciaguida's city Dante would have lived in peace and with honour; but in contemporary Florence he could not live without compromising his integrity. Thus his exile is not merely a case of temporary and isolated injustice, but a sign of the profound decadence of the city that had exiled him.

Florence last appears in the poem when Dante recalls his wonder on reaching the Empyrean: 'I, who to the divine from the human, / to the eternal from time had come, / and from Florence to a people just and sane, / with what amazement must I have been filled!' (*Par.* XXXI, 37–40). These powerful lines bear witness to the end of a long illusion. The third line ('and from Florence to a people just and sane'), suddenly inverting the syntactic order of the previous two, eloquently voices the poet's bitterness. Florence is now identified with Hell, the epicentre of the world's greed, the point in the universe furthest from peace, justice, and goodness.

In the fiction of the poem there is a journey of just a few days behind this line of poetry; in Dante's real experience there were almost twenty years of tormented and ultimately pointless waiting – pointless not for the poet, who owes the *Commedia* to his exile, but certainly for Dante the man. The poem, born to provide him with a passport home, once completed, becomes a barrier between Dante and Florence, the reason why his exile cannot end. Thus Dante reaches the ultimate 'home' and, for a moment, even beholds the face of God in the fiction of his *Paradiso*, but he does not see Florence again in his lifetime. It is the price he must pay for his moral intransigence and the creation of his great poem.

### *Epistole*

There are thirteen letters (numbered *Ep.* I-XIII), all in Latin and believed to be by Dante, four of them written on behalf of others. Some critics exclude letter XIII as totally or largely apocryphal (see below). One letter (I) is written to Cardinal Niccolò da Prato (*c.*1250–1321) on behalf of the White alliance (1304); two are of literary nature: one (III, 1306) accompanying a poem to Cino da Pistoia (*c.*1270–1336/37) and the other (IV) being a commentary on Dante's *canzone* 'Love, since after all I am forced to grieve', 1307–8); three (V, VI, VII) are political letters written respectively to the lords and peoples of Italy (1310), the Florentines (1311), and Emperor Henry VII (1311); one (XI) to the Italian cardinals, calling for the election of an Italian pope (1314); and finally the very famous one (XII) to an unidentified Florentine friend (1315) in which Dante refuses to accept the amnesty that allowed him back to Florence under humiliating conditions. Only four letters can be said to be somewhat private: a letter of condolences (II) written in 1304, and three versions of a note of thanks and best wishes written in 1311 on behalf of the Countess of Battifolle (VIII, IX, X).

Among letters lost or attributed to Dante, one letter from Venice, dated 1314 and written in vernacular to Guido Novello da Polenta (d. 1330), describes the Venetian citizens as incapable of understanding either Latin or Tuscan. The letter is generally believed to be an early sixteenth-century forgery, inspired by the Medici regime to bolster anti-Venetian sentiments in Florence.

### *Epistle to Cangrande*

Letter XIII, the longest and most controversial, includes a proper letter dedicating *Paradiso* to Cangrande della Scala (1291–1329), Lord and

Imperial Vicar of Verona (paragraphs 1–4) and a second, much longer section comprising a detailed introduction (*accessus*) to the *Commedia* as a whole (paragraphs 5–16), and an exposition of the first canto of *Paradiso* (paragraphs 17–33), which discusses in detail the first twelve lines but touches on the following ten as well. There are three main critical positions on the issue of authorship:

(1) the entire letter is by Dante;
(2) only the dedication (paragraphs 1–4) is authentic and the rest is the work of a compiler;
(3) the entire letter is a fake, assembled in its present form during the second half of the fourteenth century.

Those who believe the letter to be authentic place its composition between 1316, when Dante was in Verona, and 1320, when he was in Ravenna.

Two major objections are raised by those who do not believe that the letter can be by Dante:

(1) The letter's manuscript tradition is separate from that of the other letters, and it does not go back beyond the fifteenth century; furthermore, it is divided between three fifteenth-century manuscripts containing just the dedication (paragraphs 1–4), and six sixteenth- and seventeenth-century manuscripts that include the entire work.
(2) The commentary on the *Commedia* offered by the Epistle is too incoherent, simple-minded, or even misleading to be by the author of the poem.

However, the position of the upholders of authenticity has recently been considerably strengthened by the discovery that the Florentine notary Andrea Lancia (before 1296–after 1357) knew the Epistle and cited all its parts as Dantean as early as 1343; also, several other early commentators cite the Epistle, though without mentioning its author. Thus the 'authenticist' party seems currently to be prevailing, though there are still scholars who strongly doubt that the commentary part can be by Dante.

## *Egloge*

The *Egloge* are two compositions in Latin hexameters, based on the model of Virgil's *Eclogues*, in which Dante responds to two Latin poems by Giovanni del Virgilio (late thirteenth century–*c*.1327), professor of rhetoric at the university of Bologna, politely refusing the professor's invitation to abandon Ravenna and the vernacular Muse, and join him in Bologna.

The four poems, usually published together with the title *Egloge* in Latin, *Egloghe* in Italian, and *Eclogues* in English, were exchanged between 1319 and 1321.

The first poem was an epistle in Latin hexameters in which Giovanni del Virgilio invited Dante to stop writing for the populace and to use instead his poetic genius for the benefit of the learned public by addressing in Latin such recent epic events as the descent of Emperor Henry VII to Italy, or the war between Padua and Verona, or the siege of Genoa by the fleet of Robert of Anjou (1278–1343). Dante responds with a bucolic poem in which, interacting with Giovanni as Tityrus does with Meliboeus in the first of Virgil's *Eclogues*, he affirms the dignity of vernacular poetry and promises to send Giovanni ten cups of freshly milked sheep milk to convince him fully. Taking up the bucolic challenge, Giovanni-Mopsus responds in kind, renewing his invitation to Dante-Tityrus to join him in Bologna; if Dante will not satisfy Giovanni's thirst, the professor will be obliged to turn to Padua (where the famous Latin writer Albertino Mussato (1261–1329) lived) for satisfaction. In his reply Dante-Tityrus says that he would go and see Giovanni-Mopsus, but he fears Polyphemus, whose cruelty is described by Alphesibeus, Tityrus' friend.

The two major problems associated with the interpretation of this correspondence seem now largely solved: the ten cups of milk mentioned by Dante are very likely to be ten canti of *Paradiso*, while Polyphemus is probably Fulcieri da Calboli (d. 1340), former *podestà* of Florence and *capitano del popolo* in Bologna in 1321, hostile to Dante and the White alliance. What seems clear and very interesting about the *Egloge* is that they represent with great clarity the existence of two very different approaches to literary culture in the first half of the fourteenth century: on Dante's side the vernacular, 'comic', humble approach that favours as its subjects the social, political, and ethical issues of contemporary life; on Giovanni's side the Latin, 'tragic', proto-humanistic approach that prefers lofty subjects, such as wars and heroes, and a return to the classics. Needless to say, it was Giovanni's approach that Italian intellectuals chose, at least for the following two centuries.

## Questio de aqua et terra

Published for the first time in Venice in 1508 by Giovanni Benedetto Moncetti (d. after 1540), the *Questio de aqua et terra* (Question on Water and Earth) is a scientific treatise in Latin that Dante gave as a lecture on Sunday, 20 January 1320 in the small church of Sant'Elena in Verona. As

508 Lino Pertile

no previous manuscript tradition survives and its subject is so unexpected, the text was for a long time assumed to be apocryphal, until it was noted that Dante's son Pietro (before 1300–64), in the third version of his commentary on the *Commedia*, refers unambiguously to it. Furthermore, recent studies of its language and style have highlighted many points of contact with Dante's other works. The treatise is based on the widespread Aristotelian notion that the centre of the earth coincides with the centre of the universe and is surrounded by the four sublunar spheres of earth, water, air, and fire. The related *quaestio* – a technical term that refers to the formal treatment of doctrinal issues generating controversy – is why the land mass is visibly higher than water in so much of the earth. In response to this question, which Dante notes that he had already debated while he was in Mantua, he argues that, where the land rises above the water, as is the case in the northern hemisphere, it is because the Fixed Stars both attract the earth to themselves as a magnet attracts iron, and also draw up the subterranean vapours, which in turn force the earth to rise above the water. Such lifting was necessary, and is willed by God, so that the appropriate mixing should occur on earth among different elements to make humankind's life possible. This explanation does not match the one Virgil gives at *Inferno* XXXIV, 121–6; but while the discrepancy used to be decisive for some scholars, in particular Bruno Nardi, who would not accept the *Questio*'s authenticity, more recently it has been convincingly shown that the poetic and scientific explanations can coexist on two different planes; indeed, one complements the other.

### Notes

1 *Il Fiore e il Detto d'Amore attribuibili a Dante,* ed. G. Contini, Edizione Nazionale (Milan: Mondadori, 1984); *Fiore. Detto d'Amore*, ed. P. Allegretti, Edizione Nazionale Società Dantesca Italiana (Florence: Le Lettere, 2011); *Il Fiore e il Detto d'amore*, ed. L. Formisano, Nuova edizione commentata delle opere di Dante: Opere di dubbia attribuzione (Rome: Salerno, 2012).
2 P. Stoppelli, *Dante e la paternità del Fiore* (Rome: Salerno, 2011).
3 Hugh of St Victor, *De tribus diebus*, 94–109, ed. D. Poirel (Turnhout: Brepols, 2002), pp. 9–10; see *Paradiso* XXXIII, 85–7.
4 See J. A. Scott, *Understanding Dante* (University of Notre Dame Press, 2003), p. 225.

CHAPTER 29

# Textual transmission

### Zygmunt G. Barański

No manuscript personally penned by Dante has survived. However, we do have a description of his handwriting. In his life of the poet, the Florentine humanist Leonardo Bruni (1370–1444) states that Dante's 'script was thin and long and very accurate', as he had been able to ascertain from 'certain letters written in [the poet's] own hand'.[1] Recently, it has been suggested that the unusual calligraphy for a literary work – in technical terms the hand can be described as a semiformal late mixed gothic bookhand based on chancery cursive – and the two-column layout of many copies of the *Commedia* from the first half of the fourteenth century might reflect the appearance of the poet's original. The lack of autograph manuscripts means of course that the texts in which we read Dante's works are reconstructions based on the surviving manuscript copies and other textual evidence. Problems – as we shall see – regarding the arrangement and appearance of several works also stem directly from the loss of the authorial versions, as does the question of the formal character, namely the lexis, morphology, orthography, and even syntax, of Dante's written vernacular, since it was normal for scribes to render the texts they were transcribing into the forms of their own Italian vernacular. Thus, while the language of the *Commedia* is preponderately Florentine, Dante wrote it in exile, spending the last ten years of his life in Verona and Ravenna, so that its earliest copyists were northerners who at times adapted the poem to the structures of their respective speaking habits. In fact, when such northern copies quickly reached Dante's *patria*, which then became the major centre of production and distribution of the *Commedia*, Florentine features were reintroduced into the poem (the northern and Tuscan traditions represent the two groups under which all the surviving manuscripts can be included). The likelihood of error and confusion arising at the very start of the tradition as a result of this convoluted transmission is obvious; and, as will soon become apparent, other deficiencies mar the poem's first dissemination. Similar problems affect the form of Dante's Latin.

509

510                          Zygmunt G. Barański

Humanist copyists and editors classicized his medieval Latin, while also finding many of the abbreviations current in the early Trecento difficult to interpret.

For all Dante's monumental canonicity, his texts are marked by a disquieting 'fragility'. Indeed, in addition to the disappearance of the autographs, several other substantial complications bedevil the transmission of his *oeuvre*. Indeed, what might actually constitute that *oeuvre* continues to be a matter of dispute. The authenticity or otherwise of several works – the *Fiore*, the *Detto d'Amore*, some lyrics, and the *Epistle to Cangrande* – is far from established; while, as recently as 2002, Domenico De Robertis (1921–2011), editor of a remarkable edition of Dante's *Rime*, added eight poems to the lyric corpus and convincingly demonstrated that thirteen others exist in alternative versions, given that the poet had revised these before including them in the *Vita nova*. Ever since the fourteenth century, on account of his fame, works have been spuriously attributed to Dante, and it was only with the rise of a rigorous textual criticism of vernacular literature in the latter part of the Ottocento that a degree of consistency was brought to his corpus. Thus, the first attempt to provide an at least in part philologically reliable text of Dante's *opera omnia* dates to 1894 and the one-volume edition prepared, and then regularly revised, by Edward Moore (1835–1916) with the help of other members of the Oxford Dante Society, most notably Paget Toynbee (1855–1932). This initiative was followed by the more exacting Società Dantesca Italiana edition of *Le opere di Dante* (Dante's Works) co-ordinated by the great philologist and critic Michele Barbi (1867–1941) and published, also in one volume, in 1921 to coincide with the centenary of the poet's death. The first editions of Dante's *opera omnia* were printed in Venice in the eighteenth century (1739–41; 1757–58; and 1793). In the manuscript tradition, it is rare for works to be associated, except for the coupling of the *Vita nova* with fifteen canzoni canonized by Boccaccio (1313–75), who was the most important and influential early editor, copyist, and disseminator of Dante's texts (for instance, some of the epistles only survive in the versions he prepared; while the tradition of the *Eclogues* depends almost entirely on the copy he transcribed into his notebook, the so-called *Zibaldone Laurenziano*). Works were normally propagated individually; a noteworthy exception is the anonymous mid Quattrocento Florentine vernacularization of the *Monarchia* surviving in three manuscripts, which also contain the *Convivio*. More specifically, the lyric poetry and the epistles, which Dante, unlike Petrarch, did not bring together into organic collections, were transmitted in a fragmentary and uneven manner. Thus it was not unusual for sonnets and ballads

Textual transmission 511

to circulate alone in manuscripts, although as part of collections of late Duecento and Trecento poetry; indeed, some are attested in just a single witness. Conversely, the majority of the canzoni share the same testimonies; at the same time, the largest groupings of Dantean lyrics never number more than thirty poems. Despite being faced with a total of around 350 manuscripts containing the *rime*, De Robertis, after dedicating fifty years to the task, succeeded, for the first time, in offering a self-standing critical edition of each lyric, namely, where multiple copies exist, a text based on a reconstruction of the interconnections between the individual surviving copies and of the relationship of all these to the original.

The earliest witness of a Dantean text is the copy made by the Bolognese notary Enrichetto delle Querce (mid thirteenth century–c.1312) in 1287 of the sonnet 'No me poriano zamai far emenda' (Never can [my eyes] make amends to me), which he copied into his registry to indicate the end of a contract. On account of dissimilarities in the conditions of their dissemination and reception, the nature and history of the transmission of each of Dante's work tends to be distinct, thereby posing different editorial problems for scholars. On the one hand, the *Commedia* has always been widely read and survives in around 850 manuscripts of varying quality, approximately 600 of which transmit the complete poem; while, on the other hand, the *Fiore* and the *Detto d'Amore* are each preserved in just one manuscript, and were unknown until their discovery in the 1880s. The poems, anonymous and without titles – their designations were coined by their first editors and discoverers: *Fiore* by Ferdinand Castets (1838–1911) and *Detto d'Amore* by Salomone Morpurgo (1860–1942) – were originally part of the same codex, which is extremely accurate and thus very close to the autograph, but were separated in the nineteenth century by the bibliophile, mathematician, patriot, and notorious book thief Guglielmo Libri (1803–69), who stole the *Detto*. Furthermore, and uniquely, the *Questio de aqua et terra* is not preserved in any manuscript. Its earliest and only reliable witness is the Venetian printed edition of 1508, which was probably based on a Trecento manuscript and prepared by the theologian Giovanni Benedetto Moncetti (d. 1542–47), who had considerable difficulty in reading the copy he was utilizing, and consequently produced a seriously defective text.

Of all Dante's works, the transmission of the *Commedia* is by far the most varied, complex, and convoluted, so that many scholars doubt whether it is actually feasible to establish a critical edition of the poem. The problems relate not simply to the very high number of extant witnesses (higher than for any other medieval vernacular work); additional

Zygmunt G. Barański

serious complications stem from the peculiarities and vagaries of the *Commedia*'s earliest transmission. Although a few scholars dispute this, it is probable that the poet never prepared a complete copy of his poem for publication. This was probably done circa 1322 in Ravenna by his son Jacopo (*c*.1300–48) soon after his father's death. It is unlikely that Jacopo was working with autographs of at least the first two canticles, since *Inferno* was already circulating in 1314 and *Purgatorio* a year or so later. Indeed, there is circumstantial evidence to suggest that Dante had released batches of cantos of *Paradiso* before completing it. Disagreement exists regarding the earliest surviving manuscript of the complete text of the *Commedia*. Many scholars believe that this dates from 1336 (Piacenza, Biblioteca Comunale Passerini Landi ms. 190). However, it has recently been convincingly argued that Florence, Biblioteca Medicea Laurenziana ms. Ashburnham 828 was copied in the early 1330s, and certainly no later than the Summer of 1334. Nonetheless, there is considerable indirect evidence of the speed, popularity, and nature of the poem's dissemination in the preceding twenty or so years.

Copyists, especially those from Northern Italy, found the *Commedia* difficult to transcribe on account of its language and formal inventiveness. As a consequence, errors, misunderstandings, and simplifications were introduced into the earliest copies. To counter the corruptions, other scribes, and especially those in Florence, invented corrections and, more grievously, borrowed from other manuscripts, thereby introducing contamination, namely they undermined a direct vertical line of descent from the principal exemplars from which they were copying by introducing variants from other manuscripts. Furthermore, when preparing their versions of the poem, some copyists transcribed different canticles, and even groups of cantos, from different exemplars. Thus the 1336 Landi manuscript is contaminated throughout, thereby confirming the degree to which the defect had become entrenched in the tradition. Equally, the copyist of a lost 1330–31 manuscript, which has been reconstructed on the basis of the humanist Luca Martini's (1507–61) collation of this manuscript using as his base text a 1515 Aldine printed edition (Milan, Biblioteca Nazionale Braidense, Aldina AP XVI 25), in which he noted the variants, was clearly aware of the presence of corrupt readings, as also were the earliest commentators of the *Commedia*. In a matter of a few years after Dante's death, the relationship of the copies of the *Commedia* in circulation to the poet's original was to say the least problematic. Indeed, there is a chance that Jacopo's text itself may have been contaminated; and the situation deteriorated during the 1350s. Concerned that Petrarch did not own a copy of the

*Commedia*, Boccaccio commissioned one from a Florentine scriptorium (Biblioteca Apostolica Vaticana ms. Vat. lat. 3199), which he sent to his friend some time after 1351. Either from this or from an almost identical copy from the same source, Boccaccio made three copies of the *Commedia* between the mid 1350s and 1373. The three manuscripts are: Toledo, Biblioteca del Cabildo ms. 104 6; Florence, Biblioteca Riccardiana ms. 1035; and Biblioteca Apostolica Vaticana ms. Chigi L VI 213. Each copy is different as Boccaccio, a notoriously interventionist editor and scribe, continued to alter the text on the basis of other manuscripts he consulted and his own conjectures.

Given his authority, the tradition of the *Commedia* Boccaccio inaugurated became widely influential. It served as the basis of the Aldine edition of 1502 prepared by the great humanist Pietro Bembo (1470–1547), whose father Bernardo (1433–1519) had acquired Vat. Lat. 3199 for his personal library. The *Commedia* had first been printed in Foligno in 1472, and, given its popularity, the *princeps* was quickly followed by other incunables printed in several Italian cities. Print, however, introduced further confusion and contamination into the tradition. Indeed, the 1502 Aldine was in part a response to the linguistic hybridity and orthographical inconsistencies present in the early prints, and remained the standard text of the poem until the end of the eighteenth century. In 1775, in his *Correctiones et adnotationes in Dantis Comoediam* (Corrections and Annotations to Dante's *Comedy*), Bartolomeo Perazzini (1727–1800) claimed that, in order to establish the poem's text, scholars needed to follow the exacting criteria established by scriptural and classical textual critics. During the nineteenth century, given the relative backwardness of philological studies in Italy at the time, the major contributions in this direction were all by non-Italians. The German polymath Karl Witte (1800–83) was the first to endeavour to bring a degree of order to the confusing accumulation of *Commedia* manuscripts in preparing his 1862 edition of the poem. The vital need to classify the manuscripts and trace their interrelationships has ever since characterized the scholarly struggle to establish a reliable text of Dante's masterpiece. Witte was followed in this task, first by the Swiss Carl Taüber (1864–1945), and then, much more substantially, by Moore. Ever since the turn of the twentieth century, work on the text of the *Commedia* has overwhelmingly been undertaken by Italian philologists, reaching a noteworthy highpoint in 1966–67 with the publication of Giorgio Petrocchi's (1921–89) monumental 'national' edition. Recognizing that it was extremely difficult, if not actually impracticable, to undertake a complete recension of all the witnesses, he based his fundamental edition on a full collation – still the most extensive ever attempted – of what he considered to be the twenty-seven oldest manuscripts, all written before 1355, the date after which, Petrocchi claimed, Boccaccio's impact on the tradition meant that it became irremediably contaminated, and so of little use in preparing the text. With commendable caution, pragmatism, and methodological sophistication, Petrocchi entitled his edition *La Commedia secondo l'antica vulgata*, namely the text of the poem as it was read in the three decades or so after Dante's death, thereby acknowledging the problems in establishing the poet's original version. In recent years, scholars have increasingly questioned, not infrequently correctly, various aspects of Petrocchi's edition and its criteria, including his belief that it is not possible to prepare an edition that comes close to Dante's text. However, the textual and methodological alternatives they have proffered are often more problematic and restrictive than Petrocchi's proposals. His text thus continues to serve as the standard edition for most Dantists.

Despite the questions surrounding the text of the *Commedia*, no such doubts affect its integrity and organization. The metrical and numerological structures that Dante invented for his poem made it very hard for scribes to omit and add passages. The same is not true, however, as regards the structure and even the appearance of some of his other works. Thus, in the wake of De Robertis' edition of the *rime*, a heated debate has erupted as to whether the collection of fifteen canzoni was first brought together by Dante or, only subsequently, by Boccaccio. The evidence, which is complex, probably points to the latter's manipulation. More significantly, doubts exist as to whether the poet intended to include in the *Convivio* the texts of the canzoni that he was ostensibly glossing, and if he did, where precisely these were to be located. In any case, the tradition of the 'almost commentary' (*Conv.* I, iii, 2) is knotty. Although it was the first of the minor works to be printed, in Florence in 1490, and survives in forty-six manuscripts, no more than two of these date from the Trecento, and both are from the end of the century. The vast majority, quite uniquely, was copied 150 years after the work's composition. In the fourteenth century, except for Dante's other commentator son Pietro (before 1300–64) and a few Florentine devotees of the poet, the *Convivio* was unknown, not least because, as the faulty manuscript tradition confirms, the original was in a provisional state, strongly suggesting that Dante had not intended to publish the work. It was only beginning in the second half of the Quattrocento that, once more in Florence, serious interest in the *Convivio* developed, with particular attention being paid to its metaliterary and doctrinal aspects.

## Textual transmission

The most serious organizational uncertainties, however, affect the *Vita nova*. The *prosimetrum* is present in forty-three witnesses, the earliest, in this instance too, are relatively late, belonging to the middle of the Trecento, and hence to about fifty years after Dante had completed the *libello*. Although it is certain that the poet intended it to be divided into 'paragraphs' (*Vn* II, 10), namely what we would term chapters, the manuscript tradition is far from clear as to where such divisions ought to be introduced. Currently, the two most authoritative editions propose different solutions. Barbi's great 1932 critical edition, one of the finest examples of Italian philology, is divided into forty-two 'chapters', while Guglielmo Gorni's (1945–2010) 1996 edition has thirty-one. To confuse matters further, Barbi's text is more reliable than Gorni's, while the latter's 'paragraphing' is probably closer to the original. Very recently, questions have been posed about how Dante might have arranged the *Vita nova*'s verse and prose. Notoriously, in his two autograph copies of the *Vita nova*, in imitation of classical glossed poetic manuscripts, Boccaccio placed the prose *divisiones*, in which Dante explicated his poems, in the manuscripts' margins, thereby destroying the vital organic unity of the *libello*. Boccaccio's aim was to elevate Dante and his verse to the same rank as that of the Latin *auctores*. Yet, examining the oldest manuscripts of the *Vita nova*, it is striking that, in each one, the prose and the poetry are transcribed and laid out differently. In addition, none follows established scribal norms for prosimetrical works. To put it simply, the copyists had doubts as how best to reproduce Dante's text. This would suggest that the appearance of the autograph was unusual, and certainly did not have the layout of modern editions in which prose and poetry are clearly distinguished and conventionally printed. The evidence from the manuscripts, in fact, regardless of their individual solutions, seems to point to a text in which the two forms were probably not differentiated, in keeping with Dante's aim to forge a new type of overarching literary work.

When he copied and assembled Dante's works in his manuscripts, Boccaccio was not simply preserving the writings of an esteemed predecessor. He was also involved in a sophisticated cultural operation to canonize vernacular literature in the face of reservations expressed about its value by classicizing intellectuals. Throughout their history, the transmission of Dante's texts has been profoundly affected by external factors. For instance, the rapid and impressive growth in philological studies of his *oeuvre* in the recently unified Italy was in part driven by patriotic sentiment.

# Zygmunt G. Barański

The *De vulgari eloquentia*, too, owes its revival to changing cultural circumstances. As with the *Convivio*, Dante did not publish the treatise. Even though three of the five surviving manuscripts, of which one is a fragment, can be dated to the second half of the Trecento, the work remained largely unknown until it was made public by the humanist Gian Giorgio Trissino (1478–1550) at the beginning of the Cinquecento to help bolster his position in the debates regarding the character of written Italian. Trissino translated the *De vulgari eloquentia* into Italian and his version was printed in Vicenza in 1529; the Latin text only appeared in 1577.

On account of its controversial political views, the *Monarchia*'s transmission, more than that of any other of Dante's works, has been shaped by extratextual pressures. Another work probably not published by the poet, its fortune was first closely tied to the struggles between the emperor and the pope in the Trecento, and then, during the sixteenth century, to the disputes between Catholicism and Protestantism. Its dissemination was further complicated by its being placed on the Papal Index in 1554, from which it was not removed, according to the most recent research, until 1900. Unsurprisingly, given its troubled early reception, a minority of its twenty-one extant manuscripts date from the fourteenth century (and these are all relatively late). Conscious of the treatise's dubious orthodoxy, several scribes did not give the author's name and omitted the title, while others stressed Dante's good standing as *Christianus*. Although the *Monarchia* was popular in late Quattrocento and Cinquecento humanist circles, even being translated into the vernacular by Marsilio Ficino (1433–99), it comes as no surprise that it was first printed outside Italy, in reformed Basel in 1559. It was included in a collection of works on imperial authority, with the publisher, Johannes Oporinus (1507–68), insisting that its author was not the famous writer but a fifteenth-century Dante Alighieri. In this instance, Oporinus may well have been worried about publishing a political text by a medieval Catholic poet. The *Monarchia*, in fact, might have had a famous editor. In 1527, the imperial chancellor Mercurino Gattinara (1465–1530) invited Erasmus (1466–1536) to prepare the text so that 'the little book may be published'.[2] Nothing came of the proposal; but if it had, Dante's extraordinary transmission would have had yet another fascinating chapter, and Boccaccio would have found himself rubbing shoulders with a worthy companion in the long line of those who, over the centuries, have striven to ensure that the works of Western culture's greatest writer survive for posterity.[3]

## Notes

1 L. Bruni, *Vita di Dante,* in *Opere letterarie e politiche di Leonardo Bruni,* ed. P. Viti (Turin: UTET, 1996), p. 548.
2 Letter quoted in P. Toynbee, 'Erasmus and Dante's *Monarchia*', *Modern Language Review,* 20 (1925), 43–7, at 43.
3 I should like to thank Ted Cachey, Simon Gilson, Giulio Lepschy, Lino Pertile, Prue Shaw, and Claudia Tardelli for their comments on drafts of this chapter.

CHAPTER 30

# *Early reception (1290–1481)*

## Zygmunt G. Barański

Around the middle of the fifteenth century, on the verso of the opening page of his compilation of materials relating to Dante (Florence, Biblioteca Laurenziana ms. 90 sup. 131), the Florentine ser Piero Bonaccorsi (1410–77) copied two anecdotes that record a degree of hostility towards the poet. The first tale is constructed around the idea that 'Dante is a knave [*villano*] … because he has said everything worth saying … and has left nothing for others to say'; while the second recounts Dante's 'anger' at a 'rival' who belittles his achievements.[1] Yet Bonaccorsi's admiration for the poet was profound, not least because by the 1440s the cult of Dante's intellectual and artistic, as well as civic achievements was deeply rooted in Florence's culture. Bonaccorsi not only copied Dante's works and other texts associated with the poet, but also composed *Il cammino di Dante* (Dante's Journey, *c.*1440), which offered a careful literal summary of the *Commedia* and examined with illustrations the topography of Dante's afterlife – the latter a peculiarly Florentine interest – and a brief treatise on the poem's references to time. Nevertheless that 'knave', even if interpreted antiphrastically, given its association with the vignette of Dante irascibly defending his 'fame', and given the anecdote's strategic position in the manuscript, cannot but cast a shadow over ser Piero's appreciation. It hints at the complexity, ambiguity, and contradictoriness of Dante's reception in his native city – and indeed in the rest of Italy. On account of the extraordinary success of the *Commedia* and his widely acknowledged status as exceptional vernacular poet, thinker, and all-round exemplary individual, recourse was regularly made to Dante in literary, linguistic, cultural, and political disputes. Thus in Florence, since the latter part of the fourteenth century, the poet had become a touchstone in quarrels between defenders of the vernacular and humanist polemicists who decried the quality of his Latin and the gaps in his knowledge of the ancient world. Furthermore, by the 1430s such arguments had taken on increasingly political hues since they pitted

*Early reception (1290–1481)* 519

pro-vernacular intellectuals, most notably Francesco Filelfo (1398–1481), close to the city's ruling oligarchy against classicizing supporters of the ever-more powerful Cosimo dei Medici (1389–1464). To be a *dantista* – the earliest surviving occurrence of the appellation comes from nearly a century earlier – in mid-Quattrocento Florence was anything but straightforward; and Bonaccorsi's inclusion of the problematic anecdotes represents an interesting if minor trace of the difficulties. Moreover, ser Piero as a middlebrow aficionado of the poet, who pursued a career as a notary, and who consequently was not unlikely politically vulnerable, especially as he was regularly beset by financial troubles, must have felt such tensions with particular keenness.

The situation in Florence during the first half of the fifteenth century points both to the extent to which Dante and the *Commedia* had become central to Italian cultural life since his passing in 1321, and to the ways in which author and poem had been adapted to local needs and to the particular interests of different social groups. Dante's elevation had begun during his own lifetime, and had gathered pace immediately after his death. Unlike the waspish stories transcribed by Bonaccorsi or the more substantial strictures of some Quattrocento humanists, the bulk of fourteenth-century (and, later, fifteenth-century) evaluations of the poet tended to be positive when not actually celebratory: 'Dante, a theologian, lacking no doctrine which philosophy may cherish in her illustrious breast, glory of the Muses, the best loved author of the common people'; 'Dante Alighieri, a man of deep and renowned wisdom, a disciple of philosophy, and the loftiest poet'; 'Dante was ... distinguished in his manners and well versed in many sciences, and especially in the sciences of the poets ... indeed no mortal can be compared to him in the glory of language.'[2] Yet for intellectuals to be making such fulsome assessments of a contemporary in the late Middle Ages, even of one who belonged to the same cultural and geographical milieu as them, was remarkable. More significantly, their reactions point to the fact that, by the early Trecento, a major cultural revolution was under way in the Italian peninsula.

Before Dante wrote the *Commedia*, no post-classical author – and especially not one who, in a world dominated by Latin, had 'scandalously' decided to write using his own native language – had been celebrated with such vigour and in such evocative and culturally loaded terms. Instead, the encomiastic language used to describe Dante had, for centuries, been applied almost exclusively to the great writers and thinkers of antiquity. Dante was following tradition when he presented Virgil being 'honoured' in Limbo as 'the loftiest poet' (*Inf.* IV, 80), a conventional designation

520 Zygmunt G. Barański

for the poet of the *Aeneid*, the breadth of whose intellectual prowess was also regularly noted. Indeed, a few cantos later, Dante terms Virgil the 'courteous, all-knowing sage' (*Inf.* VII, 3). Yet, at least as far as some of Dante's fourteenth-century readers were concerned, the 'new poet' was not just on a par with but was also actually superior to his classical forebears. Although most were chary about aggressively asserting such a radical and disturbing view, that this indeed was their opinion emerges time and again in their writings. For instance, the Carmelite friar Guido da Pisa (thirteenth–fourteenth centuries) first conventionally refers to Virgil as the 'greatest poet', but then, immediately afterwards, declares that Dante 'must be judged so much greater than all the others, as he composed the greatly sublime work [the *Commedia*]'.[3] Such obviously incompatible assessments could not but undermine the traditional literary hierarchy and challenge established perceptions regarding the status of the poets of antiquity, thereby drawing attention to and augmenting Dante's burgeoning reputation. And matters of authority (*auctoritas*) – namely of who should be deemed worthy to hold cultural, intellectual, artistic, and moral sway over the present, and hence, having once been elevated to the rank of 'authoritative author' (*auctor*), serve as a model for others to imitate – were at the very core of the transformation that took place in fourteenth-century Italy. Authority controlled every area of medieval life, since, as Dante explained in the *Convivio*, ' "authority" means the same as "an activity worthy of being trusted and obeyed" ' (IV, vi, 5).

Dante's first readers, in fact, were following a trail that the poet had carefully prepared. When he first meets Virgil in *Inferno*, the wayfarer declares 'You are the one from whom alone I took | the noble style that has brought me honour' (*Inf.* I, 86–7). While praising Virgil, Dante also subtly established the distinction of his own poetic credentials – and this at the very start of the *Commedia*. In the following canto, by having Virgil speak of Beatrice, Dante drew his readers' attention to his youthful *Vita nova*, the work on which, as he began to compose the *Commedia* around 1306–07, his reputation still largely rested. Two cantos later, Dante presents himself as welcomed in Limbo by the great canonical poets of antiquity, Homer, Virgil, Horace, Ovid, and Lucan, 'so that I became the sixth amidst such wisdom' (*Inf.* IV, 102). In granting himself this exalted status – a status that no post-classical writer had previously achieved – Dante usurped the position conventionally occupied by Terence, the established authority on comedy. His new, contemporary, Christian, and vernacular 'comedía' (*Inf.* XVI, 128 and XXI, 2), building on his earlier achievements, was about to replace a centuries-old and highly respected tradition.

*Early reception (1290–1481)* 521

Nor was Dante making claims that he could not substantiate. The genius and uniqueness of his poetry immediately confirmed the validity of his assertions. Thus with the *Commedia*, Dante gave a powerful boost of confidence and energy to the nascent vernacular culture. He demonstrated that using one's own native language not only was not a bar to success, but also was not an obstacle to addressing complex theological and doctrinal topics and to being artistically innovative. The *Commedia* takes the genre to which it belongs in new and unexpected directions: its rhyme scheme, carefully partitioned structure, and linguistic and stylistic range are all unprecedented, as are its 'realism' and its 'encyclopaedic' span; and this is true as regards both the classical and the vernacular literary traditions. To put it simply, Dante offered practical confirmation that the vernacular (or at any rate his vernacular) could match, and even surpass, anything that Latin had achieved; and there were many in the fourteenth and fifteenth centuries who both agreed with him and were willing publicly to mark and canonize his extraordinary attainment.

The many commentaries that, throughout the fourteenth century, were written in both Latin and the vernacular to accompany the *Commedia* offer evident proof of this consensus. They also constitute the most important manifestation of the earliest reactions to the poet and his masterpiece. The commentaries followed the forms of scriptural and classical exegesis; however, what fundamentally distinguished them from their models was the fact that they focused their attention on a 'modern' text and author. In truth, the commentaries to the *Commedia* were not the first examples of formal exegesis of a non-classical work, or even of one composed in the vernacular – Guido Cavalcanti's (?1260–1300) notoriously difficult philosophical *canzone* 'Donna me prega' (A lady asks me) had probably been glossed during Dante's lifetime – instances of such criticism were both slight and extremely rare. The fact is that no other post-classical literary text had come even close to generating the kind of sustained, programmed, and detailed commentary that Dante's poem inspired; and, in the Middle Ages, there was no more significant recognition of an author's *auctoritas* than for his writings to be systematically explicated.

The earliest extant commentary, that by Dante's son Jacopo (*c.*1289–1348) to *Inferno*, can be dated to 1322, the year after the poet's death in Ravenna. However, Dante enjoyed considerable recognition during his lifetime. For two decades – especially after his exile from Florence in 1302 – Dante was Italy's best-known and most influential writer and intellectual. Long before he came to compose the *Commedia*, as the poet himself acknowledged in the opening two cantos of *Inferno*, the *Vita nova* had firmly established his literary reputation. Previously, in the opening chapters of the *Convivio* (I, iii–iv), Dante had offered a glimpse of the extent of his 'fame' at the start of the fourteenth century. At the same time, there is no doubt that Dante's *auctoritas* was overwhelmingly based on the *Commedia*. The history of the poet's reception in the Trecento, but also in the Quattrocento, is primarily the history of his reception as the author of the 'sacred poem' (*Par.* XXIII, 62 and XXV, 1), to such an extent that in Florence the *Commedia* became known as 'il Dante'. The obsession with the *Commedia* also helps explain the limited circulation of Dante's other works during most of the fourteenth century. It is not until the latter part of the Trecento, for instance, that the poet's lyric production begins to be copied on a regular basis.

The poem's first two canticles, *Inferno* and *Purgatorio*, and possibly batches of cantos of *Paradiso*, began to circulate in Italy during the last decade or so of the poet's life. The *Commedia*'s success was immediate; and its prestige and uniqueness, together with those of its creator, were widely recognized, as evidenced, for instance, by the many vernacular and Latin poems, powerfully celebratory in tone, written to mark Dante's passing and to honour his authorship of the *Commedia*. The opening three lines of the most famous of these, the epitaph by the early humanist scholar Giovanni del Virgilio (late thirteenth century–*c*.1327), can be read above near the start of the second paragraph (they are the first of the three laudatory quotations). Before the *Commedia* no work in the vernacular had reached most parts of the Italian peninsula. The poem's 'national' prominence is confirmed by the fact that commentaries to it were written in places as far apart as Genoa, Naples, Pisa, and Verona, as well as in Dante's native Florence and in the university city of Bologna. Furthermore, as the manuscript evidence demonstrates, in fourteenth-century Italy the *Commedia* was the most popular book after the Bible. Additionally, the quality of the manuscript tradition reveals that copies of the poem, ranging from richly illustrated codices to less ostentatious, relatively swiftly produced exemplars, were made with different audiences in mind. In particular, after 1340, to satisfy the demands of Florence's growing bourgeois-mercantile class, a flourishing market developed of quasi-serial production of the *Commedia*. The most famous copies of this kind originated from the workshop of Francesco di ser Nardo da Barberino and have become known as 'the group of the One Hundred', a designation which refers to their supposed number. Legend has it that Francesco di ser Nardo, who was active as a *scriptor* during the first half of the fourteenth century, produced so many copies not simply

*Early reception (1290–1481)* 523

to fulfil the orders of his fellow citizens but also as he had to find dowries for his several daughters.

The *Commedia*'s penetration into much of the peninsula is all the more remarkable since, given medieval Italy's linguistic fragmentation into many distinct regional vernaculars – a fragmentation that Dante was the first to record in his *De vulgari eloquentia* – the Florentine in which the poem is written would have been far from familiar to the majority of its readers. Indeed, whatever their other aims, it is certain that one of the primary functions of especially non-Tuscan commentaries was to make Dante's language accessible to readers in different regions. It is for this reason that commentators both offered detailed prose paraphrases and summaries of cantos (though both features are typical of large-scale commentaries to the *auctores*), and translated sections of the *Commedia* into Latin. Rendering the poem into Latin and analysing it using the learned language were also signs of its assimilation into official academic culture, although, as will become clearer below, Dante's position within this remained problematic throughout the fourteenth and fifteenth centuries. Furthermore, as the number of literate readers versed only in their native language steadily increased during the Trecento, commentaries originally written in Latin were translated into the vernacular. The poem's influence ranged from the schools to the pulpit and into the street. What is striking and unique about the poem's fourteenth- and fifteenth-century readers and listeners is the diversity of their backgrounds and of their social origins. The *Commedia* united preachers and university masters, theologians and artists, courtiers and artisans, princes and prelates, merchants and jurists. Indeed, behind Franco Sacchetti's (*c.*1332–1400) apocryphal short stories of blacksmiths incorrectly reciting verses from the *Commedia*, one can catch a glimpse of the degree to which Dante's masterpiece had penetrated into popular consciousness.[4]

Nonetheless, it needs to be stressed that, despite the rapid growth in literacy, especially in Florence, during the Trecento and beyond, it is almost certain that the *Commedia* was not actually read by the lower orders, and that contemporary claims regarding Dante's appeal to the vulgar crowd were normally voiced by intellectuals who, whatever else they thought about him and his work, disapproved, especially given the poem's sizeable doctrinal component, of his having written in the vernacular rather than in Latin, the established language of refined and educated communication. Giovanni del Virgilio's allusion to Dante's popularity thus introduces a note of reproof into his epitaph's tones of sorrowful appreciation; and that Giovanni should have done so is not really surprising, since, a

524                    Zygmunt G. Barański

year or so earlier, he had expressed the same reservation, and in rather more vigorous terms, in a pair of Latin poems addressed to the poet of the *Commedia*. As we have begun to see, not all reactions to the poet and his poem were positive; nor is this at all surprising if one remembers the cultural shock caused by Dante.

The diversity of the *Commedia*'s audience largely accounts for the variety, as regards their form, language, and content, of the critical responses to the poem. As well as being the focus of in-depth, organically structured commentaries in Latin and in Italian – these range from analyses of all its one hundred *canti* to interpretations of individual canticles or even of just a single canto – the *Commedia*, together with its author, inspired a plethora of other texts in both prose and verse. These include public lectures, summaries, pseudo-biographies, short stories, anecdotes, and discontinuous and connected glosses. It goes without saying that no author since classical antiquity had generated such interest; and, as a further mark of respect and canonization, it was not unusual for different texts relating to Dante to be bound together in a single codex, as occurs with the fourteenth- and fifteenth-century Italian manuscript now held in Oxford (Bodleian Library ms. Canon. Misc. 449), which contains, inter alia, the prologues of several commentaries, Alberico da Rosciate's (*c.*1290–1360) commentary to *Paradiso*, a Latin translation of Iacomo della Lana's (*c.*1278–*c.*1358) commentary to *Inferno*, and the complementary introductory poems to the *Commedia* by Bosone da Gubbio (between 1260/90–between 1349/77) and by Jacopo Alighieri.

The *Commedia*, of course, generated a literary as well as a critical reaction. Not unsurprisingly, given its range and uniqueness, it prompted few direct imitations. The most important are Petrarch's (1304–74) *Triumphi* (Triumphs, 1340–74) and Boccaccio's (1313–75) *Amorosa visione* (Amorous Vision, 1342–43, second redaction *c.*1355–60), both of which rely heavily on the *Commedia*'s metre, language, structure, and motifs to present their visionary subject-matter. Both poems are not without artistic shortcomings, although their blemishes pale to insignificance when compared to the mechanistic and ponderous attempts of other writers to compose lengthy narrative didactic poems in *terza rima* – the interlaced rhyme scheme that Dante invented for the *Commedia* – as seen in Federico Frezzi's (*c.*1350–1416) *Il Quadriregio* (The Four Kingdoms, 1394–1403). Although the *Commedia* inspired few outright imitators, its influence on the formal choices and the artistic purview of fourteenth- and fifteenth-century authors was enormous, ranging from moral-didactic writings to chronicles, and from erotic to epic poetry. It is enough to remember, to stay with

*Early reception (1290–1481)*     525

Petrarch and Boccaccio, not so much the fundamental shaping force that the poem exerted on the structure and style of the *Decameron* (1349–51), as the deep imprint it made on Petrarch's lyric language in his collection of love poems, the *Rerum vulgarium fragmenta* (Fragments of My Vernacular Things, 1336–74). In the following century, the *Commedia* left an equally powerful impression on the language and style of the *Morgante* (1460s–83), Luigi Pulci's (1432–83) exhilarating comic chivalric epic. Lorenzo de' Medici's (1449–92) writings too owe a significant debt not just to the poem, but also to the *Vita nova* and the *Convivio*, highlighting a new interest in both works.

Dante's influence also spread to the visual arts, from painting to portraiture and from sculpture to manuscript illustration. The oldest surviving illustrated manuscript of the *Commedia* is of Florentine origin and dates from 1337 (Milan, Biblioteca Trivulziana ms. 1080). It inaugurates a rich and diverse tradition of depictions of the poet and his otherworldly adventure. The drawings do not straightforwardly illustrate the poem but frequently serve as pictorial glosses. Indeed, close interconnections can be established between the images and some of the written commentaries. At times the illustrators even addressed matters that the commentators ignored or sidestepped because of their controversial nature, such as the question whether Dante had actually had a direct experience of the afterlife. The manuscript illustrators also depicted the poet in a range of authoritative guises: as prophet, as *auctor*, and as a man of learning – guises that point to the different ways in which the *Commedia* was read. Nor were Dante and his poem just a storehouse of subjects fit for artistic treatment. The *Commedia*'s vision of the afterlife influenced frescos of Hell, most notably that in the Strozzi chapel of Santa Maria Novella in Florence executed by Nardo di Cione (*c.*1320–66) during the 1350s. Moreover, the inscriptions written in *terza rima* that appear in Simone Martini's (*c.*1284–1344) fresco of the *Maestà* (Majesty, 1315–16) in the Palazzo Pubblico in Siena are based on passages from *Inferno* and *Purgatorio* – further evidence of Dante's precocious *auctoritas*.

Despite, or perhaps on account of, its popularity, the *Commedia* engendered both negative and positive reactions among intellectuals. Criticism of the poem, possibly more insistent in the Trecento than in the Quattrocento, given its immediate contemporary relevance, and that came from both secular and religious circles, centred on its language (Dante's choice of the vernacular over Latin); its lack of literary propriety (its failure to follow the customary conventions of comedy, and hence the inappropriateness of its title – the epithet 'divine', which marks a key stage in the 'divinization' of the poet, was added for the first time in 1555, to the title page of Lodovico Dolce's (1508–68) Venetian edition of the poem); its philosophical ambitions, its theological orthodoxy, its political sympathies, and its doctrinal leanings. Indeed, as recent scholarship has begun to demonstrate, all the works Dante wrote after he had begun the *Commedia*, namely the *Monarchia*, the *Eclogues*, which constitute his response to Giovanni del Virgilio's criticisms, and the *Questio de aqua et terra*, can be deemed to offer rebuttals to such attacks, thereby providing yet more proof of the speed and seriousness with which the poem was greeted. Many of the commentaries, too, by defending, for instance, the *Commedia*'s orthodoxy, its style, and its erudition, appear bent on countering efforts to discredit both the poem and its author. What unites all the extant fourteenth- and fifteenth-century commentaries is their overt desire to celebrate and monumentalize Dante and the *Commedia*. Especially in the Trecento, they constitute, as I suggested earlier, the most sophisticated overt expression of that fascination with the poem that, on its appearance, almost immediately swept through Italy – a fascination that today helps us to contextualize and appreciate the commentators and their works. For too long and anachronistically, Dante scholars have decontexualized the commentaries, considering them simply as passive appendages to the *Commedia*, useful primarily for seeing how early critics unravelled the poem's many *cruces*, rather than as independent texts in their own right.

The commentaries are products of their environment in other ways. As has already been noted, Dante was intent on vindicating himself and his great poem. This attitude stemmed from his clear awareness of the significance of the critical discourses associated with literary texts. Before he wrote the *Commedia*, in order to highlight the importance of his lyric poetry and of his poetic status, Dante composed the *Vita nova* and the *Convivio*, both of which provide detailed self-commentaries in prose to his verse and are closely modelled on the structural conventions of literary manuscripts that combined a poetic text and its commentary. In fact, the *Vita nova* inaugurates the genre of self-commentary in the Western tradition. To establish the canonical standing of his *rime*, Dante imitated a textual and critical form that, for centuries, had normally been restricted to the works of the great Latin poets. In the *Convivio*, he additionally drew on the interpretive conventions of scriptural, philosophical, and theological commentary. The commentators of the *Commedia* followed in Dante's wake, not least because in the poem, although he did not establish any explicit links with the normal conventions of exegesis as he had done

*Early reception (1290–1481)* 527

in the *Vita nova* and the *Convivio*, he did fashion a complex system of self-reflective critical allusion that was based on a judicious use of technical critical vocabulary and on the narrative action and its formal representation. Dante's aim was to explain and justify the *Commedia*'s experimentation and to establish himself as an *auctor*. In their turn, the commentators recognized and confirmed Dante's 'authoritativeness'. For the first time in centuries, a new *auctor* had been canonized; indeed, Benvenuto da Imola (1320/30–1387/88), the most incisive and original of the *Commedia*'s fourteenth-century exegetes, unambiguously declared that Dante was the greatest of all writers: 'No other poet knew how to praise and condemn as excellently and effectively as Dante, the most perfect poet'. In the late Middle Ages *laudare et vituperare* were used as an overarching formula to describe the ambit of literature as a whole, and Benvenuto wrote a monumental commentary to the *Commedia* (1375–83), based on his public lectures, to demonstrate that his critical assessment of Dante's achievement was sound.[5]

To date, Dante scholarship has found it far from easy to trace a precise history of the fourteenth-century commentators. There are several major reasons for this. The nineteenth-century editions of many of the commentaries are defective, as are some more recent ones (this situation is now being rectified, thanks especially to the sterling efforts of the organizers of the 'Edizione Nazionale dei Commenti danteschi'); it has proved difficult to establish precise dates for a large number of the commentaries (the currently most commonly accepted dates are given here); some commentaries exist in different versions; and it was not uncommon for commentators and copyists to confuse and contaminate different sets of glosses. All these reasons make it especially hazardous to try to establish the nature of the relationship between different commentaries – a problem that is especially acute as regards the so-called *Epistle to Cangrande*, labelled after its addressee the Lord of Verona between 1311 and 1329. The letter examines the *Commedia* in general by assessing its allegorical structure and by considering it under the six headings typical of one of the standard models of the *accessus* – the prologue with which a commentary to an *auctor* traditionally opened ('the subject, the author, the form, the aim, the book's title, and the branch of philosophy to which it belongs', *Epistle to Cangrande*, XIII, 18) – before offering a detailed literal reading of the opening twelve lines of *Paradiso*.

Scholars continue to disagree as to whether or not the *Epistle* was penned by Dante. Those supporting its authenticity claim that it is not only the key commentary to the *Commedia*, but also the critical text that fundamentally influences nearly all the subsequent commentaries, since these would appear to follow several of its interpretive schemes. However, the philological evidence for the *Epistle*'s authenticity is not especially compelling, and its links to the other commentaries are in fact extremely few and involve matters, such as the wording of the *accessus* headings and of the poem's ethical definition, that were commonplaces. In any case, it is not at all clear from these verbal repetitions whether the commentators depend on the *Epistle* or vice versa. The *Epistle*, in fact, is only mentioned twice during the Trecento: in the unpublished autograph glosses to the *Commedia* written by the Florentine notary Andrea Lancia (*c*.1297–1357) in the early 1340s (Florence, Biblioteca Nazionale Centrale ms. II I 39, fol. 133r) and in the preface of the last of the fourteenth-century commentaries (1391–1405), that by Filippo Villani (*c*.1325–1405).[6] This has led some scholars to hypothesize that it is a compilation of several earlier texts. The letter's status as a forgery would also seem to be supported by its conservative exegesis. It fails to assert the *Commedia*'s radical novelty – the issue at the heart of Dante's self-commentary of the poem – but treats it instead as an ordinary work of fiction with an ethically useful message. This would suggest that the *Epistle* was composed by a traditionalist intellectual troubled both by Dante's literary ambitions and by his claims that his poem was divinely inspired and hence true, a major source of disquiet even among the poet's admirers. Thus Pietro Alighieri (before 1300–64), Dante's other commentator son, while highlighting his father's erudition, insisted that the *Commedia* is a fiction.

In some religious circles, most notably the Dominicans, the idea that Dante might have been in some way divinely inspired, especially given the unorthodoxy of a number of his views, caused considerable consternation. Thus in 1335 the Florentine chapter of the order banned younger friars from reading the *Commedia* (the need for the prohibition points to the poem's popularity within the order). Already in 1328, in Bologna, another Dominican, Guido Vernani (d. *c*.1348), had censured Dante as the 'devil's vessel' and as a 'wordy sophist' for 'composing many fantastic things in poetry' and for 'leading astray not only sickly minds but also those of the learned to the ruin of salvific truth'.[7] Guido's attack opens his *Refutation of the Monarchia*, the treatise in which the poet had argued against the Church's temporal power, supporting instead the universal authority of the Holy Roman Emperor. An ecclesiastical backlash against Dante's views was unsurprising, and the work continued to be condemned as late as the end of the nineteenth century. Yet for all the Dominicans' misgivings, many other religious treated Dante and the *Commedia* as models of

# Early reception (1290–1481)

orthodoxy. Preachers drew on him in their sermons, while the Carmelite commentator of the poem, Guido da Pisa, compared the poet to the prophet Daniel as he contrived to appropriate him for his order as part of the Carmelite strategy to establish a distinct identity in opposition to both the Franciscans and the Dominicans.

All the commentaries mix apologetics, explanation, and praise. Yet beyond this, and beyond the restrictions imposed by the norms of contemporary literary criticism, it is not difficult to discriminate between the aims, and so the intellectual and cultural ambitions and profiles, of the different commentators. Thus some prefer to focus on explicating the *Commedia's* allegory and moral lessons, even as others concentrate on clarifying its literal meaning, on analysing its literary qualities, and on providing information on various aspects of Dante's career and intellectual and political sympathies. Yet other commentators pragmatically integrate literal and allegorical exposition, as in the first commentary to the entire poem (1324–28), written in Italian by the Bolognese Iacomo della Lana. Iacomo's work, which became very popular and was incorporated into early printed editions of the *Commedia*, reveals both the influence of the city's university environment and a desire to explain Dante to a broad audience. In his turn, a fellow-citizen of Iacomo's, Graziolo Bambaglioli (*c.*1290–1343), wrote a Latin commentary in 1324 highlighting the poem's high cultural standing in order to counter anti-Dante sentiment in the city. Confirming the rapid maturity and breadth of the interpretive tradition on the *Commedia*, the author of the *Ottimo commento* (1334) – termed 'best' in 1612 by linguistic purists impressed by the authenticity of its Florentine vernacular – attempted to synthesize contemporary exegesis on the poem, a clear mark of the tradition's complex, 'living', and collective textuality. The commentary also marked a growing recognition of Dante's importance within Florence, and was part of the attempt by Florentine intellectuals to recuperate the exiled poet for his native city. Commentaries were even written for personal gain, as in the case of the heavily plagiarized commentary to *Inferno* (1369–73) written by Guglielmo Maramauro (1317–after 1379) to gain favour with his political masters, as he successfully manoeuvred to be appointed to an academic post in Naples.

The variety of the commentaries and the assortment of uses to which they were put mirror the complexity and vibrancy of Dante's fourteenth-century reception. The poet and his remarkable poem affected every area of cultural life in Trecento Italy, as it would substantially continue to do in the following century. In particular, there was no major literary question, such as the relationship between Latin and the vernacular,

530          Zygmunt G. Barański

the function of poets and poetry, and the doctrinal character of literature, in which Dante's authority was not invoked. It is therefore not surprising that the reactions to Dante of the fourteenth century's two other leading intellectual figures, Petrarch and Boccaccio, were fundamentally shaped by the poet's general reception. Although Petrarch liked to present himself as largely untouched by Dante and hardly ever mentioned him in his writings, in reality both his Latin and vernacular works reveal a significant formal and ideological dependence on the works of his illustrious forerunner. Petrarch was profoundly troubled by the sway that Dante exerted over Trecento intellectual and artistic life, not least because it placed a heavy obstacle in the way of his own efforts to be treated as an *auctoritas*. Drawing on the criticisms that others had expressed regarding Dante, in the few instances that Petrarch actually did refer to his rival, he insinuated that his predecessor's reputation was largely unjustified. Petrarch's jaundiced view of Dante had a major bearing on his friendship with Boccaccio, who, although he too had some reservations about the nature and implications of Dante's authority, did more than anyone else in Trecento Italy to commemorate and canonize the older poet. Boccaccio openly borrowed from Dante in his own works; he copied and collated Dante's writings; he wrote a life of his hero that closely follows the conventions of the lives of Virgil; he composed encomiastic verse in his honour; and, in 1373, he began to write a major commentary on the *Commedia*, which, at his death in 1375, had reached the opening lines of *Inferno* XVII. Until quite recently, the accepted view was that, for all his efforts to persuade Petrarch that his negative opinion of Dante was unjustified, Boccaccio had no success in influencing his friend. This interpretation, however, has now been convincingly called into doubt. If, on the one hand, Petrarch progressively managed somewhat to attenuate Boccaccio's enthusiasm, on the other, Boccaccio's championing of Dante had a fundamental effect on Petrarch's renewed interest in vernacular poetry after 1353.

Indeed, it has been claimed, although the evidence for this is inconclusive, that Petrarch was able to dampen enthusiasm for Dante more generally, especially between 1350–70, when the composition of large-scale commentaries, even if not other marks of appreciation, undoubtedly decreased. However, the last decades of the Trecento (Petrarch died in 1374), with the appearance of the prodigious pre-humanist commentaries of Boccaccio, Benvenuto, and Francesco da Buti (*c.*1324–1406; the final version of the commentary was completed in 1396), brimming with fulsome appreciation of Dante's literary abilities, constitute one of the high points of the poet's early reception. The *Commedia*'s popularity

## Early reception (1290–1481)

also reached a peak between 1380 and 1450, as evidenced by the fact that most surviving manuscripts of the poem were copied during these years. On the other hand, the fifteenth century signals a clear decline in the number and quality of new commentaries that were written. This is likely a consequence of the authority and acceptance that, by this date, many of the Trecento commentaries had achieved. Until Cristoforo Landino's (1425–98) classicizing Neoplatonic commentary published in Florence in 1481, the other Quattrocento commentaries tend to be pedestrian and derivative. These include the brief 1466 Latin annotations, heavily dependent on Pietro Alighieri, of Niccolò Claricini (active during the fifteenth century) to the whole of the *Commedia*, the Latin marginal and interlinear 1461 glosses of Matteo Chiromono (third decade of the fifteenth century–1482) that stop at *Paradiso* VI, 37 and that draw significantly on Benvenuto da Imola, and Guiniforte Barzizza's (1406–63) vernacular synthesis of the major late-fourteenth-century commentaries to *Inferno* that he composed around 1440. Like nearly all other fifteenth-century commentaries, the aim of these three works of criticism was to make the substantial contributions of the Trecento commentators better accessible to a wider, frequently court-based public, which, with the spread of humanism, would have found much that was outdated, and hence not especially to their taste, in the previous century's readings of the *Commedia*. In addition, Quattrocento commentators sought to make the poem relevant and appealing to new generations of readers by inserting references to contemporary political, philosophical, cultural, and linguistic matters.

Although it also is a work of synthesis, once again heavily reliant on Benvenuto, Giovanni Bertoldi da Serravalle's (*c.*1350–1445) Latin commentary to the entire *Commedia* is important because it points to the poem's and Dante's steadily increasing standing outside Italy. In late 1415 or early 1416, Giovanni, who was Bishop of Fermo, had been encouraged to translate the *Commedia* into Latin by the Italian Cardinal Amedeo di Saluzzo (*c.*1361–1419) and, tellingly, by two English prelates, Robert Hallum (*c.*1377–1417), Bishop of Salisbury and former Chancellor of the University of Oxford, and Nicholas Bubwith (d. 1424), Bishop of Bath and Wells. The aim was to make Dante's poem better known to the clergy and others attending the Council of Konstanz (1414–18). Giovanni rapidly completed (May–June 1416) a literal, though inelegant, prose translation, and accompanied this with a moralizing commentary, composed also with considerable alacrity (1 February 1416–16 January 1417), which was intended to help bring about a spiritual renewal in the wake of the damaging papal schism. It is interesting to note how earlier religious anxieties

532                          Zygmunt G. Barański

regarding the *Commedia*'s orthodoxy had become relatively quickly dispelled as Dante's authoritative status, especially in Italy but also elsewhere, had continued to grow and be affirmed. Indeed, by the beginning of the fifteenth century, the Dominicans in Florence were teaching the poem in their *studium*, although there were still those in their order, such as Antonino Pierozzi (1389–1459), Archbishop of Florence from 1446 until his death, who continued to question Dante's doctrinal conformity.

In France, after Jean Froissart's (*c*.1337–*c*.1410) fleeting allusion in *Espinette amoureuse* (Loving Spinet, 1369), Christine de Pizan (1364–1429) made significant use of 'the book called Dante'.[8] Chaucer's (1342–1400) profound engagement with the *Commedia* is apparent in *The House of Fame, Troilus and Criseyde*, and *The Canterbury Tales*, confirming Dante's key role in Chaucer's development and self-definition as a vernacular poet. The poet's Spanish reception is especially noteworthy. The fifteenth century saw seven translations of the *Commedia* in both Castilian and Catalan, as well as in both prose and verse. Dante was used to legitimate and exalt the nascent Spanish vernacular literature, as the Marqués de Santillana, Iñigo López Mendoza (1398–1458), had instituted by presenting Dante as the supreme *auctoritas* for those intending to write in their own native language.

The character of Dante's intellectual, moral, and literary authority was in a constant state of flux, as it was adapted to local needs and changing cultural and historical circumstances. During the Quattrocento, humanism, the century's main intellectual movement, which emphasized the pre-eminence of poetry, moral philosophy, and history, the superiority of classical learning, and the linguistic primacy of Latin, exercised a profound effect on his reception. In the Trecento Dante had been favourably compared to the great classical poets and presented as reviving classical culture. However, already from around the middle of the century doubts had been raised, most notably by Petrarch, regarding his classical expertise. Such reservations, which focused on his unstinting preference for the vernacular, the inelegance of his written Latin, and the limitations in his knowledge of the ancient world, grew in number and vigour during the fifteenth century. The situation in Florence, as noted earlier, was especially complicated. By the start of the Quattrocento Dante's standing and that of the city had become tightly entwined. Florence increasingly presented itself and measured its reputation in light of the poet, who, as a result of public lectures, visual depictions in public spaces, and a variety of other celebratory strategies, was treated as the consummate object of civic pride. At the same time, Florence was a major centre of the *studia*

*Early reception (1290–1481)* 533

*humanitatis*, and tensions inevitably arose between the humanists' elite classicizing inclinations and the broad-based cult of Dante that gripped the city. Reactions to the poet in Florentine humanist circles ranged from almost total condemnation to unreserved celebration. Niccolò Niccoli (1364–1437), who championed an unalloyed classicism and rejected the achievements of Trecento vernacular literature, deemed Dante a poet of little worth. Conversely, Cino Rinuccini (after 1350–1417), in his *Responsiva alla Invettiva di messer Antonio Lusco* (Reply to the Invective of Messer Antonio Lusco, c.1401–5) and *Invettiva contra a certi caluniatori di Dante, del Petrarca e del Boccaccio* (Invective against Certain Slanderers of Dante, Petrarch and Boccaccio, c.1400–3), presented Dante as an outstanding poet, theologian, and philosopher, who 'surpasses all poems both Greek and Latin'.[9] Other humanist responses to Dante were more nuanced. Coluccio Salutati (1332–1406), the city's first humanist chancellor, while recognizing some problems with Dante's use of the vernacular, affirmed the breadth of his knowledge and the force of his creative powers, positively comparing these to the achievements of the ancients. Leonardo Bruni's (1370–1444) attitude to Dante shifts noticeably during the course of his life. In his *Dialogi ad Petrum Histrum* (Dialogues to Pier Paolo Vergerio, c.1404–6) he privileges Petrarch over Dante: the former prepares the way for humanism, while the latter is hampered by his poor Latin and ties to scholasticism. Thirty years later, in his *Vita di Dante* (Life of Dante, 1436), Bruni's judgement is less severe, going so far as to praise, albeit in a circumscribed manner, the quality of the poet's vernacular.

It is likely that Bruni modified his outlook as a result of the changing political situation in Florence. Dante's politics, in particular his championing of the Roman empire as providential, had created disquiet in the city ever since the latter part of the previous century. The poet's views went against the independent republicanism at the heart of Florentine civic ideology, and, around 1400, Salutati energetically justified Dante's ideas so as to protect the poet's key position within the city. By the 1430s, when Dante had become entangled in the disputes between anti- and pro-Medici factions, he was transformed by Filelfo and others into a republican civic patriot. The most sophisticated formulation of this incarnation of the poet is found in Bruni's life, in which Dante is converted into a civic humanist, active in Florentine politics and fighting on his *patria*'s behalf. By the time of Lorenzo de' Medici's accession to power in 1469, the poet had been appropriated to bolster Medicean authority. This was accompanied, after decades of criticism, by the beginnings of a positive reappraisal, led by Cristoforo Landino and Marsilio Ficino (1433–99),

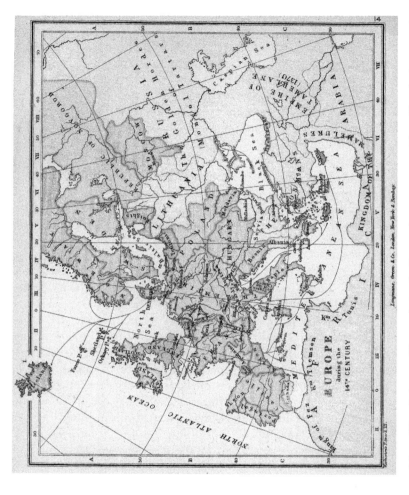

Map 1  Historical map of Europe during the fourteenth century. From *The Public Schools Historical Atlas*, edited by C. Colbeck, 1905.

Map 2 Dante's Italy around 1300.

of Dante's vernacular and of the vernacular tradition in general. Landino's role in granting new impetus to Dante's reputation, both in Florence and beyond, was fundamental. In 1480–81, he prepared the first new printed commentary to the *Commedia* – the first printed edition of the poem had

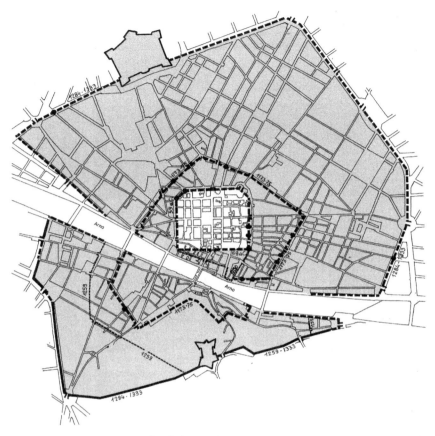

Map 3  Walls of Florence from Roman times to 1333.

appeared in Foligno in 1472 – which was published in August 1481 and which became the most important Renaissance commentary to the poem, eclipsing the work of the Trecento commentators, many of whose contributions it effectively synthesized. For Landino, the poet embodied all that was best about Florentine culture, beginning with the fact that he had shaped its language into a sophisticated literary medium. In addition, Landino humanistically portrayed Dante as well versed in classical literature and as a poetic philosopher sensitive to Platonic thought. As had occurred in the fourteenth century, Dante was once again back, if only in Florence, as the supreme poet.

*Early reception (1290–1481)* 537

Although, as the Quattrocento drew to a close, Latin culture seemed largely to have reasserted itself, its supremacy, as the emergence of a vernacular humanism confirmed, would be comparatively short-lived. Thanks in no small part to Dante, the progress and establishment of vernacular culture could be delayed but not halted. The popularity of printed editions of the *Commedia* across Italy in the late fifteenth and sixteenth centuries offers confirmation of this trend. Modern literature had arrived; and with it, in the shape of the Trecento commentaries to the poem, the modern study of literature had also dutifully appeared. Dante transformed Western literature; but it was the poet's first readers, drawing on his bold example, who fundamentally affected our reading practices and our sense of the literary. For this reason alone, Dante's early reception deserves to be much better known than it generally is.[10]

### Notes

1 All translations in this chapter are my own. The quotations are taken from G. Bruschi, 'Ser Piero Bonaccorsi e il suo *Cammino di Dante*', *Il propugnatore*, new series, 4 (1891), 5–39, at 23–4.
2 The quotations respectively come from: P. H. Wicksteed and E. G. Gardner, *Dante and Giovanni del Virgilio* (Westminster: Constable, 1902), p. 174; Graziolo Bambaglioli, *Commento all''Inferno' di Dante*, ed. L. C. Rossi (Pisa: Scuola Normale Superiore, 1998), p. 3; Guido da Pisa, *Commentary on Dante's Inferno*, ed. V. Cioffari (Albany: State University of New York Press, 1974), p. 4.
3 Guido da Pisa, *Commentary on Dante's Inferno*, pp. 30–1. The term 'new poet' is found at the very opening of Guido's commentary (p. 1).
4 F. Sacchetti, *Il Trecentonovelle*, ed. V. Marucci (Rome: Salerno, 1996), CXIV and CXV.
5 Benvenuto da Imola, *Comentum super Dantis Aldigherij Comoediam*, ed. J. F. Lacaita, 5 vols. (Florence: Barbèra, 1887), vol. I, p. 8.
6 F. Villani, *Expositio seu comentum super 'Comedia' Dantis Allegherii*, ed. S. Bellomo (Florence: Le Lettere, 1989), Prefatio 32, p. 38.
7 G. Vernani, *De reprobatione Monarchiae* in N. Matteini, *Il più antico oppositore politico di Dante: Guido Vernani da Rimini: Testo critico del 'De reprobatione Monarchiae'* (Padua: CEDAM, 1958), p. 93.
8 Christine de Pizan, *Le Débat sur le 'Roman de la rose'*, ed. E. Hicks (Paris: Champion, 1977), p. 141.
9 C. Rinuccini, *Invettiva contra a certi caluniatori di Dante, del Petrarca e del Boccaccio* in G. Gherardi, *Il Paradiso degli Alberti*, ed. A. Wesselofsky, 3 vols. (Bologna: Romagnoli, 1867), vol. I/2, pp. 303–16, at p. 313.
10 I should like to thank Ted Cachey, Simon Gilson, Paola Nasti, and Lino Pertile for their comments on drafts of this chapter.

# Further reading

## 1 Empire, Italy, and Florence

Abulafia, David (ed.), *The New Cambridge Medieval History (1198–1300)* (Cambridge University Press, 2008).

Black, Antony, *Political Thought in Europe 1250–1450* (Cambridge University Press, 1992).

Bowsky, William M., *Henry VII in Italy: The Conflict of Empire and City-State* (Lincoln: University of Nebraska Press, 1960).

Canning, Joseph, *A History of Medieval Political Thought, 300–1450* (London and New York: Routledge, 1996).

Davidsohn, Robert, *Storia di Firenze. II. Guelfi e Ghibellini, l'egemonia Guelfa e la vittoria del popolo* and *III. Le ultime lotte contro l'impero* (Florence: Sansoni, 1957 and 1960).

Davis, Charles Till, *Dante's Italy and Other Essays* (Philadelphia: University of Pennsylvania Press, 1984).

Folz, Robert, *The Concept of Empire in Western Europe from the Fifth to the Fourteenth Century*, trans. S. A. Oglivie (Westport: Greenwood Press, 1980).

Hyde, J. K., *Society and Politics in Medieval Italy* (New York: St Martin's Press, 1973).

Jones, Michael, (ed.), *The New Cambridge Medieval History (1305–1415)* (Cambridge University Press, 2000).

Jones, Philip J., *The Italian City State: From Commune to Signoria* (Oxford University Press, 1997).

Lansing, Carol, *The Florentine Magnates: Lineage and Faction in a Medieval Commune* (Princeton University Press, 1991).

Larner, John, *The Lords of Romagna: Romagnol Society and the Origins of the Signorie* (Ithaca: Cornell University Press, 1965).

Najemy, John M., *A History of Florence, 1200–1575* (Oxford and Malden, MA: Blackwell, 2006).

Paton, Bernadette and John E. Law (eds.), *Communes and Despots in Medieval and Renaissance Italy* (Burlington: Ashgate Publishers, 2010).

Runciman, Steven, *The Sicilian Vespers: A History of the Mediterranean World in the Later Thirteenth Century* (Cambridge University Press, 1958).

538

# Further reading

## 2 Economy

Dameron, George W., *Episcopal Power and Florentine Society, 1000–1320* (Cambridge, MA: Harvard University Press, 1991).

*Florence and its Church in the Age of Dante* (Philadelphia: University of Pennsylvania Press, 2005).

Davidsohn, Robert, *Storia di Firenze*, 8 vols. (Florence: Sansoni, 1956–68).

de La Roncière, Charles M., *Florence, centre économique régional au XIVe siècle: Le marché des denrées de première nécessité à Florence et dans sa campagne et les conditions de vie des salariés (1320–1380)*, 5 vols. (Aix-en-Provence: n.p., 1976).

Goldthwaite, Richard A., *The Economy of Renaissance Florence* (Baltimore: Johns Hopkins University Press, 2009).

Holmes, George, *Florence, Rome and the Origins of the Renaissance* (Oxford: Clarendon Press, 1986).

Hoshino, Hidetoshi, *L'Arte della lana in Firenze nel basso medioevo: Il commercio della lana e il mercato dei panni fiorentini nei secoli XIII–XV* (Florence: Olschki, 1980).

Lansing, Carol, *The Florentine Magnates: Lineage and Faction in a Medieval Commune* (Princeton University Press, 1991).

Pinto, Giuliano, *Il libro del biadaiolo: carestie e annona a Firenze della metà del '200 al 1348* (Florence: Olschki, 1978).

Raveggi, Sergio, Massimo Tarassi, Daniela Medici, and Patrizia Parenti, *Ghibellini, Guelfi e Popolo Grasso: I detentori del potere politico a Firenze nella seconda metà del Dugento* (Florence: La Nuova Italia, 1978).

Spilner, Paula, '"Ut Civitas Ampliatur": Studies in Florentine urban development, 1280–1400' (Ph.D. Dissertation, Columbia University, 1987).

Sznura, Franek, *L'espansione urbana di Firenze nel Dugento* (Florence: La Nuova Italia, 1985).

## 3 Law

Brundage, James A., *Medieval Canon Law* (London and New York: Longman, 1995).

*The Medieval Origins of the Legal Profession: Canonists, Civilians, and Courts* (University of Chicago Press, 2008).

Cassell, Anthony K., The 'Monarchia' Controversy. An Historical Study with Accompanying Translations of Dante Alighieri's 'Monarchia', Guido Vernani's 'Refutation of the "Monarchia" Composed by Dante', and Pope John XXII's Bull 'Si fratrum' (Washington: Catholic University of America Press, 2004).

Conte Emanuele and Sara Menzinger (eds.), *La 'Summa Trium Librorum' di Rolando da Lucca (1195–1234). Fisco, politica, 'scientia iuris'* (Rome: Viella, 2012).

Cortese, Ennio, *Il problema della sovranità nel pensiero giuridico medioevale* (Rome: Bulzoni, 1966).

540           Further reading

*Il diritto nella storia medievale. II. Il Basso Medioevo* (Rome: Il Cigno Galileo Galilei, 1995).

Costa, Pietro, *'Iurisdictio'. Semantica del potere politico nella pubblicistica medievale (1100–1433)* (Milan: Giuffrè, 1969).

Dilcher, Gerhard and Diego Quaglioni (eds.), *Gli inizi del diritto pubblico*, 3 vols. (Bologna and Berlin: Il Mulino and Duncker & Humblot, 2006–11).

Meijers, Eduard M., *Etudes d'Histoire du Droit. III. Le droit romain au Moyen Age. Publiées par les soins de R. Feenstra et H. F. W. D. Fischer* (Universitaire pers Leiden, 1959).

Post, Gaines, *Studies in Medieval Legal Thought: Public Law and the State. 1100–1322* (Princeton University Press, 1964).

Soetermeer, Frank, *'Utrumque ius in peciis': Aspetti della produzione libraria a Bologna tra Due e Trecento* (Milan: Giuffrè, 1997).

Steinberg, Justin, *Dante and the Limits of the Law* (University of Chicago Press, 2013).

Tierney, Brian, *Religion, Law and the Growth of Constitutional Thought, 1150–1650* (Cambridge University Press, 1982).

*The Crisis of Church and State, 1050–1300* (University of Toronto Press, 1988).

Ullmann, Walter, *Medieval Papalism. The Political Theories of the Medieval Canonists* (London: Methuen, 1949).

Winroth, Anders, *The Making of Gratian's 'Decretum'* (Cambridge University Press, 2000).

## 4 Justice

Blanshei, Sarah Rubin, *Politics and Justice in Late Medieval Bologna* (Leiden: Brill, 2009).

Chiffoleau, Jacques, 'Le procès comme mode de gouvernement' in A. Rigon and F. Veronese (eds.), *L'età dei processi. Inchieste e condanne tra politica e ideologia nel '300* (Rome: Istituto Storico Italiano per il Medioevo, 2009), pp. 317–48.

Chiffoleau, Jacques, Claude Gauvard, and Andrea Zorzi (eds.), *Pratiques sociales et politiques judiciaires dans les villes de l'Occident à la fin du Moyen Age* (Rome: École française de Rome, 2007).

Dameron, George W., *Florence and its Church in the Age of Dante* (Philadelphia: University of Pennsylvania Press, 2005).

Diacciati, Silvia, *Popolani e magnati: Società e politica nella Firenze del Duecento* (Spoleto: Cisam, 2011).

Fowler-Magel, Linda, *'Ordines iudiciarii' and 'Libelli de ordine iudiciorum' (From the Middle of the Twelfth to the End of the Fifteenth Century)* (Turnhout: Brepols, 1994).

Geltner, Guy, *The Medieval Prison. A Social History* (Princeton University Press, 2008).

Ikins Stern, Laura, *The Criminal Law System of Medieval and Renaissance Florence* (Baltimore: Johns Hopkins University Press, 1994).

Klapish-Zuber, Christiane, *Retour à la cité: Les magnats de Florence, 1340–1440* (Paris: Éditions de l'École des Hautes Études en Sciences Sociales, 2008).

## Further reading

Milani, Giuliano, *L'esclusione dal comune: Conflitti e bandi politici a Bologna e in altre città italiane tra XII e XIV secolo* (Rome: Istituto Storico Italiano per il Medio Evo, 2003).

Sbriccoli, Mario, 'Legislation, justice, and political power in Italian cities, 1200–1400' in A. Padoa Schioppa (ed.), *Legislation and Justice* (Oxford: Clarendon Press, 1997), pp. 37–56.

Valterza, Loren, 'Rectification, confession, torture: justice and juridical conventions in *Inferno 13*', *Dante Studies*, 129 (2011), 161–78.

Vallerani, Massimo, *Medieval Public Justice* (Washington DC: Catholic University of America Press, 2012).

Wickham, Christopher, *Courts and Conflicts in Twelfth-century Tuscany* (Oxford University Press, 2003), pp. 168–223.

Zorzi, Andrea, *La trasformazione di un quadro politico: Ricerche su politica e giustizia a Firenze dal comune allo Stato territoriale* (Florence University Press, 2008).

(ed.), *Conflitti, paci e vendette nell'Italia comunale* (Florence University Press, 2009).

## 5 Men and women

Boccaccio, Giovanni, *Famous Women*, trans. V. Brown (Cambridge, MA: Harvard University Press, 2003).

Bornstein, Daniel E. and Roberto Rusconi, *Women and Religion in Medieval and Renaissance Italy* (University of Chicago Press, 1996).

Brucker, Gene (ed.), *Two Memoirs of Renaissance Florence: The Diaries of Buonaccorso Pitti and Gregorio Dati*, trans. J. Martines (Prospect Heights: Waveland Press, 1967).

Chojnacki, Susan, *Women and Men in Renaissance Venice* (Baltimore: Johns Hopkins University Press, 2000).

Honess, Claire, *From Florence to the Heavenly City: The Poetry of Citizenship in Dante* (Oxford: Legenda, 2006).

Karras, Ruth Mazo, *From Boys to Men: Formations of Masculinity in Late Medieval Europe* (Philadelphia: University of Pennsylvania Press, 2003).

Kirkham, Victoria, 'A canon of women in Dante's *Commedia*', *Annali d'italianistica*, 7 (1989), 16–41.

Klapisch-Zuber, Christiane (ed.), *A History of Women in the West. II. Silences of the Middle Ages* (Cambridge, MA: Harvard University Press, 1992).

Origo, Iris, *The Merchant of Prato: Francesco di Marco Datini* (New York: Alfred A. Knopf, 1957).

Skinner, Patricia, *Women in Medieval Italian Society, 500–1200* (London: Pearson Education Limited, 2001).

## 6 Church and orthodoxy

Benvenuti Papi, Anna, *'In castro poenitentiae': santità e società femminile nell'Italia medievale* (Rome: Herder, 1990).

542 Further reading

Bowsky, William M., *La Chiesa di San Lorenzo a Firenze nel Medioevo* (Florence: Edizioni della Meridiana, 1999).

Dameron, George, *Florence and its Church in the Age of Dante* (Philadelphia: University of Pennsylvania Press, 2005).

Davidsohn, Robert, *Storia di Firenze*, 5 vols. in 8 (Florence: Sansoni, 1956–68).

Davis, Charles Till, *Dante's Italy and Other Essays* (Philadelphia: University of Pennsylvania Press, 1984).

de La Roncière, Charles, 'Dans la campagne florentine au XIV siècle: les communautés chrétiennes et leurs curés' in his *Religion paysanne et religion urbaine en Toscane (c.1250–c.1450)* (Aldershot and Brookfield: Variorum, 1994), pp. 281–314.

Friedman, David, Julian Gardner, and Margaret Haines (eds.), *Arnolfo's Moment. Acts of an International Conference: Florence, Villa I Tatti, May 26–27, 2005* (Florence: Olschki, 2009).

Henderson, John, *Piety and Charity in Late Medieval Florence* (New York: Oxford University Press, 1994).

Najemy, John, *A History of Florence, 1200–1575* (Malden, MA and Oxford: Blackwell, 2008).

Tacconi, Marica, *Cathedral and Civic Ritual in Late Medieval and Renaissance Florence* (Cambridge University Press, 2005).

Thompson, Augustine, *Cities of God: The Religion of the Italian Communes, 1125–1325* (University Park: Pennsylvania State University Press, 2005).

Toker, Franklin, *On Holy Ground: Liturgy, Architecture, and Urbanism in the Cathedral and Streets of Medieval Florence* (London: Harvey Miller; Turnhout: Brepols, 2009).

Trexler, Ralph, *Dependence in Context in Renaissance Florence* (Binghamton: Medieval and Renaissance Texts and Studies, 1994).

Vauchez, André (ed.), *Storia dell'Italia religiosa. I. L'antichità e il medioevo* (Rome and Bari: Laterza, 1993).

Verdon, Timothy and Annalisa Innocenti (eds.), *Atti del VII centenario del Duomo di Firenze*, 3 vols. (Florence: Edifir, 2001).

## 7 Heresy and dissidence

Angelo Clareno, *A Chronicle or History of the Seven Tribulations of the Order of Brothers Minor*, trans. D. Burr and E. R. Daniel (St Bonaventure: Franciscan Institute Publications, 2005).

Barański, Zygmunt G., '(Un)orthodox Dante' in C. E. Honess and M. Treherne (eds.), *Reviewing Dante's Theology*, 2 vols. (Oxford: Peter Lang, 2013), vol. II, pp. 253–330.

Brufani, Stefano, *Eresia di un ribelle al tempo di Giovanni XXI* (Florence: La Nuova Italia, 1989).

Burr, David, *The Spiritual Franciscans* (University Park: Pennsylvania State University Press, 2001).

## Further reading

Guarnieri, Romana, 'Il Movimento del libero spirito', *Archivio italiano per la storia della pietà*, 4 (1965), 351–708.

Le Roy Ladurie, Emmanuel, *Montaillou*, trans. B. Bray (New York: G. Brazziler, 1978).

Lambert, Malcolm, *Medieval Heresy*, 2nd edn (Oxford and Cambridge, MA: Blackwell, 1992).

Menestò, Ernesto (ed.), *Processo di canonizzazione di Chiara da Montefalco* (Florence: La Nuova Italia, 1984).

Newman, Barbara, 'The heretic saint: Guglielma of Bohemia, Milan and Brunate', *Church History*, 74 (2005), 1–38.

Orioli, Raniero, *Venit perfidus heresiarcha* (Rome: Istituto Storico Italiano per il Medio Evo, 1988).

Potestà, Gian Luca, *Angelo Clareno* (Rome: Istituto Storico Italiano per il Medio Evo, 1990).

Salimbene da Parma, *Chronicle*, trans. J. L. Baird, G. Baglivi, and J. R. Kane (Binghamton: Medieval & Renaissance Texts & Studies, 1986).

Thijssen, J. M. M. H., *Censure and Heresy at the University of Paris, 1200–1400* (Philadelphia: University of Pennsylvania Press, 1998).

## 8 Daily life

Antonetti, Pierre, *La Vie quotidienne à Florence au temps de Dante* (Paris: Hachette, 1979).

Ceccarelli, Giovanni, *Il gioco e il peccato: economia e rischio nel Tardo Medioevo* (Bologna: il Mulino, 2003).

Cherubini, Giovanni, *Signori, contadini, borghesi: ricerche sulla società italiana del Basso Medioevo* (Florence: La Nuova Italia, 1974).

de La Roncière, Charles M., *Prix et salaires à Florence au XIVe siècle, 1280–1380* (Rome: École française de Rome, 1982).

'Tuscan notables on the eve of the Renaissance' in P. Ariès and G. Duby (eds.), *A History of Private Life. II. Revelations of the Medieval World* (Cambridge, MA: Harvard University Press, 1988), pp. 157–309.

English, Edward D., 'Urban castles in medieval Siena: the sources and images of power' in K. Reyerson and F. Powe (eds.), *The Medieval Castle: Romance and Reality* (Dubuque: Kendall/Hunt, 1984), pp. 175–98.

Frugoni, Chiara, *A Day in a Medieval City*, trans. W. McCuaig (The University of Chicago Press, 2005).

Goldthwaite, Richard A., *The Economy of Renaissance Florence* (Baltimore: The Johns Hopkins University Press, 2009).

Henderson, John, *The Renaissance Hospital: Healing the Body and Healing the Soul* (New Haven: Yale University Press, 2006).

Hunt, Edwin S., *The Medieval Super-Companies: A Study of the Peruzzi Company of Florence* (Cambridge University Press, 1994).

Kovesi Killerby, Catherine, *Sumptuary Law in Italy, 1200–1500* (Oxford: Clarendon Press, 2002).

544 Further reading

Lansing, Carol, *The Florentine Magnates: Lineage and Faction in a Medieval Commune* (Princeton University Press, 1991).

*Passion and Order: The Restraint of Grief in the Medieval Italian Communes* (Ithaca: Cornell University Press, 2008).

Redon, Odile, Françoise Sabban, and Silvano Serventi, *The Medieval Kitchen: Recipes from France and Italy*, trans. E. Schneider (The University of Chicago Press, 1998).

Stuard, Susan Mosher, *Gilding the Market: Luxury and Fashion in Fourteenth-Century Italy* (Philadelphia: University of Pennsylvania Press, 2006).

Youngs, Deborah, *The Life Cycle in Western Europe, c.1300–c.1500* (Manchester University Press, 2006).

## 9 Philosophy and theology

Barański, Zygmunt G., 'Studying the spaces of Dante's intellectual formation: some problems of definition' in Z. G. Barański, A. Kablitz, and Ü. Ploom (eds.), *'I luoghi nostri': Dante's Natural and Cultural Spaces* (Tallinn University Press, 2015).

Bianchi, Luca, 'New perspectives on the Condemnation of 1277 and its aftermath', *Recherches de Théologie et Philosophie Médiévales*, 70 (2003), 206–29.

Boyle, Leonard E., *Facing History: A Different Thomas Aquinas* (Louvain-la-Neuve: Fédération Internationale des Instituts d'Études Médiévales, 2000).

Corbari, Eliana, *Vernacular Theology: Dominican Sermons and Audience in Late Medieval Italy* (Berlin: de Gruyter, 2013).

Cross, Richard, *The Medieval Christian Philosophers: An Introduction* (London: I. B. Tauris & Co., 2013).

Dronke, Peter (ed.), *A History of Twelfth-century Western Philosophy* (Cambridge University Press, 1988).

Emery, Kent, William J. Courtenay, and Stephen M. Metzger (eds.), *Philosophy and Theology in the 'Studia' of the Religious Orders and at Papal and Royal Courts* (Turnhout: Brepols, 2012).

Evans, Gillian R. and Philipp W. Rosemann (eds.), *Mediaeval Commentaries on the Sentences of Peter Lombard*, 2 vols. (Leiden: Brill, 2002–10).

Gabriel, Astrik L., 'Robert de Sorbonne', *Revue de l'Université d'Ottawa*, 23 (1953), 473–514.

Honess, Claire E. and Matthew Treherne (eds.), *Reviewing Dante's Theology*, 2 vols. (Oxford: Peter Lang, 2013).

Kretzmann, Norman, Anthony Kenny, Jan Pinborg, and Eleonore Stump (eds.), *The Cambridge History of Later Medieval Philosophy: From the Rediscovery of Aristotle to the Disintegration of Scholasticism, 1100–1600* (Cambridge University Press, 1982).

McGinn, Bernard, *Meister Eckhart and the Beguine Mystics: Hadewijch of Brabant, Mechtild of Magdeburg and Marguerite Porete* (New York: Continuum, 1994).

Masolini, Serena, 'Vernacular, politics and medieval thought: a few notes on a recent volume', *Freiburger Zeitschrift für Philosophie und Theologie*, 60 (2013), 456–67.

## Further reading

Murray, Alexander, *Reason and Society in the Middle Ages* (Oxford: Clarendon Press, 1978).

Oliva, Adriano, *Les Débuts de l'enseignement de Thomas d'Aquin et sa conception de la 'sacra doctrina'. Avec l'édition du prologue de son 'Commentaire des Sentences'* (Paris: Vrin, 2006).

Robb, Fiona, 'A late thirteenth-century attack on the Fourth Lateran Council: the *Liber Contra Lombardum* and contemporary debates on the Trinity', *Recherches de Théologie et Philosophie Médiévales*, 62 (1995), 110–44.

## 10 Moral philosophy

Bettetini, Maria and Francesco D. Paparella (eds.), *Le felicità nel Medioevo* (Louvain-la-Neuve: FIDEM, 2005).

Bejczy, István P. (ed.), *Virtue Ethics in the Middle Ages: Commentaries on Aristotle's Nicomachean Ethics, 1200–1500* (Leiden and Boston: Brill, 2008).

   *The Cardinal Virtues in the Middle Ages: A Study in Moral Thought from the Fourth to the Fourteenth Century* (Leiden and Boston: Brill, 2011).

Bianchi, Luca, 'Felicità terrena e beatitudine ultraterrena: Boezio di Dacia e l'articolo 157 censurato da Tempier' in P. J. J. M. Bakker (ed.), *Chemins de la pensée médiévale. Mélanges Zénon Kaluza* (Turnhout: Brepols, 2002), pp. 193–214.

   '"Noli comedere panem philosophorum inutiliter": Dante Alighieri and John of Jandun on Philosophical "Bread"', *Tijdschrift voor Filosofie*, 75 (2013), 335–55.

Bradley, Denis J. M., *Aquinas on the Twofold Human Good* (Washington DC: The Catholic University of America Press, 1997).

Foster, Kenelm, *The Two Dantes and Other Studies* (London: Darton, Longman & Todd, 1977).

Gauthier, René-Antoine, 'Trois commentaires "averroïstes" sur l'*Éthique à Nicomaque*', *Archives d'Histoire Doctrinale et Littéraire du Moyen Âge*, 16 (1947–48), 187–336.

   *Magnanimité. L'Idéal de la grandeur dans la philosophie païenne et dans la théologie chrétienne* (Paris: Vrin, 1951).

Gentili, Sonia, *L'uomo aristotelico alle origini della letteratura italiana* (Rome: Carocci, 2005).

Minio-Paluello, Lorenzo, 'Dante's reading of Aristotle' in C. Grayson (ed.), *The World of Dante* (Oxford: Clarendon Press, 1980), pp. 61–80.

Sturlese, Loris, 'Intelletto acquisito e divino. La dottrina filosofica di Alberto il Grande sulla perfezione della ragione umana', *Giornale critico della filosofia italiana*, 82 (2003), 161–89.

Wieland, Georg, 'The reception and interpretation of Aristotle's *Ethics*', and 'Happiness: the perfection of man' in N. Kretzmann, A. Kenny, J. Pinborg and E. Stump (eds.), *The Cambridge History of Later Medieval Philosophy* (Cambridge University Press, 1982), pp. 657–72, 673–89.

Zavattero, Irene, 'Felicitas – beatitudo' in I. Atucha, D. Calma, C. König-Pralong, and I. Zavattero (eds.), *Mots médiévaux offerts à Ruedi Imbach* (Porto: FIDEM, 2011), pp. 291–302.

546 Further reading

## 11 Natural philosophy

Asztalos, Monika, 'The Faculty of Theology' in H. de Ridder-Symoens (ed.), *A History of the University in Europe. I. Universities in the Middle Ages* (Cambridge University Press, 1992), pp. 409–41.

Clagett, Marshall, 'Some general aspects of physics in the Middle Ages', *Isis*, 39 (1948), 29–44.

*The Science of Mechanics in the Middle Ages* (Madison: University of Wisconsin Press, 1959).

Dick, Steven J., *Plurality of Worlds: The Extraterrestrial Debate from Democritus to Kant* (Cambridge University Press, 1982).

Grant, Edward, 'The Condemnation of 1277, God's absolute power, and physical thought in the late Middle Ages', *Viator*, 10 (1979), 211–44.

*Planets, Stars, and Orbs: The Medieval Cosmos, 1200–1687* (Cambridge University Press, 1994).

*The Foundations of Modern Science in the Middle Ages. Their Religious, Institutional, and Intellectual Contexts* (Cambridge University Press, 1996).

*God and Reason in the Middle Ages* (Cambridge University Press, 2001).

'Scientific imagination in the Middle Ages', *Perspectives on Science*, 12 (2004), 394–423.

Lindberg, David C., *The Beginnings of Western Science: The European Scientific Tradition in Philosophical, Religious, and Institutional Context, 600 B.C. to A.D. 1450* (University of Chicago Press, 1992).

Murdoch, John E., 'The analytic character of late medieval learning: natural philosophy without Nature' in L. D. Roberts (ed.), *Approaches to Nature in the Middle Ages* (Binghamton: Center for Medieval & Early Renaissance Studies, 1982), pp. 171–213.

Murray, Alexander, *Reason and Society in the Middle Ages* (Oxford University Press, 1978).

Thijssen, J. M. M. H., *Censure and Heresy at the University of Paris, 1200–1400* (Philadelphia: University of Pennsylvania Press, 1998).

## 12 Medicine

Agrimi, Jole and Chiara Crisciani, *Les 'Consilia' Médicaux* (Turnhout: Brepols, 1994).

Amundsen, Darrell W., 'Medieval canon law on medical and surgical practice by the clergy' in his *Medicine, Society, and Faith in the Ancient and Medieval Worlds* (Baltimore and London: The Johns Hopkins University Press, 1996), pp. 222–47.

Bullough, Vern L., *The Development of Medicine as a Profession: The Contribution of the Medieval University to Modern Medicine* (Basel and New York: S. Karger, 1966).

de Vilanova, Arnau, *Opera Medica Omnia Arnaldi de Villanova*, 12 vols. (University of Barcelona, 1975–).

# Further reading

Demaitre, Luke E., *Doctor Bernard de Gordon: Professor and Practitioner* (Toronto: PIMS, 1980).

*Leprosy in Premodern Medicine: A Disease of the Whole Body* (Baltimore: The Johns Hopkins University Press, 2007).

*Medieval Medicine: The Art of Healing, from Head to Toe* (Santa Barbara: Praeger, 2013).

French, Roger, *Medicine before Science: The Business of Medicine from the Middle Ages to the Enlightenment* (Cambridge University Press, 1993).

Jacquart, Danielle and Agostino Paravicini Bagliani (eds.), *La Scuola Medica Salernitana: Gli autori e i testi* (Florence: Edizioni del Galluzzo, 2007).

McVaugh, Michael R., *The Rational Surgery of the Middle Ages* (Florence: SISMEL, 2006).

Nicoud, Marilyn, *Les Régimes de santé au Moyen Age*, 2 vols. (Rome: École française de Rome, 2007).

O'Boyle, Cornelius, *The Art of Medicine: Medical Teaching at the University of Paris, 1250–1400* (Leiden: Brill, 1998).

Park, Katharine, *Doctors and Medicine in Early Renaissance Florence* (Princeton University Press, 1985).

Siraisi, Nancy G., *Medieval and Early Renaissance Medicine: An Introduction to Knowledge and Practice* (University of Chicago Press, 1990).

*Taddeo Alderotti and His Pupils: Two Generations of Italian Medical Learning* (Princeton University Press, 1981).

Ziegler, Joseph, *Medicine and Religion c.1300: The Case of Arnau de Vilanova* (Oxford: Clarendon Press, 1998).

## 13  Islamic and Jewish influences

Alfie, Fabian, 'Immanuel of Rome, alias Manoello Giudeo: the poetics of Jewish identity in fourteenth century Italy', *Italica*, 75 (1998), 307–29.

Battistoni, Giorgio, *Dante, Verona e la cultura ebraica* (Florence: Giuntina, 2004).

Besson, Gisèle and Michèle Brossard-Dandré (eds.), *Le Livre de l'Échelle de Mahomet / Liber Scale Machometi* (Paris: Librairie Générale Française, 1991).

Burman, Thomas E., *Reading the Qur'ān in Latin Christendom, 1140–1560* (Philadelphia: University of Pennsylvania Press, 2007).

D'Alverny, Marie-Thérèse, *La Transmission des textes philosophiques et scientifiques au Moyen Age*, ed. C. Burnett (Aldershot: Variorum, 1994).

*La connaissance de l'Islam dans l'Occident médiéval*, ed. C. Burnett (Aldershot: Variorum, 1994).

Daniel, Norman, *Islam and the West: The Making of an Image*, rev. edn (Oxford: Oneworld, 1993).

Debenedetti Stow, Sandra, *Dante e la mistica ebraica* (Florence: Giuntina, 2004).

Idel, Moshe, *Kabbalah in Italy 1280–1510. A Survey* (New Haven: Yale University Press, 2011).

Mallette, Karla, *The Kingdom of Sicily. 1100–1250. A Literary History* (Philadelphia: University of Pennsylvania Press, 2005).

548                     Further reading

Márquez Villanueva, Francisco, *El concepto cultural alfonsí*, rev. edn (Barcelona: Bellaterra, 2004).
Roth, Cecil, *The History of the Jews of Italy* (Philadelphia: JPS, 1946).
Schildgen, Brenda Deen, *Dante and the Orient* (Urbana: University of Illinois Press, 2002).
Taylor, Julie, *Muslims in Medieval Italy: The Colony at Lucera* (Lanham: Lexington, 2003).
Tolan, John, *Saracens. Islam in the Medieval European Imagination* (New York: Columbia University Press, 2002).
Vernet, Juan, *Lo que Europa debe al Islam de España* (Barcelona: Acantilado, 2006).
Ziolkowski, Jan (ed.), *Dante and Islam*, special issue of *Dante Studies*, 125 (2007).

## 14  Cosmology, geography, and cartography

Ariani, Marco, *'Lux inaccessibilis': Metafore e teologia della luce nel Paradiso di Dante* (Rome: Aracne, 2010).
Armour, Peter, 'Dante e l'*Imago Mundi* del primo Trecento' in P. Boyde and V. Russo (eds.), *Dante e la scienza* (Ravenna: Longo, 1995), pp. 191–202.
Barański, Zygmunt G., 'The mystery of Dante's *Questio de aqua et terra*' in Z. G. Barański and L. Pertile (eds.), *'In amicizia': Essays in Honour of Giulio Lepschy*, special supplement of *The Italianist*, 17 (1997), pp. 146–64.
Bemrose, Stephen, *Dante's Angelic Intelligences: Their Importance in the Cosmos and in Pre-Christian Religion* (Rome: Edizioni di Storia e Letteratura, 1983).
Bianchi, Luca, *Il vescovo e i filosofi: la condanna parigina del 1277 e l'evoluzione dell'aristotelismo scolastico* (Bergamo: Lubrina, 1990).
Boyde, Patrick, *Dante, Philomythes and Philosopher: Man in the Cosmos* (Cambridge University Press, 1981).
Cornish, Alison, *Reading Dante's Stars* (New Haven and London: Yale University Press, 2000).
Duhem, Paul, *Medieval Cosmology: Theories of Infinity, Place, Time, Void, and the Plurality of Worlds*, ed. and trans. R. Ariew (University of Chicago Press, 1985).
Gallarino, Marco, *Metafisica e cosmologia in Dante: Il tema della rovina angelica* (Bologna: Il Mulino, 2013).
Gilson, Simon, *Medieval Optics and Theories of Light in the Works of Dante* (Lewiston, Queenston, and Lampeter: Edwin Mellen Press, 2000).
Grant, Edward, *Planets, Stars, and Orbs: The Medieval Cosmos, 1200–1687* (Cambridge University Press, 1994).
Hetherington, Norriss S. (ed.), *Cosmology: Historical, Literary, Philosophical, Religious, and Scientific Perspectives* (New York: Garland, 1993).
Lewis, C. S., *The Discarded Image: An Introduction to Medieval and Renaissance Literature* (Cambridge University Press, 1964).
Moevs, Christian, *The Metaphysics of Dante's 'Comedy'* (Oxford University Press, 2005).
Scafi, Alessandro, *Mapping Paradise: A History of Heaven on Earth* (University of Chicago Press, 2006).

## Further reading

Wetherbee, Winthrop, *Platonism and Poetry in the Twelfth Century: The Literary Influence of the School of Chartres* (Princeton University Press, 1972).

Woodward, David, 'Medieval mappaemundi' in J. B. Harley and D. Woodward (eds.), *The History of Cartography. I. Cartography in Prehistoric, Ancient, and Medieval Europe and the Mediterranean* (University of Chicago Press, 1987), pp. 286–370.

## 15 Linguistic Italy

Bruni, Francesco (ed.), *L'italiano nelle regioni. I. Lingua nazionale e identità regionali* and *II. Testi e documenti* (Turin: UTET, 1992–94).

Casapullo, Rosa, *Storia della lingua italiana. Il Medioevo* (Bologna: Il Mulino, 1999).

Cavallo, Guglielmo, Claudio Leonardi, and Enrico Menestò (eds.), *Lo spazio letterario del Medioevo. I. Il Medioevo latino* (Rome: Salerno, 1994).

Lepschy, Giulio and Laura Lepschy, 'A historical view' in their *The Italian Language Today*, 2nd edn (London: Hutchinson, 1988), pp. 19–40.

Loporcaro, Michele, *Profilo linguistico dei dialetti italiani* (Rome and Bari: Laterza, 2009).

Manni, Paola, *La lingua di Dante* (Bologna: Il Mulino, 2013).

Mantello, Frank A. C. and A. G. Rigg (eds.), *Medieval Latin: An Introduction and Bibliographical Guide* (Washington DC: Catholic University of America Press, 1996).

Serianni, Luca and Piero Trifone (eds.), *Storia della lingua italiana. I. I luoghi della codificazione; II. Scritto e parlato*, and *III. Le altre lingue* (Turin: Einaudi, 1992–94).

Simone, Raffele (ed.), *Enciclopedia dell'italiano*, 2 vols. (Rome: Istituto della Enciclopedia Italiana, 2011).

Zambon, Alberto, *Alle origini dell'italiano: Dinamiche e tipologie della transizione del latino* (Rome: Carocci, 2000).

## 16 Education

Black, Robert, *Humanism and Education in Medieval and Renaissance Italy: Tradition and Innovation in Latin Schools from the Twelfth to the Fifteenth Century* (Cambridge University Press, 2001).

Davis, Charles Till, *Dante's Italy and Other Essays* (Philadelphia: University of Pennsylvania Press, 1984).

Gehl, Paul, *A Moral Art: Grammar, Society, and Culture in Trecento Florence* (Ithaca and New York: Yale University Press, 1993), pp. 82–106.

Grendler, Paul, *Schooling in Renaissance Italy* (Baltimore: Johns Hopkins University Press, 1989).

*The Universities of the Italian Renaissance* (Baltimore: Johns Hopkins University Press, 2002).

550        Further reading

Law, Vivien, 'Panorama della grammatica normativa nel tredicescimo secolo' in C. Leonardi and G. Orlandi (eds.), *Aspetti della letteratura latina nel secolo XIII* (Perugia and Florence: Regione dell'Umbria and La Nuova Italia, 1986), pp. 125–45.

Lucchi, Piero, 'La santacroce, il salterio e il babuino: libri per imparare a leggere nel primo secolo della stampa', *Quaderni storici*, 38 (1978), 593–630.

Percival, W. Keith, *Studies in Renaissance Grammar* (Aldershot: Ashgate, 2004).

Wieruszowski, Helen, *Politics and Culture in Medieval Spain and Italy* (Rome: Edizioni di Storia e Letteratura, 1971).

## 17 Rhetoric, literary theory, and practical criticism

Ascoli, Albert R., *Dante and the Making of a Modern Author* (Cambridge University Press, 2008).

Barański, Zygmunt G., '"Tres enim sunt manerie dicendi…". Some observations on medieval literature, "genre", and Dante' in Z. G. Barański (ed.), *'Libri poetarum in quattuor species dividuntur': Essays on Dante and 'Genre'*, Supplement 2, *The Italianist*, 15 (1995), 9–60.

'*Magister Satiricus*: Preliminary notes on Dante, Horace and the Middle Ages' in J. C. Barnes and M. Zaccarello (eds.), *Language and Style in Dante* (Dublin: Four Courts Press, 2013), pp. 13–61.

Camargo, Martin, *Ars dictaminis, ars dictandi* (Turnhout: Brepols, 1991).

Copeland, Rita and Ineke Sluiter (eds.), *Medieval Grammar and Rhetoric* (Oxford University Press, 2009).

Cox, Virginia, 'Ciceronian rhetoric in Italy, 1260–1350', *Rhetorica*, 17 (1999), 239–88.

Cox, Virginia and John O. Ward (eds.), *The Rhetoric of Cicero in its Medieval and Early Renaissance Commentary Tradition* (Leiden and Boston: Brill, 2006).

Faral, Edmond, *Les Arts poétiques du XIIe et du XIIIe siècle* (Paris: Champion, 1923).

Holmes, Olivia, *Assembling the Lyric Self: Authorship from Troubadour Song to Italian Poetry Book* (Minneapolis and London: University of Minnesota Press, 2000).

Kelly, Douglas, *The Arts of Poetry and Prose* (Turnhout: Brepols, 1991).

Munk Olsen, Birger, *I classici nel canone scolastico altomedievale* (Spoleto: Centro italiano di Studi sull'Alto Medioevo Italiano, 1991).

Murphy, James J., *Rhetoric in the Middle Ages* (Tempe: Arizona Center for Medieval and Renaissance Studies, 2001; reprint of 1974 edn).

Smalley, Beryl, *The Study of the Bible in the Middle Ages* (Notre Dame University Press, 1964).

Steinberg, Justin, *Accounting for Dante: Urban Readers and Writers in Late Medieval Italy* (University of Notre Dame Press, 2007).

Strubel, Armand, *'Grant senefiance a': Allégorie et littérature au Moyen Age* (Paris: Champion, 2002).

Ward, John O., *Ciceronian Rhetoric in Treatise, Scholion, and Commentary* (Turnhout: Brepols, 1995).

*Further reading* 551

Whitman, Jon, *Allegory: The Dynamics of an Ancient and Medieval Technique* (Oxford: Clarendon Press, 1987).

Woods, Marjorie Curry, *Classroom Commentaries: Teaching the 'Poetria nova' across Medieval and Renaissance Europe* (Columbus: Ohio State University Press, 2010).

## 18 Classical antiquity

Barański, Zygmunt G., '*Magister satiricus*: Preliminary notes on Dante, Horace and the Middle Ages' in J. C. Barnes and M. Zaccarello (eds.), *Language and Style in Dante* (Dublin: Four Courts Press, 2013), pp. 13–61.

Black, Robert, 'The origins of humanism, its educational context and its early development', *Vivarium*, 40 (2002), 272–97.

Camargo, Martin, 'Towards a comprehensive art of written discourse', *Rhetorica*, 6 (1988), 167–94.

Comparetti, Domenico, *Vergil in the Middle Ages*, trans. E. F. M. Benecke (London: Sonnenschein, 1908).

Reynolds, L. D. (ed.), *Texts and Transmission: A Survey of the Latin Classics* (Oxford University Press, 1983).

Reynolds, L. D. and N. G. Wilson, *Scribes and Scholars. A Guide to the Transmission of Greek and Roman Literature*, 3rd edn (Oxford University Press, 1991).

Ward, John O., 'Rhetorical theory and the rise and decline of *dictamen* in the Middle Ages and early Renaissance', *Rhetorica*, 19 (2001), 175–223.

Weiss, Roberto, *Il primo secolo dell'umanesimo* (Rome: Storia e Letteratura, 1949).
*The Spread of Italian Humanism* (London: Hutchinson, 1964).
'The dawn of humanism in Italy', *Bulletin of the Institute of Historical Research*, 42 (1969), 1–16.

## 19 Religious culture

Bornstein, Daniel and Roberto Rusconi (eds.), *Women and Religion in Medieval and Renaissance Italy* (University of Chicago Press, 1996).

Boynton, Susan and Diane J. Reilly (eds.), *The Practice of the Bible in the Middle Ages. Production, Reception, and Performance in Western Christianity* (New York: Columbia University Press, 2011).

De Hamel, Christopher, *The Book: A History of the Bible* (London: Phaidon, 2005).

Demaray, George W., *Florence and Its Church in the Age of Dante* (Philadelphia: University of Pennsylvania Press, 2005).

Farmer, Sharon and Barbara H. Rosenwein (eds.), *Monks and Nuns, Saints and Outcasts: Religion and Medieval Society. Essays in Honor of Lester Little* (Ithaca: Cornell University Press, 2000).

Frugoni, Chiara, *A Day in the Life of a Medieval City* (University of Chicago Press, 2005).

Henderson, John, *Piety and Charity in Late Medieval Florence* (Oxford: Clarendon Press, 1994).

552            Further reading

Lesnick, Daniel R., *Preaching in Medieval Florence: The Social World of Franciscan and Dominican Spirituality* (Athens, GA: University of Georgia Press, 1989).

Lund-Mead, Carolynn and Amilcare A. Iannucci, *Dante and the Vulgate Bible* (Rome: Bulzoni, 2012).

Lynch, Joseph H., *The Medieval Church: A Brief History* (London and New York: Longman, 1992).

Medieval Sourcebook: Twelfth Ecumenical Council: Lateran IV 1215 www.fordham.edu/halsall/basis/lateran4.asp.

Rubin, Miri, *Corpus Christi: The Eucharist in Late Medieval Culture* (Cambridge University Press, 1991).

Sumption, Jonathan, *The Age of Pilgrimage: The Medieval Journey to God* (Mahwah: Hidden Springs, 2003).

Swanson, Robert N., *Religion and Devotion in Europe, c.1215–c.1515* (Cambridge University Press, 1995).

Webb, Diana, *Patrons and Defenders: The Saints in the Italian City-States* (New York: St Martin's Press, 1996).

## 20 Visions and journeys

Allen, Rosamund, *Eastward Bound: Travel and Travellers, 1050–1550* (Manchester University Press, 2004).

Campbell, Mary B., *The Witness and the Other World: Exotic European Travel Writing, 400–1600* (Ithaca: Cornell University Press, 1988).

Dawson, Christopher (ed.), *Mission to Asia* (University of Toronto Press, 1980).

McGinn, Bernard, *The Growth of Mysticism: Gregory the Great to the Twelfth Century* (New York: Crossroad, 1994).

   *Visions of the End: Apocalyptic Traditions in the Middle Ages* (New York: Columbia University Press, 1998).

Wright, John K., *The Geographical Lore of the Time of the Crusades: A Study in the History of Medieval Science and Tradition in Western Europe* (New York: Dover Publications, 1965).

## 21 Historical and political writing

Balzani, Ugo, *Le cronache italiane nel medio evo*, 2nd edn (Milan: Hoepli, 1900).

Barnes, John C., 'Dante's knowledge of Florentine history' in T. Kay, M. McLaughlin, and M. Zaccarello (eds.), *Dante in Oxford: The Paget Toynbee Lectures* (London: Legenda, 2011), pp. 131–46.

Blythe, James M., *Ideal Government and the Mixed Constitution in the Middle Ages* (Princeton University Press, 1992).

   *The Life and Works of Tolomeo Fiadoni (Ptolemy of Lucca)* (Turnhout: Brepols, 2009).

Burns, James H. (ed.), *The Cambridge History of Medieval Political Thought, c.350–c.1450* (Cambridge University Press, 1988).

## Further reading

Capitani, Ovidio, 'Motivi e momenti di storiografia medievale italiana (secc. V–XIV)' in *Nuove questioni di storia medievale* (Milan: Marzorati, 1964), pp. 729–800.

Cochrane, Eric, *Historians and Historiography in the Italian Renaissance* (University of Chicago Press, 1981).

Honess, Claire E., 'Dante and political poetry in the vernacular' in J. C. Barnes and J. Petrie (eds.), *Dante and His Literary Precursors: Twelve Essays* (Dublin: Four Courts Press, 2007), pp. 117–51.

Kempshall, Matthew S., *The Common Good in Late Medieval Political Thought* (Oxford: Clarendon Press, 1999).

Lisio, Giuseppe, *La storiografia* (Milan: Vallardi, n.d.).

## 22 Vernacular literatures

Alfie, Fabian, *Comedy and Culture: Cecco Angiolieri's Poetry and Late Medieval Society* (Leeds: Northern Universities Press, 2001).

Allaire, Gloria, *Andrea da Barberino and the Language of Chivalry* (Gainesville: University Press of Florida, 1997).

Brand, Peter and Lino Pertile (eds.), *The Cambridge History of Italian Literature*, rev. edn (Cambridge University Press, 1999), esp. pp. 1–127.

Cornish, Alison, *Vernacular Translation in Dante's Italy. Illiterate Literature* (Cambridge University Press, 2010).

Gaunt, Simon and Sarah Kay (eds.), *The Troubadours: An Introduction* (Cambridge University Press, 1999).

(eds.), *The Cambridge Companion to Medieval French Literature* (Cambridge University Press, 2008).

Hainsworth, Peter and David Robey (eds.), *The Oxford Companion to Italian Literature* (Oxford University Press, 2002).

Holmes, Olivia, *Assembling the Lyric Self: Authorship from Troubadour Song to Italian Poetry Book* (Minneapolis and London: University of Minnesota Press, 2000).

Kleinhenz, Christopher, *The Early Italian Sonnet* (Lecce: Milella, 1986).

Leonardi, Lino (ed.), *I canzonieri della lirica italiana delle origini*, 4 vols. (Florence: SISMEL, 2000–01).

Segre, Cesare, *Lingua, stile, società: Studi sulla storia della prosa italiana* (Milan: Feltrinelli, 1963).

Storey, H. Wayne, *Transcription and Visual Poetics in the Early Italian Lyric* (New York and London: Garland, 1993).

Witt, Ronald G., *'In the Footsteps of the Ancients': The Origins of Italian Humanism from Lovato to Bruni* (Leiden and Boston: Brill, 2000).

## 23 Popular culture

Bronzini, Giovanni B., 'Nota sulla "popolarità" dei proverbi della *Divina Commedia*', *Lares*, 38 (1972), 9–18.

554 Further reading

'Retroterra primitivo e impiego del popolare nella *Divina Commedia*', *Lares*, 46 (1980), 5–13.

'Riflessi letterari di poesia e vita popolare nella *Vita nuova*', *Lares*, 39 (1973), 111–9.

Burke, Peter, *Popular Culture in Early Modern Europe*, 3rd edn (Farnham: Ashgate, 2009).

Campbell, Josie P. (ed.), *Popular Culture in the Middle Ages* (Bowling Green State University Popular Press, 1986).

Gurevich, Aron, *Medieval Popular Culture: Problems of Belief and Perception* (Cambridge University Press, 1988).

Naselli, Carmelina, 'Aggiunte alle tradizioni popolari nella *Divina Commedia* raccolte dal Pitré' in *Atti del Convegno di studi su Dante e la Magna Curia* (Palermo: Centro di studi filologici e linguistici siciliani, 1967), pp. 374–80.

Pertile, Lino, 'Qui in Inferno: Deittici e cultura popolare', *Italian Quarterly*, 37 (2000), 57–67.

Pitré, Giuseppe, 'Appunti su le tradizioni popolari nella *Divina Commedia*', *Nuovi quaderni del Meridione*, 3 (1965), 162–99.

Speroni, Charles, 'Folklore in the *Divine Comedy*' in F. Schettino (ed.), *A Dante Profile* (Los Angeles: University of Southern California Press, 1967), pp. 15–25.

## 24 Illumination, painting, and sculpture

Boskovits, Miklós, 'Giotto: un artista poco conosciuto?' in A. Tartuferi (ed.), *Giotto. Bilancio critico di sessant'anni di studi e ricerche* (Florence: Giunti, 2000), pp. 75–95.

Bourdua, Louise, *The Franciscans and Artistic Patronage in Late Medieval Italy* (Cambridge University Press, 2004).

Dixon II, H. M., *Arnolfo di Cambio: Sculpture*, unpublished Ph.D. thesis, SUNY Binghamton, 1978.

Kleinhenz, Christopher, 'On Dante and the visual arts' in T. Barolini and H. W. Storey, *Dante for the New Millennium* (New York: Fordham University Press, 2003), pp. 274–92.

Ladis, Andrew, 'The legend of Giotto's wit and the Arena Chapel', *The Art Bulletin*, 68 (1986), 581–96.

Medica, Massimo (ed.), *Duecento. Forme e colori del Medioevo a Bologna* (Venice: Marsilio, 2000).

Mellini, Gian Lorenzo, *Scultori veronesi del Trecento* (Milan: Electa, 1971).

Romanini, Angiola M. (ed.), *Roma nel Duecento. L'arte nella città dei papi da Innocenzo III a Bonifazio VIII* (Turin: SEAT, 1991).

Tartuferi, Angelo and Mario Scalini (eds.), *L'arte a Firenze nell'età di Dante (1250–1300)* (Florence: Giunti, 2004).

Vickers, Nancy J., 'Seeing is believing: Gregory, Trajan, and Dante's art', *Dante Studies*, 101 (1983), 67–85.

*Further reading* 555

## 25 Architecture and urban space

Braunfels, Wolfgang, *Mittelalterliche Stadtbaukunst in der Toskana* (Berlin: Verlag Gebr. Mann, 1953).

Fanelli, Giovanni, *Firenze*, 2nd edn (Rome and Bari: Laterza, 1993).

Guidoni, Enrico, *Storia dell'urbanistica: Il Duecento* (Rome: Laterza, 1990).

Istituto per gli studi storici veronesi (ed.), *Verona e il suo territorio: Verona scaligera* (Verona: Istituto per gli studi storici veronesi, 1969, 1975).

Marina, Areli, *The Italian Piazza Transformed: Parma in the Communal Age* (University Park: Pennsylvania State University Press, 2012).

Miller, Maureen C., 'Topographies of power in the urban centers of medieval Italy: communes, bishops, and public authority' in P. E. Findlen, M. M. Fontaine, and D. J. Osheim (eds.), *Beyond Florence: Rethinking Medieval and Early Modern Italy* (Stanford University Press, 2002), pp. 181–9.

Norman, Diana (ed.), *Siena, Florence and Padua: Art, Society and Religion 1280–1400*, 2 vols. (New Haven: Yale University Press, 1995).

Puppi, Lionello (ed.), *Ritratto di Verona: Lineamenti di una storia urbanistica* (Verona: Banca Popolare di Verona, 1978).

Romanini, Angiola Maria, *L'Architettura gotica in Lombardia*, 2 vols. (Milan: Ceschini, 1964).

Russell, Robert D., *Vox Civitatis: Aspects of Thirteenth Century Communal Architecture in Lombardy*, Ph.D. thesis, Princeton University, 1988.

Schulz, Juergen (ed.), *Il gotico: Regione del Veneto* (Venice: Marsilio, 2010).

Spilner, Paula, *Ut Civitas Amplietur: Studies in Florentine Urban Development, 1282–1400*, Ph.D. thesis, Columbia University, 1987.

Trachtenberg, Marvin, *Dominion of the Eye: Urbanism, Art and Power in Early Modern Florence* (Cambridge University Press, 1997).

Varanini, Gian Maria (ed.), *Gli Scaligeri, 1277–1387* (Verona: Mondadori, 1988).

White, John, *Art and Architecture in Italy, 1250–1400*, 3rd edn (New Haven: Yale University Press, 1993).

## 26 Music

Arcuri, Francesco M., 'Musica e liturgia medievale' in his '*"Asperges me" sì dolcemente udissi': Il percorso liturgico di Dante alle origini dell'innocenza* (Alessandria: Edizioni dell'Orso, 2008), pp. 1–19.

Besutti, Paola, 'Il trecento italiano: musica, "musicabilità", musicologia' in G. Salvetti (ed.), *Il mito di Dante nella musica della nuova Italia 1861–1914* (Milan: Guerini, 1994), pp. 83–193.

Cattin, Giulio, *Music of the Middle Ages* (Cambridge University Press, 1984).

Ciabattoni, Francesco, *Dante's Journey to Polyphony* (University of Toronto Press, 2010).

Ciliberti, Galliano, 'Fonti musicali per poeti e scelte poetiche di musicisti a Firenze nel tardo medioevo', *Archivio storico italiano*, 148 (1990), 767–92.

Fiori, Alessandra, 'Discorsi sulla musica nei commenti medievali alla *Commedia* dantesca', *Studi e problemi di critica testuale*, 59 (1999), 67–102.

# 556 Further reading

McGee, Timothy J. (ed.), *Instruments and their Music in the Middle Ages* (Farnham and Burlington: Ashgate, 2009).

*Musica e arte figurativa nei secoli X–XIII. Atti del XIII Convegno del Centro Studi sulla Spiritualità Medievale, Todi, 15–18 ottobre 1972* (Todi and Rimini: Accademia Tudertina, Maggioli, 1973).

Peraino, Judith A., 'Re-placing medieval music', *Journal of American Musicology Society*, 54 (2001), 209–64.

Pestalozza, Luigi (ed.), *La musica nel tempo di Dante* (Milan: Unicopli, 1988).

Pirotta, Nino, *Music and Culture in Italy from the Middle Ages to the Baroque: A Collection of Essays* (Cambridge, MA: Harvard University Press, 1984).

Stevens, John, *Words and Music in the Middle Ages: Song, Narrative, Dance and Drama, 1050–1350* (Cambridge University Press, 1986).

Ultan, Lloyd, *Music Theory: Problems and Practices in the Middle Ages and Renaissance* (Minneapolis: University of Minnesota Press, 1977).

Wilson David F., *Music of the Middle Ages: Style and Structure* (New York: Schirmer Books, 1990).

## 27 Life

Barbi, Michele, *Life of Dante*, trans. P. Ruggiers (Berkeley and Los Angeles: University of California Press, 1960).

Bemrose, Stephen, *A New Life of Dante* (University of Exeter Press, 2009).

Indizio, Giuseppe, *Problemi di biografia dantesca* (Ravenna: Longo, 2014).

Inglese, Giorgio, Vita di Dante. *Una biografia possibile* (Rome: Carocci, 2015).

Milani, Giuliano, 'Appunti per una riconsiderazione del bando di Dante', *Bollettino di italianistica*, 8 (2011), 42–70.

Najemy, John M., 'Dante and Florence' in R. Jacoff (ed.), *The Cambridge Companion to Dante* (Cambridge University Press, 2007), pp. 236–56.

Pasquini, Emilio, *Vita di Dante. I giorni e le opere* (Milan: Rizzoli, 2006).

Petrocchi, Giorgio, *Vita di Dante* (Bari: Laterza, 1983).

Santagata, Marco, *Dante. Il romanzo della sua vita* (Milan: Mondadori, 2012).

Scott, John A., *Understanding Dante* (University of Notre Dame Press, 2004), pp. 309–36.

## 28 Works

The bibliography that follows is aimed at the English-language reader. Works listed in the 'Further reading' to Chapter 27 do not reappear here. For editions and translations of Dante's works, see 'Abbreviations and note on translations'.

### General

Works in this section deal with broad questions on Dante studies, and so with more than one of the poet's texts.

# Further reading

Ascoli, Albert R., *Dante and the Making of a Modern Author* (Cambridge University Press, 2008).

Barański, Zygmunt G. (ed.), *'Libri poetarum in quattuor species dividuntur': Essays on Dante and 'Genre'*, special supplement 2 *The Italianist*, 15 (1995).

Barolini, Teodolinda, *Dante and the Origins of Italian Literary Culture* (New York: Fordham University Press, 2006).

Barolini, Teodolinda and H. Wayne Storey (eds.), *Dante for the New Millennium* (New York: Fordham University Press, 2003).

Benfell, Stanley V., *The Biblical Dante* (University of Toronto Press, 2011).

Cachey, Theodore J., *Dante Now: Current Trends in Dante Studies* (University of Notre Dame Press, 1995).

Chydenius, Johan, *The Typological Problem in Dante: A Study in the History of Medieval Ideas* (Helsinki: Societas Scientiarum Fennica, 1958).

Cornish, Alison, *Reading Dante's Stars* (New Haven: Yale University Press, 2000).

Davis, Charles Till, *Dante's Italy and Other Essays* (Philadelphia: University of Pennsylvania Press, 1984).

*Dante and the Idea of Rome* (Oxford: Clarendon Press, 1957).

Foster, Kenelm, *The Two Dantes and Other Studies* (London: Darton, Longman and Todd, 1977).

Gilson, Etienne, *Dante and Philosophy* (New York: Torchbooks, 1963).

Hainsworth, Peter and David Robey, *Dante: A Very Short Introduction* (Oxford University Press, 2015).

Havely, Nicholas R., *Dante* (Oxford: Blackwell, 2007).

Hawkins, Peter S., *Dante. A Brief History* (Oxford: Blackwell, 2006).

Hollander, Robert, *Dante: A Life in Works* (New Haven: Yale University Press, 2001).

Honess, Claire E., *From Florence to the Heavenly City: The Poetry of Citizenship in Dante* (Oxford: Legenda, 2006).

Honess, Claire E., and Matthew Treherne (eds.), *Reviewing Dante's Theology*, 2 vols. (Oxford: Peter Lang, 2013).

Iannucci, Amilcare A. (ed.), *Dante: Contemporary Perspectives* (University of Toronto Press, 1997).

Jacoff, Rachel (ed.), *The Cambridge Companion to Dante*, 2nd edn (Cambridge University Press, 2007).

Lansing, Richard (ed.), *The Dante Encyclopedia* (New York: Garland, 2000).

Marchesi, Simone, *Dante and Augustine: Linguistics, Poetics, Hermeneutics* (University of Toronto Press, 2011).

Schildgen, Brenda D., *Dante and the Orient* (Urbana: University of Illinois Press, 2002).

Steinberg, Justin, *Accounting for Dante: Urban Readers and Writers in Late Medieval Italy* (University of Notre Dame Press, 2007).

Took, John F., *Dante, Lyric Poet and Philosopher: An Introduction to the Minor Works* (Oxford: Clarendon Press, 1990).

# Further reading

## Rime

Alfie, Fabian, *Dante's 'tenzone' with Forese Donati: The Reprehension of Vice* (University of Toronto Press, 2011).

Barański, Zygmunt G., "'Nfiata labbia" and "Dolce stil novo": a note on Dante, ethics and the technical vocabulary of literature' in L. Coglievina and D. De Robertis (eds.), *Sotto il segno di Dante: Scritti in onore di Francesco Mazzoni* (Florence: Le Lettere, 1998), pp. 17–35.

Barolini, Teodolinda, 'The poetic exchanges between Dante Alighieri and his *amico* Dante da Maiano: a young man takes his place in the world' in J. J. Kinder and D. Glenn (eds.), *'Legato con amore in un volume': Essays in Honour of John Scott* (Florence: Olschki, 2013), pp. 39–61.

'Dante's lyric poetry: from editorial history to hermeneutic future' in Dante Alighieri, *Dante's Lyric Poetry: Poems of Youth and of the 'Vita Nuova'*, ed. T. Barolini (University of Toronto Press, 2014), pp. 3–28.

Boyde, Patrick, *Dante's Style in His Lyric Poetry* (Cambridge University Press, 1971).

Durling, Robert M., and Roland Martinez, *Time and the Crystal: Studies in Dante's Rime petrose* (Berkeley: University of California Press, 1990).

Honess, Claire E., 'Dante and political poetry in the vernacular', *Journal of the Institute of Romance Studies*, 6 (1998), 21–42.

Keen, Catherine, 'Florence and faction in Dante's lyric poetry: framing the experience of exile' in C. E. Honess and M. Treherne (eds.), *'Se mai continga...': Exile, Politics, and Theology in Dante* (Ravenna: Longo, 2013), pp. 63–83.

## Fiore *and* Detto d'Amore

Armour, Peter, 'The *Roman de la Rose* and the *Fiore:* Aspects of a literary transplantation', *Journal of the Institute of Romance Studies*, 2 (1993), 63–81.

Barański, Zygmunt G. and Boyde, Patrick (eds.), *The Fiore in Context: Dante, France, Tuscany* (University of Notre Dame Press, 1996).

Brownlee, Kevin, 'The conflicted genealogy of cultural authority: Italian responses to French cultural dominance in *Il Tesoretto*, *Il Fiore*, and *La Commedia*', *Forum for Modern Language Studies*, 33 (1997), 258–69.

Senior, Diane, 'The authority and autonomy of the *Fiore*', *Forum Italicum*, 32 (1998), 305–31.

Took, John, *A Translation of Dante's 'Il fiore' ('The Flower') with Introduction and Commentary* (Lewiston: E. Mellen Press, 2004).

## Vita nova

Barański, Zygmunt G., '"Lascio cotale trattato ad altro chiosatore": form, literature, and exegesis in Dante's *Vita nova*' in M. Kilgour and E. Lombardi (eds.), *Dantean Dialogues. Engaging with the Legacy of Amilcare Iannucci* (University of Toronto Press, 2013), pp. 1–40.

# Further reading

Harrison, Robert P., *The Body of Beatrice* (Baltimore: The Johns Hopkins University Press, 1988).

Hooper, Laurence E., 'Exile and rhetorical order in the *Vita nova*', *L'Alighieri*, 38 (2011), 5–27.

Gragnolati, Manuele, 'Authorship and performance in Dante's *Vita nova*' in M. Gragnolati and A. Suerbaum (eds.), *Aspects of the Performative in Medieval Culture* (Berlin and New York: De Gruyter, 2010), pp. 125–41.

Kay, Tristan, 'Redefining the *matera amorosa*: Dante's *Vita Nova* and Guittone's (anti-)courtly *canzoniere*', *The Italianist*, 29 (2009), 369–99.

Martinez, Ronald L., 'Mourning Beatrice: the rhetoric of threnody in the *Vita nuova*', *Modern Language Notes*, 113 (1998), 1–29.

Mazzaro, Jerome, *The Figure of Dante: An Essay on the 'Vita Nuova'* (Princeton University Press, 1981).

Moleta, Vincent (ed.), *'La gloriosa donna della mente': A Commentary on the 'Vita Nuova'* (Florence: Olschki, 1994).

Singleton, Charles S., *An Essay on the 'Vita nuova'* (Cambridge, MA: Harvard University Press, 1949).

## Convivio

Bemrose, Stephen, '"What is truth?" The architecture of the early chapters of *Convivio*, IV', *Dante Studies*, 121 (2003), 95–108.

Dronke, Peter, *Dante's Second Love: The Originality and the Contexts of the 'Convivio'* (Leeds: Maney, 1997).

Hooper, Laurence E., 'Dante's *Convivio*, Book 1: metaphor, exile, *epochê*', *Modern Language Notes*, 127 Supplement (2012), S86–S104.

Leo, Ulrich, 'The unfinished *Convivio* and Dante's rereading of the *Aeneid*', *Medieval Studies*, 13 (1951), 41–64.

Meier, Franziska (ed.), *Dante's 'Convivio' or How to Restart Writing in Exile* (Berne: Peter Lang, 2015).

Robiglio, Andrea, 'The thinker as a noble man (*bene natus*) and preliminary remarks on the medieval concept of nobility', *Vivarium*, 44 (2006), 205–47.

Scott, John A., 'The unfinished *Convivio* as a pathway to the *Comedy*', *Dante Studies*, 113 (1995), 31–56.

Trovato, Mario, 'Against Aristotle: Cosmological vision in Dante's *Convivio*', *Essays in Medieval Studies*, 20 (2003), 31–46.

'Dante's stand against "l'errore de l'umana bontade": *bonum*, nobility and rational soul in the fourth treatise of the *Convivio*', *Dante Studies*, 108 (1990), 79–96.

Watt, Mary A., 'Take this bread: Dante's eucharistic banquet', *Quaderni di Italianistica*, 22 (2001), 17–35.

## De vulgari eloquentia

Barański, Zygmunt G., 'Dante's Biblical linguistics', *Lectura Dantis*, 5 (1989), 105–43.

560                           Further reading

Black, Robert, 'The vernacular and the teaching of Latin in thirteenth- and fourteenth-century Italy', *Studi Medievali*, ser. III, 38 (1996), 703–51.
Cestaro, Gary P., *Dante and the Grammar of the Nursing Body* (University of Notre Dame Press, 2002).
Durling, Robert M., 'The audience(s) of the *De vulgari eloquentia* and the *Petrose*', *Dante Studies*, 110 (1992), 25–35.
Lombardi, Elena, *Dante. The Syntax of Desire: Language and Love in Augustine, the 'Modistae', Dante* (University of Toronto Press, 2007), pp. 121–74.
Phipps, Matt, 'On the presence and significance of metaphorical micro-texts in Dante's *De vulgari eloquentia*', *The Italianist*, 26 (2006), 5–16.
Rosier-Catach, Irène, 'Man as a speaking and political animal: a political reading of Dante's *De vulgari eloquentia*' in S. Fortuna, M. Gragnolati, and J. Trabant (eds.), *Dante's Plurilingualism: Authority, Knowledge, Subjectivity* (London: Legenda, 2010), pp. 34–51.
Shapiro, Marianne, *'De vulgari eloquentia': Dante's Book of Exile* (Lincoln: University of Nebraska Press, 1990).

## *Monarchia*

Bowsky, William M., *Henry VII in Italy: The Conflict of Empire and City-State, 1310–1313* (Lincoln: University of Nebraska Press, 1960).
Cassell, Anthony K., *The 'Monarchia' Controversy* (Washington: The Catholic University of America Press, 2004).
Holmes, George, *'Monarchia* and Dante's attitude towards the popes' in J. R. Woodhouse (ed.), *Dante and Governance* (Oxford: Clarendon Press, 1997), pp. 46–57.
Kantorowicz, Ernst H., *The King's Two Bodies: A Study in Medieval Political Theology* (Princeton University Press, 1997).
Kay, Richard (ed.), *Dante's 'Monarchia'* (Toronto: Pontifical Institute of Medieval Studies, 1998).
Nasti, Paola, 'Dante and Ecclesiology' in C. E. Honess and M. Treherne (eds.), *Reviewing Dante's Theology*, 2 vols. (Berne: Peter Lang, 2013), vol. II, pp. 43–88.
Trovato, Mario, 'Dante and the tradition of the "two beatitudes"' in P. Cherchi and A. Mastrobuono (eds.), *Lectura Dantis Newberryana* (Evanston: Northwestern University Press, 1988), pp. 19–36.

## *Commedia*

Armour, Peter, *The Door of Purgatory* (Oxford: Clarendon Press, 1983).
Auerbach, Erich, 'Figura' in *Scenes from the Drama of European Literature* (New York: Meridian, 1959), pp. 11–76.
    *Dante. Poet of the Secular World* (University of Chicago Press, 1961).
Barolini, Teodolinda, *Dante's Poets: Textuality and Truth in the 'Comedy'* (Princeton University Press, 1984).

*The Undivine Comedy* (Princeton University Press, 1992).

Bianchi, Luca, 'A "heterodox" in Paradise? Notes on the relationship between Dante and Siger of Brabant' in M. L. Ardizzone (ed.), *Dante and Heterodoxy: The Temptations of 13th Century Radical Thought* (Newcastle-upon-Tyne: Cambridge Scholars Publishing, 2014), pp. 78–105.

Botterill, Steven, *Dante and the Mystical Tradition: Bernard of Clairvaux and the 'Commedia'* (Cambridge University Press, 1994).

Boyde, Patrick, *Dante Philomythes and Philosopher: Man in the Cosmos* (Cambridge University Press, 1981).

*Perception and Passion in Dante's 'Comedy'* (Cambridge University Press, 1993).

Cassell, Anthony K., *Dante's Fearful Art of Justice* (University of Toronto Press, 1984).

Cogan, Mark, *The Design in the Wax: The Structure of the 'Divine Comedy' and its Meaning* (University of Notre Dame Press, 1999).

Dronke, Peter, *Dante and the Medieval Latin Traditions* (Cambridge University Press, 1986).

Ferrante, Joan M., *The Political Vision of the 'Divine Comedy'* (Princeton University Press, 1984).

Freccero, John, *Dante. The Poetics of Conversion*, ed. R. Jacoff (Cambridge, MA: Harvard University Press, 1986).

Gilson, Simon A., 'Medieval science in Dante's *Commedia*: past approaches and future directions', *Reading Medieval Studies*, 27 (2001), 39–77.

Gragnolati, Manuele, *Experiencing the Afterlife: Soul and Body in Dante and Medieval Culture* (University of Notre Dame Press, 2005).

Hawkins, Peter S., *Dante's Testaments. Essays in Scriptural Imagination* (Stanford University Press, 1999).

Hollander, Robert, *Allegory in Dante's 'Commedia'* (Princeton University Press, 1969).

Kirkpatrick, Robin, *Dante, the 'Divine Comedy'* (Cambridge University Press, 1987).

Mandelbaum, Allen, Anthony Oldcorn, and Charles Ross (eds.), *Lectura Dantis. Inferno* (Berkeley and Los Angeles: University of California Press, 1998).

(eds.), *Lectura Dantis. Purgatorio* (Berkeley and Los Angeles: University of California Press, 2008).

Mazzotta, Giuseppe, *Dante, Poet of the Desert: History and Allegory in the 'Divine Comedy'* (Princeton University Press, 1979).

*Dante's Vision and the Circle of Knowledge* (Princeton University Press, 1993).

Moevs, Christian, *The Metaphysics of Dante's 'Comedy'* (Oxford University Press, 2005).

Morgan, Alison, *Dante and the Medieval Other World* (Cambridge University Press, 1990).

Pertile, Lino, '*Paradiso*, a drama of desire' in J. Barnes and J. Petrie (eds.), *Word and Drama in Dante* (Dublin: Four Courts Press, 1993), pp. 143–80.

'The harlot and the giant: Dante and the Song of Songs' in P. S. Hawkins and L. Cushing Stahlberg (eds.), *Scrolls of Love: Reading Ruth and the Song of Songs* (New York: Fordham University Press, 2006), pp. 268–80.

# 562 Further reading

Scott, John A., *Dante's Political Purgatory* (Philadelphia: University of Pennsylvania Press, 1996).

Shaw, Prue, *Reading Dante: From Here to Eternity* (New York and London: Norton, 2014).

Singleton, Charles S., *Dante's Commedia: Elements of Structure, Dante Studies 1* (Baltimore: The Johns Hopkins University Press, 1977).

*Journey to Beatrice, Dante Studies 2* (Baltimore: The Johns Hopkins University Press, 1977).

Wlassics, Tibor (ed.), *Dante's 'Divine Comedy': Introductory Readings*, 3 vols. (Charlottesville: Printing Office University of Virginia, 1990–95).

## Epistole

Honess, Claire E., ' "Ecce nunc tempus acceptabile": Henry VII and Dante's ideal of peace', *The Italianist*, 33 (2013), 484–504.

Pertile, Lino, 'Dante looks forward and back: political allegory in the Epistles', *Dante Studies*, 115 (1997), 1–17.

## Epistola a Cangrande

Ahern, John, 'Can the Epistle to Cangrande be read as a forgery?' in Z. G. Barański (ed.), *Seminario Dantesco Internazionale / International Dante Seminar 1* (Florence: Le Lettere, 1997), pp. 281–307.

Barański, Zygmunt G., '*Comedía*: notes on Dante, the Epistle to Cangrande and medieval comedy', *Lectura Dantis*, 8 (1991), 26–55.

Ginzburg, Carlo, 'Dante's *Epistle to Cangrande* and its two authors', *Proceedings of the British Academy*, 139 (2006), 195–216.

Hollander, Robert, *Dante's Epistle to Cangrande* (Ann Arbor: The University of Michigan Press, 1993).

Kelly, Henry A., *Tragedy and Comedy from Dante to Pseudo-Dante* (Berkeley and Los Angeles: University of California Press, 1989).

## Ecloge

Annett, Scott, ' "Una veritade ascosa sotto bella menzogna": Dante's *Eclogues* and the world beyond the text', *Italian Studies*, 68 (2013), 36–56.

Davie, Mark, 'Dante's Latin Eclogues', in *Papers of the Liverpool Latin Seminar* (Liverpool: Cairns, 1977), vol. II, pp. 183–98.

## Questio de aqua et terra

Alexander, David, 'Dante and the form of the land', *Annals of the Association of American Geographers*, 76 (1986), 38–49.

## Further reading

Barański, Zygmunt G., 'The mystery of Dante's *Questio de aqua et terra*' in Z. G. Barański and L. Pertile (eds.), *In amicizia: Essays in Honour of Giulio Lepschy*, Special supplement to *The Italianist*, 17 (1997), 146–64.

Freccero, John, 'Satan's fall and the *Quaestio de aqua et terra*', *Italica*, 38 (1961), 99–115.

### 29 Textual transmission

Barański, Zygmunt G., '"Lascio cotale trattato ad altro chiosatore": form, literature, and exegesis in Dante's *Vita nova*' in M. Kilgour and E. Lombardi (eds.), *Dantean Dialogue: Engaging with the Legacy of Amilcare Iannucci* (University of Toronto Press, 2013), pp. 1–40.

Barolini, Teodolinda, 'Editing Dante's *Rime* and Italian cultural history: Dante, Boccaccio, Petrarca ... Barbi, Contini, Foster–Boyde, De Robertis' in her *Dante and the Origins of Italian Literary Culture* (New York: Fordham University Press, 2006), pp. 245–78 and 433–41.

Bologna, Corrado, *Tradizione e fortuna dei classici italiani*, 2 vols. (Turin: Einaudi, 1993), vol. I, pp. 157–99.

Canova, Andrea, 'Il testo della *Commedia* dopo l'edizione Petrocchi', *Testo*, 32 (2011), 65–78.

Ciociola, Claudio, 'Dante' in E. Malato (ed.), *Storia della letteratura italiana. X. La tradizione dei testi* (Rome: Salerno, 2001), pp. 137–99.

Folena, Gianfranco, 'La tradizione delle opere di Dante Alighieri' in *Atti del Congresso Internazionale di Studi Danteschi*, 2 vols. (Florence: Sansoni, 1965– 66), vol. I, pp. 1–78.

Gilson, Simon, 'Reading the *Convivio* from Trecento Florence to Dante's Cinquecento commentators', *Italian Studies*, 64 (2009), 266–95.

Rea, Roberto, 'La *Vita nova*: questioni di ecdotica' in R. Antonelli, A. Landolfi, and A. Punzi (eds.), *Dante, oggi*, 3 vols. (Rome: Viella, 2011), vol. I, pp. 233–77.

Richardson, Brian, 'Editing Dante's *Commedia*, 1472–1629' in T. J. Cachey Jr (ed.), *Dante Now: Current Trends in Dante Studies* (University of Notre Dame Press, 1995), pp. 237–62.

Roddewig, Marcella, *Dante Alighieri. Die göttliche Komödie: vergleichende Bestandsaufnahme der Commedia-Handschriften* (Stuttgart: Hiersemann Verlag, 1984).

Shaw, Prue, 'Introduction' in Dante Alighieri, *Monarchia*, ed. P. Shaw (Florence: Le Lettere, 2009), pp. 1–200 (especially pp. 3–23).

'Introduction' in Dante Alighieri, *Commedia: A Digital Edition*, ed. P. Shaw (Florence: SISMEL and Birmingham: SDE, 2010).

Storey, Wayne, 'Following instructions: remaking Dante's *Vita Nova* in the fourteenth century' in T. Barolini (ed.), *Medieval Constructions in Gender and Identity: Essays in Honor of Joan M. Ferrante* (Tempe: MRTS, 2005), pp. 117–32.

## 564 Further reading

### 30 Early reception (1290–1481)

Barański, Zygmunt G., *'Chiosar con altro testo'. Leggere Dante nel Trecento* (Fiesole: Cadmo, 2001).

Barański, Zygmunt G. and Theodore J. Cachey, Jr (eds.), *Petrarch & Dante: Anti-Dantism, Metaphysics, Tradition* (University of Notre Dame Press, 2009).

Bellomo, Saverio, *Dizionario dei commentatori danteschi* (Florence: Olschki, 2004).

Brieger, Peter H., Millard Meiss, and Charles S. Singleton, *Illuminated Manuscripts of the 'Divine Comedy'*, 2 vols. (Princeton University Press, 1969).

Caesar, Michael (ed.), *Dante: The Critical Heritage 1314(?)–1870* (London and New York: Routledge, 1989).

Dionisotti, Carlo, 'Dante nel Quattrocento' in *Atti del Congresso Internazionale di Studi Danteschi*, 2 vols. (Florence: Sansoni, 1965–66), vol. I, pp. 333–78.

Eisner, Martin, *Boccaccio and the Invention of Italian Literature. Dante, Petrarch, Cavalcanti, and the Authority of the Vernacular* (Cambridge University Press, 2013).

Friedrich, Werner P., *Dante's Fame Abroad 1350–1850* (Rome: Edizioni di Storia e Letteratura, 1950).

Gilson, Simon A., *Dante and Renaissance Florence* (Cambridge University Press, 2005).

  '"La divinità di Dante": The problematics of Dante's critical reception from the fourteenth to the sixteenth centuries' in R. Antonelli, A. Landolfi, and A. Punzi (eds.), *Dante, oggi*, 3 vols. (Rome: Viella, 2011), vol. I, pp. 581–603.

Griffiths, Eric and Matthew Reynolds (eds.), *Dante in English* (London: Penguin, 2005).

Havely, Nick, *Dante's British Public: Readers and Texts from the Fourteenth Century to the Present* (Oxford University Press, 2014).

Malato, Enrico and Andrea Mazzucchi (eds.), *Censimento dei commenti danteschi. 1. I commenti di tradizione manoscritta (fino al 1480)*, 2 vols. (Rome: Salerno, 2011).

Minnis, A. J. and A. B. Scott with the assistance of David Wallace (eds.), *Medieval Literary Theory and Criticism c.1100–c.1375* (Oxford: Clarendon Press, 1988).

Minnis, Alastair and Ian Johnson (eds.), *The Cambridge History of Literary Criticism. II. The Middle Ages* (Cambridge University Press, 2005), pp. 561–665.

Parker, Deborah, *Commentary and Ideology: Dante in the Renaissance* (Durham, NC and London: Duke University Press, 1993).

# Index

## Prepared by Demetrio S. Yocum

abbeys, 140, 148, 417, 427
  abbesses, 79–80, 94
  abbots, 110, 349, 420
*accessus*, 277, 282, 285, 287–8, 316, 506
afterlife, 70, 146, 153, 169, 333, 335, 339, 347,
  495–9, 502, 518, 525
age third, 107, 112–13
Albert the Great, 161–2, 165–6, 168–70, 211–12,
  227, 229, 485
Alexander of Villedieu, 264–5, 300–1
Alfonso X, 11, 204, 217
  alfonsine court, 204
allegory, 286–7, 494–5
  allegoresis, 284, 286
Angela of Foligno, Saint, 79–80
angels, 176, 178–9, 224, 230–3, 235, 239,
  352, 484, *see* intelligences: separate
  intelligences
Antichrist, 113, 147, 501
anti-classicism, 298–9, 301
aphorism, 262, 275, 393
apocalyptic expectation, 108, 112, 116, 274, 346,
  377, 470
Aquinas, T., 115, 117–18, 140, 145, 150–1,
  161–2, 165, 168–9, 171, 173, 177–9, 209,
  211–14, 225, 232, 283–5, 326, 332, 349,
  355, 485
Arabs
  Arabic philosophy/science, 127, 147, 201–4,
    209–14, 217–19, 229, 232
  arabisms, 133, 202, 395
  *see also* translations
architecture, 102, 238, 428–47
argumentation, 141, 144, 146, 148, 152, 155–6
Arianism, 208, 211
Aristotle, 10, 24, 56, 71, 75, 78, 117, 137, 140,
  144–5, 147, 153, 159–65, 167, 170–1,
  173–6, 180–7, 209, 213, 224–8, 231, 236,
  283, 313, 357, 504, 508
arithmetic, 77, 177, 183, 249, 260
Arnolfo di Cambio, 414–15

*ars dictaminis*, *see* epistolography; rhetoric
art of poetry, 281, 288–91, 310, 379, 386, 487
arts
  Lana, 34
  Calimala, 34, 41, 131, 427, 440
  major, 22, 34, 68, 131
  minor, 68, 131
astrology, 229–30, 234, 397
astronomy, 212, 222, 227–9, 231, 234, 397
*auctoritas*, 277, 287, 520–2, 525, 530, 532
Augustine, Saint, 24, 81, 138–9, 150–1, 171, 234,
  267, 279, 286, 311, 346, 348, 394, 483
Averroes, 117–18, 146, 165, 167–70, 173–4, 204,
  210, 213–14, 228, 485
Avignon captivity, 14, 23, 109–11, 471–2

*ballata*, 291, 377, 383, 391, 453, 455, 477
ban/*bandito*, 63–4, 67–9, 134, 383, 403, 433, 444,
  446, 462, 465–6, 468, 473
Bandini, Margherita, 72, 76, 81
baptism, 85, 92, 129, 320, 335, 401
Bede, the Venerable, 230, 351
*beguines*, 115, 329
Benevento, battle of, 14–15, 21, 42, 203, 280,
  361, 381
Bernard of Clairvaux, 147, 151, 154, 494
bestiaries, 397
Bible, the, 26, 48, 85, 87, 139, 147–8, 156, 202,
  279, 284, 286, 317, 324, 326, 331, 334–6,
  339, 347, 359, 393, 405, 488, 493, 495
bishops, 61, 66, 86, 88, 92–4, 102, 104
Black Guelfs, 20, 22–3, 40, 45, 69, 85, 361,
  366–7, 435, 441, 445, 465–7, 469
  *see also* Guelfs; White Guelfs
Boccaccio, G., 75–6, 140, 269, 271, 306, 317,
  375, 386, 455, 461, 492, 510, 513–16,
  524, 530
body, 149, 192, 236, 357
  physical bodies, 176–9, 181–4, 186–7, 212, 223,
  230–1, 237
Boethius, 138, 153, 156, 265–7, 269, 463

# Index

Boethius of Dacia, 163, 166–8, 171
Bologna, 16, 50, 54–5, 59, 168, 173, 190, 197,
    252–3, 255, 258, 270, 272, 274, 295, 299,
    303, 316, 320, 334, 404, 463–4, 468, 474,
    489, 506, 528
Bonaventure, Saint, 115–17, 140, 147–8, 326,
    334, 349
Boncompagno da Signa, 298–9
Boniface VIII, Pope, 14, 21, 23, 25, 45, 51,
    104, 109–10, 115, 333, 356, 358–9,
    452, 465–6
Bonvesin de la Riva, 257, 362, 378
books
    account, 119, 123, 249
    illuminated, 291–2, 403–5
    illustrated, 402
    reading, 292
Bruni, L., 446, 468, 509, 533
Buridan, J., 178, 182–4, 235
Byzantium, 9, 13, 26–7

caccia, 453, 455
Caesarism, 309
caesaropapism, 51
Caltabellotta treaty, 23
Campaldino, battle of, 15, 440, 463
Cangrande della Scala, 18–19, 124, 362, 417, 419
canzone, 294, 382, 468–9, 476–8, 484, 487,
    510, 514
capitalism, 72, 130, 502
Capellanus, Andreas, 155–6, 375
Cathars/Catharism, 87, 107–8, 118, 324–5, 328,
    332–3, 377
Cathedral chapters and canons, 21, 88–92, 94–5,
    102, 104, 441
Catherine of Siena, Saint, 80
Cavalcanti, G., 156, 255, 294, 382–3, 476, 481,
    485, 521
celestial (world), 178, 181, 212, 227, 231, 263
censorship, 111, 117, 163, 225, 528
Charlemagne, 10, 12, 26–7
Charles I of Anjou, 42, 67, 83, 414
Charles of Valois, 13, 23, 359, 366, 466
Chartres, School of, 141, 234, 281
chemistry, 177, 195
children, 73–4, 76, 101, 125, 128, 132, 260, 319, 395
Christianization, 162, 305, 307–8, 498
Church, the, 10–11, 26–7, 47–51, 64, 78–9,
    85–7, 106, 109–11, 142, 174–5, 207, 246,
    250, 252, 320–4, 358–9, 470, 488–9,
    491, 501–2
Church Fathers, 81, 138, 225, 336, 495
Cicero, 267, 310–11, 350, 463
Cimabue, 405, 408, 412, 426
Cino da Pistoia, 56, 198, 255, 361–2, 382

clergy
    regular, 94–100, 102
    secular, 87–92, 102–3, 323–4
clothes, 73, 82, 124–6, 304–17
comedy/comic, 277, 283, 287–8, 316, 361, 384,
    392, 490, 492, 494, 507, 520, 525
comets, 181, 229
commentaries, 47, 275, 277–8, 287, 316, 335,
    480, 484, 521–4, 526, 529–31, 535–6
    see also glossators
commune, 53–4, 60–1, 65–6, 78, 85, 100, 103,
    122, 125, 127, 133–4, 253, 320–1, 323, 327,
    334, 429, 434, 441, 446, 466
communication among Italians, 243–6,
    248–52
Compagni, D., 20, 22, 24, 78, 320, 366–7, 385,
    435, 440
condemnation of 1277, see Tempier, É.
confession, sacrament of, 83, 86, 95, 144, 320,
    324, 329, 331, 333, 337–8
confino, 67–8
confirmation, sacrament of, 86, 320
confraternities, 101–2, 327, 329–32, 338
consorterie, 17, 32
consuls, 60–1, 356
contado, 33, 35, 38, 45, 84, 121
contemplation/consideration, 154–5
conversion, 203, 205–6, 208, 292, 326, 332, 339,
    341, 348, 353
corruption (in public office/in Church), 11,
    22, 69, 110, 113, 224, 324, 361, 403,
    466, 501–2
cosmology, 163, 221–37, 239–40
court/courtly love, 75, 155–6, 254–5, 285, 372–3,
    380–1, 476, 480–1
creation, 54, 152, 176, 178, 186, 221, 235, 286,
    485, 489
credit market, see money-lending
crusades, 14, 201, 209, 341, 497–8
curial language, 380–1
curiosity, 151, 341, 344
cursus, 272, 281, 379

Datini, F., 72, 74, 77, 249
Decretists, 50–1, 89
Decretalists, 51–2, 56–7
decretals, 50–1, 64
deduction, 145–6, 153, 235, 284
desire to know, 15, 165, 167–8, 170–1, 226, 230,
    232, 349
devils/demons/devil worship, 14, 128, 422, 497
dialect, 244–8, 423, 486
diet, 128, 192, 194
diglossia, 246, 254
diseases, 126–8, 193

## Index

disputation, 152, 166–7, 180, 205, 207, 250, 273–5, 284, 293, 334–5, 464
*dolce stil novo, see stilnovo*
Dolcino, Fra, 87, 107–8
Dominic, Saint, 325–6, 334
Dominicans, 32, 66, 84, 95–6, 101, 106, 115, 117, 140, 144, 150, 161, 165, 205–6, 250–1, 263, 273, 284, 325–7, 334, 336, 344, 442, 464, 528, 532
Donation of Constantine, 10, 357, 489
Donatus, 261–2, 264, 266, 279
Duccio di Buoninsegna, 102, 410

earth, 177, 181–2, 184–5, 215, 223, 226, 235, 352, 495–6, 508
eclogue, 305–7, 317, 385, 498, 506–7, 510
economics, 31–5, 40–5, 72, 82, 89–90, 102–4, 129, 131–2, 379
ecstasy/ecstatic status, 155, 326, 481
education, *see* schools
elements, 16, 175, 177, 181, 221–3
Empire, Holy Roman, 10–13, 23–8, 246, 356, 377, 470, 528
Empyrean, 179, 224, 227, 230–1, 234, 239, 494, 496–7, 504
England, 11, 14, 31, 455
epic poetry/narrative, 33, 307, 341, 350, 374–5, 384, 493
Epicureanism, 107, 211
espistolography, 72, 80, 142, 249, 253, 256, 270–1, 279–81, 290, 298, 378–9, 469–70, 505
ethics, 138, 150, 159–65, 171, 230, 271–2, 283, 312, 376, 496
Eucharist, 86, 93, 321–4, 331–2, 334, 449
eudemonism, 167, 171
Everard of Béthune, 264–5, 300–1
excommunication, 10, 93, 193, 203, 324, 396
*exemplum, exempla*, 75, 203, 250, 336, 379
exile, 13, 16, 20, 22–3, 40, 59, 85, 110, 115, 119, 239, 257, 259, 361, 383, 444–6, 466–9, 472–3, 475, 477–8, 504–5
Ezzelino da Romano, 18, 302, 364, 435

Faba, G., 256, 280, 290, 378–9
faith, 137, 139, 141–2, 148, 157, 175, 187, 207, 319, 322, 326–7, 332
falconry, 203, 395
family feuds, 14, 17, 20, 22–3, 52, 89, 92, 120
fasting, 329, 337
feasts, religious, 86, 91, 93, 126, 321–3, 332, 372
flagellants, 101, 330
Florence
    art/architecture, 31–2, 84, 121, 401–2, 405–10, 415, 427–8, 430–5, 437, 440–3, 525
    Church/religion, 65–6, 84–5, 104, 319, 321

and Dante, 502, 504–5, 518–19, 522, 525, 529, 532–6
demographics/economics, 15, 30–5, 40–5, 62, 73, 84, 102–4, 120, 130–2, 490
politics, 9, 15, 20–4, 30, 35–40, 60–2, 67–70, 83, 196, 445–6, 464–73, 504–5
society/culture, 120–34, 260, 270
florin, 30, 39, 43, 467
folklore, 390–8
food, 73, 102, 122–3
Fortune, 56, 239
France, 11–12, 23, 55, 114, 246, 288, 300, 355, 373, 450, 453, 532
Francesco da Barberino, 71–3, 76–7, 79, 81, 303
Francesco da Buti, 306, 394, 530
Francis, Saint, 1, 78, 96, 112–13, 115, 117, 209, 256, 325–6, 334, 349, 377–8, 403, 412
Franciscans, 23, 32, 84, 87, 95–6, 99, 101, 106, 112–17, 140, 144, 147, 250, 274–5, 284, 325–7, 329, 334, 344, 442, 464
Franco-Venetian literature, 374
Frederick II, Emperor, 10, 12, 14, 30, 41–2, 203, 254, 258, 279, 364, 380, 421

Genoa, 13, 30, 201, 256, 372–3
genre, 55, 77, 192, 225, 233, 237–8, 265, 277, 283–4, 288, 301, 303, 306, 310–12, 316, 330, 341, 343, 346, 350, 377–8, 386, 391–2, 454–5, 477, 494, 521, 526
geography/cartography, 237–9, 344, 351
geology, 177
geometry, 177, 183–4, 229
Ghibellines, 9–10, 12, 15–17, 19–20, 23, 39, 52, 67, 70, 84, 87, 111, 280, 294, 361, 440, 462–3, 466, 468, 471, 490
Giacomo da Lentini, 293, 380
Giles of Rome, 25, 355, 357
Giordano of Pisa, 87, 251, 336–7
Giotto, 98, 102, 405, 409–13, 420, 422–4, 426, 467
Giovanni del Virgilio, 139, 275, 303, 306, 315–16, 385, 474, 506–7, 522–4
glossators, 50, 54–6, 138, 149, 165, 230, 287, 289, 303, 335, 493, 514–15, 521, 525, 527–8, 531
    *see also* Commentaries
governance, forms of, 22, 67–8, 70, 79, 95, 131, 280, 294, 354–6, 360, 429–31, 444, 504
grace, divine, 85, 138, 151, 154, 167, 357–8, 498
grammar, speculative, 144
*gramatica*, 253–4, 262, 266, 486–7
Gratian, 47–52, 139, 152, 275
Greek language, 161, 173, 387, 450
Gregory the Great, 47, 232, 338, 350
Guelfs, Blacks and Whites, 1, 9–10, 12, 15–17, 19–23, 30, 39–40, 42, 45, 67–9, 87, 281, 294, 361, 441, 445–6, 461–3, 465, 471, 490

# 568 Index

guidebooks, 343
Guido of Arezzo, 449
guilds, *see* arts
Guinizzelli, G., 255, 294–6, 382, 463, 482
Guittone d'Arezzo, 255, 285, 291, 294, 361, 379,
    381–2, 384, 477

hagiography, 338–9, 391–2
happiness, 24, 154–5, 162, 164, 166–7, 169, 171,
    357, 481, 485, 502–3
health/public health, 126–9, 191–4
    *see also* medicine
heavens, 223–4, 226–7, 229–34, 239, 484
    spheres, 49, 179, 212, 227, 229–31
    starry/crystalline, 150, 179, 235–6
Hebrew language, 202, 205, 215–16
Henry VII, Emperor, 12, 24–5, 40, 361, 470
heresy/heterodoxy, 66, 70, 87, 96, 101, 106–9,
    111, 117, 138–9, 144, 148–9, 208, 210–11,
    214, 219, 325, 336, 359, 377
Hildegard of Bingen, 348
history, 119, 147, 218, 283, 308, 354, 363–8, 375–6,
    384–5, 387–8, 471, 491, 495, 497–9
Holy Land, 209, 333, 342–3, 462, 504
Homer, 313
homosexuality, *see* sodomy
Horace, 268, 287–91, 309–10
hospitals, 99–102, 129
hours, liturgical, 83, 88, 132, 321, 324, 331, 402,
    449, 452
housing, 120–2, 444
Hugh of St Victor, 141, 495
humanism/early humanists, 78, 206, 262,
    297, 302–4
*Humiliati/Humiliate, see Umiliati/Umiliate*
humility, 151, 163, 416

immortality, 107–9, 138, 143, 162, 165, 211, 213,
    272, 494
*imperium*, 10, 12, 26–7
incarnation, 26, 207, 210
indulgences, 93, 333, 337
Innocent III, Pope, 10, 51, 323–4, 328, 356
intellect, 1, 165–6, 168–71, 213, 365
intellectualism, 149, 165, 167
intelligence, 154
    separate intelligences, 165–6, 169
Ioannes de Sacrobosco, 222–3, 230
Islamic tradition, 117, 166, 182,
    200–14, 216–19
Italian language, 243, 245, 475

Jacobus of Voragine, 338–9
Jacopone da Todi, 23, 108, 256, 330, 377–8
James of Viterbo, 357

Jerome, Saint, 202, 286, 335
Jewish tradition, 200–2, 205–7, 214–17
Jews, 125, 137, 201–2, 205, 207–8, 214, 344
Joachim of Fiore, 112, 116, 118, 147, 349
John of Garland, 75, 281–3
John of Paris, 25, 357–8
jubilee, 333, 411, 465
justice
    as social experience, 59–65
    as political conflict/tool, 65–70
Justinian, Emperor, 24, 49–50, 53–4
Juvenal, 312–13

Kabbala, 206, 215–16
knowledge, 1, 137, 145–6, 148–50, 152–4, 161,
    167–71, 187, 213, 273, 317, 341, 484–5, 501

Latin language and literature, 1, 88, 117, 137, 144,
    244, 246–8, 251–4, 256, 258, 262, 263,
    280–2, 297–9, 301–16, 322, 326, 330, 334,
    371, 380, 385, 393, 474, 484, 486, 488,
    505–7, 509, 519, 521, 523, 525, 529, 531–2
Latini, B., 20, 26, 82, 144, 204, 270, 280, 285,
    290, 294, 338, 360, 373, 379
*laudi, laudario, laudesi*, 101, 256, 330–2,
    339, 377–8
law
    canon, 47–52, 62, 89, 139, 195, 275, 338
    civil, 49, 51, 55, 274–5
    courts of, tribunals, 45, 59–63, 65–70,
        193, 197
    public, 53, 57
    Roman, 3, 24, 50–1, 53–4, 61–2, 274
    schools of, 54–8, 173, 301
lawsuit, 62
leprosy, 189, 193
letter-writing, *see* epistolography
*Liber de causis*, 214, 225, 229
libraries, 143, 160, 198, 302–3, 336, 387
light, 179, 213–14, 230, 377
literacy, 45, 249–50, 254, 260, 264, 334, 337,
    389, 523
literary theory, 277–8, 287
liturgy, 93, 252, 321–3, 331, 336, 414, 449,
    481, 490
Lombard, P., 139, 145, 176, 178
lordships/*signorie*, 11, 18–20, 111–12, 357, 360,
    430, 444
Lorenzetti, A., 125, 444, 446
Lovato Lovati, 301–3, 315, 386
love, 1, 72, 75, 77, 154–6, 168, 206, 255, 273, 278,
    284–5, 292–4, 308, 310, 323, 338, 359–60,
    372–3, 375, 378, 380–3, 462–4, 476–81,
    484–5, 496–8, 502, 525
Lucan, 308–9

# Index

Lucca, 22, 30–1, 33, 36, 83, 103, 321, 381, 469, 473
lyric poetry, 59, 252, 254–5, 277–8, 292–3, 372–3, 377, 380–3, 453, 463, 468, 476–80, 490, 510, 522, 525–6

Machiavelli, N., 16, 18
*magnati*, 10, 17–18, 21–2, 68, 464
Manfred, King, 14, 42, 203, 396
Marsilio of Padua, 28, 193, 358
martyrs, 98, 218, 413, 426, 497
  martyrdom, 209, 328
Mary, Virgin, 74–5, 84, 93, 101, 323, 325, 330–1, 339, 396
  and the visual arts, 326, 331, 402, 410, 415
masculinity, 77–8, 82
mass, *see* Eucharist
medicine, 127, 190, 192–3
  forensic, 197–8
  practitioners, 127, 191, 194, 196–7
  medicines, 128, 194
meditation, 59, 148, 335, 348
mendicant orders, 32, 94–7, 106, 140, 144, 250, 263, 273–5, 283, 325–7, 334–7, 344, 405, 442–3
  *see also* Dominicans; Franciscans
merchants, 11, 20, 30–1, 33–5, 38, 40–5, 62, 72, 74, 77, 125, 129–30, 239, 249–50, 253, 264, 292, 327, 334, 365, 367, 436, 464
metaphysics, 146–8, 150, 152, 165, 214, 230
meteorology, 177
metre, 32, 281, 302, 380, 384, 386, 454, 487, 493, 514
missionaries, 201, 205, 239, 343–4
monasteries, 38, 79, 94, 98–9, 131, 148, 336, 448
money-lending, 40, 43, 45, 130, 462
  credit market, 41, 43–5
Montaperti, Battle of, 39, 360, 362, 462
moral philosophy, *see* ethics
music, 1, 177
  monophony, 451, 453, 455
  polyphony, 449–52, 455
Mussato, A., 302–3, 367–8, 385–6
mystery plays, 331–2
mysticism, 108, 115, 149, 206, 215, 286, 329, 347–9

Naples, 15, 42, 71, 386
natural philosophy, *see* physics
nature, 141, 166, 175, 227, 291
Neoplatonism, 138, 225, 230, 234
nobility, 16, 24, 57, 153, 155–7, 212, 382, 390, 461, 464, 477, 485
notaries, 43–5, 126, 253, 367

Occitan, 244, 249, 252, 254–5, 258, 283, 291, 293, 301, 311, 371–4, 380, 391, 395, 453, 477, 486
Office, Divine, *see* Hours
Old French, 209, 217–18, 246, 252–3, 278, 371, 486
Olivi, P., 112–17, 147, 274
orthodoxy, 85–7, 114, 167, 214, 225, 516, 526, 529, 532
Ovid, 307–8, 423

Padua, 16, 168, 190, 193, 275, 297, 301–3, 316, 364–5, 368, 386, 422, 507
painting, 132, 221, 331, 402–3, 405–10, 412, 420–3, 428, 439
  painters, 224, 401, 412, 419–20
Paris, University of, 25, 140, 145, 162–3, 168, 173–6, 178, 183, 190, 214, 225, 281, 298, 334, 354
penitence, 97, 203, 329, 337–9, 497
  penitential handbooks, 338
persecution of heretics, 66–7, 87, 98, 107–9, 112, 125, 328, 346
Peter of Auvergne, 170, 355
Petrarch, 524–5, 530
Philip IV, King, 14, 23, 109–10
philosophy, 137–41, 144, 152–5, 166, 168–9, 205, 211, 225, 267, 271–3, 275, 277, 282–3, 334, 463–4, 472, 476, 483–5, 519, 527
physics, 146, 150, 173–5, 231, 283
pilgrimages, 238, 332–3, 337, 341, 346, 500
Pisa, 13, 16, 30–3, 35–7, 83, 97, 249, 366, 401, 440, 463
*plenitudo potestatis*, 111, 358–9
plurilinguism, 258–9, 374
*podestà*, 15, 59, 61, 67, 360
political theory, 25–8, 311, 317
Polo, M., 345, 374
*popolo*, 17, 20–2, 39, 66, 68–9, 83, 327, 390, 465
  *primo popolo*, 32, 67, 432–3
Porete, M., 108, 149
poverty, 79, 84, 94–6, 109, 111, 113, 115, 274, 325–7, 467–8, 489
preaching, 91, 143–4, 246, 250–1, 283, 322, 324–8, 335–9, 442
priorate, 22, 83, 123, 366, 383, 403, 433, 465
prophecy, 12, 107, 114, 116, 307, 346–7, 481, 498
  prophets, 210, 233, 305, 491, 501, 529
prostitution, 81–2, 125
providence, divine, 11, 26, 162, 239, 305
pseudo-Dionysius, 232, 348
Ptolemy, 227–9
purification, 152, 154–6, 497

570 Index

quest, 153, 157, 484–5
quodlibetal questions, 145, 176–80, 273, 335
Qur'ān, 201, 205–6, 210

*razo*, 453, 480
realism, 378, 382, 494–5, 521
reason, 117, 148, 150–4, 168, 170, 174, 206, 349,
    381–2, 479, 485, 498, 501
redemption, 138, 224, 285, 335, 498, 503
Remigio de' Girolami, 16, 23, 25, 96, 167, 171,
    273–4, 359–60
repentance, 86, 137, 155, 203, 266, 322, 330
republic, 19–20, 280–1, 356, 360, 365, 429, 431,
    444, 533
revelation, 117, 137, 141, 146, 150, 175,
    484–5, 489
rhetoric, 137, 266, 270–3, 275, 278–82, 284–5,
    289–90, 298–9, 301, 311, 317, 330,
    378–9, 484
Riccobaldo of Ferrara, 18, 27, 365
Richard of St Victor, 151
*ricordanze* (diaries), 77
Romania, 246, 248
Rome, 23, 26, 41, 52, 110, 238, 248, 309, 333,
    343, 356, 385, 411, 413–15, 426, 429, 465,
    471–2, 488

*sacre rappresentazioni, see* mystery plays
Salimbene de Adam, 9, 15, 112
Sallust, 313–14
*sapientia* (wisdom), 137, 148, 150
satire, 277, 283, 288, 291, 310, 312
scholastics, 151, 183–6, 204, 233
schoolbooks/textbooks, 139, 160, 176,
    222, 229–30, 261–2, 264–6, 270,
    297–8, 300–1
schools 53, 74, 77, 79, 96–7, 140–1, 143–5, 147–8,
    153, 161, 176, 190–1, 234, 249–50, 260–71,
    273–5, 279, 281, 283, 298–301, 304,
    306, 309, 312, 314–15, 326, 334–6, 376,
    386, 464
science, 145–6, 150–1, 153, 162, 176–8, 187, 202,
    225, 284–5, 380, 494
sculpture, 405, 413–19, 424
Seneca, 311–12
sermons, 77, 96, 149, 208, 246, 250–1, 275, 322,
    331, 336–7, 360, 529
sex, 72, 77–8, 81, 129, 163, 324, 329
Sicily, 10, 13–14, 23, 33, 200, 202–4
Sicilian–Tuscan poetry, 254–6, 334
Sicilian school of poetry, 292, 383
Siger of Brabant, 117–18, 142, 167–8, 214
sodomy, 70, 81, 269, 272
sonnet, 245, 278, 285, 290–5, 361–2, 380–1,
    383–4, 463, 477–8, 480, 511

souls, 162, 230, 320, 347, 350–2, 358, 494–5, 498
spheres, 181, 184, 223, 228
Statius, 306–7, 498
stilnovist, *see stilnovo*
*stilnovo*, 214, 255, 258, 291, 382–4, 463, 476,
    483, 494
*studium, studia generalia, see* schools
sumptuary laws, 73, 122, 125

Tempier, É., 117, 155, 163, 167, 169, 174, 185–6,
    213, 225–6, 230
temporal power, 10, 24, 47, 356–9, 488, 528
*tenzone*, 278, 291–6, 361, 477
Terence, 314–15, 520
textile industry/trade, 31, 34–5, 43, 81
theology
    monastic, 147–8, 151, 156
    scholastic, 140–5, 211
    vernacular, 149, 151–3
tragedy, 277, 283, 288, 302, 315–16, 386, 494
*translatio imperii*, 10, 12, 26–8
translations
    from Arabic, 1, 140, 160, 173, 190, 224
    of Arabic-Islamic texts, 182, 194, 202, 205,
        213, 218–19
    from Greek, 52, 160, 173, 214, 224
    from Hebrew, 192, 195, 203, 214
    Hispanic, 192, 195, 204, 217, 532
    Latin, 56, 116, 160, 168, 173, 203–6, 210, 212,
        214, 217–19, 224–5, 227–8, 232, 283,
        313, 354
Trinity, 137, 147, 151, 207, 209–10
*trobar*
    *leu*, 339
    *clus*, 381–2
*troubadours*, 291–2, 294, 371–3, 380, 453
*trouvères*, 453

Ubertino da Casale, 115–16, 274
*Umiliati/Umiliate*, 32, 34, 79, 98, 107, 328
universe, 185, 221–3, 350, 377, 383, 493, 496,
    504, 508
universities, 116, 140–2, 144, 153, 161, 173, 180,
    187, 250, 252, 264, 270, 272–5, 283, 301,
    317, 335, 464, 485
usury, *see* money-lending

Valerius Maximus, 314
vendetta, 17, 20, 62, 445
Venice, 13, 17, 80–1, 189, 191, 196–7, 201, 249,
    345, 423, 425, 430, 474
Verona, 16, 215, 303–4, 386, 394, 417–22, 430–1,
    435–40, 442–4, 467, 472–3, 507
vernacular, *see volgare*
Villani, G., 30, 77, 260, 271, 321, 367, 385

# Index

571

Vincent of Beauvais, 277, 285, 363
Virgil, 24, 154, 282, 304–7, 309, 313, 316, 342,
    345, 494–5, 498, 506, 519–20
virtues
    Christian, 163
    intellectual, 161, 164, 171
    moral, 72, 155–7, 164, 166–7, 171,
        357–8, 477
vision, beatific, 169, 231, 346, 348–9
visions, 80, 147, 217, 328, 346–53

*volgare*, 253, 385, 390, 484–8, 490, 493–4
*volgarizzamenti*, 253–4, 376, 387

Waldensianism, 107, 324
White Guelfs, 20, 22–3, 40, 45, 69, 85, 115,
    360–1, 366, 435, 441, 445–6, 465–70,
    472, 488, 505, 507
    *see also* Black Guelfs; Guelfs

zodiac, 224, 237, 403